Gambling in America

Gambling in America

An Encyclopedia of History, Issues, and Society

William N. Thompson

ABC-CLIO

Santa Barbara, California
Denver, Colorado
Oxford, England

Library of Congress Cataloging-in-Publication Data
Thompson, William Norman.
    Gambling in America : an encyclopedia of history, issues, and society /
William N. Thompson.
        p. cm.
    Includes bibliographical references and index.
    ISBN 1-57607-159-6 (hard : alk. paper)
    1. Gambling—Encyclopedias.   2. Gambling—United
States—Encyclopedias.   3. Gambling—Canada—Encyclopedias.
4. Gambling—Social aspects.   I. Title.
GV1301.T47   2001
795'.0973—dc21
                                                                                    2001003493

06   05   04   03   02   10 9 8 7 6 5 4 3 2

This book is also available on the World Wide Web as an e-book. Visit abc-clio.com for details.

ABC-CLIO, Inc.
130 Cremona Drive, P.O. Box 1911
Santa Barbara, California 93116-1911

This book is printed on acid-free paper ∞.
Manufactured in the United States of America

I dedicate this book to the librarians in my life,
especially in memory of Marion Bauschard Thompson,
and in honor of Maria White and Sidney Watson

Deal

Life is a gamble
And the days are just so many decks
The hours are cards
They deal and you play what you get

Ah! You think of the time
That you knew you could call so you raised
Ah! You think of the time
You got out when you should have stayed

So Deal, Hey maybe the next card's an ace
Deal, You ought to go home,
But you know that
A flush beats a straight

Son, you can't have a full house
The queen has been dealt to a friend
Ah! The good thing about life
Is they shuffle and they deal life again

Well the cards are all stacked
When you're hot and the women are too
It's a hard cut to take
When you raise every hand but you lose

Well I'm not complaining
It ain't like the joker to cry
And it won't do to cheat
Cause you have to cash in when you die

So Deal

By Tom T. Hall © Hallnote Music, 1975

CONTENTS

CHRONOLOGY OF GAMBLING EVENTS

At the dawn of human existence Adam and Eve gamble with the future of mankind as they disobey God and eat from the forbidden fruit on the Tree of Life.

50,000–10,000 B.C.	Indigenous populations in the Western Hemisphere gamble on the results of contests.
6000 B.C.	Dice are used in games played in the Middle East. Dice found in pyramid tombs of Egyptian pharaohs (circa 2500 B.C.) are "gaffed," that is, crooked.
4000 B.C.	Babylonian soldiers use chariots in horse races.
2800 B.C.	Dog races are held in Egypt.
2000 B.C.	Egyptians race mounted horses.
624 B.C.	There is a mounted horse race in the 33rd Olympic Games.
500–400 B.C.	Cockfighting is encouraged in ancient Greece.
A.D. 33	Roman soldiers wager to win the robes of Christ during the Crucifixion.
200	Romans organize a formal horse race meeting in England.
800	Playing cards are used in northern India.
1174	Henry II of England establishes weekly horse races at county fairgrounds.
1492	As Columbus sails to the Western Hemisphere, his crew plays card games.
1495	Columbus brings horses to the Western Hemisphere.
1530	Florence (present-day Italy) is the first European state to have a lottery.
1566	England charters its first government lottery.
1576	England holds "coursing" events, for greyhounds. These are precursors to dog races.
1612	A lottery is organized in London to support Virginia Colony in North America. Four drawings are held between 1612 and 1615. Ticket purchasers are told they are honoring both "God and Country."
1620	Twenty mares are shipped from England to Virginia Colony, and horse racing with private wagering becomes a regular activity for the settlers. A specific authorization for racing is given in 1630.
1621	The first restrictions on gambling are established in Plymouth Colony. Opposition to forms of card playing and gambling are also instituted in early Massachusetts Bay Colony. The ambiguities toward gambling are in evidence among the earliest European communities in North America.
1665	A permanent oval horse racing course is laid out on the Hempstead Plain on Long Island, New York Colony. This marks the commercial beginnings of the racing industry in North America. Racing before this time consisted of match races over long, straight courses, with betting between individuals only.
1674	Charles II of England rides a horse to a first-place finish in one of the earliest stakes races held at Newmarket.

1682	The Quaker government of Pennsylvania Colony passes antigambling legislation. The futility of prohibition is witnessed here and elsewhere as gambling continues.
1728	Goldolphin Arabian, the last of three Arabian horses, is shipped to England from the Middle East. From these three horses— Goldolphin Arabian, Darley Arabian, and Byerley's Turk—a stock of racing horses is developed. Today almost every thoroughbred racing horse can trace its lineage to one of the three horses.
1765	The British Parliament passes the Stamp Act, which provides for the taxation of playing cards. The act is one of the first of the Obnoxious Acts precipitating the eventual rebellion in North America. That the British target playing cards as a potential source of tax revenues is an indication of how much Americans love card games. A good portion of the card decks found in the colonies at the time was manufactured by the colonies' leading printer, Benjamin Franklin, who was also a frequent lottery player.
1776	Thomas Jefferson gambles as he composes the Declaration of Independence. John Rosecrance's *Gambling without Guilt* (Rosecrance 1988, 18) cites Jefferson's diary from June 1776, which details his wins and losses at backgammon and lotto during the critical days preceding the Declaration.
1777	The Continental Congress initiates a lottery game. Four games are held to raise funds for the revolutionary armies of George Washington. Massachusetts, New York, and Rhode Island legislative bodies follow suit with lotteries for the armies.
1780s–1830s	Lotteries become an economic tool for financing civic projects in the new states. They help build the new capital city on the Potomac as well as buildings for many colleges, including Harvard, Yale, Columbia, Rutgers, and Dartmouth, and even some churches. From 1790 to 1830, twenty-one state governments issue licenses for nearly 200 games.
1810	Former President Thomas Jefferson says he never gambles on lotteries, and he issues a letter very critical of lotteries and gambling.
1812	The first steamboat operates on the Mississippi River, Robert Fulton's *New Orleans*. The boat inaugurates an era of riverboat gambling in the West. Within a decade over sixty riverboats are operating with gamblers on board.
1815	New Orleans licenses casino gaming enterprises in the city. New Orleans was already a wide open "sin city" when it became part of the United States with the 1803 Louisiana Purchase. Legislation and licensing are seen as a means to control the widespread gambling and generate moneys for municipal improvements.
1826	Jefferson supports the use of lotteries as a means for persons to dispose of their property in a respectable manner so that they can pay their bills. He calls lotteries a tax "laid on the willing only." His own lottery for sale of goods at Monticello is unsuccessful.
1827	John Davis opens the first complete casino in the United States in New Orleans at the corner of Orleans and Bourbon Streets. The high-class establishment caters to aristocratic

tastes, and although it is open only until 1835, it serves as a model for modern Las Vegas– and Atlantic City–type casinos.

1828   The first Canadian horse race track opens in Montreal.

1832   The high point of early lottery play, with 420 lottery games in eight states. Scandals plague many of the games, however, leading to a reaction prohibiting lotteries and other gambling.

1833   The Jacksonian era ushers in a mood of general governmental reform. Reformers call for a cessation of gambling. Pennsylvania and Maryland are the first to prohibit lotteries, and most other states follow suit. Between 1833 and 1840, twelve states ban lotteries. By the time of the Civil War all legal lotteries have halted.

1834   Cockfighting is banned in England.

1835   New Orleans declares casinos to be illegal. John Davis's house closes, but lower-class gambling dens continue to operate illegally. The antigambling reform movement moves up the Mississippi River, where a vigilante committee torches the gambling haunts of Vicksburg, Mississippi, and lynches five gamblers.

1836   The first stakes horse race in North America is held in Quebec.

1848 and following years   The gold strike in California marks a new trend: mining camp gambling halls. Eastern reform and western opportunities redistribute much gambling activity in the 1840s and for 100 years or more. Although opportunity brings prospectors west, reform pushes gamblers in the same direction, with gamblers drawn by the opportunity to strike gold in the gambling dens themselves. San Francisco becomes a gambling center.

1855   Reformers close down open gambling in San Francisco.

1860   Riverboat gambling reaches its apex, with 557 boats operating on the eve of the Civil War. It is estimated that 99 percent of the games on the boats cheat players.

1860   Player-banked games are banned in California.

1864   The Travers Stakes horse race is run for the first time at Saratoga, New York, and is the first stakes race in the United States. Originally it was part of the Triple Crown of racing. That honor was later lost, and the Triple Crown races became the Preakness, the Belmont Stakes, and the Kentucky Derby.

1865   The totalizator is invented in France. It permits horse race bets to be pooled and odds calculated as bets are being made. The device allows for the creation of the pari-mutuel system of betting. This makes it much easier to tax horse race betting and also to collect funds for race purses. The totalizator was not used at North American tracks until 1933, but the pari-mutuel system is now in place at every major track in North America.

1867   The inaugural running of the Belmont Stakes takes place in Belmont, New York.

1868   Gambling activity gains a new momentum as the Louisiana Lottery begins a three-decade reign of abuse and corruption. Initially started in order to bring needed revenues to a war-torn bankrupt state, the lottery is soon overcome by private entrepreneurs who sustain it by bribing state officials. The lottery enjoys great success, as tickets are sold through the mail across the continent.

1873   The inaugural running of the Preakness stakes takes place at the Pimlico racetrack in Baltimore.

1875   The first Kentucky Derby is run on 17 May at Churchill Downs in Louisville. It is won by Aristides.

1876   Congress bans the use of mails for lottery advertising.

1877   Congress actually adjourns so that members can attend horse racing events at the Pimlico track in Baltimore.

1886   The first dog "coursing" events are held in the United States in Kansas.

1887   Charles Fey invents the slot machine in San Francisco. This first machine accepts and pays nickels. Soon similar devices are found throughout the city, and because patents on the concept of a gambling machine are not granted by the government at this time, other manufacturers open the door for imitation.

1890   Congress bans the sale of lottery tickets through the mail. This significantly restricts the Louisiana Lottery. Lottery advertising in newspapers is also prohibited. Two years later the Louisiana Lottery is voted out of existence, yet its operators seek to keep it operating, using foreign ports for ticket delivery.

1891   The Broadmoor Casino Resort opens in Colorado Springs, Colorado. This casino brings a new elegance to Western gaming. As many as 15,000 players visit the establishment each day. The casino fails to make money from gambling, however, as people gamble among themselves rather than playing house-banked games. The casino is destroyed by fire in 1897.

1891   The first organized regulation of horse-race courses begins with licensing of jockeys and trainers by a private board of control in New York State. The growth in popularity of race betting requires the establishment of integrity in racing.

1892   An antigambling movement takes hold in Canada as Parliament bans most forms of gambling by means of revisions to the Criminal Code.

1894   The Jockey Club of New York is established. It helps to develop national standards for horse racing.

1895   Congress bans the transportation of lottery tickets in interstate or foreign commerce. When the act is upheld by the courts, the Louisiana Lottery operations finally end.

1900   The total prohibition on gambling in Canada begins its century of unraveling as small raffles are permitted in an amendment to the Criminal Code.

1906   Kentucky becomes the first state to establish a government-run state racing commission. At the same time, other states begin to ban horse racing.

1907   The Arizona and New Mexico territorial governments outlaw all gambling as part of their quest for statehood.

1910   The era of antigambling reform seems nearly complete in the United States. Nevada closes its casinos, and legalized gambling in the United States, with the exception of a few horse race tracks, is dormant.

1910   In Canada the Criminal Code is again amended, this time to allow betting at racing tracks.

1915   Horse racing begins in Cuba.

1916   Horse-race betting is permitted in Puerto Rico.

1919   The Black Sox scandal hits professional baseball. Gamblers, including Arnold Rothstein, bribe Chicago White Sox players, who purposely lose the World Series.

1919   Casino gambling begins along with jai alai in Marianao, Cuba.

1920s   Dog racing is popularized as sixty tracks open throughout the United States.

1922   The Canadian Criminal Code is amended to ban the use of dice in any gambling activity. Some casinos simulate dice games by placing dice configurations within roulette wheels or on slot machine reels.

1922   Costa Rican law defines legal and illegal casino gambling.

1925   Limited gambling activity is permitted at fairs in Canada.

1929   A racetrack is opened at Agua Caliente near Tijuana, Mexico. A casino also has government approval.

1931   The state of Nevada legalizes wide-open casino gambling. At first, gambling is confined to small saloons and taverns and is regulated by cities and counties. Casino taxes consist of set fees on each table or machine game. Taxes are shared between local and state governments.

1933   The first totalizator is used at a U.S. horse race track in Arlington Park, Illinois. Soon legal horse-race betting returns to several Depression-bankrupt (or near bankrupt) states, including California, as a means of gaining revenues.

1933   Casinos are closed in Cuba.

1934   Casinos gain legal status in Macao, and soon the Portuguese enclave becomes the gambling center of Asia.

1935   New horse-race betting legislation is approved in Illinois, Louisiana, Florida, New Hampshire, West Virginia, Ohio, Michigan, Massachusetts, Rhode Island, and Delaware.

1937   Bill Harrah opens his first gambling hall in Reno, beginning one of the largest casino empires. In 1971 his casino interests become the first ones publicly traded on open stock exchanges.

1938   The casino in Tijuana, Mexico, is closed by the new national government headed by Lazaro Cardenas.

1940   New York legalizes pari-mutuel horse-race betting.

1940s and 1950s   Casinos reopen in Cuba under the control of dictator Juan Batista.

1941   The Las Vegas Strip begins its legacy as the world's primary casino gambling location. The El Rancho Vegas is the first casino on the Strip and is soon joined by the Last Frontier and the Desert Inn. These new-style casinos offer hotel accommodations and recreational amenities to tourists.

1944   Argentina closes all private casinos. Many reopen as part of a government corporate monopoly.

1945   Casinos in Panama are placed under government ownership.

1945   The state government of Nevada begins to license casinos for the first time. In addition to set fees on games, the casinos begin to pay a tax on the amount of money they win from players. Nevada casino activity increases as World War II ends, but operators of illegal gaming establishments throughout the country face a new wave of reform. Reform is triggered with the end of World War II as public resources and public concern turn to domestic problems. Gamblers shift operations to Las Vegas.

1946   Brazil closes its casinos. They remain closed for the remainder of the twentieth century.

1946   Gangster Benjamin (Bugsy) Siegel, financed by organized crime figure

Meyer Lansky, opens the Flamingo Casino on the Las Vegas Strip. The casino features a showroom with Hollywood entertainment.

1947   Siegel is murdered at his girlfriend's Hollywood home. The murder sensationalizes the Strip and firms up Las Vegas's reputation as a risky, naughty place where Main Street Americans can rub shoulders with notorious mobsters.

1947   The Idaho legislature passes a slot machine law that permits licensing and taxing of machines. A few years later the voters decide to outlaw machines once again.

1948   Congress permits casino gambling in Puerto Rico as part of Operation Bootstrap.

1949   The voters of Idaho decide to ban all slot machines. No other state completely bans a form of gambling again until 1999.

1949   Congress passes the Gambling Ship Act of 1949, which prohibits U.S. flag ships from operating gambling casinos.

1950   The U.S. Senate investigates organized crime and gambling casinos. Tennessee senator Estes Kefauver leads a committee that fingers Las Vegas as a "den of evil" controlled by "the Mob." Ironically, while the Senate committee is seeking a crackdown on casinos within the United States, Congress authorizes the expenditure of U.S. taxpayer funds to open a casino in Travemunde, Germany, under the provisions of the Marshall Fund for business recovery in Western Europe after World War II.

1951   The Johnson Act is passed, banning the transportation of gambling machines in interstate commerce unless they are moving to jurisdictions where they are legal.

1955   Nevada creates the Gaming Control Board under the direction of the State Treasury Commission. A process of professionalizing gaming regulation begins as an effort to convince federal authorities that the state can run honest crime-free casinos.

1955–1962   The McClelland Committees of the U.S. Congress investigate organized crime activity, including gambling activity.

1959   The Nevada Gaming Commission is created to oversee the decisions of the Gaming Control Board. Gaming regulation is removed from the State Treasury Commission.

1959–1960   Fidel Castro closes down the casinos of Cuba. He closes down a lottery as well.

1960   Dictator Jean Claude "Papa Doc" Duvalier authorizes casinos in Haiti. They are run by mobsters who have left Cuba.

1961   In response to the McClelland investigations, Congress passes the Wire Act, the Travel Act, and the Waging Paraphernalia Act in order to combat illegal gambling.

1962   Congress amends the Johnson Act of 1951 to include all gambling devices.

1962   Mathematics professor Edward Thorpe writes *Beat the Dealer,* which describes the card counting system for blackjack play. Almost instantly, blackjack becomes the most popular casino table game in Las Vegas.

1963–1964   The legislature of New Hampshire authorizes a state-run sweepstakes game, which becomes the first government lottery in the United States since the closing of the Louisiana Lottery. The state sells its first lottery ticket in 1964.

1964   The voters of Arkansas defeat a measure that would have allowed casino gambling in Hot Springs, a location of much illegal gambling in recent years.

1965–1967   The President's Commission on Law Enforcement and the Administration of Justice meets. Little attention is given to gambling.

1966   Billionaire Howard Hughes moves to Las Vegas and begins to purchase Nevada casinos from owners with suspicious connections to organized crime. This helps to improve the city's image. Hughes has a flamboyant image but also a reputation as an entrepreneur with integrity.

1966   Jay Sarno opens Caesars Palace in Las Vegas. This is the first "themed" casino on the Las Vegas Strip. He follows this with the opening of the Circus Circus Casino in 1970.

1967   Alberta permits charity casinos at the two-week Edmonton Exhibition. This is the first authorized casino gambling in Canada.

1967   New York begins a lottery, but it fails to meet state officials' budget expectations. Similar to the New Hampshire games, the lottery's monthly draw game proves to be too slow. Few other jurisdictions take notice of the lottery.

1968   The federal government initiates actions to prohibit Howard Hughes from purchasing any more Las Vegas casinos (specifically the Landmark) on antitrust grounds. Hughes is angered and initiates a plan to win federal approval by allegedly bribing presidential candidates Richard Nixon and Hubert Humphrey (see Michael Drosnin's *Citizen Hughes* [1985]). Kennedy family confidant Larry O'Brien is on Hughes's staff at the time.

1969   Nevada permits ownership of casinos by public corporations. This action is prompted by the industry's need to maintain and upgrade facilities and by a continuing need to improve the state's image.

1969   The World Series of Poker is established at Binion's Horseshoe Casino in Las Vegas.

1969   Kirk Kerkorian opens the International Hotel and Casino in Las Vegas. With its 1,512 rooms it is the largest hotel in the world. He soon sells it to Hilton Corporation, and he builds the MGM Grand with 2,084 rooms. It becomes the largest hotel in the world. He sells it to Bally's.

1969   New Jersey authorizes a lottery. In 1970 the state begins sales of weekly lottery tickets using mass marketing techniques. The New Jersey operation is successful from the beginning, and other states realize that large revenues can be realized from lotteries if ticket prices are low and games occur regularly. Lotteries begin to spread quickly.

1969   The Canadian Criminal Code is amended to permit lottery schemes to be operated by governments and charitable organizations. Soon many of the provinces have lotteries, and the door is wide open for the charities and governments to offer casino games.

1970   The Yukon Territory permits the Klondike Visitor's Association to conduct casino games from mid-spring through the summer at Diamond Tooth Gerties in Dawson City.

1970   Loto Quebec, an agency of the Quebec provincial government, initiates the first lottery gaming in Canada.

1970   Congress passes the Organized Crime Control Act. Among other provisions it authorizes a study of gambling activity. The study does not begin until 1975.

1970   New York City creates the Knapp Commission to investigate police corruption, much of it tied to illegal gambling operations.

1970   Don Laughlin opens the first casino in Laughlin, Nevada.

1970   Genting Highlands resort and casino opens in Malaysia. With a gambling floor of 200,000 square feet, it is the largest casino in the world for several decades.

1970s and 1980s   Casinos with unauthorized games begin operation in Costa Rica despite laws defining legal and illegal casino gambling.

1971   New York authorizes offtrack betting. New York City creates a public corporation to conduct the operations within its boundaries.

1972   Richard Nixon orders a break-in of Larry O'Brien's office in the Watergate Building in Washington, D.C. It is suggested that Nixon wants to find out what information O'Brien has about alleged bribery by Howard Hughes in 1968. O'Brien is the national Democratic party chairman.

1973   Following disastrous forest fires, the Tasmanian government authorizes casinos as a means of gaining revenues to deal with the calamity. The Tasmanian casinos are the first ones allowed in Australia.

1974   New Jersey voters defeat a proposal for local-option casinos, which would be operated by the state government.

1974   Massachusetts becomes the first North American jurisdiction to have an instant lottery game. This becomes the most popular lottery game of the decade, and all other lotteries begin to sell instant games.

1974   Maryland authorizes the creation of an interest-only lottery program like one used in England. The player buys a no-interest bond and may cash it in at full purchase price at any time. As long as he or she holds the bond, however, he or she is eligible to win lottery prizes, which are awarded in lieu of interest payments. The system is never implemented.

1975   The Western Canada Lottery Corporation initiates the first intergovernmental lottery anywhere. The provinces of Manitoba, Saskatchewan, Alberta, and British Columbia operate these games together. British Columbia later drops out of the joint operation in order to have its own lottery games.

1975   New Jersey starts the first "numbers game" with players selecting their own three-digit numbers. The game is offered with hopes that it will drive the popular illegal numbers games out of business. Other lotteries adopt the numbers game as well, often adding a four-digit numbers game. There is little evidence that illegal games stop.

1975–1976   The Commission on the Review of the National Policy toward Gambling meets and issues a report affirming the notion that gambling activity and its legalization and control are a matter for the jurisdictions of state governments. The Commission concludes, however, that casinos should be located in remote areas far removed from metropolitan populations.

1976   New Jersey voters authorize casino gambling for Atlantic City by a margin of 56 percent to 44 percent.

1976   The Atlantic Lottery Corporation is formed by action of the provinces of Newfoundland, Prince Edward's

Island, New Brunswick, and Nova Scotia. Lotteries are begun in these four provinces, thereby bringing the games into each Canadian province.

1977   The New Jersey legislature creates a regulatory structure for casino gaming.

1978   Casino gaming begins in Atlantic City with the opening of Resorts International on Memorial Day weekend.

1978   The Interstate Horse Racing Act is passed, providing standards for operating offtrack betting as well as intertrack betting.

1979   Sam's Town Casino opens on Boulder Highway in Las Vegas, ushering in an era of casinos that cater to the local residents of the gambling community.

1979   High-stakes bingo games begin on the Seminole Indian reservation in Hollywood, Florida, signaling a new period of Native American gambling. In subsequent federal court litigation the Indians retain the right to conduct games unregulated by the state.

1979   Scandal rocks the Pennsylvania lottery as its numbers game is rigged. Although the culprits—who were paid by the government—go to prison, the state continues all its lottery games without interruption.

1979   The province of Ontario initiates the world's first lotto game, called Lottario. The game requires players to select six numbers, and all play is entered into an online computer network. A jackpot prize is given to any player who picks all six numbers. If there is no winner, more prize money is added to the next drawing. Jackpots in North American lotto games have grown to exceed $250 million.

1979   Casino gambling is authorized by the corrupt regime of General Lucas Garcia in Guatemala. The casinos are closed after a Christian Fundamentalist, General Rios Montt, overthrows Lucas Garcia in 1982.

1981   The New York legislature rejects measures to authorize casino gambling after a major attack on gambling by state attorney general Robert Abrams.

1981   Charity blackjack games are given formal authorization in North Dakota. The success of the games leads the charities to successfully campaign against lotteries for the state. North Dakota is the only state to vote against lotteries until Alabama joins it in 1999.

1984   Arkansas voters defeat casinos a second time.

1984   California voters authorize a state lottery.

1984   Donald Trump opens Harrah's Trump Plaza, the first of his three Atlantic City casinos.

1985   The Canadian national government agrees to place responsibility for the administration of all gambling laws with the provinces in exchange for a $100 million payment to offset the costs of Calgary Winter Olympics of 1988.

1985   The President's Commission on Organized Crime meets but fails to issue a report on gambling, as it now considers gambling to be, for the most part, a legitimate industry.

1986   Congress passes the Money Laundering Act, requiring casinos to record large gambling transactions.

1986   Donald Trump opens his second casino, Trump Castle, in Atlantic City.

1987   The U.S. Supreme Court upholds the rights of Indian tribes to offer unregulated gambling enterprises as long as operations do not violate state criminal policy. The case, *California* v. *Cabazon Band of Mission Indians,* determines that any regulation of noncriminal matters must come from the federal government or be specifically authorized by Congress.

1987   One century after its invention, slot machine gaming becomes the number one form of gambling in U.S. casinos.

1988   The Indian Gaming Regulatory Act is passed by Congress in response to the *Cabazon* decision. The act provides for federal and tribal regulation of bingo games and for mutually negotiated Indian–state government schemes for the regulation of casinos on reservations.

1988   The voters of South Dakota authorize limited (five dollar) stakes casino games of blackjack, poker, and slot machines in casinos in the historic town of Deadwood.

1989   Stephen Wynn of the Mirage Corporation opens the Mirage, the first new Las Vegas Strip casino in over a decade.

1989   Donald Trump opens the Taj Mahal in Atlantic City, the third of his three Atlantic City casinos.

1989   The South Dakota legislature passes enabling laws, and limited casino gambling begins in Deadwood. A state lottery also begins operation of video lottery terminals throughout South Dakota.

1989   The Iowa state legislature approves riverboat casino gaming with limited (five dollar) stakes betting on navigable waters in the state. Boats begin operations in 1990.

1989   The state of Oregon starts the first sports game–based lottery in the United States. Proceeds of the gambling are assigned to support college athletics in Oregon.

1989   The Manitoba Lottery Foundation, a government-owned entity, opens the first year-round permanent casino facility in Canada. The Crystal Casino is located in the classic Fort Garry Hotel in Winnipeg.

1989   The jackpot prize in the Pennsylvania lotto game exceeds $115 million. It is won, and shared, by several lucky ticket holders.

1990   Alaska voters defeat a proposal for local option casino gambling. Ohio voters refuse to authorize casino gaming.

1990   Riverboat casinos begin operation in Iowa. Riverboat casinos are also approved by the Illinois state legislature.

1990   The voters of Colorado approve limited casino gaming for the historic mountain towns of Blackhawk, Cripple Creek, and Central City.

1990   West Virginia permits slot machines to operate at racetracks. This action is later imitated by five other states and by many Canadian provinces during the 1990s.

1990   Casinos are authorized in New Zealand.

1991   Riverboat casinos are approved by the Mississippi legislature. It is determined that the boats may be permanently docked. Casino boats begin operation in Illinois, and limited casinos start in Colorado.

1991   Oregon and Colorado introduce keno as a lottery game.

1992   The Atlantic Provinces—New Brunswick, Prince Edward's Island, Nova Scotia, and Newfoundland— authorize video lottery terminals for locations throughout their territories.

1992   The Louisiana legislature approves riverboat casinos and one land-based casino in New Orleans. Missouri voters also approve riverboat casinos. Colorado voters refuse to expand casinos to additional towns.

1992   Congress prohibits the spread of sports betting beyond four states currently authorizing it: Nevada, Oregon, Montana, and Delaware. New Jersey is given one year to approve sports betting for Atlantic City casinos but declines to do so.

1992   Congress passes an act allowing U.S. flag ships to have casino gambling.

1992   Rhode Island and Louisiana permit slot machines to operate at racetracks.

1993   The Ontario government approves a casino for the city of Windsor. The casino is to be government owned but privately operated. The provincial government selects a consortium of Las Vegas casino companies, including Caesar's Palace, Circus Circus, and the Hilton, to operate the casino. The province of Quebec opens a government-owned and -operated casino in Montreal at the site of the French Pavilion of the Montreal World's Fair. Quebec also approves gaming sites at Charlevoix and Hull.

1993   The Nova Scotia government removes video gaming machines from all locations that are accessible to young people.

1993   The Indiana legislature approves boat casinos. Five boats are authorized for Lake Michigan ports, five for ports on the Ohio River, and one for an interior lake.

1993   Georgia establishes a lottery and devotes revenues to university scholarships for all high school graduates with B averages or better. The scholarship program is very popular and becomes a model for other states desiring to win approval for gambling enterprises.

1993   Kirk Kerkorian opens the new MGM Grand, with 5,009 rooms, making it the largest hotel in the world.

1994   Florida voters defeat a proposal for "limited" casino gambling. The proposal would have authorized about fifty major casinos for many locations around the state. Colorado voters again defeat efforts to expand casino gambling. Riverboat casinos begin operation in Louisiana and Missouri.

1994   Congress passes the Money Laundering and Suppression Act.

1994   The government of the province of Nova Scotia authorizes casino gambling.

1995   A temporary casino opens in New Orleans. It is operated by a group including Harrah's Casinos and the Jazzville Corporation. Riverboat gambling begins in Indiana. Slot machine gaming is authorized for racetracks in Iowa on a local government option basis.

1995   Provincially owned casinos open in Halifax and Sydney, Nova Scotia, and also in Regina, Saskatchewan.

1995   The voters of the Virgin Islands approve casinos.

1995   Costa Rica changes its laws to permit most forms of casino games.

1995   Delaware and Iowa permit slot machines to operate at racetracks.

1996   The new government of South Africa authorizes the establishment of forty casinos.

1996   The New Orleans casino project closes and declares bankruptcy. The casino reopens in 2000.

1996   The U.S. Supreme Court rules part of the Indian Gaming Regulatory Act of 1988 unconstitutional. The Court determines that the act's provision allowing tribes to sue states over compact negotiations violates the 11th Amendment.

1996   Congress passes a law setting up a nine-person commission to study the social and economic impacts of gambling on U.S. society.

1996   Congress gives a blanket approval to "cruises to nowhere" out of state ports into international waters for gambling purposes unless states specifically prohibit the cruises.

1996   In November, the voters of several states speak out on gambling, but they give quite mixed messages. Michigan voters approve a law that authorizes three major casinos for the city of Detroit. Ohio and Arkansas voters defeat casinos; West Virginia approves machine gaming for racetracks, and Nebraska voters say no to track machines. Colorado also says no to new casino towns. Washington state voters defeat slot machines for Native American casinos, but Arizona voters mandate that the governor sign compacts for new Native American casinos.

1996   Two historical casinos on the Las Vegas Strip—the Hacienda and the Sands—are imploded to make way for newer and bigger gambling halls. Three new casinos open up in Las Vegas: the Monte Carlo, the Orleans, and the Stratosphere. The Stratosphere boasts having the tallest free-standing tower on the North American continent.

1996   Casino Niagara opens in Niagara Falls, Ontario, in December. It is owned and operated by the Ontario Casino Corporation, a government corporation. The Ontario government also permits a Native casino to open in Rama near Orilla.
    The Saskatchewan government opens Casino Regina.

1997   Major casino expansions take place in Las Vegas. These include the opening of the New York, New York resort casino and expansions of the Rio, Harrah's, Caesars, and Luxor.

1997   The National Gambling Impact Study Commission begins operations.

1998   California voters pass Proposition 5, designed to allow Native American tribes to have unlimited casino gambling. The tribes of the state invest over $70 million in the campaign for Proposition 5, and Nevada casinos spend $26 million in opposition. It is the most expensive referendum campaign in history.

1998   New Mexico permits slot machines to operate at racetracks.

1999   The Ontario government abandons a plan for forty-four charity casinos in all parts of the province and instead authorizes four new "charity" casinos in Thunder Bay, Sault Ste. Marie, Point Edward, and Brantford. A Native casino also operates near Port Erie. Gambling machines are authorized for provincial racetracks.

1999   The Canadian ban on the use of dice in any gambling activity ends as Ontario casinos seek to compete with new Detroit casinos.

1999   The voters of Alabama defeat a lottery. This is only the second state in which voters say no to lotteries.

1999   The state Supreme Court orders that the slot machines of South Carolina be shut down. On 30 June 2000, over thirty thousand machines stop. It is the first major shutdown of a form of statewide gambling since Idaho voters closed down machines in 1949.

1999   Expansion in Las Vegas continues with the opening of the Bellagio, Mandalay Bay, Venetian, and Paris casinos.

1999   The National Gambling Impact Study Commission issues its report.

1999   The Supreme Court of California rules Proposition 5 to be unconstitutional.

2000   Kirk Kerkorian's MGM Corporation purchases the Mirage Corporation and all its properties—including the Golden Nugget of Las Vegas and Laughlin, the Mirage, and the Bellagio.

2000   The new Aladdin Casino opens in Las Vegas.

2000   A casino opens in the Virgin Islands, the first since casinos were approved by voters in 1995.

2000   California voters approve Proposition 1A, which allows Native American casinos with some regulations and limits. The ban on player-banked games in California is lifted.

INTRODUCTION

Gambling in America: An Encyclopedia of History, Issues, and Society examines people, places, events, laws and policies, and concepts concerning gambling as well as gambling equipment. The focus is on gambling in the Western Hemisphere—the Americas. It is recognized, however, that the phenomenon of gambling is global, so entries will treat matters of interest on other continents that do have a bearing on American gambling either directly or for comparative reasons.

The indigenous peoples of the North American and South American continents certainly participated in gambling activities throughout their history prior to European settlement, and their practices form part of the basis of modern-day gambling. Much of the essence of modern gambling in the Americas, however, can be traced to European Old World origins. This gambling has been nurtured and developed by descendants of the European settlers from across the Atlantic. In addition, modern forms of gambling as well as ideas about gambling have also borrowed from African and Asian activities.

Although gambling is indeed worldwide in scope today, gambling activity is driven by such Western Hemisphere forces as entrepreneurs and enterprises. It is appropriate then to build an encyclopedia on gambling around its manifestations in the Americas. In doing so, we are able to cover the most essential concepts. Although there will be specific references to linkages with Old World gambling operations, I will maintain the delimiting geographical framework. Other works cited may be utilized by the reader who wishes to extend a reach beyond these boundaries. I suggest the third edition of *International Casino Law* (Cabot, Thompson, Tottenham, and Braunlich 1999) as a good starting point for orienting a reader with gambling throughout the world.

I use the term *gambling* in the encyclopedia title as well as throughout the text for all entries (unless another term appears in previously published materials). Leaders in the gambling industry today tend to use the word *gaming* instead of *gambling*. They do so for public relations purposes, believing that the word *gaming* has a more pleasant tonal sound and that the word can be associated with the types of play in which every person has participated, for instance, softball, jacks, hopscotch, Monopoly, or checkers. The word is also associated with hunting and fishing. For historical reasons and because the word *gambling* is tied to the word *gamble* instead of the much less identifying word *game,* I use the word *gambling*.

Today opponents of legalized gambling almost invariably use the word *gambling* instead of *gaming*. Proponents use the word *gaming*. In this encyclopedia, my use of *gambling* is not intended to suggest to the reader that I am either a proponent or an opponent of legalized gambling activity. The truth is that I have both supported and opposed various campaigns for legalization of gambling. I purport to have done so with a consistency that is discussed in the text (see especially The Economic Impacts of Gambling; Economics and Gambling).

It is my true desire to present ideas in a neutral and nonbiased way. There is no doubt that in some places individual or selected commentary may imply favoritism or animosity toward gambling activity. Be that as it may, I have striven for objectivity, realizing that at different times the entries may be utilized by both opponents and supporters of gambling.

It is my belief and contention that the words *gambling* and *gaming* are essentially synonymous. For the most part the words have been used to mean the same thing in the law, although debates over usage persist. Other words that have been applied to the gambling phenomenon include *betting, wagering,* and *risk taking.* Again, although the words may carry different connotations for some readers, they all have the same common core elements in their definitions.

The most recent comprehensive dictionary of gambling is *The Dictionary of Gambling and Gaming,* written by the late professor Thomas Clark of the University of Nevada, Las Vegas (Clark 1987). Most definitions of gambling cited by Clark find three elements to be essential in the activity: consideration, chance, and reward. (1) Consideration is the money put up—or staked. It represents something of value. (2) A game involves at least some degree of chance—a randomly occurring risk that may or may not be calculated. (3) A reward is something of value that may be in excess of the value of the consideration. Clark defined *gambling* as "of or pertaining to risking of money or something of value on the outcome of a chance event such as a card or dice game"(Clark 1987, 88). He defined *gaming* as "the playing at games of chance for stakes." *Game* is defined as short for gambling game and in a verb form as "to stake a wager on the outcome of an event, as at cards or dice; to gamble." All the definitions encompass notions of "risk taking," although Clark chose not to offer a definition of *risk.* Additionally, Clark defined a *bet* as "to wager or stake, usually between two parties, on the outcome of an event" (16–17).

The activities he utilized in refined definitions include casino games and horse-racing events. *Wager* is also defined as "a stake placed on the outcome of an event, such as a horse race or hand of a card game or roll of the dice" (Clark 1987, 246).

Again, it is not my point to seek very specific legal distinctions of the terms used most often to describe activity in the games of chance focused upon in this volume. Whether the games involve races, lotteries, bingo, slot machines, cards, dice, or other casino play, the terms may appear interchangeably. The term *gambling,* I repeat, will be the preferred term for use. The text will devote attention to specific aspects of individual games and discuss the notions of skill and luck in their play.

Gambling is a risk-taking activity, but this encyclopedia will not be devoted to a comprehensive discussion of all risk-taking activities. Rather attention is given to risk-taking activities involving games of some chance outcomes, the placing of stakes on the outcomes, and the awarding of prizes for those who have put their money (consideration) on the outcomes that actually occur.

This encyclopedia is not about risky activities such as mountain climbing, sky diving, deep sea diving, surfing, ski jumping, or high speed automobile racing. It is not concerned with business activities and businesspeople who are sometimes described in macho terms as ones who "swim with the sharks." A discussion of investments and trading on securities markets is included in order to make distinctions from (or to point out some similarities with) activities that are more universally described as gambling activities.

Much of the business world devotes attention toward minimizing risky activities. These risky activities may have been a part of the human condition before modern developments occurred. Spencer Johnson recently penned *Who Moved My Cheese,* an interesting book that describes contrasts between modern worlds and worlds of nature—albeit the book comes down on the side of the latter—as a guide for behavior (Johnson 1998). The premise of the book is that two human beings from the civilized world discovered their "cheese"; that is, they discovered what was of value to them. So too did two mice. All lived in comfort, having all that their hearts could possibly desire. One day, however, the stash of cheese upon which they all feasted disappeared—perhaps it was depleted by their excessive consumption, perhaps a stock market crashed, or other "investors" found it.

To briefly recap Johnson's discussion, the reactions of the humans and the mice to the loss of the cheese were quite different. The two little mice were initially stunned, but they soon rushed back out into the cruel world (the "real world") and once again engaged in the risky activity of hunting down "new cheese." The humans reacted differently. After looking at each other in stunned astonishment, they held a discussion (they could think, and they were civilized). They came up with the same thought almost at the same time and expressed it out loud: "Who moved my cheese?" Their subsequent thoughts and activity were ones of complete denial. They thought that they were entitled to the cheese. They wanted reparations of various kinds for having had it taken from them. When one suggested they engage in a new search, the other howled about the risk that they faced if they ventured out into the "real world."

Eventually the two humans split up, and one yielded to his inner feelings and began a new quest for cheese. Perhaps Johnson's story is illustrative of a deep-seated feeling within our genetic makeup that leads us on a quest for a prize, even if that quest involves dangers and unknown factors. Yet society may work against this natural force. We humans often have to first brush aside societal tendencies that tell us to stay in place before we can undertake risk. For other animals the impulse is much closer to their surface behaviors. Perhaps people have an impulse to gamble—to reach out and accept a fate that awaits them if they "let the dice roll."

As a species we have a dichotomous history: We took the risk of hunting, but our civilizing tendencies also urged us to abandon the hunt and settle in one place—to stop searching, to avoid risk and chance. Abt, Smith, and Christiansen began their book on gambling by suggesting that the first gamblers were Adam and Eve in the garden (1985, 1). They took a risk and as a result either won or lost something, but afterward with a new-found knowledge they developed conventions and rules and regulations over their activities.

Over time the games played by people became less and less related to "the hunt" and more and more contrived exercises with artificial rules. Their games were controlled by laws of society. As governments became more formal organizations, the laws of games became more formal as well. Although almost every society ever recognized by anthropologists has had some sort of gambling activity in its games, organized societies also have had rules that either prohibited gambling or limited gambling to specific occasions and specific games.

The story of gambling in the Americas begins with pre-Columbian societies of indigenous peoples, variously called First Nations, American Indians, Indians, Inuits, or Native Americans. These indigenous, original populations had a wide variety of games and contests upon which people would place wagers. They used objects that had similarities to dice, lottery balls, and even cards in the games.

The crews who served with Columbus engaged in card games during his first voyage across the Atlantic. Some accounts suggest that the sailors on the *Pinta, Niña,* and *Santa Maria* became quite fearful as the voyage went on and on and on and land was not sighted. They threw their playing cards overboard, thinking God was punishing them for gambling. Once they found the island of San Salvador and safely stepped onto its shores, however, they quickly made up new decks of cards. The first Europeans to make permanent settlements in North America introduced European games to the continent. Other Europeans that followed also gambled.

Although lottery games were played during the glorious days of ancient Rome, the first government-organized lotteries were conducted in the sixteenth century in the Netherlands and Italy. This form of play spread rapidly, and soon after English colonists settled in Jamestown, Virginia, the lottery was part of their lives. In 1612 a lottery was conducted in London on behalf of the economically struggling colony. Horse racing dates back over six millennia, and betting on the races is probably just as old. Race betting came to the American colonies in the 1660s when a track was built in New York.

Casinos—permanent places for gambling activities in the form of games—were probably in existence in some form during the Roman Empire. They were certainly reestablished during the Renaissance era, and they were exported to the Americas as the European settlers reached the shores of the New World. The casino-type games followed as settlers moved to the interior and then to the west. The games were prominent on riverboats traveling the Mississippi, and western prospectors and miners were drawn to gambling as a leisure activity. They were drawn by cardsharps who saw their gold rush in sleight-of-hand play. Many came to become casino entrepreneurs. Although the thousands of Asian immigrants who were drawn westward by the available work in the mines or on the railroads did not operate open commercial gambling establishments serving the general public, they certainly brought their games and their gambling spirit with them. Many did start clandestine Asian gambling houses that persist even today in large cities.

Professor I. Nelson Rose of Whittier Law College has envisioned legalized gambling in the United States as occurring in three waves (1980). In one generation legal gambling would flourish openly, only to be restricted during an ensuing period of reform. The first wave occurred in the colonial and early nation and was highlighted by widespread lotteries and horse racing. Ironically, a champion of the horse set, President Andrew Jackson, led the cry for the reforms that closed down most of the gambling in the 1830s. The second wave of legal gambling came after the Civil War and was found mostly in southern states eager for revenues that could be secured through lotteries. Horse racing was also revived. The infamous Louisiana Lottery represented the high-water mark of this era. When it was closed down at the turn of the twentieth century along with other gambling in response to the pressures of the Progressive movement (which also sponsored Prohibition), the second wave ended. Although some gambling reemerged during the Great Depression—for instance, horse-race betting and wide-open casino gambling in Nevada—the third wave was truly manifested only after modern government-run lotteries were authorized by the state of New Hampshire in 1963. Canada opened the door to charity and lottery games with a basic change in its criminal code in 1969.

Today all the provinces of Canada as well as the Yukon and the Northwest Territories have lotteries and allow horse racing. The new territory of Nunavut has discussed starting a lottery and participating in other Canadian lotteries. Casino halls are in operation in seven of ten provinces as well as in the Yukon. Machine gambling is permitted in nine provinces.

Some form of gambling is permitted by legal authorities in forty-eight of the fifty states in the United States. Only Utah and Hawaii prohibit all forms, while Tennessee permits horse racing but has no tracks in operation. Eleven states have commercial casinos. Another twenty have casinos on Native American lands within their boundaries.

All other jurisdictions of the Western Hemisphere have gambling. Most have casinos; almost all have lotteries. Horse racing is prevalent, as is cockfighting, in several Latin American countries.

The pervasiveness of gambling activity throughout the millennia of time and across the world suggests that the activity serves some basic functions for the human species as well as for the social order. The gambling phenomenon in its generic as well as its commercial forms may add a vitally needed quality to lives. It may help connect people to a sense of community or to a rationale for existence. Gambling is related to religious experiences in some ways and to magical exercises that allow people to gain a notion that they can have some control over lifetimes that otherwise might seem futile.

Activities encompassed in the modern gambling industry may also present positive economic benefits for a society. Where the activity has become routine and has been organized with commercial ends in mind, gambling can produce jobs for many people. Additionally it is possible that where society gives a legal endorsement to the activity, gambling can become a source of revenues for governments. Legalization can also lead to controls on the activity to ensure its honesty and fairness.

Even though risk taking and game playing are endemic and in ways probably functional for individuals and society, there are dysfunctional aspects to gambling as well. Gambling can become habitual and all-consuming for persons engaging in play. Certain individuals develop pathologies around their gambling behaviors. The pathologies can become destructive to their well-being, leading to financial ruin, physical deterioration, and in some cases self-destruction through suicide. The pathologies also may impose great costs upon the society at large.

Concomitant with the problems of uncontrolled habitual gambling are criminal behaviors that may be associated with gambling. The locations of gambling endeavors become attractive to persons with criminal motivations. Some may sieze opportunities for financial gain by cheating at games; others regard the constant flow of cash in some games as a chance for stealing money. Also, players who lose money at legitimate games may be propelled into thieving behaviors in order to regain their losses. Gambling enterprise also attracts unsavory characters such as loan sharks, prostitutes, and drug dealers. On the other hand, the employment opportunities in the gambling industry can give hope to some individuals who might otherwise be drawn into criminal activities.

The job production and other economic benefits of regulated gambling operations, while obvious, may be offset by economic losses as well. Profits and taxes may be taken away from communities where gambling occurs, causing an overall economic decline in a community.

In a global sense, gambling activity may be beneficial or not beneficial for specific geographical areas, but it is at best a neutral economic phenomenon overall. Wealth changes hands through gambling, but wealth is not created through gambling. Moreover, the critics of gambling argue that the activity engenders certain attitudes that are antithetical to attitudes necessary for the creation of wealth in society. The attitudes that success follows from hard work, delayed gratification, and investments and innovation may be short circuited by contrary notions that success really comes from a lucky roll of the dice or a spin of a wheel or a slot machine reel.

By emphasizing gambling in the Western Hemisphere, I recognize a certain prejudice in my outlook on gambling. I am, after all, writing from Las Vegas, which I recognize as the central gambling community on the globe. The geographical point of view presents an artificial boundary that is certainly not impervious to outside influences. Some of these outside influences will be included in the entries; others will be only mentioned. In selecting the Americas (North, Central, and South) as the main locus of concern, I have manifested a bias in the volume. I have personally explored gambling enterprises in Europe, Asia, North America, Central America, and South America. Events in Europe and Asia have influenced American gambling. At this point, however, it is gambling enterprise in the Americas that is moving most development of operations in many important ways throughout the world. Las Vegas represents the model for commercial casinos everywhere. Important gaming machine technologies come out of the United States. So also do innovations in Canadian and U.S. lotteries direct the course of activities elsewhere. American investments are found in gambling operations throughout the world. Just how dominant American interests are on the world gaming scene is debatable, but the debate will have to take place elsewhere. A bias is recognized, and I will proceed accordingly with the task at hand.

I also recognize that this is not the first encyclopedia of gambling. One would have to go back many years to find the first such effort in this field. Certainly John Scarne's *New Complete Guide to Gambling* in 1986 stands out. More recently, Carl Sifakis prepared a very comprehensive *Encyclopedia of Gambling* (1990). He covered more than games, featuring discussions of properties and personalities as well. Rather than seeking to become a rival for that excellent volume, I recommend it highly. The Sifakis encyclopedia covers gambling throughout the world and also offers the kind of detail on games found in Scarne's work. This encyclopedia complements Sifakis's work by providing more detailed analyses of gambling laws and operations and venues in the Americas as well as providing updated information on many topics that will be found in both encyclopedias.

The items in the encyclopedia are arranged alphabetically. As I found it difficult to scatter information on selected items among several subitems, the subitems are drawn together for a more unified presentation. Hence several items regarding pathological and problem gambling, for instance, appear under the main heading. Before the entries, a chronology of major gambling events is provided. After the entries come two appendixes: one of articles on topics related to gambling and one on law cases. Next comes a Glossary. Following that is an Annotated Bibliography that includes summary (as well as critical) reviews of more than sixty books selected as important books on the subject and books that will be especially helpful to the individual wishing to learn much more about the topic of gambling than can be learned in this volume. Finally, there is a Nonannotated Bibliography.

Abt, Vicki, James F. Smith, and Eugene Martin Christiansen. 1985. *The Business of Risk: Commercial Gambling in Mainstream America.* Lawrence: University Press of Kansas.

Cabot, Anthony N., William N. Thompson, Andrew Tottenham, and Carl Braunlich, eds. 1999. *International Casino Law.* 3d ed. Reno: Institute for the Study of Gambling, University of Nevada, Reno.

Clark, Thomas L. 1997. *The Dictionary of Gambling and Gaming.* Cold Spring, NY: Lexik House Publishers.

Dombrink, John D., and William N. Thompson. 1990. *The Last Resort: Success and Failure in Campaigns for Casinos.* Reno: University of Nevada Press.

Johnson, Spencer. 1998. *Who Moved My Cheese.* New York: G. P. Putnam.

Rose, I. Nelson. 1980. "The Legalization and Control of Casino Gambling." *Fordham Law Review* 8: 245–300.

Sifakis, Carl. 1990. *Encyclopedia of Gambling.* New York: Facts on File.

ACKNOWLEDGMENTS

Just as I have utilized many printed sources in order to put together this encyclopedia, so I have also relied heavily upon the help of many other persons. A great number of these are people I met during travels to examine gambling operations in Asia and Europe as well as throughout North, Central, and South America. Many, many people have helped me as I gathered materials and put this encyclopedia together. I appreciate the important support of my wife, Kay, and family members all—Laura, Tim, Steve, and Siqin, and brothers Bob, John, and Fred, as well as Ruth and Leota, David, Sally, Nellie, and Hermine. They were all neat friends while I was into this project.

I am very appreciative of the help I received from the editors and staff at ABC-CLIO in Denver and Santa Barbara for first inviting me to do this volume, then encouraging me always through the project, providing critical input to the process of writing and organizing, and then producing the final product. Key individuals deserving recognition are Alicia Merritt, Michelle Trader, Vince Burns, Allan Sutton, and Liz Kincaid.

I certainly wish to acknowledge all those who have helped write sections and helped gather materials for sections. Their names appear at the ends of entries. Gracious thanks are offered to my Canadian gambling authorities and helpers, including Colin Campbell in British Columbia; Garry Smith and Harold Wynne in Edmonton, Alberta; Shirley Tomovic in Niagara Falls, Ontario; and Christian Marfels at Dalhousie University in Halifax, Nova Scotia. University of California–Irvine professor John Dombrink's counsel was also prized. I drew extensively upon our coauthored book—*The Last Resort: Success and Failure in Campaigns for Casinos*. The coauthors of *International Casino Law*, especially coeditors attorney Tony Cabot of Lionel, Sawyer and Collins in Las Vegas, London gaming consultant Andrew Tottenham, and Professor Carl Braunlich of Purdue University are thanked.

I wish to note that I have sought to place as complete a set of references for materials in each entry as has been readily available to me. Some entries do not have references, however, and others have incomplete references. Quite frankly, I have gathered and used much uncited information on gambling through my life experiences over the past twenty years. I have personally visited over 500 casinos, and I have conducted interviews with their personnel. Every semester I invite industry representatives to my classes along with gambling regulators. I especially thank Nevada regulators Bill Curran, Steve DuCharme, Bobby Siller, and John O'Reilly. Each year for nearly a decade I have received approximately 200 telephone calls from news media and others interested in my perspectives about various gambling issues in various places. I always probe my callers for information about the gambling situation in their locales. I read gambling journals, both academic and trade, and I follow the gambling industry through various news outlets, including ones on the Internet. I am very grateful that Walter C. Abbott provides me with a daily e-mail collection of newspaper stories on gambling from around the country. I have also consulted for the industry and for others interested in gambling. I have worked for Native American tribes regarding gambling issues in Ontario, Michigan, Wisconsin, Texas, New Mexico, Arizona, California, Montana, Idaho, and Washington. I have given speeches on gambling in over thirty states and provinces. I purposely seek out some of the information on gambling; other information simply comes through osmosis. I suspect that I am trying to make an excuse for not giving the reader better documentation, but any reader who wishes to discuss an entry should feel free to telephone or write me, and I will be glad to give background information.

I should note many others who have been helpful. A note is due in recognition of colleagues at the University of Nevada, Las Vegas (UNLV), including the staff of the Center for Business and Economic Research: Professors Keith Schwer and Mary Riddle, and Bob Potts and Bruce Pencek (two who helped me so much through my inevitable computer glitches and frustrations at being a true computer dummy), and Center support staff Sharon Green, Peggy Jackman, and Eddie Rivera. Other helpful university staff include Mike Geary, Richard Blair, Robert White, and Nicole Koon-Heward. Thanks are offered to Dean Jim Frey and to UNLV Professors Hal Rothman, Eugene Moehring, Vern Mattson, Pat Goodall, Soonhee Kim, Karen Layne, Anna Lukemeyer, Lee Bernick, Bradley S. Wimmer, Darrell Pepper, Bob Boehm, and to soon-to-be-professor Bo Bernhard. I owe a debt of gratitude to former students who worked with me on various gambling research projects. Standing out are Dr. Diana Dever of Mohave College, who worked with me studying Native American gaming; attorneys Craig Kenny and Brad Kenny, who gave research time on gambling operations in Illinois and Louisiana; and David Nichols, whose travels to Latin America were helpful. Jim and Nancy Hoy of Marietta, Ohio, D. John and Carol Holms of Portage, Michigan, and Tony and Linda Juliano of Lansing, Michigan, provided helpful information on Midwest gambling. I also thank Michigan friends George Kempf of Ann Arbor, Clem and Margo Gill of Ann Arbor, Sam and Nancy Morgan of Chelsea, and Leo and Peg Kennedy of East Lansing. Thanks always to Dr. Valerie Lorenz, director of Harbour Center facility for compulsive gamblers, Baltimore, and to Dennis Piotrowski and Roy Kawaguchi of Las Vegas, and Ichiro Tanioka of Osaka, Japan.

I save my special thanks for our librarians, who are truly the sine qua non for all my work. During my entire career these special people have given me the essential support needed to finish term papers, write a thesis and dissertation, and gather materials for myriad research papers and articles. I like librarians. I like the idea that our nation's First Lady is a librarian; so was the "first lady" of my life. My mother was on the staff of the University of Michigan Libraries. Mention a topic, and my mother would be off and running, hunting and gathering until I yelled "Stop!" or more likely, offered her another project needing her assistance. So too have been the librarians of other colleges and universities with which I have been associated as a student and as a professor. At the University of Nevada, Las Vegas (UNLV), we are fortunate to have a Special Collections Library that features works on gambling. Helpful staff members include Kathy War, Jonnie Kennedy, Su Kim Chung, Susan Jarvis, David Schwartz, and director Peter Michel. Librarians Tom Mirkovich and Marta Sorkin of the UNLV Research Library were also of great assistance. Howard Schwartz of the Gambler's Book Club has been almost like another gambling librarian to me over the past two decades.

I reserve my highest measure of thanks for Sidney Watson and Marie White, who have played several roles in my scholarly life—librarians (Maria is the circulation librarian of the University's Lied Library, and Sidney is the director of the Curriculum Materials Library), students (while working full time plus), colleagues, and friends. After Maria and Sidney finished master's degrees in public administration (I was their adviser), they just could not get graduate school out of their systems. They told me they felt something was missing—they had been taking classes and writing research papers for five years, and now it was over. They asked me (out of the blue—no kidding) if I had any project on which they could offer assistance. That was about three months before I had finished my draft of this encyclopedia. I could not believe this "gift from heaven." After a very long pause, I brought up this project. They were off and running, hunting and gathering, but mostly organizing and editing, reading each page once, twice, and more. They helped me gather my many files together, track down bibliographic sources, convert materials from WordPerfect to Word, and back again. And they wrote one section also. Truly their eagerness to contribute was a godsend for me, and I am exceedingly grateful. They even said it was fun—now that might have been a bit too much.

My thanks go to all colleagues, students, family, and friends who have helped me in this quest, but especially to the very important librarians in my life.

Gambling in America

A

Adelson, Sheldon

During the 1990s, Sheldon Adelson became one of the leading entrepreneurs in the gambling industry as the primary developer and owner of the Venetian Casino resort on the Las Vegas Strip.

Adelson was born in 1933 in Boston, the son of a cab driver. He worked hard and studied hard as a youth. He received a bachelor's degree in real estate and corporate finance from the City University of New York. After a period of service in the United States Army, Adelson set upon a plan to make himself fabulously rich. He succeeded more than one time. As a venture capitalist in the 1960s, he acquired scores of companies, only to see his budding financial empire fall as the stock market took a plunge in 1969. He came back by developing a series of trade shows, the most important of which was COMDEX, the leading computer dealers' exposition, and by the 1980s, the leading annual convention in Las Vegas each year. The success of the show led to other ventures such as developing airlines. That success also focused his attention upon Las Vegas. The convention was a gold mine for Adelson, but even Las Vegas did not have enough convention space. He privately built a facility next to the Las Vegas Convention Center and gave it to the county, realizing that his revenues from his big show would cover his capital costs in a few years. But he wanted more—his own convention center.

The Venetian Casino owned by Sheldon Adelson is the first two-billion-dollar casino property anywhere.

In the late 1980s, Sheldon Adelson was able to finance the purchase of the Sands Casino Hotel from its owner, Kirk Kerkorian. In 1989, it was licensed by the Nevada Gaming Commission, and Adelson became a casino magnate. Actually he was just holding on to the property waiting for something bigger. In 1993, he built the Sands Exposition Center, a one-million-square-foot convention facility on the Sands property. But he was still waiting for something bigger. His chance to "do something" with the Sands came in 1995 when he was able to sell the COMDEX show and sixteen other trade shows for $860 million. The next year he imploded (blew up) the Sands, and he devoted his new resources to the construction of the Venetian Hotel. The Venetian opened in April 1999 with a 113,000-square-foot casino, a shopping mall set alongside canals with gondolas, and 500,000 feet of new convention space. The hotel's thirty-three-story tower and 3,000 rooms featured luxuries not found elsewhere. The basic room was over 700 square feet, making it the largest standard room for a hotel anywhere. The total square footage of the rooms actually exceeded that of the MGM Grand, with its 5,009 rooms. The facility had a first-phase price tag of $1.5 billion "plus." The "plus" was the result of the fact that others paid the price. Adelson leased all the space for shops and restaurants, keeping only the casino, hotel, and meeting areas under his financial control. As the new century began, the revenues for the casino were meeting all expectations and then some, and Adelson was planning a phase-two construction of a museum and a new casino and hotel tower with 3,036 rooms adjacent to the Venetian.

Sources: Burbank, Jeff. 2000. *License to Steal: Nevada's Gaming Control System in the Megaresort Age.* Reno: University of Nevada Press, 128–135.

Africa

Africa, the world's largest continent, with 20 percent of the land mass of the world, includes more than fifty nation states. Almost all permit some gambling activities, lotteries, and racing, and about half allow casino gambling. Casinos in the various regions of Africa differ considerably. In the

northern African Muslim countries there are limited numbers of casinos: two in Morocco, one in Tunisia, and fourteen in Egypt. Local residents of Egypt may not enter the country's casinos, as they are specifically designed to attract foreign currency from tourists and foreign businessmen. The casinos are in major hotels; they require identification for entrance and impose dress codes. Egypt is one of the few African jurisdictions where casinos are lucrative investments.

The other area of Africa where casino gambling is attracting considerable interest is South Africa. Prior to the establishment of full democracy, the government of the Union of South Africa had a firm ban on casino gambling. That all changed in 1993 and 1994. A newly elected congress passed an act establishing lotteries and gambling. In 1996, a National Gambling Act was passed. The act created a board that was empowered to draw up rules for the creation of forty new casinos. Licensing began in 1999. Prior to the new eras of multiracial democracy, casinos had been permitted in the segregated areas known as "homelands." The Sun City casino organization had been instrumental in establishing several casinos in the four areas that have now been integrated into South Africa under the new constitution.

East Africa has casinos that also seek to market to tourists. For instance, in Zambia there are seven casinos, with two at Victoria Falls. The other casinos are in international hotels. Kenya has twelve casinos in the capital city area of Nairobi and another nine in the coastal resort of Mombasa, all of which are quite small. There are also casinos on the tourist islands of Seychelles, Reunion, Madagascar, and Mauritius, as well as in Ethiopia, Djibouti, and Uganda. Without tourism, the casinos could not be profitable, as local populations are extremely poor.

Such is also the case with the properties in West Africa, which are found in countries such as Benin, Cameroon, Congo, Gabon, Gambia, Ghana, Liberia, Niger, and Nigeria. Senegal, Zaire, Togo, Senegal, and Sierra Leone have also had casinos, although one has to wonder how gambling activities can proceed within the atmosphere of national, political, and economic disintegration that is all too often present in some of these countries.

Casinos in very poor countries have trouble developing markets. Their ability to recruit casino staff is limited by workforce deficiencies, coupled with national rules demanding that locals be hired. These would often be locals with political connections that precluded their being properly trained or supervised and making it unthinkable that they could be disciplined if they violated the trust that must go with casino jobs. Where there are workforces in place, casino operators find that it is necessary to pay workers every day, as they might not return to work for several weeks if they received a large labor payment. A shocking sight witnessed by more than one European casino owner has been a group of local residents coming to a casino and pooling their wealth so that they could make a single pull on a slot machine handle. In Togo, the national government was so poor that it could not provide sufficient coinage to use in the operation of the slot machines. Most of the African countries between the northern Muslim region and the new South Africa state are in desperate need of economic development, but casino gambling is simply not the tool they need to establish economies that can participate in the global economy.

Sources: Cabot, Anthony N., William N. Thompson, Andrew Tottenham, and Carl Braunlich, eds. 1999. *International Casino Law.* 3d ed. Reno: Institute for the Study of Gambling, University of Nevada, Reno, 483–511.

Alabama

Even though Mobile, the first city of Alabama, has had a rich history of pirates, houses of ill repute, Mardi Gras celebrations, and gambling dens of inequity, most sinful activities in the state have been effectively suppressed in modern times. One major exception was the illegal enterprises of Phoenix City, which during and after World War II catered to a clientele made up mostly of soldiers from nearby Fort Benning. A major cleanup was instituted in the 1950s by state attorney general John Patterson. Patterson was propelled into the crackdown activity after his father, a candidate for attorney general at the time, was murdered by local mobsters who were running the town. In 1954 John Patterson was elected in place of his father.

Gambling activity resurfaced in the 1980s; however, it now operated on a legal basis—for the most part. Charitable games were permitted under the control of local governments, and the state also authorized the establishment of dog- and horse-race betting. The largest track in the state opened near Birmingham, and it pioneered an unusual event. The track featured both dog and horse racing on the same day and on the same card. The experiment with racing was not overly successful, as it was initiated just a few years before the state of Mississippi authorized commercial casino gambling as well as Native American casino gambling. Several of these facilities were near the Alabama border. Also, two other states bordering Alabama—Florida and Georgia—started very active lottery games that drew players from Alabama. The Alabama Porch Creek tribe of Native Americans led by Eddie Tullis reacted to the new gambling ventures by creating two large bingo halls and by seeking a compact for casino games. State officials refused to negotiate a casino compact, but the tribe began using gambling machines anyway.

As the twentieth century ended, the legislature gave serious consideration to legalizing new forms of gambling, including table games, and machine gambling for racetracks. There are now four dog tracks in existence, as Birmingham closed its horse-race activities. The legislature was able to authorize a public vote on the question of having a state lottery. In 1998, the governor was elected on a platform that included the lottery proposal. In October 1999, however, the voters of the state shocked not only Alabama but also the whole nation when they said no to the lottery by a vote of 54.3 percent to 45.7 percent. The lottery proposal was designed to duplicate the Georgia experience in that it designated revenues for a plan of free college scholarships for Alabama high school graduates with good records. With the negative vote, Alabama became only the second state (the other being North Dakota) to receive a negative vote on a state-operated lottery proposal.

Sources: "Bible Belt Suffers Big Losses on Gambling Issue." *Crossfire.* CNN Television, 15 October 1999; Peck, John. "Focus Helps CALL Leader Lure Churches to Activism." *Birmingham Times,* 17 October 1999, 1;

www.ag.auburn.edu/ads/ExtPrograms/horsebreeding (and racing).

Alaska

Native Alaskans and Native Americans in Alaska conduct bingo operations. There are also many bingo games sponsored by charitable organizations. Much of the revenue for the games' sponsors comes from the sale of pull-tab tickets. Alaska permits many raffle-type games for a variety of nonprofit interests. One of the most interesting games allows people to pick the time for the first breakup of ice floes in the spring each year. In recent years there has been interest in developing some casino gambling. The proposals for increased gambling have not found support in the legislature, however, or among the general population. In 1990, a ballot initiative to permit limited stakes casino games in bars and taverns was soundly defeated by a 60 percent to 40 percent margin.

Sources: Thompson, William N. 1997. *Legalized Gambling: A Reference Handbook.* 2d ed. Santa Barbara, CA: ABC-CLIO, 163–166, 186; www.AlaskaInterior/NenanalceClassic.html; www.gov.state.ak.us/elections.

Alberta

Alberta can lay claim to having the first legalized casino gaming in Canada, albeit in a temporary form. In 1967 the provincial government initiated several laws that seemed to open the door to casino games even though they were forbidden by the Penal Code. In the summer, during the Edmonton Exhibition, the Silver Slipper Saloon was opened as part of the two-week celebration. The general manager of the exhibition later indicated that he had taken payoffs from the carnival company that ran the games, that is, the Silver Slipper. Amendments to the national code in 1969 helped regulate Alberta gaming. The attorney general took control over licensing charitable bingo games and raffles. In 1975, the attorney general's office opened the door to casinos once again as it first approved a casino for a charity event supporting a summer camp. A license was then given for a casino at the Calgary Stampede. A flood of applications for casino events overwhelmed the attor-

ney general, and he quickly created a special Gaming Control Section to regulate the gaming. Rules were set into place over the next two years. In 1981, a new Alberta gaming commission took over all licensing powers.

As gaming developed, Alberta adopted the model used in British Columbia. Charities could have casino events, but they had to be held in permanent facilities that were operated by private parties. In the 1990s, the number of such facilities grew to nearly a score. There are five casinos in Edmonton; four in Calgary, and others spread around the province. Until 1998 they were not allowed to have slot machine gaming, and the charities paid a fixed fee for having an event. When the government installed machines, a new revenue division based upon play was instituted. As the government owns the machines, it keeps a majority of machine revenues. Although no serious consideration is being given to the creation of large commercial casinos, proposals have been made for wide-open, large-scale casino gaming on the First Nations reserve lands.

Alberta has many other types of gambling, including all forms of pari-mutuel operations, both on-track and offtrack. Raffles and pull tabs are sold by charities. The most prevalent form of gambling, however, is found in the bars and taverns of the province. By 1999 more than 6,000 video lottery terminals were operating in 1,200 locations, producing about $300 million in revenue, which is about 70 percent of the gaming revenue produced in the province. In that year the popular machines (which provide an average gaming revenue of $50,000 a year) accounted for a per capita gaming participation of about $1,300 per adult, the largest in Canada and North America, with the exception of Nevada. Studies have also revealed that Albertans have the highest rate of problem gambling in Canada. Efforts to ban the terminals have been concerted, with local elections called in 1998 in most of the cities. Only in a few smaller cities did the voters choose to ban the machines.

—coauthored by Garry Smith

Sources: Cabot, Anthony N., William N. Thompson, Andrew Tottenham, and Carl Braunlich, eds. 1999. *International Casino Law.* 3d ed. Reno: Institute for the Study of Gambling, University of Nevada, Reno,

172–173; McCall, William W. 1989. "Operational Review of Gaming in Alberta 1978 to 1987." In *Gambling in Canada: Golden Goose or Trojan Horse?* edited by Colin Campbell and John Lowman, 77–92. Burnaby, B.C.: Simon Fraser University; Smith, Garry, Bonnie Williams, and Robert Pitter. 1989. "How Alberta Amateur Sports Groups Prosper through Legalized Gambling." In *Gambling in Canada: Golden Goose or Trojan Horse?* edited by Colin Campbell and John Lowman, 323–333. Burnaby, B.C.: Simon Fraser University.

Alberta Gaming Research Institute. *See* Gaming Institutes: Research and Political

American Gaming Association. *See* Gaming Institutes: Research and Political

Antigua

Antigua and Barbuda, in the Leeward Islands of the West Indies, constitute an island nation that was formerly under the control of Great Britain. The government allows casino gambling, bingo halls, horse-race betting, a lottery, offtrack betting, and sports betting on the Internet. There are five casinos in the capital city of St. John's and one in the city of Deep Bay. The minister of finance licenses all the casinos. A license may be given to any person who owns a hotel that markets rooms to tourists.

The Antiguan government encourages casino development and is willing to offer new licenses to those wishing to start casinos. Larger hotels pay an annual licensing fee of $300,000; smaller hotels pay $100,000. Additionally they pay a tax of 15 percent of their gaming revenue. Although local residents may come to the casinos, the casinos are prohibited from advertising gaming to the local public.

In 1985, one of the largest properties, the Halcyon Cove, instituted a small gambling junket program in which tourists fly in from cities in the United States on inclusive tours. Because checking credit players incurs an element of risk, the Halcyon Cove does not subscribe to a credit check service based in the United States (unlike other junket destinations in the Caribbean). Therefore, to ensure against potential problems, the hotel has received written guarantees from junket organizers, who cover debts owed by the players they bring to the casino.

In operating the casinos on Antigua, the gaming management must realize that vacationers do not travel to the island in order to gamble. They come to relax, rest, and enjoy the weather and scenery. Gambling is only one amenity to fulfill the entertainment needs of the guests. It is not a major profit center for the management or government.

Sources: Cabot, Anthony N., William N. Thompson, Andrew Tottenham, and Carl Braunlich, eds. 1999. *International Casino Law.* 3d ed. Reno: Institute for the Study of Gambling, University of Nevada, Reno, 236–237.

Argentina

Argentina has all major forms of gambling: casinos, slot machine parlors, lotteries, bingo halls, racetracks, and a variety of lotteries. The 34 million citizens occupy a land base about one-third the size of the United States. The country is divided into twenty-eight provinces, plus the national district of Buenos Aires City. Both the provinces and the national government have authorized lotteries, casinos, and other forms of gambling. Until the 1990s, the government operated almost all of the gambling; since then a privatization drive has brought many new casino organizations to the country, upgrading that form of gambling. Until very recently, no casino gambling was allowed in the national city of Buenos Aires; however, a dockside ship now offers over 300 slot machines and nearly fifty tables for gamers.

Casino gaming has been common in Argentina, starting in colonial days of the eighteenth and early nineteenth centuries when viceroys from Spain governed the land. At that time and even after national independence in 1810, casinos were privately owned and locally licensed. This structure of minimal regulation and local control changed drastically in the mid-twentieth century.

As in most Latin American politics, a chief executive and his appointed council, as opposed to a broad representative legislative chamber, control

A view of Mar Del Plata, the largest casino in South America, located 200 miles south of Buenos Aires.

government. This pattern of executive rule derives from colonial traditions and cultural expectations. Military governments also have been common in the region. Argentina's governmental structures fit these patterns. In 1943, General Edelmiro Farrell assumed the role of "keeper of the national conscience" after deposing the civilian government. His selected council included General Juan Peron, who was the minister of war, the vice president, and the secretary of labor. General Peron succeeded to the presidency as the head of the new Argentine Labor party in 1946. His election resulted from widespread support from the working classes and the Catholic Church. He remained the leader and virtual dictator until other military officers deposed him in 1955. Many changes occurred under the leadership of Farrell and Peron, including the structure of casino operations. Peron advanced industrialization programs requiring increased national control at the expense of provincial powers. He also fostered public ownership of enterprise.

In 1944, a presidential decree closed all private casinos in Argentina. The national government controlled all casinos from then on. One consequence of this action, remaining to this day, was the closure of casinos in the national capital city of Buenos Aires and its suburbs. This decision influenced the development of South American gaming. Casinos in Argentina, Uruguay, Chile, Ecuador, Colombia, and Surinam now market their properties to wealthy Buenos Aires players. The other major target area is Brazil, which also lacks legal casinos.

The National Lottery Administration (La Lotteria de Beneficial) has operated a national drawing since 1893. It now oversees the publicly owned casinos for the national government. In 1947 the administration created a casino commission to direct operations. The commission consists of representatives of the Ministries of Finance and Labor and the National Bank.

The first casinos authorized to be part of this organization opened in the beach resorts in the province of Buenos Aires, about 200 miles from the capital city. Casinos operating as private casinos in Mar del Plata, Necochea, and Miromar (December 1944) continued as national government casinos. In 1945, the government nationalized the casino at Termas de Rio Hondo, a hot springs resort in the province of Santiago del Estero. A decree in 1946 reiterated that all casinos were under the jurisdiction of the national government but recognized that provinces could prohibit gaming within their borders.

The international hotel overlooking the Iguasu Falls on the Argentina-Brazil border.

Despite a decree in 1947 that placed the National Lottery Administration under the minister of the interior, two years later the minister of finance assumed the responsibility. Casino revenues were to be spent on social work, health, and urban sanitation programs. Later additions to the list of gaming recipients were schools, universities, local governments, tourism programs, medical foundations, and the Eva Peron Foundation. The government set admission charges for players and fees for exchanging checks and purchasing chips. In 1951, the government assessed a fee of 0.5 percent of the drop but later eliminated it.

The national casino system expanded by nationalization of a private casino in Mendoza in 1947 and the creation of a casino annex at Mar del Plata in 1949. In 1954, casinos opened at the snow skiing and lakes resort of Bariloche in Rio Negro Province and at Termas de Reyes in Jujuy Province. Another casino opened at Termas de Rosario de la Frontera in Salta Province in 1959.

In 1963, a national casino opened at the edge of the great Iguazu Falls in Misiones Province. Casinos came to Alta Gracia and La Cumbre in Cordoba Province in 1971. The provinces of Corrientes and Chaco and the city of Parana in Entre Rios Province received authorizations for casinos in 1972. In the same year, a new national casino opened in the seaside resort of Piromar in Buenos Aires Province. Later in the decade, the remote coastal cities of Rivadavia and Puerto Madryn in Chubut Province and the interior city of Tandil in Buenos Aires Province established casinos. A seasonal casino in the oceanside resort of Las Grutas in Rio Negro Province also began operations.

After the fall of the final Peron government in the mid-1950s, the interior provinces tried to reassert autonomy over many public policy areas previously dominated by Peron officials. Several provinces wanted their casinos back.

In 1960, the national casino at Mendoza closed, and the provincial government assumed control of gaming. In 1961, the casino at Termas de Rio Honda was transferred to the provincial government of Santiago del Estero. In 1962, a presidential decree authorized provincial participation in all revenues from the national casinos. Subsequently, the provinces acquired the casinos in Salta and Jujuy. These and other provincial governments started province-operated casinos. The interior provinces of San Luis, San Juan, La Rioja, Tucuman, Santa Fe, Misiones, and Corrientes now have such casinos.

A movement toward privatization on a national level began in the mid-1980s. The public treasuries of the nation faced trouble from Argentina's continuing economic crisis. The incentives for

The Salta Argentina Casino.

levels. Other new private casinos were also authorized, and the Mirage organization of Las Vegas was instrumental in starting a major facility at Iguasu Falls at the Brazilian border.

The National Lottery Administration also controls and administers other gaming. A major track near Buenos Aires offers horse racing. Three tracks along with fifty offtrack betting facilities had a total handle of around $300 million a year in 1997, the most recent year for which information is available. Another form of legal gaming is parlay betting on soccer games. The administration also offers various lottery products. Additionally, the provincial governments run lottery operations.

—coauthored by Andrew Tottenham

Sources: Cabot, Anthony N., William N. Thompson, Andrew Tottenham, and Carl Braunlich, eds. 1999. *International Casino Law.* 3d ed. Reno: Institute for the Study of Gambling, University of Nevada, Reno, 277–284.

Arizona

In 1908, all gambling activity was banned in Arizona Territory in an effort to win congressional support for statehood. By mid-century, the state of Arizona had legalized pari-mutuel horse-race and dog-race betting and had also established active charity gambling operations. The state has also had a lottery since 1991. When Las Vegas Nights were authorized, commercial gambling suppliers actually took slot machines around to the events. The state also permitted the sale of slot machines, and in the 1980s, several businesses were importing used machines from Nevada and repairing and reselling them throughout the country. The businesses were supplying many of the machines to illegal operators, yet the state took no direct actions to stop the sales.

The many Native American tribes of the state were therefore set back when the state refused to negotiate a compact for casino gambling. After several years of legal maneuvering, the tribes won a federal court order mandating negotiations, and in the early 1990s tribal bingo halls were converted into tribal casinos. Eventually over twenty tribes established casinos; the largest ones, in the Phoenix area, are operated by the Ft. McDowell, Ah-Chin, and Salt River Pima tribes.

generating revenues by sales of casino properties were present.

The central government negotiated with the province of Rio Negro to transfer the national casino at Bariloche. In the early 1980s, the government of Mendoza Province had been anxious for resort developments. Ernesto Lowenstein saw the possibility of developing a world-class ski resort at Las Lenas on the edge of the Andes. In exchange for taking a risk with his development, he asked for a casino concession. The province was happy to comply with his desires. The resort opened in 1985, and two years later, a casino began operations. The Lowenstein Resort Company owns the casino, which Casinos Austria operates under a management contract. In 1989, the provincial government granted a second private casino concession to the developers of the new Ora Verde Hotel in Mendoza City. These two private casinos, the first in over forty years in Argentina, were the impetus for the privatization of the existing government casinos at both the national and provincial

Sources: Dombrink, John D., and William N. Thompson. 1990. *The Last Resort: Success and Failure in Campaigns for Casinos.* Reno: University of Nevada Press, 158–161; Thompson, William N. 1997. *Legalized Gambling: A Reference Handbook.* 2d ed. Santa Barbara, CA: ABC-CLIO, 165.

Arkansas

In terms of legal gambling, Arkansas is best known for the Oaklawn Park horse racing track in Hot Springs and also for a dog track in West Memphis. Yet the real story of gambling in Arkansas involves wide-open illegal casinos in Hot Springs (in Garland County) that operated for over a century with connections to many of the leading mobsters in the land. In the mid-1950s, reform governor Orval Faubus sought to close down the gaming. Local Garland County judges overruled his efforts, however, and Faubus dropped the issue. After a staunch antigambling Baptist minister was elected to the legislature, the issue was reopened. He pushed a resolution demanding that the governor shut down the casinos. In 1963 the governor responded. After he did so, the citizens of Hot Springs circulated petitions to legalize casinos. The question was put on the ballot in 1964. The campaign for casinos was led by the local chamber of commerce; however, it was opposed by both Faubus and his 1964 opponent, Winthrop Rockefeller. Arguments that the state could experience a financial windfall from casinos fell on deaf ears, and the voters defeated casinos by a vote of 318,000 to 215,000. The doors of the casinos have been closed since then, but the casino proponents keep trying to win public support. In 1984, another petition was presented to the voters. Again, Garland County residents led the campaign. The state's young governor, Bill Clinton, opposed it. His wife, Hillary, led the campaign against casinos with a statewide speaking tour. Voters said no by a 71 percent to 29 percent margin. In 1996, voters said no again by the same overwhelming margin. This time, the appeal had been not to produce state revenues but rather to meet the competition from riverboat casinos in surrounding states. The dreams of returning to the glory days of gangsters and excitement in Hot Springs remain, but

all the gambling is confined to the short racing season each summer.

A proposal was put forth in the 2000 election that would have allowed six counties to have local option votes on casino gambling. The voters of Arkansas defeated casinos one more time.

Sources: Dombrink, John D., and William N. Thompson. 1990. *The Last Resort: Success and Failure in Campaigns for Casinos.* Reno: University of Nevada Press, 144–151; Rose, I. Nelson. "2000 Election Results." www.gamblingandthelaw.com.

Aruba

Aruba has been the most successful casino jurisdiction in the southern Caribbean. The island, now an independent nation, lures tourists who enjoy the warm climate along with gaming opportunities. Casinos reach into South America, particularly to Venezuela, for players. Many people also come to Aruba from the United States via the gambling junkets offered by the casinos. The lack of adequate lodging, however, limits the potential for gaming development. Profit margins are small, as expenses are very large. Also the government extracts a 2 percent drop tax, meaning that when a player buys $100 in chips, the casino is obligated to pay a tax of $2. That amount is rather high. In addition, there is a gross gaming tax.

The casinos of Aruba are self-regulated; the island nation has no gaming board. The Ministry of Justice provides inspectors who monitor the doors of the casinos to ensure that no persons younger than eighteen years of age enter.

Sources: Cabot, Anthony N., William N. Thompson, Andrew Tottenham, and Carl Braunlich, eds. 1999. *International Casino Law.* 3d ed. Reno: Institute for the Study of Gambling, University of Nevada, Reno, 234–235.

Asia

From my studies and personal observations, I believe that the Asian continent has produced the world's best gamblers. Persons of Asian heritage attack the games of the casinos all over the world with a vigor and zest not found coming from other ethnic groups. The explanations for Asians' love of gambling are explored in Appendix A in the section "The Best Gamblers in the World." Here we consider the irony that the most prevalent religions of the Asian continent—Muslim, Hindu, Buddhist, and Shinto—all frown upon gambling activity. The religious activities have greatly limited the scope of legal gambling that is permitted, although there are exceptions to the rule. Many countries permit lotteries and horse racing. The major jurisdictions—indeed the two most populous countries in the world, China and India—totally ban gambling, however. (The enclave known as Macao is now part of China, and its casino gambling will be reviewed over the next few years by authorities in an effort to decide whether it will stay or go. *See* Macao.) India has allowed gambling boats, and there are also horse racing tracks and lotteries, but there is no casino gambling.

In the area known as Asia Minor (and the Middle East), Turkey has had casinos since 1969. The legality of the facilities has been under constant scrutiny, however, and the gambling has not been able to be focused toward any societal goals such as economic development. For many decades before the 1970s, Lebanon offered the finest casino in the Middle East. Internal warfare totally destroyed the entertainment value of gambling in the country. When the Palestine state gained a measure of sovereignty in the 1990s, it authorized a casino that sought much of its patronage from Israeli citizens.

Nepal has small casinos for foreign visitors to the hotels in Kathmandu. Most of their patrons are Indians. The only other casinos on the soil of mainland Asia are in Korea. Casinos have operated there since 1967 as a way to attract foreign capital. Local residents are not permitted into the casinos. Among the foreign patronage are the 40,000 U.S. military personnel stationed in the country.

A government organization in the Philippines runs twelve casinos. Additionally, the organization has contracts with foreign investors who operate private casinos in several large hotels. The Philippines have not been subjected to the religious restraints of most of the Asian countries, as the islands were under Spanish and U.S. control with strong, gambling-tolerant Catholic influences for nearly four centuries before independence came in 1946.

Malaysia offers an interesting casino environment. The Genting Highlands resort, located thirty-five miles from the capital city of Kuala Lumpur, is the only permitted casino. It has been in operation since 1970, with a complex of 3,500 hotel rooms and 200,000 square feet of casino space. Until the Las Vegas MGM and Foxwoods in Connecticut opened casinos in the 1990s, Genting Highlands was the largest casino in the world. (Indeed, when the Pequot tribe of Native Americans wished to build Foxwoods, it was refused financing by every U.S. source because it was too big a risk. The tribe eventually received its loan from the Genting Highlands Gaming Corporation.) As the Muslim faction among the Malaysian population has considerable political influence, it has permitted the casino only under the condition that only non-Muslim Malaysian residents may enter the casino. The Muslim religious organization is allowed to patrol the casino with a police arm. It has the authority to drag out any local Muslims it finds, and the religious authorities mete out punishment.

Japan offers many gambling experiences; however, casinos as such are not permitted. The Japanese government lottery is the largest single lottery in the world in terms of revenues. There is also horse racing. Unique forms of gambling include pari-mutuel wagering on bicycle and motorboat racing. Although there are no gambling halls with casino table games, there are 18,000 gambling halls featuring machines. Most of the machines are pachinko machines (*see* Japan and Pachinko).

Sources: Cabot, Anthony N., William N. Thompson, Andrew Tottenham, and Carl Braunlich, eds. 1999. *International Casino Law.* 3d ed. Reno: Institute for the Study of Gambling, University of Nevada, Reno, 515–540.

Atlantic City. *See* New Jersey (and Atlantic City Casinos)

The Atlantic Lottery Corporation

The four Maritime or Atlantic provinces of Canada—New Brunswick, Newfoundland, Nova Scotia, and Prince Edward Island—joined together in 1976 to form the Atlantic Lottery Corporation. The purpose of the corporation is to serve as a central marketing agency for lottery products in the provinces. An eight-member board of directors is composed of two representatives from each province. The corporation offers several different games, including traditional weekly and daily draws, instant games, and lotto games.

Sources: Cabot, Anthony N., William N. Thompson, Andrew Tottenham, and Carl Braunlich, eds. 1999. *International Casino Law.* 3d ed. Reno: Institute for the Study of Gambling, University of Nevada, Reno, 170.

Australian Institute for Gambling Research. *See* Gaming Institutes: Research and Political

B

Baccara, Chemin de Fer, and Baccarat-type Games

There are several variations of a game called baccara. The word *baccara* means "zero" in Italian. The game originated in Italy and developed during the Middle Ages. The game was exported to France, where it became known as *baccarat* and also as *chemin de fer*. The latter term means "railroad" and refers to the fact that the bank for the traditional game was passed around the table from player to player. Other variations of the game are called *punto banco* and minibaccarat.

Although the manner of play in the games varies, the strategy is quite similar. The goal of all the games is to get a series of two or three cards that total 9 in value or as close to 9 as possible. The side that is closer to 9 wins the game. Cards are typically drawn from a six-deck shoe. Cards are alternately given face down to one side, called the "bank," and to the other side, called the "player." The cards are then turned over—first the player's cards, then the bank's cards. The ace is counted as 1; each numbered card is counted as its value, except for the ten, which is counted as 0; the face cards are counted as 0. When the numbers are added up, 10 (or 20) is subtracted from any number over 9 (or 19). If the player's first two cards add up to 8 or 9, it is considered a "natural," and no more cards are drawn for either side. The bank's cards are revealed, and the winner is determined. If both hands have the same number, it is a tie. If the player's hand is not a natural, the bank hand is examined to be sure it is not a natural. If it is a natural, there is no draw for the player's hand. The player's hand draws another card if the hand adds up to 0, 1, 2, 3, 4, or 5. If the player's hand adds up to 6 or 7, it gets no more cards. Whatever the player's hand has, the bank must draw if it has a 0, 1, or 2. It stands on a 7, and of course on a natural

8 or 9. If the bank has a 3, 4, 5, or 6, it takes cards depending upon the cards of the player. In the baccarat game played in most casinos today, there are absolutely no possibilities for deviating from these rules. In some variations of the game, there is an option of drawing or standing when the player's hand is 5.

The games now played find all players betting against the house—against the casino. The players may bet either that the bank hand wins or that the player hand wins. Players receive even-money payoffs if their bets are correct. If there is a tie, neither hand wins or loses. The players may also wager on a tie, however, and they are paid eight to one if the game is a tie.

In some European casinos now as well as traditionally, there would be a double table for baccarat. This game gives the casino dealer a degree of discretion. Three hands are dealt. One hand, the bank hand, is the casino's hand. Two hands—one for each side of the table—are designated as player's hands. The casino (bank) competes one-on-one against each of the player's hands. In this game the casino patron may bet only on the player's hand at his side of the table. As the player's hands are revealed (both before the bank's hand is revealed—except to check for naturals), the casino dealer must then within strict limits decide whether to play in a way to maximize winning against one or the other side of the table. The dealer considers the amounts wagered at each end of the table if choices are possible to draw or stand.

Casinos in the United States use only a single-table baccarat table for games, although players are spread all around the table. In the commonly played game (which is universally played in the United States), the players who bet on the bank and win must pay a 5 percent commission fee on the amount of their winnings. With this commis-

Frank Sinatra dealing Baccarat at the Sands, 1959. (UNLV Special collections)

sion, that casino maintains a 1.17 percent advantage over the player who bets on the bank and a 1.36 percent advantage over players betting on the player hand. In the European chemin de fer game, the advantage actually belongs to one of the patrons at the table. He or she bets against all other players, who must bet on the player's hand. That patron keeps the bank as long as the bank hand wins. On each such bank win, however, he or she must give the casino a 5 percent commission on all winnings. It is in this game that the player hand (actually played by the largest bettor against the bank) has the option of standing or playing on a five.

There is also a popular variation of the baccarat game that is played at a small table (the size of a blackjack table). All players face the dealer, who handles all the cards, dealing both hands, turning over the cards of each hand, and making set bets without any options. A minibaccarat game typi-

cally allows low-stake bets, whereas the casino baccarat game has gained a reputation for being the casino's most elegant game, as it has the highest table limits permitted in the casino.

Except when played at the minitable, there is great ritual at the baccarat game. Cards are turned over by the player (one player in turn represents the player's hand) with great suspense. The casino's dealers mimic this style as they reveal the bank's hand and then draw new cards. Casinos find the highest bets at these tables. The highest rollers to be found in the world gravitate to the baccarat tables of the leading casinos. They may play several hundreds of thousands of dollars per hand. The games are favored especially by the most wealthy Asian and European players wherever they may be found. The games may be separated from other tables by ropes. Dealers wear tuxedos at baccarat tables, but only standard casino uniforms at others. In European casinos where drinks and food are not allowed on casino floors, exceptions are made for the baccarat players.

System players using simple methods, ranging from the Martingale strategy to much more elaborate schemes, also seek out the baccarat tables for their even-money bets, as these tables offer the best odds to players on even-money choices. Casinos compete with each other to win the loyalty of the baccarat high rollers. Gifts of every type imaginable are offered to these special players. From month to month, Las Vegas Strip casinos see their bottom-line revenues go up and down considerably, depending upon how much is played at the baccarat tables and whether or not one or several of the richest players hit a prolonged winning streak. Occasionally, a casino will experience a monthly loss because of a run of player luck at baccarat. This cannot be said of any other game (unless there is cheating). Another attraction of the baccarat table is that the players can act as a social group and bet together—whether on the bank or player—and can cheer and console each other, as the case may be.

Sources: Miller, Len. 1983. Gambling Times Guide to Casino Games. Secaucus, NJ: Lyle Stuart, 157–160; Scarne, John. 1986. Scarne's New Complete Guide to Gambling. New York: Simon and Schuster, 459–489; Sifakis, Carl. 1990. Encyclopedia of Gambling. New York: Facts on File, 10–15; Silberstang, Edwin. 1980. Playboy's Guide to Casino Gambling. Chicago: Playboy Press, 349–448.

Baccarat-type Games. *See* Baccara, Chemin de Fer, and Baccarat-type Games

Backgammon. See Craps and Other Dice Games

The Bahamas

The Bahamas consist of two islands with population concentrations (Nassau on New Providence Island and Freeport on Grand Bahamas Island) and many smaller islands, the closest ones lying about fifty miles off the Atlantic coast of Florida.

The country was under the political control of Great Britain until 1973. Tourism has been the dominant product of the islands for most of the past century. The islands' resorts now employ over 40 percent of the workforce. Casino properties dominate the tourist offerings.

Prior to the 1960s, there was very little gambling in the Bahamas. The Penal Code in colonial statutes declared all gambling to be illegal. In the 1920s, however, the small Bahamian Club opened in Nassau on New Providence Island, having been given an exemption by the governor. Another small casino won an exemption to operate on the tiny island of Cat Key. Efforts to establish major casino facilities had been advanced by Sir Stafford Sands as early as 1945. Sands was a private attorney seeking opportunity, but he was also the minister of finance and tourism for the island colony. The timing was not right, but Sands did not go away.

Sands was still a critical player in island politics in the early 1960s when the Castro revolution in Cuba caused many gaming interests there to look in the direction of the Bahamas. Meyer Lansky was purported to have visited Sands in 1960 with a $2 million offer for the right to have casinos. The offer may have been rebuffed, but soon Sands, in a "partnership" with two Americans—Wallace Groves (a convicted stock swindler) and Louis Chesler (a major Florida land developer and compulsive gambler)—pushed a proposal for a casino in Freeport through the Executive Council. The Monte Carlo Club at the Lucayan Beach Hotel began operations in 1964. A second casino in Freeport—El Casino—opened in 1966. Lansky had a direct interest in the property, as several of his associates in Cuba took management roles. These included brothers Dino and Eddie Cellini, who also shared management in a Lansky-controlled London casino and in a casino dealers' school that furnished employees for casinos in England as well as the Bahamas. Initially, all casino employees had to be nonresidents, a rule that has since changed. From the beginning, no local resident has been allowed to be a player at any of the casinos in the Bahamas. A local resident is fined $500 if caught playing.

Sands was also instrumental in pulling together the principals who negotiated to establish a casino near Nassau. These included James Crosby and Jack Davis of the Mary Carter Paint Company, Wallace Groves, and Huntington Hartford, a millionaire with grandiose dreams for development of Paradise Island, which was very near Nassau. A silent partner in the organization was Lynden Pindling, whose political party had won control of the government in the parliamentary elections of 1967. It was the first time in the history of the island that the Black party had won an election. The effort to gain a license for a new property included the purchase of the license that had been held by the Bahamian Club. In 1968, the Mary Carter partnership was reorganized as Resorts International, and they opened the Paradise Island Resort and Casino. The company had to actually move the Bahamian casino building onto their grounds to gain its license. Today the old casino facility is the restaurant within the new casino structure. Resorts International also took over the management of the El Casino in 1978. In 1983, the license for the El Casino was sold to the London-based casino company (Lonhro) that built the Princess Casino in Freeport.

A second casino in Nassau was licensed on Cable Beach in 1978. It operated as the Playboy Casino until 1983. Then the license was transferred to Carnival Cruise Lines, who opened the Crystal Casino; subsequently it has become a Marriot property. In the 1990s, the Paradise Island Resort was sold to Sun International and renamed the Atlantis. Also, the Gentings Casino company of Malaysia purchased the Lucayan Beach Resort. A fifth casino license has been given to the Club Med, which operates the Columbus Isle Casino on San Salvador Island, the location where Columbus first set foot on land in the Western Hemisphere in 1492.

Earlier patterns of organized crime involvement in Bahamas casinos have essentially been eliminated through a process of effective regulation. Moreover, the operators' connections to other jurisdictions where they must face vigorous checks for licensing preclude connections with organized crime. The Bahamas have one of the most interesting taxation systems for casino gaming—a reverse progressive tax system. The island nation wishes to use casinos to promote tourism. Because the political leaders realize that it is expensive to market gaming to high rollers and persons who will spend considerable vacation dollars in the islands, the goal is to attract players who will stay in the hotels and take full advantage of the beaches and other tourist amenities. Larger properties have a better chance to market to these players. Also, it costs more to bring in such players than it does to advertise to low-roller day trippers who take boats from the Florida coast. Hence, the reverse-progressive tax system. Casinos pay a 25 percent tax on gaming revenues up to $10 million per year. As the earnings go up, the tax rate goes down. For earnings between $10 million and $16 million, the tax is only 20 percent. It is reduced to 10 percent for earnings between $16 million and $20 million. Annual earnings above this amount are taxed at a rate of only 5 percent. Casinos pay other fees as well.

—coauthored by Larry Dandurand

Sources: Cabot, Anthony N., William N. Thompson, Andrew Tottenham, and Carl Braunlich, eds. 1999. *International Casino Law.* 3d ed. Reno: Institute for the Study of Gambling, University of Nevada, Reno, 224–228; Mahon, Gigi. 1980. *The Company That Bought the Boardwalk.* New York: Random House.

Bank Secrecy Act of 1970. *See* Cash Transaction Reports and Money Laundering

Bennett, Bill

Bill Bennett and Bill Pennington purchased the Circus Circus casino from Jay Sarno in 1974. They immediately transformed a losing property into a "winner," as they parlayed the investment into one of the most successful casino companies in the world.

Bennett was born in Glendale, Arizona, on 26 November 1924. Following his service in World War II as a pilot, he returned to Phoenix to run a furniture store. Soon, however, a friend coaxed him into investing in a financial firm. The firm went broke and so did Bennett. Luck was on his side, however, as his friend L. C. Jacobsen was president of the Del Webb Construction Company. Jacobsen was looking for personnel who could

The Circus Circus Casino dominated the Reno skyline for many years. The property was developed by William Bennett and William Pennington.

help in the company's newly acquired casino properties. Bennett signed on and worked his way up to a top management post with the Mint Hotel in Las Vegas. In 1971, he cashed in his stock options with Webb and entered into a partnership with Bill Pennington. The two established a company that distributed gaming machines to casinos. In 1974, they found Jay Sarno in deep financial trouble, and they helped bail him out by taking over the Circus Circus casino in a lease option deal.

Bennett and Pennington liked the Circus Circus idea, but the two saw that the property was not being managed properly. They first made plans for a tower of hotel rooms and cleaned up many carnival games that at best would be considered sleazy. Circus acts were moved away from the gambling tables. They marketed the property heavily through radio advertisements and dropped Sarno's notion that Circus Circus could appeal to high rollers. Instead, they nurtured and developed the idea of marketing the property to middle-class patrons—lots of them. The new owners placed a much greater emphasis on their slot machine department than it had received previously. The property also began sponsoring many sporting events. Bennett was a stunt pilot,

and he rode motorcycles and speedboats. Soon Circus Circus had a hydroplane boat on the professional racing circuit.

Bennett and Pennington also reached out to develop new properties. They built Circus Circus–Reno in 1978, and they purchased the Edgewater Casino in Laughlin, Nevada, in 1983. Later they added the Colorado Belle. In 1983, Circus Circus became a public company. Over the next ten years, the stock outperformed all others in the casino gambling field. Values of shares increased 1,400 percent.

The 1990s were good to Circus Circus, although the company was not always good to Bill Bennett. At the beginning of the decade, the company opened the largest hotel casino in the world. The Excalibur featured a medieval court with the knights of the round table. The facility had 4,000 rooms and was built at a cost exceeding $250 million. In 1993, the Luxor, a pyramid-shaped casino hotel with 2,500 rooms, opened, and the next year a Circus Circus casino opened in Tunica, Mississippi. In 1994, several management changes accompanied lower-than-anticipated revenues at the upscale Luxor property, and Bennett was roundly criticized by an organized opposition at an annual stockholders' meeting. He decided to step down as chairman of the board, and then to leave the company altogether. He sold his stock for $230 million and promptly purchased the Sahara Hotel for $193 million. He knew the Sahara, as it had originally been a Del Webb casino. Now it was aging and in bad repair. Bennett invested millions more in improvements and in the construction of a new tower of hotel rooms.

Las Vegas needs dreamers and builders like Sarno, and it needs people like Howard Hughes, who will purchase properties others wish to get rid of. But it especially needs persons who take others' dreams and convert them into reality for stockholders and customers. In the gambling industry, Bennett has not been a dreamer, but he has been one who makes dreams come true.

Sources: Hopkins, A. D., and K. J. Evans. 1999. *The First 100: Portraits of the Men and Women Who Shaped Las Vegas.* Las Vegas: Huntington Press, 212–213.

Big Wheel (Wheel of Fortune or Big Six). *See* Roulette and Wheels of Fortune

Bingo

Bingo has been the quintessential charity game in the United States for most of a century. Expansions of the game (in terms of hours played and prize amounts) led to the court cases culminating in decisions that generated the initiation and widespread proliferation of Native American gambling in the United States. Bingo is also played in many commercial casinos. The game demands vigilance and attention from the players, who may form a collective audience of a dozen or several thousand (or more with satellite connections among several bingo halls).

Bingo is played on two basic styles of cards. A bingo card in the United States has 25 spaces: 5 rows and 5 columns. Numbers are on 24 spaces; the center space has a star or another mark, designating it as a "free space." The columns are designated as B, I, N, G, and O. Under the respective letters are numbers between 1 and 15, 16 and 30, 31 and 45, 46 and 60, and 61 and 75. In simple games, the ob-

ject is to get 4 or 5 numbers called to fill a column, a row, or a diagonal line through the center or to fill in each corner of a card. More complex games may require filling in a pattern (for example, a letter T—top row and center N column; filling the outer edge—top and bottom rows and B and O columns) or covering all 24 numbers on the card.

The second type of card, popular in Europe, is called a tombola. The card has 3 lines and 5 columns. Each individual card has 5 numbers on a line, for 15 numbers in all. Eighty-one numbers are used in the game. Each game has 2 winners. The first winner is the one who first calls "bingo" when all 5 numbers of any one line are filled. The second winner is one who gets all 15 numbers on the card filled.

Although casinos and bingo halls may offer guaranteed prizes for winners of certain games, traditionally the prize pool has been taken from player purchases of cards, making the game a pari-mutuel player-banked exercise in gambling. If two or more persons win at the same time, the prize is divided. On big cover-all games, a bingo hall may offer a big prize if the cover-all is reached within a certain number of calls, for instance, forty-five numbers. If it is not, a part of the prize pool may be carried over to another day, and the big prize increased in a progressive manner.

In many Las Vegas casinos that cater to senior citizens, bingo offers a large return to the players. That practice is used as an incentive to draw in customers who are expected to play slot machines and other games between and after the bingo games.

The numbers called at the bingo game usually appear on Ping-Pong balls that blow about in a sealed cage. When a small tunnel to the cage is opened, one ball is sucked up into an area where a caller can take it. The number on the ball is called and then recorded on a board that all can see. The ball is usually held up so that it can physically be seen as well. If a player has a win, he (more appropriately she, as more players of bingo are women than men—quite different than almost all other games) must call out "bingo" before the next number is called. The bingo card is then verified to ensure that all numbers are on it and that it contains the last number called.

A Bingo game in a Las Vegas casino, ca. 1940. (UNLV Special Collections)

The percentage payout varies considerably, depending upon the desires for an operator to get a certain return from the players by setting prizes at a certain level. The bingo game utilized today is an outgrowth of a private Italian game called *lotto*. This in turn was derived from a national lottery game that began in the sixteenth century. Forms of bingo (called by other names) were played in the United States in the mid-nineteenth century. The popularity of the game was developed in the 1920s, when movie halls used it for raffle prizes given to those attending shows.

The American card used today in bingo is traced to the 1920s. The name *bingo* had been used as a reference to beans that players used to mark winning numbers.

Bingo has maintained a wide popularity due to its simplicity, its almost "pure luck" form, and the fact that it is a very social game that can be easily set up for commercial or charitable functions.

Sources: Scarne, John. 1986. *Scarne's New Complete Guide to Gambling.* New York: Simon and Schuster, 205–223.

Binion, Benny

For over four decades, Benny Binion was a local hero in Las Vegas; actually, he was a hero among the gambling community worldwide. He was the "Cowboy Gambler," who—like his image in bronze on a horse at Second and Ogden streets in downtown Las Vegas—always rode "high in the saddle." His casino, Binion's Horseshoe, gained the reputation for being the "gamblers' casino" in Las Vegas. His casino started the World Series of Poker, and his casino was the only casino that would take a "hit" for any amount of money. Here, a hit is a single bet on a single play (see Glossary). It is a bet where both sides let it all ride, one time, one spin of the wheel, and one whirl of the dice—no next time, one time. Most casinos will limit "hits" to the normal table limits—several thousands of dollars. Binion's had no limit. The limit was what the player was willing to lay down on the table in hard cash. Hits are risky business, because the laws of probability are based upon large numbers—large numbers of bets. One time a gambler came in with a suitcase of money. He opened the suitcase and

Benny Binion and daughter, with his $1 million collection (of money in a horseshoe). (UNLV Special Collections)

poured $777,000 on the table. He bet on "don't pass" on the craps table. The dice rolled a few times, and the boxman called out "don't pass wins." The cage prepared a stack of cash worth $1,554,000, and the gambler took the money and left. If a casino that was owned by a publicly traded corporation did something so risky, a stockowner lawsuit might just be successful. But the Binion family privately held Binion's. And maybe they were not being too risky, because the publicity they received for paying off a bet like that was also worth a whole lot of money. Actually, the same man came back and later bet $1,000,000 and lost. So in the long run, it had been good business. Three months later the man committed suicide. He was broke, but the police said he had romantic problems, too.

I did a few shots for the PBS show "Going Places: Las Vegas." When we went into a casino on the Strip, people were crowding the cameras, waving their hands and calling out "Hi, Mom" and the like. But when we went into the Horseshoe, we shot an interview with the poker pit directly behind us.

The producers did not have to make a double take, nor did they have to wait for the place to be quiet or for a distracting guest to move on. We shot the interview and not one single bettor even lifted his eyes to observe the network cameras. The bettors were more interested in the action on the table. On the Strip, the action might have been a television camera; in the Horseshoe, the action was the next card being dealt. Over the decades that Benny Binion reigned as the cowboy gambler, and when he and his wife and sons ran the casino, other gambling entrepreneurs came to Binion's when they wanted to gamble. It was their local casino. Called the "most popular gambler" in the United States, Binion was especially popular with his fellow casino owners. He did not cater to tourists, except the hard-core gambling kind. He had no show, no music, and no two-for-one "fun book." He did not have people out in the streets hawking the wares, trying to get the sucker in the door. His players were not suckers. He gave the best odds on the table games, offering all the options in blackjack and giving ten times odds for even bets at craps. His machines were programmed to give the largest payouts in Las Vegas—and Las Vegas gives the best payouts of any gambling city in the world.

Benny Binion's one concession to the tourists was a plastic-covered horseshoe display of one million dollars in cash; he had mounted 100 ten-thousand-dollar bills. He invited the public to come in and look and to have their picture taken with the money at no cost. When I saw that, my head began to spin numbers around, figuring that he was losing a couple hundred dollars a day just in the interest the money could be earning in a bank. But then, maybe the money was in a bank, and maybe he could not be earning the interest. The Nevada gambling regulators demand that large casinos have several millions of dollars on hand at all times in order to cover any large win that a player (perhaps with a suitcase) may have at any moment. Las Vegas builds its reputation on paying off, and the reputation could disappear quickly if there was a pattern of casinos making players wait until the "other" banks opened before they got their money. After all, when the player loses, the casino takes the money right away (well, there are credit gamblers too). The million on display may just have been part of the cage requirement, and Binion would also have been out the interest if he had had the money locked in a vault. Moreover, with the extra security (and the money was well guarded) of having the displayed million dollars, other casinos could always count on Binion's having surplus funds. When other casinos hit a run of bad luck and their reserves fell below what the law requires, very often they would send a special security detail up to the Horseshoe to borrow a million or two, just to tide them over until the "other" banks opened. Rumor has it that Steve Wynn, as the executive of the Golden Nugget across the street from the Horseshoe, had to do just that.

Benny Binion was born in Pilot Point, Grayson County, Texas, in 1904. When he was fifteen years old, he dropped out of school and ran away, first to El Paso and then to Dallas. He got a job in the St. George Hotel, and there he learned about gambling. When in his later years he was asked if he would do it again, he said yes, he would have had to become a gambler: "What else could an uneducated person do?" Dallas was a wide-open town, a place of opportunity. At age twenty-two, Benny opened a casino game at the Southland Hotel, and two years later he established a leadership role in the Dallas numbers games. Things in Dallas were rough, and the competition could be tough. Although the government tolerated games for a price (he paid ten dollars a gambler to the politicians in order to stay open), others wanted him closed. In two separate instances he was in gun battles over just who would stay open; he survived. Two others died and were never able to spin the wheels of fortune again. One of those times Binion received a suspended sentence; he was acquitted on grounds of self-defense the other time. During World War II he bought a casino in Fort Worth, but its time was limited. There was a crackdown on Texas gambling after the war. There had been twenty-seven casinos in the Dallas area during the war, and some felt they could stay and try to ride it out until another election could bring the right people to office. Binion did not; he packed up his family in 1946 and went to Las Vegas.

In Las Vegas, Benny Binion opened a casino on Fremont Street along with Kell Houssels, a man who was actively involved in many casinos. As time went on, however, Binion felt that he was being restricted on doing things the way he wanted to do things. Houssells did not like the idea of allowing the players to have high limits. Some professional operators figure that with high limits, the players can use a system called the Martingale, which allows them to keep doubling their bets when they lose, and eventually they will win. But Binion knew (and it was a risk as to when) that streaks or runs of a wheel on black or red, odd or even very often can go five, six, seven, or more in length. Increasing the odds only allows one or two more bets against a fate of losing.

Binion broke up the partnership, and in 1951 he bought the Apache Hotel, renaming it Binion's Horseshoe. His limits became the highest limits in town. On one occasion the Mob leaders at the Flamingo did persuade Binion that he should not try to compete with them too vigorously, and Binion lowered his keno limit for a while.

Binion's problems with the law did not end when he came to Las Vegas. In the mid-1950s, he was convicted of income tax evasion and served forty-two months in a federal prison. When he was released in 1957, the state of Nevada suspended his casino license, and management of the Horseshoe was given to his wife and his son Jack. Jack carried on the tradition of Benny Binion when he established the World Series of Poker in 1969. The tournament has grown considerably since that time. All players must put up $10,000 to enter. The winner collects a million dollars. Amateurs from every corner of the globe come to compete with the most professional of all gamblers. I was in Birmingham, England, touring casinos, when I came upon the Rainbow. There I found a big sign and a program for Binion's World Series. The casino ran the British Poker Championship, and the first prize was an all-expense paid trip to Las Vegas with the stakes to enter Binion's World Series.

On 1 June 1988, the Horseshoe empire spread out a bit, and the Binion family purchased the next-door Mint Casino from the Del Webb estate for $27 million. The Horseshoe casino expanded its gambling area and also gained 300 hotel rooms. Previously, the Horseshoe had fewer than 100 rooms. The Horseshoe also took over the restaurant at the top of the Mint, and it became the Steakhouse. There the finest beef, nurtured on Binion's Montana ranch, was served. The casino was also able to expand its complimentary services with the larger facility. Over one-million-dollars worth of free food was given to selected players each month. Rarely did the casino charge a full price room rate. Most rooms were frequently occupied by very good players.

On Christmas Day 1989, Benny Binion went on to "cowboy heaven," and he left his family in charge of the gambling on Fremont Street. Jack Binion, who was born in 1937, carried on. He also branched out, establishing the number-one riverboat casino in Louisiana and then the number-one revenue-producing casino in Tunica, Mississippi. He has since become a partner in an Illinois riverboat. Family fights consumed the business after Benny's wife, Teddy, died in 1994. Jack's brother, Ted, was involved with substance abuse problems and lost his casino license. He later died suspiciously, murdered by a former girl friend and her new boyfriend, who were seeking Ted's wealth. According to the *Las Vegas Review Journal* of 20 May 2000, the couple was tried and convicted of the murder in 2000. Two sisters fought Jack over control of the casino, and finally Jack sold the property to one of his sisters and devoted his full attention to gambling interests in the Mississippi Valley. The legend of the "cowboy gambler" is still found in Las Vegas under the canopy of the Fremont Street Experience.

Sources: Binion, Lester (Benny). 1973. *Some Recollections of a Texas and Las Vegas Gambling Operator.* Reno: University of Nevada Oral History Project; Hopkins, A. D. 1997. "Benny Binion: He Who Has the Gold Makes the Rules." In *The Players: The Men Who Made Las Vegas,* edited by Jack Sheehan, 48–67. Reno: University of Nevada Press; Hopkins, A. D., and K. J. Evans. 1999. *The First 100: Portraits of the Men and Women Who Shaped Las Vegas.* Las Vegas: Huntington Press, 165–167; *Las Vegas Review Journal,* 20 May 2000, 1.

Blackjack

Blackjack is the most popular card game in casinos throughout the world. The game is an Ameri-

can creation in its present form, although it has origins in European games such as the French *vingt-un* (translated as "twenty-one") and the game *trente et quarante* (or "thirty-one") as well as the English game of pontoon. The form of twenty-one used in the United States was modified in 1912 when play at some card rooms in Indiana added an additional three-to-two payoff for winners who had a "natural twenty-one," that is, a twenty-one count on their first two cards.

The popularity of the game was greatly enhanced by the publication of Dr. Edward O. Thorpe's book, *Beat the Dealer,* in 1962 (*see* Annotated Bibliography). The book presented solid evidence that with proper playing techniques and structures, the odds for this game can actually change and be in the favor of the player.

Blackjack is a house-banked game in which a house dealer seeks to have cards valuing 21 or a number closer to 21 (without being over 21), but higher than the values of cards held by players. The player makes an initial bet according to the house limits. A dealer gives two cards (one at a time) to each player and also takes two cards himself or herself. The blackjack table may accommodate up to seven players, each of whom individually competes with the dealer. The object of the game is to get cards totaling 21. The cards from 2 through 10 count as their number value. The jack, queen, and king each count as 10 points. An ace may count as 1 or as 11. If a hand has a value of 22 or more it is a "bust," a losing hand for a player, and in most cases for the dealer as well. Although there are variations, in general the two player cards are dealt face up, whereas one dealer card is dealt down and one face up. The player may ask for additional cards in hopes of getting a 21, or closer to 21 than the dealer's hand. If an extra card makes the player's hand go to 22 or over, however, the player immediately loses the hand, regardless of what happens to the dealer's hand. A player who is satisfied with the hand's value and has not "busted" indicates that he or she wants no more cards. After all players are done taking cards, the dealer exposes the facedown (or hole) card. He or she takes extra cards if that total is 16 or less but stands (that is, takes no more cards) if the value of the cards is 17 or more. In some casinos, a dealer

A gambling table before opening hours in a Santa Domingo casino.

will take more cards when he or she has a value of 17, which includes an ace that is counted as an 11. (This is called hitting a soft 17).

Winners are paid at even money; if they bet $5, they win $5, a return of $10. If both the player and the dealer have hands with the same value, it is a tie, and the player's bet is returned to him or her. A player who busts loses even if the dealer later busts in the same hand.

The situation is altered if the player or the dealer has a natural blackjack. A natural blackjack consists of an ace and a card valued at 10 (10, jack, queen, or king). If the player's first two cards are a blackjack, he or she wins and is paid three to two; that is, a win of $7.50 plus $5, or a return of $12.50. This win is negated if the dealer also has a two-card blackjack, in which case the play is a tie. If the dealer has a blackjack, he or she beats all players who do not also have a blackjack. In the case of a dealer showing an ace or a 10-value card, the dealer looks at his other card; if it makes a blackjack, he or she reveals it and collects the bets from the losing players without giving them the opportunity to draw cards. If the dealer is showing an ace, how-

ever, he or she first offers all players a chance to make insurance bets, which are described later.

Certain special plays and bets are allowed to the players. For instance, if both of the player's first two cards are the same, he or she may split them into two hands by making an equal bet on the second hand. Some casinos also allow resplitting. New Jersey casinos and many in other jurisdictions, Nevada excluded, allow the player to make a "surrender" play. After the player looks at the dealer's one card and his or her own two cards, the player may forfeit the hand immediately for only half of the original bet. The player may also like the situation so much that he or she doubles the bet. After "doubling down," the player may be given only one more card—if he or she desires more cards. Some casinos allow a player to double down if showing cards with values of 10 or 11. Other casinos allow any player to double down.

If the dealer is showing an ace, the player may make a bet called "insurance." This is a side bet that does not affect the main bet on the value of the player's and dealer's hands. The player bets up to half of his or her original bet and wins a two-to-one payoff if the dealer reveals that he or she has a natural blackjack. With this side bet, the casino has an 8 percent edge over the player, as there are sixteen ten-valued cards (which can make the insurance bet a winner) and thirty-six other cards.

The casinos may use from one to eight decks of cards for play at blackjack. As players use strategies that may depend in part upon the cards that have already been bet (counting strategies), some players like single-deck blackjack. This is a game dealt from the dealer's hand with both of the player's cards being dealt face down. Most casinos shy away from single-deck games as hand dealing introduces opportunities for cheating and hence requires more monitoring. In multideck games, the cards are dealt from a shoe. A shoe is a box, usually plastic, into which the shuffled decks of cards are placed. They are dealt as the dealer slides cards from one end of the box through an opening. Shoes are also used with baccarat games and other card games.

The popularity of blackjack derives from the fact that, in addition to allowing a strategy that can give the player the edge, the game is a simple game in concept but also allows for very personal strategies. As a variety of strategies and playing styles is used by players, it is not possible to assess the odds-advantage possessed by the house (casino). In one strategy, the player seeks simply never to bust. Hence, he or she stands on any cards giving him or her a value of twelve or more, regardless of the card shown by the dealer. Under this strategy, the casino has a 6.35 percent edge over the player. If the player instead mimics the rules followed by the dealer—taking cards when he or she has a sixteen or less and holding on seventeen or more, then the casino's edge is reduced to 5.90 percent. A more complicated, but more effective, strategy called "basic blackjack strategy" can reduce the house edge to below 1 percent, and to even, or a slight player edge, with a single-deck game. With properly executed card counting (the Thorpe strategy), the player can gain a 1 or 2 percent edge over the house.

Sources: Miller, Len. 1983. *Gambling Times Guide to Casino Games.* Secaucus, NJ: Lyle Stuart, 25–39; Scarne, John. 1986. *Scarne's New Complete Guide to Gambling.* New York: Simon and Schuster, 342–392;

Sifakis, Carl. 1990. *Encyclopedia of Gambling.* New York: Facts on File, 33–39; Silberstang, Edwin. 1980. *Playboy's Guide to Casino Gambling.* Chicago: Playboy Press, 125–244; Thorpe, Edward O. 1962. *Beat the Dealer.* New York: Random House.

Bolivia

The remote, landlocked, mountainous country of Bolivia is not at all distinguished for its gambling activities. The preponderance of the almost 8 million citizens are of indigenous heritage and do not live prosperous lives. The country has had a lottery, as do all of the independent countries of South America, and there is pari-mutuel racing.

Although casinos do not operate within the confines of a legal framework, a large portion of the population of the national city of La Paz has nevertheless had occasion to visit local casinos. Casino owners have been operating casinos for years on a quasi-legal basis. In 1993, the president issued an executive order declaring the facilities to be illegal. A 1994 city statute in La Paz permitted lotteries, however, and local entrepreneurs used it as a ruse for opening casinos. After a federal raid had closed down thirteen of the country's casinos, the mayor of La Paz authorized the opening of two in the city, holding that the casino games were municipally approved lotteries. The wrangling between the city and national authorities has scared off many potential foreign investors. As a result, pressure has increased for the National Congress to take action on a casino bill that was first introduced in 1991. No action was taken before the end of the twentieth century, and matters of the casino front remain in limbo.

Sources: Cabot, Anthony N., William N. Thompson, Andrew Tottenham, and Carl Braunlich, eds. 1999. *International Casino Law.* 3d ed. Reno: Institute for the Study of Gambling, University of Nevada, Reno, 286.

Boulder City, Nevada: Nongambling Oasis

Boulder City, Nevada, is the only community in the state of Nevada where gambling is not permitted in any form. The small city of about 15,000 residents lies twenty-five miles southeast of Las Vegas and abuts the Colorado River. Boulder City was not part of Wild West mining days of the Silver State. Rather, it was a government creation, established in 1931 as a city to house workers for the building of the Hoover Dam. The Boulder Dam Project had been authorized by an act of Congress in 1928. Almost immediately thereafter, the state of Nevada and the federal government sought to exercise their separate authority over the parcel of land selected for a new workers' community. The federal government, even in the years right before Nevada legalized casinos in 1931, recognized the state as a rogue among the members of the union. Gambling was openly operating in Las Vegas, as were houses of prostitution, which actually were in conformity with the local law. Las Vegas was also considered to be the location where violations of the national prohibition against alcoholic beverages were most apparent. In 1929, some thought was given to making Las Vegas the base camp for the construction workers. After Secretary of the Interior Ray Wilbur visited the "sin city," however, he recoiled at the notion of workers living among saloons and prostitutes and being tempted to spend their salaries in casinos. Wilbur declared that a "model" community be constructed closer to the site of the construction.

Secretary Wilbur invoked the provisions of the Reclamation Act of 1902 and created a 144-square-mile enclave out of unappropriated federal lands surrounding the site of the dam. The enclave included a town site for Boulder City. The city was made a federal reservation much in the same legal form as the Native American reservations of the same era. Federal law dominated city life, and Nevada law was unenforceable. A prohibition against liquor was put firmly into place and remained in place even after the 21st amendment ended national prohibition in 1933. Prostitution was strictly forbidden, as was gambling, even though it was soon made completely legal by the Nevada legislature.

Boulder City, the first "planned community" of the twentieth century, was to be an isolated oasis of morality and "quality life," albeit surrounded by the many diversions of Nevada society. Author Dennis McBride writes that "everything was designed and blueprinted long before the first spadeful of earth was turned at the site. The government

decided how many people would live in Boulder City, and which businesses would be allowed to operate" (McBride 1981, 16–17). The city was built on desolate desert lands. It transformed the lands into a hospitable environment for workers who desperately needed quarters for themselves and their families. The same consortium of companies that was chosen to build the dam built the city. They hired an architect to lay out the streets. He did so and also designated lands for parks and golf courses. The architect incorporated desert landscaping into his plan. The need for quick construction led to modifications, however, and the golf course idea was abandoned. Also, the almost unbearable heat prompted the government to bring in a landscape gardener, aptly named Wilbur Weed, to begin a project of planting grasses, shrubbery, and trees everywhere. He selected the correct species of each after much study, and miraculously, his plantings survived to bring a measure of coolness and shade to the streets of the community. The plantings also broke up the wind and dust storms that had otherwise swept through the town as a result of all the construction activity. The autocratic city managers appointed by federal authorities did not let the landscape gardener's work go unnoticed. They decreed that all residents would have to maintain their lawn and garden areas, and if they did not, the city would do so and deduct the cost from the residents' wages at the dam.

The government decided that Boulder City would not be just a place for workers to live temporarily but that it would be a true community. A variety of civic institutions and organizations was sponsored, and churches were invited to join the community. By 1932, four were constructed and well attended.

Dennis McBride writes that by

the end of 1932, most of Boulder's principal buildings were finished, and her institutions established. The streets were paved, the boulevards and parks landscaped. There were no more tent neighborhoods; hundreds of houses stood in monotonous rows, each identical to the next. Plaster on the new Bureau of Reclamation Administration Building, the dormitory, and the Municipal Building was smooth and white, reflecting the powerful afternoon sun. Fords, Chevys, and other working-class cars lined the streets. New stores in the business district displayed goods behind big polished windows. Arcades with graceful plaster arches shaded the downtown sidewalks. . . . Where before there had been barren desert, there was now a modern American city. Wives shopped in clean, well-supplied stores and ate lunch in fine cafes; their husbands worked all week, and brought home a good paycheck. Children went to school taught by bright innovative teachers, and played on green, front lawns and in shady parks. While families in the rest of America went hungry, the people who lived in Boulder City on the federal reservation lived quiet, insulated domestic lives. Boulder today still looks remarkably like it did fifty years ago. (McBride 1981, 45–46)

A fence surrounded the city, with a gate manned by guards who would only let in workers and residents, who had to carry passes. Eventually over 5,000 workers lived in the dam-building community. The decision of Secretary Wilbur to create the enclave of "clean living" had several consequences for the development of Las Vegas as a gambling Mecca. First, by banning gambling and other "entertainment" from the vicinity of the dam, Wilbur ensured that a large number of federal employees would venture into Las Vegas and support its newly legalized casinos in the 1930s. Further, the restrictions on life in Boulder City—in terms of entrance and exit from the town—precluded a development of hotel accommodations until well into the construction schedule. Only one hotel was available during construction. Accommodations developed in Las Vegas instead. Moreover, as a private center of enterprise, Las Vegas attracted a share of the capital resources that were directed into the construction project. Las Vegas became a major transportation center for materials because enterprise was not allowed to develop in Boulder City.

When the Hoover Dam project was completed, Boulder City declined in population as workers moved away. The town persisted as a government center during the years of World War II, however, as a military force was stationed in the area to guard the dam, considered by authorities to be a target for the Japanese enemy. After the war, the city began to attract workers of the newly develop-

ing casino industry of Las Vegas. In the 1950s, the residents moved to have the city removed from federal control. In 1958, for the very first time, residents were permitted to vote for local governing officials. First a commission was elected to write a home rule charter for the city. After a charter was written, it was approved by a vote of the citizens. Then in 1960, Congress passed legislation releasing the land for private sale to the citizens whose city now came under the jurisdiction of the state of Nevada. The first charter banned both gambling and hard alcoholic beverages, probably in recognition that the charter would not become effective unless ratified in an act of Congress. The state of Nevada had banned prostitution in Clark County (the county including both Las Vegas and Boulder City), so this was no longer an issue. After the city emerged as a home rule town under Nevada law, there were several attempts to legalize both alcohol and gambling. In 1958, the city charter was amended to allow the sale of alcohol both by the bottle and by the glass. In vote after vote, however, the residents have remained firm in the position that they do not want gambling. This adamant standing does not mean that residents do not frequent casinos. The residents, now 15,000 strong, patronize two major casino complexes on their borders; one at the Railroad Pass area on the road to Las Vegas and another on a private enclave of land outside the city limits on the road to the dam and the Arizona state line.

As a resident of nearby Las Vegas, I can attest that Boulder City, the state's only nongambling city, has maintained much of the culture that was imposed upon the city by its federal mentors during the construction of the dam. The city seeks to be a quiet community with good schools and churches, a city that enjoys the very green parks and tree-lined streets cultivated by the federal government in the 1930s. The city adopted anti-growth policies in the 1960s and 1970s and maintains a policy of limited and controlled growth. The latter policies help maintain high values of residential properties. They also maintain a buffer to the urban sprawl prevalent throughout the rest of the Las Vegas metropolitan area. A small town character prevails. Within this atmosphere there are events such as the autumn art fair that attracts both artists and art patrons from throughout the southwestern United States. The city is also a tourist center, as it is the first motel area near Hoover Dam and the Lake Mead recreational area that was created with the completion of the dam in the 1930s. Visitors to the city who stay in the local motels have access to the many entertainment venues of the Las Vegas area, while at the same time they can enjoy quiet walks through un-crowded green parks beneath trees, much as if they were in a small Midwestern city.

Sources: McBride, Dennis. 1981. "Boulder City: How It Began." Manuscript. Special Collections Library, University of Nevada, Las Vegas.

Boule. *See* Roulette and Wheels of Fortune

Boyd, Sam

Local casino owner John Wolfram has told me how he sat in a car way out of town, on the Boulder Highway where Flamingo Road began. He was with Sam Boyd, and Sam asked him to look at the cars and count them. Sam told John that each of those cars was worth a dollar, or some such num-ber. A certain number of cars would pull into a casino if it were located right there. As the story goes, Wolfram said that he was not into that kind of speculation and that he would pass on the offer to buy a piece of the action. Wolfram has been suc-cessful in his own smaller casinos; in later years, he owned the Klondike at the far south end of the Strip. Sam Boyd not only was successful, but he be-came a phenomenon in Las Vegas gambling. But it did not start when Sam's Town Hotel and Casino opened at the corners of Nellis, Flamingo, and the Boulder Highway; the seeds of success were planted decades before.

Sam Boyd was an "Okie," born in Enid in 1910. His father did well as the owner of a small town taxicab company, but he died when Sam was only nine years old. Sam's mother was a nurse who felt that to support her family, she needed a job in a more prosperous location. Eventually, the family relocated to Long Beach, California. Not only did Long Beach have better jobs for those in the med-

ical fields, but it also offered opportunities for other people who liked to "hustle." And Sam Boyd as a teenager came to like hustling a lot. He worked as a barker and a carnival games operator on the Pike. The lessons he learned on how to draw peo-ple into games were lessons he would use through-out his lifetime. He came to use "fun books," flags, balloons, parties, anything to make the player feel the game was exciting. He also learned that the op-erator could make a lot of money if he went after the masses—a few dollars from everyone was worth the same as many dollars from a single player. After the carnival gaming experience, Sam Boyd learned all about casino games on one of the gambling ships that worked out of southern Cali-fornia. He dealt each game. He also became a bingo game operator.

He married Mary Neuman in 1931, and the fol-lowing year their only child, Bill, was born. Sam al-ways emphasized to Bill that his career would be much better if he received a formal college educa-tion. Bill got an undergraduate education, and then he received a law degree. His "enhanced" ca-reer began in a law office, but soon he found that he could be helpful as the attorney for his father's casino interests, and then he could be even more helpful as a casino executive himself. He eventu-ally helped the Boyd organization make the transi-tion to a corporate property with interests in many locations besides Las Vegas.

In the late 1930s, Sam Boyd spent five years in Hawaii involved with a variety of bingo establish-ments. In those short years he came to appreciate the Hawaiian population with its Asian heritage and love for gambling. This appreciation became the nexus of his marketing efforts when he set up operations in Las Vegas several years later.

Sam came to Las Vegas in 1941, in response to a federal crackdown on gambling in California. His first jobs were in small casinos on Fremont Street. He went on to work at the El Rancho Vegas, the first casino on the Las Vegas Strip. After a tour of duty with the army in World War II, he was em-ployed at the Flamingo, after "Bugsy" Siegel. He also worked in northern Nevada at Lake Tahoe. His son, while a student at the University of Nevada in Reno, worked with him during sum-mers. Sam also held positions at the Sahara and the Thunderbird. Sam Boyd loved working, and he was very diligent about saving as much of his salary as possible. In 1952, he had a chance to buy 1 percent of the Sahara. Hard work habits now became a compulsion. Sam purchased more shares when the Sahara developed the Mint downtown. He kept working and saving. In 1962, Sam, his son, and two others purchased the casino that became the El Dorado in downtown Henderson. In 1971, he became a partner in the Union Plaza casino at the end of Fremont Street. There he was innovative, as he used women as dealers at blackjack games. His goal was to build a player base. He also brought musical plays onto the property.

Sam Boyd took his money out of the Plaza so that he could become the major investor in the California Hotel just off Fremont Street. Quickly the California Hotel became the venue for Hawaiian players. His controlling interests in the California and the property in Henderson necessitated that he drive the thirteen miles that separated the two properties each day. (This distance is significant to me, as the Boyds sponsored an official minimarathon race in which I participated, between the doors of the two hotels.) It was on one of these drives that he realized there might be a market among the many cars that were on Boulder Highway each day.

Realtor Chuck Ruthe was on the board of directors of Boyd Casinos and used his expertise to put together the land deal that allowed the construction of Sam's Town and its opening in 1979. Many establishments had previously tried to target local gamblers for their market—most were on Fremont Street, but there was also the Showboat, at the top of Boulder Highway. The Sam Boyd touch, however, made his efforts to get the local gamblers especially lucrative. His Sam's Town ushered in a new genre of Las Vegas casino—the locals' casino. Without Sam's Town showing the way, it is unlikely there would have been an Arizona Charlie's, Santa Fe, Texas, Boulder Station, Fiesta, or Sunset Station. As the 1980s went on, however, Sam Boyd realized that the old management styles would not be totally effective if Boyd's were to expand into a public company and go into new jurisdictions. He yielded corporate power to his son and enjoyed his final years as an elder statesman representing the days of the

personal touch in Las Vegas. He was able to see his company set higher goals under Bill's leadership. Sam Boyd died in 1992 before the company entered the Tunica, Mississippi, market with the largest hotel in the state, established a riverboat in Missouri, and made a management agreement with a large casino for the Choctaw tribe in Mississippi.

Sources: Sheehan, Jack. 1997. "Sam Boyd's Quiet Legacy." In *The Players: The Men Who Made Las Vegas,* edited by Jack Sheehan, 104–119. Reno: University of Nevada Press.

Brazil

Brazil is by far the largest country in Latin America, with a land mass larger than that of the forty-eight contiguous states of the United States and a population approaching 180 million. The country boasts two of the largest cities in the hemisphere: Rio de Janeiro and São Paulo.

Although casino gambling is currently illegal in the country, the population participates in many forms of gambling, including illegal casino-type games. The wealthy, among a population with a wide gulf between the rich and poor, support the casinos of the surrounding countries with a great share of their patronage. They also frequent the casinos of the United States.

Casino gambling throve in Brazil in the 1930s and 1940s; however, it was prohibited by presidential order in 1946. Remnants of casino-type games remain. Machine gaming of a video variety is prevalent in the country's many bingo halls. Sports betting and football pools are also popular, as are cockfighting, horse racing, and all forms of lottery games. A private and only quasi-legal lottery called *jogo do bicho* ("the animal game") is played to support the activities of the Mardi Gras celebrations in Rio de Janeiro.

Through the 1990s and up to the present, there have been efforts to legalize casinos in some form. A casino bill was narrowly defeated in the 1991 session of the national legislative body. In 1995, a special committee was set up to study gambling and casino games. The issue remains controversial. Some organizations consider casinos to be a threat to their own financial interests. There is considerable political, economic, and cultural support, however, for the reconsideration of legalizing casinos.

The anticasino lobby is led by church forces advancing moral arguments. Pro-casino legalization arguments include the globalization of casino gaming, the reduction of trade barriers, the opening of markets, and the pressures and opportunities associated with multinational, integrated market groupings, such as MERCOSUL (the Southern Cone Common Market of Brazil, Argentina, Paraguay, and Uruguay). All the other members of MERCOSUL have legalized casino gaming, and Brazilian tourists often visit their gaming facilities, such as Punta del Este, Uruguay, and Mar del Plata, Argentina.

One perpetual major proposal for casino gaming legislation would allow luxury hotel-casinos in officially designated tourism zones. A government agency, EMBRATUR (the Brazilian Institute of Tourism), would determine the gaming zones. A Federal Gaming Commission would be established to ensure the integrity of the games.

—coauthored by Larry Dandurand

Sources: Cabot, Anthony N., William N. Thompson, Andrew Tottenham, and Carl Braunlich, eds. 1999. *International Casino Law.* 3d ed. Reno: Institute for the Study of Gambling, University of Nevada, Reno, 285.

British Columbia

Most forms of legalized gambling are permitted in British Columbia, Canada's westernmost province. Pari-mutuel racing was permitted before the Canadian Penal Code was amended in 1969. Now telephone betting, offtrack betting, and intertrack betting are allowed for gamblers. At first, lottery games were conducted under the auspices of the Western Canadian Lottery Corporation, but British Columbia established its own independent lottery organization in 1985. The province has permitted bingo and raffle events for charities since 1970. Charities have been permitted to conduct casino events since 1978.

The casino events grew quickly in number and volume of activity. In 1984, the province issued regulations that governed private companies that were offering casino management services for

The "dice" wheel in a British Columbia casino. Dice were not allowed in Canada until 1999.

In British Columbia casino dice games were played by rolling balls. The editor makes his play.

charities. The charities were restricted in their ability to pay staff to operate games, but the management companies could do so. Gradually a pattern emerged of having casino events all located in permanent casino facilities that were privately owned. There are now seventeen such casino buildings. Most are in Vancouver and its suburbs. The private companies are permitted to keep 40 percent of the gaming profits from a casino event of two days; the charity gets 50 percent and the government 10 percent. The private company pays the salaries of dealers and other gaming personnel, as well as all other costs. The charity only provides personnel to watch the cage.

Initially, the casinos could offer only table games, with roulette and blackjack being the most popular. In 1997, the casinos were allowed to install up to 300 slot machines each under a new revenue-sharing formula. Technically, the government owns all the slot machines.

Until national law removed the ban on dice games in 1999, the casinos had unique devices for sic bow, a three-dice game. The player rolled three balls into a roulette wheel that had thirty-six slots representing face-sides of the dice. Craps and sic bow are now played with actual dice.

For many years, there have been top-level discussions regarding the introduction of destination-type casino resorts. In the early 1990s, a plan to have the Mirage resorts of Las Vegas build a casino on the Vancouver waterfront was advanced by the premier of the province. Another plan called for a casino at the Whistler Ski Resort north of Vancouver. When the plans were announced publicly, there was a major outcry of protests from several citizen groups. The premier backed down, but the idea of having major casinos is still a matter of conversation in the province.

In 1997, the government, without sites being designated, again initiated a local option plan for twenty-one larger casinos. The First Nations of the province, however, were supposed to be given thirteen sites on their reserves. In the process of jockeying with persons wishing to control sites, the premier was forced to resign in 1999 when he was exposed for having taken favors from some of the applicants for site licenses. Also in 1999, slot machines were permitted in the charity casinos under local option. Additionally, a casino boat was permitted to operate off a dock in New Westminster.

—*coauthored by Garry Smith*

Sources: Cabot, Anthony N., William N. Thompson, Andrew Totttenham, and Carl Braunlich, eds. 1999. *International Casino Law.* 3d ed. Reno: Institute for the Study of Gambling, University of Nevada, Reno, 174–179.

See also Craps and Other Dice Games

C

California

California, the nation's most populous state, is on the verge of becoming the leading gambling jurisdiction in the Western Hemisphere. The state has several of the largest horse racing tracks. It also has one of the largest lotteries, hundreds of poker clubs, and several dozen Native American casinos.

Shortly before California became a state in 1850, gold was discovered at Sutter's Mill on the American River. The news spread quickly, and soon a "rush" of forty-niners was on the way west. Between the time gold was discovered and 1860, over 350,000 immigrants had come to the Golden State. They were miners and prospectors who had free spending habits when they made their personal discoveries—or whenever they got money in their hands. Gambling was pervasive, as San Francisco became a center for a wide variety of "sin" activities. Gambling was also widespread in smaller cities and in the many mining camps of the state. Soon both the state and the local communities were charging fees for operating gambling halls.

The sinful nature of California did not last. Mining opportunities lessened as gold veins were depleted. But California offered many other opportunities—good agricultural lands and ports for commercial activity. Waves of nonmining people—"good" people—came to the state looking for normal business activities and also for opportunities to raise families and cultivate futures for their children. The dominant interests of the state—the mine owners and railroad interests—did not see that their roles in society were incompatible with those of the newer immigrants. The power elite responded to cries of public outrage and demands to clean up the sinful activities prevalent in the state. Actually, the first state constitution had contained a ban on lotteries, but

casino gambling had been accepted by local authorities, until the citizens acted. Gamblers in San Francisco were lynched in 1856, and the legislature took notice. In 1860, all banking games were banned, but poker games could continue to be played.

The rule against banking games remained until 2000, when the final effort to win legal status for Native American casinos was successful, and the constitution was changed. The slot machine was invented in California in the 1890s, and machines operated in the open until state laws specifically made them illegal in 1911.

Wagering on horse races was legalized in 1933; however, the major distinguished form of gambling in California from the 1860s through the 1980s was the poker club. Many debates in court and in the legislature revolved around definitions of different kinds of games that were legal or not and whether certain poker clubs could be considered public nuisances. Courts ruled that the clubs could exist only under the authority of local ordinances. The 230 poker and card clubs of California produce revenues approaching $1 billion a year. The private clubs are not allowed to participate as players in the game, nor are they allowed to take a percentage of the money bet by the players. The card club furnishes a dealer and then charges players a participation fee per hand or a fee based upon how long the player sits at the table—the fee is collected each half-hour. There are over 2,000 tables in the clubs of the state. The largest clubs are in southern California. These include the Commerce Club (in Commerce) with 233 tables and the Bicycle Club (in Bell Gardens) with 180 tables. The clubs were, for the most part, unregulated until 1999, when the legislature activated a state gambling control commission. The commission makes decisions on new licenses and rules for the games that may be played and also makes recommendations regarding taxes.

California also permits charity gambling. There are many bingo halls in the state. The charity gambling and the poker clubs opened the door for Native American casino gambling in the state in the 1980s, precipitating an ongoing controversy that by the year 2000 had been mostly resolved.

There have been continuing efforts to legalize casinos in California since the mid-twentieth century. In 1950, the voters decisively defeated a plan for creating a state agency that could have authorized all forms of gambling, including casinos. In 1975, a legislative bill for casino gambling in Placer and El Dorado Counties, near Lake Tahoe, died in committee. A 1977 plan called for three casinos along highways leading into the state of Nevada. A 1979 proposal to have casinos in Jackson failed, as did a 1982 plan to put casinos in the towns of Adelanto in San Bernadino County and Clear Lake in Lake County. The sponsor of the plan was arrested for holding illegal games to get funds to run his campaign.

The opposition to casinos became an element of the campaign for a state lottery in 1984. Sensing that the public was adverse to the notion of having casinos and that they might fear that a successful lottery vote could strengthen efforts to get casinos, the lottery sponsors put a provision into their constitutional initiative that stated casinos would be banned in California. The measure passed, and this meant the constitution would have to be amended if there were to be any casino gambling—similar to that in Nevada.

The ban did not stop the Native American quest for casinos, but it certainly "muddied the waters." Several tribes set up bingo and poker games, but they did not follow the local rules governing them. This precipitated a series of cases leading to the U.S. Supreme Court's ruling in *Cabazon v. California,* which said that the Native Americans could run games according to their own rules as long as the games did not violate the general public policy of the state. Hence, since poker and bingo were allowed, they did not violate the general public policy of the state. The case, in turn, caused the U.S. Congress to pass the Indian Gaming Regulatory Act of 1988.

The Native Americans of California are located on over 100 small reservations, called rancherias. The Native Americans wanted casino games, but the governor would not make an agreement with them to allow the games. Nonetheless, the Native Americans installed a variety of slot machines, and they also played nonbanking versions of Nevada casino games. Legal squabbles seemed endless, until the tribes sponsored a legislative initiative to mandate that the state give them an agreement to have some casino games. The 1998 campaign on Proposition 5 turned out to be the most expensive initiative campaign in U.S. history, as the Native American interests invested almost $70 million in their effort. Nevada casinos that opposed the Native American casinos invested $26 million in the campaign.

The proposition passed overwhelmingly. A court challenge struck it down, however, on the basis that the 1984 amendment to the constitution said casinos were banned. The Native Americans returned to the campaign. In March 2000, they won passage of Proposition 1A, which amended the constitution to allow Native American casino gambling in California. It is predicted that as many as sixty tribes will open casinos and that their collective revenues will approach those of the casinos in Nevada after they are in full operation. Controversies will persist, however, as there are "vague" limits on the amount of gambling devices that each tribe may have. In any case, California is poised to become the leading gambling state in overall volume of gambling.

Sources: Cabot, Anthony M., William N. Thompson, Andrew Tottenham, and Carl Braunlich, eds. 1999. *International Casino Law.* 3d ed. Reno: Institute for the Study of Gambling, University of Nevada, Reno, 9–16; Dombrink, John D., and William N. Thompson. 1990. *The Last Resort: Success and Failure in Campaigns for Casinos.* Reno: University of Nevada Press, 162–164; Dunstan, Roger. 1997. *Gambling in California.* Sacramento: California Research Bureau, California State Library; Lutrin, Carl, and William N. Thompson. 2000. "A Tale of Two States: Political Cultures Converge around a Divisive Issue: California, Nevada, and Gambling." Paper prepared for the Western Political Science Association, 26 March, San Jose, California; *Sacramento Bee,* 9 March 2000, 1; *Sacramento Bee,* 9 March 2000, 1.

See also Native American Gaming: Contemporary

Canada

The Canadian nation and its ten provinces and several territories offer a full range of gambling opportunities. Lottery games operated by the government are available in all ten provinces, Yukon Territory, and the North West Territories. (The new Nunavut Territory has not yet developed its own lottery.) Charity gaming is also pervasive. Parimutuel horse-race betting (on-track, intertrack, and/or offtrack) is permitted in all jurisdictions, and casino-style gaming is legal in most of the provinces and Yukon Territory. All the provinces except British Columbia have video gaming available in noncasino settings, such as bars and hotels.

The lotteries and casino gaming in Canada developed during the last three decades of the twentieth century. Initially, casinos were either temporary or small organizations operated on behalf of charities or provincial exhibitions. (One exception was the seasonal casino called Diamond Tooth Gerties in Dawson City, Yukon Territory, in 1970.) The nature of casino gaming changed when Manitoba decided to consolidate many small operations and open a permanent gaming hall in the ballroom facilities of the Fort Garry Hotel in Winnipeg in 1990. Quasi-commercial casinos along the order of ones found in the United States soon were authorized in Quebec. Casino du Montreal opened in 1993, and Casino Charlevoix in 1994. Ontario licensed a casino for Windsor in 1994 and one at Niagara Falls in 1997. Casinos were opened in Saskatchewan and Nova Scotia in 1995. In all cases, the provincial governments "own" the casinos; management and operations in some cases are by regular government employees (Quebec, Saskatchewan, Manitoba) or by private companies (Ontario, Nova Scotia).

The Native Americans (First Nations) of Canada also are involved in numerous gaming facilities either as owners, operators, or beneficiaries of operations. The initial First Nation casino of considerable size is the Casino Rama facility at Orilla, Ontario.

By the middle of the 1990s, Canadian provinces gained C$4.7 billion in revenue from gambling in 1995, and charities and other operators won perhaps another billion dollars. The development of Canadian gambling into a multi-billion-dollar business, albeit mostly controlled and operated by provincial governments, followed a major change in the national law in 1969. Prior to that time, most gambling had been prohibited. The laws of Canada have incorporated the common law of England, and without positive legislation passed by the national parliament, the laws of England at the time of national confederation in 1867 remain in force. Hence, the first Canadian law on gambling is traced back to a 1338 statute passed because Edward III feared that his military was wasting valuable training time on idle pursuits, including "dice games." All games and contests except those involving archery were banned. The prohibition on the use of dice in gambling remained in place in Canada until 1999. It was eliminated in England and Scotland in 1968.

The English laws, which generally eliminated most gaming, were enacted into the statutory law of Canada when the first Criminal Code was passed into law in 1892. For the last century and a decade, that statutory prohibition on gambling has been nibbled away at by lawmakers. First in 1900, the code was amended to permit charitable raffles with small prizes. In 1910, on-track horse-race betting was allowed. It has remained legal with the exception of a short period during World War I. A 1922 statute specifically banned the use of dice in games, a ban that had never been lifted out of the common law. Limits on various other games of chance were relaxed in 1925 for fund-raising events at agriculture fairs.

In the 1950s, a parliamentary committee studied the gambling restrictions and in 1956, issued a report recommending major changes. These, however, did not come to pass for over a decade.

Financial commitments rising out of the Montreal World's Fair of 1967 provided legislative support for opening up more gaming opportunities for government budget makers. The fact that south of the border, the states of New Hampshire, New York, and New Jersey legalized lotteries added to the support. This support led to the passage of the Criminal Code Amendments of 1969, providing the major breakthrough for the development of a modern gambling industry in Canada. The 1969 law added a new Section 190 to the Criminal Code that allowed the provincial governments and the national government to conduct and manage a "lottery scheme." Several provinces could also operate lotteries together. Provinces were permitted to license charitable, religious, or exhibition and fair organizations and bona fide social clubs to conduct lottery schemes. The concept of lottery schemes soon came to encompass many casino-type games. Section 190 repeated the ban on the use of dice in games, however, and also prohibited betting on single sports events. Gaming machines were allowed only if the provincial governments operated the machines.

Lotteries were quickly established in the provinces and territories. The national government also utilized a lottery to underwrite the costs of the Montreal Olympics in 1976. A national sports lottery funded the winter Olympic Games at Calgary in 1988. In 1985, the provinces rejected the competition of the federal games. In exchange for $100 million from the provincial lotteries (enough money to fund the debt from the 1988 games), the federal government agreed to a law relinquishing its authority to operate any gambling at all. Present policy on gambling is held entirely in the hands of provincial governments and in territorial legislatures. One area of gambling has developed without benefit of a clear jurisdictional framework, however. Policy on affairs regarding the First Nations is still held in the hands of federal authorities, yet gambling policy is not a matter for federal law. To date, the bands of First Nations have had to resolve their rights to have gambling operations on an ad hoc basis in consultation with provincial authorities.

Sources: Cabot, Anthony N., William N. Thompson, Andrew Tottenham, and Carl Braunlich, eds. 1999. *International Casino Law.* 3d ed. Reno: Institute for the Study of Gambling, University of Nevada, Reno, 169–216; Campbell, Colin, ed. 1994. *Gambling in Canada: The Bottomline.* Burnaby, B.C.: Simon Fraser University, v–x; Campbell, Colin, and John Lowman. 1989. "Gambling in Canada: Golden Goose or Trojan Horse?" In *Gambling in Canada: Golden Goose or Trojan Horse?* edited by Colin Campbell and John Lowman, xvii–xxxvii. Burnaby, B.C.: Simon Fraser University.
See also specific provinces; Yukon Territory

Canadian West Foundation. See Gaming Institutes: Research and Political

Canfield, Richard

Richard Canfield (1855–1914) rose out of poverty in New Bedford, Massachusetts, to become the leading gambling entrepreneur in the United States at the turn of the twentieth century. He was the leading casino owner in New York City, and in 1902 he purchased and rebuilt the Saratoga Club House in Saratoga, New York, bringing it back to the elegance it had displayed when it was the private preserve of Jack Morrisey. As an operator, Canfield never gambled; instead, he enjoyed the finer things of life—wine, art, top fashion clothing, and carriages. He gambled in his youth, and although the activity helped him economically and gave him a social standing, it also earned him a short stay in prison as a result of operating a poker joint in Providence, Rhode Island.

Canfield was a student of many things, and when he decided that casino gambling would be a business pursuit, he decided to study gambling in its finest settings. He actually took a year to travel to Europe and examine the many elegant gambling halls of England and the continent. He was able to utilize his new knowledge when he moved the venue of his operations to New York City. New York was friendlier than Providence, as the police seemed to make their system of noninterference more regularized and reliable.

In New York, Canfield determined that the best gambling money to be made would be money spent by wealthy players, not money spent by immigrants in dives. He offered games to the upper classes, and was able to woo this clientele with his fine tastes and intellectual banter. Canfield was self-educated and extremely well read, could converse with the most renowned scholars of the day, and certainly was a welcomed host by the best business minds. He gathered partners, and they financed the most exclusive rooms in New York City for gambling. After a decade of operations, however, reformers Charles Parkhurst and Anthony Comstock pressured the city to close down Canfield's casinos.

Rather than resist the police action of 1901 and 1902, Canfield shifted his sights to Saratoga. There he acquired a stable of the finest racehorses, and he stood above all the local casino operators by running the finest casino—the Saratoga Club

House. A main feature of his house was the cuisine: the best offered in the United States. He discovered the value of loss leaders. Each summer he would lose $70,000 on food operations, much of it going for "comps" to high rollers, but he more than made up for the losses at his tables.

The Saratoga Club House remained in operation as a gambling hall par excellence for only five more years, as the reform movement reached into northern New York in 1907. This time Richard Canfield did not fight history. Rather, he retreated to a life as a Wall Street investor and a collector of fine art works. He was a friend of James Whistler, and the famous artist did Canfield's portrait. Canfield's collection of Whistler and other well-known artists was often displayed in major museums. A man of distinction and fine taste, he died in 1914 in a rather mundane manner, after falling on the steps leading to the New York subway.

Sources: Asbury, Herbert. 1938. *Sucker's Progress: An Informal History of Gambling in America from the Colonies to Canfield.* New York: Dodd, Mead, 419–467; Chafetz, Henry. 1960. *Play the Devil: A History of Gambling in the United States from 1492 to 1955.* New York: Potter Publishers, 318–339; Gardiner, Alexander. 1930. *Canfield: The True Story of the Greatest Gambler.* Garden City, NY: Doubleday-Dornan; Hotaling, Edward. 1995. *They're Off! Horse Racing at Saratoga.* Syracuse, NY: Syracuse University Press, 175–184; Longstreet, Stephen. 1977. *Win or Lose: A Social History of Gambling.* Indianapolis, IN: Bobbs-Merrill, 234–238; Sifakis, Carl. 1990. *Encyclopedia of Gambling.* New York: Facts on File, 54–55.

See also Comstock, Anthony; Morrisey, Jack

Cards, Playing

Many gambling games utilize playing cards. Although games can be traced to prehistoric times, the use of cards did not become prevalent until the invention of paper in China about 2,000 years ago. It is likely that Chinese and Koreans were the first to use cardlike objects for gambling. Systematic decks or series of cards can be traced to Hindustan (northern India) in about A.D. 800. Chinese and Koreans probably had cards during the same era, and Europeans developed card games in the Middle Ages, aided especially by the development of the printing arts. Cards were present in Italy in

1279. The nature of today's deck of cards was gradually established over the fifteenth and sixteenth centuries.

The sailors on Columbus's first voyage to the New World played cards on board the *Pinta, Niña,* and *Santa Maria.* Except for graphics, cards have not changed much since those times. The modern deck has the same fifty-two cards divided into four groups or suits of thirteen cards each. Two suits are red; in the French system they were named *couer* ("hearts") in honor of the clergy and *carreau* ("diamonds") in honor of the merchants. Two black suits were named swords or *pique* ("spades") in honor of the nobility and *trefle* ("clubs") representing the peasants. In each suit, there are cards numbered from one (an ace) to ten, and there are also three picture cards—the jack, queen, and king.

In the American colonies, there were many card players, and printers such as Benjamin Franklin were happy to supply them. The cards were so popular that when the British found they needed more revenue to support their administrative activities in the colonies, they decided to tax playing cards. Franklin quickly became a tax protester, then a tax rebel, and finally a revolutionary demanding independence for the colonies. The British would have been best advised to leave the card industry alone when they were choosing items to tax.

The wide proliferation of cards led to an ever-expanding number of games and a great variety of rules for those games. Confusion reigned supreme over gaming before Englishman Edmund Hoyle (1672–1769) began composing a series of books on the manner of playing games. In his early career, Hoyle was a barrister. He was also a gambling instructor. After the age of seventy, he wrote *A Short Treatise on the Game of Whist.* He also published books on the games of brag, quadrille, and piquet, along with guides on the dice game of backgammon and also chess. By the time he died at the age of ninety-seven, he was "the authority," and whenever a dispute arose over the rules of a game, someone would begin the declaration of the solution with the words, "according to Hoyle." In the twentieth century, several game rulebooks incorporated his other works and honored him in their titles. (e.g., *The New Complete Hoyle* [Morehead, Frey, and Mott-Smith 1964] and *According to Hoyle* [Gaminara 1996]).

By the twentieth century, there were many new games such as poker and blackjack that had not been played during Hoyle's life. Nonetheless, he remains one of the greatest card experts of all time.

Sources: Gaminara, William. 1996. *According to Hoyle.* London: Nick Hern Books; Morehead, Albert H., Richard L. Frey, and Geoffrey Mott-Smith. 1964. *The New Complete Hoyle.* Garden City, NY: Doubleday; Scarne, John. 1986. *Scarne's New Complete Guide to Gambling.* New York: Simon and Schuster, 625–636; Sifakis, Carl. 1990. *Encyclopedia of Gambling.* New York: Facts on File, 56–57.

Caribbean Casinos

Many Caribbean jurisdictions have casino gaming facilities. Lotteries are also in operation on larger islands that have major population concentrations. Casino gambling is offered in approximately twenty jurisdictions. Major events in the expansion of casinos in the region include the closing of casino operations in other places—a crackdown on illegal casinos in the United States in the 1950s, Castro's Cuban revolution in 1959, London's casino reforms in 1968. Each of the casino locations follows different regulations for casinos with different taxation structures and different enforcement policies. Overall, it might be suggested that there is considerable laxity in regulation. A tradition of laissez-faire oversight has been generated by the fact that casino gaming was, in several places, initiated by operators from other jurisdictions—such as Cuba and early Nevada—who had operated with limited enforcement in those jurisdictions. Also, the purpose of gaming in the Caribbean region has been to draw in tourists whose economic activity outside the casinos provided the greatest level of benefits to the jurisdiction—greater than could be provided by direct taxation. Casinos are seen as an added attraction that fills an entertainment void for the majority of tourists, particularly in evening hours. The tourists come for beach attractions and occupy daytime hours outside the casinos. The nature of their travels suggests that they have only limited hours for gaming activity. The relatively high expenses for hotel rooms and transportation also provide impediments to the development of the region as a place for mass crowds of gamblers.

Although efforts to establish casinos persist in the noncasino jurisdictions of the region, several factors seriously obstruct the opportunities for successful casinos. One factor is government stability. Financial institutions that are necessary for capital investments generally lack confidence in the island locations owing to traditional and ongoing political problems. As governments change, taxation policies also change, adding to the instability of business conditions. A second problem is that most of the jurisdictions do not have formal specialized gaming control boards. In most cases, a minister of finance oversees gambling along with his or her other duties. Without specialized government regulation, casino management controls the honesty of games. The managers also control the size of the bank—how much money they have on hand. Cases of cheating against the players or failing to pay off wins have occurred. A third difficulty arises from a lack of a coherent policy on development of the casino industry. Governments (or politicians) may greedily desire the fees that come with licenses for casinos, and accordingly, they may license too many facilities. Markets can be saturated, making profits very difficult for most casinos.

Several of the island nations are newly independent, and as such, the local populations resent the notion of having foreign entrepreneurs on their soil. They may resent any suggestions that the casino operators offer regarding the manner in which the casino conducts business. This situation has an impact on the labor forces available for the resorts. Jurisdictions may require that hires be taken from a native workforce that might be totally inadequate for the tasks at hand. Many of the populations have been agriculturally based, and commercial work habits, such as following daily work schedules, have been lacking. This means that the casinos have to engage in conducting long training sessions. Also, it may be very difficult for a casino operated by "foreigners" to fire or discipline local workers if they are inefficient or even if they are dishonest. The concept of *mañana* has become very much a part of some operations, causing customer service goals to trail the recreational inter-

El Rancho Casino, Port-au-Prince, Haiti.

ests of the employees. Sometimes resentment against foreign casino owners is transformed into resentment against the customers.

Another factor that causes some difficulties to gaming operatives in the Caribbean region is currency exchange. This is usually overcome by having all gambling transactions conducted in dollars. Problems may then be posed by government policies restricting exportation of dollars (either in player wins or owner's profits). Import duties can be overwhelming to the casinos during construction and furnishing phases of start-ups.

The casinos encounter marketing problems, as costs can be very high. The costs of travel are high owing to a lack of direct flights into major U.S. cities; all tourist products are expensive, as they must be imported. Moreover, tourism is seasonal in all the jurisdictions. One additional seasonal difficulty is presented by severe (and potentially catastrophic) weather at the end of the summer season each year. The weather problems only exacerbate the inadequacies of island infrastructure—airports, roads, water, and power supplies.

All the above factors make casino gambling a risky commercial business in most of the Caribbean region. Nonetheless, many operators seem willing to give gambling a try in most places where it is legal. One exception seems to be the Virgin Islands, which legalized casinos as a result of an election in 1995. No company has presented an application for a license in this new "wide-open" venue. The intervening years have witnessed two major hurricanes that have dampened investor optimism.

The Virgin Islands are at the eastern end of the Greater Antilles. On the western end, Cuba has no casinos, and Jamaica has permitted slot machine gaming but has resisted other casino gaming. Haiti has had several casinos, but severe political turmoil culminating in a U.S. military invasion and occupation in 1994 has effectively ended casino operations. There is some effective casino gaming in both Puerto Rico and the Dominican Republic. To the north of the Greater Antilles (technically outside of the Caribbean basin), the Bahamas have some profitable operations as well. Also to the north, Grand Turks Islands and the Caicos Islands have one small casino in a resort hotel. Most of the islands in the Caribbean region welcome operators of Internet gaming beamed toward the United

States and focusing upon gambling on sports events.

In the Lesser Antilles, the Leeward Islands of St. Martin, St. Kitts (formerly St. Christopher)–Nevis, and Antigua and Barbuda all have casinos. St. Martin is a divided island, one-half being a subprefecture under French control; the other part—the Netherlands Antilles—is under control of The Hague. The Windward Islands of Martinique, Saint Vincent, Saint Lucia, and Guadeloupe have casino gaming, as do each of the "ABC" islands in the south Caribbean—Aruba, Curaçao, and Bonaire.

There have been unsuccessful efforts to place casinos on other island nations and dependencies of the Caribbean, including Trinidad and Tobago, Barbados, the Cayman Islands, the Grenadines, and Grenada. Either investors with ample resources to make it all work would not step forth (considering the multiple disadvantages listed above), or the governments could not be persuaded that they wanted this kind of foreign investment and potential foreign control over their island economies.

> Source: Cabot, Anthony N., William N. Thompson, Andrew Tottenham, and Carl Braunlich, eds. 1999. *International Casino Law.* 3d ed. Reno: Institute for the Study of Gambling, University of Nevada, Reno, 221–272.
> See also specific Caribbean nations; The Bahamas

Caribbean Stud Poker. *See* Poker

Cash Transaction Reports and Money Laundering

Gambling enterprises, both legal and illegal, have long been considered to be integrally involved with criminal elements in various ways. In recent decades, concerns have revolved around the use of casino organizations as banking institutions that could aid criminals in what is called money laundering. The Bank Secrecy Act of 1970, with amendments; the Money Laundering Act of 1986; and the Money Laundering Suppression Act of 1994 address the problem of money laundering.

Money laundering involves various activities. One is simply changing one set of cash bills for an-other set of cash bills. Many criminal enterprises rely upon patronage of ordinary people at the street level—purchasers of drugs, illegal bettors, customers of prostitutes. Such people pay for their products and services with small denomination bills—ones, fives, tens, and twenties. As a result, criminal enterprises have very large quantities of paper money. It is difficult to carry the money, and it is especially hard to transport the money outside of the country in order to put it into secret bank accounts in other countries. When a bank or a casino willingly changes many small bills for a few large bills, they may be laundering money for criminal elements.

Laundering also occurs when financial institutions convert the criminals' cash deposits into different forms—traveler's checks, cashier's checks, or money orders. The institutions may also assist laundering efforts by initiating a series of wire transfers of money to foreign bank accounts or to other peoples' accounts in a series of transactions that make it difficult for law enforcement to identify the true source of the money.

Casinos are also vulnerable for use by criminals who simply wish to establish a legitimate source for their funds so that they may use them openly. Theoretically, it would be very easy for a criminal to come to a casino, change cash into casino chips, wager with a confederate at roulette (one playing black, the other red), and then claim all the chips they end up with as income—keeping record only of their wins and not of their losses. If a casino would cooperate in such a ruse, the criminals would be very happy to let the casino have its 5 percent edge in the game (both players would of course lose when the roulette ball fell into the zero or double zero slot of the wheel.

In the case above, the gamblers (criminals) are happy to pay income tax on their winnings, freeing them from the fear of being subject to investigation from the Internal Revenue Service. The situation is even better in Canadian and European casinos, where no income tax is imposed upon winnings. All the "laundry" operation needs is a verification that the money was "won" at the casino. When I asked the manager of a large casino in Germany about the possibilities of money laundering in his casino, he smiled and quietly said, "that is a service we provide." He was happy to have the player's action, as the casino could not lose. Today, however, casinos in the United States can lose by laundering criminal money. They can be fined or closed down (Burbank 2000).

In 1970, Congress enacted the Bank Secrecy Act. Initially the act applied to traditional bank-type institutions only. Banks were required to report to the U.S. Treasury Department any single-day transactions that involved $10,000 in cash. The bank was required to be vigilant and to track smaller transactions to make sure that a single party was not violating the law through multiple transactions. In 1985, regulations of the Treasury Department extended the provisions of the act to the casino industry. Casinos with over $1 million in annual revenues had to abide by the reporting and other requirements. In 1986, the Money Laundering Act criminalized violations of the procedure. The act specified a very large number of criminal activities that generated money that would likely be laundered. If any person attempted to launder any such money through a bank or casino, that person would be committing a criminal offense. Anyone knowingly assisting such a person in moving that money would also be guilty of a criminal action. In 1994, the Money Laundering Suppression Act extended the provisions of the acts to Native American casinos.

The banks and other financial institutions, Native American casinos, and commercial casinos in all states except Nevada make reports to the U.S. Treasury Department. The state of Nevada made a plea to Treasury officials to allow state casino regulators to implement the requirements. Accordingly, Nevada gaming agents spend over 20,000 hours a year collecting reports, checking records, visiting casino cages, and investigating complaints regarding cash transactions. Nevada authorities have also levied much higher fines for violations of the procedures than have been levied elsewhere. One casino had to pay fines in excess of $1.5 million for multiple infractions discovered by state agents.

The casinos must track all gamblers to ensure that none is exchanging over $10,000 in a day without making a full report involving positive identification of the gambler. Reports must be given to authorities within fifteen days of the transaction. They must also keep records of every transaction over $3,000 so that they can later assess whether a single-day transaction of $10,000 has been made. The requirements apply to bringing cash into the casino for any reason—to buy chips, deposit money for later play, make cash wagers. They also apply to money coming out of the casino—as prizes, withdrawals from deposits, cashed checks. Nevada casinos are also required to report events involving suspicious activities by players or by employees.

The money laundering laws, as amended, require all casino organizations to conduct special training for all employees to ensure that they are familiar with reporting and recording requirements. They also must have an accounting plan to conduct the required activity.

Sources: Burbank, Jeff. 2000. *License to Steal: Nevada's Gaming Control System in the Megaresort Age.* Reno: University of Nevada Press, 35–103; Cabot, Anthony N. 1999. *Federal Gambling Law.* Las Vegas: Trace, 247–281.

Casino

A casino is a singular location where gambling games are played. The word *casino* can be modified with many adjectives narrowing its scope. In this encyclopedia, attention is focused upon government-recognized or legal casinos, ones authorized by law, and ones that share their revenues with public treasuries through commission fees or taxation. Casinos considered here also have permanence. They are places where games are played on a regular basis as distinguished from places that offer only occasional gambling events, such as Las Vegas Nights. A casino operation is also one in which the house establishment is an active participant in the games. It participates as a player (e.g., in house-banked games), or it conducts player-banked games by furnishing house dealers and using house equipment. Again, a casino is more than a mere place where independent players can conduct their own games, as they did, for instance, on Mississippi riverboats in the nineteenth century.

A person studying gambling casinos as I have done over the past twenty years must be wary of

The Perelada Casino in Catyluna Spain. The casino has been built into a fourteenth-century castle.

other uses of the word *casino*. In a generic sense, the word *casino* means "a small house" (from the Italian *casa,* meaning "house," and *ino,* meaning "small") or room in a house that is "used for social amusement" (according to the tenth edition of *Merriam Webster's Collegiate Dictionary*). From other dictionaries, we can find casinos identified as "Italian summer villas," "brothels," and "social clubs." The word also means "dancehall." The large casino on the southern California resort island of Catalina is a movie house. I made several inquiries in Santiago, Chile, in search of a regulatory authority for gambling "casinos." Admittedly, I had trouble with the Spanish language, but I had the word pronunciation down perfectly. In any event, I kept being referred from one government office to another. At the end of my journey, I found myself in offices outside a large cafeteria for government employees. Indeed, I had found the "national casino."

In order to distinguish their *gambling* casinos from other casinos, the Spanish (of Spain) call their casinos *casinos de juegos* or "casinos of games." In Germany, the gambling casinos are called Spielbanken ("play banks"). (Perhaps too many had been getting requests from visitors from Italy for certain nongambling services).

A real casino should have some distinction from places that merely have a side room for games within a larger establishment devoted to other activities. The Las Vegas Supermarket casino is really a supermarket with machine gambling; in smaller stores with machines, the machines can provide the dominant flows of revenue for the establishment. The gambling area that is a casino is a focal point for social activity wherever it is located.

The first gambling casinos appeared in ancient historical times, probably across the vast Eurasian land mass. The record of Asian gambling halls of the distant past is rather incomplete. It is known, however, that Greeks and Romans of the privileged classes traveled to beach resorts or resorts that were adjacent to natural spas and mineral waters with health-giving powers. Today's casino resorts at Spa, Bad Aachen, and Trier were also Roman gambling centers. Roman authorities actually taxed the wagering activity of these resorts. During the Middle Ages, gambling flourished at these same places and also at houses for overnight stays along the roads traveled by the commercial and the privileged elites.

Venice became one of the first sites for a government-authorized casino in the 1600s. In 1626, the government gave permission for the Il Ridotto (the Redoubt) to have games, provided it paid a tax on its winnings. Part of the rationale for granting what was at first a monopoly casino franchise was the fact that the government was having a hard time controlling many private operators. It was hoped that they would lose their patrons to the "legal" house. The Il Ridotto then did what many "high-roller" houses do now—it protected the privacy of the players. Indeed, the players all wore carnival masks as they made their wagers. Unfortunately, this practice allowed many cheats to ply their trades without fear of easy discovery. The Spa casino in present-day Belgium reopened in the early eighteenth century, as did casinos at Bad Ems, Weisbaden, Bad Kissingen, and Baden Baden. Organized play at various houses near the

The New Caesar's Tower on the Las Vegas Strip.

Palais Royal in Paris also flourished. The nineteenth century saw a great proliferation of casinos across Europe. The most prominent developers of the century were the Blanc Brothers, Louis and François. They started games at the Palais Royal and then moved to Bad Homburg, where they managed the house until the Prussian government banned gambling in the 1850s. The Blancs followed opportunity and accepted an invitation to take over a failing facility in Monaco, and they developed it into what is even today the world's most famous casino, the one at Monte Carlo.

The entry on European casinos (*see* The European Casino) provides a look at reasons why European gambling failed to maintain a leadership role in world gambling into the twentieth century. The 1900s instead saw the central interest in casino gambling shift to the Western Hemisphere and especially the United States. Illegal houses in cities and resorts such as Richard Canfield's first drew attention, and then Nevada came on the scene, where Las Vegas has come to dominate the world casino scene for more than fifty years.

European halls remain, and many newer major casinos have come to be established in a large number of the countries of the world; however, the model—the yardstick—for analyzing all casinos in the world today is found in Las Vegas. (It may be that I have a parochial bias toward the "hometown" that I have adopted, along with 90 percent of the other local residents!)

There is a wide variety of casinos in Las Vegas. They cover just about all the types of casinos found on the world scene, save the exclusive private membership casinos of England and some European jurisdictions. The Las Vegas casinos must all be open to the public, and no admission charges are permitted at the doors to the gambling rooms—indeed, if you could find such doors they would be open *all* of the time. There are several categories of casinos in Las Vegas. First, there is the major resort hotel casino that caters to patrons from all over the world. Some of these properties include the Bellagio, Mandalay Bay, Caesars Palace, Flamingo Hilton, Mirage, and the MGM Grand. Second, some resort hotels seek convention business from business personnel. Two such major properties are the Venetian and the Las Vegas Hilton. A third category consists of other Strip casinos that market more to a middle-class crowd that seeks a reasonably priced (even low-cost) resort vacation with all the trappings of gambling and Las Vegas sights. The Imperial Palace, Ballys, Riviera, and Sahara fill this bill, as well as the Excalibur and the Circus Circus, two establishments that have made a success out of niche marketing to vacationers who want to bring their children with them (see the section "The Family that Gambles Together" in Appendix A). Fourth, there are several smaller downtown casinos, including the Union Plaza and Lady Luck, that appeal to a drive-in audience from California and Arizona, and they keep the customers coming back with low-cost facilities. Fifth, the California Hotel focuses its marketing efforts on Asian-Americans, especially those living in Hawaii.

On the edge of the city and in the suburbs there is a genre of casinos that seek the patronage of local residents. They have very large gambling floors, but not many hotel rooms (they have to meet a minimum requirement of 200 or 300 rooms). They emphasize machine gambling and bingo. They offer good food at low prices, as well as movie theaters, bowling alleys, dance floors, and even ice rinks; anything that will keep the people coming back. Many rely on construction workers and senior citizens to keep them going. They actually run buses to senior living centers. Then there are smaller slot joints and a very wide array of bars and taverns that rely on the money from machine gambling (they are allowed fifteen machines) in order to be profitable. Convenience stores, liquor stores, drug stores, restaurants, and even grocery stores also have machines, although it would be somewhat of a stretch to call these places casinos. They do, however, come close to matching the atmosphere of some of the casinos in the small towns of Colorado and in Deadwood, South Dakota.

There are Native American casinos on the periphery of Las Vegas. Across the country the Native American casinos and the riverboat casinos mimic the types of casinos in Las Vegas. Most of them are similar to the casinos that go after the local residents. They also expect their patrons to drive to the casinos many times for repeat visits. A few may seek to become vacation resorts, but it so rarely happens that none come to mind. As California tribes develop their casinos under the provisions of Proposition 1A, however, many will strive to become resort properties where guests spend more than one day at play. This might occur in some selected locations such as Palm Springs. For the reasonably near future, however, the big casino-hotel resorts offering full vacation opportunities will continue to be found in Las Vegas and other Nevada sites, such as Reno and Lake Tahoe.

Sources: Cabot, Anthony N., William N. Thompson, Andrew Tottenham, and Carl Braunlich, eds. 1999. *International Casino Law.* 3d ed. Reno: Institute for the Study of Gambling, University of Nevada, Reno, v–vi; Tegtmeier, Ralph. 1989. *Casinos.* New York: Vendome Press; Thompson, William N. 1998. "The Economics of Casino Gambling." In *Casino Management: Past, Present, Future,* 2d ed., edited by Kathryn Hashimoto, Sheryl Fried Kline, and George Penich, 305–320. Dubuque, IA: Kendall-Hunt.
See also Boyd, Sam; The European Casino

Casino Employees

Well over 400,000 persons work in the casino properties of the United States. Over half of these are in Nevada and Atlantic City facilities where casinos are attached to very large hotel complexes. Even nonhotel casinos, however, have large numbers of employees. Casino resorts are labor-intensive enterprises. For instance, one blackjack table will require the labor of five or six dealers, one and one-half supervisors, and one-half of a pit boss (assuming a pit of six tables.) Line authority extends upward from a dealer, to a game supervisor who will watch two or three tables, to a pit boss, to a shift manager, to a casino manager, to a general manager. There are also many other important jobs on the casino floor. Slot machines require attendants and technicians. There are drink service personnel (where jurisdictions permit drinking on the floor) and change personnel who furnish coins to slot machine players, although their role has lessened with dollar bill accepters on most machines. There are also change booth personnel who sell both coinage and casino chips, and there are the casinos cage and casino security. There are accounting departments and marketing departments behind the scenes.

Traditionally, persons working the games received very little pre-job training. Now, however, many complete courses at private training schools, at community colleges, or within the casinos. As the labor situation has tightened, casinos try to make the entry process as easy as possible, given the strict demands for casino integrity. In New Jersey and some other jurisdictions, the gaming employees must all be licensed. In Nevada, however, full licensing is required only for key employees or those above the pit boss level. Dealers must obtain "sheriff cards" that ensure they do not have a disqualifying criminal record. In several jurisdictions, strict licensing requirements have disqualified many lower economic status applicants for jobs, making public policies of trying to employ the unemployable very difficult to realize.

Casino workers operate in an atmosphere of great pressure. First of all, while the learning curve may be of short duration for a job as a dealer, the job involves several skills that many people do not have. Of course, blackjack dealers have to be able to count to twenty-one. But it is not just counting: It is constant quick counting of hand after hand while keeping track of bets, shuffling cards, keeping an even disposition, and maintaining the integrity of the table; all of this while being watched constantly by a hidden camera that records every move. Moreover, keeping an even disposition is not always easy, as players who lose money can be quite rude. Even nice players can fill the atmosphere with cigarette smoke, and alcohol flows more freely than may be desirable. Breaks do not occur often enough, but when they do, it may be in an atmosphere where drug use is prevalent and cigarette smoking is almost universal. Meals are taken "on the run."

Along with these difficulties, the dealers are subject to casino policies (in Nevada and several other jurisdictions) mandating that they can be fired at will. A new pit boss may come in at any time and decide he or she has to give a dealer's job to someone as a favor. The result is, one dealer has to be fired. No cause need be given, especially if the dealer is a white male (that is, not a member of a protected class). The compensation situation also exacerbates the pressure-filled environment of dealing. Dealers in Nevada receive little more than a minimum wage with a good benefits package. Most of their compensation comes from tips that are distributed to the dealer staff each day. The tips can fluctuate greatly from day to day, as the business volumes of most casinos are not uniform throughout the year. The tip situation has also led to a high degree of surveillance of dealers by Internal Revenue Service officials, making life even more uncomfortable.

The fluctuations and uncertainty about tips make it difficult for most dealers to gain good credit ratings. They tend not to become homeowners, and they tend to have overall low job satisfaction scores on surveys. Two Las Vegas sociologists found in a survey that 86 percent of the dealers reported that they "never knew when they might be fired," and 80 percent said they would rather be working someplace else. Nearly four in five saw themselves working in another job within five years, and three in five saw "no future" in dealing; 69 percent found it a boring job; 70 percent disliked the lifestyle of their job; and 68 percent felt they were less happy than workers in other jobs (Frey and Carns 1987, 38). Unfortunately, the money from tips in good casinos makes their overall compensation packages quite lucrative, and few find the initiative to give up their jobs for better jobs that might require, at least at first, a reduction of their income.

The tip system varies from casino to casino. Only a rare casino in Nevada will let dealers keep their individual tips. In almost all casinos tips are pooled. In some places, for instance the Mirage, the pool consists of every dealer of every game for the entire day. In other places, such as Caesars, the tip pool goes to dealers on particular pits of games for their particular shift on one day. The different methods of tip distribution can cause wide differences in compensation, as certain games and pits attract better (more affluent) players, as do certain shifts and days of play. An example of the differentials was offered when a billionaire gambler from Australia made two visits to Las Vegas. On each occasion, he made a $100,000 tip for the blackjack dealers—actually, he played $50,000 for the dealer. He won both times. At Caesars, each blackjack dealer for the shift was given $300 in tips as a result. When the exercise was repeated at the Mirage, all dealers of all games for the day received a cut, and the individual result was a $110 tip (Thompson and Comeau 1992, 170–174).

In many jurisdictions of the world, casino dealers are unionized. Many dealers with unions have gone on strike. This has happened in Winnipeg and Windsor, Canada; in Spa, Belgium; and in casinos in southern France; this is not the case in Las Vegas. The leading union, the Culinary Union, organized all the other nonmanagement workers in the casinos and the hotels, and they agreed that they would leave dealers alone. The Nevada casinos have firmly established the notion that they need direct control over workers in order to maintain tight security at the casinos. Dealers are subject to drug and lie detector tests, at least at the hiring stage.

Supervisory personnel in the casinos—pit bosses and casino managers—have general responsibilities for monitoring the flow of the games and the flow of money in and out of the games. They also are the key casino employees with the responsibility for ensuring that the top players receive complimentary services. They work with hosts to ensure that good players get free rooms, free transportation, free meals, show tickets, and other "services" that may be appropriate—that is, from a casino economics standpoint. The pit boss is responsible for ensuring that the high-roller player is actually making the wagers that he or she is obligated to make in order to qualify for the free services.

Change personnel for slot players are not as prevalent as they were in the past. Much of their job function has been automated. Where they do exist, they are usually the lowest of the low among regular casino employees. Shills, persons paid to sit at tables and essentially pretend they are playing, are the really lowest, but they are not regular employees. Change persons are still very much needed, as the majority of the casino wins (even on the Strip) are from machine gamblers, and without change persons they lose most of the human contact that a casino can give them. Change persons and other slot personnel are necessary as ambassadors to the group that is collectively the best-playing group in the casino.

The work situation in casinos varies from jurisdiction to jurisdiction. In Las Vegas, with the onslaught of many new properties, good treatment of dealers and others is essential if the casino is to be successful. Labor is in such demand that firings without cause have become much more rare. Enlightened management is also learning a corollary to the golden rule of good customer service: "Treat your employees the way you would like your employees to treat the customer."

Sources: American Gaming Association. 1996. *Economic Impacts of Casino Gaming in the United States.* Las Vegas: Arthur Andersen; Christiansen, Eugene Martin. 1998. "Gambling and the American Economy." In *Gambling: Socioeconomic Impacts and Public Policy* (special volume of *The Annals of the American Academy of Political and Social Science),* edited by James H. Frey, 36–52. Thousand Oaks, CA: Sage; Frey, James H., and Carns, Donald E. 1987. "The Work Environment of Gambling Casinos." *Anthropology of Work Review* 8, no. 4 (December): 38–42; Thompson, William N., and Michele Comeau. 1992. *Casino Customer Service = The WIN WIN Game.* New York: Gaming and Wagering Business, 170–174; Thompson, William N. 1998. "The Economics of Casino Gambling." In *Casino Management: Past, Present, Future,* 2d ed., edited by Kathryn Hashimoto, Sheryl Fried Kline, and George French, 306–319. Dubuque, IA: Kendall-Hunt.

Casino Nights (Las Vegas Nights)

Casino Nights are also called Las Vegas Nights, Monte Carlo Nights, Millionaire Nights, and other such names in various states and provinces. Although rules for operations of the games vary, the basic elements of Casino Nights are the same in the more than twenty-five states and provinces that permit the events. Nearly $2 billion goes from gamblers to various causes as a result of these events each year. Data are very sparse on Casino Nights, as many are governed entirely by local regulations, with perhaps only a general permissive statute on the state books. Very few states have any record keeping on games revenues.

The existence of Charity Nights gambling and similar gambling has been considered to be "permitted" casino gambling for the purposes of negotiating Class III casino gambling compacts for Native American casinos in many states. These states include Arizona, Connecticut, Michigan, Minnesota, Montana, New Mexico, New York, North Dakota, and Washington.

Children play freely at a charity casino event attended by the editor in El Paso, Texas.

A (Casino) Night on the Town

The following account is based upon my visit to an El Paso, Texas, charity Casino Night on 15 January 2000. It would have been the seventy-first birthday of legendary civil rights leader, Dr. Martin Luther King Jr. Members of the El Paso chapter of Alpha Phi Alpha, a predominantly African American social fraternity, were celebrating. They were serving as volunteer dealers and croupiers at the North East El Paso Optimist Club's Casino Night. The players were a multiracial group that would have made Dr. King proud. There were whites (some affluent, but mostly working class), Latinos (Hispanics from Mexico and the United States), Native Americans, and African Americans. They were of all age groups, although most seemed to be over fifty, or even sixty. There were also at least a dozen children, preteens and youngsters in their early teens, in the Optimist Hall.

The twelve Alpha Phi Alpha volunteers were selling their services as dealers and were loaning their equipment—tables, cards, chuck-a-luck cage—to the Optimist Club in order to raise money for college scholarships for young African Americans. They charged $700 to run six blackjack tables, one poker table, a craps table, and a poker table. The North East Optimist Club cleared another $2,000 or more for its work with youth. Pictures of scout troops, Little League sports teams, summer camps, and fishing trips were in a case on the wall. At least one of the players, a thirteen-year-old, was in his scout uniform. A six- or seven-year-old girl was sitting next to her mother, and both were playing blackjack hands. The mother seemed to know the Optimist sponsors of the game.

The approximately 100 players had paid $20 each to enter the gambling hall. They began to gather at 6 P.M., and gambling started at 7:30 P.M. They were given a beef brisket meal that would have cost $6.95 down the street at the Village Inn. The meal was put together by Optimist volunteers (members and spouses) at one-third that cost. The persons entering the hall were also given $10,000 in casino cash in addition to their meal. The "cash" could be exchanged for chips, the smallest value of which was $1,000. In other words, the players were sold single lowest-value chips at a cost of approximately $15 for ten ($20 minus the cost of the meal), or $1.50 each. The players were also permitted to purchase additional chips at a cost of $5 for $10,000, or $ .50 each. One man was observed writing a $50 check for $100,000 in casino money, or 1,000 "$1,000" chips. Later in the evening—the gambling went beyond 10 P.M.—an Optimist volunteer was giving bonus chips to anyone spending more than $100 (real money) for extra chips.

During the gambling session, Optimist members were drawing numbered ticket stubs for door prizes. The biggest prize was a round trip air ticket to Las Vegas, Nevada. Other prizes were for meals at local restaurants and free bowling games and movie tickets. At the end of the gambling session, the players gathered for an auction of prizes. The money they won at gambling could now be offered in bids for their prizes. The biggest prize was a 1999 model television set, probably carrying a retail value of $300. Other prizes included four automobile tires of similar retail value, as well as smaller appliances, tool sets, and various kitchen dishes. Organizers of the event indicated that merchants had donated the prizes or sold them to the Optimists for cost. They could also discount the full retail value from business revenues for taxation purposes.

The players were gambling by any definition of the term. They were advancing something of value—real money—in order to make wagers at games of chance. As a result of the play at the games of chance, they were able to claim prizes that had values greatly in excess of the money they had individually wagered. They also had participated in raffles that involved buying a ticket, having numbers drawn by chance methods, and winning prizes of greater value than the cost of tickets.

The games were played in the same manner as they would be played in a Las Vegas casino, albeit hands were dealt more slowly, and the dealers advised players on the game rules as well as expectations for certain kinds of play. (They generally advised players to assume that cards to be dealt at blackjack would likely be ten-value cards—something that is true 31 percent of the time). The blackjack cards were dealt in the same sequence as

in Las Vegas, and players were allowed to split and double down. The dealer hit on sixteen and held on seventeen. A four-deck shoe was used. The craps rules were identical to casino craps, and the three-dice game of chuck-a-luck was played as it used to be played when it was popular in Las Vegas several decades ago. All these games were clearly house-banked gambling games. In the poker game, the dealer competed with the players on an even odds basis, as his hand was but one of the several played, and the best hand won the pot played by all the players. The dealer contributed to the pot the same as the players did.

The Alpha Phi Alpha fraternity ran about one game a month through the year in El Paso and also in nearby New Mexico. They would often have ten blackjack tables, as well as poker, chuck-a-luck, craps, and roulette—for a service cost of $1,000. In the summer, they ran their own game and drew over 300 players. Their biggest month was May, when they ran games for high school graduation classes. The president of the fraternity indicated that twenty years ago they had a lawyer go closely over all the rules in Texas to ensure that everything being done was legal. He certainly agreed that the games were casino games and that they were gambling games. The event was clearly advertised in the El Paso newspaper as a Casino Night. Some may question whether it was legal in all aspects, but there can be no doubt that the state of Texas permitted the gambling games at the event. They were publicly advertised, and the public was invited in. An armed law enforcement officer from the police force of the city of El Paso was present at the event from the beginning to the end. Auxiliary police personnel were also present at all times. A former El Paso city councilman was prominently present, smiling and shaking hands with players and dealers. The Alpha Phi Alpha's president indicated that there was no local or state license or fee for the event.

The auction at the end of the session added an extra element to the gambling that is not present in other casinos. The players would have to assess their relative wealth vis-à-vis other players in order to decide how to bid. It is quite likely that only the tires and television carried money values higher than the money values of the amounts wagered by most individual players. At the end of Las Vegas games, winners and losers are clearly identified, and players need not go through another gambling session in order to find out if they are winners.

Sources: Cabot, Anthony N., William N. Thompson, Andrew Tottenham, and Carl Braunlich, eds. 1999. *International Casino Law.* 3d ed. Reno: Institute for the Study of Gambling, University of Nevada, Reno, 158–168. Christiansen, Eugene Martin. 1999. "The 1998 Gross Annual Wager." *International Games and Wagering Business* (August): 20ff.

Casinos, Caribbean. *See* Caribbean Casinos

Casinos, European. *See* The European Casino

Centre for the Study of Gambling and Commercial Gaming. *See* Gaming Institutes: Research and Political

Cheating Schemes

Cheating at games is part of the history of gambling enterprise. The terms *gambler* and *riverboat gambler* have rightly or wrongly become closely associated with dishonesty over time. Jewish courts would not recognize the testimony of a gambler because his veracity was always suspect. *The Gamblers,* in the Time-Life series on the Old West, asserts that 99 percent of the riverboat gamblers cheated at one time or another (Time-Life, Inc. 1978, 61). Graphics of Old West poker games invariably show pistols on the table, reminders to one and all that cheating was to be frowned upon.

Carnival games and private games are most susceptible to cheating, as there is inadequate outside supervision. Licensing authorities for casinos, however, usually mandate that surveillance systems be installed and activated during play. Security rooms have monitors, and personnel watch play as monitors record action. Usually videotapes are kept for a period of time (week or month) in case any question arises over the integrity of the games. State racing authorities are always present at tracks to make sure that the racing is legitimate, to the extent that they can.

Customer service begins with the "win-win" game: Winners talk and losers walk. That is an essential ingredient for the marketing and advertising of gambling meccas such as Las Vegas. Winners love to tell of their Vegas triumphs, whereas losers tout the wonderful weather and bargain rates for slop food at the buffets or for their rooms. Everyone wins, and only the winners talk about gambling. This great deal fails when players feel they are cheated or exploited. For the latter reason, it is in the self-interest of casinos to minimize and mitigate the volume and effects of compulsive gambling. But they must also make sure that the games are honest. A loser who feels that the games were not honest will be very willing to tell the world about it, whereas other losers are quite content knowing that no one else knows the results of their gambling activity.

Indeed, the games in Las Vegas are honest. There could be no Las Vegas if the games were not honest. Certainly, the gambling city would not be able to attract 33 million visitors each year. But gambling games have always attracted persons who would want them to be something other than honest. Cheating has been perpetrated by parties running the games, and also by players.

There are many forms of cheating. The instruments of gambling have been manipulated so that they do not give honest results. Dice are sometimes weighted and shaved so that certain numbers will fall. Shaved dice have been found in Egyptian tombs dating back thousands of years. Crooked dice can also be weighted to influence their falls. Metal pieces have been put into dice, and tables have been magnetized to affect falls as well. One reason that dice are of a clear plastic is so that they can be seen through. A clear die will also reveal if the numbering on the cube is correct.

Card decks can also be altered. Extra aces can be slipped into a game. More likely, however, is that a cheater can misshuffle and misdeal, taking cards from the bottom of the deck or middle of the deck in order to help or hurt a particular player. Quick hands can result in the placement of cards where the dealer can retrieve them at will and deal them without discovery—of course, then there are those pistols at the table. Other cheaters at card games can become adept at peeking at cards about to be dealt, or they can have confederates peeking over the shoulders of their opponents and sending them signals. It has often been said that if you have been at a private poker game for an hour and you are still wondering who the patsy (victim) is, it is you.

Roulette wheels have been magnetized to stop at certain numbers. Bias wheels have also been constructed not to cycle evenly. Dealers or others can also use techniques (from friction to electric stoppers) to cause the wheel to end its spin on certain numbers. The big wheel (wheel of fortune) is quite exposed and vulnerable to being nudged by a foot, hand, or one's hind quarters.

The Ping-Pong balls that have been used in devices producing numbers for bingo games and lotteries can also be manipulated. In one case, balls were weighted down with lead paint so that other balls would be selected—hence, producing certain numbers for the prizes. Although that case was detected, one can certainly wonder if such cheating had not occurred many times before and since.

Number randomizers in modern machine-driven games—slot machines, keno games, computerized bingo games—can be manipulated if one can get access to them. State casino regulators carry devices that can quickly check if the chip in a slot machine or keno machine is identical to the one that has been registered to ensure fully random play. One of the agents of the Nevada Gaming Control Board who was given the responsibility for inspecting the chips at the factory saw his opportunity, however, to be a dishonest person. He took a chip and reprogrammed it to distribute numbers in a certain sequence if a machine was played with a certain pattern of multiple coins in on consecutive plays. He enlisted confederates to play the machines. Fortunately for the regulators, when his friends won the big prizes, they refused to identify themselves (as big winners must do for tax purposes), and their behavior revealed that they were not playing honestly. Of course, one thing led to another and then another, and the scheme was found out. Unfortunately, the culprit had probably gotten away with his cheating for some time before he was caught.

Ironically, the same regulator had broken another case in which American Coin, a major slot route company, was revealed to have programmed its poker machines so as not to allow royal flushes if a player put in maximum coins for a play. The discovery resulted in the company's immediately losing its license. Before a criminal trial of company officials took place, an employee who was to be a key witness was murdered. This happened in the 1990s, and Las Vegas residents shuddered at the realization that the old days had not all gone away.

Regular casino chips are also subject to counterfeiting. As a chip can represent up to $100 in value (or more), casinos must be very vigilant against this possibility. Special companies make chips that can be observed by detectors that can verify their legitimacy. Slugs have always been used in slot machines. Modern machines have comparators, which can detect the size, weight, and metal composition of coins or slot tokens to make sure they are proper. Nonetheless, as a token may cost only twenty cents to make, but might represent one dollar (or as much as $500), thieving persons will always seek to find a perfect (or workable) match for a machine.

Throughout history, many ways have been used to manipulate slot machines. The handles of old mechanical machines could be pulled with a certain rhythm, and reels could be stopped by design. After a cheater began giving lessons on how to do this, machine companies quickly retrofitted the machines with new handles.

Other simple, silly-sounding schemes were used to compromise machines. A hole would be drilled into a coin, and a string attached to it. The coin would then be dropped into the machine, and after play was activated, the coin would be pulled back out to be played over and over again. Slot cheats would also use spoonlike devices to reach up into the machine from the hopper tray in order to make coins flow. Other schemes involved groups that would distract casino security agents as they opened a machine or drilled holes in the machine in order to affect the spinning of the reels.

Probably the most prevalent type of cheating still going on in casinos is past posting. Quite simply, a player will make his bet after the play has stopped—after the dice have been rolled, or the cards dealt. Where a dealer is trying to work a busy table, he can be naturally or purposely distracted as the cheater slips the extra chip on the winning number. If done very quickly, past posting can go undetected. A suspicious dealer or games supervisor can quickly ask officials in the security room to review their videotapes to check what has happened.

Much of the gambling cheating at casinos involves collusion between dealers and dishonest players. The simple technique of paying off a loser will work if there are no supervision and no camera checks. Dealers and players may also work together by using false caps that are placed over chips. A player will play a stack of white chips (one dollar) covered by a cap that makes them look like black chips ($100 value). The dealer will pay off bets as if the higher amount was bet, and the cameras may not catch the deception.

Another kind of cheating is not cheating of the game, but rather cheating of government authorities. Unauthorized or unlicensed owners will seek to get their share of the profits by "skimming." Legitimate owners may also try to "skim" profits in order to avoid their taxation obligations. One way they do this is to give credit to certain players who then simply fail to pay off their debts. Another quite ingenious means of "skimming" at one casino involved the use of miscalibrated scales that displayed the wrong value of coins when they were weighed. A thousand dollars in coins was weighed and declared to be $800, and the owners put the extra $200 in their pockets, while they paid taxes on only $800 in profits.

There are as many techniques for surveillance of cheating as there are techniques for cheating; nonetheless, the cheating will continue as long as some see an opportunity. Casinos work together and trade photographs, names, and descriptions of known cheaters and then ban them from the casinos. The State of Nevada also keeps a black book list of excluded persons.

In horse racing, cheating can be as simple as collusion among jockeys to have a certain horse win. In other situations, ringers are used. A good horse is slipped into a race disguised as a horse with a bad record so that the payoff odds are much better. Horses may be drugged for better performances as well. Horsemen may have their steed run

slowly in a few races to establish it as a loser. Then when it gets long odds, they bet heavily on it and have it run out at its full potential. There is the story of the horse owner who told his jockey to hold back during a race. The jockey did so and the horse finished fifth, out of the wagering and the prize money. The owner then asked the jockey if the horse had anything left in him at the end of the race, and if the jockey thought he could have beaten the four horses in front of him. "Sure," said the jockey. "The horse had much left in him, and had I turned him loose around the corner, we could have sprinted by the four horses." The owner thanked him for the good ride and indicated they would run against the same field in a few weeks, and he was sure the horse could win. The jockey then revealed the truth. "Sir, I'm sure we can beat the four horses that were ahead of us, but we are going to have a lot of trouble with several of the horses that were behind us." The trouble with cheating is that it is not just a game for one cheater.

Sources: Farrell, Ronald A., and Carole Case. 1995. *The Black Book and the Mob: The Untold Story of the Control of Nevada's Casinos.* Madison: University of Wisconsin Press; Scarne, John. 1986. *Scarne's New Complete Guide to Gambling.* New York: Simon and Schuster, 74–78, 420–428; Sifakis, Carl. 1990. *Encyclopedia of Gambling.* New York: Facts on File, 59–62; Thompson, William N. 1997. *Legalized Gambling: A Reference Handbook.* 2d ed. Santa Barbara, CA: ABC-CLIO; Time-Life, Inc. 1978. *The Gamblers.* The Old West Series. Alexandria, VA: Time-Life Books.
See also Lotteries

Chemin de Fer. *See* Baccara, Chemin de Fer, and Baccarat-type Games

Chile

Chile permits horse-race and casino gambling as well as lottery games. The Loteria de Concepcion is the oldest lottery still operating. Begun in 1921, it devotes its profits to several charities, including the Red Cross and the Universidad de Concepcion.

The southernmost country on the South American continent, Chile has a population of 11.1 mil-

Vina del Mar Casino, the largest casino in Chile.

lion on 292,258 square miles of land. The country is a strip of land 2,650 miles long and no wider than 225 miles. It is nestled between the Pacific Ocean and the high Andes. A variety of climates and terrain appeals to all categories of tourists. Desert beaches, Mediterranean breezes, magnificent glaciers, ski resorts, and mountain grandeur welcome the visitors. Still the isolated geography restricts the country's ability to utilize its gambling facilities as a means of attracting outside revenues.

The struggle for Chilean national independence from Spain, led by Bernardo O'Higgins, lasted for many years during the first decades of the nineteenth century. When the local forces emerged with political control, they sought to deal severely with the sinful acts that were remnants of the days of Spanish colonial rule. The "sin" of gambling was high on the "hit list." An 1812 law proclaimed all games to be illegal. The law stated that gambling "compromised, demoralized, prostituted, and ruined" civilian members of society by corrupting the innocent. Gaming was a "genuine crime" and a "detestable occupation." An 1818 decree by the liberator O'Higgins saw gambling as

the "worst scandal." Cafe owners were subject to fines for permitting games in their establishments. Another decree in 1819 labeled gaming "repulsive" and promised to punish violators of the prohibition to "the full severity of the law" (Cabot et al. 1999, 287–289).

Yet, as the days of independence unfolded, Chilean lawmakers were aware they could not fully suppress old habits from colonial times. In 1847, the national legislature recognized that "people gambled anyway." Instead of a full prohibition, they opted for controlled legalization by authorizing municipalities to designate areas for gaming. An 1852 statute provided for local councils to grant two-year licenses for casinos. Later in the century, however, all gaming was again made illegal after a new wave of moralism swept over the lawmakers.

Modern casino gaming in Chile dates back to 1913 and the vision of the city leaders of Vina del Mar. This seaside resort community (now a city of 300,000) just north of the major port of Valparaiso successfully drew tourism with its racetrack. Local facilities were inadequate, however, to use tourism to foster growth. Council members debated about creating a lake and reclaiming land from the sea to build a municipal baths center, the *balneario*. From this debate came the idea of casino gaming. There was no casino at the balneario when it originally opened. Shortly after its opening, the idea of a casino gained momentum. Vina del Mar is only eighty miles from the capital city of Santiago, and its newly developed baths and beaches attracted many urban dwellers. The Vina politicians turned their attention to the lawmakers in the large capital city.

It took until 1924 before the national government decreed a new policy that would allow selected resort cities to establish casinos. In 1928, new legislation specifically designated the creation of the first nationally recognized casino at Vina del Mar. It authorized a new local government corporation to spend up to 14 million pesos on a casino at the oceanfront near the balneario. The corporation could also select a private concessionaire to operate the casino. The initial concession agreement would last for twenty-five years. It has been renewed several times (Cabot et al. 1999, 286–288).

Casino gross profits were taxed and the proceeds designated for public works. Taxes are now on a scale up to 70 percent of gross gaming win. Of this tax, 30 percent goes for road construction and improvements in the region around Vina del Mar. The remainder goes to the city government to develop tourism facilities. The initial casino, and the three subsequently authorized, also pay a 7 percent gross win tax directly into the national government's general fund. In 1988, the national government gained 4,005,989,000 pesos (US$20,000,000) from casinos and other gaming (lotteries and horse racing). Entrance fees charged to patrons go directly to the municipal governments.

The national Ministry of Finance provides auditors who regularly visit the casinos. Local government officials conduct all other gaming inspections. The gaming laws and regulations at Vina del Mar and the other locations require the exclusion of certain people from gaming. These include those under twenty-one, those under the influence of alcohol, those with bad behaviors, and persons known (through previous experiences) not to have

sufficient funds. Gaming employees and public employees who deal with public funds also may not gamble. Under the law, women cannot gamble without permission of their husbands. Residents of the casino towns can only gamble if they get prior approval from their municipal governments. An anachronism in the national law, which is not enforced, requires that any unaccompanied women must have the written permission of their husbands, or former husbands, if they wish to enter the casino. Nonetheless, all patrons must still show identification and pay an entrance fee as they come into the casino. Foreigners must show their passports. Te Vina del Mar casino has a restaurant and bar facility, but the other casinos do not. Patrons cannot drink in gaming rooms.

The municipality constructed the current buildings at Vina del Mar in 1929 and 1930. On New Year's Eve, 31 December 1930, the wife of the mayor of Vina del Mar cast a ball into a spinning wheel. A croupier called out "Negro y Ocho" ("black and eight"), and the casino was open.

The casino now draws as many as 2,000 players a day in the summer season. During the high tourist time, the casino has twenty-eight baccarat and *punto banco* tables, eighteen American roulettes (with two zeros), four blackjack tables, and two craps tables in the main gaming room. The casino gives credit to selected players known to have sufficient means to gamble. They will also cash checks. Complimentaries are limited to restaurant and bar services available within the casino. There are no hotel facilities or complimentaries for rooms or transportation. The casino arranges group tours, but there are no gambling junkets. During the summer season, many players come from Brazil, Argentina, and the United States. In other seasons, most players come from the Santiago region.

The casino has 500 employees. During my visit to the casino in the early 1990s, all the dealers in the main room were men. Women could work only the lower-stakes games in the other rooms. The entrance fee is 800 pesos (US$2.50). The casino waives the fee for persons wishing only to observe the art collections regularly displayed in a gallery and hallways or to attend events in the 700-seat showroom.

National laws designated a casino for Arica in 1965. Arica, 1,100 miles north of Santiago, is a hot desert city of 150,000 residents located beside the ocean and near the Peruvian border. Its sandy beaches attract many tourists. In 1969, a casino was approved for Puerto Varas, a town of 25,000 that is 600 miles south of Santiago. Puerto Varas is on a beautiful lake and provides tourists access to magnificent glaciers farther to the south. The beach resorts of Coquimbo, an oceanside city of 75,000 that is 300 miles north of Santiago, won approval for a casino in 1976. In 1990, casinos were also approved for Pucoa, Puerto Natales, and Iquiqe.

The municipal governments own the casinos and contract with private organizations to operate them. All concessions, except in Vina del Mar, run for five years. The concession for the casino at Vina del Mar runs for twenty years. It was renewed in 1989. The concession agreements set the rules of the casino, the games, limits, and the taxation arrangements. Casino operators must also provide entertainment, shows, and other cultural events for the community. There have been continuing discussions regarding the establishment of new casinos in new locations.

Source: Cabot, Anthony N., William N. Thompson, Andrew Tottenham, and Carl Braunlich, eds. 1999. *International Casino Law.* 3d ed. Reno: Institute for the Study of Gambling, University of Nevada, Reno, 287–289.

Chips, Gambling

Gambling chips are used in games to represent money being wagered by players. Here the word is used generically and also includes references to gambling checks, tokens, jetons, and plaques. The chips are used to make play more convenient, as well as more routine and more secure.

From the earliest times, it has been necessary to have objects that represented wealth wagered, rather than having the actual wealth put forth in the games. Native Americans had very good control over excessive gambling, in that the players in a game would have to physically place the thing being wagered into an area near the place of the game. If they were betting a horse and a sad-

dle, the horse and saddle would be brought to the game. With these rules of engagement, the players would never wager more than they possessed, nor would they incur a debt because of their gambling. The development of money currencies simplified gambling activity considerably.

One of the latent functions of the use of chips in games has been to help the player "pretend" that the game was just a game and not about the risking of real wealth. This self-delusion has led many players into wagering amounts way beyond their means. The introduction of markers and the use of personal checks in exchange for chips has led many players into serious debt situations as a result of gambling. One casino executive applauded the value that chips have given to casinos and game operators, saying that the "guy who invented the chip was a genius" (Sifakis 1990, 65). No one knows who that guy was.

The earliest use of chips for games may have been in ancient Egypt. In the Western world, chips have been used for many centuries. European (French-style) chips were found in the eighteenth-century casinos such as Bad Ems and Wiesbaden. They were engraved in mother-of-pearl and later made of bone or ivory. In nineteenth-century games in the United States, chips were made from other materials. Ivory was used until it became too scarce and too expensive. In the 1880s, clay chips with a shellac finish were developed. A great advance in chip technology came in the 1950s, as plastic became a major component of the chips. Mixed materials were sometimes used with clay and plastic compositions surrounding metal centers for the chips. In the 1980s, the compositions led to multicolored chips of very distinctive appearances that could not only be picked out by the trained eyes of dealers and pit bosses but could also be electronically read to ensure their genuine character.

The first gambling chips in the United States did not have indications of value marked upon them. They could be used interchangeably for low-stakes and high-stakes games, merely by designating their value at the start of a game. These "plain" chips were especially popular in early illegal casinos because they could not be used as evidence if there was to be a police raid. Legitimate casinos soon found a need to control the flow of chips, however, and they did so by distinctively marking the chips with values and also with casino logos. Today, the only unmarked chips are those of different colors that are used by different players at U.S. roulette games in order to indicate which bet belongs to which player.

European (French-style) chips are different from basic U.S. casino chips in two ways. The European chip (called a jeton) is usually of a plastic composition that has a rounded surface and an oval or round shape. The chips cannot be placed on top of one another but must be spread out to determine their value and to count them. Europeans also use squared plaques for higher denominations—as do some U.S. casinos with substantial play from high rollers. The U.S. chip is invariably circular but has a flat surface. Although European chips of different values vary in size, all U.S. chips are of the same size, with the exception of plaques and some very high-value chips that are larger circles. The U.S. chip can be easily stacked and moved about. Side color markings allow casino personnel and cameras to see their values and check for authenticity. Most of the U.S. chips are the same size as an old silver dollar. Games in the United States move faster than those in Europe, and the stacking chips facilitate game speed.

The value chips in U.S. casinos today are referred to by their colors. A one-dollar chip is white, a five-dollar chip is red, a twenty-five-dollar chip is green, a one-hundred-dollar chip is black, and a pink chip is worth five hundred dollars. The notion that a high roller is a "blue chipper" or that a solid value stock on Wall Street is a "blue chip stock" is apparently a term left over from another day.

U.S. slot machines began using tokens instead of actual coins when the silver dollar started to go out of circulation in the 1960s. The earliest machines used tokens as a way of hiding the fact that they were gambling machines, but law enforcement authorities did not fall for the ruse for long. Federal laws regarding the use of tokens other than official coinage for value transactions were modified so that casinos could have machines accept the tokens. Today, many casinos outside of Nevada accept only tokens for slot play—in machines with coin acceptors. The token-accepting devices have sophisticated mechanisms with comparators that can observe the token shape, size, weight, and metal composition to ensure its validity, for the most part. Slugs or counterfeit tokens and coins are still a problem. The problem is lessened somewhat by the fact that most of the machines have dollar bill acceptors that are gradually replacing coin-in usage for slot and video slots. The players should now have that ultimate reality check each time they put a twenty- or fifty-dollar bill into a machine. They should know they are playing "real money." Once the bill is in, however, the player starts hitting a button and playing not money but "credits"—the newest gimmick to separate the player from reality.

Sources: Herz, Howard, and Kregg Herz. 1995. *A Collector's Guide to Nevada Gaming Checks and Chips.* Racine, WI: Whitman Products; Sifakis, Carl. 1990. *Encyclopedia of Gambling.* New York: Facts on File, 65; Spencer, Donald D. 1994. *Casino Chip Collecting.* Ormond Beach, FL: Camelot Publishing.

Chuck-a-Luck. See Craps and Other Dice Games

Cockfighting

Cockfights are banned throughout most of the world, including Canada and the United States, with the exception of Oklahoma. No European, African, or continental Asian country allows the sport; the only Pacific jurisdictions that permit cockfighting are the Philippines and Guam. Most of the "action" is found in Latin America and the Caribbean, including Puerto Rico, Mexico, Panama, Honduras, the Dominican Republic, Aruba, Guadeloupe, Martinique, and Haiti. Although banned almost everywhere, the fights are also found in many clandestine locations throughout North America.

Cockfighting dates back to the ancient world. Greeks and Romans bred birds especially for fighting purposes. J. Philip Jones's history of gaming, *Gambling: Yesterday and Today, a Complete History* (Jones 1973), tells of a Greek commander who was inspired by two fighting birds on his way to a victorious battle against the Persians in the fifth century B.C. In giving thanks for his triumph, he declared that there would be cockfighting everywhere in a celebration recognizing the victory (Jones 1973, 97). The activity spread throughout Europe.

At first the birds fought on tabletops, but later enclosed pens were used. The Romans brought fighting birds to England, and cockfighting developed into a popular activity there during the seventeenth century. In the American colonies, the cockfight was a regular side attraction at a horse race meeting. As birds are bred, they are closely watched for signs that they could be fighters. The training process is as elaborate as that used for racing horses or dogs. Each "cockmaster" directs the bird in rituals and practice fights using leather guards over their spurs. Before they are engaged in contests, they may be allowed to remove their spur covers and attack other chickens in order to keep their instincts intact. They are isolated so they can rest and fast before the match to ensure that they are "fresh and ready" for battle.

Betting at the cockfight is usually conducted privately on a one-on-one basis among the players. There are also bookies who will cover the action of many bettors. The heaviest betting is between the owners of the birds, with the loser losing not only money but also his prize fighter. The vicious nature of the fight to the death causes animal protective groups to vigorously oppose the sport. It was banned in England in 1834, and in most U.S. jurisdictions not long afterwards. Clifford Gertz offers a poignant description of the emotions of participation in the cockfight in his essay, "Deep Play: Notes on the Balinese Cockfight."

Sources: Gertz, Clifford. 1972. "Deep Play: Notes on the Balinese Cockfight." *Daedalus* 10 (Winter): 1–37; Jones, J. Philip. 1973. *Gambling: Yesterday, and Today, a Complete History.* Devon, England: David and Charles, 97–100.

Colombia

Tourist magazines boast of Colombia's beaches on the Caribbean, ports on the Pacific, mountain grandeur, and Amazon jungles that yield the world's finest emeralds. Colombia is a beautiful land. Democracy has prevailed in its political institutions since 1957. With a one-term limit on the office, free elections for president occur every four years. Each election has seen a peaceful transition. With its 35 million residents, it could be an ideal country.

But Colombia has its problems. A new agricultural commerce developed around the illegal drug industry, and drug activity has created a level of violence not witnessed since the days of the Spanish conquistadors. The problems of developing tourism based on the casino industry in Colombia are monumental, and perhaps insurmountable.

Bogota, the capital city, has over 5 million residents and a feel similar to New York and Paris. Still, the prominence of soldiers guarding street corners with high-powered weapons confirms unrest and uneasiness. In 1987, the murders of judges and other political officials who battled the drug lords of the Medellin Connection left no doubt as to who controlled the country. The very word *Colombian* has become synonymous with negatives that bode no good will for a national tourism industry.

Nevertheless, there is a gambling industry. Horse racing is authorized, there is a national lottery and local lotteries, and there are casinos. Somehow they have managed to get customers, but few would expect that high-rolling tourists could be found among their customers.

Colombia has had many casinos, but until very recently, there was little cohesiveness among their owners and operators. The commercial games were not subject to common rules or regulations. Until 1990, the national law was of little practical significance for the casino industry. There were references to taxes for tourism development, but national taxes were not collected. In a visit with national officials in 1989, I gained the impression that the national government wished to avoid any political controversy that might attend a debate on casino policy. With so many other more troubling problems, casino policy was one "can of worms" that could remain closed.

In 1990 a process of change began. The Colombian government undertook national health care reform and looked toward gaming revenues to fund health programs. A private company was

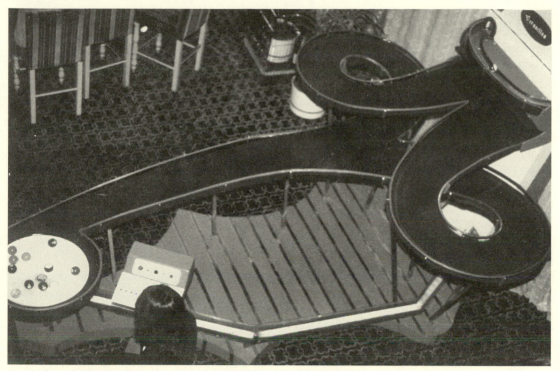

A most funny looking game: Espherodromo, the Bogata variation of Roulette.

begun under the auspices of federal authorities. Called the ECOSALUD, it holds an exclusive government charter to license and/or to operate directly or through franchising arrangements almost all forms of gaming in Colombia. Lotteries are outside of its purview and may continue to be operated by the national government and its provinces. Since the creation of ECOSALUD, laws have been passed to specify the rules for blackjack games, machine gaming, and racetrack betting. As of 1995, there were fifteen larger casinos operating under the official policies of the national government. Each had about eight to ten tables and 100 to 125 slot machines. Other venues also had slot machines. There were perhaps 30,000 machines in the country.

The phrase "casino industry" needs qualification. Colombia has casinos, but there is little cohesiveness among their owners and operators. Commercial games have few rules. Most casinos are not subject to the national casino law. The law references the use of taxes to promote tourism, but there are no national casino taxes. Learning the casino policy of Colombia is difficult, not just

for an outsider but also for the highest government officials in Bogota. Carlos Marulanda Ramirez was the cabinet minister of economic development in 1989. His ministry oversees tourism and casino policy. When I interviewed him in Bogota on 12 January 1989, he admitted that "there is no clear policy as I can see it, and I am the minister." He was studying the matter because the country should have some direction for its casinos. Ramirez acknowledged that casinos were low-priority items for a government caught up in the broader issues of economy, violence, and justice. Politicians are wary of gambling, and although they support a national lottery and horse-racing establishment, they are hesitant to endorse casino gaming officially. They believe casino policy is best developed outside the legislative process.

Casino gaming is legal under legislation passed in 1943 and 1944 and presidential decrees issued in 1977 and 1978. An earlier law passed in 1927 had prohibited casino gaming. Under the 1977 decree, a national tourism corporation within the Ministry of Economic Development would authorize casinos for a term of twenty years in the cities of Cartagena, Santa Marta, and Cali and within the region of Guajira. The 1978 decree specified that a national tourist investment company would own the Cartagena casinos. All casinos would exist according to agreements between the owners and the alcalde (or mayor of the city). Fifty percent of the public revenues from the casinos would go to promote tourism. Yet, the laws and decrees do not dictate the types of games played, the rules of the games, the taxation of gaming activity, or the inspection of the gaming halls and their personnel. The laws are simply broad statements saying that there could be casino gaming. Although the laws mention four jurisdictions, casinos exist in locations not specified by the national "policy." The industry and the national minister believe the alcaldes and the councils of the city governments should control gaming. Local governments now decide the style of gaming and any taxation.

A national policy could have emerged. Before the mid-1980s, the national government appointed the local government officials. The alcaldes are now popularly elected. Still, the development of gaming policy never influenced appointments of local officials. Because of the local nature of casino licensing and control, there is no definitive list of casino properties in Colombia. In 1989 the National Tourist Board identified casinos in Santa Marta, Cali, Cartagena, Medellin, Barranquilla, Bogota, and San Andreas Island. Santa Marta, the first European-settled community in South America, has casinos in the Hotel Rodadero and the Tamaca Inn. The Caribbean port city of Barranquilla, the second-largest city in Colombia, has a casino in the Hotel Cadebia. Cali, another city of over one million, offers five gaming houses. Medellin, a city whose name is synonymous with the violence of the illegal drug trade, has three casinos, only one of which is now open to the public. There are over ten casinos in Bogota, two in Cartagena, and two more on the Island of San Andreas.

The Bogota alcalde will license casinos, but he will not allow roulette. Yet, the game of roulette is a game of choice among Latin players. Therefore, the local casino operators used their ingenuity to develop *espherodromo,* an alternative game. Eleven

billiard balls, ten with numbers and one solid white, are released from a high platform and rolled down a chute. The chute splits into two, and part of the balls go in each direction as their descent follows a path not unlike paths on a meandering water slide. The two chutes then meet and the balls go into a large bowl, hitting each other. They descend until one enters a hole at the bottom of the bowl. This ball has the winning number. The concept is, of course, the same as for roulette. The payoff on the ten-to-one risk is nine to one. The house wins with the white ball, giving it a 10 percent edge over the players. Espherodromo has been taken to its ultimate form in Eugenio Leal Pozo's four casinos—the Versailles and Gallery 21 in the Tequendama Hotel and the Club Diversiones and Ambassador. He developed an automatic elevator system that returns the balls to their starting platform for the next play. Two dealers work the game. One dealer conducts betting activity, and the other oversees the machine. Eugenio Leal Pozo is a Cuban expatriate who worked in the Gran Casino of Havana and the Colony Club of London. He formerly owned the casino at the Hotel Hispaniola in Santo Domingo. He came to Bogota in 1975 and to the Tequendama in 1985. His two hotel casinos are small, but very plush, and they offer a few blackjack tables, one baccarat game, one *punto banco* table, four slots, and espherodromo.

The other Bogota casinos are on its main streets and cater to local walk-in traffic. There are no dress codes. Some of their names conjure up gaming images for potential players: the Atlantic City Casino Club, the Mar Del Plata, and the Palacio Del Cesar Club. Bogota casinos pay no special taxes on gaming wins, but they pay a monthly fee for each table. They also pay normal business profits taxes.

Eugenio Leal Pozo also owns a casino on San Andreas Island. The island is two hours from Bogota by air (one hour from Cartagena). National tourists do not come to gamble; almost all players in the island's two casinos are locals. As in Bogota, Leal has been an innovator on the San Andreas casino scene. He has introduced a roulette wheel with ten numbers and one zero. In his International Casino, the players suffer the same odds disadvantages as they do at espherodromo. Yet, many like the action more than that provided by his two standard wheels with thirty-six numbers and two zeros.

Tourist magazines all consider Cartagena de Indias to be one of the most fascinating cities of the continent. It was founded in 1533 and soon became a walled fortress guarding Spanish shipping that used the harbor as a point of debarkation for wealth of all kinds. The present city has two parts: the walled old city and the new resort beach community called El Laguito. The two casinos are in the new area. The drug wars of 1990 resulted in the temporary closing of the two casinos; however, they have since reopened. The Casino Turistico de Cartagena was a "down market" property. If it had many customers, it would be a grind joint (see Glossary). An outside entrance way on St. Martin's Street was lined with two rows of Bally mechanical slots that were always exposed to the salty sea air. The four roulette and six blackjack tables also showed the effects of being exposed to the elements. At 6:00 P.M. on a Saturday in January 1989, only one table was open. The property may exist today only as a repository for a license that can later be moved or sold for a lucrative profit.

The other casino, the El Caribe, has been the premier gaming property in Colombia. Its licensing status is also confusing. The casino started in the Caribe Hotel. Then, fifteen years ago, a major emerald company based in Bogota constructed an office and shopping complex near the hotel. It also envisioned having a 300-room hotel in the office-shopping complex and would build a foundation to support a hotel tower. The company gained control of the casino license and moved the gaming facility to its property. The hotel was never built. Meanwhile, the Ministry of Economic Development supported the construction of a new Hilton Hotel (the government owns 46 percent of the property). The deluxe hotel with 298 rooms offers full facilities for all tourist activities. During his interview with me in January 1989, the minister of economic development stated that the hotel would have a casino in the future. But others suggest that such talk has been going on ever since the hotel opened. The managers of the El Caribe casino affirmed that they based their agreement to operate the facility on an understanding that Cartagena would have no more than two licenses. The minister's position is that he is the government, and he can have a license if he decides there should be one. The managers suggest that the local government must approve all licenses, and the local government said "only two" casinos. On the other hand, the Hilton possibly could take the license from the Casino Turistico, or it could negotiate to have the El Caribe operate a Hilton casino under its license.

The El Caribe developed into a major casino property only after a new U.S. management team took charge in 1985. It introduced U.S.-style gaming, retrained dealers, replaced French roulette with the faster U.S. roulette games, remodeled the facility, installed a prive sala (private room) with four full games of baccarat, and opened a craps table. A special feature of the casino was a series of cockfights that were held in a special ring just outside of the main gambling area. Players could watch the fights and place private wagers on the birds. A low ceiling over the gambling area permitted the installation of a system of mirrors (affectionately called the Cartagena Catwalk) that permits security personnel to observe action on all tables in a pit simultaneously. There are no security cameras except in the cage area. The U.S. managers also set up a gambling junket program for East Coast high rollers. Yet, as the drug crises deepened, players refused to come from the United States. In 1989, most foreign play came from Canadians.

In that same year, the casino drew about 200 patrons a night, with weekend crowds as high as 500. The casino had eighty dealers. All were Colombians, as it was very hard for a foreigner to get a work visa. As in Honduras, a system of private loan agents existed to circulate money to patrons. The agents borrowed funds from the casino and loaned it to players. The agents repaid the casino each evening. They charged the players 10 percent for their services and took all the risks of collecting the debts.

Local police moved in and out of the casino to maintain order. When Colombian drug lords visited the casino, the understanding was that they came unarmed and did not engage in drug business in the casino. Although their activity destroyed the casino's best foreign markets, the casinos hoped that with such understandings, they would not destroy remaining markets.

The government has also encouraged a revitalization of the other smaller urban casinos in Bogota, Cali, Medellin, Santa Marta, and other cities, as it has authorized the importation of additional machine games for the facilities. As the twentieth century ended, authorities were successful in attracting capital for a new casino in Bogota. The Hollywood Casino featured fourteen tables and 180 machines.

Source: Cabot, Anthony N., William N. Thompson, Andrew Tottenham, and Carl Braunlich, eds. 1999. *International Casino Law.* 3d ed. Reno: Institute for the Study of Gambling, University of Nevada, Reno, 290–295.

Colorado

Colorado offers a state lottery, charity games and raffles, pari-mutuel horse- and dog-race betting, and casino gambling activities. The modern era of gambling began when the lottery was initiated in 1983 for the purpose of raising funds for parks and environmental projects. As with many other lottery states, the normal legislative funding for these projects was reduced in accordance with the lottery gains, however, and in effect the lottery money simply went into the general fund of the state. The experience only confirmed that it is very difficult to have lottery funding for any ongoing programs that are normally funded by legislative action. The "modern" situation of using lotteries for regular government programs is contrasted with the experience in colonial times when lotteries were utilized to fund specific capital projects—college buildings, roads, bridges, military arms.

There was one difference that citizens noticed in Colorado after the lottery was initiated. Many of their state parks had signs proclaiming that the park was being supported by the lottery, which of course was true, but possibly also false. In some states the lottery money is added to budgets; however, it is difficult to trace the funds. Often they are merely shifted from one program to another one.

In November 1990, the voters were persuaded to approve limited-stakes casino gambling for three mountain towns—Blackhawk, Central City, and Cripple Creek. The gambling rules were patterned after those in South Dakota—five-dollar maximum bets on blackjack and poker games and on slot machines. One of the motivations for voter approval was the fact that the casinos of Deadwood were marketing their gambling to players from Denver, the largest city within a one-day drive of Deadwood. Even though the governor opposed the proposition, it passed with a 57 percent favorable vote. The number of casinos in existence at one time has fluctuated considerably from over eighty to fewer than sixty—the approximate number as the new century began.

Subsequent to the successful vote, several other towns in Colorado have sought voter approval for casinos, only to have their propositions lose by big margins. Two of the three towns with casino gambling, Blackhawk and Central City, are located on winding mountain roads about one hour west of Denver, and the third town, Cripple Creek, is one hour west of Colorado Springs. How the three towns were picked for the ballot proposition in 1990 is no mystery. In 1989, leaders from a group of about a dozen communities approached the legislature and requested passage of a law permitting casino gambling in their venues. They received very serious consideration; the legislative votes were close, but the proposal was defeated. Afterwards, a few of the leaders decided that the only way they could succeed would be to circulate petitions and secure a statewide vote on a constitutional amendment permitting casinos. Since these campaigns are expensive, the leaders of the effort asked the dozen communities to fund the election. Most of the towns declined to make a financial contribution to the campaign. Blackhawk, Central City, and Cripple Creek, however, agreed to make the financial commitment necessary for a successful campaign. The leaders decided that if this were the case, the casino proposition would apply only to these three towns.

Casino policies—rules and regulations, taxation and licensing actions—are determined by a five-member Colorado Limited Gaming Control Commission. The policy enforcement activities are conducted by the Colorado Division of Gaming, an

The storefront casinos of Cripple Creek, Colorado.

agency within the Colorado Department of Revenue. The amendment approved by the voters permitted the taxation rate to be as high as 40 percent of the casino win. The top rate in a progressive tax structure, however, is 20 percent of the gambling revenue. There are also extensive fees charged by both the state and local governments. For instance, the local governments charge between $750 to $1,500 annually for each gambling device (machine or table). The state requires each employee to go through a licensing process and pay a $200 fee before working in a casino.

The slot machines in the casinos must pay out in prizes at least 80 percent of the money that is played. Unlike South Dakota, the state has no fixed limit on the number of machines in a casino. Many have several hundred machines. There are over 13,000 machines in the sixty or so casinos.

The ostensible purpose of the Colorado gambling has been to aid in tourism development. State taxes, however, go to the general fund directly. Moreover, the overwhelming numbers of players—certainly over 90 percent—are from the two metropolitan areas located near the casinos.

Source: Cabot, Anthony N., William N. Thompson, Andrew Tottenham, and Carl Braunlich, eds. 1999. *International Casino Law.* 3d ed. Reno: Institute for the Study of Gambling, University of Nevada, Reno, 17–25; Dombrink, John, and William N. Thompson. 1990. *The Last Resort: Success and Failure in Campaigns for Casinos.* Reno: University of Nevada Press, 152–158.

Commission on the Review of National Policy toward Gambling (1974–1976)

The 1970 Organized Crime Control Act authorized the president and Congress to appoint a commission to examine gambling in the United States. The commission was charged with conducting a "comprehensive legal and factual study of gambling" in the United States and all its subdivisions and was instructed to "formulate and propose such changes" in policies and practices as it might "deem appropriate." At its conclusion, the commission included four U.S. senators (Democrats John McClellan of Arkansas and Howard Cannon of Nevada and Republicans Hugh Scott of Pennsylvania and Bob Taft of Ohio) and four members of the House (Democrats James Hanley of New York and Gladys Spellman of Maryland and Republicans Charles Wiggins of California and Sam Steiger of Arizona). Seven "citizen" members included Commission chairman Charles Morin, a Washington, D.C., attorney; state attorney general Robert List of Nevada; Ethel Allen, a city council member in Philadelphia; Philip Cohen, director of the National Legal Data Center; prosecutor James Coleman of Monmouth County, New Jersey; Joseph Gimma, a New York banker; and professor of economics Charles Phillips of Washington and Lee University. Former federal prosecutor James Ritchie served as the executive director of the commission. The commission had a life of almost three years. The first meetings were in January 1974, and its final report was presented on 15 October 1976.

The commission staff of nearly thirty professionals, twenty student assistants, and twenty-six consultants prepared several dozen research studies. Additionally, the Survey Research Center of the University of Michigan was engaged to conduct the first national survey of gambling behavior ever taken. It also conducted a gaming survey of the Nevada population. The commission also held forty-three days of public hearings in Washington, D.C., as well as in several other cities, including Las Vegas. Testimony was received from 275 law enforcement personnel; persons involved with gambling enterprises, both legal and illegal; and persons representing the general public.

The report presented conclusions suggesting a much more relaxed view of gambling than had been found in earlier federal investigations. Indeed, the commission seemed to be urging the federal government to remove itself from the regulatory process almost entirely. A certain mixed message was given—a recognition that gambling has a downside, but a frustration that legislation seeking to totally outlaw gambling is simply unenforceable. Hence citizens and governments were urged, for the most part, to "roll with the punches."

The sense of the commission's feelings is presented in Chairman Morin's Foreword to the final report: "[We] should carefully reflect on the significance of the fact that a pastime indulged in by two-thirds of the American people, and approved of by perhaps 80 percent of the population, contributes more than any other single enterprise to police corruption . . . and to the well-being of the Nation's criminals. . . . Most Americans gamble because they like to, and they see nothing wrong with it." He then highlights a statement from the report: "Contradictory gambling policies and lack of resources combine to make effective gambling law enforcement an impossible task. . . ." He adds, "Not 'difficult'—not 'frustrating' not even 'almost impossible'—but *impossible*. And why not? How can any law which prohibits what 80 percent of the people approve of be enforced?"(Commission on the Review of the National Policy toward Gambling 1976, ix).

The commission made a firm recommendation that gambling policy be a matter that is determined by the states. Indeed, it urged that Congress enact a statute "that would insure the states' continued power to regulate gambling" (Commission on the Review of the National Policy toward Gambling 1976, 5). Moreover, the federal government was asked to take care that its regulations and taxing powers not interfere with states' rights in this area. The commission urged that player winnings from gambling activities not be subject to federal income taxes and that the federal wagering tax and slot machine tax be removed. State authorities were asked to devote law enforcement energies against persons operating gambling enterprises at a "higher" level and to relax enforcement against "low-level" gambling offenses. Prohibitions against public social gambling should be removed. If a state had a substantial amount of illegal gambling, however, the federal government should be authorized to use electronic surveillance techniques not authorized before, and judges were urged to give longer prison terms and more substantial fines to convicted offenders.

The report suggested that states use considerable caution before they legalized casinos. If they did so, the state regulatory law should provide a series of player protection provisions. Moreover, casinos should be private, not government, enterprises. Casinos should not be built in "urban areas where lower income people reside" (Commission on the Review of the National Policy toward Gambling 1976, 3). The commission recommended that racetracks and offtrack betting facilities lower the take-out rate on wagers (the amount the track removes from its betting pool). If the bettors were able to keep more of their wagers at legal betting facilities, they would be less inclined to turn to illegal operators when placing bets. The states should also determine if players were allowed to make wagers on out-of-state races. The commission felt that state lotteries were often unfair to players and that full information about true odds for the games should be presented to the public. Advertisements by the lotteries should also be more honest and accurate. States were discouraged from allowing wagers on single-event sports games, especially on games involving amateur teams. The commission recommended that states not have sports betting without a referendum vote of the citizens.

Source: Commission on the Review of the National Policy toward Gambling. 1976. *Gambling in America: Final Report.* Washington, DC: Government Printing Office.

Commission to Investigate Allegations of Police Corruption and the City's Anti-Corruption Procedures. *See* The Knapp Commission

Compulsive Gambling. *See* Gambling, Pathological

Comstock, Anthony

Anthony Comstock was one of the most prominent reformers in the Victorian era of the later nineteenth century. Other biographies included in this encyclopedia look at the leading gamblers, certainly rogues of the time, but some attention should be given to one who might be truly considered the greatest rogue of all. Comstock did not cheat the innocent, naive, and greedy out of their money. Rather, he purposely cheated society out of personal freedoms, and his vehicle for doing so was government policy and police enforcement powers. His target was sin—all types of sin, especially those of a sexual nature, but also the sins of

drinking alcohol and gambling. The impact of the laws he pushed toward passage is still felt today.

On 7 March 1844, Anthony Comstock was born in the small town of New Canaan, Connecticut. He was raised in a very religious family, and he had a disciplined childhood shielded from sinful activities. He came out of this cocoon in 1863, when he joined the 17th Connecticut Company for service in the Civil War. He felt an obligation to serve in place of his brother, who had fallen in battle. The 17th Company saw firefights in South Carolina before it withdrew for passive duty in St. Augustine, Florida. Comstock's real battles began there. He confronted the foul language and base habits of his fellow soldiers, and he resolved that he would have to change their behaviors. He found the means to change other people in the Army's Christian Commission and the Young Men's Christian Association (YMCA). After the war, he moved to New York City and found that once again he was surrounded by sins of all kinds. He actively involved his YMCA comrades in harassing the sinners at every opportunity. He pressured police forces to enforce laws against prostitution and wide-open drinking and gambling.

His politics of enforcement put him in direct opposition to feminist groups. He gained considerable attention in seeking to win a prosecution against Victoria Claffin Woodhall, a free-love advocate who ran for president in 1872. As the result of the following he gained in the battle, he went to Washington, D.C., and secured passage of what became known as the Comstock Obscenity Law. The law prohibited the mailing of any materials with a sexual message of any type. In 1873, he secured a position as the chief inspector of the Postal Service, so the enforcement of the law was in his hands. He went after the job with vigor.

Soon afterwards, he persuaded the New York legislature to charter the New York Society to Suppress Vice. The charter act gave officials of the society "arrest" powers as if they were police officers. Comstock won support from several leading entrepreneurs who wanted to root out the influence of sin over their workforce. Among his supporters was J. P. Morgan. Comstock pushed the New York legislature to act as well. In 1882, state laws were recodified, and all gambling except for horse racing was made illegal. Anthony Comstock went to work against gambling. He harassed the police into some prosecutions against casinos that operated openly in New York City. In this fight he was not successful until 1900 and 1901, when he forced Richard Canfield to close down his city casino, the most glamorous in the country at the time. Comstock was less successful in closing down the Canfield casino in Saratoga.

During Comstock's later career, he did not emphasize his disdain for gambling, but he pushed where he could. He rivaled, but also allied, Rev. Charles Parkhurst and the Society for the Prevention of Crime in his fights. He was with Parkhurst in 1890 as the reformers persuaded Congress to pass the law banning the use of the U.S. mails by lotteries and other gambling interests. Comstock's activities were also blended into those of the Progressive movement, and he was aboard the ride that found all gambling, except racing, banned everywhere. Soon after his death, all alcoholic beverages were banned throughout the United States as well.

Sources: Bates, Anna Louise. 1995. *Weeder in the Garden of the Lord: Anthony Comstock's Life and Career.* Lanham, MD: University Press of America; Broun, Heywood, and Margaret Leech. 1927. *Anthony Comstock, Boundsman of the Lord.* New York: A and C Boni; Comstock, Anthony. 1967. *Traps for the Young.* Cambridge: The Belknap Press of Harvard University Press; Longstreet, Stephen. 1977. *Win or Lose: A Social History of Gambling.* Indianapolis, IN: Bobbs-Merrill, 234–238.

See also Canfield, Richard

Connecticut

Modern gambling came to Connecticut swiftly and almost completely in 1971. A lottery, offtrack betting, and horse-track betting all became legal at the same time. In 1972, dog-racing and jai alai betting were legalized. Only casinos and sports betting remained, and efforts to bring about legalization started in the 1970s. Bills allowing a casino in the depressed community of Bridgeport were introduced in 1981. The measure died in a state legislative committee. Bills were also defeated in 1983 and 1984. The momentum for casinos seemed to die. But Connecticut permitted casino games for charities; they could hold Las Vegas Nights. Connecticut also had Native American tribes. The one organized reservation belonged to the Mashantucket Pequots. They started bingo games and then requested negotiations for casino gaming. After several court battles, the state negotiated to allow the tribe to offer casino table games. In 1992, the tribe asked for slot machines even though they were not permitted in other entities in the state. Without going through the negotiation process, the state agreed to allow the machines if the tribe would give the state 25 percent of the revenues from the machines. The National Indian Gaming Act prohibited state taxation of tribal gaming; therefore, the state and tribe called the "fee" a contribution exchanged for the right to have a monopoly over machine gaming in the state. When a second Native casino opened on a new reservation created by the Mohegans, the Pequots renegotiated the amount of money from the machines that they give the state. In 1999, nearly $300 million went to the state as a result of the agreement.

The Pequot casino, called Foxwoods, is located near the town of Ledyard. The casino is the largest in the world, with 284,000 square feet of gambling space, a bingo hall, 4,585 machines, and 312 tables. It produces gambling wins of approximately $1 billion a year. The Mohegan Sun casino is managed by Sun International, a company with gambling experience in South Africa and the Bahamas that had earlier acquired and later sold the Desert Inn Casino in Las Vegas. The casino, which is near Uncasville, has a gaming area of 150,000 square feet, 3,000 tables, and 180 tables.

Sources: Dombrink, John D., and William N. Thompson. 1990. *The Last Report: Success and Failure in Campaigns for Casinos.* Reno: University of Nevada Press, 127–129; WEFA Group (with ICR Research Group, Henry Lesieur, and William Thompson). 1997. *Study Concerning the Effects of Legalized Gambling on the Citizens of the State of Connecticut.* Eddystone, PA: WEFA Group.

Costa Rica

Costa Rica has both lottery games and casino games. Until very recently, the casinos operated on a basis that most charitably would be called Third

World. The casinos purportedly operated under the provisions of a 1922 law that indicated which games were legal and which games were illegal. For instance, craps was illegal, but dominos was legal. Blackjack was illegal, but rommy (a variation of the word *rummy*) was legal. Moreover, roulette gambling was illegal, but if a game was not gambling, it was legal. Slot machines were also illegal.

Not too much notice was given to gaming in Costa Rica before the 1960s. Games were played, but both the operators and the players were Costa Ricans, so it was all a local thing. Then residents of the United States discovered the country. It was close to the United States, and it seemed to be quiet and peaceful. It was the perfect place to retire or to run away if your name was Robert Vesco (a fugitive financier of the Nixon era) or you had the Internal Revenue Service chasing after you. Costa Rica refused to extradite fugitives to the United States. A growing population from the United States was accompanied by growing tourist interest in Costa Rica. The casino activity reached out to foreign "visitors." In 1963, an ex-dealer from Las Vegas named Shelby McAdams saw an opportunity. He tied a roulette wheel on top of his Nash Rambler car and headed south on the Pan-American Highway. He introduced a new style of casino gaming. And along with a German expatriate named Max Stern, he offered "first class" gaming. McAdams and Stern were accepted by appreciative local residents, and soon others imitated their operations. In the 1970s and 1980s, casino gaming spread to all the major hotels in San Jose, as well as to outlying resort hotels such as the Herradura, Irazu, Cirobici, and Cariari.

The casino operators knew that the patrons wanted blackjack, roulette, and craps games, so they read and reread the 1922 law. Collectively they came up with their solution, and for two decades, they alternatively sought alliances with government officials or fought the efforts of government officials who wanted to read the law another way. I was stunned when I visited most of the gaming facilities in 1989. One casino was named Dominos. Indeed, in the middle of the gaming floor there was a long table and over it was a sign that said "dominos." Inside the table there was a layout that showed the field, the big six, come, don't come,

A casino hotel in San Jose, Costa Rica.

pass, don't pass, and other familiar-looking dice table configurations. The players held two little cubes with white dots on each of their six sides, and they rolled the cubes into the corner of the table. As they did so, they yelled such things as, "Baby needs some new shoes," "eighter from Decatur," and "seven come eleven." I asked the manager just what they were playing. With a straight face, he said, "Dominos." I looked at the table, and inside the play area there was indeed a stack of dominos. I said, "What are those for?" He said, "Oh, if an investigator or stranger comes in and we think he wants to cause us trouble, we ask the players to put the cubes down and throw the dominos." As play continued at the "craps," also known as "dominos" table, a police officer came in. But he was not there to cause trouble, merely to see the manager, who spoke to an assistant. Momentarily the assistant returned with a carton of cigarettes, and the policeman left (with the cigarettes.)

The casinos also offered the game of rommy. Rommy was played with a shoe of six decks. Two cards were dealt to players, and the dealer also took two cards. The players then either "stood" or asked for more cards. If the player's cards added up to a number closer to twenty-one (without going over twenty-one) than the dealer's cards, then the player won. All payoffs were on an even-money basis. The casino managers insisted that this was not "blackjack" because blackjack was prohibited by the law. This was "rommy." There was no blackjack payoff of 5–2; there were payoffs of 10–1 if the player had three sevens and 3–1 if the player had a 5–6–7 straight in the same suit. Rommy was a legal game.

I noticed a small roulette wheel in the back of a casino. I was told that they tried this but the government at the time did not accept it (perhaps they had not given the authorities enough cigarettes?). The roulette game they tried was one called golden ten or observation roulette in Holland and Germany, where it was popular at the time. The wheel was stationary, with its number slats in the middle of a big metal bowl. The dealer would roll the ball slowly so it would make wide ellipses as it rolled to the center. While the ball was slowly moving downward, the player would observe it closely and predict where it would land. With great skill, the predictions could be correct. Hence, argued the casinos, the game was not a gambling game, but a skilled game. The argument worked better in Holland than it did in Costa Rica. The casinos also set up a roulette layout and called the game canasta (a legal game). In this "canasta" game, a single number was drawn out of a basket of Ping-Pong balls (similar to a bingo basket). The number was the winning number for a game played on a roulette layout.

The casino very much wanted to have slot machines, but there was no way they could read them into the 1922 law. In the matter of taxes, the casinos seemed to pay what the government demanded, and that amount was quite flexible and certainly much less than per-table fees stipulated in municipal ordinances.

In 1995, the casinos stopped trying to fight the law. The law was changed, clearly permitting casino games of craps, roulette, and blackjack. Slot machines were also authorized. As of 2000, the number of casinos had been reduced; there were approximately twenty in the country, a dozen being located in the capital city of San Jose. They must be in resort hotels, and the hotel must own the casino.

—*coauthored by David Nichols*

Source: Cabot, Anthony N., William N. Thompson, Andrew Tottenham, and Carl Braunlich, eds. 1999. *International Casino Law.* 3d ed. Reno: Institute for the Study of Gambling, University of Nevada, Reno, 296–299.

Craps and Other Dice Games
Hazard

Hazard is an old English dice game that contains elements of today's craps game. Knights played hazard as early as the twelfth century during the crusades to Arabia and the Middle East. It was not until the seventeenth and eighteenth centuries, however, that hazard became the most popular English casino game.

In basic hazard, a shooter throws two dice. He throws and rethrows until he gets a 5, 6, 7, 8, or 9. This number then becomes his "point." He rolls again (and again), until a game-ending number comes up. He wins if he makes the point and also if he rolls an 11 or 12 (with some exceptions). He loses if he rolls a 2 or 3 (called a crabs). With a 4 or 10, he rolls again. If he rolls a 5, 6, 7, 8, or 9 that is not his point, it now becomes his "chance," and he loses if he rolls it again (which means he rolls it before he rolls his point or a 2, 3, 11, or 12).

For a player making rolls over and over, the game was not difficult to understand, although it certainly seems to be a complicated game. To make matters more confusing, many variations were added to the game as time passed. When the game was brought to the North American colonies, the craps version was introduced, and this version was accepted as the standard two-dice game in North America. A three-dice game called grand hazard was also widely played in the colonies. The games of chuck-a-luck and sic bo became a variation of grand hazard.

Chuck-a-Luck

Chuck-a-luck is a three-dice game also known as "bird cage." Three dice are placed into a large cage

A game of craps in a Las Vegas casino, ca. 1940. (UNLV Special Collections)

Chuck-a-luck is a three-dice game. Here it is played by the editor and David Nichols (in author biographies) at a charity casino event in El Paso, Texas.

Casino Craps layout. Many different bets are allowed in this most popular dice game.

shaped like an hourglass. The cage is on an axis, and it is rotated several times by a dealer. The dice fall, and their numbers total from 3 to 18 (each die showing a 1 to 6). A player may bet that a certain number (1 to 6) will show on at least one die. If it does, he or she receives an even-money payoff; if the number appears on two dice, the payoff is two to one; if all three dice show the number, the payoff is three to one. Although the bet appears to most casual observers to favor the player, the house actually has a 7.87 percent advantage.

Other bets could also be made. For instance, a player could wager that there would be a three of a kind on a particular number, or any three of a kind. A player could also bet on a high series of numbers or a low series of numbers.

Sic Bo and Cussec

Sic bo and cussec are two variations of chuck-a-luck. Sic bo is popular in Canada; cussec is played in many Asian countries, as well as in Portugal. Until 1999, no dice were allowed in Canadian games. Sic bo was played in some rather unique ways. A casino in Vancouver had players roll three small balls into a roulette wheel marked with the faces of two dice on each num-

ber area (thirty-six markings). At the charity casino in Winnipeg's Convention Centre (open for a few years during the 1980s), there was an actual slot machine that had three reels. On each reel was the face of a die. The three die faces became the player's "roll."

French Bank

French bank is a very fast three-dice game played in Portugal. It is one of the most popular games in Portuguese casinos. The three dice are thrown rapidly until a low series (5, 6, or 7) or a high series (14, 15, or 16) comes up. Players wager even money on low or high. If three aces (1–1–1) come up, all players lose, except those betting on the three aces—they win a sixty-to-one payoff.

Backgammon

Backgammon is a game played with two dice and a board. It involves moving tiles around a playing surface and also blocking movements by one's opponents. The game is considered by some to be the oldest board game, as it dates back to Roman times. In the eighteenth and nineteenth centuries, it was very popular with English nobility and involved very high gambling stakes.

Sources: Jensen, Marten. 2000. *Secrets of the New Casino Games.* New York: Cardoza, 127; Miller, Len. 1983. *Gambling Times Guide to Casino Games.* Secaucus, NJ: Lyle Stuart; Scarne, John. 1986. *Scarne's New Complete Guide to Gambling.* New York: Simon and Schuster, 259–330; Sifakis, Carl. 1990. *Encyclopedia of Gambling.* New York: Facts on File, 15, 65–66, 77–82; Silberstang, Edwin. 1980. *Playboy's Guide to Casino Gambling.* Chicago: Playboy Press, 19–123.

Credit and Debts

In 1990, I visited the Casino Copanti in San Pedro Sula, Honduras. The casino owners were an American, Eddie Cellini, and his sons. Members of Cellini's family had previously worked in casinos in Havana, Cuba, and Lagos, Nigeria. I was talking with one of his sons when a player approached the cage and seemed to purchase a full tray of tokens. I thought nothing about it until the same man returned ten minutes later and purchased another full tray of tokens. I commented to the younger Cellini that the man appeared to be a "high roller." He laughed and said, "No, he is buying tokens to loan to the players." He went on to add that the tokens were sold at a discount to certain individuals. Those individuals would then know which players they could loan them to with a good expectation of being paid back. The individuals made their own loan and collection arrangements with the players. The casino management endorsed the practices. They had learned several things when they first opened up and made loans directly to the local players. They learned that they were "the ugly Americans" when they tried to collect repayments from players who had been losers. Often the players would say, "I gave you your money back at the tables." Then they would suggest that the casino's request for repayment was an affront to their "manhood" and dignity. When the Cellinis went to court to collect the debts, they found judges who were quite reluctant to support the cause of the foreigners from the casino who were now seeking to "exploit" the local players. The casino's solution was simple—let the locals borrow from each other. I questioned if this might represent casino support for loan sharking but was assured that the loan agents were respected local businessmen and that the

casino had never heard of a complaint that their collection procedures were anything but fair.

The Jaragua Casino of Santo Domingo loaned chips to players directly. They had two sets of chips, however. The set of chips that were loaned to players had white stripes across them. The casino manager told me that they had had problems with players borrowing funds to gamble and then cashing in the chips and not repaying the loans on time. Credit players could only win striped chips. The players could not cash these until their debts were fully paid.

Gambling credit and indebtedness pose many issues for the gambling industry. There are simple business decisions, such as: Can the person borrowing money from the establishment be trusted to pay it back? There are also legal questions. For instance, can an establishment go to court to force repayment of a gambling debt? Moral issues confront the industry when casinos may offer loans to players who are not in control of their play (e.g., compulsive gamblers). Other questions concern the use of credit card machines and automated teller machines (ATMs) in gambling places. There is also concern expressed in gambling jurisdictions about the presence of "loan sharks" representing organized crime interests.

Without credit, many large gambling casinos would not be able to sustain ample profits to support their operations in a viable manner. Perhaps half of the table play at Las Vegas Strip casinos is credit play. High rollers appreciate being able to set up accounts with casinos upon which they can draw and also be able to draw upon credit allotments as well. As with the credit card machines or an ATM, this ability permits the player to come to the casino without having to carry large sums of money. Also, winnings can be placed back into accounts instead of being converted into cash that would have to be carried out of the casino on one's person. This latter situation remains a major problem for casino ATMs, as they allow only withdrawals but no deposits.

By establishing accounts with a casino, a high roller can begin to establish a record of play activity. This enables the casino to award the good player with complimentaries such as free transportation (air flights), free hotel rooms, meals, beverages, and show tickets. Additionally, by engaging in straight credit play, the player and the casino can avoid the necessity of reporting large cash transactions as required by the Bank Secrecy Act of 1970. This may give the player an added sense of anonymity.

In jurisdictions where gambling credit is permitted (as in Nevada and New Jersey), there are usually detailed rules surrounding the loans. In Nevada, regulations require casinos to check the credit history of players seeking loans. They must also look at the previous loans given to the player to be assured that they were repaid. They must also check with other casinos regarding the player's activity. Casinos are required to check identifications when players cash checks. In actuality, the credit loan from the Nevada casino is like a bank counter check. The credit instrument is called a marker, and it contains information about player bank account numbers and authorizes loan repayments for the accounts. It also acknowledges that the loan was made entirely within the state of Nevada and that the player is willing to be sued in courts, including Nevada courts, for repayment if necessary. The player also agrees to pay the cost of collection.

"In the old days," casinos may have resorted to ugly tactics to retrieve money owed by players. Nowadays such tactics as threatened physical harm or embarrassments bordering on blackmail are hardly ever used. If they were used and discovered, casinos would be severely disciplined. Most players truly want to replay loans. One major consideration many have is that they will not be able to return to the casino to play again with VIP (very important person) treatment unless they repay the loans. If they are temporarily without sufficient funds, casinos will give them a "long leash"—that is, adequate time to get the necessary resources. Casinos will also discount loan amounts to ensure quick repayment.

Discounts may be as much as 25 percent of the value of the loan. Of course, the casino would have a record that the debtor actually lost the money while playing in the casino. Casino loans that are repaid in a reasonable time do not carry any interest. This factor distinguishes the casino loans from those received from loan sharks. Typically,

the loan shark requires a repayment with 10 percent interest per week. If the person cannot make the total repayment, then only the 10 percent is accepted (that is mandatory), and the full loan plus the 10 percent interest carries over until the next week. Casinos in Nevada may use collection agencies that are bonded and licensed; in New Jersey, casino organizations do all the collection activities themselves.

The casinos must make a bona fide effort to collect all debts. Otherwise, they will be assessed taxes as if they had collected the debt in full. New Jersey limits the amount of "bad debt" that can be deducted from their casino win for taxation purposes.

Most North American jurisdictions follow the edict of the Statute of Anne (1710), which became part of the common law of England. The statute holds that debts incurred because of gambling represent contracts that are unenforceable by courts of the realm. Before 1983, Nevada also followed the Statute of Anne. As the Nevada law would apply anywhere as long as it pertained to a Nevada debt, the casinos could not collect debts from out of state, even if the debtor's state permitted collection of gambling debts through the courts. In 1982, a federal tax court ruled that uncollected Nevada debts could no longer be subtracted from casino wins for tax purposes. Although the decision was overruled by other courts, Nevada was stimulated into action for change. Also, with the advent of New Jersey casinos and the fact that New Jersey courts allowed collection of gambling debts, Nevada casinos found themselves at a disadvantage. Players with debts in both states were paying off the New Jersey debts and ignoring the Nevada debts when they did not have sufficient funds to cover both. In 1983, Nevada repealed the Statute of Anne, and now gambling debts may be collected through courts in Nevada as well as New Jersey.

Even with the Statute of Anne repealed, both states found that other states' courts would still refuse to order repayment of the loans. Hence, casino operators in Nevada and New Jersey have adopted another method for collection. In Nevada, casinos take their cases only to Nevada courts. There, the facts support them; the courts give judgments in favor of the casino against the debtors. The court ruling is then entered into the courts of the debtor's home state. Those courts then will issue orders supporting the Nevada court rulings and will not consider the gambling issue. Fortunately for the casinos, debt matters do not have to go to court very often.

A gambling debt is, in effect, the result of a contract between the casino and a player. When a player is taken to court to repay the debt, he or she may offer several defenses regarding the contract, perhaps making a case that the gambling activity in question is illegal. If proven, that would make the contract for a loan illegal and unenforceable. The gambling debtor may also claim that the debt is excessive and that the casino should not have allowed him or her to incur such a large debt. Puerto Rican courts have entertained such defenses and have actually reduced the amount of the debt they ordered to be repaid.

If the player is too young to gamble, age is a complete defense against compulsory repayment of the loan. In a reverse case, a nineteen-year-old was denied a $1-million jackpot he "won" at Caesars Palace in Las Vegas. Even though Caesars was in a sense indebted to the player to pay the amount, the casino did not do so. The gaming control board and the courts voided the casino's obligation to pay the jackpot, because the player was too young to gamble.

Some have argued that the debts from gambling should not have to be repaid if the player was intoxicated. Courts have heard such cases, although they have not ruled in favor of such a debtor. A special defense heard in many cases today is that the player was a compulsive gambler. In such situations, the player must have proof that the casino knew of the compulsive condition prior to the debt. There have also been third-party suits from family members or victims of embezzlement seeking recovery of moneys gambled by compulsive gamblers. There have been some out-of-court settlements in these cases, but as of yet, no major decisions have disallowed collection of debt or given recovery because of compulsive gambling. Efforts continue, however, to bring such cases to court.

Sources: Cabot, Anthony N., ed. 1989. *Casino Credit and Collection Law.* Las Vegas: International Association of Gaming Attorneys; Lionel, Sawyer and Collins. 1995. *Nevada Gaming Law.* 2d ed. Las Vegas, NV: Lionel, Sawyer and Collins; Thompson, William N. 1991. "Machismo: Manifestations of a Cultural Value in the Latin American Casino." *Journal of Gambling Studies* 7 (Spring): 143–164.

Crime and Gambling

The crime issue has been and will continue to be an essential issue in debates over the legalization of gambling. Opponents of gambling make almost shrill statements about how organized crime infiltrates communities when they legalize gambling. They also suggest that various forms of street crimes—robberies, auto-thefts, prostitution—come with gambling, as do embezzlements, forgeries, and various forms of larceny caused by desperate problem gamblers.

On the other hand, proponents of gambling contend that the evidence of any connections between crime and gambling is rather weak. They contend that the stories of Mob involvement with gambling are a part of the past, but not the present, and that even then the involvement was more exaggerated than real. Most cases of increased street crime are passed off as owing to increased volumes of people traffic in casino communities. Moreover, proponents of legalized gambling even argue that because gambling may lead to job growth in gambling communities, crime may actually go down, the reason being that employed people are less inclined to be drawn to criminal activities than are people without jobs. They also suggest that by legalizing gambling, society can fight the effects of illegal gambling.

Opportunities for Crime

Criminologists have identified opportunity as a factor in explaining much criminal activity. The kinds of crimes that are purportedly found in association with gambling indicate the efficacy of "opportunity" theories of crime. For instance, the several types of crime that might be associated with the presence of casinos include inside activity concerning casino owners and business associates and employees, crimes tied to the playing of the games, and crimes involving patrons. Organized crime elements may try to draw profits off the gaming enterprise through schemes of hidden ownership or through insiders who steal from the casino winnings. Managers may steal from the profit pools to avoid taxes or to cheat their partners.

Organized crime figures may become suppliers for goods and services, extracting unreasonable costs for their products. Crime families have been the providers of gambling junket tours for players and, in New Jersey, for various sources of labor in the construction trades. Organized crime figures also may become involved in providing loans to desperate players, and the existence of the casinos may facilitate laundering of money for cartels that traffic in illegal activities such as prostitution and the drug trade.

Another set of crimes attends the actual games that are played. Wherever a game is offered with a money prize, someone will try to manipulate the games through cheating schemes. Cheating may involve marked cards, crooked dice, and uneven roulette wheels. Schemes may involve teams of players or individual players and casino employees. Cheating is also associated with race betting and even with lotteries. In some cases, the gambling organization may attempt to cheat players.

The greatest concern about crime and gambling involves activities of casino patrons. On the one hand, they present criminals with opportunities. Players who win money or carry money to casinos may be easy marks for forceful robberies as well those by pickpockets. Hotel rooms in casino properties are also targets. Players are targeted by prostitutes and also by other persons selling illicit goods, such as drugs. On the other hand, desperate players may be drawn to crimes in order to secure money for play or to pay gambling debts. Their crimes involve robberies and other larcenies, as well as white-collar crime activity—embezzlements, forgeries, and so on.

Studies of Crime and Gambling

The issue of crime and gambling has been well studied for generations. Virgil Peterson, director of the Chicago Crime Commission, issued a scathing attack on gambling in his *Gambling: Should It Be Legalized?* (1951). He asserted that "legalized gambling has always been attractive to the criminal and racketeering elements" (120). . . . "[C]riminals, gang-

sters, and swindlers have been the proprietors of gambling establishments" (137). . . . "[M]any people find it necessary to steal or embezzle to continue gambling activity" (120–121). . . . "The kidnapper, the armed robber, the burglar and the thief engage in crime to secure money for play" (123).

In a 1965 article that seemed prophetic, considering future events in New Jersey, Peterson wrote, "The underworld inevitably gains a foothold under any licensing system. If state authorities establish the vast policing system rigid supervision requires, the underworld merely provides itself with fronts who obtain the licenses, with actual ownership remaining in its own hands; and it receives a major share of the profits" (Peterson 1965, 665).

Other stories of the relationships between organized crime and gambling are plentiful. While Peterson was gathering information for his book, the Senate Committee on Organized Crime was holding hearings under the leadership of Estes Kefauver in 1950 and 1951. The committee was specific in identifying gambling as a major activity of organized crime.

In the 1960s, Ovid Demaris and Ed Reid wrote the *Green Felt Jungle* (Reid and Demaris 1963), a shocking account of the Mob in Las Vegas. Demaris continued the saga with his *Boardwalk Jungle* (Demaris 1986), an early account of casinos in New Jersey. His story was built upon a journalistic account of crime involvement in Atlantic City's first casino by Gigi Mahon, *The Company that Bought the Boardwalk* (1980). The role of organized crime was tangential to the activities of the first company that won a casino license in New Jersey and persisted with involvement in labor unions that served companies constructing the casino facilities.

The issue of organized crime and gambling has lost much of its punch over the past thirty years, however, as major corporations have emerged as the most important players in the gambling industry. Nonetheless, gaming control agents and other law enforcement agencies from the local, state, and federal levels must remain vigilant lest organized crime elements return to the gambling scene. In reality they have never completely left the scene. In the 1990s, they were still found seeking inroads to the management of casino operations in one San Diego County Native American casino. They actually infiltrated the operations of the White Earth Reservation casino in Minnesota, and the tribal leader was indicted for wrongdoing in connection with his Mob ties. The slot machine operations in restaurants and bars of Louisiana were compromised by organized crime elements, and indictments ensued. As the twentieth century ended, organized crime interests maintained ties with several Internet gambling enterprises operating in other countries.

The major concern over gambling has, however, turned toward ambient crime—personal crime that appears in the atmosphere around gambling establishments. In September 1995, L. Scott Harshbarger, Massachusetts state attorney general, commented to the U.S. House Judiciary Committee that "one of the noted consequences of casino gambling has been the marked rise in street crime. Across the nation, police departments in cities that have casino gambling have recorded surges in arrests due to casino-related crime. In many cases, towns that had a decreasing crime rate or a low crime rate have seen a sharp and steady growth of crime once gambling has taken root . . ." (Quoted in *Gambling under Attack* 1996, 785). Although there were many statements from law enforcement officials that echoed Harshbarger's thoughts, there were also those who disputed the claims.

Empirical Studies

Much of the data for the studies mentioned above was anecdotal or came from personal testimony of law enforcement personnel. Other entries into the literature have been based upon similar kinds of evidence. Such studies may be interesting, but they have only a limited value. Anecdotes may not always be precise or accurate.

More solid data have come from analyses of criminal statistics. George Sternlieb and James Hughes's study of Atlantic City revealed that crime increased rapidly in the community after the introduction of casinos in 1978. Pickpocketing activity increased eighty-fold, larceny increased over five times, and robberies tripled, as did assaults (Sternlieb and Hughes 1983, 192). Simon Hakim

and Andrew J. Buck found that the levels of all types of crime were higher in the years after casinos began operations. The "greatest post-casino crime increase was observed for violent crimes and auto thefts and the least for burglaries" (Hakim and Buck 1989, 414). As one moved farther from Atlantic City in spatial distance, rates of crime leveled off (415). On the other hand, Joseph Friedman, Simon Hakim, and J. Weinblatt found that increases in crime extended outward at least thirty miles to suburban areas and to areas along highways that extended toward New York and Philadelphia (Friedman, Hakim, and Weinblatt 1989, 622).

Similarly a study of Windsor, Ontario, found some crime rates increasing after a casino opened in May 1994. Overall, previous decreases in rates of crime citywide seemed to come to an end, whereas rates in areas around the casino increased measurably. The downtown area near the casino found more assaults, assaults upon police officers, and other violent crimes. Particularly noticeable were increases in general thefts, motor vehicle thefts, liquor offenses, and driving offenses (Windsor Police 1995).

Not all the evidence points in the same direction. Several riverboat communities in Iowa, Illinois, and Mississippi saw decreases in crime rates following the establishment of casinos. Moreover, several scholars, including Albanese (1985, 44) and Chiricos (1994), demonstrated that higher incidents of crime in Atlantic City were a result, in large part, of increases in visitor traffic. If numbers of tourist visitors were included in permanent census figures, crime rates would be stable or might even be less than they were before casinos came to Atlantic City. A study by Ronald George Ochrym and Clifton Park compared gaming communities with other tourist destinations that did not have casinos. They found that rates of crime were quite similar. Although crime statistics soared following the introduction of casinos in Atlantic City, so too did crime in Orlando, Florida, following the opening of Disney World. If the casinos themselves were responsible for more crime, gaming proponents suggest that Mickey Mouse also must cause crime (Ochrym and Park 1990).

Casino proponent Jeremy D. Margolis, a former assistant U.S. attorney, discounts the crime factors as well. In a December 1997 study for the American Gaming Association, he summarized the literature of crime and gambling studies by pointing to these conclusions: "Las Vegas, Nevada has a lower crime rate and is safer than virtually every other major tourist venue. Atlantic City, New Jersey's crime has been falling dramatically since 1991. Joliet, Illinois [a casino community] is enjoying its lowest level of crime in 15 years. Crime rates in Baton Rouge, Louisiana have decreased every year since casino gaming was introduced" (Margolis 1997, 1).

My study (Thompson, Gazel, and Rickman 1996) found a mixed pattern of crime and gambling associations in Wisconsin. We examined crime rates for major crimes and arrest rates for minor crimes in all seventy-six counties from 1980 to 1995. Our analysis compared counties with casinos to other counties. We also considered the impacts of crime on outlying nearby counties. We considered all crime data prior to 1992 to be data from counties without casinos. We looked at the incidence of crime in fourteen counties with casinos for 1992, 1993, and 1994 as data from casino counties, whereas 1992, 1993, and 1994 data from other counties was considered non-casino county data. We utilized a technique called linear regression for our analysis.

The introduction of casinos did impact the incidence of serious crimes in the casino counties and counties adjacent to two casino counties. For each 1 percent increase in the numbers of major crimes statewide, the numbers of major crimes in the casino and adjacent counties significantly increased an additional 6.7 percent. Reduced to simple language, the existence of casinos (or nearness of casinos) in the selected counties explains a major crime increase of 6.7 percent beyond what would otherwise be experienced in the absence of casinos. As there were approximately 10,000 major crimes in these counties in 1991, we can suggest that casinos brought an additional 670 major crimes for each of three years after casinos came. The largest share of casino-related crimes were burglaries (10).

Our analysis of Part II (minor crimes, as defined by the Federal Bureau of Investigation [FBI])
looked at data on the numbers of arrests in each county of the state. Overall, we found that increases in arrests for all Part II crimes in casino counties and counties adjacent to these counties constituted a number 12.2 percent higher than that found in other counties. Although Part II arrest numbers overall are related to the presence of the casinos in Wisconsin, not all categories of Part II arrests could be linked to the casinos. Relationships could be demonstrated for arrests for assaults, stolen property, driving while intoxicated, and drug possession (15).

Assaults increased 37.8 percent more in these counties than for the state as a whole. Arrests for stolen property increased 28.1 percent more in the casino-adjacent counties. Certainly this finding complements the demonstrated increase in incidents of burglary. Drunk driving arrests increased 13.9 percent more in the casino and adjacent counties than in the other ones, and drug possession arrests increased an extra 21.9 percent. Although the percentage increase was not as great as for some other categories, the most significant relationship between the presence of crime and casinos was driving while intoxicated (17).

Although the general comments and anecdotal evidence suggest ties between casinos and forgery, fraud, and embezzlement, no strong linkages were found in our data. We did find significant associations between casinos and forgery and fraud within the casino counties, but these relationships did not extend to surrounding counties. No relationships were established with embezzlement arrests. This does not mean they might not exist at a future time. This kind of crime, when it is linked to gambling, takes time to develop. This type of crime is also associated with problem or pathological gambling. First, the cycle of pathological gambling takes time to develop. Second, as the cycle is developing, the pathological gambler is using all possible legal means to get funds for gambling. Only in later desperation stages will the gambler turn to illegal means for funds.

The presence of additional crime also imposes additional costs on the society. We used standard criminal justice costs of arrests, court actions, probation, and jail time, as well as property losses, in our analysis. We concluded that an additional

5,277 serious crimes per year cost the public $16.71 million, and an additional 17,100 arrests for Part II crimes cost society $34.20 million each year. The data suggest that casinos may be responsible, directly or indirectly, for nearly $51 million each year in societal costs due to crime generated as a result of their existence (18).

Political Crimes and Gambling

Gambling interests (and potential gambling interests) have money. Often their profit margins may be very large, especially in monopoly or semimonopoly situations. The interests are willing to spend their money to advance their causes. The very open bribery of Louisiana legislators in the late nineteenth century by operators of the state's lottery led to the reforms that ended that lottery and precluded the reestablishment of any state lottery until 1964. Gambling interests will still invest large sums of money into political action. Often their targets are referenda campaigns. The California Proposition 5 campaign of November 1998 was the most expensive ballot initiative campaign in U.S. history. Nevada casino interests put $26 million into the campaign, and tribal gambling interests in California invested nearly $70 million. Prior to 1998, a 1994 campaign to legalize casinos in Florida that drew almost $18 million from the casino industry had been the most expensive referenda campaign in history.

The casinos and other gambling enterprises also invest large sums of money in lobbying campaigns and public persuasion campaigns. This is the political process in the United States, one that thrives on the clash of interests and the clash of issues. It is a Madisonian system in which rival interests protect their turf by making their positions known and by commandeering the facts that will help them persuade policymakers that they are on the correct side when the issues rise to decision points on the public agenda.

Some of the interest might go too far. After all, the potential benefits can be extraordinary. In some jurisdictions, forces desiring casino licenses or contracts with government-controlled gambling operations have crossed the line. A former governor of Louisiana, Edwin Edwards, was a leader in the efforts to get casinos and gambling machines into his state. Rumors about bags of money being brought into state offices filled the air from the beginning—but those are just rumors. Federal Justice Department officials gathered the facts, and he was indicted more than once for taking bribes. The new century began with the former governor on criminal trial; since then he has been convicted and awaits incarceration. Officials in Missouri were charged with the same kind of wrongdoing, and several resigned during the 1990s. One Las Vegas gambling interest withdrew from pursuing casino activity in Missouri because of the exposure of political activities considered inappropriate. Another company remained an active Missouri player but only after removing key company officials. In the 1980s, both Atlantic City and Las Vegas were rocked by FBI sting operations, which involved undercover agents offering bribes to influential public figures in exchange for their intervention in the casino licensing process. The Atlantic City operation—called ABSCAM (a code name based on *Arab* and *scam*)—resulted in the resignation of U.S. senator Harrison Williams (D-New Jersey) from office. Several local officials in Nevada saw their political careers also end when they were exposed for taking bribe offers.

Lines between acceptable and even honorable political activity and unacceptable or even illegal activity can be blurred. The incentive remains, however, for continued activity and even intense activity. Citizens, political leaders, law enforcement officials, and industry operatives must always be on watch for wrongdoing; if they are not, the industry will suffer in the long run.

Legalization as a Substitute for Illegal Gambling

Advocates of legalizing gambling suggest that there is a certain quantity of illegal gambling existing in any society and that the process of legalization will serve to eliminate the illegal gaming and channel all gambling activity into a properly regulated and taxed enterprise. As with the other evidence, the research here is also mixed. Nevada certainly had a large amount of illegal gambling before "wide-open" casino gambling was legalized in 1931. Since 1931, there has been very little evidence of illegal casino gambling games in Nevada.

Illegal operators simply obtained licenses from the state government.

Similarly, David Dixon found that illegal book-making was effectively replaced by legal betting when Great Britain passed legislation in 1960 permitting betting shops (Dixon 1990). Opposite results have been found elsewhere, however. An examination of casinos in Holland by William Thompson and J. Kent Pinney found that legalization in 1975 seemed only to promote an expansion of illegal casinos that had operated before laws were passed for government-operated casinos (Thompson and Pinney 1990). Clearly the illegal operators were not permitted to win licenses. Also, the government placed many restrictions on its own casinos—they had to be located (at first) outside cities; they could not advertise, give complimentary services, or operate around the clock. Illegal casinos found new places to advertise—at the doors of the legal casinos when they closed at 2 A.M. David Dixon also found that when Australia established its government-operated betting parlors, illegal sports and race betting underwent a major expansion (Dixon 1990). Additionally, Robert Wagman explained that the efforts to get rid of the illegal operators in the United States might actually have achieved an opposite effect (Wagman 1986).

Some law enforcement officials are now saying that indications are that the lottery may actually be helping the illegal game. Players are being introduced to the numbers concept in the state-run game, and then they switch to the illegal game when they realize they can get a better deal. The legal state game has solved the perennial problem faced by the illegal games of finding a commonly accepted, and widely available, three-digit number to pay off on. Most of the illegal street games now simply use the state's three-number pick (Wagman, 1986).

Sources: Albanese, Jay S. 1985. "The Effect of Casino Gambling on Crime." *Federal Probation* 49 (June): 39–44; Chiricos, Ted. 1994. "Casinos and Crime: An Assessment of the Evidence." Manuscript; Demaris, Ovid. 1986. *Boardwalk Jungle: How Greed, Corruption and the Mafia Turned Atlantic City into the Boardwalk Jungle.* New York: Bantam Books; Dixon, David. 1990. *From Prohibition to Regulation: Bookmaking, Anti Gambling and the Law.* Oxford: Clarendon Press; Dombrink, John D. 1981. "Outlaw Businessmen: Organized Crime and the Legalization of Casino Gambling." Ph.D. diss., University of California, Berkeley; Friedman, Joseph, Simon Hakim, and J. Weinblatt. 1989. "Casino Gambling as a 'Growth Pole' Strategy and Its Effects on Crime." *Journal of Regional Science* 29 (November): 615–624; Hakim, Simon, and Andrew J. Buck. 1989. "Do Casinos Enhance Crime?" *Journal of Criminal Justice* 17(5): 409–416; Kindt, John. 1994. "Increased Crime and Legalized Gambling Operations." *Criminal Law Bulletin* 43: 538–539; Mahon, Gigi. 1980. *The Company that Bought the Boardwalk.* New York: Random House; Margolis, Jeremy. 1997. *Casinos and Crime: An Analysis of the Evidence.* Washington, DC: American Gaming Association; Miller, William J., and Martin D. Schwartz. 1998. "Casino Gambling and Street Crime." In *Gambling: Socioeconomic Impacts and Public Policy* (special volume of *The Annals of the American Academy of Political and Social Science*), edited by James H. Frey, 124–137. Thousand Oaks, CA: Sage; Ochrym, Ronald George, and Clifton Park. 1990. "Street Crime, Tourism and Casinos: An Empirical Comparison." *Journal of Gambling Studies* 6 (Summer): 127–138; Peterson, Virgil W. 1951. *Gambling: Should It Be Legalized?* Springfield, IL: Charles C. Thomas; Peterson, Virgil W. 1965. "A Look at Legalized Gambling." *Christian Century* 82 (26 May): 667; Reid, Ed, and Ovid Demaris. 1963. *The Green Felt Jungle.* New York: Trident Press. Reprint, 1994. New York: Pocket Books; Skolnick, Jerome. 1978. *House of Cards: Legalization and Control of Casino Gambling.* Boston: Little, Brown; Sternlieb, George, and James W. Hughes. 1983. *The Atlantic City Gamble: A Twentieth Century Fund Report.* Cambridge: Harvard University Press; Thompson, William N. 1997. *Legalized Gambling: A Reference Handbook.* 2d ed. Santa Barbara, CA: ABC-CLIO; Thompson, William N., Ricardo Gazel, and Dan Rickman. 1996. *Casinos and Crime: What's the Connection?* Mequon, WI: Wisconsin Policy Research Institute; Thompson, William N., and J. Kent Pinney. 1990. "The Mismarketing of Dutch Casinos." *Journal of Gambling Behavior* 6 (Fall): 205–221; Wagman, Robert. 1986. *Instant Millionaires.* Washington, DC: Woodbine House; Windsor Police. 1995. *Crime and Casino Gambling: A Report.* Windsor, Ont.: Windsor Police Department; Worshop, Richard L. 1996. "Gambling under Attack." 1996. *CQ Researcher* 6 (33): 771–791.

See also California; Cash Transaction Reports and Money Laundering; Cheating Schemes; Gambling, Pathological

Cruise Ships

There are several categories of shipboard casino gambling. Gambling on riverboats or other vessels

A casino cruise ship moves through the Panama Canal.

within the waters of a specific jurisdiction is discussed under the entries covering the various jurisdictions (e.g., Illinois). The two categories discussed in this entry include ocean or high seas cruises and voyages and what have come to be known as "cruises to nowhere."

Voyages on the High Seas

The shipboard cruises encompass destination vacation activities for passengers. Typically, the cruises last several days or even weeks. The ships are luxurious, the cruises are expensive, and the amenities aboard the ships are many—food, dancing, sports activities. Casino gambling has been an activity on more and more of the cruises. The leader among the cruise companies having casinos aboard their ships is Carnival Cruise Lines, with more than forty ships offering casino games. Carnival has a gambling staff exceeding 1,000 individuals for its ships. The ships offer linked slot machines among several vessels, permitting megajackpots. Other major cruise lines with casinos include Holland American Line, Norwegian Cruise Line, Princess Cruises, and Royal Caribbean International.

These ships must operate their games on the high seas, and their voyages are essentially inter-national. They stop at several seaport cities on their venture—at least two of which are in different jurisdictions (countries). While in port, no casino gambling is allowed.

The ship lines listed above are not U.S. companies. Indeed, very few U.S. ships have casino gaming, and very few have luxury cruises either. In 1949, the U.S. Congress passed very strict prohibitions banning gambling on U.S. flag vessels no matter where they were operating, whether in territorial or international waters. The ban affected vessels registered as U.S. and also ones principally owned by U.S. citizens. Although the point of the law was clearly to regulate the type of gambling ship discussed as cruises to nowhere, the effect was general. Even though the law was to apply to ships that were used "principally" for gambling (a rather vague term); U.S. ships ceased to have casinos on their voyages.

The Johnson Act of 1951 made possession of gambling machines illegal except under certain circumstances (e.g., they were legal in the jurisdiction where they were located). This law gave an emphasis to the notion that U.S. ships could not have machine gambling and come into any U.S. port where state law prohibited the machines (which included every port city in the United States in 1951). Foreign vessels could stop the use of the machines in these ports and not be in violation of the 1951 law, as they were still under foreign or international jurisdiction to some degree while in port.

By 1990, the cruise ship industry was flourishing. Over eighty cruise ships utilized U.S. ports. All but two flew foreign flags. Moreover, the general state of U.S. shipbuilding and U.S. companies operating sailing vessels was one of deterioration. In 1991, the U.S. attorney general ruled that a ship was not a "gambling ship" if it provided for overnight accommodations and/or landed in a foreign port on its cruise. U.S. shipping companies renewed an interest in offering gambling on cruises. As a result, Congress passed the Cruise Ship Competitiveness Act on 9 March 1992 in order to establish "equal competition" for U.S. ships. Now the U.S. flagships can have gambling on their cruises while in international waters.

The international cruise ships are, for the most part, not subject to the regulation of any jurisdiction regarding their gambling activities. There are few limitations on licensing of casino managers or employees and few guidelines on surveillance and player disputes. Nonetheless, the major cruise ship companies have considerable internal regulations. Most have definite limits on the amounts of money that can be wagered, as they do not wish to take opportunities for spending money on other amenities away from the passengers, who may have to remain on the ship for several days after their gambling venture has ended. As Carnival Cruise Lines and other ship casino companies (Casinos Austria runs several of the casinos) have land-based operations in other jurisdictions (Carnival is in Louisiana and Ontario), they do not want to have their licenses there jeopardized by any unacceptable practices within their shipboard casinos.

There is one ship on the high seas that has been subjected to the direct regulation of a state. Nevada requires its casino license holders to secure permission of the Nevada Gaming Commission and the Gaming Control Board if they are operating gambling operations outside of the state. Prior to 1993, the permission had to come from the state authorities before out-of-state operations could begin. Accordingly, in 1989 Caesars Palace applied for approval to manage the casino on board the *Crystal Harmony,* an exclusive Japanese-owned ship flying the flag of the Bahamas. The approval was granted under the condition that Caesars establish a fund for the Nevada gaming authorities so that the state could conduct background investigations of the ship owners, operators, and crew. Internal auditing controls also had to meet state standards, with independent accountants conducting regular reviews of the books. Nevada agents were given full access to the casino's records, as well as to the facilities. Caesars absorbed all costs of regulation. The *Crystal Harmony* was the first and only international ship to have a casino regulated by the jurisdiction of a state of the United States.

Cruises to Nowhere

The 1949 act banning gambling on U.S. flagships resulted from a controversy lasting several decades in California and other coastal states. Starting in the 1920s, floating barges appeared in the waters off of San Francisco and Los Angeles, as well as off the Florida coast. The ships anchored in international waters—three miles off the coasts. They had brightly lighted decks that could be seen from shore and beyond. Each day and evening they would provide boat taxi service for customers from nearby docks. The ships had entertainers, food, drinks (it was Prohibition time), and gambling. They operated through the 1930s without much opposition from law enforcement. When Earl Warren became attorney general of California, however, he decided to crack down. Raids were conducted, but the issue of what was definitely legal or illegal persisted until U. S. senator William Knowland of California persuaded his congressional colleagues to pass legislation in 1949. The law now had teeth and was enforced until there was pressure for change in the 1990s.

Even before the passage of the 1992 Cruise Ship Competitiveness Act, vessels began to test the resolve of states and the federal government regarding coastal gambling operations. The actions of one company seemed to be the catalyst for the legalization of riverboat and coastal casinos in Mississippi in 1990. After the 1992 legislation passed, the states were given the opportunity to opt out of the Johnson Act prohibition on machines in their waters. Hence, they could allow boats to have cruises out to international waters for gambling even if the boats did not stop at foreign ports. In 1996, the U.S. Congress acted again. This time Congress gave a blanket approval to the international waters' "cruises to nowhere" unless the state (of debarkation and reentry) specifically prohibited the gambling ships. The state could only prohibit them if the ship did not make port in another jurisdiction. The ship's gambling operations would not be subject to any jurisdiction unless, again, the state took specific action for regulation.

Since the 1996 law was passed, a large number of ships have begun operations off of Florida and also in the northeast. The state of California specifically passed a ban on the ships. Over twenty-two ships operate off of Florida, generating collective revenues of well over $200 million a year. Ships also have used South Carolina ports. Several ships attempted to gain docking rights in New York City, but local officials, including Mayor Rudolph Giuliani, fought the efforts and demanded that the boats go out to at least twelve miles off the coast before they could have gambling. After many months of negotiations, the city agreed to establish a gambling regulatory board for the ships through passage of an ordinance. One major vessel, the *Liberty I,* agreed to follow the local regulations.

Several states, including South Carolina and Florida, have found opponents of the boats seeking legislation against them, but so far their efforts have been to no avail. Even California has succumbed to the realization that regular gambling cruises for local residents have come to be. On 15 April 2000, the *Enchanted Sun* began voyages out of San Diego. The ship goes out three miles and hugs the coast until it reaches Rosarito Beach, south of Tijuana, Mexico. It hits the dock, briefly drops anchor, and then returns. The ship is at sea for a total of less than eight hours. In each trip, over 400 passengers enjoy a meal, entertainment, drinks, and gambling. Commercial success of such operations is not guaranteed. Passengers have to pay a cruise fee of $68, and as with other ships,

there is always the problem of rough seas. An interesting twist to the *Enchanted Sun* casino is the fact that the California Viejas Band of Native Americans is an operating partner in the venture on the high seas.

—*coauthored by Anthony N. Cabot and Robert Faiss*

Sources: Cabot, Anthony N., William N. Thompson, Andrew Tottenham, and Carl Braunlich, eds. 1999. *International Casino Law.* 3d ed. Reno: Institute for the Study of Gambling, University of Nevada, Reno, 605–612; Doocey, Paul. 1997. "A Mixed Forecast." *International Gaming and Wagering Business* 18, no. 12 (December): 1, 18–40; Lionel, Sawyer and Collins. 1995. *Nevada Gaming Law.* 2d ed. Las Vegas, NV: Lionel, Sawyer, and Collins.

Cruises to Nowhere. *See* Cruise Ships

Cuba

During the 1950s, Cuba offered the gambler several of the leading casino facilities in the world. There was little doubt, however, that the gaming was connected to organized crime personalities in the United States as well as to military dictator Fulgencio Batista, and both entities skimmed considerable sums from the operations. Cuba also had both public and private lotteries, a first-class racing facility, and jai alai fontons. All the gambling activity came to a halt after Fidel Castro engineered a successful rebellion and took over the reins of power in January 1959. Repeated attempts to negotiate a continuation of casino gaming were unsuccessful, and it has been suggested that U.S. crime interests were involved in attempts to overthrow the Castro regime, both in the abortive Bay of Pigs invasion and in several assassination attempts on the new dictator's life. The entire tourism infrastructure has slipped into decay during the four decades of Castro rule. Today there are voices suggesting that Cuba may seek to restore its tourism industry and may even contemplate reopening casinos.

The island of Cuba was colonized and controlled by the Spanish government for four centuries, until a revolution developed to a major scale in the 1890s. When the United States declared war on Spain in 1898, the revolution became successful, and independence was gained for the Cuban people. Authorities in the United States, however, sought to keep many controls over the Cuban people. War troops were not removed until 1902, and even after the Cubans elected a new government under President Jose Miguel Gomez that year, the United States "negotiated" to have a major naval base at Guantanamo Bay. Other commercial interests in the United States also maintained an economic domination over much of Cuba, but these interests had been in Cuba for many years before the revolution. Many Americans looked at the seaside location called Marianao, ten miles outside of Havana, and found it to be a desirable place to live, engage in real estate transactions, and start tourism resorts.

A local group known as the 3 C's (named for Carlos Miguel de Cespedes, Jose Manuel Cortina, and Carlos Manuel de la Cruz) formed a tourism company that sought to build a casino in Marianao. In 1910, they proposed legislation in the National Congress that would permit the casino and would also grant them an exclusive thirty-year concession to operate it. At a time when the Americans in Cuba saw the casino as "opportunity," Americans in the United States were in a wave of anti-sin social reform. This was the same year that the casinos of Nevada closed their doors and the Prohibition movement was in high gear. U.S. president Howard Taft was lobbied hard by church interests to not allow gambling so close to our shores. During the Spanish American War, President William McKinley had decreed that there be no more bullfighting in Cuba, calling the activity a disgraceful outrage. Taft was expected to bully the Cuban Congress to follow U.S. wishes as well. The legislation failed to pass. A second attempt was made to have casino-tied revenues to support $1.5 million in construction of facilities for tourism in Marianao. One New Yorker, who had a contract to build a jai alai fonton and a grandstand for racing, sought to change Taft's mind on the issue, but again, casinos were defeated as a result of a moralist campaign in the United States.

Gambling was in the cards for Cuba, however. In 1915, Havana's Oriental Park opened for horse racing. In 1919, the casino promoters promised that they would build the streets and plazas for Marianao if they could have casinos. President Mario Menocal, who had been elected in 1917, supported a bill for casinos. The national legislature authorized a gambling hall for the resort on 5 August 1919. The 3 C's group ran the facility. In addition to land improvements for tourism, they agreed to a national tax that was designated for the health and welfare of poor mothers and their children. At the same time, President Menocal's family won the concession to have jai alai games in Marianao. The tourism push was on, and the United States was the primary market, especially after Prohibition began for the whole country in 1919. The Roaring Twenties roared outside of Havana. Several new luxurious hotels opened, each having a gaming room. Each successive presidency endorsed tourism and welcomed all investors. Even Al Capone opened a pool hall in Marianao in 1928. Then the Depression came.

The 1930s in Cuba were years of reform thinking. Leaders openly condemned the degradation of casino gaming and other sin activities that had been widely offered to tourists. In 1933, the casinos were closed, and Prohibition ended in the United States. The economy floundered. The next year, army sergeant Fulgencio Batista was able to oust President Ramon Grau San Martin and install his own government. He ruled as chief of staff of the army while another held the presidency. At first Batista tried to bolster the notion of cultural tourism, but he could not resist allowing casinos to reopen—under the control of the military. Batista was very concerned about the honesty of the games. For sure, he would be skimming. If players were being cheated, however, there soon would be no players. The house odds could give the casinos enough profits to pay off the generals and the politicians, but not enough to pay off all of the dealers. Games had to be honest. He turned to a person who understood this and other dynamics of the casino industry very well—Meyer Lansky. Lansky took over casino operations, and he imported dealers who would work for him and not behind his back. The Mob cleaned things up. Because of World War II and postwar disincentives for foreign travel by Americans, however, the casino activity was rather dormant through the

1940s. Nonetheless, Havana attracted more persons of bad reputation. In 1946, Salvatore "Lucky" Luciano moved in to conduct heroin trade and to be involved with the Jockey Club and the Casino Nacional. Lansky was influential in persuading the government to expel his competitor.

Fulgencio Batista won the presidency on his own in 1940. In 1944 and 1948, he permitted Grau San Martin and Carlos Prio Socarras to win open elections; however, he remained very much a controlling element. In 1952, while a candidate for the presidency, he sensed he had no chance of victory. Batista executed a coup and took the reins of power. Subsequent elections were rigged, and he remained in power until the beginning of 1959. During this latter period of rule, casino development accelerated.

The 1950s started out slowly for the casinos. Prior to 1950, only five casinos were in operation, and a brief reform spirit in 1950 led the government to close them. Commercial pressures, however, led to a reopening before Batista conducted his coup. The casinos now offered large numbers of slot machines for play. By the mid-decade, new Cuban hotels were attracting large investments from the United States, as the gambling operations were quite lucrative. Foreign operators, however, still had ties to organized crime members. A major incentive for a renewed interest in Cuban gaming came from the Senate Kefauver investigations that were exposing illegal gambling operations in the United States. Organized crime members were being run out of places such as Newport, Kentucky; Hot Springs, Arkansas; and New Orleans, Louisiana. At first, they gravitated toward Las Vegas; then Nevada instituted licensing requirements that precluded their participation in operations there. Cuba, the Bahamas, and Haiti became desired locations. Four of the five largest Havana casinos were in the hands of U.S. mobsters. As newer properties such as the Havana Hilton, the Riviera, Hotel Capri, and the Intercontinental Hotel came on line, Mob hands were involved in the action. Meyer Lansky was always the leader of the group. He kept the games honest, and he kept the political skim money flowing in the correct directions. When someone got out of line, he gave the word, and Batista could make a great show about throwing a mobster out of the country. In addition to enhancing casino gambling, Batista also improved revenues of the national lottery by inaugurating daily games.

In 1958, things seemed to be on a roll just when Fidel Castro gathered strength for his military takeover. Revelations in the *New York Times* about Mob involvement in Cuban casinos dampened tourist enthusiasm, as did the fear of impending violence. The names of Jake Lansky, Salvatore Trafficante, and Joseph Silesi were added to the lists of unsavory participants in the industry.

Fidel Castro was born in 1926, the son of an affluent sugarcane planter. He attended a Catholic school in Santiago de Cuba before entering the University of Havana as a law student in 1945. There he began his career as a political activist and revolutionary. He participated in an attempt to overthrow the government of Dominican Republic strongman Rafael Trujillo and disrupted an international meeting of the American states in Bogota in 1948. He sought a peaceful way to power in 1952 as he ran for Congress; however, the contest was voided as Batista seized power and cancelled the election. In 1953, Castro took part in an unsuccessful raid on the government; he was captured and imprisoned for a year. He was released by Batista as part of a general amnesty program but kept up his revolutionary efforts, leading another unsuccessful raid in 1956. His third try was his charm, as he successfully moved through rural Cuba during 1958, attacking Havana at the end of the year and driving Batista from office.

When Castro's forces descended on Havana on New Year's Eve 1958, there were thirteen casinos in Havana. The hotel casinos represented a collective investment of tens of millions of dollars. Lansky's Riviera alone cost $14 million. Owners and operators did not want to join Batista in his hasty exile out of the country, even after revolutionary rioters had smashed up many of their gaming rooms. They wanted to hold on to what had been a very good thing. That would be difficult, however. Castro had waged a revolutionary media campaign that condemned the sin industries of Cuba and their connections to the Batista government. Castro had pledged that he would close down the casinos.

Castro was true to his word on this score, at least at the beginning. He also stopped the national lottery from operating. Meyer Lansky, on the other hand, pledged that he would work with the new government, and casinos were temporarily reopened, ostensibly to protect the jobs of their 4,000 workers. The reopenings were short-lived, however. The casinos closed for good (under the Castro regime) in late 1960. Castro's frontal attack on the Mob and its casino interests in Havana had political consequences in the United States, where the Central Intelligence Agency planned the 1961 Bay of Pigs invasion to overthrow Castro and also may have contracted with organized crime operatives to attempt to assassinate the new leader.

The fall of the Batista regime and the end of Cuban casinos had repercussions throughout the gaming industry. Nevada lost its strongest competitive market, and Cuban operatives and owners had to move. The ones that could be licensed went to Las Vegas, as did many of the dealers and other casino workers. Others had to find unregulated or underregulated jurisdictions. Haiti and the Dominican Republic were close at hand, as were the Bahamas. Most of the gaming entrepreneurs in these jurisdictions had Cuban experiences, as did many who went to London to open casinos after 1960 legislation gave unregulated charity gaming halls a green light. Lansky, George Raft, and Dino Cellini were principals in London's Colony Club until they were expelled from the country. Former Nevada lieutenant governor Cliff Jones of Las Vegas had been active in Cuba. He had made a choice between Nevada gaming and foreign gaming when the "foreign gaming" rule was adopted in Nevada. He chose to be involved in foreign gaming and therefore could not return to Las Vegas. Instead, he began campaigns in one small country after another to legalize casinos and then began operations that he would later sell to (or share with) local parties for high profits. Clearly, the activity of Castro in closing down Havana gaming caused a major spread of gaming elsewhere.

Sources: Lacey, Robert. 1991. *Little Man: Meyer Lansky and the Gangster Life*. Boston: Little, Brown; Schwartz, Rosalie. 1997. *Pleasure Island: Tourism and Temptation in Cuba*. Lincoln: University of Nevada Press, chaps. 6, 12; Sifakis, Carl. 1990. *Encyclopedia of Gambling*. New York: Facts on File, 85.

Cussec. See Craps and Other Dice Games

D

Dalitz, Morris

Moe Dalitz started his career in the shadows of the law, but as that career unraveled in Las Vegas, his life became one of community development and philanthropy. More than any other of the "founding fathers" of Las Vegas, Moe Dalitz converted a questionable past into an honored status as a community icon.

Morris "Moe" Barney Dalitz was born on 24 December 1899 in Boston, Massachusetts. When Moe was very young, his family moved to Michigan. There his father started Varsity Laundry near the University of Michigan campus. The laundry business expanded, and soon the Michigan Industrial Laundry in Detroit was in son Moe Dalitz's control. The laundry had certain symbiotic relationships that opened doors for Dalitz's new business interests. When Prohibition descended upon the nation, bootleggers needed delivery mechanisms. Dalitz had trucks. The laundry trucks served customers at hotels and could also be put onto barges that could be transported across the waters of the Detroit River, Lake St. Clair, Lake Huron, and Lake Erie from Canada. One of the favorite places of entry for liquor as it came from Canada to the bootleggers in the United States was the point where Mayfield Road near Cleveland ended at the shores of Lake Erie. Dalitz became the leader of a group called the Mayfield Road Gang operating in Cleveland, Detroit, and Ann Arbor.

Moe Dalitz continued from the earliest days of his bootlegging activities to take the profits and convert them into legitimate businesses: more laundry businesses, the Detroit Steel Company, and even a railroad. He also had his eye out for what his liquor customers wanted, especially when Prohibition ended. He concluded that gambling was a natural business for a follow-up. Dalitz became a principal owner for several illegal casinos throughout the Midwest, including several in Cleveland and northern Kentucky.

Moe Dalitz was too old to be drafted when the United States entered World War II. He had a strong sense of obligation, however, and he enlisted as a private. His business acumen landed him in the quartermaster corps, when he received a commission. He served stateside running army laundry services. His assignment allowed him to keep in touch with his private investments.

Moe Dalitz remained active in the Detroit laundry business into the 1950s. Inevitably, he came face-to-face with Jimmy Hoffa in negotiations with the International Brotherhood of Teamsters (the Teamsters' union). At first it appeared that there would be a monumental confrontation, with both sides calling out their "muscle" to make their position stronger. But their cooler heads prevailed as they found that mutual benefits could flow from friendly relationships. Later, Hoffa negotiated major loans for several Dalitz gambling projects and for other things as well. The first Teamsters' loan to Las Vegas went to Dalitz so that he could finance Sunrise Hospital. Later loans also financed the Winterwood Golf Course, the Las Vegas Country Club, and Boulevard Mall—the largest shopping center in Nevada, even today.

Dalitz had come to Las Vegas in the aftermath of the crackdowns on illegal gambling that had been prompted by the Kefauver investigations. Dalitz himself was a witness in front of the Kefauver Committee. When asked if he had made money bootlegging, he told Senator Kefauver that he had not inherited his money, and "if you people wouldn't have drunk it, I wouldn't have bootlegged it."

In the 1950s, Dalitz had had to choose between Las Vegas and Havana, and after trying Cuba, he decided to leave that territory to his friend Meyer Lansky. In actuality, Fidel Castro's takeover of the island ended Dalitz's thoughts about Havana casinos. If he had pursued the Havana idea, the Nevada gambling regulators would have informed him that no Nevada casino license holder could have a casino interest elsewhere.

The leaders of organized crime families in the United States had declared Las Vegas an "open city" after Benjamin Siegel finished his Flamingo in 1946. This meant that groups of entrepreneurs, such as those with whom Dalitz was associated, were welcome to come into Las Vegas and compete alongside Meyer Lansky, Lucky Luciano, Frank Costello, and other eastern Mob leaders. The Dalitz group found its opportunity on the Strip with Wilbur Clark's Desert Inn Resort. Clark had gathered resources for his "dream" in 1947, but he was way short of what he needed. Dalitz and his Cleveland group made Clark an offer he "couldn't refuse." Clark gave up 74 percent of the ownership (that is, majority control) in return for seeing the project with his name still on it. Later the name was dropped. Dalitz added a special touch that changed marketing approaches for casinos in the future. He added a championship golf course next to the Desert Inn. Then he created a major tournament on the Professional Golf Association's tour: the Tournament of Champions in which only winners of other tour events could compete.

In 1955 Tony Cornero died. This West Coast crime figure had made his name running casino ships off the coast of California until authorities such as Gov. Earl Warren closed down the gambling. Cornero moved to Las Vegas and started the Stardust. When he died, the remaining ownership group was very scattered and lacked the funds to complete the project. Dalitz moved in and secured a loan from Jimmy Hoffa's Teamsters union and finished the job. He took control of management when the property opened in 1958. The Stardust added a golf course with another Champions Tournament. The casinos increased the glitz level of the Las Vegas Strip by having the largest and most noticeable sign. The Stardust also brought in the Lido Show from Paris, which featured a chorus line of fifty well-costumed but still topless showgirls.

Moe Dalitz's interests also went to downtown Las Vegas, where he bought and sold the Fremont

and also constructed the Sundance (now the Fitzgerald), which was the tallest building in the state for many years. His investment in a California resort called Rancho La Costa brought a lot of attention, as he again used Teamsters' loans and his partners were people with questionable backgrounds. Dalitz sued *Penthouse* magazine for writing a very critical article about his participation with mobsters. He lost the suit, but the Nevada Gaming Commission began to examine the question of whether or not he should hold casino licenses. He had by this time already sold the Desert Inn, and he sold other casino interests as well, keeping the properties and leasing them to the holders of the gambling licenses. He became content to be an elder statesman for Las Vegas. Other business interests satisfied all his financial needs, and his many charities made him a leading citizen.

Moe Dalitz had organized a group of casino owners in the mid-1960s to develop a strategy to make casinos more legitimate in the eyes of the power holders in the state. The Nevada Resorts Association was established as a lobbying arm of the casinos. One of their first projects was to support the creation of a hotel school at the new University of Nevada, Las Vegas. In personal actions Dalitz gave additional contributions to the new university to furnish its first building—Maude Frazier Hall. He was also a major contributor to many charities. His money was instrumental in starting a major temple for his faith. He was named Humanitarian of the Year by the American Cancer Society and in 1982 received an award from the Anti Defamation League of B'nai B'rith. When he died on 31 August 1989, he had completed the transition from being an outlaw businessman to being the most respected citizen of his city.

Dalitz's career had a very personal impact on my life. I grew up in Ann Arbor, Michigan, where my family patronized the Varsity Laundry started by Moe Dalitz's father. Neighbors' houses were sold by Dalitz Realty. I never heard that name again until I moved to Las Vegas in 1980. When my father visited me, he asked if there was a Moe Dalitz in Las Vegas, and I replied that yes, he was one of the founders of the Las Vegas Strip. My father then related that he had played cards with Moe's father,

Barney, in the 1920s and that they had lived just two blocks away from us on Granger Street. In the late 1980s I went to Ohio to study a campaign for casinos in Lorain, near Cleveland. As I drove off the interstate highway into town, I noticed the name of the road was Mayfield Road, famous from Prohibition days. I had come to another spot in Moe Dalitz's career. Now in Las Vegas I shop at the Boulevard Mall; one year my boys went to the school at Temple Beth Shalom; I visited the emergency room at Sunrise Hospital when the kids needed a stitch or two; I walk by Frazier Hall on the University of Nevada, Las Vegas, campus five days a week—all places associated with Dalitz. My office is in the building that houses the Hotel College. On occasion I have had the pleasure of dining at the Las Vegas Country Club as a guest of one "important" person or another. I feel that the shadow of Moe Dalitz has covered many of my footsteps.

Sources: Hopkins, A. D., and K. J. Evans. 1999. The First 100: Portraits of the Men and Women Who Shaped Las Vegas. Las Vegas: Huntington Press, 120–124; Smith, John L. 1997. "Moe Dalitz and the Desert." In The Players: The Men Who Made Las Vegas, edited by Jack Sheehan, 35–47. Reno: University of Nevada Press.
See also Hoffa, Jimmy

Dandolos, Nick

Nick "the Greek" Dandolos was born in Crete in 1893. Over a career of great renown, he secured the reputation as the last of the gentlemen gamblers and a man of great personal integrity, although some suggest the latter honor was not entirely deserved. Nick was the son of a rug merchant and the grandson of a shipowner. His grandfather sponsored Nick's coming to the United States, and he became a citizen in 1902, when he was eighteen. His grandfather also gave Nick an allowance of $150 a week. Although he also gained a job selling figs, with his guaranteed stake he quickly moved to gambling action wherever he could find it. First he followed the horses and then turned to cards and dice.

During a career that made him one of the major celebrities of Las Vegas, Dandolos often gave his assessment of the gambling life: "The greatest pleasure in my life is gambling and win-

ning. The next greatest pleasure is gambling and losing" (Alvarez 1983, 115) He might have added the rest of the compulsive gambler's mantra: "Whatever is in third place ain't even close." Over his career he won and lost over $50 million—actually he lost quite a bit more than he won.

Nick the Greek won his reputation as the greatest player of his day and a gentleman from the fact that he would play for the highest stakes available anywhere. When he came to Las Vegas, he gained a cult following among Greek Americans with his big bets. He was a gentleman because he always showed grace when he lost, whether it was a few hundred dollars or several hundreds of thousands of dollars. He could afford to be graceful, because for most games he was staked—he was playing with other people's money. Many times it was money given to him by compatriots of Greek heritage. Some writers have suggested that his frequent losses, for which his Greek sponsors would forgive him because he was one of them, were caused because he made arrangements with his adversaries across the tables. It has been alleged that he would lose on purpose and receive a kickback after play was over.

Dandolos came to Las Vegas before the Mob had taken over the Strip. He played at the Flamingo when Bugsy Siegel was still alive. A few years later he became a national figure when Benny Binion of the Horseshoe invited Dandolos to play in a poker game against Johnny Moss. Moss and Dandolos went at it one-on-one in the front window of the Horseshoe. The game, or series of games, lasted five months and was a precursor to the establishment of the later World Championship of Poker. The lead went back and forth, but in the end Moss, fourteen years the Greek's junior, "outlasted" Dandolos.

Although his reputation remained for another decade, Nick the Greek began slipping in the 1950s. He started borrowing heavily, and his losing continued. A collection had to be taken to pay his funeral costs after he died on Christmas Day in 1966. To the end he was a gambler in his heart. When he was asked why people gambled, he responded, "Why? Because they find ordinary life a swindle, a sellout, a ripoff. It's just eating, working, dying. The nose to the ground and the boss chewing out your ass. Attached to one woman, she growing wrinkled and mean before your eyes. Okay, okay; most people accept it. Most people accept anything and do not balk. But the few who don't accept, that's your lifelong gambler" (quoted in Longstreet 1977, 236).

Sources: Alvarez, A. Alfred. 1983. *The Biggest Game in Town.* Boston: Houghton Mifflin, 20–24, 115, 123, 164; Chafetz, Henry. 1960. *Play the Devil: A History of Gambling in the United States from 1492 to 1955.* New York: Potter Publishers, 420; Longstreet, Stephen. 1977. *Win or Lose: A Social History of Gambling.* Indianapolis, IN: Bobbs-Merrill, 234–238.

Davis, John

John Davis is considered to be the first casino entrepreneur in the United States. But gambling was not the essential part of his life, as he was a patron of the arts. He was born in Santo Domingo (his date of birth is not known) and educated in French colleges, studying music and art. When he came to New Orleans his attention was on the arts. He gained much social prestige as he built the Theatre d' Orleans where operatic performances were given. He also opened an exclusive ballroom. John Davis gave the raucous frontier community its culture.

John Davis associated with the "best" people of New Orleans, and when the opportunity to have a gambling hall arose, he sensed that his group of friends would not want to be playing games among the street hoi polloi in saloons and brothels. Therefore in 1827 he applied for a license for a different style of gambling hall, one that was not just an annex to a saloon. His emporium of games was located beside his ballroom on Orleans near Bourbon Street. Perhaps he anticipated the style of Steve Wynn's Bellagio in Las Vegas, as the casino was carpeted; featured fine furniture, fine food, and the best of liquid refreshments; and was adorned with fine music and its walls lined with art works. The amenities—all the food, drink, and entertainment—were free to his valued customers. Perhaps he can be credited with inventing the "comp" (complimentary), at least in the United States. In a sense his casino was comparable to the best in Las Vegas, without the slot machines and without the masses of people wandering in and

out. When he was given his license, his was the only exclusive hall for games. He only had to compete with the dives of New Orleans, that seem even today not to have gone away. As his upmarket clientele kept growing, he branched out and started a second casino in suburban Bayou St. John.

During the early 1830s, others attempted to imitate his establishments, but they fell short of his standards. His offerings were the most elegant of any gambling facility for decades to come. His "run," however, was not a long one. In 1835, a reform movement—perhaps taking its cues from the antigambling mobs upriver in Vicksburg—pressured the city government to rescind all of the gambling licenses. Davis's reaction was not to try to operate underground, nor was it to run off to another jurisdiction where he could seek accommodations with legal authorities. He was a social leader in New Orleans, and he was an operator of integrity. The classy John Davis was also a man of wealth. He merely closed the doors to his gambling operations, and he returned to a full-time pursuit as the city's primary patron of the opera and the arts. For Davis gambling had always been the amenity.

Sources: Asbury, Herbert. 1938. *Sucker's Progress: An Informal History of Gambling in America from the Colonies to Canfield.* New York: Dodd, Mead, 113–118; Chafetz, Henry. 1960. *Play the Devil: A History of Gambling in the United States from 1492 to 1955.* New York: Potter Publishers, 195–196; Sifakis, Carl. 1990. *Encyclopedia of Gambling.* New York: Facts on File, 87–88.

Delaware

Delaware instituted its lottery in 1975. Because the state was very small and also surrounded by other jurisdictions with very active lotteries—Pennsylvania, New Jersey, and Maryland—state leaders sought a mechanism to win play from neighboring states. They decided to let players try to pick the winners of professional football games. Rather than incur the expense of professional consultants to advise them on appropriate point spreads for the games, they tried to develop that expertise in-house. It was the bureaucrats against the wise guys for Philadelphia and "Jersey." The "big guys" (professional gamblers) also bet actively with the illegal bookies who used the "Las Vegas" line, that is, the line set by Las Vegas casinos (see Glossary). With a few quick phone calls, the true experts could discover which Delaware lines were faulty. The players continuously beat the game, and the state abandoned it before it could put the entire state budget into a deficit. Nonetheless, in 1992, when Congress passed the bill banning sports betting across the United States, Delaware was one of the four states that was given an exemption. There has been no cry from the Blue Hen State to give it another go. The state continues to operate other lottery games, including instant tickets, numbers, and Powerball lotto games.

Delaware has one thoroughbred racetrack and two harness tracks. The state authorized all types of slot machines and other gaming machines for its racetracks in 1995. Delaware Park offered the machines first, but Harrington Raceway and Midway soon followed them, and GTech won a contract to furnish the machines. Delaware Park pursued a strategy somewhat different from that of other states, as it sought to make a strong separation between the machine gaming and the track wagering. Track efforts to bring slot players to the track windows were simply unsuccessful. A track manager commented that people got too confused and that clearly Delaware had a dedicated group of slot players who had no interest in racing. An unused 60,000-square-foot section of the grandstand was converted to slots. No racing monitors were placed in the room, and players had to go to another room to make racing wagers.

Sources: www.lotttery.state.de.us(history).
See also The Racino

Demographic Categories of Players
Gambling and Ethnicity
Players in the African American Community
African American players are not distinguishable by quality of play from most other players; however, particular cultural, historical, and situational factors may be related to certain gambling behavior in some circumstances. Minority people and persons of lower income who live together in poorer communities have often been targeted by

gambling entrepreneurs as being good potential players. Government lotteries have been faulted for directing marketing campaigns at minority communities with advertisements suggesting that gambling is "the way out" of the ghetto. Also, as states such as Illinois purposely located casino facilities in communities needing economic development, they caused casinos to be very near minority people. Such being the case, African Americans and others living close to the casinos had a much higher level of participation in gambling than did other people.

Historically, the African American community, especially in urban settings, has embraced the numbers game. The games, which were first operated by members of the community (and later taken over by white organized crime groups), served many functions for the community. First, the numbers game provided employment for residents. Local people were given jobs as salespersons and numbers runners. They managed groups of runners, and they were also the entrepreneurs, or owners, of the games.

Second, the numbers game was functional in that it provided a mechanism for capital accumulation in the community. Historically (and even today), financial institutions such as banks redlined urban minority communities and refused to make loans to residents or businesses in the designated districts. In turn, the members of the minority community would not patronize the banks—to do so would involve the inconvenience of traveling some distance and meeting with persons who discriminated against them. The numbers entrepreneurs took moneys from their profits and made investments in the local area and also made loans to local businesspeople, a practice that stimulated business activity. They were absentee owners who extracted money from the poor communities—as the later Mafioso game owners did. The entrepreneurs also provided many charity gifts at a time before there was a well-developed welfare system in place.

Third, the numbers game provided a savings function for persons who did not have bank accounts. Each week—or day—they would "invest" a small amount, maybe just a dime or a dollar, on a number. They acted much like a person in the suburbs putting a few dollars away in a Christmas Club account at a branch bank. By playing a number over and over, the resident, or at least many of the residents, could be assured of having an occasional win. That win could represent a time for a major purchase and a celebration. The numbers game also contributed to community solidarity, as residents would share dreams with each other.

General Colin Powell wrote about these functional values of the numbers game in a New York City community. "The secret dream of these tenement dwellers had always been to own their own homes. My father also dreamed about numbers. He bought numbers books at the newsstands to work out winning combinations" (Powell 1995, 301). Every day his father would combine thoughts with Aunt Beryl, and they would buy a number together. One Saturday night, Aunt Beryl dreamed of a number. The next day in church the first hymn had that number in it. "This, surely, was God taking Luther Powell by the hand and leading him to the Promised Land. Pop and Aunt Beryl managed to scrape up $25 to put on the number" (303). They hit the three-digit number. It was worth a payout equaling three-years' pay. "And that's how the Powells managed to buy 183–68 Elmira Avenue in the . . . boroughs of Queens" (303). The numbers represented the Powells' "way out." Colin Powell was just entering college, and perhaps a pressure of having to help his family out an extra bit was lifted from his shoulders, enabling him to pursue his education and career goals in a more focused way.

The gambling establishment knows the value of games to poor people and to persons such as General Powell's father and aunt. Very few African Americans have become leading entrepreneurs on the legitimate side of commercial gambling, however. No casinos in Las Vegas are predominantly owned or controlled by African Americans, and few of the casino executives are minorities. Prior to the 1960s, most of the major casinos on the Strip would not let African Americans play at their tables or stay in their hotel rooms. For a short time, a casino called the Moulin Rouge in the northern part of Las Vegas became the venue for African American players from low rollers to high rollers. It was also the place where leading black entertainers would stay, even though they were performing on the Strip. The barriers of discrimination were broken down in the early 1960s when James Macmillan, a local young dentist from the minority community, became head of the local National Association for the Advancement of Colored People. He refused to acquiesce to the policies of "going along to get along." He threatened a major protest parade that seemed to have all the news elements in it that would make it a national story in a media looking for civil rights protest stories. The casinos agreed to integrate almost overnight. By the time federal legislation on public accommodations was passed in 1964, Las Vegas was fully integrated in that sense.

Employment was something else, and still is. Prior to the 1970s, there was overt employment discrimination in Las Vegas, but a court decree accepted by the industry opened doors for general employment. Nonetheless, much of the employment is still secured through a process called "juice," or "who you know." The bulk of entry-level jobs in hotels are now held by Hispanic Americans, who are very adept at using family connections to make sure their friends know about job openings and have the right introductions to those making hiring decisions. African Americans are still not represented in the industry to the extent that their numbers would suggest they should be, given that they make up approximately 10 percent of the population of Las Vegas.

New casino projects in other urban centers such as Detroit and New Orleans carry very specific obligations for hiring target percentages of minorities and women. Groups applying for licenses also are encouraged to enlist local minority members among their ownership ranks. The extent to which the local policies for minority participation are successful remains to be assessed after the casinos enjoy their first years of operation.

Asian Players

Asians and Asian Americans have a reputation of being very active gamblers. They enjoy playing in groups and sharing the excitement of winning or even coming close to having a win. In my travels to Great Britain, I was informed that play from the Asian sector of the population essentially kept the casinos in business. Although this is not the case in most U.S. jurisdictions, the play of the Asian high roller is critical for the profits of many of the casinos on the Las Vegas Strip. Moreover, in urban communities on the West Coast of the United States and Canada, the Asian play is often a majority of the play. People who have studied gambling sense that there are cultural values that make gambling a part of Asian community life. Numerology and a mystique about fate and luck propel people into gaming. There is also a great desire to participate in games of all sorts, so the drift to gambling games is not unusual.

Asians may be susceptible to developing gambling problems. Their subcommunities may encourage some play that might be considered reckless and harmful. One facet of this is that most of the Asian players have strong families, and they are also tied to family businesses, which have cash flows that can be utilized for daily gambling. When the play begins, the player may feel that he or she can risk everything on the game because of having a safety net that other Americans may not have. No matter whether the player loses all or wins, a member of the extended family will always have a place for him or her to stay. Thus homelessness is not the problem that it is for some other compulsive gamblers. Moreover, someone in the family structure will have a job for a player who is broke. Such a tight family structure, which is a positive force in other situations, tends to present barriers for programs of recovery, as there is a notion of "shame" attached to any social problems. To go outside the family for help, especially to persons outside of the ethnic nationality group, may be considered an embarrassment to the entire group.

Asian gamblers are discussed further in "The 'Best' Gamblers in the World" in Appendix A.

Latino and Hispanic American Players

There are many separate Latino and Latin American communities throughout the Western Hemisphere. Generalizations can never be totally accurate. Nonetheless, at the risk of making ethnic behavioral associations that certainly will not apply to all peoples, I authored an essay on gambling in Latin America (see "Machismo and the Latin American Casino" in Appendix A). My

Young men show their "style" at the Salta Argentina Casino.

study was the result of personal visits to casinos in fourteen Caribbean and Latin American jurisdictions. During the visits, I found a casino that held cockfights, another that banned women players unless they had written permission from their husbands (or former husbands), and another that used local loan agents (perhaps "sharks") because local players would not pay back debts to "foreign" owners. Many of these situations seemed to be a manifestation of the cultural value of *machismo* in many aspects of the daily life and certainly in the daily life of the gambling operations.

Gambling and Age

There appear to be age correlations with gambling behavior. Gambling activity occurs among all age groups, but it seems to increase with age through the adult years until the sixties, when a decline starts. Nonetheless, at both ends of the age spectrums there are conditions that suggest that excessive gambling may be a major concern for society. We will look in turn at youth gambling and then gambling during the golden years.

Youth Gambling

The childhood years are devoted to much play activity, as it is through such play that basic social values can be learned: competitiveness and striving for goals, camaraderie and team involvement, adherence to rules and notions of fair play, acceptance of defeats and a sense of renewed efforts, gracefulness in enjoying victory. Certainly an emphasis on playing games, an encouragement for playing one or another kind of game can cause children to desire participation in games and contests where the reward—the goal—is money. Gambling has to have a natural draw for persons who are compelled to engage in fantasy play as part of their socialization. And indeed, where children are given the opportunity to gamble, they do so.

A wide range of studies indicates that young people may be very involved in gambling (see Goodman 1995, 43–44; Arcuri, Lester, and Smith 1985, 935–938). For instance, one study found that 90 percent of young people in the United States had purchased lottery tickets by the time they were seniors in high school. Another found that 77 percent of high school students had gambled

Amusement games—such as this crane pull—that cater to children have the three elements of gambling: players advance money to play, there is at least an element of luck in determining the winner, and the winners receive prizes.

sometime (Goodman 1995, 44). A survey in Atlantic City found that over 60 percent of high school students had played slot machines in casinos. In most cases, parents were aware of this activity (Arcuri, Lester, and Smith 1985, 938).

The surveys suggested that youthful gambling and gambling problems occurred at times before young people turned to alcohol or drug use. Early gambling was associated with parental gambling and parental problem gambling. In later adolescence, gambling was associated with peer group acceptance. The studies suggested that young people craved acceptance and saw gambling as a means toward that goal. Those who persisted at gaming tended to do it alone, however, in order to escape either a bad home environment or their failure to participate in social activities with their peers. The availability of gambling in the community was related to youth participation, even though in most of the surveys the young people were gambling illegally.

The youthful gamblers will play whatever game is available, but because they must be wary of being excluded from a facility because of age, they gravitate toward hidden-away slot machine areas of casinos. They also participate in sports betting, usually making their wagers with a bookie or with an intermediary who is not concerned with the fact that they are young—only that the costs of the gambling will be paid.

Youthful gamblers exhibited the same rates of pathological gambling as, or even higher rates than, the adults who were surveyed. The survey for the recent National Gambling Impact Study Commission suggested that as many as 6 percent of teenagers had characteristics of pathological gamblers, a percentage several times higher than that for adults (NGISC 1999, 7–23). The issue of youth gambling is important because many surveys of pathological gamblers find that they started their gambling activity while they were teenagers, due to an exposure to the activity and in part to parental support of their participation. Henry Lesieur's book *The Chase* portrays a critical time in the development of a compulsive gambling career as an early "big win" (Lesieur 1984). Psychologically, young people are less able to handle the emotional rush coming with that "early win" than

are adults seasoned in life's many ups and downs. As a result of the research information gathered, the National Gambling Impact Study Commission urged that youth not be exposed to gambling opportunities (NGISC 1999, 7–30).

Senior Gambling

The great expansion of gambling opportunities has also attracted many senior citizens to situations that may not be socially beneficial. Senior gambling has not been extensively studied, but there is an indication that where casinos are available, seniors do play in large numbers. Overall their gambling participation rates are not as high as those of other adults but are growing. A 1975 survey found that 38 percent of the elderly (over sixty-five) had gambled during the previous twelve months (Commission on the Review of the National Policy toward Gambling 1976, 59); a 1998 survey found that more than 60 percent had done so (NGISC 1999, 730). Gambling is a growing recreation among the elderly, as in contrast with the past they now collectively have better health and

Las Vegas "locals" casinos appeal to senior citizens.

more resources. Of course they also have more time available for gambling than do other adults. In Las Vegas, the locals-oriented casinos target seniors as players to fill the casinos' daytime hours and their soft weeknights as well as their down-seasons when tourists are not as plentiful. The casinos feature special buffet meals at low costs, they offer their regular players bargains through "slot clubs," and they even offer a regular bus service into senior neighborhoods (Sun City–type communities) and senior housing developments.

One study from Las Vegas found that elderly men gambled less than younger men did, but the opposite was the case for elderly women. For the latter, the gambling opportunity was seen mostly as a social event and a chance to escape the boredom of daily life, often in an apartment-type setting. Among men, those who rented apartments gambled much more than did homeowners.

As with youth, the seniors have their games of choice. In the casino, they are ardent video-poker machine players as well as bingo players (Schwer, Moseley, and Thompson 2001).

Gambling and Gender

Traditionally, gambling has been a male-dominated activity. The same can be said of sports and other competitive games that even reach into the business world. But gradually, women are participating in gambling activities at higher and higher levels. This reflects the growing importance of women in the workforce and also the fact that more and more women are financially independent. On the downside of the equation is the fact that many women find themselves in abusive situations, and they turn to gambling as an escape mechanism, much as they have also turned to alcohol and drugs. As gambling is more available in communities across the country, it is becoming an addiction of choice for many escape-prone women.

In the recent past women played bingo more than men did, as it was a social event and a very acceptable activity. Most players were excitement oriented rather than escape prone. The casinos that first welcomed women found that they preferred machine play to table play. This is still the case, as the bravado of the tables fits male traits more closely. Women may sense that the action at the tables is too fast or too competitive and that players

are too serious about the competitive nature of the games. These psychological barriers persist, but they are falling to a large extent. Nonetheless, today the favorite game for the woman player in the Las Vegas casino is the slot machine, especially the video-poker machine. And of course, as is discussed in the entry on slot machines, this is a device that can get gamblers into trouble rather quickly. Indeed, one person who counsels problem women gamblers in Las Vegas told me that 95 percent of his clients were playing the video poker machines. Nonetheless, problem gambling is still a greater problem among the male gender. The national survey for the National Gambling Impact Study Commission found that the rate of problem and pathological gamblers among men was double that of women (NGISC 1999, 4–8).

Sources: Arcuri, Alan F., David Lister, and Franklin O. Smith. 1985. "Shaping Adolescent Gambling Behavior." *Adolescence* 20 (Winter): 935–938; Commission on the Review of the National Policy toward Gambling. 1976. *Gambling in America: Final Report.* Washington, D.C.: U.S. Government Printing Office, p. 59; Goodman, Robert. 1995. *The Luck Business: The Devastating Consequences and Broken Promises of America's Gambling Explosion.* New York: Free Press, 43–44; Lesieur, Henry R. 1984. *The Chase: Career of the Compulsive Gambler.* Cambridge, MA: Schenkman Publishing; Moehring, Eugene. 1989. *Resort City in the Sunset: Las Vegas 1930–1970.* Reno: University of Nevada Press; Mok, Waiman P., and Joseph Habra. 1991. "Age and Gambling Behavior: A Declining and Shifting Pattern of Participation." *Journal of Gambling Studies* 7, no. 4 (Winter): 313–336; National Gambling Impact Study Commission [NGISC]. 1999. *Final Report.* Washington, DC: NGISC, 7–30; Schwer, R. Keith, Charles Moseley, and William N. Thompson. 2001. "Gambling and the Elderly in Las Vegas," Draft Manuscript, Center for Business and Economic Research, University of Nevada, Las Vegas; Stinchfield, Randy, and Ken C. Winters. 1998. "Gambling and Problem Gambling among Youths." In *Gambling: Socioeconomic Impacts and Public Policy* (special volume of *The Annals of the American Academy of Political and Social Science*), edited by James H. Frey, 172–185. Thousand Oaks, CA: Sage; Strachan, Mary Lou, and Robert Custer. 1989. "The Female Compulsive Gambler in Las Vegas." Paper presented at the 4th International Conference on Compulsive Gambling, 19 October, Las Vegas.
See also Japan and Pachinko; Lotteries; Slot Machines and Machine Gambling; Appendix A: "The Best Gamblers in the World," "The Family That Gambles Together," "Machismo and the Latin American Casino"

Dice Games. *See* Craps and Other Dice Games

Dog Racing

Dog racing began in the United States in 1919 with the opening of a greyhound track in Emeryville, California. Although gambling on dog races is permissible under the law in eighteen states, today there are tracks in only fifteen states. Since 1919, there have been tracks in over forty states at one time or another, although in most cases betting on races was not formally sanctioned by the law. Currently in the Western Hemisphere there are also tracks in the U.S. dependency of Guam, in Mexico (two states), and in Panama. Previously there were tracks in Puerto Rico, Haiti, the Dominican Republic, Barbados, and Montreal, Canada. The forty-nine operating tracks in the United States employ 30,000 people and generate approximately 13 percent of the pari-mutuel betting in the United States. In 1998, the tracks won $494 million (including offtrack and intertrack wagering, and after prizes given to players). Wagering totals have remained stable, increasing an average of 1 percent a year since 1982. All legal wagering at dog tracks today is through pari-mutuel betting systems. Systems operate both on track and through offtrack or intertrack parlors (Christiansen 1999).

Today racing is confined essentially to one breed of dog, the greyhound. Evidence of the domesticated greyhound is found in Egyptian carvings that have been dated back to 2800 B.C. Early Greek civilizations probably named the dog Greekhound, and a corruption of that word yielded its present name. Others suggest that the dog has a grey tone in its face and on its head as it ages—almost a human-like quality. The Egyptians may have used the greyhound for hunting hares and gazelles, but the first recorded evidence of this activity came from the Roman era. The Romans also began the sport of "coursing." Hares would be placed in a large field, and the dogs would be in contests to see which one could run the poor animal down the fastest. In England, coursing events were formalized. As early as 1576, meetings were held in which two greyhounds would race across a field to reach a trapped animal in a fixed spot. Dogs were bred for the events. A certain breed of greyhound resulted from a cross and

A racing dog rescued by an adoption program. The dog hurt its foot and could no longer race. Without the adoption program the dog would have been put to death.

recross with English bulldogs. A resulting dog named King Cob excelled, and today all the racing greyhounds worldwide can show lineage back to this one dog. In 1836, the Waterloo Cup competition began, and by 1858, a National Coursing Association was established in England to govern the events.

Coursing began in the United States with an event in Kansas in 1886. Animal rights activists stifled growth in the competition, however, as they protested the killing of jackrabbits that were used in the events. Their protests led dog enthusiasts to seek out alternative, nonanimal lures or bait. Owen Patrick Smith answered their call. He experimented with stuffed jackrabbits that he mounted on motorcycles. By 1920, he had received a patent for an artificial mechanical lure that he used in Salt Lake City. Finally he contrived a mechanical rabbit that could be run around a track in front of a pack of greyhounds. He put his device into use at the country's first dog track, which he called the Blue Star Amusement in Emeryville, California,

Starting gate on a dog-racing track in Wisconsin.

near the present-day Oakland Bay Bridge. Smith's first venture was not successful, but he did better as he took the idea of greyhound track racing to other locations. In 1921, tracks opened in Tulsa, Oklahoma; East St. Louis, Illinois; and Hialeah, Florida. A track that opened in Chicago in 1922 proved to be successful. In 1925, there were seven tracks; by 1930, there were over sixty tracks in the United States. In 1926, Smith founded the International Greyhound Racing Association, which works with the American Kennel Club to register dogs and regulate racing. Owen Smith lived long enough to see his sport flourishing, but he died in 1927, before he could reap major profits from its success.

Coursing activity waned with the introduction of dog track racing; however, coursing is still found in the United States and elsewhere, but no live lures are used. Events are governed by the American Sighthound Field Association and the American Kennel Club.

Although dog racing was here to stay after the 1920s, in many places it did not stay long. Of the tracks that opened before 1930, only four can be counted among the active tracks today. To be profitable, the tracks allowed bookies to come in and set up shop next to the racing areas. They gave a healthy fee to the track for the right to do business, but they also had to bribe the local sheriff in many places, as the betting was not legal. As political tides would turn, the sheriff would be persuaded to ban events. Opponents also seized upon opportunities to discredit the sport with revelations that mobsters, such as Al Capone, were involved in track operations. He reportedly owned an interest in the Hawthorne (dog) Race Track in Chicago. The political forces of opposition would sometimes be directed by horse track interests who did not enjoy the competition. A Miami track initiated the innovative use of night racing in order to placate the horsemen, and other dog tracks imitated the practice. Pari-mutuel racing was initiated with greyhound events in Montreal in 1928, and when Florida legalized the betting system for its horse tracks, the dog track owners sought and won legislative approval for pari-mutuel betting as well.

Dog tracks struggled through the Depression years and the early 1940s as the nation's attention was consumed by economic and war matters. But racing survived. According to Thomas Walsh (1991, 8–9), in the early 1940s, a Massachusetts operator actually used monkeys as jockeys, mounting them on the greyhounds' backs. He had his monkeys tour throughout the East as a serious effort to make the races more interesting. The experiment was novel and drew some spectator interest, but it proved not to be at all functional. Racing was closed down in the later war years but was revived after peace resumed, and in 1946, an American Greyhound Track Owners Association started operations. Today this organization joins with the National Greyhound Association in setting forth the rules for all races. The latter organization registers all dogs and maintains records. Dogs must be tattooed (on their ears), and breeding is regulated. Artificial insemination is permissible, whereas it is banned for horse breeding. A National Greyhound Hall of Fame opened in 1973 in Abilene, Kansas.

Dog races have the same kind of officials—secretaries, paddock judges, patrol judges, and so on—that are found at horse tracks. Ownership and training functions are also similar. Of course there is no jockey, and exercise workers are not significant at the kennels. The structure of betting is very similar to that on horse racetracks. Newborn greyhounds are given about sixty days of general freedom before their training begins. Then they are tattooed, registered, and started in walking and running exercises. When the greyhound is fourteen months old, it is either sold to a racing kennel or placed there by the owner. Dogs start racing several months after training begins. Both male and female greyhounds run, but the males tend to have longer careers—up to five years. The dogs race from 5/16th mile to 7/16th mile. The dogs have a grading system that is used by racing secretaries to create well-matched races. Dogs will race every two to three days during the peak of their careers. Some stakes races have prizes running into the hundreds of thousands of dollars; however, as with horse racing, dog ownership is not a good business venture. It is an activity tied to excitement, and many owners are in the game to be in the game, not to reap financial rewards.

A severe problem facing the dog racing industry has been the discarding of dogs that do not win. They are generally not put to pasture, sold as pets, or put to stud; they are killed. Over 8,000 dogs were killed during one five-year period in the 1970s. In response to the issue, an organization called Retired Greyhounds as Pets (REGAP) was formed in 1982 by Ron Walsek, an employee at a racetrack, to facilitate the adoption of the animals. Today there are 100 groups associated with REGAP. They have brought about over 15,000 adoptions. The adoption costs are very low—less than fifty dollars. The animals are extremely gentle, well mannered, intelligent, and affectionate. Thousands of people are finding that they are wonderful pets around children and in the home (Walsh 1991, 121).

Sources: Branigan, Cynthia A. 1997. *The Reign of the Greyhound.* New York: Howell Book House, Simon and Schuster; Christiansen, Eugene Martin. 1999. "The 1998 Gross Annual Wager." *International Gaming and Wagering Business* (August): 20ff; Walsh, Thomas. 1991. *Greyhound Racing for Fun and Profit.* Deerfield Beach, FL: Liberty Publishing.
See also Horse Racing

Dominican Republic

The Dominican Republic shares the Greater Antilles island of Hispaniola with Haiti, with which it has shared many attributes, especially an impoverished condition. In the early 1800s, the country was ruled in succession by French, Spanish, and Haitian military forces. When not ruled by foreign forces, the Dominican Republic has suffered at the hands of indigenous dictatorial rule as well as having been dominated by commercial interests of the United States, aided by the U.S. military. During the rule of strongman Raphael Trujillo (1930–1961), foreign casino interests established properties that were essentially governed by the dictator, largely for his benefit as well as that of the owners. The years from 1961 to 1966 were turbulent and unstable. In 1965 U.S. troops invaded as a measure to preserve order and preclude intervention by Cuba. The troops left in 1966, and the stage was set for the installation of a democratic government. Democracy has survived over the remaining years of the twentieth century and into the twenty-first century.

The legislature of the Dominican Republic formalized a set of rules for casino operations in a law that was passed in 1968. Under the 1968 law, the casinos must be in top-rated tourist hotels that have 200 rooms. Exceptions were made for two casinos in smaller hotels that had been operating

The Jaragua Casino of Santo Domingo features major Las Vegas–style shows.

before 1968. All licensed hotels since the law was passed are in larger hotels that market their rooms to foreign tourists.

The 1968 act outlawed slot machines. Slot machines had operated in casinos before that time; however, the government felt that the machines appealed too much to poorer local residents, who did not have the resources to meet minimum play requirements of the table games. The machines were permitted to come into the casinos with a new law passed in 1988; however, the government imposed a higher tax on machine wins than on other wins. The government wished to encourage the casinos to have only higher-denomination machines (one dollar per play or more) rather than nickel and dime machines that would appeal to the poorer people. In contrast, poorer people can purchase passive lottery tickets each week in order to satisfy their gaming urges. Besides that, the lottery directs its profits to programs for the poor and also employs many poor people to sell the tickets.

The casinos have two sets of books, one for play in U.S. currency and the other for play in Dominican currency. There is no currency exchange.

There are two sets of chips—U.S. and Dominican. There are also specifically designated chips for credit play. This provision for special chips enables the casino to ensure that loans are repaid at the time a winning player would be "cashing-in." The casinos follow two methods of taxation. For casino wins in Dominican currency, the casinos pay a tax of 20 percent on the gross win. For players using chips valued in U.S. dollars, the tax is paid when the chips are purchased. It is a 2 percent drop tax; that is, for each $100 of chips purchased, the casino pays $2 in tax. There is no win tax. The casinos are reluctant to offer credit to players, especially local players. They had a history of players refusing to pay back the casino owners who, for the most part, are foreigners—usually Americans (*see* Honduras for a discussion of the same problem). Locals have considered it an affront to be challenged in court by "rich foreigners" for repayment of money they have "already returned" to the casinos via their losing play. Therefore, the casinos contract with local residents who will "guarantee" repayment of the loans. If the player loses and does not repay the loan in a rapid fashion, the

A major resort casino hotel in Santa Domingo—Embajador.

casino asks the guarantor to collect the loan. The guarantor then pays 70 percent of the loan and is given the right to collect the entire loan and to keep the 30 percent differential as a commission. The guarantor is also empowered to take the loan obligation to court, where he is well acquainted with the judicial personnel and is not subject to antiforeign accusations.

There are several premium casinos in Santo Domingo, the capital city—a city that was settled by Bartholemew Columbus, the brother of the explorer. The leading casino is the Jaragua, which is owned by Americans. It features a Las Vegas–style floorshow and a set of fountains that was designed by the architect who designed the fountains at Caesars Palace. Koreans own the next leading property, which is located at the Embajador Hotel. Most of the dealers in these facilities are citizens of the United States, and many have had experience in Las Vegas casinos. There is no restriction on such foreign labor. Other major casinos are in the Sheraton, Concorde, Lina, and Centanario hotels. Altogether, there are a dozen hotels in the Santo Domingo area.

Santo Domingo is a historical city that should appeal to a tourist with a craving for evidence of the founding of the oldest European-settled city in the hemisphere (1496) and a desire to see buildings still standing at the oldest university in the hemisphere (founded in 1538). Most casino-oriented tourists, however, like things such as beaches and room amenities. Santo Domingo falls short. It has no sandy beaches, and its electrical supply is challenged. Every day the power in the hotel—casino and rooms—goes out for some time. The casino keeps essential functions going with backup facilities; however, tourist facilities such as Jacuzzis, television, restaurant areas, and telephones temporarily go down. For tourism, however, the Dominican Republic is fortunate to have another location with ample power and with top-class natural beaches—the north island shore called Puerto Plata. Its golden beach extends for nearly sixty miles. Several new casino hotels have been constructed in Puerto Plata within the last decade, the leading one being a Jack Tar facility with 300 rooms and a 40,000-square-foot casino area.

The Dominican Republic competes with Puerto Rico for casino players—each has its advantages and disadvantages. In Puerto Rico, English must be spoken at the casinos, whereas it is not mandated in the Dominican Republic. Puerto Rico has superior airline service, whereas the Dominican Republic has limited direct flights to the United States. On the other hand, labor costs are much lower in the Dominican Republic, which translates into lower hotel costs for tourists—and lower costs for casinos that are offering free rooms to players. The other advantage of gaming in the Dominican Republic is shared with other Caribbean venues: No reports are given to the Internal Revenue Service of the United States regarding players activities—how much they wager and how much they win.

The Dominican Republic was one of the first offshore jurisdictions to enter the market for sports bettors. They now offer bets through telephone service as well as over the Internet.

Sources: Cabot, Anthony N., William N. Thompson, Andrew Tottenham, and Carl Braunlich, eds. 1999. *International Casino Law.* 3d ed. Reno, Nevada: Institute for the Study of Gambling, University of Nevada, Reno, 229–231.
See also Credit and Debts

Draw Poker. *See* Poker

E

The Economic Impacts of Gambling

Does gambling help the economy? This question has been asked over and over for generations. Economic scholars such as Paul Samuelson have suggested that since gambling produces no tangible product or required service, it is merely a "sterile" transfer of money. Therefore the energies (and all costs) expended in the activity represent unneeded costs to society. Further, he points out that gambling activity creates "inequality and instability of incomes" (Samuelson 1976, 425).

On the other hand, a myriad of economic impact studies have concluded that gambling produces jobs, purchasing activity, profits, and tax revenues. Invariably, these studies have been designed by, or sponsored by, representatives of the gambling industry. For instance, the Midwest Hospitality Advisors, on behalf of Sodak Gaming Suppliers, Inc., conducted an impact study of Native American casino gaming. Sodak had an exclusive arrangement to distribute International Gaming Technologies (IGT) slot machines to Native American gaming facilities in the United States. The report was "based upon information obtained from direct interviews with each of the Indian gaming operations in the state, as well as figures provided by various state agencies pertaining to issues such as unemployment compensation and human services" (Midwest Hospitality Advisors 1992, 1).

The study indicated that the Minnesota casinos had 4,700 slot machines and 260 blackjack tables in 1991. Employment of 5,700 people generated $78.227 million in wages, which in turn yielded $11.8 million in social security and Medicare payments, $4.7 million in federal withholding, and $1.76 million in state income taxes. The casinos spent over $40 million annually on purchases of goods from in-state suppliers. Net revenues for the tribes were devoted to community grants as well as to payments to members, health care, housing, and infrastructure. The report indicated that as many as 90 percent of the gamers in individual casinos were from outside Minnesota; however, there was no indication of the overall residency of the state's gamblers (Midwest Hospitality Advisors 1992).

The American Gaming Association (AGA) ignores the question of where the money comes from as it reports that "gaming is a significant contributor to economic growth and diversification within each of the states where it operates" (Cohn and Wolfe 1999, 7). An AGA survey talks of the jobs, tax revenues, and purchasing of casino properties in 1998: a total of 325,000 jobs, $2.5 billion in state and local taxes, construction and purchasing leading to 450,000 more jobs, and $58 million in charitable contributions for employees of casinos. The report indicates that the "typical casino customer" has a significantly higher income than the average American, with 73 percent setting budgets before they gamble (there was no indication about how many of these *kept* their budgets), making them a "disciplined" group. The report made no attempt to see if the players were local residents or not (Cohn and Wolfe, 7–10).

Likewise, another study sponsored by IGT and conducted by Northwestern University economist Michael Evans found that "on balance, all of the state and local economies that have permitted casino gaming have improved their economic performance" (The Evans Group 1996, 1–1). Evans found that in 1995, casinos had employed 337,000 people directly, with 328,000 additional jobs "generated by the expenditures in casino gambling"(4–1). State and local taxes from casinos amounted to $2 billion in 1995, and casinos yielded $5.9 billion in federal taxes. Yet Evans did not consider that the money for gambling came

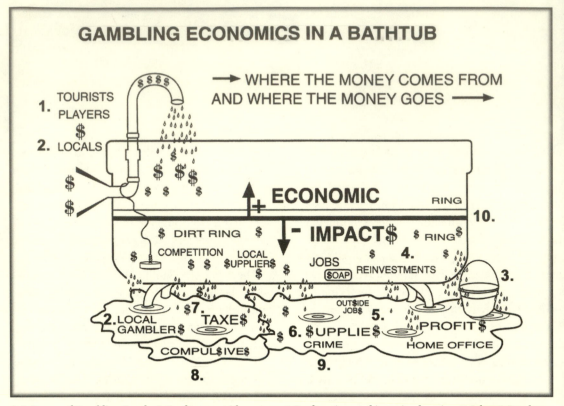

GAMBLING ECONOMICS IN A BATHTUB

1-2. Source of Gambling Funds; 3. Profits to outside owners; 4. Profits reinvested in casino location; 5. Jobs; 6. Purchase of supplies; 7. Taxes; 8. The social cost of pathological gambling; 9. The costs of gambling-related crime; 10. The dirt ring—we don't see it if the water level is rising.

from anywhere, or that the money could have been spent elsewhere if it were not spent in casino operations, or that if spent elsewhere, it would also generate jobs and taxes. The studies by industry-sponsored groups also neglect the notion that there could be economic costs as a result of externalities to casino operations—namely, as a result of the increased presence of compulsive gambling behaviors and some criminal activity. Evans brushed aside the possibilities with a comment that "the sociological issues that are sometimes associated with gaming, such as the rise in pathological gamblers who 'bet the rent money' at the casinos, are outside the scope of this study. Nonetheless, it seems appropriate to remark at this juncture that occasional and anecdotal evidence does not prove anything" (6–3).

Whatever is produced by a gambling enterprise does not come out of thin air; it comes from somewhere, and that "where" must be identified if we

are to know the economic impacts of gambling operations. The impact studies commissioned by the gambling industry fall short.

So what is the impact of gambling activity upon an economy? This is a difficult question to answer, as the answer must contain many facets, and the answer must vary according to the kind of gambling in question as well as the location of the gambling activity. Although the question for specific gambling activity poses difficulties, the model necessary for finding the answers to the question is actually quite simple. It is an input-output model. Two basic questions are asked: (1) Where does the money come from? and (2) Where does the money go? The model can be represented by a graphic display of a bathtub.

Water comes into a bathtub, and water runs out of a bathtub. If the water comes in at a higher rate than it leaves the tub, the water level rises; if the water comes in at a slower rate than it leaves, the water level is lowered. An economy attracts money from gambling activities. An economy discards money because of gambling activity. Money comes and money goes. If, as a result of the presence of a legalized gambling activity, more money comes into an economy than leaves the economy, there is a positive monetary effect because of the gambling activity. The level of wealth in the economy rises. If more money leaves than comes in, however, then there is a negative impact from the presence of casino gambling. Several factors must be considered in what I will call the Bathtub Gambling Economics Model. We must recognize the source of the money that is gambled by players and lost to gambling enterprises, and we must consider how the gambling enterprise spends the money it wins from players.

Factors in the Bathtub Gambling Economics Model

- Tourist players: Are players/persons from outside the local economic region (defined geographically)—and are they persons who would not otherwise be spending money in the region if gambling activities were absent? A tourist's spending brings dollars into the bathtub unless they otherwise would have spent the money in the region.
- Local players: Are the players from the local regional economic area? If so, does the presence of gambling activities in the region preclude their travel outside the region in order to participate in gambling activities elsewhere? If they are locals who would not otherwise be spending money outside the region, their gambling money cannot be considered money added to the bathtub.
- Additional player questions: Are the players affluent or people of little means? Are the players persons who are enjoying gambling recreation in a controlled manner, or are they playing out of control and subject to pathologies and compulsions?
- Profits: Are the profits from the operations staying within the economic region, are they going to owners (whether commer-

cial, tribal, or governments) who reside outside the economic region, or are they reinvested by the owners in projects that are outside of the region?
- Reinvestments: Are profits reinvested within the economic region? Are gambling facilities expanded with the use of profit moneys? Are facilities allowed to be expanded?
- Jobs: Are the employees of the gambling operations persons who live within the economic region? Are the casino executives of the companies who operate (or own) the facilities local residents?
- Supplies: Does the gambling facility purchase its nonlabor supplies—gambling equipment (machines, dice, lottery and bingo paper), furniture, food, hotel supplies—from within the economic region?
- Taxes: Does the facility pay taxes? Are profits leading to excessive federal income taxes? Are gambling taxes moderate or severe? Do the gambling taxes leave the economic region? Does the government return a portion of the gambling taxes to the region? How expensive are infrastructure and regulatory efforts that are required because of the presence of gambling that would not otherwise be required? Do the gambling taxes represent a transfer of funds between different economic strata of society?
- Pathological gambling compulsive or problem gambling): How much pathological gambling is generated because of the presence of the gambling facility in the economic region? What percentage of local residents have become pathological gamblers? What does this cost the society—in lost work, in social services, in criminal justice costs?
- Crime: In addition to costs caused by pathological gamblers, how much other crime is generated by gamblers because of the presence of a gambling facility? How much of this crime occurs within the economic region, and what is the cost of this crime for the people who live in the economic region?

• The construction factor: If a gambling facility is a large capital investment, the infusion of construction money will represent a positive contribution to the economic region at an initial point. The investors must be reimbursed for the construction financing with repayments and interest over time, however. The long-range extractions of money from a region will more than balance the temporary infusions of money into a region. An application of the model must recognize that the incomes eventually produce outgoes. The examples that follow therefore ignore the construction factor—although more refined examples may see it as positive for initial years and negative thereafter.

Some Descriptive Applications of the Model

The Las Vegas Bathtub Model

The Las Vegas economy has witnessed phenomenal growth in the past few years. This has occurred even in the face of competition from around the nation and world, as more and more locations have casinos and casino gambling products. As of the end of 2000, the Las Vegas economy was strong because the overwhelming amount of gambling money (as much as 90 percent) brought to the casinos came from visitors. According to 1999 information from the Las Vegas Convention and Visitors Authority, visitors stay in Las Vegas an average of four days, spending much money outside of the casino areas. Las Vegas has money leakage as well. State taxes are very low, however, and much of the profits remains, as owners are local. Or if not, they see great advantages in reinvesting profits in expanded facilities in Las Vegas. The costs of crime and compulsive gambling associated with gambling are probably major; however, many of these costs are transferred to other economies, as most problem players return to homes located in other economic areas. Las Vegas is not a manufacturing or an agricultural region, so most of the purchases (except for gambling supplies) result in leakage to other economies. Gambling locations in Las Vegas such as bars, 7-11 stores, and grocery stores represent very faulty bathtubs—bathtubs with great leakage.

Other Jurisdictions in the United States

Atlantic City's casino bathtub functions appropriately, as most of the gamblers are from outside the local area. Players are mostly "day-trippers," however, who do not spend moneys outside the casinos. Most purchases, as with those in Las Vegas, result in leakage for the economy. Like those in Las Vegas, state gaming taxes are reasonably low. Other taxes, however, are high.

Most other U.S. jurisdictions do not have well-functioning bathtubs, because most offer gambling products, for the most part, to local players. Native American casinos may help local economies because they do not pay gambling excise taxes or federal income taxes on gambling wins, as they are wholly owned by tribal governments who keep profits (which are in the form tribal taxes) in the local economies.

Two Empirical Applications of the Model

Illinois Riverboats. In 1995, I participated in gathering research on the economic impacts of casino gambling in the state of Illinois (Thompson and Gazel 1996). Illinois has licensed ten riverboat operations in ten locations of the state. The locations were picked because they were on navigable waters and also because the locations had suffered economic declines. We interviewed 785 players at five of the locations. We also gathered information about the general revenue production of the casinos and the spending patterns of the casinos—wages, supplies, taxes, and residual profits. The casinos were owned by corporations; most of them were based outside of the state, and none of them were based in the particular casino communities.

The focus of our attention was the local areas within thirty-five miles of the casino sites. The data were analyzed collectively, that is, for all the local areas together.

In 1995, the casinos generated revenues of just over $1.3 billion. Our survey indicated that 57.9 percent of the revenues came from the local area, from persons who lived within thirty-five miles of the casinos. From our survey we determined, however, that 30 percent of these local gamblers would have gambled in another casino location if a casino had not been available close to their home.

Therefore, in a sense, their gambling revenue represented an influx of money to the area. That is, the casino blocked money that would otherwise leave the area. We considered a part of the local gambling money to be nonlocal money, in other words, visitor revenue. On the other side of the coin, as a result of our surveys, we considered that 22 percent of the visitors' spending was really local moneys. Many of the nonlocal gamblers indicated that they would have come to the area and spent money (lodging, food, etc.), even if there were no casino in the area.

By interpolating the income for one casino from the total data collected, we envision a casino with $120 million in revenue. The share of these revenues that came from within the thirty-five-mile economic area (after adjustments for the 30 percent retained from other casino jurisdictions) equaled $60 million. In other words, we can represent this as local money lost to the casino. The question then is, how much of the money from the casino revenues of $120 million was retained in the thirty-five-mile area (see Table 1).

The direct economic impact was negative $8.367 million (that is, $60 million of revenues came from the local thirty-five-mile area, but only $51,632,200 of the spending was locally retained). A direct economic loss for the area of $8,367,800 may be multiplied by approximately two, as the money lost would otherwise have been able to circulate two times before leaving the area economy. The direct and indirect economic losses due to the presence of the gambling casino therefore equaled $16,735,600.

Added to these economic losses are additional losses due to externalities of social maladies. For each local area, there will be an increase in problem and pathological gambling, and there will also be an increase in crime due to the introduction of casino gambling. The presence of casino gambling, according to one national study (Grinols and Omorov 1996), added to the other social burdens of society, such as taxes, per-adult costs of $19.63 due to extra criminal activity and criminal justice system costs due to related crime. The National Gambling Impact Study Commission found that the introduction of gambling to a local area *doubled* the amount of problem and pathological

Table 1 Economic Impacts of Illinois Casinos

Casino Expenses	$ Thousand	
Wages	$30,000	
Payroll taxes	2,000	
Promotional activities	2,000	
Purchases	22,500	
Gaming and local taxes	27,500	
Illinois corporation tax	1,800	
Federal corporation tax	11,628	
Retained profits	22,572	

Retained Money from Casino Operation/Portion Retained within 35-mile Radius	$ Thousand	% of Total
Wages	$27,000	90
Promotions	2,000	10
Purchases	13,500	60
Gaming and local taxes	6,875	25
Retained profits	2,257.2	10
Total	$51,632.2	

Source: Thompson, William N., and Ricardo Gazel. 1996. *The Economics of Casino Gambling in Illinois.* Chicago: Chicago Better Government Association.

gambling (National Gambling Impact Study Commission 1999, 4–4). Our studies of costs due to compulsive gambling find adults having to pay an extra $56.70 each because of extra pathological gamblers (0.9 percent of the population) and an extra $44.10 each because of extra problem gamblers (2 percent of the population). This additional $120.43 per adult translates into an extra loss of $12,043,000 (or $24,086,000 with a multiplier of two) for an economic area of 100,000 adults when the first casino comes to town.

Wisconsin Native American Casinos. A similar impact study was made for Wisconsin Native American casinos in 1994 (Thompson, Gazel, and Rickman 1995). We interviewed 697 players at three casinos. Using casino descriptions as well as player information, we calculated that the state's casinos won $600 million from the players. Interpolating data for one casino with $120 million in revenues we determined how much of the gambling revenue was attracted to and retained in the area of thirty-five miles around the casino.

The players' interviews indicated that 37.2 percent were from the thirty-five-mile area surrounding the casino. Of their $44.64 million in gambling revenues, 20 percent is money that would otherwise be gambled elsewhere. On the other hand, 10 percent of the $75.36 million gambled by "outsiders" would have otherwise come to the area in other expenses by these players. Hence we consider that $43.248 million of the losses are from the local area and $76.752 million comes from the "outside."

The expenses of the casino are as shown in Table 2. With a multiplier of two, the direct positive impact of such a Native American casino is $88,776,000.

The positive impacts are lessened by the social costs due to crime and compulsive gambling. As most of the casinos are in rural areas, the population rings of thirty-five miles will not contain in excess of 200,000 or 300,000 adults, making these costs considerably less than the positive benefits shown.

A Comparison of the Empirical Applications. The positive local area economic impacts of Native American casinos in Wisconsin contrast to the negative impacts in Illinois for several reasons. The Illinois casinos are purposely put into urban areas as a matter of state policy. As a result, a higher portion of gamers are local residents; therefore, fewer dollars are drawn into the area. The urban settings also exacerbate social problems, as the negative social costs are retained in the areas. The two major factors distinguishing the positive from negative impacts are (1) the fact that the Native casinos do not pay taxes to outside governments and (2) the fact that the ownership of the casinos by local tribes keeps all the net profits (less management fees) in the local areas.

Other Forms of Gambling
The economic model can be applied to all forms of gambling. Other findings may arise from studies, however. For instance, for horse-race betting, there would have to be a realization that commercial

Table 2 Economic Impacts of Wisconsin Casinos

Casino Expenses	$ Thousand
Wages	$25,600
Payroll taxes	1,700
Promotions	2,000
Purchases	29,240
Management fees	8,000
Tribal share (66,540)	53,460

Money Retained from Casino Operations/Portion retained within 35-mile Radius	$ Thousand	%
Wages	$20,480	80
Promotions	2,000	100
Purchases	11,696	40
Tribal share	53,460	100
Total retained	$87,636	

Direct economic impacts: $87,636,000 – $43,248,000 = $44,388,000

Source: Thompson, William N., Ricardo Gazel, and Dan Rickman. 1995. *The Social Costs of Gambling in Wisconsin.* Mequon, WI: Wisonsin Policy Research Institute.

benefits of racing are spun off to a horse breeding industry. Today those benefits could be seen merely in terms of dollars. In the past, however, those benefits were seen in terms of a valued national resource. Because breeding was encouraged, the nation's stock of horses was improved in both quality and quantity, and that stock was a major military resource in times of war. Even though the Islamic religion condemned gambling as a whole, exceptions were made for horse-race betting precisely because it would provide incentives for "improving the breed." Another consideration affecting race betting is the source of funds that are put into play by widely dispersed offtrack betting facilities, and then how those funds are distributed. The employment benefits of racetracks are also more difficult to put into a geographical context, as many employees work for stables and horse owners whose operations are far from the tracks.

Lotteries also draw sales from a wide geographic area. Funds are all given to government programs; however, the funds are often designated for special programs. The redistribution effects are difficult to trace and are dependent on the type of programs supported. When casino taxes are earmarked, the same problem exists; however, a casino tax will be much less than the government's share of lottery revenues. Lotteries do not provide the same employment benefits for local communities as are provided by casinos, as they are not as labor intensive. Benefits from sales tend to go to established merchants, often large grocery chains, in the lottery jurisdiction.

National lottery games, such as Lotto America, only further complicate the economic formulas. Such is also the case with Internet gambling. For race betting and lotteries, there is very little activity by nonresident players.

What Do Negative Gambling Economic Impacts Mean for a Local Community?

Negative direct costs, imposed on an area by the presence of a casino facility, simply mean there can be no economic gains for the economy. There can be no job gains, only job losses. Purchasing power is lost in the community; local residents play the gambling dollars, and those residents do not have funds for other activities. Our survey of Wisconsin players found that 10 percent would have spent their gambling money on grocery store items if they had not visited the casino. One-fourth indicated they would have spent the money on clothing and household goods. Additionally, there can be no real government revenue gains, except at a very high cost imposed upon local residents in severely reduced purchasing powers and high social costs. Negative impacts simply mean the facilities are economically bad for an area.

Sources: Cohn and Wolfe. 1999. *The 1999 Industry Report.* Washington, DC: American Gaming Association; The Evans Group. 1996. *A Study of the Economic Impact of the Gaming Industry through 2005.* Evanston, IL: Evans Group; Grinols, Earl, and J. D. Omorov. 1996. "When Casinos Win, Who Loses?" *Illinois Business Review* 53, no. 1 (Spring): 7–11, 19; Midwest Hospitality Advisors. 1992. *Impact: Indian Gaming in the State of Minnesota.* Minneapolis, MN: Marquette Partners; National Gambling Impact Study Commission [NGISC]. 1999. *Final Report.* Washington, DC: NGISC; Samuelson, Paul A. 1976. *Economics.* 10th ed. New York: McGraw Hill, 425; Thompson, William N. 1999. "Casinos in Las Vegas: Where Impacts Are Not the Issue." In *Legalized Gambling in the United States,* edited by Cathy H. C. Hsu, 93–112. New York: Haworth Hospitality Press; Thompson, William N. 1998. "The Economics of Casino Gambling." In *Casino Management: Past, Present, Future* 2d ed., edited by Kathryn Hashimoto, Sheryl Fried Kline, and George Fenich, 306–319. Dubuque, IA: Kendall-Hunt; Thompson, William N., and Ricardo Gazel. 1996. *The Economics of Casino Gambling in Illinois.* Chicago: The Chicago Better Government Association; Thompson, William N., Ricardo Gazel, and Dan Rickman. 1995. *The Economic Impact of Native American Gaming in Wisconsin.* Milwaukee: Wisconsin Policy Research Institute.
See also Crime and Gambling; Gambling, Pathological

Economics and Gambling

The essence of gambling is economics—gambling involves money. Money is put at risk, and money is won or lost. Money goes into the coffers of organizations such as racetracks, casinos, lotteries, or charities, and that money is redistributed in taxes or public funds, profits, wages, and various supplies. The money of gambling can help economies of local communities and regions grow, but gambling operations can also cause money to be drawn out of communities. The existence of gambling represents an opportunity to express personal freedoms, and these have values, although they are not easy to measure in a precise manner. On the other hand, gambling can also impose costs upon societies because of problem behaviors of persons who cannot control gambling impulses.

Gambling enterprises, specifically casino resorts and racetrack operations, involve major capital investments. These may come through expenditures of individual entrepreneurs, sale of stock at equity exchange markets (e.g., the New York Stock Exchange), bond issues, or other borrowing mechanisms. Gambling enterprises are subject to a wide range of competitive forces. Participants in each form of gambling compete against one another, but they also compete against other entertainment providers as well as all other services and products that can be purchased with the consumers' expendable dollars.

The vast array of economic attributes tied to gambling has led to many studies that focus upon gambling economics. Most concentrate upon positive sides of the gambling equation, and they tend to overlook a very basic fact: Gambling revenues must come out of the pockets of players. In my lectures on gambling, I like to point out that Las Vegas was the fastest-growing city in the United States during the 1980s and 1990s, with the greatest job growth and wage growth. Yet Las Vegas is in a desert—it does not have trees. On the other hand, the wooded areas of the United States have suffered economic declines—albeit during a prosperous period for the general economy. The point is, quite simply, that "money does not grow on trees." A large casino may generate great revenues that can be translated into many jobs; however, those revenues do not fall out of the air. They come from people's pockets. I also like the story of the man whose life is falling apart. As he is driving to church, he sees a sign that says "Win the Lotto, and Change Your Life." In church he prays that he will win. He hears the voice of God telling him, "My Son, you have been good; you shall win the lottery." Convinced his problems are over, the man is much relieved. But he does not win the lottery. The next week, instead of praying to God, he is angry and asks God why He lied, why He has forsaken him. God replies, "Yes, my son, I understand your anger, because I did promise. But my son, you have to meet me half way. You have to buy a ticket." All the money that is discussed in studies of the economics of gambling is money that has to come out of people's pockets. Unless individuals "buy the ticket," there is no gambling phenomenon—no lotteries, no racetracks, and no casinos. The formula for understanding gambling economics is not difficult. It can be expressed in but a few words: It involves where the money comes from and where the money goes. In the second section of this entry, we will return to this basic formula. First we will look at the revenues in gambling.

Gambling Revenues

In 1998, gambling players spent (another way of saying "lost") $54.4 billion on legal gambling products in the United States (this is called the gambling "hold") (Christiansen 1999). The $54.4 billion represents the money that gambling enterprises retained after players wagered $677.4 billion dollars (this is called the gambling "han-

dle"). In other words, casinos, lotteries, and tracks kept 8 percent of the money that is played. The greatest share of these players' losses was in casino facilities of one kind or another, followed by purchases of lottery tickets.

Table 1 draws information from the annual report of revenues published by Eugene Martin Christiansen in *International Gaming and Wagering Business* (Christiansen 1999).

Since the statistics of all legal gambling began to be compiled in 1982, the gambling revenues have increased an average of 10.4 percent every year. Overall, the growth in revenues has been more than 530 percent, compared with a 150 percent increase in the Gross Domestic Product (Christiansen 1999). The gambling growth has been seen in all areas, although only minimally in the pari-mutuel sector of gambling. Much of the growth is due to the fact that new jurisdictions have legalized forms of gambling and that new gambling facilities have been established.

If all gambling were conducted in one enterprise, the business would be among the ten largest corporations in the country. Gambling revenues in the United States represent the largest share of entertainment expenditures. Indeed, the revenues surpass those of all live concerts; sales of recorded music; movie revenues, theater and video; and revenues for attendance at all major professional sporting events combined! The revenues surpass the sales of cigarettes by 13 percent. The gambling revenues approach 1 percent of the personal incomes of all Americans.

In 1998, the commercial casinos attracted 161.3 million visits from customers representing 29 percent of the households (or 28.8 million households) in the United States. The average visitor made 5.6 trips to casinos. The visitors spent an average of $123 during each of those visits. Visits to venues in Las Vegas, Atlantic City, and other resort gambling areas will be for days in length, accounting for larger expenditures, whereas those visiting casino boats usually confine their gambling to two or three hours of time; many boats impose time limits. A typical boat visitor will lose $50–$60 per visit. With approximately 200 million adults in the country, each spends an average of $100 per

Table 1 Gambling Revenues (player losses, or "hold"), 1998, United States

	$ Million	%
Casino Gambling		
Land-based commercial casino	$12,614	
Riverboats	7,294	
Cruise ships/"cruises to nowhere"	539	
Native American (all class III)	7,213	
Noncasino machines	1,830	
Total	**29,490**	**54.3**
Lotteries		
Lottery tickets	15,399	
Video lottery	1,282	
Total	**16,681**	**30.7**
Pari-mutuel Wagering		
Horse racing	3,307	
Dog racing	494	
Jai alai	45	
Total	**3,846**	**7.1**
Charity and Bingo		
Charitable bingo	972	
Native American bingo (all class III)	954	
Other charitable games	1,598	
Total	**3,524**	**6.5**
Other Gambling		
Card rooms	739	
Bookmaking	72	
Total	**811**	**1.5**
Grand total (rounded)	**54,352**	**100**

Note that Internet gambling revenues were estimated to be $651 million for the year; however, much of the wagering was outside the United States and hence not included in the table. *Source:* Based on information in Cabot, Anthony N. 1999. *Internet Gaming Report III.* Las Vegas: Trace, 3; and Christiansen, Eugene Martin. 1999. "The 1998 Gross Annual Wager." *International Gaming and Wagering Business* (August): 20ff.

year in commercial casinos, but $147 in all casinos, including those operated by Native Americans and charities.

A higher percentage of households participates in lottery games—54 percent (or 53.5 million households). They play on a regular basis, buying tickets each week; hence they do not lose as much to this form of gambling at a single time. The average American adult spends $84 a year on lottery tickets or video lottery play.

Approximately 11 percent of the households participate in bingo games and 8 percent in racetrack betting. Considering all the forms of legal gambling, the average adult spends (loses) $272 on gambling each year. When that amount is spread over the entire population of 270 million, the per capita expenditure is $200 (Christiansen 1999).

Employment and Gambling

Employment is considered one of the leading benefits of gambling enterprise. Proponents of gambling initiatives usually make "job creation" a central issue in their campaigns. Gambling provides jobs. There is no doubt about that. Estimates suggest that well over 600,000 people are employed by legal gambling enterprises in the United States. Critics of gaming suggest, however, that specific gambling interests may not provide net job gains for communities, as gambling employees may be people who simply moved from other jobs. Moreover, gamblers themselves may lose jobs because of their behavior, and their gambling losses may also result in a loss of purchasing power in a community, leading others to unemployment. Critics also suggest that gambling jobs are not necessarily "good" in that they may offer low salaries, low job security, and poor working conditions. Gambling proponents counter these claims and add that jobs produced lead to indirect jobs through economic multipliers.

The different gambling sectors produce different job circumstances. Casinos are labor-intense organization. Racing provides fewer jobs at track locations but generates many direct jobs in the agriculture sector on horse breeding farms. Modern lotteries in North America are not job providers in a major sense. Government bureaucracies increase employment; however, a lottery distribution system using existing retailers adds few jobs to society.

The casino and racing sectors provide jobs in North America in the same manner as they do elsewhere. Lotteries, however, are quite different.

Slot machines accept dollar bills—eliminating jobs for many slot change persons.

In Europe as well as in traditional societies, poor people and handicapped people find employment through selling tickets. For instance, over 10,000 blind and handicapped persons support themselves through selling tickets in Spain. They are able to have incomes of about $30,000 a year through their activities. Moreover, administration of a special lottery organization is staffed by the handicapped, and all of the proceeds from ticket sales are designated for programs for the handicapped. In many poorer countries, persons who could not otherwise secure employment buy discounted lottery tickets on consignment and resell them in order to support themselves and their families. In Guatemala City, Guatemala, and Teguicalpa, Honduras, the lottery sales force gathers in squares near cathedrals or government buildings and creates market atmospheres with its activities. The lotteries in these countries produce revenues for charities. In the United States,

Canada, and other modern lottery venues, the sale of tickets is directed almost exclusively to provide general revenues for government activities. Therefore, the goal of the lottery organization is to maximize profits through efficient procedures. Sales are coordinated through banks and major retail outlets, which conduct lottery business along with other product sales. As the tickets are simply added to other purchases made by the gamblers, there is little if any employment gain through the activity.

Big corporations usually control the lottery retailers. In many cases, however, they are small businesses that may be aided considerably by volumes of ticket sales. Ticket sales may provide them with margins of profits enabling their businesses to compete with larger merchants. Video lottery machines (gambling machines) also provide revenues that allow bars and taverns to remain competitive with other "entertainment" venues and, hence, remain as employers in society.

According to industry reports, pari-mutuel interests that run horse and dog tracks as well as jai alai frontons employ about 150,000 workers in the United States. Less than 2 percent of this number are working at the nation's ten frontons. 30,000 work at dog tracks and 119,000 at horse tracks. The numbers for tracks include 36,300 employed at track operations, 52,000 as maintenance workers, and 30,800 in the breeding industry (National Gambling Impact Study Commission 1999, 2.11–2.12).

Casinos are responsible for most of the gambling employees. A report of the American Gaming Association showed that in 1999 casinos in the United States directly employed almost 400,000 (Cohn and Wolfe 1999; National Gambling Impact Study Commission 1999, 7–6).

The Nevada gaming industry indicates that the tourism in Nevada in 1998 employed 307,500, with 182,621 directly in gaming. In that same year, the state led the nation in job growth. Unemployment in Las Vegas was a very low 2.8 percent. Indirect employment led analysts to observe that in 1998 casinos were responsible for 60 percent of the employment in the state. Each of the casino jobs in Nevada leads to the employment of 1.7 persons in all—that is, an extra 0.7 employee (or seven em-

Slot machines have themes familiar to players. Machine games bring the greatest amount of revenue to casinos today.

ployees for every ten casino employees). This multiplier factor (1.7) is considered rather low. It is low because Nevada is not a manufacturing state. In fact, with a 3-percent manufacturing sector, the state manufactures less per person than any other state. As the state produces few products, almost the entire casino purchasing activity is directed to imported goods and, accordingly, not to goods produced by Nevada workers (Cohn and Wolfe 1999; Schwer 1999, 4).

New Jersey casinos employ approximately 50,000 workers. The industry claims that this employment creates employment of 48,000 workers through purchasing activities of casinos and casino employees. In 1998, the 50,000 jobs produced a payroll of $1 billion, or $20,000 per job. Many of the jobs are not full time. Although the employment in Atlantic City gambling halls is extensive (averaging over 4,000 per casino), the casinos have not solved the problems of poverty and unemployment in the community, a city of 38,000. The population of Atlantic City has continually declined since the introduction of casinos in 1978,

and its unemployment rate was 12.7 percent in 1998, a time when the national average and state of New Jersey average were approximately 4 percent (Cohn and Wolfe 1999).

Mississippi casinos employed 32,000 in 1998. As the casinos of the state were established in the 1990s, the effects of construction employment have been noticeable. For instance, from 1990 to 1995 an additional 1,300 construction jobs existed in Biloxi, one of the state's casino centers. The jobs persisted through the end of the century; however, construction jobs must be tied to specific projects, and when the projects are finished, the jobs are finished. Although Mississippi experienced a boom with the introduction of casinos in 1992, the new employment witnessed in the state did not alter unemployment rates to a degree that was any different than that for the entire country. The 1990s were prosperous, and casino communities in the state experienced the same prosperity felt by noncasino communities (Cohn and Wolfe 1999).

A similar phenomenon has taken place in the Native American community. There, scores of casi-

Many of the daily visitors to Atlantic City casinos come on tour buses.

nos have generated about 100,000 jobs. Most of the jobs, however, are found in casinos on very small reservations. Overall Native Americans still experience the worst economy of any subsector of the U.S. population, with unemployment rates over 50 percent. Lots of people, mostly non-Native Americans, have obtained jobs in casinos, and small tribes have became extremely wealthy, but generally the Native American community has not "cashed-in" (*see* Native American Gaming: Contemporary)

Other sectors of the gambling industry have not caused job creation. The National Gambling Impact Study Commission reported that there was no evidence whatsoever that convenience store gambling (machine gambling) created any jobs. Charity gambling has produced considerable funding for myriad projects, but it has not produced jobs either (National Gambling Impact Study Commission 1999, chap. 2).

A study of jobs produced by the onset of riverboat casino gambling in Illinois found that the multiplier of each job was less than one, but still more than zero. That meant that most of the new jobs were only shifted away from other enterprises, and the vacant jobs were not filled in all cases. Indeed, a multiplier of approximately 0.2 resulted as the casinos added 10,000 jobs, but the numbers employed overall increased by only 2,000. The unfilled vacant jobs were possibly not filled because the casinos extracted purchasing power away from the residential populations. Casino jobs can also cause undesired impacts for a community by depriving other businesses of workers. Atlantic City casinos drew many new employees from local school districts and local police forces. In free markets, people can make job and career choices on their own, and such job shifts indicate that some people may see casino jobs as better than other available jobs (Grinols and Omorov 1996, 19).

The industry jobs have been both praised and criticized. The positions run the gamut, from stable hand to chief executive, from minimum wage without benefits to seven-figure positions with golden parachutes. A stable hand working with horses may be residing in very substandard housing conditions, perhaps ever sharing quarters with the animals he or she cares for. The largest number of "good" positions is found in commercial casinos. The bulk of these jobs are unionized and carry very good fringe benefit packages, including full health coverage for families of workers. Dealer positions, for the most part, are not unionized, although they do have good fringe benefits. The dealers usually make low salaries, but they share tips. Where tips are not good (or not permitted, as in Quebec), salaries are higher. The best tip situations are found in Atlantic City and on the Las Vegas Strip. A typical dealer at a casino such as Caesars might expect an additional $50,000 a year in tips.

Working conditions in gambling facilities are often not the best. There is high job turnover due to job dissatisfaction and also to policies that sometimes allow firing at will. Traditionally, people were hired in Las Vegas casinos through friendship networks; however, this practice is now less pervasive, as the industry has grown considerably and it is more a "buyers," that is, an employees', market. Nonetheless, other adverse conditions surround casino employment. For years the casino atmosphere was one that was dominated by "male" values. Women employees were often placed into situations where they were degraded. This behavior came from fellow employees as well as from customers. It is unacceptable behavior today, yet in some ways it is still tolerated in the casino atmosphere. That atmosphere also has downsides from a health standpoint, as most casinos permit open smoking—and many players smoke—as well as drinking. Casinos can be very loud, and of course, employees work shifts over a twenty-four-hour schedule.

Most workers in the United States have indicated in surveys that job security and salaries are no longer the leading motivators, but rather that factors such as "ability to get ahead," "recognition for work accomplished," and "having responsibility" are more important. A survey of casino dealers found, however, that they desired security and financial compensation over the other factors. This is an indication of the insecurity that persists among the workforce (Darder 1991).

—*coauthored by Ricardo Gazel and Dan Rickman*

Sources: Bowen, John, Zheng Gu, and Vincent H. Eade. 1998. *The Hospitality Industry's Impact on the State of Nevada.* Las Vegas: UNLV International Gaming Institute; Christiansen, Eugene Martin. 1998. "Gambling and the American Economy." In *Gambling: Socioeconomic Impacts and Public Policy* (special volume of *The Annals of the American Academy of Political and Social Science*), edited by James H. Frey, 36–52. Thousand Oaks, CA: Sage; Christiansen, Eugene Martin. 1999. "The 1998 Gross Annual Wager." *International Gaming and Wagering Business* (August): 20ff; Cohn and Wolfe. 1999. *The 1999 Industry Report: A Profile of America's Casino Gaming Industry.* Washington, DC: American Gaming Association; Darder, Richard. 1991. "An Assessment of a Motivational Environment as Viewed by Dealers in the Casino Industry." M.A. Thesis, University of Nevada, Las Vegas; Grinols, Earl L., and J. D. Omorov. 1996. "When Casinos Win, Who Loses?" *Illinois Business Review* 53, no. 1 (Spring): 7–11, 19; National Gambling Impact Study Commission [NGISC]/ 1999. *Final Report.* Washington, DC: NGISC; Schwer, Keith. 1989. "Why the Las Vegas Multiplier Is Less Than 3." *Las Vegas Metropolitan Economic Indicators.* Las Vegas: Center for Business and Economic Research, University of Nevada, Las Vegas, 1–4; Thompson, William N. 1998. "The Economics of Casino Gambling." In *Casino Management: Past, Present, Future,* edited by Kathryn Hashimoto, Sheryl Fried Kline, and George Penich, 306–309. Dubuque, IA: Kendall-Hunt; Thompson, William N. 1999. "Casinos in Las Vegas: Where Impacts Are Not the Issue." In *Legalized Gambling in the United States,* edited by Cathy H. C. Hsu, 93–112. New York: Haworth Hospitality Press.

Espherodromo. *See* Roulette and Wheels of Fortune

European Association for the Study of Gambling. *See* Gaming Institutes: Research and Political

The European Casino

The institution that we call the casino had its origins in central and western European principalities in the seventeenth and eighteenth centuries. It was here that governments gave concessions to private entrepreneurs to operate buildings in which games could be legally played in exchange

The Casino Honensyburg-Dortman (Germany), one of the most modern in Europe.

for a part of the revenues secured by the entrepreneurs. Whereas from time immemorial, players had competed against one another in all sorts of private games, here games were structured to pit the player against the casino operators—known as the "house." These gambling halls were designed to offer playing opportunities to an elite class in an atmosphere that allowed them to enjoy relaxation among their peers. Even though casinos in the United States seek to achieve goals that are primarily financial by offering gaming products to as many persons as possible, the notion of having a European casino often resonates where proponents meet to urge new jurisdictions to legalize casinos.

In some cases, casino advocates actually believe they can somehow duplicate European experiences, but rarely do they meet such goals, for a variety of reasons. If they indeed knew about the way European casinos operate, they would not want any of the experience repeated in casinos

they controlled. Other times, they may actually try to establish some of the attributes of these casinos, only to realize later that the attributes are quite adverse to their primary goals—profits, job creation, economic development, or tax generation.

The European casino is offered in campaigns for legalization as an alternative to having a jurisdiction endorse Las Vegas–type casinos. In reality, however, it is the Las Vegas casino that the advocates of new casino legalizations in North America wish to emulate. Among all the casino venues in North America, Las Vegas best delivers on the promise of profits, job creation, economic development, and tax generation. Even though this encyclopedia is devoted to gambling in the Western Hemisphere, the imagery of the European casino is so often used in discussion of casino policy outside of Europe that a descriptive commentary is pertinent here.

In June 1986, I visited the casino that operates within the Kurhaus in Wiesbaden, Germany. In an interview, Su Franken, director of public relations for the casino, was describing a new casino that had opened in an industrial city a few hours away. With a stiff demeanor, he said, "They allow men to come in without ties, they have rows and rows of noisy slot machines, they serve food and drinks at the tables, and they are always so crowded with loud players; it is so awful." Then with a little smile on his face, he added, "Oh, I wish we could be like that."

The reality is that, even with the growth in numbers of casino jurisdictions and numbers of facilities, Europe cannot offer casinos such as we are used to in North America—those in Las Vegas and Atlantic City; the Mississippi riverboats; those operated by Canadian provincial governments or by Native American reservations—because a long history of events impedes casino development based upon mass marketing. Actually, the rival casino to which the Wiesbaden manager was referring, the casino at Hohensyburg near Dortmund, was really just a bigger casino, where a separate slot machine room was within the main building as opposed to being in another building altogether. Men usually had to wear ties, but the dress code was relaxed on weekends, and the facility had a nightclub, again in a separate area. It was crowded simply because it was the only casino near a large city, and the local state government did not enforce a rule against local residents' entering the facility.

Table 1 shows a pattern of differences between the prototypical European casino and the Las Vegas Strip casino.

The casinos of Europe are very small compared to those in Las Vegas. The biggest casinos number their machines in the hundreds, not the thousands. A casino with more than twenty tables is considered large, whereas one in Las Vegas with twice that number would be a small casino. Even the largest casinos, such as those in Madrid, Saint Vincent (Italy), and Monte Carlo, have gaming floors smaller than the ones found on the boats and barges of the Mississippi River. The revenues of the typical European casino are comparable to those of the small slot machine casinos of Deadwood, South Dakota, or Blackhawk, Colorado. The

Table 1 American and European Casinos: Prototypical Comparisons

	American	*European*
1. Bottom line	Revenue for private enterprise; job creation; tourism as a goal	Community enhancement; tourism as amenity
2. Ownership	Private	Mixed; typically government-owned
3. Location	Concentrated	Diffuse; typically small town; monopolies
4. Taxation	Minimal; consistent with need for private investment; 6–8 percent	High to excessive; 50–90 percent
5. Access	Open, free; no dress codes; no identification; minimal exclusion lists	Restricted; fee charged; dress codes; passport identification; no locals; restricted occupations; voluntary exclusion lists
6. Hours	Continuous	Limited; evenings; closed holidays
7. Clientele	National; international; high volume	Local and regional; low volume
8. Promotions	Many; advertisements; junket tours; complimentaries	Few; no advertisements; no junkets; few complimentaries
9. Credit	Credit operations; open check cashing	No credit; limited check cashing
10. Community involvement	Mixed	Essential
11. Decor	Loud; large; glitzy; bright; red; closed in (no windows)	Quiet; small; elegant; calm; blue; open (windows)
12. Alcohol	Free; open distribution	Limited; restricted distribution
13. Games	Slots and tables mixed; blackjack dominates; craps; poker; some baccarat; limited roulette	Tables dominate; slots nonexistent or separate; roulette dominates; baccarat; some blackjack
14. Labor	High turnover; trained outside; salaried plus large tip volume controlled by dealers individually and in small groups; nonunion	Career employment; all hired at entry level; promotions from within; no salaries; tips controlled by casino, share with all employees; union
15. Compulsive gamblers	Not considered a factor or concern	Discouraged; excluded
16. Crime	Pervasive in atmosphere; ongoing problem in casino control	Not a factor or concern

Source: William N. Thompson

Baden Baden (Germany)—The most luxurious casino in the world.

largest casinos would produce gaming wins similar to those of average Midwestern riverboats.

Another distinguishing feature of the European casino is that most are local monopoly operations. Where casinos are permitted, a town or region will usually have only one casino. The government often has a critical role in some facet of the operation, either as casino owner (or directly or through a government corporation) or as owner of the building where the casino is located. Where the government does not own the casino, it might as well. Taxes are often so high that the government is the primary party extracting money from the operations. For example, some casinos in Germany pay a 93 percent tax on their gross wins. That means for every 100 marks the players lose to the casino, the government ends up with ninety-three marks. In France the top marginal tax rate is 80 percent; it is 60 percent in Austria and 54 percent in Spain. Nowhere are rates below the top 20–30 percent rates in U.S. jurisdictions (the Nevada rate is less than 7 percent—that is, for each $100 players lose to the casino, the government receives just $7 in casino taxes.)

The European casinos typically restrict patron access in several ways. (1) Several will not allow local residents to gamble. (2) They require identification and register patron attendance. (3) They have dress codes. (4) Many permit players to ban themselves from entering the casinos as a protection from their own compulsive gambling behaviors. They also allow the families of players to ban individuals from the casinos. The casinos themselves also may bar compulsive gamblers. (5) The casinos operate with limited hours, usually evening hours. No casino opens its doors twenty-four hours a day. (6) The casinos, as a rule, cannot advertise. If they can, they do so only in limited, passive ways. (7) Credit policies are restrictive. Personal and payroll checks will not be cashed. (8) Alcoholic beverages are also restricted. In many casinos (for instance, all casinos in England), such beverages are not allowed on the gaming floors. Only rarely is the casino permitted to give drinks to players free of charge. (Other free favors such as meals or hotel accommodations or even local transportation are also quite rare.)

The clientele of the European casino is generally from the local region. Few of the casinos rely upon international visitors. Moreover, very few have facilities for overnight visitors, although several are located in hotels owned by other parties. The casinos feature table games, and where slot machines are permitted, they are typically found in separate rooms or even separate buildings. The employees at the casinos are usually expected to spend their entire careers at a single location. The employees are almost always local nationals.

There are myriad reasons why the European casino establishment has remained in the past, while modern casino development occurred in the United States, specifically in Las Vegas. First, Europe is a continent with many national boundaries. The future may see more and more economic and even political integration, but national separateness has been strong and will remain as a factor retarding casino development. The European Union has, at least at its initial stage of decision making, decided to allow casino policy to remain under the jurisdiction of its individual member states. Although a central congress may decree that all European states must standardize other products, usually following the most widely attainable and profitable standards, there will be no decrees that the entire continent should follow the most liberal casino laws. Each country retains sovereignty in this area.

Language and religious differences separate the various nations of Europe. No European congress can decree away these differences. National rules of casino operation have emphasized that entrepreneurs and employees be local residents. Such rules remain in place in most jurisdictions. In the past, movement of capital has been restricted among the states, making the possibilities of accumulating large investments for large resort facilities and for large promotional budgets difficult. Additionally, it was difficult for players to move their gaming patronage across borders, as they also would have to be able to move capital with that patronage. Advertisement restrictions also tied casino entrepreneurs to local markets. These small local markets never beckoned as attractive opportunities for foreign investors even when they could move funds.

The roulette table at the Sam Remo Casino in northern Italy.

Second, employment practices have not fostered the kind of cross-germination that is present in the North American casino industries. Typically, the employees of European casinos are local residents, and they are expected to stay with one casino property for an entire career. Promotions come from within. The work group is very personal in its interrelationships. The work group is also unionized and derives much of its wage base from tips given by players at traditional table games. The employment force is simply not a source for innovative ideas.

Third, as almost all of the casinos are monopoly businesses, the industry has had little incentive to develop competitive energies that could be translated into innovations. Also, the entrepreneurs have not been situated to take advantage of the forces of synergy, which are quite obvious in the Las Vegas and the U.S. gaming industry.

Fourth, the basic political philosophy that dominates government policymaking in Europe

A player must show identification and purchase a ticket to enter most European Casinos.

has its roots in notions of collective responsibility. Americans threw off the yoke of feudalism and its class system of noblesse oblige when the first boats of immigrants reached its Atlantic shores in the seventeenth century. The colonies fostered a spirit of individualism. Conversely, a spirit of feudalism persists in European politics. Remnants of monarchism remain, as the state has substituted official action for what was previously upper-class obligation. Socialist policies now ensure that the working classes will have their basic needs guaranteed. The government is the protector as far as personal welfare is concerned, and those protecting personal welfare (that is, the government officials) also are expected to guide personal behavior, even to the point of protecting people from their own weaknesses.

In the United States, and especially in the American West, the expectation was that people would control their own behaviors; such was not the case in Europe. In Europe, but not in the United States, viable Socialist parties developed. Coincidentally, Christian parties also developed. They too fostered notions that the state was a guardian of public morals. Christian parties saw casinos as anathema to the public welfare and permitted their existence only if they were small and restricted. Socialists also saw casinos as exploiting-bourgeois enterprises that had to be out-of-bounds for working-class people.

Fifth, and perhaps the overriding force against commercial development of casinos, there has been an almost perpetual presence of wartime activity in Europe over the past three centuries. The many borders of Europe have caused a constant flow of national jealousies, alliances, and realignments, all of which contributed to one war after another. Often the wars engulfed the entire continent: the Napoleonic wars, the Franco-Prussian wars, and World Wars I and II. A modern casino industry cannot flourish amid wartime activity. Casinos need a free flow of people as customers, and people cannot move freely during wartime. Casinos need markets of prosperous people, but personal prosperity is disrupted for the masses during wartime. Wartime destruction consumes the resources of society. Moreover, a society does not allow its capital resources to be expended on leisure activities when the troops in the field need armaments. And wars change boundaries, governments, and rules. Casinos need stability in the economy and in political policy in order to grow; Europe has lacked stability over the last three centuries.

The United States has benefited from not being a war battlefield for over a century. Following World War II, the new industrial giant of the world accepted an obligation to help European countries rebuild their industrial and commercial bases. The Marshall Fund was created to infuse U.S. capital into European redevelopment. The Marshall Fund could have been a vehicle for infusing the individualistic American spirit of capitalism into European commercial policy as well. The fund stipulated, however, that the new and revitalized businesses of Europe had to be controlled by Europeans. U.S. entrepreneurs were not allowed into fund-supported businesses. The fund actually supported the reopening of a casino at Travemunde, Germany. But the policy of the U.S. government in not allowing Americans to directly participate in the commercial enterprise of rebuilding Europe blocked U.S. casino operators from legitimately entering Europe with the modern spirit they were utilizing in Las Vegas gambling establishments. On the other hand, less than fully legitimate Americans sought to bring slot machines to the continent. They were rooted out, however, and as these "operators" were deported, the image of the slot machine as a "gangster's device" became firmly rooted into casino thinking in Europe.

The impacts of these many forces are felt today even though the existence of the forces is not as strong. There is much expansion of casino gambling in Europe. It is generally an expansion in the number of facilities, however, not in the size or scope of the facilities. Each of the former Eastern Bloc countries now has a casino industry, but restrictions on size and the manner of operations are severe, as are tax requirements. France authorized slot machines for its casinos for the first time in 1988. But a decade later, its largest casinos were producing revenues less than those of a typical Midwest riverboat, revenues measured in the tens of millions of dollars—nowhere near the hundreds of millions won by the largest Las Vegas and Atlantic City casinos. In Spain, casino revenues have been flat as the industry begs the government for tax relief. Austria has developed a megacasino at Baden bi Vien, but it would be almost unnoticeable on the Las Vegas Strip. Casinos Austria and Casinos Holland, two quasi-public organizations, are viewed as two of the leading casino entrepreneurs of the continent. But both derive much of their revenue from operations of casinos either on the sea or in Canada. Twenty Las Vegas and a dozen Native American properties exceed the revenues of the leading casinos in Germany.

The European casinos have a style that would be welcomed by many North American patrons. In achieving that style, however, the casinos must forfeit what most entrepreneurs, governments, and citizens want from casinos—profits, jobs, economic development, and tax generation.

Sources: Thompson, William N. 1998. "Casinos de Juegos del Mundo: A Survey of World Gambling." In *Gambling: Socioeconomic Impacts and Public Policy* (special volume of *The Annals of the American Academy of Political and Social Science*), edited by James H. Frey, 11–21. Thousand Oaks, CA: Sage.

F

Faro

The game of faro was played in France as early as the seventeenth century. The game came to North America through the colonial port of New Orleans. As Louisiana was transferred to the new nation, the game became very popular on Mississippi riverboats and on the Western frontier. The game survived late into the twentieth century in Nevada casinos. Its slow action combined with its low return for the casinos, however, caused houses to drop faro in favor of games such as the increasingly popular blackjack.

The word *faro* was derived from the word *pharaoh,* as the winning card was seen as the "king." The rather simple luck game is played on a layout called a faro bank. The table has pictures of cards on two sides, the ace through six on one side, the seven at the end in the center, and the eight through the king on the other side. There is also an area marked as "high" on one side. Cards are dealt from a fifty-two-card deck. Suits are not considered, only the card values. After a first card is exposed and discarded, twenty-five two-card pairs are dealt, leaving one remaining card that is not played. The pairs are dealt one card at a time. The first card is a losing card, the second one a winning card. Basically, the players bet that a certain numbered card will appear as the winning or losing card in a pair when the card is next exposed. Correct bets are paid even money. If the card comes up and the other card of the pair is the same, the house wins half of the bet. If a pair does not con-

A faro game at the Old Las Vegas Club in Las Vegas. (UNLV Special Collections)

tain the card, the bet remains until the card comes up in a future pair. For instance, if the bet is that a six will lose, cards are dealt in pairs until a six comes up, either as a winning or losing part of the pair. If two sixes come up, the player loses half the bet. The dealer records which numbers have been played, and so the player can make subsequent bets with a knowledge about chances that a pair will be dealt with that number. The house edge starts at about 2.94 percent when the first pair is dealt and increases against players betting on subsequent pairs if the card bet upon (for example, a six) has not yet appeared. If three of the four sixes have appeared, however, the house edge is gone if the player bets the six will either be a winner or loser when it comes up the fourth time. Players betting on the high can bet that the winning or the losing card will be a higher-valued card.

There is also a variety of combination bets, many of which give the player a very bad disadvantage. The changing odds structures of the game can be calculated as play progresses, giving the game many strategies. The game attracted many systems players, and their many deliberations caused play to be slow compared to other casino games. In early times, systems were probably to no avail as games at the mining camps and on the riverboats were known to often be run by cheaters and sharps.

Sources: Lemmel, Maurice. 1966. *Gambling: Nevada Style.* Garden City, NY: Dolphin Books, 105–124; Scarne, John. 1986. *Scarne's New Complete Guide to Gambling.* New York: Simon and Schuster, 234–235; Sifakis, Carl. 1990. *Encyclopedia of Gambling.* New York: Facts on File, 113–115.

Federal Lottery Laws

In the early days of the republic, gambling policy was considered the prerogative of state governments. The new government was structured to be one of delegated powers. The government of the constitution was created by "We the People," and officials of the government were empowered to make policy only in the areas designated by the "People." Congress was delegated certain powers in Article I, Section 8, and nowhere on the list were powers to regulate gambling activity. Moreover, the

10th Amendment of the U.S. Constitution specifically reserves the "powers not delegated to the United States . . . [nor] prohibited" to the states to the "States, respectively, or to the people." Accordingly, the federal government stayed away from gambling for nearly a century—that is, except for the few lotteries actually run by the government or authorized by the government. Congress was empowered to raise money.

Congress was also given the power to "establish post offices" and to "regulate commerce . . . among the several States." Congress turned to these powers when concerns were raised, first about illegal lotteries, and then about the legal but disrespected Louisiana lottery. In 1872, the use of the mails was denied to illegal lotteries. This was followed by a series of laws aimed at curbing the interstate activities of the Louisiana Lottery.

On 19 July 1876, President Grant signed an act that provided legal sanctions against persons using the mails to circulate advertising for lotteries through the mails (44th Congress, Chapter 186). On 2 September 1890, an act was signed, proscribing any advertisements in newspapers for lotteries. (51st Congress, Chapter 980). The Louisiana Lottery managers saw a loophole in these antilottery laws, and they moved their operations to Honduras. They were only a few years ahead of the law, however. On 27 August 1894 (53d Congress, Chapter 349), legislation was passed prohibiting the importation "into the United States from any foreign country . . . [of] any lottery ticket or any advertisement of any lottery." All such articles would be seized and forfeited. Penalties of fines up to $5,000 and prison time of up to ten years, or both, would be assessed against violators. The next year (2 March 1895; 53d Congress, Chapter 191), Congress passed an act for the suppression of all lottery traffic through national and interstate commerce. Very specifically, the mails could not be used by lotteries to promote their interests.

These federal laws had a desired effect. They put severe restrictions upon the operators of the Louisiana Lottery. Also, the citizens of Louisiana came to recognize that the operators were bribing state political leaders and extracting exorbitant profits from the lottery, whereas state beneficiaries were being shortchanged. There were also exposures of dishonest games. Under pressure from citizens, the legislature ended the state sponsorship of the lottery in 1905.

In two U.S. Supreme Court decisions, the acts of Congress were determined to be constitutional. That is, they were passed within the scope of the powers of Congress. In 1891, the Court ruled in the case of *In re Rapier* (143 U.S. 110) that the 1872 prohibition was a valid exercise of congressional power to regulate the use of the mails. In 1903, the justices held in *Champion* v. *Ames* (188 U.S. 321) that Congress had the power to pass an appropriate act against a "species of interstate commerce" that "has grown into disrepute and has become offensive to the entire population of the nation."

Although there were no other legal state-authorized or -operated lotteries until New Hampshire began its sweepstakes in 1964, there were lotteries that sought markets in the United States. There were illegal numbers games in all major cities, and there was the Irish Sweepstakes. The Irish Sweepstakes was created by the Irish Parliament in 1930 as a means of benefiting Irish hospitals. The Irish were well aware that they did not have a substantial marketing potential if they aimed only at customers within the Free State, so they looked outward to Europe and to the United States. At first, they used the mails to promote and sell tickets to customers in the United States; however, the U.S. Post Office successfully intervened with legal action to stop this blatant violation of the 1895 law. Then the Irish Sweepstakes operators turned to smuggling tickets onto U.S. shores. Using ship-to-shore operations, as well as Canadian border cities, they were quite successful into the 1960s and 1970s, when U.S. states began to meet them with competition from their own lotteries.

When radio became established as a viable entertainment media, the federal government found that it was necessary to create the Federal Communications Commission (FCC) and to establish uniform regulations for operations of radio stations across the country. The Communications Act of 1934 stipulated rules for advertising "on the air." Within a few decades, the rules applied also to television signals.

The broadcasting law held that persons would be subject to fines of $1,000 or penalties of one year in prison, or both, if they used radio stations to broadcast or knowingly allow stations to broadcast "any advertisement of, or information concerning, any lottery, gift enterprise, or similar scheme, offering prizes dependent in whole or in part upon lot or chance . . ." (Federal Communications Act of 1934, Public Law 416, 19 June 1934).

But that was 1934, when no government in the United States had its own lottery. That situation changed in 1963, when New Hampshire authorized a lottery that began operations the next year. By 1975, eleven states had lotteries. The limitations on advertising seemed to be adverse to the fiscal interests of state budget makers. Congress responded to a demand for exemptions to the 1934 act.

In 1975, Congress passed legislation that allowed a state-run lottery to advertise on radio and television stations that only sent signals within the state. Courts later held that the substantial portion of the signals had to be within the state. In 1976, the exemption was expanded to allow advertisements on the air that extended into adjacent states as long as the other states also had state-run lotteries.

In 1988, the exemption included signals into any other state that had a lottery. (Nonprofit and Native American gaming was also exempt from the 1934 act; in 1964 the FCC issued rules allowing horse race interests to advertise "on the air" as long as the advertising did not promote illegal gambling.)

By the last years of the century, the application of the law was in reality an anomaly, with only commercial casino gambling subject to the ban on "lottery" advertising. Lotteries were fully exempt. The anomaly was short-lived, as the 1934 provision was deemed unconstitutional as a violation of freedom of speech after a 1996 U.S. Supreme Court case in a related matter (44 *Liquormart* v. *Rhode Island;* 517 U.S. 484 [1996]).

Sources: Cabot, Anthony N. 1999a. 39–80; Thompson, William N. 1997. *Legalized Gambling: A Reference Handbook.* 2d ed. Santa Barbara, CA: ABC-CLIO, 130–134.

See also Louisiana Lottery Company

The Federal Wire Act of 1961

The Federal Wire Act of 1961, passed with the support of Attorney General Robert F. Kennedy, was aimed at illegal horse race bookies and bettors on sports events. The law prescribed penalties of up to two years prison time and $10,000 fines for persons who "knowingly" use "a wire communication facility for transmission" of bets, wagers, and information assisting betting and wagering on any sports event or contest. Telephone companies could be ordered to cut off service from betting customers when notified of the activity by law enforcement agencies.

Legitimate reporting on sports events by newspaper media was exempt from the act. Similarly it was permissible to transmit messages for betting from one state to another as long as the betting activity was legal in both the states.

The Federal Wire Act was written at a time when telephones with physical wire lines represented the major avenue for interstate communication. Also, horse-race betting was the most prevalent form of illegal gambling. Attorney General Kennedy's testimony to Congress on the bill mentioned only sports and race betting. Since 1961, telephones have used wireless signals, and there are also other forms of satellite communication signals. The Internet is replacing the telephone for many communicators. Moreover, the Internet carries many kinds of wagering activity in addition to bets on races and sports events. The imprecise fit of the act to current gaming forms has necessitated discussion regarding new legislation to clarify the application of the law. A bill sponsored by Senator Jon Kyle of Arizona won approval in the U. S. Senate but had not come to a floor vote in the House of Representatives as of the end of the 2000 session. That bill would make all gambling on the Internet illegal. Amendments were added to make exceptions for legal race betting and lottery organizations. The bill would give the Department of Justice and the Federal Trade Commission power to enforce the law.

Sources: The Federal Wire Act of 1961 (Public Law 87–216, signed 13 September 1961); Kelly, Joseph M. 2000. "Internet Gambling Law." *William Mitchell Law Review* 26: 118–177.

Florida

Florida has the third-most-profitable lottery and the third-most-active pari-mutuel enterprise in the United States. The pari-mutuel industry features horse racing, dog racing, and jai alai games. The state has had a long history with underground gambling and with elements of organized crime that ran gambling operations throughout the country and in many other places as well.

Miami had been designated in the 1930s as an "open city" by the Mob. That meant all organized crime families were welcome to live in Miami and to conduct their business operations, whether they involved sex, drugs, or gambling. During the 1940s, illegal casinos flourished in the southern part of Florida. Meyer Lansky made Miami Beach his headquarters for much of his adult life.

From there he guided his activities in Cuba, the Caribbean, and Las Vegas. In 1970, he actually initiated a campaign to legalize casinos in Miami Beach. His contrived arrest on a meaningless drug charge was timed, however, for just before Election Day. The passage failed by a large margin even though some polls showed it ahead a few weeks before the election.

The presence of organized crime figures in Florida also contributed to the defeat of a campaign for casinos in 1978. Before Atlantic City opened its casinos, Floridians initiated a ballot proposition for gambling. Although polls showed this proposition with a chance to pass, an active campaign against the casinos led by Governor Reuben Askew caused a major defeat of casinos by a 73 percent to 27 percent margin. In 1986 another vote defeated casinos by a 67 percent to 33 percent margin. In the same election the voters approved a lottery for Florida. Casino forces, this time linked to Las Vegas gambling entrepreneurs, tried again in 1994. They spent over $17 million in their campaign, the most money spent on any ballot proposition in U.S. history up to that date. It was expensive, but again they oversold their product, and the measure went down to defeat with less than 40 percent of the voters favoring casinos. Efforts continued through the rest of the decade to get machine gaming at tracks or other forms of casino gambling into Florida.

The Florida lottery was very successful from its inception. So were the bingo games at the halls of the Native Americans in Florida. It was the Seminoles who generated the initial federal lawsuit over Native gambling. The Seminoles' first facility was in Hollywood, just north of Miami. They built a second hall in Tampa when the city gave them lands, supposedly for the purpose of having a Native American museum. After the land was put into trust status for the tribe, the Seminoles initiated gambling at the site. A third Seminole gambling hall is in Okechobee. The Miccosukee Tribe developed a gambling hall on the Tamiami Trail west of Miami. The tribes installed various video gambling devices in their halls under the pretense that they were lottery devices. The courts have not agreed. The tribe never won an order forcing the state to negotiate a casino agreement. Nonetheless, the gambling halls each have from 200 to 600 machines, as well as dozens of table games, in addition to their legal bingo games.

Sources: Dombrink, John D. 1981. "Outlaw Businessmen: Organized Crime and the Legalization of Casino Gambling." Ph.D. diss., University of California, Berkeley; Dombrink, John D., and William N. Thompson. 1990. *The Last Resort: Success and Failure in Campaigns for Casinos.* Reno: University of Nevada Press, 42–82, 132–138, 166–167.

See also Lansky, Meyer

French Bank. *See* Craps and Other Dice Games

G

The Gambler's Book Club

The Gambler's Book Club is perhaps the only bookstore devoted exclusively to selling books about gambling and gambling-related topics. The store is located near downtown Las Vegas just one mile north of the famous Las Vegas Strip. With over a thousand titles in stock, it is also the largest gambling bookstore in the world. The bookstore's founder was John Luckman, who began his gambling career as a player and then a bookie in California. He moved to Las Vegas in 1955 to work as a blackjack and baccarat pit boss. From that experience, he became convinced that the players did not know the games and that business could be increased in the casinos if players were more knowledgeable. He started writing pamphlets describing each casino game. From that start he developed a mail order book business for his pamphlets, as well as books that others wrote on gambling. With his wife, Edna, he secured his location and bought a printing press. Soon he was publishing 120 titles and stocking them for sale.

John Luckman died in 1987, but his store remains under the operation of his wife and Howard Schwartz, a true scholar of Las Vegas gambling history. Schwartz not only knows the name of every important gambler in Las Vegas history, but he has met and interviewed every one of them who was alive in the last twenty years. Edna Luckman and Howard Schwartz make most of their sales now through a mail order catalog and the Internet; however, the store itself is a marvel. It is a place where all gather: players, local historians, the intelligentsia of gambling, casino entrepreneurs as well as dealers, FBI agents, and all sorts of other people just interested in some aspect of gambling. The store has several local competitors who do well but tend to concentrate their sales efforts on other gambling merchandise from chips to antique machines. The Gambler's Book Club remains the essential bookstore for the industry.

Sources: Hopkins, A. D., and K. J. Evans. 1999. "John Luckman." *The First 100: Portraits of the Men and Women Who Shaped Las Vegas.* Las Vegas: Huntington Press, 232–233; Barrier, Michael. 1991. "How Bookmaking and Bookselling Came Together in Las Vegas." *Nation's Business,* November, 29: 4–8.

Gamblers' Motivations: Why Do They Gamble?

In *Legalized Gambling: A Reference Handbook,* I present a discussion of reasons why people gamble (Thompson 1997, 25–32). A clear majority of American adults participate in legalized gambling activities each year. Many reasons can be suggested for the activity. The results of a random national survey of 1,522 respondents taken by a research group at Mississippi State University in 1995 provide a substantive base for the reasons offered. Before looking at the results of that survey, we will reexamine the reasons as discussed in the earlier book.

People may gamble because it is a logical thing to do. It simply makes economic sense to do so—sometimes, with some games. Sometimes players have skills that permit them to outperform other players in games played for money. Certainly this is the case with most live poker games—not poker machines. This is also the case with horse-race betting and sports betting. The player who has the necessary skills to outperform other players may choose to make wagers because it is a way to make money. Also, some blackjack players may be able to memorize and count cards that have been played and thus discern moments at which the remaining cards in a deck will give advantages to the players and disadvantages to the casino. If these players can use their special memory skills in the

The "Slide for Life" for those who don't want to take real risks on the Las Vegas Strip.

games, they may play the games for the very logical reason of making money.

At other times, the odds of a game may also favor players. In slot machine and lottery games where there is a progressive jackpot, a point may be reached where the jackpot offered may exceed the odds of winning the jackpot. For instance, the odds may be a million to one, but because part of the losses of earlier players is put into the jackpot, the jackpot may be $2 million. Although the game is a long-shot chance game, the playing of the game is logical and rational from an economics point of view. Even when, as is normally the case, the odds do not favor the player, however, the play can make some economic sense. A lottery player may wager a single dollar. That dollar has very little value (marginal value) to the player. It might represent a cup of coffee in a cafe or six cigarettes. The player may forgo the pleasure of the cigarettes or coffee in order to play, and in such a case, the player does not suffer any in his or her quality of life. In practical terms, nothing is risked. On the other hand, no matter how remote the possibility of a large jackpot is, the large jackpot represents a

major factor that could drastically improve a person's quality of life. The logical player who calculates this proposition must be wary not to make excessive wagers that could subtract from his or her quality of life.

Although players can play for logical economic reasons, most of the players must know that even at games of skill, more players lose than win. Also there are not very many big lottery winners whether or not the odds, relative to the jackpots offered, favor the player. If players are approaching gambling activity from a more logical point of view, they should see the activity in exchange terms. As they are most likely giving up money, they should expect something in return for the money. Gambling offers things of value for the money invested. Gambling offers a source of entertainment. The entertainment industry is very large in the United States. People pay money to be entertained by movies, television, music, and sports events. Entertainment helps people achieve a distraction from the boredom and the difficulties of daily life. People use entertainment outlets as hobbies. Gambling entertainment can be seen in the same way.

The gambling opportunity can be an opportunity for social interaction for people who crave interaction. People socialize around gambling activities. Also, gambling can bring an excitement to lives. One professor at my university suggested that gambling opportunities should be brought into homes for senior citizens. The thrust of her argument was that gambling could give meaning to lives of seniors, a hope for the future, and something to look forward to. The excitement can have positive health consequences for otherwise sedentary people.

Some people may participate in gambling activities because they wish to support causes of a group sponsoring a gambling event. Private schools, amateur athletics, health care facilities, and many other causes sponsor gaming events, and people can be drawn to gambling to support those causes. Many people, especially first timers, may gamble just for the curiosity of gambling. As new forms of gambling are coming to many areas of the country, people may be drawn to the activity just simply to see it and try it out.

Having looked at the reasons for gambling, we can now look at the study previously mentioned. In early 1995, the Social Science Research Center at Mississippi State University formed a gambling study group. The group is directed by Arthur Cosby. I have been a member of the group. We designed a survey questionnaire that covered many aspects of gambling. We asked what games people played. We also asked why they played. Information was collected on the backgrounds of the respondents. The questionnaire was administered through telephone calls to a national random sample. Of the 1,522 respondents, 937 (61.6 percent) had made a wager during the previous twelve months (Thompson 1997, 25–32).

These respondents were asked to indicate why they gambled. They were permitted to offer more than one response. Even though only a very few gamblers can use their talents and skills to regularly win money from gambling, as discussed earlier, a clear majority indicated that the reason they gambled was "to win money." The second category—"for entertainment"—was offered by one-third of the gamblers. Fewer than one-fifth said "for excitement"; "curiosity," "socializing," "worthy

Table 1 Why People Gamble (N = 937)

	No.	%
To win money	473	50.5
For entertainment	313	33.4
For excitement	172	18.4
For curiosity	99	10.6
To socialize	89	9.5
For worthy causes	38	4.1
As a distraction	38	4.1
As a hobby	34	3.6

Source: Thompson, William N. 1997. *Legalized Gambling: A Reference Handbook.* Santa Barbara, CA: ABC-CLIO, 31.

causes," "distraction," and "hobby" followed. The responses given are reported in Table 1.

The overall responses are somewhat disturbing, as they indicate that the general population is buying into a false concept of the true product of the gambling industry. Of course, winners and winning are featured in advertising about gambling, but the simple truth is that most cannot win. There may be consequences for the gambling industry because of these attitudes. A collective disillusionment may soon encompass the industry if majorities persist in being drawn to the activity as a way of gaining money. Indeed, some of the recent defeats of gambling propositions may spring from such disillusionment. The overall numbers need to be examined more closely, however, before such conclusions are evident.

Respondents were asked which games they had played during the previous twelve months. Again, they were permitted to name one or more form of gambling (as well as more than one reason for gambling). Of the gamblers, 817 (87.2 percent) had played the lottery. Casino players (both in commercial and Native American casinos) numbered 367 (39.2 percent); 127 (13.6 percent) had wagered at horse races or dog races, and 117 (12.5 percent) had played bingo games.

The survey indicates that players at different kinds of games play for different reasons. Without trying to isolate persons who played at only one kind of game, I sought to compare those playing different games. The differences shown are probably smaller than the real differences, because people will be reported in more than one category. Nevertheless, the differences appear to be major ones in many cases. Table 2 reports the leading categories of responses of players of each type of game. Table 3 indicates other responses.

Clearly the lottery players appear to be the most unrealistic of the gamblers. Over half (53.7 percent) gamble to "win money." Yet, the lottery game is the one in which skill plays the smallest role— basically no role at all—in determining the winner. Moreover, except for special times when lotto jackpots exceed the odds of winning, the lotteries give the lowest return of any of the games. Only about half of the money gambled at lotteries is returned to the players in money prizes. Even in the case of large lotto jackpots, the number of players who win is extremely low—one in hundreds of thousands. Playing the lottery "to win" is indeed an unreason-

able fantasy, even if on occasion it may be economically logical. Only 31.7 percent see lottery play as "entertainment," and only 17.7% find it exciting.

The next most luck-oriented game is bingo. Here, the skills of listening and paying attention help, but the luck of the draw really determines the winner. Payoffs are only marginally better than lottery payoffs. Yet 43.6 percent of bingo players play "to win money." An equal portion indicated "entertainment" as their motivation, and 20.3 percent said they played bingo for "excitement."

Casino players and race bettors indicated that the desire for "entertainment" was the leading reason for gambling. Of the race bettors, 48.8 percent cited "entertainment" as the first reason; 36.2 percent said it was "to win"; 30.7 percent indicated "excitement" as the reason for gambling. Of casino players, 48.8 percent sought "entertainment," 37.3

Table 2 Players' Games and Reasons for Play

	To Win	Entertainment	Excitement	Hobby
Lottery (N = 817)	439	259	145	84
	53.7%	31.7%	17.7%	10.3%
Casino (N = 367)	137	177	100	38
	37.3%	48.8%	27.2%	10.4%
Race bets (N = 127)	46	62	39	16
	36.2%	48.8%	30.7%	12.6%
Bingo (N = 117)	51	51	24	9
	43.6%	43.6%	20.3%	7.7%

Source: Social Science Research Center, Mississippi State University. 1995. *National Gambling Survey.* State College: Mississippi State University.

Table 3 Players' Games and Reasons for Play

	Curiosity	Socialize	Worthy	Distraction
Lottery (N = 817)	66	33	35	31
	8.1%	4.0%	4.3%	3.8%
Casino (N = 367)	52	19	17	17
	14.2%	5.2%	4.6%	4.6%
Race bets (N = 127)	13	5	5	10
	10.3%	3.9%	3.9%	7.9%
Bingo (N = 117)	20	8	8	10
	16.9%	6.8%	6.8%	8.5%

Source: Social Science Research Center, Mississippi State University. 1995. *National Gambling Survey.* State College: Mississippi State University.

percent played for the purpose of "winning," and 27.2 percent played "for excitement." The casino card games and the race betting allow players the greatest opportunity to exercise skill. The ambience of the games, however, puts a premium on their entertainment value. The responses suggest that most of the people drawn to the games are not chasing false dreams or false promises of easy wealth. Rather they are exchanging their time and money for entertainment experiences.

Curiosity seekers are marginally more likely to be drawn to racetracks. Bingo is clearly seen as the game most likely to draw those desiring a social experience (6.8 percent). Casinos follow closely (14.2 percent), whereas lottery players are least likely to be drawn to the games for social reasons (4.0 percent). Bingo players are most likely to play in order to support "worthy causes." They are also most likely to play as a "hobby" and as a "distraction" from the problems of daily life.

Gender differences reveal that males are more likely to gamble "to win" than females (54.4 percent to 46.4 percent) but less likely to play games for entertainment (27.7 percent to 39.0 percent) or for social reasons (7.8 percent to 11.3 percent). Males show a greater inclination to game for "excitement" (20.4 percent to 16.3 percent), whereas females are more likely to play as a distraction from daily problems (5.0 percent to 3.2 percent).

Whites and nonwhites express many of the same reasons for gaming. They can be distinguished on two factors, however. Nonwhites are more likely to gamble "to win money" (58.1 percent to 49.3 percent); they are less likely to gamble for social reasons (4.7 percent to 10.6 percent).

We also asked if people had traveled in order to gamble. Of those who had, a much greater portion gambled for entertainment (39.4 percent to 29.5 percent%) and for excitement (26.8 percent to 12.8 percent). Persons who indicated that they had gambling opportunities in their communities were less likely to gamble out of curiosity (10.2 percent to 21.4 percent) and more likely to gamble to "win money" (50.8 percent to 41.4 percent). Local gambling was also more socially oriented (9.7 percent to 3.6 percent).

The bottom line? People gamble for many reasons. With the exception of a small portion of skilled players, those who do so for the purpose of winning money are quite simply fooling themselves. It appears that some gamers are more likely than others to fall under the false allure of the notion that they can win. It is regrettable that the lottery players are most prone to these feelings. Lotteries are not only the most luck-oriented games, but they also give the player the worst odds of any of the games. What is even worse is the fact that only the lotteries, of all the games, are offered by government entrepreneurs. At a time when the politicians are seeking to raise their voices against gambling in Washington as well as several state capitals, it is disconcerting that the one gambling game directly operated by politicians is the game most apt to be sold for something it is not—an opportunity to win money. Casino gambling is the target of gambling's political opposition. Yet the casino players appear to have the most realistic rationale for their play. The gambling industry offers many games. Some offers are more responsible than others. Policymakers examining the impacts of gaming on society should be very mindful of the differences among different games and among the way the games are offered to the public.

Sources: Social Science Research Center. 1995. *National Gambling Survey.* State College: Mississippi State University; Thompson, William N. 1997. *Legalized Gambling: A Reference Handbook.* 2d ed. Santa Barbara, CA: ABC-CLIO, 25–32.

Gambling, Compulsive. *See* Gambling, Pathological

Gambling, Pathological

. . . Ah, I have a premonition—I can't miss! . . . If I start very carefully. . . . Why am I really such an irresponsible infant? Can't I see that I am a doomed man? But why can't I come back to life? All I have to do is to be calculating and patient once, and I'll make it! I have to hold out for just one hour, and then my whole life will be different. Just remember what happened to me seven months ago in Roulettenburg, before I lost everything. Oh, it was a beautiful instance of determination . . . I lost everything I had then . . . I walked out of the Casino, and suddenly discovered that I still had one gulden in my waistcoat pocket. Well, that'll pay for my dinner at least, I said to myself. But after I had taken a hundred steps or so, I changed my mind and went back to the roulette table . . . I won, and twenty minutes later I left the Casino with one hundred and seventy gulden in my pocket. It's the absolute truth! That's what your very last gulden can do for you! But suppose I had lost heart then? What if I hadn't dared to risk? . . .

Tomorrow, tomorrow, it will all be over!
—Final lines from Dostoyevsky's *The Gambler*

[Dostoyevsky] knew that the chief thing was gambling for its own sake—*le jeu pour le jeu.*
—Sigmund Freud, analyzing Dostoyevsky in *The Psychology of Gambling*

Freud and Dostoyevsky are but two of the most famous of those who have been intrigued by the peculiar phenomenon currently known as pathological, compulsive, or problem gambling. Although it is clear that thinkers have long contemplated those who gamble excessively and problematically, at no

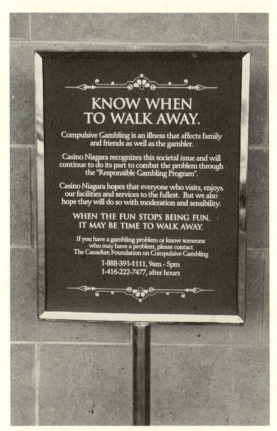

Casino Niagara advises pathological gamblers to "walk away."

time in history has the phenomenon of pathological gambling been studied with more widespread rigor or enthusiasm than it is today. In this entry, some of the past, present, and future challenges facing those who care about the well-being of problem gamblers will be examined. Keep in mind, however, that this is a young and rapidly evolving field of study and that many of the following issues are still vigorously debated.

Historical Challenges for Problem Gamblers
Historically, two institutions have been primarily responsible for describing, defining, and interpreting problem gamblers. These institutions—religion and psychiatry—merit further discussion here, as tracking their historical trajectories reveals some interesting parallels. Both religious and psychiatric institutions have reserved some of their harshest vocabularies for pathological gamblers. More recently, both have begun to alter their original diagnoses. Even though both have abandoned their previous positions to a certain degree, however, remnants of these prior characterizations continue to shape the social milieu in which pathological gamblers live their lives today.

Religious Tirades and Transformations:
From Sinners to Somebodies
Throughout history, churches have often criticized gambling and gamblers, and those who gambled to excess have generally been subject to the harshest of criticisms. Of course, religious thinkers have not always been interested in discriminating between "pathological" gamblers and "normal" gamblers. Although complications abound when attempting to project current-day definitions onto the past, it is interesting to examine the ways that those in the pulpit have described those who today would most likely be labeled as pathological gamblers.

For a long time, religious leaders were in effect the Public Stigmatizer Number One for gamblers of all stripes. In fact, many of the earliest references to gambling activity can be found in sermons that have survived over the years. To cite one example, on 19 April 1835, Samuel Hopkins, pastor of the First Congregational Church in Montpelier, Vermont, gave a sermon entitled "The Evils of Gambling." Remarkably, Hopkins articulated quite

Quick Cash and Choctaw Baskets: A pawn shop near the Choctaw's Silver Star Casino in Philadelphia, Mississippi.

clearly behavioral phenomena that psychologists today have come to term *tolerance, preoccupation,* and *loss of control.* In fact, in describing the generic "gambler," he alluded to many of the current diagnostic criteria for pathological gambling. He noted that:

> [T]he victim continually craves the stimulus of his depraved habit, till, by and by, life becomes insupportable without it and insupportable with it . . . this is . . . a gambler in the last stages of his progress, a gambler whirling upon the lowest, swiftest, narrowest convolution of the whirlpool . . . drunken [note the early reference to the perils of alcohol] with infatuation. How much more detestable, then, does [he] appear when [he] has passed the point of initiation and become a living passion which *will* and *must* be fed! How much more hateful when it has taken such hold of its victim . . . that he *hungers* and *thirsts* for the excitement of his secret sin! Then see how quickly he is a man of habitual frenzy—how soon it comes to pass that he cannot abide life save in the tumult, the stormings . . . of this maddening passion. And see how he is first led, then coaxed, then driven, then lashed, and at length, goaded by its power. I do not speak of what might be. I speak of . . . what has been proved . . . they have betrayed the confidence of unsuspicious friendship; embezzled the treasure entrusted to their keeping, to feed therewith their own passion . . . O! It is foul . . . let the gambler know that he is watched, and marked; and that . . . he is loathed. Let the man who dares to furnish a resort for the gambler know that he is counted a traitor to his duty, a murderer of all that is fair, and precious, and beloved among us. Let the voice of united, incensed remonstrance be *heard*—heard until the ears of the guilty tingle. (Hopkins 1835)

Hopkins's rhetoric is harsh and unequivocal, and it reveals much about the social environments of his day. More recently, however, these types of condemnations have softened somewhat in favor of a gentler approach, and religious leaders have begun to co-opt the problem gambler in their attempts to curb the expansion (and in some cases, ban entirely) gambling in jurisdictions around the United States. Additionally, houses of worship have long been important to twelve-step groups such as Gamblers Anonymous, whose meetings are often held in churches.

The Evolution of Psychological Assessments: From Sociopaths to Somebodies
For a long time, to the extent that the psychological community paid attention to pathological gam-

blers, its members concluded that the afflicted suffered from personality disorders or sociopathy. Medical professionals noted that these folks seemed to be "possessed" when they played and that they usually committed horrible acts of destruction affecting both persons and property. They destroyed their home lives as well, acting as human wrecking balls to all things personal and familial. Moreover, these people's problems usually came to light after they had been incarcerated for any number of offenses, from writing bad checks to bank robbery.

Until recent times, this was the predominant view. In the 1960s and 1970s, though, the late Dr. Robert Custer, the founding father of pathological gambling treatment in the United States, began to notice a vital trend. Although sociopaths leave a path of destruction in their wake and then display no remorse, the pathological gamblers that Custer encountered were feeling tremendous remorse—and in many cases were committing suicide. Custer's efforts, which led to the inclusion of pathological gambling in the third edition of the *Diagnostic and Statistical Manual of Mental Disorders,* will be further discussed in other sections of this entry.

Comparing Religious and Psychological Trends
A number of parallels emerge, then, when examining the history of these two institutions' interpretations of the lives of pathological gamblers. Seemingly despised by those in the pulpit, and for all intents and purposes labeled as uniquely evil by the science destined to supplant religion as the ultimate labeler, pathological gamblers have faced no shortage of individuals and institutions willing to unleash their harshest vocabularies upon them. Today, pathological gamblers, after a multicentury roller coaster ride, are starting to receive a bit more private and public sympathy, in large part because both religious and psychiatric institutions have cooled on the concept of the gambler as a uniquely evil or sociopathic individual.

To be fair, these religious and psychological shifts reflect broader trends that took place in both of these institutions. On the other hand, it should be noted that despite the "conversion" of psychologists and religious leaders, potentially harmful

remnants of these historical labeling processes are alive and well today. Although many would debate the merits of various labels and definitions for the pathological gambler, it is difficult to dispute that these two "labeling powers" have exerted and continue to exert a powerful influence on the social milieu in which pathological gamblers have existed. Furthermore, many problem gamblers today would recognize leftovers from both religious (as egregious sinner) and psychiatric (as a uniquely flawed personality type) perspectives as continuing influences on the degree to which they are accepted socially.

Current-Day Challenges: Definitions of Pathological Gambling
Despite the fact that professionals in the field of problem gambling have moved beyond the historical characterizations just discussed, it would be unwise to ignore the ways that the public has settled into its own less-sophisticated assessments of this population. In this section, various clinical, research, and nonprofessional (e.g., Gamblers Anonymous) definitions of pathological gamblers will be discussed in greater detail.

As is often the case in maturing fields of study, experts on pathological gambling are currently sifting through complex definitional issues in order to arrive at a more cogent and effective terminology to describe the pathological gambler. In a field in which perhaps the most common description—compulsive gambling—makes many clinicians cringe, arriving at a consensus is no easy task. For the purposes of this discussion, the term *pathological gambling* will be used, except in cases in which other terms are explicitly chosen by others attempting to define these phenomena.

The "Bible" of Psychiatric Assessments
Although pathological gamblers have been alluded to in the medical literature for years, the most important definitional developments have occurred in the past two decades. Thanks largely to the groundbreaking work of Dr. Robert Custer, the *Diagnostic and Statistical Manual of Mental Disorders* (DSM) first included pathological gambling in its third volume (DSM-III) in 1980. As the diagnostic "Bible" among psychologists and psy-

Do casinos sell drugs? A sign advertising the Motor City Casino in Detroit.

chiatrists, inclusion in the DSM represents a major step forward for the recognition and acceptance of any psychological affliction as a legitimate disorder.

Although the presence of pathological gambling in the DSM-III was significant in and of itself, the definitions provided soon became controversial. Most notably, some pathological gambling experts regretted that the criteria focused on behavioral actions or *effects* of pathological gambling. It was decided by those responsible for putting together the criteria for the updated DSM-III-R (revised) that the new diagnostic criteria should reflect pathological gambling's apparent similarity to other addictive behaviors (National Research Council 1999, 25). As such, the DSM-III-R, published in 1987, represents a significant step for those seeking professional and public acceptance of pathological gambling as an addictive affliction (a connection suggested long ago by Freud [1974], among others). Equally significant for pathological gamblers themselves was the evolution of the criteria to access and emphasize underlying causes and cognitive processes as much as behavioral effects of their problem. The similarity to other addictions—as well as the increasing emphasis on internal, causal, or cognitive factors—can be observed in its criteria.

Because of the overhaul of the criteria—reflecting a desire to embrace a new "addiction" terminology—it could be argued that the DSM III-R is as historically significant as its groundbreaking predecessor. The newer criteria were still problematic for many practitioners (for an in-depth discussion, see National Research Council 1999, 26), however, and many of them resented the "parroting" of other addiction terminologies. This dissatisfaction, coupled with an increasing desire to incorporate the growing body of empirical research into the DSM definitions, led a handful of researchers to attempt to differentiate pathological gamblers from those suffering from other types of addictions. As a result of these empirical forays, a new set of criteria emerged for the DSM-IV in 1994. According to the DSM-IV, pathological gambling was the diagnosis when a person exhibited four or more of a list of characteristics: progression and preoccupation, tolerance, withdrawal, escape, chasing, denial, illegal activity, jeopardizing family or career, and bail out.

The DSM-IV criteria are significant for at least three reasons. For one, the shift to a more empirically based diagnostic science is one that will continue to shape definitional controversies in the future. Second, the addition of criterion 5 (the "escape" criteria) is significant because it began to address a "new" pathological gambler: the individual who engaged in (primarily machine) gambling for an "escape"—rather than for a "high." This distinction (the "action" versus the "escape" problem gambler) remains one of the most promising in the field today. Interestingly, these escape pathological gamblers—many of whom gamble on increasingly popular video machines—often follow a different trajectory compared to their "action-seeking" counterparts who so dominated the early literature on pathological gambling. Many practitioners—including pioneering clinician Durand Jacobs—insist that these "escape" elements are the key factors in diagnosing problem gambling. It could well be, then, that as the face of gambling across the United States changes, so too will the pathological gambler. Third, the DSM-IV represents the most widely accepted standard for pathological gambling diagnosis, a distinction reflected in the National Gambling Impact Study Commission's heavy reliance on these newest criteria to ascertain pathological gambling prevalence rates across the country (National Gambling Impact Study Commission 1999).

The South Oaks Gambling Screen

The *Diagnostic and Statistical Manual* is far from the only measure used to define pathological gamblers. Anyone who journeys into the pathological gambling literature is bound to encounter the ubiquitous South Oaks Gambling Screen (SOGS), an instrument developed by Henry Lesieur and Sheila Blume in 1987 (Lesieur and Blume 1987). The SOGS is notable both for its widespread use as well as for its admirable initial attempt to develop a valid and reliable clinical screening measure. Despite its widespread use, the SOGS was eventually criticized in the research community. Some have pointed out that as a screening device, the SOGS is designed to identify *possible* pathological gamblers as well as definite pathological gamblers. This "wide-tent" approach allows clinicians to reduce the chances of obtaining false negatives, that is, determining that an individual is not a pathological gambler when he or she actually is one. Some have lamented that this emphasis can result in inflated estimates of pathological gambling in a general population. As a result, the SOGS has re-cently fallen out of favor among demographers seeking to determine rates of pathological gambling in general populations.

The NORC DSM Screen for Gambling Problems

Although the SOGS has served as a foundation for most of the pathological gambling prevalence studies conducted in this field, those studying pathological gambling for the National Gambling Impact Study Commission in 1999 sought to employ newer instruments based on the most recent advances in the field. A National Opinion Research Center (NORC) research team at the University of Chicago addressed this issue by developing, testing, and implementing its own new instrument for problem gambling assessment: the NODS (short for the NORC DSM Screen for Gambling Problems). This new instrument adheres closely to the DSM-IV criteria for pathological gambling diagnosis. The NODS contains seventeen items measuring both past-year and lifetime gambling activity: When respondents indicated that they had engaged in the behavior in the past year, they were then asked about their lifetime behaviors (National Opinion Research Center 1999, 18).

The NODS addresses concerns about the tendency of prior instruments to overestimate pathological gambling rates by making its criteria "more demanding and restrictive" than those used in previous studies (National Opinion Research Center 1999, 18). The NODS is scored using a unique terminology, which is determined by the respondents' scores on the instrument. Scores corresponded with the DSM-IV system and ranged numerically from zero to ten (National Opinion Research Center 1999, 21) Respondents answering in the affirmative to one or more of the DSM-IV criteria were labeled as follows. Gamblers scoring a one or two on the NODS instrument are classified as "at-risk gamblers." Those who answer yes on three or four DSM-IV criteria are labeled as "problem gamblers." Finally, those scoring a five or higher on the NODS are classified as "pathological gamblers." These distinctions reflect a growing trend among researchers to recognize individuals who do not qualify under the most stringent guidelines but who nevertheless may be in need of identification and/or treatment.

The "Twenty Questions" of Gamblers Anonymous
Although the so-called experts of pathological gambling have long debated the merits of a number of different definitions of pathological gambling, the definitional approach of Gamblers Anonymous (GA) has remained remarkably stable over the years. Gamblers Anonymous has listed its Twenty Questions for those who believe that they may have a gambling problem. GA suggests that those answering seven or more of its criteria in the affirmative may have a gambling problem.

Although the Gamblers Anonymous questions may not have the "official stamp" of the instruments discussed previously, this by no means should suggest that they are any less meaningful to the lives of pathological gamblers. On the contrary, it could be suggested that those responsible for creating the twenty questions represent an organization that has been treating pathological gamblers for far longer than virtually all of the professional clinicians in practice today. (For a discussion of how GA operates, see the later section "How to Help? Treatment and Awareness Programs" in this entry.) Furthermore, in light of suggestions that only a very small percentage of those identified as "pathological gamblers" by other instruments ever show up in treatment centers or other societal "safety nets," professional practitioners may be well advised to respond to the definitions developed by nonprofessionals. After all, as is the case in any young field of study, the truest of experts can often be found among those who happen to suffer from the phenomenon in question.

Prevalence Rates: How Many Problem Gamblers Are There?
Closely linked to the concepts of defining problem and pathological gambling are the issues pertaining to locating and counting the individuals who suffer from this affliction. In this section, the important attempts to measure pathological gambling in the general population will be discussed. Within the past few years, the two most comprehensive quantitative studies ever conducted on pathological gambling behaviors in the United States have been completed: the Harvard Medical School Division on Addiction's meta-analysis of 120 prevalence studies of "disordered" gambling

behaviors (Shaffer, Hall, and Vander Bilt 1997) and the National Gambling Impact Study Commission's research report (conducted by the National Opinion Research Center at the University of Chicago).

At the very least, it is impossible to dispute that the metaphorical bar has been raised in pathological gambling research. Indeed, it is difficult to envision any future prevalence study that does not of necessity engage and incorporate these two comprehensive attempts to count pathological gamblers.

Harvard Medical School's Metanalysis
In 1997, Shaffer, Hall, and Vander Bilt conducted a comprehensive metanalysis of the prevalence studies that had already been conducted in North America. Meta-analyses are attempts to combine previous research efforts into one coherent whole. After looking at studies incorporating a wide variety of methodologies, the authors made the important conclusion that the construct they refer to as "disordered gambling" represents:

> an apparently robust phenomenon that research can identify reliably across a wide range of investigative procedures that vary in quality of method. Robust phenomena tend to be reliable, occurring in almost all study settings; these phenomena may be found with almost any research methodology, even those that are widely disparate. (Shaffer, Hall, and Vander Bilt 1997, ii)

In other words, after examining 125 prevalence studies in jurisdictions across the United States and Canada, the contention made here is that disordered gambling is far from an illusion. In fact, in study after study—and regardless of methodology, setting, or population—this phenomenon has proven to be a widespread societal problem that large numbers of individuals experience in everyday life as well as over the course of a lifetime.

In order to incorporate all of the different prevalence studies that fit the parameters of their study, the authors implemented a three-level typology that distinguishes among various manifestations of normal and problematic gambling activity. According to this classification system, Level 1 gamblers are individuals who "gamble with little or no consequences." These gamblers make up the majority of individuals in North America. Among individuals who have experienced problems with their gambling activity, Level 2 gamblers are those who have had problems, but who possess "subclinical levels of gambling disorders." This level is variously defined in different studies, depending on the diagnostic threshold of the instrument in use. Finally, Level 3 gambling "refers to disordered gambling that satisfies 'diagnostic' criteria and, therefore, is clinically meaningful." These are individuals who surpass the various diagnostic thresholds for pathological gambling in these studies (National Gambling Impact Study Commission 1999, 4–6).

Finally, the study examined respondents' disordered gambling behaviors over the course of a lifetime as well as over the past year. The study found that 1.60 percent of the adult general population in the United States were lifetime Level 3 gamblers, and 1.14 percent fell into the past-year Level 3 category. Among individuals in the same populations, 3.85 percent qualified as lifetime Level 2 gamblers and 2.80 percent as past-year Level 2 gamblers.

The National Opinion Research Center's Survey
In April 1998, the National Gambling Impact Study Commission hired the National Opinion Research Center to conduct a nationwide poll to track gambling behaviors in the adult population of the United States. (The resulting NODS survey was discussed in the section on the South Oaks Gambling Screen.) NORC used telephone survey methods to interview a "nationally representative" sample of 2,417 adults (National Opinion Research Center 1999, 1). Because it was expected that a survey of this size would not identify enough pathological gamblers to conduct any significant statistical analysis, NORC supplemented this research with another survey of 500 randomly selected "patron interviews" in various gambling locations. NORC categorized respondents' gambling activities using the typology outlined in the earlier definitions section (e.g., "at-risk," "problem," or "pathological" gamblers). In addition, NORC examined these behaviors over the course of a lifetime and over the previous year.

The NORC survey found that 7.7 percent of individuals qualified as "at-risk" gamblers at some point during their lifetime, and another 2.9 percent were categorized as "at-risk" gamblers based on their past-year activity. Meanwhile, 1.5 percent of respondents were "problem" gamblers at some point in their lives, and 0.7 percent were labeled as past-year problem gamblers. Finally, 1.2 percent of Americans qualified as "pathological" gamblers at some point during their lifetime, and 0.6 percent of the sample qualified as pathological gamblers for the past year.

The survey also studied the effects of problem and pathological gambling among different demographic groups. These results are listed in Table 1.

One final subgroup that deserves to be mentioned here pertains to geography: NORC found that problem and pathological gambling rates within fifty miles of a casino are roughly double the rates found elsewhere. It would seem, then, that proximity to casinos does affect prevalence rates in a given location.

These data provide some interesting insights into the phenomenon popularly described as "pathological gambling." At the very least, the conclusion by Shaffer, Hall, and Vander Bilt that these activities are very much real—and not merely some figment of our current-day imagination—deserves serious attention. After all, even though these percentages may appear small, in absolute numbers they represent millions of lives—more, in fact, than the number of individuals who suffer from more notorious afflictions such as Alzheimer's disease.

How to Help? Treatment and Awareness Programs

Having briefly discussed the history, definitions, and prevalence of pathological gambling, we now proceed to the obvious question of how to help pathological gamblers. This section covers pathological gambling treatment approaches and outlines approaches to public awareness and education.

Professional Treatment Programs
Today, a diverse number of treatment strategies are employed to alleviate the suffering of the pathological gambler. The first treatment program

Table 1 Prevalence of Gambling Problems among Selected Populations

Demographic	Problem Gambling		Pathological	
	Lifetime	Past Year	Lifetime	Past Year
Gender				
Male	2.0	0.9	1.7	0.8
Female	1.1	0.6	0.8	0.3
Race				
White	1.4	0.6	1.0	0.5
Black	2.7	1.7	3.2	1.5
Hispanic	0.9	0.7	0.5	0.1
Other	1.2	0.5	0.9	0.4
Age				
18–29	2.1	1.0	1.3	0.3
30–39	1.5	0.8	1.0	0.6
40–49	1.9	0.7	1.4	0.8
50–64	1.2	0.3	2.2	0.9
65+	0.7	0.6	0.4	0.2
Education				
Less than high school	1.7	1.2	2.1	1.0
High school graduate	2.2	1.1	1.9	1.1
Some college	1.5	0.8	1.1	0.3
College graduate	0.8	0.2	0.5	0.1

Source: National Opinion Research Center. 1999. "Gambling Impact and Behavior Study." *Report to the National Gambling Impact Study Commission,* 26–27.

was developed at the Brecksville, Ohio, Veterans Administration hospital by Dr. Robert Custer. Custer, whose background was in alcohol and drug addiction, was approached by Gamblers Anonymous members about creating a treatment program for those whose problems stemmed from a different type of excessive behavior. Custer's emphasis on the similarities to other addictions is still widely respected and implemented in treatment programs across the country. In this type of program, a three-pronged "attack" is used to battle the disorder. Psychoeducational programs let the pathological gambler learn about his or her affliction—in much the same way that individuals suffering from any disorder are educated. Psychotherapeutic approaches deal with the inevitable interpersonal and psychological problems of the pathological gambler. Finally, a peer counselor (generally a recovering problem gambler) incorporates the twelve-step approach of Gamblers Anonymous to teach the pathological gambler "one-day-at-a-time" strategies to avoid gambling.

More recently, a diverse series of treatment approaches has built upon these historical foundations. Other professional clinical approaches incorporate psychoanalytic, behavioral, cognitive, and even pharmacological strategies (for an in-depth discussion of these treatment processes, see National Research Council 1999, 192–236). Many treatment professionals are excited about the groundbreaking biogenetic research currently being conducted, as advances in the biological understanding of this disorder will no doubt bring added attention to the field.

Gamblers Anonymous
Outside of the professional treatment community, Gamblers Anonymous is a private self-help group devoted to assisting individuals whose lives have been adversely affected by a gambling problem. The program is modeled after Alcoholics Anonymous and other twelve-step groups.

The history of GA is an interesting one. "Jim W." started playing cards as a young child, and by the time he was a teenager he was an accomplished poker player. In early adulthood, he began to bet on the tracks at Santa Anita. He then went into the service during World War II, an experience that exposed him to an even more expansive world of gambling. It was during these years, however, that Jim began to lose heavily. These losing streaks continued after he returned to the United States after the war. By the mid-1950s his life was consumed by what many (most notably Lesieur 1984) have called the "chase." His business failed, and his marriage faced increasing troubles.

"Jim W." had previously experienced success in an Alcoholics Anonymous group, and that success inspired him to pursue a similar program for pathological gamblers. From 1954 through 1956, Jim W. tried in vain to organize group meetings with other pathological gamblers. Finally, in 1957, he was invited to participate as a guest on a Los Angeles radio show to publicize his dream of a twelve-step program for gamblers. Soon after, he began to receive phone calls from others sharing his plight and his desire to get help. At first, the group was of modest size, but that original group served as a model for what has become a worldwide movement.

The following year a Gamblers Anonymous group began in San Francisco. GA headed east in 1960, with new chapters in New York, Boston, Philadelphia, and Washington, D.C. By the end of 1960, there were 16 chapters, and by the end of the next decade there were 130. By 1992 there were over 700 chapters in nearly every state (in addition to chapters in some of the Canadian provinces). In 1973, GA went international with a chapter in Sydney, Australia.

It was agreed at the outset that there would be no dues, no affiliations with other groups, no GA-sanctioned political activity, no acceptance of gifts from nonmembers, and no organizational officers. GA groups are loosely held together by a National Service Organization that provides literature, holds meetings, and gives advice on setting up groups. Individual chapters have members who serve as coordinators and make arrangements for meetings.

In GA meetings, members share their stories in order to help others resist their urges to gamble.

Though some psychiatric groups (notably in areas with significant numbers of stock traders, such as Chicago and New York) have designed "controlled gambling" programs, GA claims that the belief that the pathological gambler can return to gambling is an illusion. Accordingly, GA insists that members abstain from gambling for the rest of their lives.

The National Council on Problem Gambling
In 1972 the Board of Trustees of Gamblers Anonymous moved to establish a council for awareness and education. As a twelve-step-program, GA had stringent secrecy requirements that precluded public advertising efforts and open lobbying for support of programs for troubled gamblers. Many felt that as a consequence of this political inactivity, the idea of counseling help for gamblers was left out of federal legislation passed in 1970 (and funded to the tune of $40 million) to help those with alcohol and drug abuse problems. In 1972 interested parties created the National Council on Compulsive Gambling (which later changed its name to National Council on Problem Gambling [NCPG]) and worked to rally support for awareness, education, and counseling programs. Early efforts of the national council also resulted in public funding of treatment and educational programs in several states. Today, thirty-four states have councils affiliated with the NCPG, and offices can also be found in a handful of other countries worldwide.

Future Challenges: Where to Go from Here?
It has been suggested here that it would be beneficial to acknowledge more seriously that unlike alcohol, for instance, access to gambling games is very different in different jurisdictions. As a result, it could well be that pathological gamblers who happen to live in different areas have experienced very different trajectories along their "downward spiral." While a universalizing tendency was necessary—and perhaps even noble—when the field of study was young and desperately seeking the acceptance of a medical community that yearns for universality, this stage has long since passed.

The implications for future research and clinical work are as numerous as they are vital. Claiming, for instance, that the majority of pathological gamblers are male or middle-aged—when gender and age breakdowns can and do vary widely according to location—would appear to be irresponsible. To extend this argument, it might be called into question whether it is excusable to group female retirees whose game of choice is video poker with eighteen-year-old males whose gambling problems result from excessive interactions with the campus bookie. These types of groupings lead us to one amorphous and monolithic (but ostensibly neat and tidy) "pathological gambler" category. This tendency is much like the formerly popular pastime of stuffing as many human beings into a phone booth as possible: intriguing, and even intoxicating to a certain degree, but in the end one has to wonder whether anyone is being suffocated in the process.

Although psychological and biological explanations are certainly vital and continue to be promising, they cannot be exclusively endorsed at the expense of explorations of the sociocultural. In many academics' (often noble) quest to universalize the experiences associated with this affliction, many nuances of local communities have been overlooked, and New Orleans, Louisiana, becomes Detroit, Michigan, becomes Las Vegas, Nevada, and so on. The resultant haze—in which we can be certain of neither the micro nor the macro—has plagued countless works over the years.

It does us no good, for instance, to speak of "pathological gambling" when we really mean "video poker addiction," as the two labels potentially represent very different phenomena. Continuing to use a "big-tent" approach to incorporate all of these subtypes of pathological gambling activities is no longer defensible in light of continuing observations that different types of gamblers potentially have very different experiences during their gambling and social activities.

In keeping with this plea, a number of future directions might be suggested for those interested in pursuing studies in this field. In particular, a number of important distinctions among pathological gamblers might be pursued in the future. Again, it is essential for researchers and policymakers to address the potentiality that as gambling seeps further into the mainstream of life in the United States, so too could pathological encounters with this recreation increase.

Assessing and Addressing Social Costs

A number of social costs are associated with pathological gambling. The pathological gambler imposes a wide range of burdens not only onto himself or herself but also onto family members, friends, co-workers, those with whom he or she has business relationships, and the general public as well. It has been estimated that between ten and fifteen persons are directly and adversely affected by the pathological gambler (Lesieur and Custer 1984, 148). These gamblers often will borrow from close associates and even resort to stealing or "creatively rearranging funds" when the money runs out. Unfortunately, the popular notion that pathological gamblers somehow have a financial "cap" on the damage they inflict is flawed; in fact, these individuals often are able to locate funds far beyond their own means. And finally, when the individual or family can no longer pick up the pieces, the entire society may have to pay for welfare, for treatment costs, for police service, for jails and prisons.

Unfortunately, it is not easy to come up with definitive money figures that can discern the exact social costs caused by each compulsive gambler. There are definitional issues in deciding exactly what a "social" cost is, and there are methodological problems in calculating costs, even where one knows the specific cost item. Several experts have offered opinions about the societal costs associated with pathological gambling. Lesieur and Puig (1987) examined several illegal behaviors in general and insurance frauds in specific. They indicate a monumental cost for society from this fraudulent activity; in their analysis, they conclude that one-third of insurance fraud can be attributed to pathological gamblers. On 1 September 1994, John Kindt testified to the Committee on Small Business of the U.S. House of Representatives that the social costs of an individual compulsive gambler was between $13,000 and $52,000 a year. In 1981 Robert Politzer, James Morrow, and Sandra Leavey (1981) made an analysis of the annual costs to society of untreated pathological gamblers. These costs included lost productivity, criminal system costs, and "abused dollars," an illusive term that included not only bad debts but also all money lost at gambling. Their information was gathered from ninety-two persons receiving treatment at the Johns Hopkins Compulsive Gambling Counselling Center. They found that the average "bottomed-out" gambler imposed a cost of $61,000 upon society over the last year of gambling. A "more average" problem gambler imposed an annual cost of $26,000 upon society. A study in South Carolina found that the social costs of a pathological gambler are less—only $6,299 each (Thompson and Quinn 2000). (See Box 1).

Other Policy Remedies

Current-day gaming companies are realizing that if the gambling industry is to survive as a benefi-

cial provider of economic development, with good jobs and with revenues for worthy public (and private) causes, it must confront its "unfriendly" side and deal with it in a responsible manner. Though it is not always comfortable with the analogy, the gambling industry is in a position analogous to that of the tobacco and alcohol industries. Although both of these industries are roundly condemned for the social ills they generate, tobacco's posture of denial has led to major law suits and judgments that could potentially threaten its imminent profitability. Alcohol industry leaders, on the other hand, have addressed social costs associated with their product, and they have devised tools to mitigate problems (e.g., sup-

---

Box 1: Putting a Dollar Figure on Impacts of a Pathological Gambler

How much does the activity of a pathological gambler cost his or her fellow citizens? How much does it cost the governments to provide for service needs resulting from the activity? How much does it cost the entire society? Several studies have attempted to find answers by surveying gamblers in treatment. A study by William N. Thompson and Frank L. Quinn found the costs shown in the accompanying table per pathological gambler in a South Carolina survey of seventy persons in treatment. The gamblers were asked how much of each area was the result of gambling. Of this amount, $3,161 becomes a burden to the total society—meaning that the wealth in the entire society is reduced.

Costs per Pathological Gambler (annualized)

Unpaid debts	$464
Lost productivity/missed work	2,156
Unemployment compensation	178
Reduced productivity/unemployment	1,082
Theft of property	1,035
Costs of arrests	116
Costs of criminal trials	124
Jail and prison	334
Probation	117
Costs of civil cases	241
Bankruptcy cases	118
Divorce court costs	111
Welfare/food stamps due to gambling	140
Therapy	83
Total	$6,299

Of the total, $3,161 each year is because of one pathological gambler, and $3,137 in costs are transferred to other people who are not part of the gambling transaction (creditors, theft victims). The general society also pays here with higher interest rates, hiring of more police, buying of locks, and administrative costs of otherwise unneeded insurance. On top of these costs are ones borne by the gambler and his or her family. Gambling losses take $9,687 from each pathological gambler each year, divorce actions and attorneys $703, therapy $83, lost property value through forced sale $937—for a total cost of $13,566 to the gambler and family. The National Gambling Impact Study Commission also found that the costs of problem gamblers were 53 percent of those of pathological gamblers. When one considers that as many as 4 million Americans are either current pathological or problem gamblers, the high social costs of gambling begin to come into focus. Indeed, if only 1 percent of the adults in the United States are pathological gamblers at one time, and only 1 percent are problem gamblers, the cost exceeds $19 billion. The 1 percent or 2 million adults who are pathological cost their fellow citizens $12.6 billion a year, and the 2 million problem gamblers impose a cost of another $6.7 billion on society. These annual amounts exceed the total tax revenues all governments receive from the gambling industry in the United States.

Source: Thompson, William N., and Frank L. Quinn. 2000. "South Carolina Saga: Death Comes to Video Machine Gambling: An Impact Analysis." Paper presented to the National Conference on Problem Gambling, 6 October, Philadelphia.

port for the concept of the designated driver and stiffer drunk driving laws). As a consequence, alcohol companies are not often a prime target of reformers. Recent efforts by the gambling industry—such as the establishment of the Responsible Gambling program under the auspices of the American Gaming Association and support of education and treatment programs—are headed in the right direction if the industry wishes to think in the long term.

As discussed previously, public education efforts, which up to this point have been relatively modest, need to be expanded. Public awareness of problem and pathological gambling lags far behind awareness of the alcohol and drug abuse fields. This responsibility needs to be shared by both public and private institutions. In fact, investigators involved in the NORC study estimate that the total federal expenditures on pathological gambling studies over the past twenty-five years are equivalent to the weekly expenditures on drug abuse surveys (National Opinion Research Center 1999, 51).

Research and education programs would appear to be the best starting point for future projects. Information can serve as a powerful weapon against the perils of these problems. Even if the pathological gambler is not reached through educational programs, if just one individual in the pathological gambler's social circles learns enough about the affliction to provide a "safety net," these individuals may receive attention and help before their problems become too severe. In treatment centers across the country, clinicians relate that few things are more frustrating than listening to pathological gamblers whose downward spiral was accompanied by a complete lack of awareness of the potential financial, legal, and psychological help that is available to the public.

Individuals need to be made aware that treatment is available and that they are not alone in their suffering. Because intensive psychological treatment is expensive and because pathological gamblers often find themselves in severe debt, it is a good idea to make sure that these types of programs are supported or subsidized in some way by public and private monies.

As gambling expands, mental health practitioners need to be educated about the nature of this affliction. The National Council on Problem Gambling reports that there are fewer than one hundred outpatient and only one dozen inpatient treatment centers for problem gamblers in the entire country. By contrast there are 13,000 programs for alcohol and drug abusers. Most mental health professionals have not been exposed to information about gambling problems and lack training in dealing with gambling addicts.

In sum, there are many ways we can educate individuals about this affliction, and none needs to make any sky-is-falling claims. To conclude, an analogy first suggested by Dr. Robert Custer is perhaps most appropriate.

In many ways, casino gambling is much like a ski slope. Millions upon millions of people worldwide enjoy skiing and have a wonderful time shooting down the slopes. Skiing brings in all kinds of revenue to various economies. Skiing provides jobs. Skiing can certainly rejuvenate a stagnant economy. Skiing is not completely safe for all individuals, however, and hence these potential benefits do not come without a cost. File it with the "sad but true:" While skiing, some people are bound to break their legs. Unfortunately, some people are also going to break their necks.

Because of this inevitability, it is imperative that ski slopes have a well-trained ski patrol as well as a hospital (which one hopes will have a degree of expertise in broken legs and necks) at the base of the mountain to take care of the injured. And of course, care must be taken to make sure that the communication lines among the ski patrol, the lift operators, and the hospital are streamlined and top-notch.

In effect, treatment professionals, casino operators, and researchers need to continue to cooperatively investigate the ways this population can be helped. At this point, gambling "slopes" remain a popular destination for both locals and tourists alike. What remains to be seen is the degree to which businesses and communities will be able to serve the needs of both the masses of recreational users as well as the individuals who fall.

—*primary author is Bo Bernhard*

Box 2: Two Giants in Treatment and Research

Robert L. Custer (1927–1990)

Dr. Robert L. Custer must be recognized as the true pioneer of modern treatment and modern perspectives on pathological and problem gambling. He was born in Midland, Pennsylvania, in 1927, attended Ohio State University, and received his medical education at Western Reserve University with psychiatric training following at the University of Missouri. In 1955 Custer and his wife, Lillian, began careers treating persons with addictions. Soon they were seeing gamblers who had problems. Custer joined the Veterans Administration (VA) in 1974 and began a tour at the VA hospital in Brecksville, Ohio. There, in 1972, he developed the first inpatient treatment program for pathological gamblers combining individual therapy with group counseling. His work with his patients convinced him that Freudian approaches in treatment would not be effective. Instead, he saw the gambling affliction as a disorder that could best be treated as if it were a disease. He pushed his notions within the medical community and as a result of his efforts, the American Psychiatric Association accepted his perspective toward pathological gambling and included the malady along with a list of symptoms in the third edition of the *Diagnostic and Statistical Manual of Mental and Nervous Disorders* in 1980. The fourth edition refined the definition of what was designated as an "impulse control" disorder. After leaving the VA, Custer organized the Taylor Manor psychiatric center in Ellicott, Maryland, to treat pathological gamblers. Dr. Custer's advocacy for problem gamblers was evidenced by his many appearances as an expert witness in criminal trials and also by his book *When Luck Runs Out,* coauthored with Harry Milt (see Annotated Bibliography).

Henry Lesieur

Henry Lesieur learned about problem gambling as a teenager while working in a gas station near a horse-racing track. He heard story after story from the gamblers, and he started to engage the bettors in conversations. As a graduate student at the University of Massachusetts in Amherst, he formulated discussions with gamblers in Gamblers Anonymous groups and gamblers in the student body into the body of a master's thesis. This in turn led him to expand his studies, resulting in the 1977 publication of *The Chase.* His book (republished in a second edition in 1984) has been recognized as the first sociological study into the lives of serious problem gamblers. Lesieur soon joined the criminology faculty of St. John's University in Jamaica, New York. There he became the founding editor of the *Journal of Gambling Behavior* (now the *Journal of Gambling Studies*). Dr. Lesieur teamed with Sheila Blume to develop the South Oaks Gambling Screen, the most utilized instrument for assessing the prevalence of gambling problems in society. He also developed tools for assessing social costs of gambling. Lesieur's research and his perspectives on gambling have been presented to scores of academic conferences as well as to government policy-making groups. His influence on the modern study of problem gambling has been monumental.

Sources: Comings, David E. 1998. "The Molecular Genetics of Pathological Gambling." *CSN Spectrums* 6 (November): 26–37; Custer, Robert, and Harry Milt. 1985. *When Luck Runs Out: Help for Compulsive Gamblers and Their Families.* New York: Facts on File; Gamblers Anonymous. 1964. *The GA Group.* 2d ed. Los Angeles: Gamblers Anonymous; Gamblers Anonymous. 1984. *Sharing Recovery through Gamblers Anonymous.* Los Angeles: Gamblers Anonymous; Hopkins, Samuel. 1835. *The Evils of Gambling: A Sermon.* Montpelier, VT: E. F. Walton and Son; Lesieur, Henry R. 1984. *The Case: The Career of the Compulsive Gambler.* 2d ed. Cambridge, MA: Schenkman Publishing; Lesieur, Henry R., and Sheila Blume. 1987. "The South Oaks Gambling Screen (SOGS)." *American Journal of Psychiatry* 144, no. 9: 1184–1188; National Gambling Impact Study Commission [NGISC]. 1999. *Final Report.* Washington, DC: NGISC; National Research Council. 1999. *Pathological Gambling: A Critical Review.* Washington, DC: National Academy Press; Rosecrance, John. 1988. *Gambling without Guilt: The Legitimation of an American Pastime.* Pacific Grove, CA: Brooks-Cole; Shaffer, Howard J., Matthew N. Hall, and Joni Vander Bilt. 1997. *Estimating the Prevalence of Disordered Gambling Behavior in the United States and Canada: A Meta-analysis.* Boston: Harvard Medical School.

American Psychiatric Association. 1980. *Diagnostic and Statistical Manual of Mental Disorders.* 3d ed. Washington, DC: American Psychiatric Association; American Psychiatric Association. 1994. *Diagnostic and Statistical Manual of Mental Disorders.* 4th ed. Washington, DC: American Psychiatric Association; Comings, David E. 1998. "The Molecular Genetics of Pathological Gambling." *CNS Spectrums* 6(1): 26–37; Custer, Robert, and Harry Milt. 1985. *When Luck Runs Out.* New York: Facts on File; Freud, Sigmund. 1974. "Dostoyevsky and Parricide." In *The Psychology of Gambling,* edited by Jon Halliday and Peter Fuller, 157–174. London: Allen Lane; Gamblers Anonymous. 1964. *The GA Group.* 2d ed. Los Angeles: Gamblers Anonymous; Gamblers Anonymous. 1984. *Sharing Recovery through Gamblers Anonymous.* Los Angeles: Gamblers Anonymous; Hopkins, Samuel. 1835. *The Evils of Gambling: A Sermon.* Montpelier, VT: E. F.

Walton and Son; Lesieur, Henry R. 1984. *The Chase: Career of the Compulsive Gambler.* Cambridge, MA: Schenkman Publishing; Lesieur, Henry, and Sheila B. Blume. 1987. "The South Oaks Gambling Screen (SOGS)." *American Journal of Psychiatry* 144(9): 1184–1188; Lesieur, Henry R., and Robert L. Custer. 1984. "Pathological Gambling: Roots, Phases, and Treatment." In *Gambling: Views from the Social Sciences* (special volume of *The Annals of the American Academy of Political and Social Science*), edited by James H. Frey and William R. Eadington, 146–156. Beverly Hills, CA: Sage; Lesieur, Henry R., and Kenneth Puig. 1987. "Insurance Problems and Pathological Gambling." *Journal of Gambling Studies* 7 (Spring): 5–39; National Gambling Impact Study Commission [NGISC]. 1999. *Final Report.* Washington, DC: NGISC; National Opinion Research Center. 1999. "Gambling Impact and Behavior Study." Report prepared for the National Gambling Impact Study Commission: 89pp.; National Research Council. 1999. *Pathological Gambling: A Critical Review.* Washington, DC: National Academy Press; Politzer, Robert M., James S. Morrow, and Sandra B. Leavey. 1981. "Report on the Social Cost of Pathological Gambling and the Cost-Benefit Effectivenss of Treatment." Paper presented to the Fifth National Conference on Gambling and Risk Taking, 22 October, Reno, Nevada; Rosecrance, John. 1988. *Gambling without Guilt: The Legitimation of an American Pastime.* Pacific Grove, CA: Brooks-Cole; Shaffer, Howard J., Matthew N. Hall, and Joni Vander Bilt. 1997. *Estimating the Prevalence of Disordered Gambling Behavior in the United States and Canada: A Meta-analysis.* Boston: Harvard Medical School; Thompson, William N., and Frank Quinn. 2000. "South Carolina Saga: Death Comes to Video Machine Gambling: An Impact Analysis." Paper presented to the National Conference on Problem Gambling, 6 October, Philadelphia; Walker, Michael. 1992. *The Psychology of Gambling.* Oxford: Pergamon Press.

Gambling, Problem. *See* Gambling, Pathological

Gambling and Crime. *See* Crime and Gambling

Gambling and Economics. *See* Economics and Gambling

Gambling and Insurance. *See* Insurance and Gambling

Gambling and Religion. *See* Religion and Gambling

Gambling and Sex. *See* Sex and Gambling in Nevada

The Gambling Devices Acts (the Johnson Act and Amendments)

One of the primary accomplishments of the Kefauver Committee's investigations of organized crime was the passage of the Gambling Devices Act of 1951, also known as the Johnson Act (Public Law 81–906, passed 2 January 1951) (*see* The Kefauver Committee). The act prohibited the transportation of slot machines across state lines, except where they could legally be used in the state of destination.

No slot machines were permitted on federal enclaves such as domestic military bases, national parks and forests, and Indian reservations. The machines were also prohibited for use in waters under the maritime jurisdiction of the United States, unless they were on vessels authorized for legalized gambling by state governments. As U.S. flag ships were prohibited from having gaming operations on international waters by 1949 legislation, the Johnson Act made the transportation of machines to these ships also an illegal act.

Under provisions of the act, every manufacturer of machines had to register with the U.S. attorney general. All machines had to be especially marked and numbered for identification. Records of all sales and distributions of machines had to be filed with the attorney general each year.

The Johnson Act of 1951 gave a specific definition to "gambling devices." They were mechanical devices "an essential part of which is a drum or reel . . . which when operated may deliver, as the result of the application of an element of chance, any money or property." They also included other machines activated by coins for purposes of gambling. The act applied to parts of these machines as well.

In 1962, the Gambling Devices Act was amended to include gambling machines other than traditional slot machines (such as video games, digger or crane machines, quarter drop machines, and pinball machines that allow free replays) and also devices for gambling such as roulette wheels and wheels of fortune. The act did not apply to nonmechanical devices such as paper products for bingo games. Pari-mutuel equipment was also exempt, as were certain games designed especially for carnivals.

Subsequent legislation such as the Indian Gaming Regulatory Act of 1988 and the Cruise Ship Competitiveness Act of 1992 added further exemptions to the act.

Sources: Gambling Devices Act (Public Law 81–906, signed into law 2 January 1951).

See also Gambling on the High Seas, the Laws of

Gambling on the High Seas, the Laws of

For seventy-five years, the subject of gambling on the high seas has been a policy concern for U.S. officials. In 1926 operators anchored barges three miles off the coast of California and welcomed gamblers from San Francisco and later Los Angeles, who would take smaller speedboats from the shores to the boats. The barges were well lit and could be seen from the shores. State officials did not like the boats, but they were frustrated in attempts to enforce state anticasino laws, as the boats were considered to be in international waters. The boats could accommodate as many as 600 players, and they soon appeared off the Atlantic Coast as well.

In 1948, U.S. senator William Knowland (R, California) introduced legislation aimed at these barges. In the process he won passage of a bill that stopped all gambling on the high seas by U.S. flag-bearing ships worldwide.

The law was supposedly applied to vessels used "principally" for gambling, but in actuality, it applied to all ships whether gambling was the major activity of the ship or merely a side activity—as gambling is on most cruise ships. Gambling was prohibited on the vessels if they were registered under the laws of the United States or if they were "owned by, chartered to, or otherwise controlled" by citizens or residents or corporations of the United States. Persons violating the law could be fined up to $10,000 and jailed for two years and also could lose their vessel.

The law also made it illegal to transport passengers from the shore to a gambling ship in international waters, regardless of whether the ship was under the American flag or a foreign flag.

In 1951 (and as amended in 1962), the Johnson Act made it illegal to transport gaming equipment onto any U.S. ship. There was no change in the law until 1992. Over these intervening decades, U.S. shipping interests seemed to have suffered considerably. Although gambling activity provided only a small part of the revenues of cruise ships, the extra revenues probably helped the ships achieve overall net profits. As of 1991, there were eighty-two cruise ships that docked at U.S. ports. Only two of these were U.S. ships.

In 1992, as part of the Flower Garden Banks National Marine Sanctuary Act, Congress amended the Johnson Act to remove the prohibition on transporting gambling equipment to U.S. ships and also authorized those ships to permit gambling in international waters or in national waters if permission was granted by states. Under the new law, states could still stop such international waters gambling if the ships simply made "cruises to nowhere." States could prohibit the gaming unless the ships docked in ports of other states or countries before they returned to the port in the state of origin.

In 1996, the federal law of gambling ships changed again. Now ships were permitted to have gambling on Lake Michigan if they were authorized to do so by the state of Indiana. Voyages to Alaska were also allowed to have gambling if they stopped twice in Alaska and also either in Canada or another state. The ability of states to prohibit the gaming was also restricted. The boats could have gambling if they returned to the original state without going to another state or country as long as the cruise was tied to a longer cruise. The new law stimulated new interest in what were referred to as "cruises to nowhere," as these were allowed without specific state action stopping them. That state action had to be expressed in new legislation, and cruise boat interests were adept at lobbying against the restrictions.

The growth in the number of gambling ships caused the 1997–1999 National Gambling Impact Study Commission to recommend new legislation to allow states to more easily stop the "cruises to nowhere" that did not have explicit permission to operate under the state law.

—coauthored by Anthony N. Cabot and Robert Faiss

Sources: Cabot, Anthony N., William N. Thompson, Andrew Tottenham, and Carl Braunlich, eds. 1999.

International Casino Law. 3d ed. Reno: Institute for the Study of Gambling, University of Nevada, Reno, 605–612; National Gambling Impact Study Commission [NGISC]. 1999. *Final Report.* Washington, DC: NGISC; Thompson, William N. 1997. *Legalized Gambling: A Reference Handbook.* 2d ed. Santa Barbara, CA: ABC-CLIO, 131–132.

See also Cruise Ships; The Gambling Devices Act (the Johnson Act and Amendments)

Gambling Systems

As gambling is as old as human existence, so too are the attempts to beat the game. Players have used cheating schemes and have also used more or less legitimate systems and strategies for winning from the first moment that cards were dealt or dice were rolled. Although the basic truth is that an honest random game cannot be beaten, systems can indeed be effective. At times they can produce wins that are beyond normal expectations. But more often systems can be used to protect a player from excessive losses or to maximize playing time when the player is seeking game play for entertainment.

The most effective winning systems are tied to games in which skill is a greater factor than luck in determining winners. Applications of systematic play can produce results in live poker games, at blackjack tables, and with sports and horse-race betting. The most important part of systematic play is having a full knowledge of the odds in the game; for instance, knowing the likelihood that particular cards will be dealt at a particular moment. In a player-banked game such as poker, the systematic player will also be cognizant of his or her bankroll and the bankroll of opponents. Systematic skills at poker also involve being able to "read" the other players; that is, finding "tells" or mannerisms that might reflect the strength of their hands. Another essential skill at poker or at other games involving calculations and interpretations of situations is the ability to have a clear head; for instance, the skill to remain fully sober during play. In blackjack, good playing strategies keep the house edge down to one or two percentage points. Card-counting strategies, however, if properly executed, can give the player a positive return, as discussed in Edward Thorpe's book, *Beat the Dealer* (1962).

Sports bettors can gain an edge over the casino by carefully studying records of teams and game situation histories. The sport bettor can use information to assess the likelihood that one team will win a game or the likelihood that it will win by a certain margin. The sports bettor has an advantage over the casino in that the casino oddsmakers are not assessing the results they feel will occur in the game but rather are assessing how the betting public will play the game. For instance, the casino knows that players will favor teams such as Michigan and Notre Dame in their betting. Given this situation, the casino will add greater handicaps to these teams. When the oddsmakers think Notre Dame will beat Northwestern by eleven points, they put the point spread at fifteen points, knowing that half of the public will bet on each side of the game at that level. The true student of the game with no emotional attachment to either team will see that Northwestern has a definite advantage in the betting situation. That player is getting an extra four points by betting on Northwestern. As long as the betting is balanced on both sides, the casino does not care who wins or loses. The casino is hurt only if the betting is heavily on one side. In such cases, it will move the point line to seek an adjustment. If the casino move the line too much—more than two or three points—the smart, skillful bettors will bet when the spread is low on one team and when it is high on the other team and hope they can win on both sides.

In horse-race betting, most systems are also based upon having full information and records about a horse's pedigree and prior experiences in similar situations (dry track, muddy track, long race course, short race course). Again, the odds that will be given on a particular horse are balanced, according to how other bettors are making wagers on the race. If one bettor gets better information or can better analyze information, he or she can make money on the wagers. One system assumes that the bettors on first-place horses—the win bets—are knowledgeable. Therefore, the system player analyzes betting on the board (at the track or at an offtrack betting parlor). He or she sees the possible return on the favorite. It might be two for one—a $4 payout for a $2 wager. The next best horses may pay off $10, $12, or $14. The bettor then looks at the bets to show—that is, that the horse will finish in one of the first three places. This is a different pool. The other bettors might overlook the favorite here, and that horse's return could be $3 compared to $4, $5, and $6 on the other horses. This is proportionally much more favorable to the favorite. Under the system, a bettor placing his or her money on the favorite to finish in one of the top three places can gain a very good edge on the others and even on the track, which takes away up to 20 percent from the pool of bets.

In games involving skillful choices, systems can provide an edge, as most of these games—even when house banked (as sports betting is)—pit one player's skill against that of other players. In luck games such as roulette, baccarat, or craps, however, the player is foolish to believe he or she can sustain an edge over the house with any system. Of course, with luck, any system can provide short-term winnings, but so too can luck do that for a nonsystem player. Systems can help with managing the player's money, but every system first directs the player toward finding the best bets on the table. For instance, system players at craps would avoid all but the pass/come bets combined with the odds bets. Blackjack betters would avoid insurance bets, and roulette bettors would seek out wheels with only one zero and would not bet on a five-number combination at a double-zero wheel. The optimum bet would be one offering *en prison* on a single-zero wheel, preferably in England, where tipping is prohibited.

Bettors playing total chance games have pursued several systems with some frequency over the centuries wherever the games have been played. One very simple system is called flat betting. Under this system the bettor simply bets the same amount every time. At games such as blackjack, the player would double down and split when it was advantageous to do so. At a roulette game, such players would bet on even-money choices such as red and black. Which way they bet would make no difference. They could bet pass or no-pass on a craps table whether they thought the table was hot or cold, but it would make no difference. Using this system or strategy, the player can be assured that over the long run, he or she will lose at the rate of the house percentage. As the house edge is 5 percent or less, the system can sustain a long time of play. A streak of luck can pro-

vide the player with a win. And the one big advantage all players have, but reluctantly use, is that they can walk away from the game at any time. The casinos really cannot do that.

The most popular system, one that has broken many players but never a casino, is called the Martingale Progressive System. In this system the player raises bets by doubling them after losses. If the first bet is $1 on red and it is a loss, the player next bets $2 on red. A player who wins goes back to betting $1 dollar the next time. If he or she loses again, the next bet is $4. Another loss and he or she bets $8, then $16, then $32 if there are five losses in a row. The player is now putting $32 at risk. A player who wins is $1 ahead. A player who loses is risking in turn $64 and then $128, all in order to get ahead by $1. This system is very much dependent upon the nerve of the gambler. Will he or she really be willing to put out $64 in a bet after losing six in a row, when he or she started out with a $1 bet in hopes of winning $1? But even more than nerve, there is the question of house limits. The limits usually involve a spread of 100 times or less. In this case, if the player has seven losses, he or she is forced to bet $128 to get the $1 win. A $1 table will probably have an upper limit of $100 for bets, so the system can no longer be used. The laws of probability and streaks indicate that with thousands of rolls of dice or wheels, there will be streaks occurring with some regularity. Wheels turn up red seven or eight times every night. The same is true for odds and evens and for high and low numbers. The streak can kill the system player, wiping out his or her bankroll very quickly. If, on the other hand, the player is betting with the streak, he or she wins only $1 each time. In a streak of seven, the player loses $131 if he or she is on the wrong side but wins $7 on the right side.

Cognizant of these facts and the fact that wheels and dice do indeed follow streaks, some of the Martingale Progressive System players will watch a wheel (or dice table) several minutes and wait for a streak to develop. Then depending upon their disposition, after five or six reds in a row, they will start their system by playing black, or if they sense a wheel bias, by continuing to bet on red. All of this is a futile exercise, assuming that the casino does monitor its wheel against biases, because the wheel does not remember what it has rolled the previous five times, ten times, or ten thousand times. The casinos with roulette and baccarat games encourage these Martingale System players by furnishing them with pencils and paper so they can track the numbers on the wheels. They also publish books of numbers for the past month, or past year, to try to get players to practice their systems. Evidently, the casinos are not afraid of the Martingale. Nor are they afraid of Great Martingale systems that find the bettor tripling bets after losses.

A cancellation system is offered as a sure winner. The bettor writes down three numbers, 1, 2, and 3. He or she now bets $4, the total of the first and third digits (1+3). A player who wins cancels out the 1 and 3 and bets $2. A winner cancels out the 2 and starts over. If he or she loses, he or she adds the $2 loss to the 2 and now bets $4. A player who wins crosses off 4 from the total and starts over. A player who loses adds the 4 to the 1, 2, and 3 and bets 5 (4 + 1). Wins bring the player back to the 1, 2, 3. Although under this system one can show a profit with an even number of wins and losses, streaks can be as deadly as with the Martingale.

Another more simple system suggests that the player should go with the flow, raising bets one unit whenever there is a win and lowering them one unit (or keeping the original bet amount) when there is a loss. Under this method, over the span of play the player should be able to keep his or her losses within the house percentages.

Casinos as an entertainment experience offer play at house games. The best systems cannot change that fact. Good money management demands the ability to set limits. The player should determine his or her budget before play begins and be willing to walk away from the tables when the budget is spent. If the player wishes to sustain play over a period of time for enjoyment of the games, the initial bet should not exceed 1 percent of his or her bankroll. The player should also consider a winning limit. If with a $100 bankroll the player achieves wins of $20, he or she should remove this amount from the bankroll and play it no more during that session. A player who experiences a streak of more than five or six bets should pause and consider going to another table or game.

Sources: Scarne, John. 1986. *Scarne's New Complete Guide to Gambling.* New York: Simon and Schuster, 409–420;

Sifakis, Carl. 1990. *Encyclopedia of Gambling.* New York: Facts on File, 24–27; Thorpe, Edward O. 1962. *Beat the Dealer.* New York: Random House.
See also Cheating Schemes

Gambling Taxes. *See* Taxes, Gambling

Games, House-banked. *See* House-banked Games

Games, Player-banked. *See* Player-banked Games

Gaming Institutes: Research and Political

The rapid growth of legalized gambling, both domestic and international, has been responsible for the number of organizations being formed in recent years to analyze, teach, manage, and research many areas of the gaming industry and to train personnel to work in the industry. There is a great need for understanding and planning when evidence of social, economic, and political effects is seen as a result of gambling. The associations and institutes presented in this entry vary in purpose and size, but all of them have the common objective of managing information related to the gaming industry.

University of Nevada, Las Vegas, International Gaming Institute

The International Gaming Institute (IGI) is part of the College of Hotel Administration located on the campus of the University of Nevada, Las Vegas (UNLV). The institute was started in 1993 to provide executive development programs, seminars, training, classes, and conferences for the gaming industry and for gaming regulators. The IGI utilizes experts in gaming and hospitality industries to provide a unique learning environment in its casino lab and support facilities as well as in Las Vegas casino/resorts and gaming-related businesses. The institute has five centers: Gaming Regulation Center, Publication and Information Center, Hospitality Research and Development Center,

Gaming Management and Development Center, and the International Gaming Technologies (IGT) Gaming Resource Center.

Gaming Regulation Center

The purpose for the Gaming Regulation Center at IGI is to create a venue where gaming regulators can meet to discuss topics on public policy and the regulation of gaming. The center conducts seminars on law enforcement for gaming regulators, background and licensing investigation procedures, casino auditing, surveillance, and financial issues relating to casinos.

Publication and Information Center

The IGI has authored or sponsored several publications relating to the casino industry, and these are made available through the Institute's Publication and Information Center. One objective of the IGI is to conduct research for the gaming industry, and toward this end, the IGI publishes a biannual academic journal, the *Gaming Research and Review Journal*. This professional journal is dedicated entirely to research and management of gaming operations, and it is designed to benefit gaming operators, industry consultants and researchers, government policymakers, and regulators.

Hospitality Research and Development Center

The Hospitality and Development Center (HRDC) is part of the University's College of Hotel Administration, a situation that allows the HRDC to draw upon the experience of faculty members who are experts in the hospitality industry. HRDC provides nongaming educational seminars and workshops, customized executive programs, market research and customer surveys, expert witness testimony, and sessions on time management and team building.

Gaming Management and Development Center

The Gaming Management and Development Center designs, coordinates, and markets seminars as well as contracting conferences, seminars, and symposia for the gaming and casino industry. Seminar topics include table game management, mathematics of table games, slot volatility, game protection, casino marketing, analysis of customer game participation, rebates on losses, gaming financial issues, managing human resources in the gaming industry, several general management and leadership issues, and customer service. The center also offers a fast-track, rigorous Gaming Management Certificate Program, which focuses on several key areas of casino management.

The International Gaming Technologies Gaming Resource Center

The IGT Gaming Resource Center offers reference and referral services for researchers, businesspeople, and students. Referrals for questions beyond the resources of the center sometimes lead to gaming professors, government agencies, gaming organizations, and gaming resources in other libraries. The core of the IGT Gaming Resource Center is the Gary Royer Gaming Collection, an extensive compilation of documents and information relating to gaming.

Sources: http://www.unlv.edu/Research Centers/ International Gaming Institute/.

Gaming Studies Research Collection, Special Collections Department, Lied Library, University of Nevada, Las Vegas

The Special Collections Department at UNLV's main campus library serves as a central research repository for information relating to gambling and commercial gaming as it developed in Las Vegas and became an international model for the industry. Special Collections houses materials that provide important documentation of the history of gaming, casinos, and entertainment in Las Vegas. The collections document the history and statistical basis of games and gambling; the economics and regulation of the gaming industry; psychological, social, and political effects of gambling; and the history of specific Las Vegas hotels and casinos. Significant collections have been developed in the related fields of organized crime and prostitution. Cultural aspects of gaming are represented in collections of literature and periodicals concerning Las Vegas and gambling, as well as in photographs and motion pictures. The *Taxe Collection* is an important resource for the study of nineteenth-century gaming.

The International Institute of Gaming Studies, University of Nevada, Las Vegas.

Sources: University of Nevada, Las Vegas. 1999. *Graduate College Catalog.* Las Vegas: University of Nevada, Las Vegas, 13.

Institute for the Study of Gambling and Commercial Gaming

The Institute for the Study of Gambling and Commercial Gaming was established by the University of Nevada, Reno, in 1989. It was the first academically oriented program of its kind. The institute promotes the understanding of gambling and the commercial gaming industries and encourages research and learning.

William Eadington is director of the institute. He has international recognition as an authority on the legalization and regulation of commercial gambling and is a prolific author concerning economic and social impacts in the commercial gaming arena. Professor Eadington organized several conferences, including the International Conferences on Gambling and Risk Taking, between 1974 and 1997. He has also edited a variety of gaming publications.

The institute serves as an important resource for Nevada's major industry. It also responds to public information and research requests, main-tains contact with domestic and International media, and directs an annual Executive Development Program, as well as gaming management education for the College of Business Administration.

Sources: http://www.unr.edu/unr/colleges/coba/game/.

Centre for the Study of Gambling and Commercial Gaming

Located at the University of Salford, Manchester, England, the Centre for the Study of Gambling and Commercial Gaming was established by a consortium of companies to actively research and encourage serious discussion of the gaming industry and to offer university students options for pursuing careers in gaming. The increasing attention to the national lottery in England has led to the perception that the country is deficient in academic- and government-sponsored research on gambling. The centre is a response to the need for examining policy alternatives and economic issues with respect to the gaming industry.

The objective of the centre is to encourage scholarly research and teaching in all aspects of gambling and commercial gaming. It provides a reference point for individual scholars and researchers interested in the economic, social, cultural, and mathematical studies of gaming, and emphasis is given to its policy, regulatory, and organizational aspects. The centre provides a sequence of courses at the undergraduate and postgraduate levels that fall under the area of business economics with gambling studies. The series of courses introduces students to some of the practical problems associated with gaming and gambling and provides a firm foundation in the basic principles of economic theory and quantitative economics. The degree course of economics and gambling is designed to establish a good base for a career in management, finance, or marketing.

Sources: http://www.salford.ac.uk/gambling/.

National Indian Gaming Association

The National Indian Gaming Association (NIGA) was established in 1985 as a nonprofit organization. As of 2001, its members include 168 Indian nations and 55 nonvoting associate members representing organizations, tribes, and businesses engaged in tribal gaming enterprises from around the country. NIGA has an executive committee headed by a chairman and other officers, including delegates from tribal nations around the United States. The association's headquarters are located in Washington, D.C. NIGA's common commitment and purpose are to advance the lives of Indian peoples economically, politically, and socially. Its stated mission is to protect and preserve the general welfare of tribes striving for self-sufficiency through gaming enterprises in Indian country. To fulfill its mission, NIGA works with the federal government and the U.S. Congress to develop sound policies and practices and to provide technical assistance and advocacy on gaming-related issues. NIGA also seeks to maintain and protect Indian sovereign governmental authority in Indian country.

NIGA operates a Library and Resource Center that houses and provides educational research materials related to Indian gaming and other issues affecting Native Americans. To facilitate its research objectives, the center is attempting to gather data to document the historic impacts of Indian gaming on tribal communities and governments as well as on their non-Indian neighbors

via the development of a National Indian Gaming Survey. The National Indian Gaming Library's education goal is to become the most comprehensive library of printed material on Indian gaming in the country. The center also has a web site that includes basic information about Indian gaming, a searchable database, and an impressive set of links to other Native American web sites. Its "virtual library" has more than fifty research and impact studies related to Indian gaming available online. NIGA also publishes a monthly newsletter that provides updates on legislative activities, Indian gaming casinos, and related national events.

Sources: http://www.indiangaming.org/.

American Gaming Association

In 1993, major gaming/casino executives discussed forming a trade association to represent their industry to the nation and the powers that be in Washington. As a result of these talks, the office of the American Gaming Association (AGA) opened in Washington, D.C., in June 1995. Its primary purpose is to promote a better understanding of the gaming entertainment industry by providing the general public, elected officials, other decision makers, and the media with facts about the industry through education and advocacy.

The AGA represents the commercial casino entertainment industry by speaking to federal legislative and regulatory issues that affect its members and their employees and customers. Some of these issues include federal taxation, regulation, and travel and tourism.

The AGA has an aggressive public education program designed to convey the industry's message to key audiences in Washington and throughout the country. It provides leadership and guidance when new issues emerge and in developing industry-wide programs in response to important issues such as problem and underage gambling. As the industry's first national clearinghouse, the AGA provides timely and accurate gaming industry data to the media, elected officials, other decision makers, and the general public.

The association has approximately eighty members from different organizations affiliated with the gaming industry, including casinos and equipment manufacturers, suppliers and vendors, companies that provide professional and financial services, a pari-mutuel/sports book, and a variety of associations, publications, and unions. The AGA's membership also includes some of the most recognizable names in the industry, including Harrah's Entertainment, International Game Technology, Mandalay Resort Group, MGM Mirage, Park Place Entertainment, Gtech, and the Nevada Resort Association. The AGA is supported by dues from its member casinos and organizations.

The AGA's web site has a section on its publications, which includes selected articles from the AGA's membership newsletter, *Inside the AGA,* and third-party newsletter, *AGA Ally.* There is a library of AGA documents and studies, which can be received through the mail. The web site also includes gaming industry videos available for viewing online; Media Updates, which contains the AGA's latest press releases, speeches, op-eds, letters to the editor, and archival materials from 1995 to 2000; and Member Services, which contains information about member benefits. The American Gaming Association was also instrumental in establishing the National Center for Responsible Gaming (NCRG) in 1996.

Sources: http://www.americangaming.org/.

National Center for Responsible Gaming

The National Center for Responsible Gaming (NCRG), located in Kansas City, Missouri, is an independent nonprofit organization founded in 1996. It is the first and only funding source dedicated solely to scientific research on gambling disorders, particularly problem and underage gambling. Its mission is to assist individuals and families affected by problem gambling disorder and eliminate underage gambling by:

Supporting the finest peer-reviewed basic and applied research on gambling disorders.

Encouraging the application of new research findings to improve prevention, diagnostic, intervention and treatment strategies.

Enhancing public awareness of problem and underage gambling.

The NCRG is a division of the Gaming Entertainment Research and Education Foundation and is governed by a board of directors. The membership of the board includes representatives of the gaming industry and leaders from the civic, charitable, educational, community, and public service sectors.

The center is supported financially by the commercial casino industry and has received pledges of over $7 million from gaming and gaming-related organizations. The NCRG administers its research grant program using peer review panels. Panel members, who are recognized as experts in their areas, follow review procedures and criteria guided by rigorous standards established by the National Institutes of Health to evaluate the scientific merit of proposals submitted to the NCRG (a list of members who have served on the panel from 1997 to 2000 is available on the NCRG's web site). The center has granted $2.5 million to renowned research and medical centers, such as Harvard Medical School, in support of research in the fields of neuroscience, behavioral and social science, and epidemiology. Ideally, these research projects will help to expand our knowledge about gaming disorders and lead to effective prevention and treatment programs.

Sources: http://www.ncrg.org/.

The National Coalition against Legalized Gambling

The National Coalition against Legalized Gambling (NCALG) is the creation of its executive director, Tom Grey. Grey, a Vietnam infantry veteran and a United Methodist minister, became concerned about gambling in 1991. Grey was a graduate of Dartmouth College and the Garrett Evangelical Theological Seminary, and he had led four congregations. He was pastoring a Methodist church in his hometown, Galena, Illinois. Illinois has authorized riverboat casinos, and an operator expressed interest in running a boat out of Galena. Grey supported a local referendum vote against the proposal. Over 80 percent of the local voters said no to the idea of a local casino. Nonetheless the county commissioners supported the casino, and in 1992, the Illinois Gaming Board ignored local opinion and awarded a license for the Galena

Tom Grey is the leading spokesperson against the spread of gambling in North America. He is director of the National Coalition against Gambling.

bling. The e-mail net of the NCALG serves as a clearing house for antigambling information.

Tom Grey and his groups have challenged gambling proponents wherever they have appeared. The campaigns are ongoing, and Grey finds himself traveling about the country, usually driving by himself, popping into communities, dining at church suppers, and being a house guest of local clergy. He then energizes the local population by providing facts and speaking with the local media and key community leaders. He offers a zeal that is usually associated with the pulpit. One political consultant labeled the sixty-year-old Grey (born in 1941) as the gambling industry's nemesis: "Our most dangerous man in America" (*U.S. News and World Report,* 15 January 1996, 52). Grey and his coalitions have seen major victories as well as defeats. He was instrumental in getting Congress to establish the National Gambling Impact Study Commission, which began work in 1997. The efforts of the groups defeated casino gambling in Ohio, Arkansas, and Florida but fell short in Michigan. They were key in the fights to defeat a lottery in Alabama and to close down slot machine operations in South Carolina.

Sources: http://www.ncalg.org.

site. Grey was incensed, and very soon he found that a lot of people around the country were faced with the same problem—having casinos placed near their communities in face of local opposition. Grey decided to organize these opposition forces.

In May 1994, Grey brought together a group of opponents as the NCALG, and he structured a network of people in almost every state as well as in Canada. He began holding annual conferences and issuing a newsletter. The NCALG established the National Coalition against Gambling Expansion to serve as its political activity arm. The NCALG makes education its top priority. It provides research, information, and technical support to those battling the expansion of gambling. Staff leaders—especially Grey—travel the country helping local groups organize in grassroots efforts to oppose gambling. They help build bridges to other local groups that do not want legalized gam-

Alberta Gaming Research Institute

Recommendations came from the Alberta Lotteries and Gaming Summit '98 for the government to spend more money on gaming research. The Alberta Gaming Research Institute was established in November 1999 in response to those recommendations. The purpose of the institute, which is a consortium of the Universities of Alberta, Calgary, and Lethbridge, is to sponsor research of gaming-related topics such as the social impacts of gaming, aboriginal gaming issues, and trends in gaming.

The institute supports the collaborative research efforts of faculty researchers, graduate students, visiting scholars, and postdoctoral fellows. The Alberta Gaming Research Council directs most of the Institute's research activities. Its fourteen members, who represent both the public and government sectors, have been appointed to serve for three years.

For the first three years, $1.5 million per year has been allocated to the institute from the Alberta

Canadian gambling scholars Harold Wynne (left) and Colin Campbell at a conference in Whistler, British Columbia.

Lottery Fund. The Alberta government earmarked an additional $3.4 million from the Alberta Lottery Fund for 1999–2000 to go to the Alberta Alcohol and Drug Abuse Commission (AADAC) to provide support for the prevention of problem gambling, education, and treatment programs.

The Alberta Gaming Research Institute has a web site that provides some basic information, including historical background, the purpose of the institute, its organization, budget, and how it operates. The site also has links that provide access to information about gaming in Alberta, research and education, legislation, various reports, business plans, news releases and updates, and forms.

Sources: http://www.gaming.gov.ab.ca/what/ agr_institute.html.

The Canadian West Foundation

The Canadian West Foundation (CWF)—a nonprofit research institute—was established in 1970 to pursue research and to promote civic education in Canadian public policy. The CWF sponsors conferences on myriad policy issues and has an active publication program. In 1998, the CWF embarked upon a three-year "gambling in Canada" project. They have explored: (1) the impact of gambling on the nonprofit sector; (2) opinions, attitudes, and public policy implications of gambling; (3) the history and scope of gambling in Canada; and (4) the socioeconomic impact of gambling on communities. A series of monographs has been published as a result of the project.

The CWF is headquartered in Calgary, Alberta. The gambling research project has been directed by Jason J. Azmier and has been supported by researchers including Garry Smith, Harold Wynne, and Colin Campbell.

Sources: www.cwf.ca.

Australian Institute for Gambling Research

The Australian Institute for Gambling Research (AIGR) is a research center located at the University of Western Sydney (UWS). It is the only independent national center of gambling studies in Australia. The AIGR has an advisory board with representatives from both the community and academia. It has a worldwide reputation for in-depth gaming research, including the areas of policy and social impacts.

The AIGR was established in 1993 with a grant from UWS and was supported through the collaborative efforts of experienced Australian researchers. UWS was instrumental in appointing Australia's first faculty Chair of Gaming, and in January 1997 Prof. Jan McMillen was named executive director of the AIGR, broadening the research focus of the Institute.

The AIGR has received various research grants from the Australian Research Council as well as Australian and international governments. This has resulted in the publication of articles in scholarly journals, as well as books and research reports. The AIGR is involved in community service and engages community groups in its research programs. AIGR researchers also provide voluntary service to the community.

The Library and Information Services of UWS supports the needs of the AIGR. Its gambling collection has over 1,000 items, including reports, videos, journals, games, books, and newspaper clippings. The AIGR sponsors various annual conferences related to gaming issues.

Sources: http://fassweb.macarthur.uws.edu.au/AIGR/.

European Association for the Study of Gambling

The European Association for the Study of Gambling (EASG), located in the Netherlands, strives to improve communication among its members, who represent many different areas of the European gaming industry. It also provides a forum for the study, discussion, and dissemination of knowledge about European gambling issues.

The EASG is concerned with promoting comparative studies of questions regarding: historical, economic, and social impacts of gambling; developmental and regulatory gambling issues; ethical management and marketing of gaming; and pathological gambling issues, including prevention and treatment programs.

EASG membership is open to both individuals and institutions affiliated with the gaming industry, either within or outside Europe, as well as to academic researchers. The association is governed by an executive committee, which includes a chairman and several subordinate officers.

The association's web site provides some pertinent information about gambling and gaming literature. It also highlights several international gaming conferences and provides links to related web sites.

Sources: http://www.easg.org/.

Lionel, Sawyer, and Collins

Lionel, Sawyer, and Collins, a Las Vegas law firm, is the world's leading gaming law firm. The firm was founded in 1967 by Samuel Lionel and Grant Sawyer, the retiring governor of the state of Nevada (*see* Sawyer, Grant). One of their first functions was conducted under the leadership of attorney Robert Faiss. He helped pen significant amendments to the Nevada Gaming Control Act. In subsequent years, the firm continued its assistance in drafting gambling regulatory bills for legislative consideration. The firm has also been the leading sponsor creating the International Gaming Law Association, and attorney Anthony Cabot served as a coeditor of the *Gaming Law Review* (with Joseph Kelly). No other law firm has published as many law materials on gambling. Cabot is a leader in the publication efforts, having served as the senior coeditor on three editions of *International Casino Law.* He also has been the author or senior contributor to *Nevada Gaming Law, Federal Gaming Law, Legalized Gambling in Nevada, Casino Gaming Policy, Economics and Regulation,* and *Casino Credit and Collection Law.*

Sources www.lionelsawyer.com.

Conclusion

As worldwide interest in gaming grows, it is expected that many more institutions will be formed to study, teach about, and manage the industry. Proponents and opponents of gambling will continue to coexist and to debate the social, political, and economic gaming issues. Gaming research education, regulation, and lobbying by gaming organizations will continue.

—coauthored by Sidney Watson and Maria White

Gaming Studies Research Collection. *See* Gaming Institutes: Research and Political

Gates, John W.

John W. "Bet a Million" Gates, who was born in 1855, became a fabulously wealthy man as a producer of barbed wire as the West was opening up for farmers and ranchers. He was also a big player and winner on the stock market, controlling the flows of wheat in the economy. Gates was not happy just being a businessman; he wanted more action. He found it in gambling activity. During the Gay Nineties and the few years afterwards, he became known as the biggest player anywhere. Gates would bet on anything: the flip of a coin, which piece of sugar would draw the most flies, which raindrop on a window pane would fall to the bottom first. He would bet up to a dollar a point at bridge. Although he probably never bet a million dollars on a single play, he certainly won and lost several hundreds of thousands of dollars at a single sitting. A 1902 game of faro at Richard Canfield's Saratoga Casino cost Gates $400,000 one afternoon. The same evening he won back $150,000.

Gates dressed like the millionaire he was (until his later years), wearing several diamonds on his shirt. He played with other millionaires, such as Cornelius Vanderbilt and Diamond Jim Brady, usually on cross-country train, or in exclusive hotel rooms. He also loved the horses.

Gates was very philosophical about his play. He explained why he had to wager such large amounts of money: "For me there's no fun in betting just a few thousand. I want to bet enough to hurt the other fellow if he loses, and enough to hurt me if I lose" (Chafetz 1960, 363). A lot of people got hurt when he played. He hurt the most. Like the other "big players," he lost more than he won, and he often was "the sucker." He played the stock market heavily until he lost most of his fortune in the panic of 1907. Soon afterwards, he swore off all gambling, suggesting of the stock market that "sometimes the bulls win, sometimes the bears win, but the hogs never win" (Longstreet 1977, 166). In 1909, he testified to a group of Methodist ministers in Texas, pleading: "Don't gamble, play cards, bet on horses, speculate on wheat or the stock exchange, and don't shirk honest labor. Don't be a gambler, once a gambler, always a gambler" (Asbury 1938, 451). Preaching to the choir. Tom

Grey, of the National Coalition against Legalized Gambling, could not have expressed it any clearer. "Bet a Million" Gates died a humble man at the age of fifty-six in 1911.

Sources: Asbury, Herbert. 1938. Sucker's Progress: An Informal History of Gambling in America from the Colonies to Canfield. New York: Dodd, Mead, 446–451; Chafetz, Henry. 1960. Play the Devil: A History of Gambling in the United States from 1492 to 1955. New York: Potter Publishers, 324–325, 362–367; Longstreet, Stephen. 1977. Win or Lose: A Social History of Gambling. Indianapolis, IN: Bobbs-Merrill, 73, 164–166; Sifakis, Carl. 1990. Encyclopedia of Gambling. New York: Facts on File, 132–133.

Golden Ten. See Roulette and Wheels of Fortune

Gaughan, Jackie

Jackie Gaughan is very much Mr. Downtown Las Vegas. He is the principal owner of two anchor properties at the ends of the Fremont Street Experience: the Jackie Gaughan Plaza (formerly called the Union Plaza before he bought out his partners) where Fremont Street ends at Main Street and the El Cortez, a property built in 1941 and the oldest property in Las Vegas still bearing its original name. In between these gambling halls he owns the Western, the Gold Spike, and the Las Vegas Club. He operates only in downtown Las Vegas, where his five properties offer 37 percent of all the slot machines, 36 percent of the casino floor space, and 24 percent of the hotel rooms. He is a hands-on manager; he walks through each property every day, and he even lives in the penthouse of one of his casino-hotels—the El Cortez. The measure of his success is customer service.

Jackie Gaughan was born in Nebraska on 20 October 1920. He learned his gambling in the Midwest, and even today he especially caters to middle-class players from the Midwest. He is considered the biggest Nebraska Cornhusker football fan in Las Vegas. His grandfather had been a policeman who grew up in Ireland. His father strayed a bit from the line of law-abiding behavior—just a bit. He owned race horses, and he was a bookmaker. One of Jackie's brothers was a bootlegger.

When Jackie was only sixteen years old and working as a messenger for other bookies, he started to take action on his own. He has been in the gambling business ever since. Soon he owned two bookie shops in Omaha. He also participated in casino gaming in the area. A change in the course of the Missouri River had left an enclave of Iowa on the Omaha side of the river. Therefore, the Iowa authorities had to travel an inconvenient distance to patrol the area. A wise entrepreneur established the Chez Paris—an illegal casino. It was run by Jackie's uncle. Jackie participated in the business.

Gaughan attended Creighton University before he joined the Air Corp in World War II. His gambling activity did not skip a beat, as he was soon running his games on a base near Tonopah, Nevada. That assignment brought him close to Las Vegas, and in 1943 he visited the city, stayed at the El Cortez, and established some lifelong contacts. By 1943 he was married; his son Michael was born the same year. In 1946, after the war ended, he borrowed money from his mother to purchase a small stake in a little Fremont Street casino called the Boulder Club. He remained in Omaha, keeping his fingers in "the business" there until 1951. When he came back to Las Vegas, he purchased a small piece of the Flamingo, which he held until 1968.

His tale became one of working incredibly long hours at several properties and slowly acquiring shares of the businesses where he worked. He especially liked sports betting, and he started the first exclusive sports and race book in the downtown area. Sports betting was always a part of each of his ventures.

In 1959, he bought the Las Vegas Club, and in 1963 he acquired the El Cortez. In 1971 he joined with several other local interests—Sam Boyd, Frank Scott, Kell Houssels, and Walter Zick—to create the Union Plaza casino. This was the most expensive new property up to that time in the downtown—costing $20 million. It was also the largest, with over 500 rooms and a 66,000-square-foot gaming floor. It was themed as a railroad casino, because it actually was (and still is) the station for the railroad that ran through Las Vegas. In the early 1980s the property added a second tower with a convention center and another 500-plus rooms. Until the Golden Nugget added two towers and a convention center, the Union Plaza was the only convention property downtown. In 1990 Gaughan acquired full control of the Union Plaza and changed its name. By then he also had the Western and Gold Spike—two smaller downtown casino hotels.

As a hands-on customer-oriented casino owner-operator, Jackie Gaughan has been an innovator. If he did not invent the Las Vegas Fun Book (a coupon book with bargains such as low-cost meals, free souvenirs, and chances for double money bets), he certainly perfected it and made it a basic tool for promotions in the community. He also started a constant line of promotional giveaways. He discovered that there were "professional" contest players who seemed to win most of the prizes while his out-of-town players and other regulars were left out. So he devised a special contest that has become synonymous with the El Cortez—the Social Security number drawing. By definition, no player could have more than one entry in the contest, and the players would have to come in every day to check the prize list. He also developed what he calls the Season Pass for players who win jackpots on his machines. The pass holders are given three weeknights free at one of his hotels quarterly for the next twelve months. It keeps 'em coming back.

Jackie Gaughan is one of the "old-timers" of Las Vegas. His methods are tried and true, and they still work in the market he goes after. The new breed of corporate gamers looks at operations a little differently. Michael Gaughan, Jackie's son, has moved his attention to the Strip and also to the edges of town where he appeals to a new kind of "local" gambler and tourist. He has partners in his Coast Casino's operations. He also has a major riverboat in the St. Louis market. Michael Gaughan is college educated, holding a master's degree in business administration from the University of Southern California, where he also studied computers. Computers drive Michael's operations, but perhaps he is the bridge to the future, as he has not abandoned the basic lessons his father has taught—Michael talks the corporate game, but he walks the old timer walk with hands-on management. Despite the difference in their education, there is little doubt but that Michael is his father's son.

Some time ago when I encountered Michael Gaughan at the Barbary Coast Casino in order to interview him for a customer service book, he was breathing hard and speaking rapidly in stop-and go-phrases. He had just completed his daily walk-through of the casino, and he was reviewing and explaining the daily computerized report on each of his slot machines. He was indicating how each part of his property contributed to the bottom line, but mostly he was telling about the individual players he had just greeted by name. He told how he was striving to keep them happy and to keep them coming back time and time again. It was the kind of personalized service that one would not expect at a casino on the Las Vegas Strip, let alone a casino on the major corner of the Strip—Flamingo Road and Las Vegas Boulevard South.

Michael Gaughan carries on a strong family tradition—his younger brother works with his father's properties—of being strong contributors to good causes in Las Vegas. The Gaughans are not only good gamers; they are good citizens for Las Vegas.

Sources: Moody, Bill, and A. D. Hopkins, 1977. "Jackie Gaughan: Keeping the Faith on Fremont Street." In *The Players: The Men Who Made Las Vegas,* edited by Jack Sheehan, 120–132. Reno: University of Nevada Press.

Guadeloupe

The island of Guadeloupe in the French West Indies is a department of France. With 687 square miles of land, it has 330,000 residents. Casino gaming appears to be a very small part of its tourism attractions. One gaming facility is located near the Meridien St. Francois and Hamak hotels and another on the grounds of the Hotel Arawak. The Gosier Beach Community also offers the Casino de Gosier Les Baines. The casinos do not have slot machines, and players must pay a fee to enter the gaming rooms.

Sources: Cabot, Anthony N., William N. Thompson, Andrew Tottenham, and Carl Braunlich, eds. 1999.

International Casino Law. 3d ed. Reno: Institute for the Study of Gambling, University of Nevada, Reno, 325.

Guatemala

Guatemala's penal code of 1880 prohibits all gambling. One exemption to the law is given to the National Lottery organization that conducts a monthly game that benefits poor persons (both as employees of the lottery and as beneficiaries of programs supported by the lottery).

The penal code has also been totally ignored by others running gambling operations. In 1979 the brutal and corrupt regime of General Lucas Garcia authorized the opening of Club Monja Blanca in the penthouse of the Hotel Guatemala Fiesta in Guatemala City. A private group of operators consisted of expatriates from Cuba and Costa Rica. General Garcia's military "henchmen" were quite interested in the daily revenues of the casino, as they took their "share" along with the government's tax share. Very little of the take filtered down to the poverty programs that the casino was ostensibly supporting. The casino remained opened for three years. In 1982 General Rios Montt overthrew the Garcia government. Montt was a Fundamentalist Christian and was morally opposed to casino gambling. Even when he was overthrown by Mejia Victores in 1983, the casino remained closed. There is no casino gaming today, although certain business interests seek to keep the issue alive with the current civilian government.

Although casinos are closed, there is other authorized gambling that seems to violate the letter of the penal code. Private charities are permitted to run raffles and lottery games that include weekly drawings and instant tickets. Also, there is a large private bingo hall on the Avenida Reforma just one block from the Hotel Guatemala Fiesta.

Sources: Cabot, Anthony N., William N. Thompson, Andrew Tottenham, and Carl Braunlich, eds. 1999. *International Casino Law.* 3d ed. Reno: Institute for the Study of Gambling, University of Nevada, Reno, 302.

H

Haiti

Haiti achieved its independence in a revolution against the French army in 1804. Haiti is the oldest black republic in the world, and, next to the United States, it is the oldest independent country in the Western Hemisphere. The "independence" must be qualified. The people of Haiti have not enjoyed a democratic freedom during many of its years. Most of its rulers have been dictators, and the country has remained under the commercial domination of many nations during its history.

In 1915 U.S. President Woodrow Wilson feared that other countries might invade Haiti because of its foreign debt. He sought to enforce the Monroe Doctrine before it could be breached. Therefore, he had the U.S. Marines invade Haiti. They occupied the country until 1934. Although depriving the people of their autonomous status, the presence of U.S. troops did lead to an eradication of yellow fever and also to the construction of roads and a sewerage system. Governmental instability ensued when the marines left, but in 1957 stability returned with the election of François "Papa Doc" Duvalier as president. In 1964 he declared himself president for life. Upon his death in 1971, his son, Jean-Claude "Baby Doc" Duvalier, became the dictator.

In 1960 Papa Doc Duvalier guided the national legislature in passing a casino law. The timing was appropriate. Operators who were being thrown out of Cuba were seeking new venues. In truth the 1960 legislation was just a piece of paper that would justify Duvalier's invitation for new casino entrepreneurs to come on in and make an offer. One casino, the International, had been established on the waterfront in Port-au-Prince in 1949. It had a reputation of being a Mob house from the start.

The 1960 law was not intended to be followed to the letter, if at all. The law provided that casinos could only be in hotels with 200 rooms. There were no such hotels in the entire country then, and there are none now. At least two casinos, in addition to the International, were free-standing gaming halls unattached to any hotel. The casinos could have only seven table games, and the games allowed were specified. The major casinos in operation in 1989 during my tour of the country had fifteen or more table games. They also had games that were not authorized. Additionally the casinos had slot machines.

Licenses for casino gaming were supposed to be granted by the minister of commerce. At the time of licensing the operators were supposed to present a deposit of $50,000 to the government to be held in the Central State Bank. This earnest money was to be returned to the operators when the casino actually began conducting gaming activity. One of the operators in 1989 had gone through the licensing procedure for his property. When I asked about the law, he laughed. He said the deposit was not $50,000, it was $250,000. The deposit was not given to the minister of commerce; it was given directly to Baby Doc Duvalier (when he was in power). The deposit was not returned to the casino when it began operations; it was never seen again.

The law provided that the casinos would pay an annual fee of $1,000 plus a tax of 40 percent on the gaming win. Individual casinos would work with the government to negotiate certain expenses that could be deducted from the tax obligation. The tax had been paid in the past. When Baby Doc was deposed in a coup d'état in 1985, the tax collectors no longer came to the casinos. The operator that I interviewed in 1989 indicated that he had not paid taxes since the Duvaliers had been exiled. During the earlier years of the law, an additional 5 percent tax had been levied on players when they cashed

The Chaucon, a thatched roof casino in Petionville, near Port-au-Prince, Haiti.

in their chips—when they won. This tax was earmarked for the construction of the Duvalier International Airport in Port-au-Prince. When the airport was finally constructed, the tax collector no longer asked for the player win tax.

Foreigners were permitted to own the casinos; in fact, that was the desire of the government. They could have foreign dealers, but to do so, they had to get special work cards from the government for an undetermined price.

In 1989, during my visit, there were five casinos in the Port-au-Prince area. One, the Club 54 in the suburb of Petionville, was owned by Haitians. It was operating but in poor condition. As I entered the gaming area, a hen and four little chicks walked across the floor. The leading property was the El Rancho. It was also located in Petionville and was attached to a hotel with 125 rooms. A thatched-roof casino without a hotel was located on the main square of Petionville. The Chaucon was owned by Mike McLaney, an American who had previously been involved with Cuban and Bahamian casinos. He had held the concession for the International from 1969 to 1976. In the capital city a small casino operated at a Holiday Inn, and a

larger casino was at the eighty-five-room Royal Haitian Hotel. The casino, which opened in 1973, was also owned by McLaney. The International, enclosed by a chain-link fence, was in disrepair and out of business. It had been closed since McLaney gave it up in 1976.

In 1989 there were very few players at any of the facilities. In previous times—during the stable years of the Duvalier dictators—cruise ships touring the Caribbean would stop in Port-au-Prince, but by 1989 they no longer did so. A few stopped on the northern coast of Haiti, but there were no casinos there. Cruise ships ceased stopping in Haiti at all later in 1989. One week after my tour of the casinos, there was a coup d'état, and gunfire filled crowded streets on which I had walked from the national palace to the International. Any chance of growing markets for the casinos ended with the gunfire.

Since 1989 there have been almost no tourists in Haiti. I may have been the last casino tourist. The government disintegrated into near anarchy, and in 1994, the U.S. Marines once again landed in order to preserve something—certainly not the U.S. casino property. The marines are still there.

Casino gaming is no longer of any importance. There may be some play from local residents, but the outward signs of poverty suggest things would be otherwise.

Sources: Cabot, Anthony N., William N. Thompson, Andrew Tottenham, and Carl Braunlich, eds. 1999. *International Casino Law.* 3d ed. Reno: Institute for the Study of Gambling, University of Nevada, Reno, 232–233.

Harrah, William F.

Harrah's Casino Corporation has more gambling facilities across the United States than any other casino company. There is a Harrah's casino in each major casino jurisdiction and in many other places as well—Atlantic City, Laughlin, Lake Tahoe, Las Vegas, Reno; the states of Mississippi, Louisiana, Missouri, and Colorado; and New Zealand. Harrah's operates many Native American casinos as well. Until the Hilton casino group (Park Place Gaming) and Caesars Casinos merged in 1999, Harrah's was the biggest gambling company in the world. Harrah's gambling revenues are well over $1 billion a year. Harrah's markets to middle America and features many tour packages for its customers.

The founding father of Harrah's casinos started his gambling activities at Venice Beach, California. William F. Harrah was born in southern California in 1911. His father ran bingo halls and carnival gambling games in Venice Beach. Father and son discovered that gambling activities in a jurisdiction that really did not want gambling could be rather tenuous. The Depression years were also hard on them. They sought to practice their business activities elsewhere. When Nevada legalized casino gambling in 1931, it certainly appeared to be the place to go. Both Harrahs came to Reno in 1937, but by the time they did, young Bill had bought out his father's interest in the business. Bill

William Harrah and his car collection. (UNLV Special Collections)

Harrah first opened a bingo parlor, but then turned to casinos.

Bill Harrah had learned lessons in California that he applied in Reno, lessons that the rest of the casino industry had to also learn if survival in a competitive world was desired. When others were operating downmarket "joints" that sought to extract money from players any way they could, including cheating, Harrah made customer service a top priority. He also was the first to put carpets on the casino floors. He sought to make casinos more respectable by having windows to the outside and by having women dealers. He also took new measures to control all flows of money at a time when other properties were victims of skimming by employees and others.

In 1955, Bill Harrah built a casino on the south shores of Lake Tahoe. He was warned that the location was too remote, but he took the chance that people would enjoy staying near the most beautiful lake in the Sierras. Harrah did find that the casino had a seasonal problem, as winter could restrict travel for all but those coming to the area to ski. In response to the problem, Bill Harrah developed a busing system to bring in players from all over California. This was an innovation that has now been imitated in almost all other U.S. jurisdictions.

Bill Harrah was a solitary owner of his property, and he mixed his private life into the business. He had been indulged by his father from the time he was a small child, and with the casino profits he continued to indulge himself. He was a playboy (he was married seven times), he built personal retreats, and he developed an exquisite collection of automobiles that he maintained as a business expense. As he became older, he neglected his properties, and his excesses affected his bottom-line profits. In desperate need for funds, in 1971 he converted his personal empire into one of the first publicly traded corporate gambling properties. This gave him the funds to develop a high-rise tower at his Lake Tahoe casino. Every room in his tower had windows facing the lake and its surrounding mountains.

His personal excesses hurt his company through the 1970s, however. Harrah's associates tried to persuade him that he should sell his assets, but he steadfastly refused. Months after he died in 1979, his executive attorney, Mead Dixon, negotiated a deal to sell all of Harrah's properties to Holiday Inn for $300 million. Much of the money was used to pay estate taxes. Although the price was considered excessive at the time, Holiday Inn was able to realize over $100 million from selling Harrah's car collection. A new management team led by Holiday's Michael Rose and Dixon introduced management controls and policies that emphasized both financial responsibility and property upgrades. Existing casinos in Las Vegas and Atlantic City that carried the Holiday Inn name changed their signs to carry the Harrah name, and the empire began to move into every major casino jurisdiction in the United States and many beyond the borders of the country.

Sources: Douglass, William A. 1999. "William F. Harrah: Nevada Gaming Mogul." In *The Maverick Spirit: Building the New Nevada*, edited by Richard O. Davies, 58–73. Reno: University of Nevada Press; Kling, Dwayne. 2000. *The Rise of the Biggest Little City: An Encyclopedic History of Reno Gaming, 1931–1981*. Reno: University of Nevada Press; Longstreet, Stephen. 1977. *Win or Lose: A Social History of Gambling*. Indianapolis, IN: Bobbs-Merrill, 182–183; Mandel, Leon. 1982. *William Fisk Harrah: The Life and Times of a Gambling Magnate*. Garden City, NY: Doubleday, chap. 2.

Hawaii

Tourism is one of the mainstays of the Hawaiian economy. Therefore, many interests have sought to bring casinos into the state. The efforts go on unabated. The efforts have never won the support of the important decision makers, however, so Hawaii does not have casinos. Also, Hawaii has avoided having lotteries, charity gambling, or pari-mutuel wagering. There certainly is an underground offering gambling products in an illegal form, but leaders fear that bringing gambling into the open air of legality would only encourage bad elements. Hawaii is one of two states (the other is Utah) in which no form of gambling whatsoever is permitted under the law.

Sources: Dombrink, John D., and William N. Thompson. 1990. *The Last Resort: Success and Failure in Campaigns for Casinos*. Reno: University of Nevada Press, 161–162.

Hazard. *See* Craps and Other Dice Games

Hoca and E-O. *See* Roulette and Wheels of Fortune

Hoffa, Jimmy

James Riddle Hoffa became an essential part of the Las Vegas casino industry when he arranged the financing of several new properties in the late 1950s and early 1960s with the use of pension funds of the International Brotherhood of Teamsters.

Hoffa was born in Brazil, Indiana, on Valentine's Day in 1913. He was the son of a coal driller who died when Jimmy was seven years old. His mother soon moved the family to Detroit, where she secured employment in an automobile factory. Jimmy got his first job when he was eleven years old. Life was tough, and Hoffa responded to it with his fists, fighting and scrapping all the way. Through experiences in many hard jobs, Hoffa was drawn into the union movement. He organized a strike at a Kroger's grocery store where he worked in the stockroom. That successful effort resulted in his first affiliation with the International Brotherhood of Teamsters (often referred to as the Teamsters' union). He went on to work for the union, first in 1932 as a recruiter, then as a business agent, and soon as a leading organizer. In the mid-1930s, he became the president of Detroit Local 299. Hoffa rose in the Teamsters' ranks, and in 1952 he became the chairman of the Michigan Conference of Teamsters. He joined in the efforts to help make David Beck the Teamsters' president, and Hoffa got the vice presidency of the union as a result.

David Beck was the first victim of the U.S. Senate's McClellan Committee hearings on union corruption. It was revealed that Beck had misused Teamsters' pension funds, and he had to step down from the presidency in 1957. Hoffa became union president. The McClellan Committee, with its counsel Robert Kennedy, never ceased its attacks on the Teamsters' union, now making Hoffa its target of choice. An ongoing battle between Kennedy and Hoffa ensued that lasted for almost a decade.

During his union presidency, the Teamsters' union's Central States Pension Fund became the leading source of funds for capital financing of Las Vegas casinos. Moe Dalitz turned to Hoffa for the money needed to build La Costa Country Club in California, the Sunrise Hospital in Las Vegas, and the Stardust Casino in Las Vegas. Hoffa financed the Dunes Casino through his personal attorney, Morris Shenker, and also the Landmark, the Four Queens, Aladdin, Circus Circus, and Caesars Palace. Caesars received the biggest Teamsters' loans, over $20 million. The money was critical, as it came into Las Vegas at a time when organized crime interests tied to Meyer Lansky were pulling back from investments because they were coming under more and more scrutiny from federal investigators. The Hoffa pension fund money provided an interlude between Lansky capital and Howard Hughes capital financing. The Teamsters' loans came at a price, even though interest rates were not high—actually quite the opposite. Through a variety of means, however, Hoffa reportedly received kickbacks and also access to casino operations. He could place his people in the casino, and he also could demand a piece of the action through different skimming-type mechanisms.

Although Hoffa lived a very modest middle-class lifestyle, the charges of corruption and misuse of funds came to rest at his doorstep. Robert Kennedy pursued a prosecution of Hoffa with a vigor that probably transcended notions of due process or adherence to constitutional liberties or values. After one unsuccessful prosecution in 1962, Hoffa was finally nailed with a conviction for tampering with the jury. In 1964 he was convicted again of misappropriating union funds. His appeals ran out, and in 1967 he stepped down from union office and went to prison for fifty-eight months.

President Nixon commuted Hoffa's sentence in 1971 with a pardon decreeing that he could not hold union office again until 1980. In 1975 Hoffa was purportedly cooperating with federal authorities who were still investigating the misuse of Teamsters' pension funds. Perhaps he was seeking to have his pardon changed so that he could reclaim the union presidency. That was not to be. On 31 July 1975 he disappeared. The presumption is that he was murdered, although his body was never recovered, and the crime has never been solved.

In 1936, Hoffa married Josephine Poszywak. They had a daughter, born in 1938, and a son, James Hoffa Jr., in 1941. The son is now the president of the Teamsters' union.

Sources: Brill, Steven. 1978. *The Teamsters.* New York: Simon and Schuster; Kurland, Gerald. 1972. *James Hoffa.* Charlotteville, NY: SamHar Press; Moldea, Dan E. 1979. *Interference: How Organized Crime Influences Professional Football.* New York: William Morrow; Sloane, Arthur A. 1991. *Hoffa.* Cambridge: MIT Press.

Honduras

In Honduras the "action" is found in two casinos at night, and in the plaza of the Tegucigalpa Cathedral by day. The poor people visit the marketplace each day. There they buy and sell groceries and lottery tickets. As with many less developed as well as several forward-looking countries, the lottery operations are of the poor, by the poor, and for the poor. People with no other jobs—and maybe no job possibilities—can sell tickets on consignment. The profits from the lottery are also designated to go to programs for the poor.

Honduras is a very poor country, and Tegucigalpa certainly does not have the airs of a national capital. Its streets are narrow and dusty, and many people seem to wander them without a sense of their destination. Cows graze on garbage that is thrown into a dry riverbed. The most visible commercial sign in the city is the Coca Cola sign on the side of a mountain just above the central business and government district. It seems to be a reminder to all that their independent sovereign country may not be totally in control of its own affairs—maybe people in Atlanta have as much control over their lives as they do. Although many Third World countries have towns and cities that could be called "quaint," the presence of machine guns on each corner and outside of each major store or office building keeps the word *quaint* from entering the mind.

U.S. commercial interests are in Honduras, selling Coca-Cola and also running large banana plantations. They and their employees, as well as military personnel, provide a marketing base for the casinos. Unfortunately, the poverty of the country as well as the devastation of Hurricane Mitch in 1998 has weakened prospects for strong casino revenues.

A Honduran man carries his lottery tickets as he begins his daily rounds for sales.

The Royale Casino is at the Honduran Maya Hotel in Tegucigalpa, Honduras.

to them. Courts were also reluctant to order locals, many of whom may have been living on modest means, to pay money to the "rich" American casinos owners. The casino decided to cut off all credit play, but then discovered that their crowds decreased considerably. The operators came up with a solution. They found local agents who would be happy to purchase chips from the casino cage at a discount, and then loan the chips to the players. They would have all responsibility for collection on the loans, and if they made the collection, they of course would realize a good profit—as they purchased chips at a discount and also charged the players a loan fee. The loan agents were local residents in good standing and usually with good connections to judges and other local officials. The patrons borrowing chips from them would be sure to pay them back, as their standing as honorable citizens was at stake with these loans. The casino operators assured me that the loan agents did not use any unacceptable methods to collect loans.

Sources: Cabot, Anthony N., William N. Thompson, and Andrew Tottenham, eds. 1991. *International Casino Law.* Reno: Institute for the Study of Gambling, University of Nevada, Reno, 191–193.

Two casinos operate in Honduras: one in Tegucigalpa at the Honduran Maya Hotel; the other in the country's business capital, San Pedro Sula, near the Hotel Copantl Sula. Private entrepreneurs from the United States operate the two hotels. One of the management teams is also active in the casino industry in Curaçao; the other operator has a history of old ties to Cuban and London casinos.

Both casinos have roulette games, blackjack, and slot machines, and the casino at San Pedro Sula also has poker games, *punto banco,* and bingo sessions. The casino tax represents 20 percent of the gaming win.

I visited Honduras in January 1989 and discovered that the Casino Copan in San Pedro Sula had a feature unique among Western Hemisphere casinos. In the past the casino had difficulties in granting credit to players. Most of the players were local residents. When they were approached to pay back their loans, they considered it an affront to have an American demanding repayment of a loan

Horse Racing

Horse racing is one of mankind's oldest sports, going back to the earliest days of recorded time. There has been a variety of types of racing and breeds of horses engaged in racing. Thoroughbreds are the most recognized breed of racehorses, but there are also quarter horses, Arabians, and standardbreds.

There are races over straight courses and oval tracks, from one-fourth mile to several miles. The standard distance of races is measured in furlongs; one furlong is one-eighth of a mile. Tracks may be grass or dirt. In addition to mounted races (called flats) and harness races, there are obstacle races called steeplechases.

Certain races command much more attention than others. These include the championship races known as the Triple Crown or Breeders Cup for thoroughbreds, the Breeders Crown and the Hambletonian for standardbreds (harness horses), and the American Futurity for quarter horses. There

Legal bookmakers taking bets at the famous New Market race course in England.

are horse races for two-year-olds, three-year-olds, and older horses. There are also maiden races for horses that have never won a race before. Other varieties of races include allowance and handicap races, stakes races, and claiming races.

The majority of states have some forms of race betting. Thirty-seven states allow thoroughbred racing, 27 states allow quarter horse racing, and 26 states have harness racing. Additionally, 25 states allow offtrack betting, and 39 states have intertrack betting facilities. Every Canadian province has pari-mutuel betting on horse races. The ten provinces and the Yukon permit harness racing, seven provinces and the Yukon allow thoroughbred racing, and nine provinces and the Yukon allow quarter horse race betting. All provinces and the Yukon permit intertrack betting as well as telephone betting and offtrack betting. There are also tracks in Mexico, Puerto Rico, the Dominican Republic, and the Virgin Islands and the Caribbean island states of Antigua, Bar-

bados, Guadeloupe, Jamaica, Martinique, and Trinidad.

In the United States approximately 6 percent of all gambling losses in 1998 were by pari-mutuel horse bettors (Christiansen 1999). Track winnings (and other moneys taken out of betting pools) totaled $3.3 billion in 1998. Although on-track betting has declined a great deal over the past three decades, the total amounts bet on horse races have increased slightly, going up an average of 2.3 percent a year since 1982. All gambling in the United States has increased 10.4 percent each year since 1982. There are approximately 150 tracks in the United States, with several of these operating only during short fair seasons. Canada has approximately forty tracks; most of them for harness racing events (National Gambling Impact Study Commission 1999, 2–11; www.HorseRacing.Gambling.com).

Gambling operations have supported racing ever since it became a popular form of entertainment. There is a variety of betting systems, but in modern times, the pari-mutuel system has replaced almost all other systems at the track in North America. Other systems included pooled and auction betting, as well as betting with bookies who guarantee odds of horses at time of bets. In recent years betting revenues have shown only minuscule growth, and tracks have sought other opportunities to gain revenues. They have benefited from intertrack, offtrack, and even telephone betting. Many tracks see their future in converting facility use to slot machine and video machine gambling (*see* The Racino).

History of Racing

Records of horse racing date back to 4000 B.C. or earlier. At that time Babylonian soldiers used chariots not only in wartime battles but also in staged races. By 1500 B.C., Assyrians incorporated chariot races into their recreational lives. The early breeds of horses that were available to the peoples of known Western "historical" societies were small in size. It would take two or more to pull a chariot, and individual horses could not be mounted by riders. A statue in a New York museum shows an Egyptian racing a mounted horse, however. The statue dates to 2000 B.C. In 624 B.C.

there was a mounted horse race during the 33d Olympic games in Greece. Records suggest that the Greeks captured stronger horses from Arabs and Persians.

There was very likely betting on the Greek races, as gambling was part of their society. There is little question that the Romans bet on horse races. Races were held in Rome very soon after the city was founded. Racing events became an essential part of the entertainment of the masses of Roman citizens. Racing was also seen as a way of encouraging the development of a better, stronger, faster stock of horses for military uses. Romans are also credited with bringing their horses to the British Isles, where they raced against and also mixed with Celtic ponies. In about A.D. 200, the Romans held their first formal race meeting in England.

During the first millennium, racing captured the attention of all the civilizations throughout the Mediterranean world and farther east. The Arabian societies, which fell under the influence of Islam, adhered to prohibitions against gambling, but they made two exceptions. It was permissible to bet on scholarship contests involving children, as doing so encouraged learning the Koran, and it was permissible to bet on horse races, as doing so encouraged improvements in breeding that would result in better horses that could be used in holy battles with the infidel.

In England, horse racing and betting flourished. In the Middle Ages, horse-race betting took on its identity as the Sport of Kings. Henry II established weekly races at fairgrounds about 1174, and his son John kept a royal stable of racehorses. Serious breeding efforts and formal racetracks date back to the sixteenth century. Henry VIII passed laws that sought to isolate racing stallions from ordinary horses. He also demanded that each of his dukes and archbishops keep at least seven stallions. The oldest sponsored British race was probably the Chester Cup, which was run in 1512 during Henry's reign. The first stakes race (a race requiring owners to pool money for the winner's prize) was held during King James's reign in the early seventeenth century. Under James's direction, the racetrack at Newmarket initiated racing. During the Cromwell interlude a Puritan dominance of England precluded racing, but the activity came back with a vengeance with the Restoration and Charles II. He established new stakes royal races, and in 1674, the king himself mounted a steed and ran to a first-place finish at Newmarket.

Racing developed over the course of the seventeenth century in England as breeding practices were regularized, lineages were recorded, and tracks were improved. The notion of accurate lineage became even more critical with the arrival of three special horses in England toward the end of the seventeenth and beginning of the eighteenth centuries. Every thoroughbred horse running in the world today is descended from these three horses: Byerley's Turk, Darley Arabian, and Godolphin Arabian.

In the seventeenth century, the purest breeds of horses were to be found in Turkey and Arabia. In 1688, British captain Byerley captured a horse from a Turkish officer at Buda. The horse that became known as Byerley's Turk was probably born in 1680. He was brought to England, where his breeding career began. The second horse was called Darley Arabian. He was twenty years younger than Byerley Turk. He was bought by Englishman Thomas Darley at Aleppo in 1704 and sent to a farm in Yorkshire, where he performed stud duties until 1730. One of his sons was sent to North America. The third horse, Godolphin Arabian, was born in Yemen in 1724. He was first exported to Syria and then to Tunis, where he was given to the king of France. Englishman Edward Coke of Derbyshire purchased the horse in Paris and later sold him to the second earl of Godolphin for stud at his estate near Newmarket.

The first horses to arrive in the Western Hemisphere came west with the second voyage of Columbus in 1495. Columbus used horses in his conquest over indigenous populations in the Caribbean region. Thereafter, every ship from Spain carried horses. Their numbers multiplied in the Caribbean islands, and Cortez took horses from Cuba to Mexico in 1519 and used them as he overwhelmed his Aztec Native adversaries. Horses soon were being exported to the far reaches of South America. Many were also captured by Native Americans, and some ran off to start a wild horse population that was found on the American plains and into the Southwest. On some occasions the horses became a part of the food supply for desperate conquistadors and explorers. But the Spanish also raced the stock in Cuba and Mexico during the sixteenth century.

English settlers came to Virginia and New England in the early decades of the seventeenth century. The first horses arrived at Jamestown Colony in 1610, but the six mares and one stallion were eaten as other food supplies dwindled during the next winter. Subsequent ships brought more horses, including twenty mares in 1620, and a solid permanent stock of horses was established. The Virginia colonists also purchased horses, which had descended from Spanish imports, from Native peoples. As soon as horses were in the American colonies, horse racing began. The Virginia colony passed a law allowing racing in 1630. The previous year horses arrived in New England. By mid-century, racing was common all along the eastern seaboard, as the stock of horses was pervasive.

Cleared land was at a premium in these early colonial years, so most of the racing was on village streets or on narrow paths through woods. The notion of the sprint race developed, a precursor of quarter horse racing, which was popularized in the American West. Originally the betting on races was conducted among the owners of the horses. Disputes over betting and the results of the races were submitted to the law courts for resolution. The first race track in the Americas was established by Richard Nicholls, the British governor of New York, immediately after his countrymen had taken hostile possession of New York (New Amsterdam) from Dutch settlers in 1665. Nicholls built a large, oval, wide-open, grass track in present-day Jamaica, Long Island.

Other colonies followed by building their own tracks. The tracks allowed for much longer races. Indeed, the four-mile race became common. Racing was formalized, and large purses were offered to winners. At first, all betting had been among players, but with tracks, entrepreneurs developed systems of pooled betting. A pool seller would offer a wager at set odds, and then he would seek to sell chances on all the horses. If he could not sell all the horses and all the bets in the pool, he would be subject to taking losses on the races. The popularity of the tracks led more and more people to betting, including members of the less wealthy classes. As a result, several colonies passed laws banning racing.

Nevertheless, betting continued through the years leading up to the Revolutionary War. Then the stock of racing horses became critical to the war effort, and racing stopped. Prior to the war, several colonies had developed jockey clubs that would establish the rules for all the races and to a degree would replace the civil law courts as the arbiters of disputes regarding wagers and race results.

The development of the breed and racing stock in Canada has been related to events in other countries as well as indigenous factors. The French began settlements in Quebec City in 1608. As the weather was quite severe there and also in other French Canadian settlements, horses were viewed as work animals. They ate and they worked, performing tasks on the farm and also in transportation. The population did not see them as frivolous objects that could be raced for fun. The motherland in Europe—France—did not send horses to Quebec for racing purposes. In France racing was an activity of royalty. During the French Revolution the rebels who brought down the royalty purposely killed all the racehorses in France, as they were a symbol of autocracy. There the activity of racing was lost for generations and also lost as an activity that could be exported to cousins in North America. By the time of the American Revolution, Quebec was part of a British colonial system. Some French farmers experimented in developing trotters; however, most of these horses were sold to be run in the United States. Nonetheless, a horse track opened in Montreal in 1828. Most of the thoroughbreds running in Montreal were initially from the United States. In 1836, however, King William IV of England commissioned a flat race (alternatively called the King's Plate and Queen's Plate) for Canadian-bred horses. Montreal remained the center of Canadian racing for a quarter-century.

Ontario (Upper Canada) developed steeplechases, as an elite aristocratic population familiar with fox hunting had migrated northward during the American Revolution. With increased populations, Ontario turned its sights to thoroughbreds. In 1860 the Toronto Jockey Club was able to persuade racing officials and horse owners to move the Queen's Plate race to the Woodbine Track, where the race is still run. The Civil War in the United States years saw many horses from the South being moved into Ontario. More Canadian tracks developed. Canadian racing also received a boost when moral authority in the United States caused much racing to be declared illegal in all but a few states in the first decade of the twentieth century. This boost, which had resulted in many small Canadian tracks' being opened, also brought in many corrupting elements. An epidemic of rigged races and other untoward practices resulted in Canada's banning racetrack betting in the 1920s. In the 1930s racing was revived with a pari-mutuel system of betting in place.

In the United States, racing had a revival after the Revolutionary War, with most of the action being found in the South. Kentucky established itself as the premier location for horse breeding. Newly settled Western areas attracted racing interests. The era brought an end to long endurance races, as one-mile dashes and quarter-mile runs became popular. Quasi-official "stud books" were initiated to record the identities of all racing horses.

The Civil War devastated racing in the South. Only in the border state of Kentucky did racing continue without interruption. In the meantime, New York reestablished its earlier predominance in the sport. The Saratoga track opened in 1863 and became the country's leading facility. Major stakes races were started, the first being the Travers Stakes run at Saratoga in 1864. Three new stakes races took on the aura of America's Triple Crown. These were the Belmont Stakes, first run in New York City in 1867; the Preakness, first run at Baltimore's Pimlico Track in 1873; and the Kentucky Derby, which had its initial run at Louisville's Churchill Downs in 1875.

In 1894 the Jockey Club of New York was formed by the leading horse owners. The club set down rules for all thoroughbred racing, and the next year the state legislature decreed that the rules would be enforced on all tracks. Other states'

lawmakers also accepted the New York Jockey Club's rules for their own tracks. The Jockey Club also took over the American Stud Book and thereby made it the universal book of registry for all thoroughbreds in the country. The rules and organization of regulation helped racetrack betting survive in New York at the turn of the century, whereas it was being rendered illegal in most other states. In Kentucky racing survived with state intervention in the form of the creation of the first state racing commission in the United States in 1906.

A wave of reform at the turn of the twentieth century that led to the demise of lotteries and the closing of casinos in New Mexico Territory and Arizona Territory and the state of Nevada also brought most racing to a standstill. Kentucky and Maryland survived as the only states allowing horse race betting through the reform era; policy in New York vacillated between tolerance and prohibition. Racing began its comeback in the 1920s and 1930s as states looked toward the gambling activity as a source for taxation revenues. The charge for a return to racing was helped with the introduction of the pari-mutuel system, as it centralized all betting, facilitating both control and also the extraction of taxation. Florida opened the Hialeah racetrack in 1925. A course opened in 1929 at Agua Caliente, Baja California, near Tijuana, serving the desires of California bettors before that state joined nine other states in legalizing pari-mutuel betting in 1933.

Other innovations also strengthened the growth of the sport. Power starting gates ensured that all horses were given an even beginning. Saliva tests were developed that could ensure that horses were not drugged. They were first used at Saratoga in 1932. In 1936 the photo finish was first used. The popularity of racing was also facilitated by illegal betting, which was encouraged by national bookie organizations that used wire services to instantaneously send information across the country to local street bookies and bookie shops.

During World War II racing remained a sport demanding public attention. Two horses, Count Fleet and Citation, won the Triple Crown in 1943 and 1948, respectively. Their presence made racing

Running to the finish line.

activity common conversation throughout the land. Horse racing peaked in the 1950s and 1960s with performances of star thoroughbreds such as Nashau, Swaps, and Native Dancer.

In 1966 Walter D. Osborne wrote, "The United States today is in the midst of the greatest boom in horseflesh since the invention of the gasoline engine" (Osborne 1966, p.11). What goes up sometimes comes down, however, and since the end of the 1960s, horse racing has been in a steady decline. Attendance at races has plunged drastically, and betting at on-track pari-mutuel windows has suffered accordingly. In the last three decades betting on racing at the tracks has gone from being the most popular form of gambling, with almost a legal monopoly of gambling activities in the United States, to being a very small sector of legal gambling—producing revenues under 8 percent of all legal gambling revenues. Only two factors have saved the betting sport from almost certain oblivion: (1) the introduction of revenues gained from off-track wagering and telephone betting and (2) the introduction of revenues from other gambling activity taking place on tracks and in

card rooms (Hollywood Park, California), gambling machines (six states and four provinces), and sports betting (Tijuana).

There have been many suggestions for why racing has declined. Many have suggested that racing lost its edge by clinging to old "proven" methods that worked in an atmosphere of no competition. Racing rejected opportunities to put its entertainment products on television as that media swept American culture in the 1950s and 1960s. Other professional sport events rushed to television. The public gave endorsements to baseball, football, and basketball as never before.

The baby boom generation that began to reach the age of majority in the 1960s did not relate to horses as did their fathers, or grandfathers. They were more focused upon automobiles as their form of transportation. More important, this emerging and now middle-aged generation was action oriented. Its members wanted their entertainment now, and they wanted entertainment to be constant. They did not see the excitement in watching horses run at a twenty-five-mile-per-hour clip for two minutes and then having to sit for thirty minutes before the action began again. They might ask why a sports fan would prefer horse racing to an auto race where cars spin around a track at 200 miles per hour for several hours.

The entertainment consumer of the latter part of the twentieth century did not want to have to devote time and energy to understanding what he or she was watching. It was not easy to understand the fine points of horse racing—that is, understanding enough for becoming a reasonably astute bettor-handicapper. When other forms of gambling—lottery, most casino games—became available to these consumers, their desire for racing products naturally declined.

Gaming competition is generally considered to be the major factor in the decline of racing. Additional factors surrounding the decline include the declining and aging condition of racing facilities—stands, betting areas, rest rooms. The tax "reform" legislation in the mid-1980s also took investment incentives away from businesspeople interested in racing.

The decline also fed upon itself, as prizes for horse race winners were taken from a betting pool. As bets were reduced in size, so too was money available for prizes. Lower prize money discouraged investors and also kept many from entering their horses into races. The quality of racing was affected as lesser-quality entries were led to the post gates. In turn, public interest in racing lessened again. The state (and provincial) governments made the situations worse as they often responded to lower betting activity by increasing their tax take from the betting pool. This not only affected prizes but also made the return for bettors less desirable, hence reducing the incentive for betting.

Although tracks realize these factors, they find that reforms are at best stopgap measures only allowing them to barely survive. They must run faster and faster just to stay in place.

Types of Races

In addition to races of various distances and races for certain kinds of horses (races for mares only, races for horses that have never won before—called maiden races, or races only for two-year-olds or for three-year-olds), there are four basic kinds of races: claiming races, allowance races, handicap races, and stakes races.

Claiming Races

Most races are claiming races. An owner who puts a horse into a claiming race is, in effect, putting the horse up for sale. Registered persons can claim the horse for a price equal to the purse of the race. The claimers must present cash or a certified check to a race official before the race starts. If two or more persons claim the same horse, a roll of the dice decides who purchases the horse. The ownership of the horse changes when the race begins; however, the old owner retains the purse for the race if the horse is a winner. Claiming races are a mechanism for selling horses that have not met the expectations of their owners. The prices received for the horses are generally below those that are exchanged in horse auctions.

Allowance Races

Allowance races are usually a step above claiming races in quality. The track secretary accepts applications for entry and then balances the qualifying horses by adding or subtracting weights carried by individual horses. For horses that have performed well in the past, winning races and bigger purses, weights are added to the saddles, making the horse have to work harder in the race. Horses that have not won or have won only maiden races or claiming races might be able to take weight loads off. The weights are assigned by a specific formula. There could be as much as a ten-pound difference or more between the horses with the best and worst records.

Handicap Races

As in allowance races, the track secretary assigns extra weights to favored horses in handicap races. The weights, however, are assigned not according to a fixed formula but in accordance with how the secretary feels the horse would perform without extra weights. The secretary is seeking to truly make the contest "a horse race," that is, a race in which all horses stand relatively the same chances for reaching the finish wire in the lead. In handicap races, the trainers and jockeys know that the racing secretary is seeking to have a balanced race. Therefore, if they gain a very large lead in the race, they tend to adopt a strategy of holding back somewhat so their victory will not appear as large as it otherwise could be. By winning closely instead of running away with the race, they win favor with the secretary, who may not assign as much weight to them in the next race run by the horse.

Stakes Races

The most important races are stakes races. In these races the owners pay a set of fees beginning at the time they apply to enter a horse in the race, then another fee when the track secretary accepts their entry, and a subsequent fee or fees when they appear at the track on the day of the race. All the fees are added into the purse. The leading stakes race in the United States is the Kentucky Derby; other races such as in the Breeder's Cup series have large fees. The entrant to the Kentucky Derby may incur fees as large as several hundred thousand dollars. The track may also add money into the purse for a stakes race. These races attract the best horses, and they all run carrying the same weights. Most run all out and seek to win by the biggest margins possible. Strong wins in stakes races can be translated into very good prices if the owners wish to sell the horse and also for stud services if the horse is retired.

In all the races mares are given a five-pound discount—that is, they run with a weight load five pounds lighter than all the other horses in stakes races or claiming races, or five pounds less than they would otherwise carry in allowance or handicap races. There are special races just for mares; however, there are no races that are exclusively for stallions.

Racing Participants

Owners

Owners of horses purchase horses and cover all costs for their maintenance and training, as well as track entry fees for stakes races. Although owners may be serious businesspeople who see racing as a way of accumulating wealth, few owners can actually make money in horse racing. Costs for maintaining a racehorse approximate $30,000 a year,

whereas the average racehorse achieves winnings that are below $10,000. In the past, racing attracted many moderately successful businesspeople who calculated the excitement of being in the "racing game" and assumed there would be losses but that the losses could be subtracted from their business income for tax advantages. The 1986 tax reforms made such write-offs much more difficult; hence many otherwise willing businesspeople moved out of racing. Racing also attracts the rich, who wish to be in the game without serious qualms about losses they might incur because their horses cannot win races. Some of these owners willingly pay the very high fees to have their horses in the major stakes races, thus giving the best fields of horses several "sure losers," running against odds of 50–1, 60–1, 70–1, or even greater. But then, maybe one out of seventy times their horses can score a major upset. The winning owners are given 80 percent of the purse of the race if their horses are winners. In most cases, to be a winner—of some of the purse—the horse must finish in one of the first four spots. In major races, part of the purse may go to the fifth-place horse. One of the major jobs of the owner is to select a trainer for the horse.

Trainers

The trainer is in charge of the horse twenty-four hours a day, every day. He or she has been called the "Captain of the Stable" (Scott 1968, 47). The trainer is responsible for doing everything that gets the horse ready to come to the track and race, makes decisions regarding the races in which the horse will run, and advises owners when to sell the horse or when to buy horses. Of course, in these decisions—and the decision to put a horse into a claiming race—he or she must have the approval and confidence of the owner. Usually if there is not a good relationship when these major decisions are made, the trainer will refuse to work for the owner. The trainer picks the facilities for training and keeping the horse and also makes another big decision: He or she chooses the jockey for the races. A trainer receives 10 percent of the purses won by the horses he or she has trained, as well as fees from the horse owner for the activities involved.

Jockeys

Jockeys have to be small, or at least light in weight. The upper weight of a jockey should be less than 120 pounds. There are no real qualifications for getting a job as a jockey other than size. Most jockeys just appear at tracks and ask for the work. They are first given menial tasks around the stalls. A person who shows the appropriate amount of dedication, wins the support of stable personnel, and, most important, can get close to a trainer or assistant trainer may move toward being a jockey. The first step in that movement would be to become an "exercise boy." This is a low-status job consisting of walking a horse, either for exercise or for cool downs after an exercise run or race. When the jockey is able to get mounts for races, he or she must usually start with horses that are not expected to win. The jockey is given a minimal fee for running each race in addition to 10 percent of the purse. On the other hand, jockeys incur expenses. They must invest in all their equipment and outfits including boots, pants, and saddles. They do not have to pay for the specific colors they wear, as these represent the owner. The job of the jockey is very dangerous, and often careers are cut very short with small or major injuries. Many jockeys return to earlier roles such as that of being an exercise boy or being a groom—essentially a stable hand. Others, of course, become very famous. Those in the latter category use agents who also take part of their winnings.

Race Officials at the Track

Stewards

Every race meet at a track has three stewards. One is appointed by the track—that is, the racing association; another by the state racing commission; and a third by the local jockey club. The three are essentially the "supreme court" of the track. They resolve all disputes arising from races. They also enforce rules, certify the identification of horses, and conduct investigations into any perceived misconduct. For instance, if horses do not run up to their performance, or if a long shot mysteriously finishes in the lead, the stewards will examine the matter closely. They also authorize drug tests for horses, either with reason or on a random basis. All winning horses must be subjected to saliva and urine tests after races. Stewards are empowered to fine or suspend jockeys or trainers for misconduct. Their suspension takes effect on all tracks in the country.

The Racing Secretary

The track secretary creates the races. He or she seeks out the horses and in allowance and handicap races is the one who assigns weights to horses. The goal is to produce races that are well matched and even. Sometimes when strong favorites are selected for races, the secretary will use considerable powers of persuasion with trainers and owners to fill a field of horses. The secretary also arranges for stable accommodations for the racehorses.

The Paddock Judge

The paddock is the area between the stables and the track. The grooms bring the horses out of the stable and walk them around the paddock ring for the entire world—the owners, bettors, and officials—to see. After a walk around the ring the jockeys mount the horse, and again they walk around the ring. Then they walk off to the track. The paddock judge inspects each horse, examining its appearance, markings, and a tattoo on its lip in order to ensure that there is no "ringer" in the race. In the history of racing, substitute horses have many times been secretly put into the field in order to give selected insiders betting advantages.

The Starter

The starter oversees the entrance of the horses into their starting gates. He encourages the jockeys and grooms to settle the horses down and to ready them for the start. When he is satisfied that all the horses are set, he pushes the button that releases the gate, and "they're off."

Patrol Judges

Each track has at least four patrol judges who closely watch all facets of the race. They watch to see if one horse bumps another or one jockey commits unfair actions, such as grabbing another horse or prodding his mount illegally. They alert other officials to examine a film of the race if they discern irregularities. They also help the steward resolve complaints registered by race participants.

Placing Judges

Three judges watch the finish line and independently declare which horse finishes first, second, third, and fourth (or fifth if that spot is "in the money.") If they do not have a unanimous agreement, they request a photo of the finish. They also seek photos if the race is close for any of the four positions.

Track Veterinarians

There are veterinarians at each track. The official one must certify that each horse is physically able to compete in the race. He determines that no illegal drugs have been put into the system of the horses if he suspects they might have been.

The Racing Hall of Fame and Museum

The National Museum of Racing and the Thoroughbred Racing's Hall of Fame have been established and located in Saratoga Springs, New York, near the historic Saratoga track. The museum opened its doors in 1950, and the Hall of Fame was created at the site in 1955. As of 1998, the most recent year for which statistics are available, the Hall of Fame included 154 thoroughbreds, 77 jockeys, and 71 trainers. They are selected by a special panel of 125 experts from nominations made by leading media writers and commentators (www.Hall.racingmuseum.org). Among the leading members of the Hall of Fame are the following horses and competitors.

A Selected List of Leading Thoroughbred Horses

Affirmed

Affirmed, the great-grandson of Native Dancer, won the Triple Crown in 1978 under the saddle of Steve Cauthen. In a three-year career, Affirmed won twenty-two of twenty-nine races and finished out of the money only one time. Affirmed was owned by Louis Wolfson and trained at his Harbor View Farm in Florida. As two-year-olds, Affirmed and Alydar began a series of ten races that captured the attention of all horse enthusiasts. They raced six times as two-year-olds, with Affirmed victorious four times. As three-year-olds, Affirmed finished first and Alydar second in all Triple Crown races—the only time two horses have done

that. In a subsequent race, Affirmed won again but was disqualified. Affirmed also finished his Triple Crown year with a loss to the previous year's Triple Crown winner, Seattle Slew, and then had an out-of-the-money finish in a race where his saddle slipped. Nonetheless, Affirmed was proclaimed to be the horse of the year. As a four-year-old he repeated the honor of being horse of the year.

Cigar

Cigar ran to nineteen victories in thirty-three starts over a four-year career. His mark of fame came in 1996 as a six-year-old when he galloped to his sixteenth consecutive win, tying a record set by Citation. Cigar was raised at Allen Paulsen's Brookside Farm in Kentucky, after being born in Maryland. He was the great-grandson of Northern Dancer. The future record-running horse did not race until he was three years old, and he bypassed the Triple Crown. He won only two of nine races as a three-year-old, and it was discovered that he had chips in the bones of each knee. Arthroscopic surgery corrected the trouble, but he still won only two of six races as a four-year-old. The wins were his last two races that year, and they were the beginning of a streak. In 1995 in the Donn Handicap, his leading challenger was Holy Bull, the horse of the year for 1994. Holy Bull took a misstep and incurred a career-ending injury. Critics discounted Cigar's victory even though he was leading when Holy Bull's accident happened. Soon, however, Cigar was defeating other "Grade I" fields in the Pimlico Special Handicap, the Massachusetts Handicap, and the Hollywood Gold Cup Handicap, also the Woodward Stakes, the Jockey Gold Cup, and most impressively, the 1995 Breeder's Cup Classic. The season was a perfect ten for ten, and Cigar's winning streak was at twelve. Cigar won horse of the year honors as well as the Eclipse Award as the older male champion. In 1996 Cigar raced to four straight victories at the Dubai World Cup, the Donn Handicap, the Massachusetts Handicap, and the Arlington Citation Challenge. That sixteenth win came in a race especially created for a national television audience.

Cigar tied Citation's record, but the chance for seventeen victories in a row was lost when his jockey, Jerry Bailey, could not slow his pace, and he succumbed to exhaustion and a second-place finish three and a half lengths behind Dare and Go in the Pacific Classsic at Del Mar. He won one more time before being turned out to stud. His career produced prizes of $9,999,815. The prize money was his crowning glory, as he was a failure at stud. He was sterile. Cigar was moved to the Kentucky Horse Park in Lexington so that his many admiring fans could come and look him over—another kind of pleasurable retirement.

Citation

Citation, a bay colt, won the Triple Crown for Calumet Farms in 1948. He competed four years: 1947, 1948, 1950, and 1951. He ran 45 times, with 32 firsts, 10 seconds, 2 thirds, and only 1 out-of-the-money run. Injuries kept Citation off the track in 1949, and the horse never regained his Triple Crown form afterwards, but his owner, Warren Wright, requested that he keep running in order to become the first one-million-dollar purse winner. He did that for his owner, retiring in the middle of the 1951 season. In the course of his race career, Citation put together a string of sixteen wins, a record that held for over five decades until it was equaled by Cigar. Citation was a horse with both speed and staying power and a "killer's instinct" that craved victory.

Count Fleet

Count Fleet ran only two years, competing in 21 races, winning 16, placing second in 4, and third in 1. Among Count Fleet's victories were the Triple Crown races in 1943, in which he was ridden by the legendary Johnny Longden. Count Fleet was the offspring of the 1928 Kentucky Derby winner, Reigh Count, and Quickly, a sprint filly. Because he had suffered a hoof injury during the Wood Memorial, Count Fleet was challenged by several horses in the Kentucky Derby. He was still the favorite, and he won over Blue Swords by three lengths. That did it for most of the others. Only three challengers showed up at the Preakness, where he galloped to a win over Blue Swords by eight lengths. That made the Belmont only a three-horse race, and Count Fleet flew by the competition, winning with a twenty-five-length lead, unsurpassed in any Triple Crown event until

Secretariat's Belmont run of 1973. Count Fleet's time was a record for the Belmont, and he actually won with an injured ankle. He was immediately retired to stud. There he continued his greatness, as he became racing's leading sire. He fathered thirty-eight stakes winners, as well as female offspring that produced another 119 stakes winners, including Kelso. Count Fleet was retired from stud in 1966 and lived until age thirty-three, dying in 1973.

Eclipse

The "first champion" English thoroughbred, Eclipse, was foaled in 1764. Eclipse was a great-great-grandson of Darley Arabian. He began training and racing at age five and ran matched heats of four miles each. He won every race he entered, but his true fame is for posterity. Over 80 percent of all racing thoroughbreds today can trace their bloodlines to this champion.

John Henry

John Henry started 83 races over an eight-year career. He won 39 and was second 15 times while amassing $6,591,860 in prizes. He was not a fast starter as a career horse. While a three-year-old, he was purchased sight unseen for $25,000. He was born in 1975 at Kentucky's Golden Chance Farm, and seemingly no one wanted the horse. In 1980, however, he hit his stride as he won 6 straight stakes races. In 1981, he won 8 of his 10 starts. In the most recognized of his runs that year, he was ridden by Bill Shoemaker as he won the first Arlington Million. John Henry won the Eclipse Award for older horses and also was named horse of the year. Over the next two years, injuries kept his starts down, but in 1984 he returned to prominence with 6 victories in 9 races. In 1985 he retired to the Kentucky Horse Park, as the leading money winner of all time.

Kelso

In 1960 Kelso was voted the champion male three-year-old and also the horse of the year. He won 8 of 9 races. The honors came even though he did not run that year until after the Triple Crown cycle had ended. But once running, he kept running for six more years, amassing a total of 39 victories, 31 in stakes races, as well as 12 seconds in his 63 starts. He won $1,977,896 in prizes. Kelso was durable, winning a record five designations as horse of the year. He also set track records at eight different courses. Often he ran with the disadvantage of extra weights as race organizers tried to give the competition a chance. Kelso was born in 1957 on the Claiborne Farm of Paris, Kentucky. He retired after running only one start in 1966 at the age of nine. He lived to be twenty-six, dying at the du Pont's Woodstock Farm in Maryland in 1983.

Man O'War

Man O'War was designated to be the greatest horse of the twentieth century by *Blood-Horse Magazine*. All agree that he was the "super horse" of 1919 and 1920, winning all of his eleven races the latter year. As he was not entered in the Kentucky Derby, he did not achieve the Triple Crown. Nonetheless Man O'War, called "Big Red," is still considered by some to be the greatest racehorse in history. In his two-year career he had twenty first-place finishes and only one second place. His second-place finish came in the 1919 Sanford Stakes. He lost to a decided underdog by the name of Upset. As a result of that race a new word, *upset,* was introduced into the vocabulary of sports enthusiasts and applied to victories by underdogs. Man O'War's record of twenty victories in twenty-one starts has only once been surpassed. In his final race, the Kenilworth Gold Cup, he defeated Sir Barton, the previous year's Triple Crown winner, by seven lengths. Man O'War also was accomplished in stud, as he fathered War Admiral, the Triple Crown winner of 1937. Man O'War lived to be thirty. He died in 1947, and his funeral was broadcast by radio to the nation. The site of his grave, now at the Kentucky Horse Park, is marked by a 3,000-pound sculptured likeness.

Native Dancer

In 1952 as a two-year-old, Native Dancer ran to nine straight victories, sharing horse of the year honors with One Count. Native Dancer was born on the Scott Farm near Lexington, Kentucky, in March 1950, and he was raised on his owner's— Alfred Vanderbilt's—Sagamore Farm in Maryland. He won his first race at Jamaica in April 1952, and his second race only four days later. The speed of his entries was probably a training error, as he had to be rested for three months with bruised shins. He again picked up his frantic pace, however, winning the Flash Stakes at Saratoga and then three more victories within the next three weeks. He added four more victories before the end of the season. In 1953 he picked up the pace with two more victories in the Gotham Stakes and the Wood Memorial. He became the heavy odds-on favorite to win the Kentucky Derby going away. That victory proved to be elusive, however. In the first turn of the race he was bumped by a long shot, and he ended up in heavy traffic. Finally he burst loose from the crowd and charged at the leader, Dark Star, gaining on him all the way. Alas, "all the way" was not long enough; the finish line came too soon. Native Dancer finished second by a head. Two weeks later, Native Dancer defeated Dark Star and the field in the Preakness. He kept on winning—the Belmont Stakes, the Dwyer Stakes at Aqueduct, the Arlington Classic, and the Travers Stakes. At age four, he added three more victories, and he was designated as the horse of the year, after which he was retired. He had won a record twenty-one of twenty-two races. At stud at Sagamore Farm, he sired forty-four stakes winners, including Kentucky Derby winner Kauai King. Native Dancer was the grand sire of Mr. Prospector—the greatest sire of all time, and he also sired the mother of Canada's greatest horse, Northern Dancer. Native Dancer died in 1967.

Secretariat

Secretariat was a very strong chestnut colt born on 30 March 1970. He was known as "Big Red," the same nickname as Man O'War had. Secretariat's father was Bold Ruler, horse of the year in 1957, and his mother Somethingroyal, a horse who never ran a race. The greatest horse of the last half-century was owned by the Penny Chenery and Meadows Stable and carried blue and white colors. He was trained by Lucien Laurin and ridden by jockey Ron Turcotte. As a two-year-old he lost his first race but then showed dominance in the next eight runs, winning all but the last, which he lost as a result of a disqualification. He was named horse of the year in 1972, the first two-year-old to win the honor. In 1973, he was ready for the Triple Crown. His warm-up races went fine until he had a weak performance in the Woodward Memorial owing to a painful abscess. Although many doubted that he had the stamina, he was ready for the Kentucky Derby. He won going away with a Derby record time, 1:59:40, the only time a horse has run the one and one-quarter miles under two minutes. In the Preakness he won by two and a half lengths, in what would have been a record time had the track clock functioned. His competition was intimidated. There were only five horses in the Belmont. Secretariat left them in the dust, winning by a phenomenal thirty-one lengths, in a record time of 2:24, more than two seconds faster than the track record. His final race was at the Canadian International at Woodbine Track in Toronto, after which he again was named horse of the year. He retired to stud at Claiborne Farm in Lexington, where in addition to the mares, he attracted over 10,000 visitors a year until he died in 1989. The source of Secretariat's extraordinary stamina was discovered after his death, when an autopsy revealed that his heart was 50 percent larger than normal size.

Leading Thoroughbred Jockeys

Eddie Arcaro

Eddie Arcaro was born in Cincinnati in 1916. He ran his first race at the age of fifteen in Cleveland, but he had to wait almost a year for his first victory, which came at the Agua Caliente track in Tijuana. He soon won a contract to ride exclusively for Calumet Farms and then with the Greentree Stable of the Whitney Family. In 1946 he became an independent. Arcaro was the first and only jockey to have mounted two Triple Crown winners—Whirlaway in 1941 and Citation in 1948. Over a career of thirty years he ran 24,092 races, winning 4,779 of them and finishing in the money almost 12,000 times. He won the Kentucky Derby five times, the Preakness and the Belmont six times each. His success was earned with a riding style that seemed to have horse and rider always as one. It also came from the quality of his many mounts: Kelso—five times horse of the year, Bold Ruler, Native Dancer, Nashua, and of course, the two Triple Crown winners.

Jerry Bailey

Jerry Bailey was born in Dallas in 1957. He was drawn into racing when his father purchased several horses at claiming races. Bailey started racing quarter horses when he was only twelve. When he was seventeen, he turned to thoroughbreds and took his first mount in a professional race. He has been racing ever since and doing very well. Three times he has been selected as the winner of the Eclipse Award for jockey of the year. He won two Kentucky Derbys with Sea Hero in 1993 and Grindstone in 1996. He also rode nine winners in Breeder's Cup races. In 1995, he was inducted into the racing Hall of Fame. One of his most notable claims to fame came as the jockey who rode Cigar in 1994 and 1995, as the horse was horse of the year both years. Bailey has been the president of the Jockeys' Guild. He is still an active rider in 2001.

Steve Cauthen

Steve Cauthen became a sports "phenom" as a teenager. He was named *Sports Illustrated* Sportsman of the Year in 1977 at the age of seventeen. Steve began riding when he was only five. He began racing in 1976, immediately setting track records. At River Downs he won ninety-four races in his first fifty days of racing. From there he moved on to Arlington Park, Aqueduct, and Belmont. In his second year, records continued to fall as he won a record $6.1 million in purses. But the best came in 1978 as he guided Affirmed to the Triple Crown. He was the youngest jockey ever to win any Triple Crown race. In 1979, however, he experienced a losing streak and then accepted an offer to move to England, where he rode for the rest of his career. While fighting weight problems and also alcohol dependency, he was still able to win, becoming the number-one English rider in 1984, 1985, and 1987. A severe fall in 1988 kept him out of action for most of a season; nevertheless he returned to race for another year, after which he retired at age thirty. He moved back to his home state of Kentucky, where he raises horses.

Angel Cordero

Angel Cordero Jr. was born on 8 May 1942 in Santurce, Puerto Rico. In a career of thirty-one years he registered 7,057 wins in 38,646 starts and won purses totaling $164 million. He is fourth on the all-time list for numbers of winners. His wins included three at the Kentucky Derby, two at the Preakness, and one at the Belmont Stakes. He also had four winners in Breeder's Cup races, with over $6 million in Breeder's Cup earnings. Cordero was named the Eclipse Award winner two times, in 1982 and 1983. An inspirational figure, he once remarked "If a horse has four legs, and I'm riding it, I think I can win" (www.cybernation.com).

But he could not win them all. In 1992 he retired after almost dying in a spill at Aqueduct track in New York. He then became an agent and trainer. Tragedy struck the Corderos again in January 2001, when Angel's wife, Marjorie, was killed in a hit-and-run accident while jogging at night. Marjorie herself had been a very popular jockey, winning seventy-one races between 1982 and 1985 (www.canoe.ca).

Pat Day

Pat Day was born on 13 October 1953 in Brush, Colorado. He was drawn into racing after competing in high school and amateur rodeos. He thought he should turn to racing because of his slight build. At age nineteen he moved to California and started riding thoroughbreds. He won his first race in 1973. Since then he has had more than 7,000 wins, including the Kentucky Derby aboard Lil E. Tee in 1992, the Preakness five times, and the Belmont twice. He has also become the leading winner among Breeder's Cup race jockeys with eleven wins. He has led the country in number of wins six different times. He won the Eclipse Award for being the leading jockey in 1984, 1986, 1987, and 1991. He was inducted into the racing Hall of Fame in 1991. He is ranked third in all-time winning among jockeys, and in 2001 he is still racing.

Bill Hartack

Bill Hartack was born in Blacklick Valley, Pennsylvania, in 1932. He took up riding in his late teenage years, and in a professional career from 1952 to 1974 he won 4,272 races, capturing purses of $26 million. His many winners included five mounts at the Kentucky Derby, a feat equaled only by Eddie Arcaro. Hartack was the leading winner

in four different years and the leading money winner twice. He was known as a stickler for many details and an antagonist to the press and the general public. He was always at his best while steering his horse around the track and at his worst in the winner's circle, refusing to give interviews and making caustic remarks to those around him. It was reported that he hated the media because they insisted on calling him "Willie." After retirement in 1974 he worked as a steward at California tracks.

Julie Krone

Julie Krone was born in Benton Harbor, Michigan, in 1963. She is a Hall of Fame member with the most all-time wins of any female jockey—3,454. She accomplished this record over an eighteen-year career from 1981 to 1999. Her most notable win was at the Belmont Stakes. She is the only woman to win a Triple Crown race. She also matched Angel Cordero's and Ron Turcotte's record of having five winners on the same day at Saratoga. Besides winning the Belmont, Krone rode winners in the Arlington Classic, Meadowlands Cup, Jersey Derby, Carter Handicap, and Delaware Handicap. Her career was marred by several accidents that eventually led to her retirement in 1999. The next year she was elected to the Hall of Fame.

Johnny Longden

Johnny Longden was born in England in 1907. He was raised in Canada. He became the leading jockey of his era. He was the first jockey to win 6,000 races; by the end of his riding career at the age of fifty-nine in 1966 he had won 6,032 races. This stood as a record until Willie Shoemaker surpassed the number in 1970. Longden's purses totaled $24.6 million. His most notable achievement was riding Count Fleet to the Triple Crown in 1943. His career demonstrated his great spirit and love of horses. He broke both arms, both legs, both ankles, feet, and collarbones in racing accidents along with six ribs and several vertebrae. His arthritis slowed him down enough to cause his retirement as a jockey. But his maladies could not keep him away from the track. Three years after retiring as a rider he was a trainer, leading Majestic Prince to a Kentucky Derby win. He is the only person to have Kentucky Derby wins as both a jockey and a trainer. But there was more—he was also Majestic Prince's exercise boy, groom, and stable-cleaner.

Laffit Pincay

Laffit Pincay is now the jockey with the most wins in history, having reached the plateau of 8,034 races in December 1999. He passed Willie Shoemaker's accomplishments in a thirty-five-year period. Pincay was born in Panama City, Panama, on 29 December 1946. He started racing professionally at the Presidente Ramon racetrack in Panama at age seventeen. Two years later he moved to the United States. Success followed as he became the all-time leading jockey at Hollywood Park, Santa Anita, and Del Mar. One day he rode a record seven races at Santa Anita. He led the nation in jockey earnings seven times, and in five years he was given the Eclipse Award as the top jockey. He biggest win came at the 1984 Kentucky Derby. He also won the Belmont Stakes three times in a row and had seven wins in Breeder's Cup races. He took several spills with his victories, showing great fortitude. He broke his collarbones eleven times and his ribs ten times; he had two spinal fractures, two broken thumbs, and a sprained ankle. He is still racing in 2001, riding in his twentieth Kentucky Derby; some suggest he is hoping to win 10,000 races (www.canoe.ca).

Willie Shoemaker

Willie Shoemaker was born in 1931 in Fabens, Texas, moving to California as a child, where he started riding. At age seventeen he rode in his first professional race, and after a month he rode his first winner. By age twenty-two he had ridden a record 485 wins in a single year. He just kept winning and winning. On six occasions he won six races in a single day. In 1970 he passed Johnny Longden as the leading winner as he rode across the finish line in first place for the 6,033d time. By the end of his forty-one-year riding career in 1990 he had ridden 8,833 winners. In ten different years he was the leading money winner among jockeys. Overall he produced purse wins of $123 million for his mounts, being the first jockey to have wins of over $100 million. He won 1,009 stakes races. On four occasions he won the Kentucky Derby, the last time in 1986 at age fifty-four. He was the oldest jockey ever to win the race. He also had two wins in the Preakness and five wins in the Belmont stakes. After retiring, he became a trainer. His career success came at serious costs. He suffered broken legs and hips from falls during races. His most devastating injury came in a car accident in 1991, however, the year after he retired as a rider. The accident left him paralyzed below the neck. He continued an advisory role until 1997 as a trainer at Santa Anita, where he had had so many victories over his career.

Ron Turcotte

Ron Turcotte will always be known as the jockey who rode the great Secretariat to the Triple Crown in 1973. But he did more than just that outstanding feat. He also won the Kentucky Derby and Belmont aboard Riva Ridge in 1972, giving him five of six Triple Crown race victories in two years. He also rode Tom Rolfe to victory in the Preakness in 1965, and he rode Northern Dancer as a two-year-old. Turcotte was a French Canadian, born in Drummond, New Brunswick, on 22 June 1941. He was one of twelve children. He dropped out of school at the age of thirteen in order to work as a logger. In that work, he began to ride horses. As a result, he was drawn to racetracks and set his sights on becoming a jockey, but he had to work up to it. He moved to Toronto and its Woodbine track in 1959 and started cleaning stables, then walking horses, and then giving them work-out rides. In 1961 he became an apprentice jockey. Success followed each step of the way. In 1962 he had 180 wins, and in 1963 he was the leading Canadian jockey. In that year he also began racing in the United States at Laurel and Saratoga. His U.S. career received a big boost with his Preakness win on Tom Rolfe, and he was hired to ride for Meadows Stable, where he was given the reins of Secretariat when the horse was a two-year-old and won horse of the year honors. He retired in 1978 and was elected to the Hall of Fame the next year (www.Hall.racingmuseum.org).

Trainers

Bob Baffert

Bob Baffert was born in Nogales, Arizona, on 13 January 1953. He was a professional jockey before turning to training quarter horses. He trained Gold

Coast Express, the champion quarter horse of 1986, before turning his attention to thoroughbreds. Within his first decade as a thoroughbred trainer he guided the victories of five national champions. He won the Eclipse Award as the leading trainer in 1997. In both 1997 and 1998, he won the first two legs of the Triple Crown with Kentucky Derby and Preakness victories with Silver Charm and Real Quiet. He has also won two Breeder's Cup races. His earnings have already surpassed $25 million.

Jim Fitzsimmons

James E. "Sunny Jim" Fitzsimmons was born in 1874. He began exercising horses when he was ten, and he paid his dues by cleaning stables, grooming horses, and then becoming a jockey. He went on to become one of the most famous trainers of all time, not retiring until he was eighty-nine years old in 1963. In a training career spanning three-quarters of a century, his horses won 2,275 races and purses exceeding $13 million. His most notable claims to fame were his two Triple Crown winners, Gallant Fox in 1930 and Omaha in 1935. He also won the Kentucky Derby with Johnstown in 1939, and trained Eclipse Award winners Bold Ruler, Granville, High Voltage, Misty Morn, Vagrancy, and Nashua. Fitzsimmons was inducted into the Thoroughbred Racing Hall of Fame in 1958. He died at the age of ninety-two in 1966.

Ben Jones

Ben Jones was born in 1882. He spent forty-seven years as a trainer. He was the key figure in building Calumet Farms into the leading owner of winning horses eleven times in the 1940s and 1950s. He trained Triple Crown winner Whirlaway for Calumet, and he took over the general managership of the farm in 1947, just as Citation's racing career began. He gave the reins of Citation to his son Jim, to train for his successful run at the Triple Crown in 1948. Ben Jones produced 1,519 winners as a trainer, earning purses of nearly $5 million. Counting Citation, his six wins at the Kentucky Derby are the most ever for a trainer.

Lucien Laurin

Lucien Laurin trained 1973 Triple Crown winner Secretariat and also 1972 Kentucky Derby and Bel-

mont winner Riva Ridge for the Meadows Stable. His four consecutive victories in Triple Crown races stood as a trainer's record until D. Wayne Lucas won five in a row. Laurin also trained horses that won thirty-two other stakes races. Laurin was born in 1912. He began his career with horses as a jockey, riding 161 winners before he turned to training in 1942. He was an active trainer for forty-five years. Lucien Laurin died in May 2000 at the age of eighty-eight.

D. Wayne Lucas

D. Wayne Lucas was born in Antiga, Wisconsin, in 1935. By the mid-1980s he emerged as the leading contemporary trainer. He has also been important as the purchasing agent selecting several champion horses. Lucas graduated from the University of Wisconsin, where he was also an assistant basketball coach. He began training horses in the late 1960s. Lucas was inducted into the racing Hall of Fame after having been the top money-earning thoroughbred trainer in fourteen different years. His wins have included the Kentucky Derby on four occasions, the Preakness five times, the Belmont, and fifteen Breeder's Cup races. He won the Eclipse Award as the leading trainer in 1985, 1986, 1987, and 1994. In 1994, 1995, and 1996 he set a trainer's record when he won five Triple Crown races.

William I. Mott

William I. Mott was born in Mobridge, South Dakota, in 1953. He started training horses while he was still in high school, winning many races in the unrecognized meets of South Dakota. In 1978 he joined the stable of trainer Jack Van Berg, where he worked until 1986. Then he became the trainer for owners Bert and Diana Firestone before becoming independent. At age forty-five, Mott was the youngest trainer ever to be inducted into the racing hall of fame. His major claim to fame was supported by the record of Cigar—two times the horse of the year. During the 1990s, Mott was the second leading money winner among trainers.

Woody Stevens

Woodford Cefis "Woody" Stephens was born a sharecropper's son on 1 September 1913 in Midway, Florida. He died in 1998 just before his eighty-fifth birthday. Woody Stephens started his career with horses as a jockey in 1930. Ten years later he became a trainer, a trade he continued for fifty-seven years. Stephens's most notable achievement was his five consecutive wins at the Belmont in the 1980s. He also had two Kentucky Derby winners and one Preakness win. He trained eleven national champions—only D. Wayne Lucas trained more. Before Stevens retired in 1997, he was elected to the Hall of Fame in 1976 and was given the Eclipse Award as the leading trainer in 1983.

Charlie Whittingham

Charlie Whittingham was born on 13 April 1913. He lived eighty-six years and came to be known to some as the greatest trainer ever. It was certain that he was the oldest trainer ever to have a Kentucky Derby winner. He was seventy-three when Ferdinand claimed the roses, and he was seventy-six when Sunday Silence was the first to cross the finish line in Louisville. Whittingham's leading rider during his career was Willie Shoemaker. Whittingham followed horses from the age of eight, as his older brother was a jockey. He began training horses in 1934. His sixty-year career brought him three Eclipse Awards as the leading trainer and Hall of Fame induction in 1974. He trained eleven national champions and three horses named as horse of the year—Ack Ack, Ferdinand, and Sunday Silence. He was the all-time most winning trainer at both Santa Anita and Hollywood Park. His amazing career also included a tour of duty with the marines in the South Pacific during World War II. He died in California on 20 April 1999.

Nicholas Zito

Nicholas Zito was born in New York City in 1948. When he was nine years old he started attending the horse races with his father, who had done service as an exercise attendant. At the age of fifteen, Nicholas got a job as a handyman in the racetrack stables. He moved up the career ladder as an exercise boy, then a groom, and slowly worked toward being a trainer. He learned every step of the way. In the early 1970s, he won his opportunity, training his first horse in 1972. But even then success came

slowly. In the 1980s, he teamed up with owner B. Giles Brophy and the keys to success were in his hands. In 1991 he won the Kentucky Derby with Strike the Gold and again in 1994 with Go for Gin. He was only the fifteenth trainer ever to have two Kentucky Derby winners.

Tracks and Track Organizations

Churchill Downs, Inc.

Churchill Downs is the premier thoroughbred racing track in North America. The track is part of a larger organization (Churchill Downs, Inc.) that includes Hollywood Park, Arlington International, Ellis Park, Hoosier Park, and Calder Race Course as well as the Churchill Downs Sports Spectrum (an offtrack facility) and other interests.

Churchill Downs is located within the city of Louisville, Kentucky, close to the bluegrass horse farms that breed a majority of racing stock in the United States. Racing started at Churchill in 1875, and that was also the inaugural year of the Kentucky Derby, the most famous race in the United States and the lead event in the Triple Crown. The Kentucky Derby is run over a one and one-quarter-mile distance. Colonel M. Lewis, who was the president of the track for twenty years, established the race. As racing fell into disrepute around the turn of the twentieth century (as did all gambling-related activities), the Derby declined in prominence. Its rejuvenation became the life work of Matt Winn. Winn had been with the track in 1875 and saw all of the first seventy-five Kentucky Derby races before his death in 1949. The Derby now draws in excess of 150,000 fans each year. The track's icon is its twin spires that were built atop its stands in 1895.

Hollywood Park was organized by the Golden State Jockey Club in 1936 and began offering races on 10 June 1936. Although the 350-acre park and track facility is located in Inglewood, California, it was called Hollywood because its founders included film industry celebrities Jack Warner, Walt Disney, Sam Goldwyn, Al Jolson, and Bing Crosby. The track has been open except for World War II years, when the land was used for military purposes. The track was also closed for the 1949 season owing to a fire that destroyed the grandstand. Today the track is the premier West

In the clubhouse at Churchill Downs—serious players study the racing charts before placing wagers.

Coast racing venue during the summer months with the one-million-dollar Hollywood Gold Cup. The track also has a short fall season. Hollywood Park had the honor of holding the first Breeder's Cup races in 1984. They also hosted the event in 1987 and 1997. In 1994 the facility became a racino, as it opened a cardroom casino (*see* The Racino). Recently the operations were taken over by Churchill Downs, Inc.

In 2000 the Arlington Park International Racetrack was merged into the Churchill Downs Corporation. The Chicagoland Arlington Park has enjoyed a history of glamour and a reputation for elegance. Yet the track that opened in 1927 has had its problems. In 1985 the original grandstand was devastated by fire. Four years later, however, the course made its comeback, reopening with the word "International" in its title and having even more elegant facilities. Arlington track has been a pioneer in several track developments. In 1933 the track installed the first all-electric totalizator that projected ongoing betting activities onto a board that could be followed by patrons. In 1936, the track used the first photo-finish cameras, and in

1940, the first electric starting gates were installed. The track banked its turns in 1942—another first. Arlington also initiated the trifecta bet (a bet on which horses will finish first, second, and third in a race) in 1971. In the same year Arlington began a commercially sponsored race that offered a prize of $100,000. Ten years later, Arlington hosted the first race with a one-million-dollar purse. The inaugural Arlington Million race was won by John Henry. In 1996, Arlington was the site of the Citation Challenge, the race in which Cigar matched Citation's record for sixteen consecutive wins.

Churchill Downs purchased Ellis Park in 1998. The racecourse had been built in 1922 by the Green River Jockey Club. It is located in Henderson County, Kentucky, just across the Ohio River from Evansville, Indiana. The track suffered a decline after the opening of the Aztar Riverboat Casino in Evansville, but with an influx of Churchill capital, it is attempting to increase its viability.

Churchill Downs, Inc., won a license to open Indiana's first racetrack, Hoosier Park, which is located north of Indianapolis in Anderson. The track began racing with standardbreds in 1993.

The paddock at Churchill Downs, the most famous of all racetracks.

The first thoroughbred races were held one year later. The leading race is the Indiana Derby, held in October.

Churchill Downs purchased Florida's leading venue, Calder Race Course, in January 1999 for $86 million. The course had begun operations near Miami in 1970, featuring a special formula track surface designed by the 3M Company. Churchill is dedicated to returning Florida to the glory days of racing that were enjoyed in the mid-twentieth century.

Del Mar

The Del Mar Racetrack is located near the ocean, just north of San Diego. The track's season opens just as Hollywood Park's summer season closes down. The two tracks do have a short overlap of seasons during the Hollywood fall meeting. Del Mar opened on 3 July 1937. The track was founded by Hollywood celebrities Bing Crosby and Pat O'Brien. Many outstanding events have taken place at Del Mar, including a famous match race between Seabiscuit and Ligaroti in 1938 and Bill Shoemaker's 1970 ride for win 6,033—surpassing Johnny Longden's record. New grandstands were built in an $80 million renovation during the early 1990s to make the facility one of the most modern and comfortable in the world. Bing Crosby immortalized the track with his song, "Where the Surf Meets the Turf."

El Comandante

El Comandante is Puerto Rico's only horse racing track. It is located twelve miles east of the San Juan tourist and casino district, on the edge of the Yunque Rain Forest National Park. It is a rare track in that racing is ongoing throughout the year five days a week. In the early twentieth century, there were several tracks in the commonwealth. In 1954, however, the government gave the San Juan Racing Association a monopoly over track operations, and they developed El Comandante in 1959 as a modern facility. A newer facility was built in 1976, offering a one-mile oval, 257 acres of landscaped property, a 65-foot-wide exercise track, and a 12,000-seat six-level grandstand. Eight thousand cars can park in the lot. Puerto Rico offers 675 off-track outlets for online television betting.

Keeneland Race Track and Sales Operations

The Keeneland Race course is in the heart of the Kentucky bluegrass country, just six miles away from Lexington. Keeneland offers a beautiful track with a short season that features the Bluegrass Stakes, an event for three-year-olds that is a warm-up for the Kentucky Derby. Fourteen Derby winners have won the race. Keeneland is also a year-round training facility and a research center with a library collection of 2,000 volumes on pedigrees, breeding, and racing information. The key activity at Keeneland is horse sales. The track holds five sales annually. The January sale is for all horses, the April sale for two-year-olds, a yearlings sale in July and September, and a sale of breeding stock in November. Sales began in the 1930s, but they gained their premier standing during World War II. Prior to the war, horses would be transported by trains from Kentucky farms to Saratoga Springs, New York, for auctions. The military precluded such heavy use of trains during the war, however, and sales activity remained close to the source—at Keeneland. Many stories revolve around the sales. Foals of Northern Dancer sold for over $2.8 million; John Henry was sold for $1,100 in the sale for all ages in 1976 and for $2,200 in 1977. A late bloomer, he commanded only $25,000 as a three-year-old. The gallant steed went on to win $6,591,860 in his amazing career. The Keeneland organization is unique, as it is a non-dividend-paying corporation. All profits are reinvested in capital improvements, used as purses in races, or distributed to charitable or educational operations.

The New York Racing Commission Tracks

The New York Racing Commission owns and operates three major tracks—Saratoga, Belmont, and Aqueduct.

Saratoga Race Course in Saratoga Springs, New York, opened its race card in 1864 to a jampacked crowd of 10,000. The president of the track was William Travers. The first major race at the track was named in his honor—the Travers Stakes. It was originally part of the Triple Crown. A detailed history of the track and also the other gambling (casino) activity of Saratoga Springs is found in Ed Hotaling's book *They're Off,* which is described in the Annotated Bibliography. Saratoga has been known for many of the great surprises of racing. In 1919 Upset defeated Man O'War in the Sanford Stakes at Saratoga. In 1973, Secretariat lost to Orion in the Whitney Stakes. The 1930 Travers Stakes provided that year's only defeat for Triple Crown winner Gallant Fox. That race was won by a 100–1 long shot named Jim Dandy. Until World War II, Saratoga was the leading venue for horse sales; however, transportation restrictions caused that honor to pass to Keeneland.

Belmont Track is the home of the Belmont Stakes, the Triple Crown's last and longest event. Like that race, the track is a one and-a-half-mile oval. The course was named after banker and horseman August Belmont. It opened in 1905 but had to suffer through an era of prohibition on race betting that closed down its 1911 and 1912 seasons. The Belmont Stakes was begun in 1867 and run at Jerome Park and Morris Park before coming to Belmont in 1905. Belmont has undergone several renovations, the major one being a $30 million grand stand construction project in 1968. During the period of construction activity, the Belmont Stakes was run at Aqueduct. Belmont has another mark of historical significance. In 1910, the Wright Brothers held an international air flight tournament at the track and drew 150,000 people.

Aqueduct Racecourse began operations in Queens, New York, in 1894. The track facilities were completely rebuilt in 1959. In 1975 an inner track was designed, and a winter meet is held at that track. The facility runs a summer meeting each season featuring two major handicaps—the Brooklyn Handicap and the Suburban Handicap.

Pimlico

The Pimlico track in Baltimore is the home of the middle race of the Triple Crown—the Preakness. The track opened in 1870. The major race of the 1870 season was the two-mile Dinner Party Stakes, which was won by an impressive colt named Preakness. When a stakes race for three-year-olds was established in 1873, former governor Oden Bowie, the track president, chose to name the race after the popular horse. The Preakness was run at Pimlico between 1873 and 1889. Then for fifteen years the race was moved to the Gravesend track in Brooklyn, New York. From 1889 until 1909, Pimlico racing was confined to standardbred and steeplechase events as scandals touched thoroughbred race gambling. The Maryland Jockey Club brought respectability back to the Baltimore track, and in 1909, they once again held the Preakness. Since 1925 the race has been one and three-sixteenths miles in length. The winner receives the Woodlawn Vase, which was created by the Tiffany Jewelers in 1860. The Pimlico track features sharp turns that have proved to be very demanding for horses that have won other Triple Crown events.

Santa Anita

Santa Anita first began its racing program on Christmas Day 1934. Now it opens each season the day after Christmas. The track offers a very beautiful setting, as it is situated in the San Gabriel Mountains in the city of Arcadia, twenty miles northeast of Los Angeles. The track was founded by the Los Angeles Turf Club led by Dr. Charles Strub. Strub ran the operations until his death in 1958. Santa Anita runs the top stakes races in the country during the winter months. The leading events are the million-dollar Santa Anita Derby and the Santa Anita Handicap. The handicap gained instant fame when it offered a $100,000 purse at its first running in the midst of the Depression years. The race has a list of winners the likes of Spectacular Bid, Affirmed, Seabiscuit, Ack Ack, and two-time winner John Henry. The Santa Anita Derby has been won by eight Kentucky Derby winners, including Sunday Silence, Affirmed, Majestic Hill, and Swaps, the first California-bred horse to win the Churchill classic. Both Johnny Longden and Bill Shoemaker rode their last mounts at Santa Anita, and Laffit Pincay had a record seven wins in one day in 1987. Santa Anita hosted the 1986 and 1993 Breeder's Cup and also the equestrian events for the 1984 Olympic Games. The track facility has been in continuous operation since its 1934 beginnings except for the years of World War II, when it served as the staging area for the removal of Japanese Americans from their homes and into internment camps in the desert. Not all the millions of visitors to Santa Anita over its eight decades have been able to fully appreciate its luxury and elegance during racing seasons—certainly not these unwilling visitors.

Woodbine and the Ontario Jockey Club

Canada's leading race venue, Woodbine, is located northwest of Toronto. It began racing with trotters in 1874. The track was developed on Joseph Duggan's horse farm. As elsewhere, the era found bad elements congregating around the racers. In a reaction against the negative reputation that was gathering, Duggan and others formed the nonprofit Ontario Jockey Club in 1881. The club took over the track. The Ontario Jockey Club has also been active in the operation of other tracks, including Fort Erie and Mohawk.

The Woodbine facility was originally in the city of Toronto. A new facility was built in 1956, however, on the outskirts of the metropolitan area. In 1959 the old track was renovated and became Greenwood Race Course. The Fort Erie track across from Buffalo, New York, was developed by the Ontario Jockey Club, but it was sold to private interests in 1997. Today it is the second thoroughbred track in Ontario. The Mohawk track, twenty-five miles west of the Lester Pearson International Airport at Toronto, offers only standardbred racing. Mohawk is the home of the one-million-dollar North American Cup and the Breeder's Crown, the standardbred version of the Breeder's Cup. Woodbine itself offers seasons of both thoroughbred and standardbred racing. The track was the home for the Breeder's Cup in 1996, but its most famous race was the 1973 Canadian International that was won by Secretariat—the famous steed's last contest. Racing's popularity in Canada has waned somewhat, as it has elsewhere. The Ontario tracks, including Woodbine, have gained economic strength, however, by becoming racinos. The Woodbine facility now operates approximately 2,000 slot machines.

Owners: Farms and Individuals

Brookside Farms/Allen E. Paulson

Iowa native Allen Paulson made his fortune by creating the Gulfstream Aerospace Corporation. Horses have become his passion, and he has his Brookside farms in Kentucky, California, Florida, and Georgia. Since the Breeder's Cup began in 1984,

Paulson has had a horse start in every race. He won the Eclipse Award for top owner in 1995 and 1996 and for top breeder in 1993. His most notable product has been Cigar, horse of the year in 1995.

Calumet Farms

In 1924 William Monroe Wright, a man who made his fortune with Calumet Baking Powder, purchased a horse farm outside of Lexington. He named it after his company. Until his death in 1931, the farm was devoted to the preparation of standardbred horses for racing. Wright was able to produce the winner of the Hambletonian in 1931. His son took over the farm that year and converted it into a thoroughbred racing farm. Warren Wright Sr. had his first major winner with Nellie Flag in 1934. Over the sixty-eight years that the farm was in the Wright family, it became synonymous with winning. In twelve separate years Calumet horses had more wins than those of any other owner. They had eleven years in a row as the leading breeding farm. The farm produced thirty-eight divisional winners of horse of the year designations. Of course, their most notable feats were with Triple Crown winners Whirlaway and Citation. The property was held by Warren Monroe Wright's widow until her death in 1950 and then by their son-in-law until 1992. Substantial economic setbacks caused the farm to be sold at a public auction. It was purchased by Henryk de Kwaitkowski.

Coolmore Stud

The most sought-after studs in the horse industry are found at Coolmore Stud Farm, a 350-acre spread near Lexington, Kentucky, and at the Coolmore facilities on four other continents. The Coolmore operations were established in 1975 as a partnership among owner-breeder Robert Sanster, trainer Dr. Vincent O'Brien, and stallion master John Magnier. The organization uses a dual-continent notion of sending stallions from the Northern Hemisphere to Australia for the Southern Hemisphere breeding season. Fifty stallions are under Coolmore management on the five continents.

Golden Eagle Farm

John and Betty Mabee, founders of the Big Bear Grocery chain, used profits from the sale of that business and earning from the sale of the Golden Eagle Insurance Company to purchase and stock a 560-acre farm near San Diego in 1997. They now have more than 500 horses at the farm as well as a stable of broodmares they keep in Kentucky. The farms have bred in excess of 140 winners of major races. They also have produced the leading California-bred horses over several years. In 1992, the Golden Eagle Farm was the leading North American owner of racehorses. Their purses exceeded $5 million that year. The farm also led the nation in breeding fees, earning over $7 million. The Mabees earned the Eclipse Award for the leading breeders of 1991, 1997, and 1998. John Mabee was an original member of the Breeder's Cup board of directors.

Robert and Beverly Lewis

The Lewises own Silver Charm, who won the Kentucky Derby and the Preakness in 1997. Beverly and Robert Lewis started their ownership of horses in 1990. Since then they have produced Silver Charm and other champions. They have fifty-five horses that are trained for racing and another twelve broodmares. Their horses have been in training with such notables as D. Wayne Lucas, Bob Baffert, and Gary Jones. Their operations are in California, where Robert is the chairman of the Thoroughbred Owners of California and also a director of the National Thoroughbred Racing Association.

Overbrook Farm/William T. Young

Lexington, Kentucky, native William T. Young made a fortune developing Jiffy Peanut Butter and selling the brand to Procter and Gamble. These and other business ventures have enabled him to pursue Overbrook Farm in Lexington as an avocation. The farm is a 1,500-acre breeding facility that has a number of the leading horses in the nation. One leading sire is Storm Cat. Two Overbrook horses have been Kentucky Derby winner Grindstone and Belmont Stakes winner Editor's Note. Young's two-year-old, Boston Harbor, was the Eclipse Award winner in 1996, and Young also won the award as the outstanding breeder in 1994.

The Sheikhs of Dubai

The ruling family of oil-rich Dubai has been involved in horse racing for several generations.

Among their members is Sheikh Hamdan bin Rashid al Maktoum, who has more than 300 thoroughbred stables in England, Ireland, Australia, Dubai, and the United States. He also owns 155 broodmares. In the United States, the sheikh owns the 1,350-acre Shadwell Farm in Lexington. He was the leading owner of winning mounts in England in 1995. Sheikh Maktoum al Maktoum is the current ruler of Dubai. He came to notice in horse racing circles in 1981, when he and his brothers spent $6.5 million at the Keeneland July yearling sale. His major U.S. possession is the Gainsborough Farm near Versailles, Kentucky. The sheikh has 110 broodmares as well as 200 horses in training.

Stronach Stable/Frank Stronach

Frank Stronach was born in Austria, but he generated his fortune as a Canadian industrialist with Magna International, Inc. In 1998, Stronach purchased Santa Anita Park and 300 nearby acres for $126 million. He stables about 100 racing horses. One leading horse is Awesome Again, who won the $5 million Breeders Cup Classic in 1998. His Touch Gold (which he owned in a partnership) won the Belmont Stakes, keeping the Triple Crown away from Silver Charm. Stronach was the given the Eclipse Award for being the outstanding owner in 1998.

The Thoroughbred Corporation/Prince Ahmed Bin Salman al-Saud

Prince Ahmed Bin Salman al-Saud, a member of the royal family of Saudi Arabia, and four other partners lead the Thoroughbred Corporation. Salman and his Saudi partners have forty-five horses in training in the United States and an equal number of broodmares that are kept at the Mill Ridge Farm in Kentucky. Other horses are kept in England and Saudi Arabia, as well as at a sixteen-acre facility near Santa Anita in California. The corporation's horses include the leading stallion, Skip Away; Breeder's Cup winner Distaff; and Sharp Cat. The corporation's purchase of a yearling for $1.2 million at Keeneland's September sale in 2000 was an all-time record price for the sale.

Colors: The Jockey and the Mount

Colors are an important part of the tradition and mystique of horse racing. Each major stable is identified by the registered colors worn on the silks of their jockeys. For example, jockeys for the Calumet Stable horses wear red and blue; those riding for the Meadows Stable wear blue and white. This practice of using colors dates to England's New Market track in 1762. Bettors who favor certain owners may clearly see which numbers are carried by their champions.

Bettors may also seek to look at the colors of the horses themselves for clues about performance; however, their luck is bound to fail them if they bet that way for long. Although I have heard seasoned bettors exclaim that four white hooves are very good, three worse, and no white hoof bad, such coloring is unrelated to performance. So, too, is the general coloring of the horse. Bay and chestnut horses are the leading colors, and accordingly they register the most wins. In the Kentucky Derby, bays have won 58 times, chestnuts 40, dark bays or browns 17, gray or roans 6, and black horses 4 times.

Colors are important in that they are used in the registration of thoroughbreds for identification purposes. The following color definitions are used by the Jockey Club:

- Bay: A horse with a coat of yellow-tan to bright autumn, with black main, tail, and lower legs. Some white markings may be present.
- Black: A horse with an entirely black coat, but some white markings may be present.
- Chestnut: The coat is red-yellow to golden-yellow, with some white markings.
- Dark bay/brown: The coat varies from brown to dark brown, with areas of tan. Mane, tail, and legs are black, with some white markings present.
- Gray/roan: A horse with combined colors of the gray and roan.
- Gray: The majority of the horse's coat has a mix of white and black colors.
- Roan: The majority of the coat has a mix of red and white colors.

—written with the research assistance of Bradley Wimmer

Sources: "Angel Cordero." 1975. *Current Biography Yearbook.* New York: H. W. Wilson, 90–92; Bolus, Jim.

1990. *The Insider's Pocket Guide to Horse Racing.* Dallas: Taylor Publishing; Christiansen, Eugene Martin. 1999. "The 1998 Gross Annual Wager." *International Gaming and Wagering Business* (August): 20ff; Churchill, Peter. 1981. *Horse Racing.* Dorset, England: Blandford Press; Everson, R. C., and C. C. Jones. 1964. *The Way They Run.* Los Angeles: Techno-Graphic Publications; Hollingsworth, Kent. 1976. *The Kentucky Thoroughbred.* Lexington: University of Kentucky Press; Hotaling, Edward. 1995. *They're Off! Horse Racing at Saratoga.* Syracuse, New York: Syracuse University Press; "Julie Krone." 1989. *Current Biography Yearbook.* New York: H. W. Wilson, 314–317; Litsky, Frank. 1975. *Superstars.* Secaucus, NJ: Derbibooks; National Gambling Impact Study Commission [NGISC]. 1999. *Final Report.* Washington, DC: NGISC; "Ron Turcotte." 1974. *Current Biography Yearbook.* New York: H. W. Wilson, 418–420; Scott, Marvin B. 1968. *The Racing Game.* Chicago: Aldine; Smith, Sharon B. 1998 *The Complete Idiot's Guide to Betting on Horses.* New York: Alpha Books; "Willie Shoemaker." 1966. *Current Biography.* New York: H. W. Wilson, 373–375.

House-banked Games

A house-banked game is conducted by a gambling enterprise such as a casino, a lottery, a bingo hall, or an organized charity. The game is one in which the player opposes the gambling enterprise, and either the player or the enterprise wins the bet (unless there is a tie). There may be many players (thousands as in a lottery) or a single player (e.g., one player at a blackjack table), but there is only one house—one gambling enterprise. The house (enterprise) runs the game and puts its resources (money) against the resources (money) of all of the players.

Most, but not all, casino games are housed-banked games. These include blackjack, craps, roulette, baccarat, *punto banco* (minibaccarat), and the big wheel. Las Vegas sports betting on football, basketball, baseball, and hockey games is also house banked. In all of these games, each player at the game is individually wagering money against the house. Most commercial (and Native American) bingo games are house banked, although the players are pitted against each other to see which one (or several) is the first to fill a card or line full of numbers. The game is banked if the house guarantees a specific winning prize to the players regardless of how many players are playing or how much money the players have wagered. If there is a predetermined prize, the house is engaging in gambling, as it is putting its resources at risk—it may lose money if too few players are in the game or if it has a high prize for a player covering a card in so many calls of numbers, and the player does so. The house would not have to give out the prize if no players accomplished that goal, however, and its winnings would be higher than otherwise.

Some charity bingo games are not house banked. In these the house awards a prize based upon the money that is actually wagered by the players when they purchase cards. The house may take out a percentage of the money as its share and then divide the rest of the money among the winners (or winner) of the bingo game. In this case the game is player banked, and the house is merely an agent managing the players' money for a fee.

In most lottery games, a player is guaranteed a prize of a certain amount of money if the player has a winning number. In the case of instant tickets, a finite number of tickets are sold. If all of a batch are sold, the lottery is like the bingo organization, as it merely manages the players' money, shifting it from losers to winners and taking out a fee. Instant ticket games are not house-banked games. On the other hand, if the player (or a random number generator) picks a number that is played (for instance, in a pick three, pick four, or pick five game), and a winner is guaranteed an individual prize that is given regardless of the actual number of players or winners in the game, then the game is house banked. The lottery is risking its money against the play of each individual player. The house-banked nature of the pick-three game was highlighted in 1999 when the Pennsylvania lottery attempted to close down play on certain popular numbers (777, 333, 666) in order to avoid high financial losses if the popular numbers were selected. The lottery knew it was in a risky house-banked situation, and it wished to minimize its risk. Indeed, the lottery officials knew what they were doing. In 1979 one game was rigged by a contract employee of the lottery who controlled the number-generating machine. The number 666 was chosen as the winner. Not only did an inside group of cheaters win a lot of money, but so did regular players who always played the popular 666—known as the devil's number because of references in the Bible's Book of Revelation. The state of Pennsylvania took a severe loss on that day (*see* Crime and Gambling).

Lotto games have giant prizes that are based upon amounts of money that have been wagered by the players. There is a superprize that is usually awarded to a player (or all players on a shared basis) who selects all six winning numbers (numbers may include one through fifty). If no player selects all the winning numbers, a pool of money is gathered from ticket sales and transferred to the superprize for a subsequent game the next week. In a way, the giant lotto prize can be considered a player-banked game, but this is not truly the case. Only if the money played in the single drawing contributed to the giant prize would the game really be player banked. No lotto game is played this way. The starting game after a giant prize has been given away the previous week offers a guaranteed superjackpot prize, regardless of how much is wagered during that first game. In Texas, the state sets the superprize for the starting week at $4 million. If a player selects all the winning numbers in the first drawing, the state is definitely a loser. The lottery organization is banking the game. The fact that superprizes are shared does not change the house-banked nature of the game. Also, there is no legal requirement that the government continue to have new games after superprizes reach multi-million-dollar levels, although so far no major games have been discontinued. Moreover, each lotto game has guaranteed prizes for players who correctly pick only some of the winning numbers, again making the game essentially a house-banked game.

Often a lottery will put a cap (ceiling) on the amount it gives to big winners without changing smaller prizes and without guaranteeing that there will be a superwinner at all. These are house-banked games, as the lottery is risking its money against the wagers of the players. The lottery is either a small winner, a big winner, or occasionally a loser. An example of such a game is run in Texas. There the Texas Millionaire Game asks players to pick four numbers between zero and ninety-nine.

Guaranteed prizes of specific dollar amounts are given to players who select either two or three correct numbers. Players matching all four numbers win $1 million. If no one correctly picks the four numbers, the lottery is the winner pure and simple. If more than ten people pick the correct four numbers, they must collectively share a prize of $10 million. The lottery caps its losses, but the game is still a house-banked game just the same as a blackjack game in a casino.

The most typical games that are player banked rather than house banked include live games of poker, pari-mutuel games on activities such as horse and dog races, jai alai games, and lottery instant ticket games—when all tickets in a batch of tickets are sold (*see* Pari-mutuel Wagering Systems; Player-banked Games).

Sources: Thompson, William N. 1997. *Legalized Gambling: A Reference Handbook.* 2d ed. Santa Barbara, CA: ABC-CLIO.

Hughes, Howard

More than any other individual, Howard Robard Hughes stamped the seal of legitimacy upon a Las Vegas casino industry that had been labeled as corrupt and Mob-invested in the general public mind. Hughes paved the way for corporate America to invest in gambling properties that had previously been controlled to a large degree by pension funds of the International Brotherhood of Teamsters and assorted underworld characters. Hughes did not necessarily transform Las Vegas from a profit center for organized crime in the favorite resort in the United States on purpose. Moreover, there were many unanticipated consequences of his drive to dominate Las Vegas gambling, not the least of which was the scandal that will go down in the history books as Watergate.

Hughes was born in Houston, Texas, in 1905. Four years later his father, Howard Hughes Sr., helped develop a drilling bit that could penetrate hard rocks with ease. The tool revolutionized oil drilling and made the Hughes family wealthy. At age eighteen, the younger Hughes became the majority stockholder of Hughes Tool Company when his father died in 1924. Having been warned by his father never to have partners, he immediately set plans into motion for acquiring all the stock in the company from his relatives. He also began to diversify his interests. He maintained a stake in mineral extraction in addition to developing experimental aircraft, producing movies, and designing military hardware. Very soon he became a multimillionaire and also a playboy working the Hollywood scene. For excitement he flew many of his experimental aircraft. In 1938 he flew around the world, setting various speed records. The downside of his flying came with several crashes. Perhaps the most serious one was in 1946, after which doctors expected him to die. They gave him excessive dosages of morphine to kill his pain, not thinking of consequences if he lived. He lived and developed a lifetime addiction to drugs. It is also suggested that his plane crashes caused many head injuries that left a mark on later behavior that would have to be called "bizarre," to say the least.

During the 1940s Hughes was a frequent visitor to Las Vegas, and several times prior to 1966 he had attempted to move his corporate interests to the desert. He purchased 28,000 acres of land on the west side of the city with the notion that the land would be used for aircraft development and testing. It remained undeveloped until the 1980s, when it became the essence of Summerlin, a residential expanse that filled as Las Vegas became the fastest-growing city in the United States. During the 1950s Hughes's fortune approached $2 billion, and he became the principal owner of Trans-World-Airlines (TWA). Hughes hired Robert Maheu, a former Federal Bureau of Investigation agent, to be his chief business agent, and from 1957 on, Hughes became a recluse unwilling to meet any business associate on a face-to-face basis. All his contacts with Maheu from 1957 to 1970 were by telephone or on note pads. In the early 1960s, Hughes relocated his operations to the Bahamas, but he still yearned to be in Las Vegas. On Thanksgiving Day 1966, he moved to Las Vegas. Soon he was buying casinos.

The 1960s had been hard on Las Vegas. Bobby Kennedy had pushed the McClellan Committee of the U.S. Senate in its investigation of Teamsters' union money in Las Vegas. As attorney general, Kennedy carried on ongoing probes into Mob ac-

tivity in Las Vegas. No new casinos were being built because the Mob was fearful that the federal government might shut down gambling. Public corporations were precluded from owning casinos (unless every single stockholder was licensed), and legitimate lenders—banks and other institutional financial houses—would not touch the industry. Las Vegas was looking for a miracle, and here came Howard Robard Hughes—with money to spend. In May 1966 Hughes refused to appear before a congressional committee investigating aspects of the operations of TWA. To avoid having to appear in public, he willingly agreed to divest himself of all his holdings in the company—78 percent of the stock. He received $546.5 million for an investment that had originally cost him $80. For purposes of avoiding excessive taxation, he had to quickly reinvest the money. Las Vegas was waiting.

Fiction and fact became mingled and confused as the story of Howard Hughes unwrapped in Las Vegas. Some say events just occurred; others see a masterful plan behind Hughes's entrance into the gambling community. In November 1966, Maheu rented the top two floors of the Desert Inn for Hughes's living quarters. He was supposed to stay for ten days, but after he entered his hotel suite, he stayed there for almost four years—until 5 November 1970. He may have been secretly taken out of the room on a few occasions, but no one outside a very small group of personal attendants saw him over these four years. A whole litany of strange behaviors, manias, phobias, delusions, and obsessions afflicted Hughes during his Las Vegas stay, but crazy or not, he made an impact on the town.

When Hughes refused to leave the Desert Inn after his ten-day stay, Maheu began to negotiate a deal with Moe Dalitz and the other owners of the property. On 22 March 1967, the parties agreed that Hughes would purchase the Desert Inn for $13.2 million. The licensing process for casino ownership entailed many hurdles. These included financial statements, personal statements, fingerprints, photographs, fees, and a personal appearance in front of the Gaming Control Board and the Nevada Gaming Commission. There was no way that Howard Hughes was going to endure such procedures. On the other hand, there was no way Nevada was going to allow Hughes to slip away.

Howard Hughes poses with his plane, ca. 1930s. (UNLV Special Collections)

Governor Paul Laxalt and the gaming officials waived many requirements and allowed Maheu to appear on behalf of Hughes in the licensing hearing. The license was not opposed by anyone. Said board chairman Alan Arber, "After all, Mr. Hughes' life and background are well known to this Board and he is considered highly qualified" (Garrison 1970, 52–53). The truth was quite different. Neither Hughes nor anyone in his organization had any experience managing a gambling facility.

Safely brought into the business, Hughes and the state of Nevada wanted more. In July 1967, Hughes purchased the Sands Hotel and Casino and 183 acres of land beside it for $14.6 million, and in September he acquired the Frontier. He quickly followed this with purchases of the smaller Castaways and Silver Slipper casinos. He also bought Harold's Club in Reno. Then he set his sights on the Stardust and the Landmark. But by then, the federal government had its sights set on Hughes as well.

U.S. Attorney General Ramsey Clark thought Hughes had bought enough. Clark contended that any further purchases would make Hughes a monopolistic owner on the Las Vegas Strip. Hughes did not like to be told no. Clark and the president, Lyndon Johnson, were due to leave office soon, and so Hughes maneuvered to control the next president's capacity to refuse his desires. In 1968 Hughes hired Larry O'Brien, a family friend and political confidant of the Kennedy family, to be on his legal team. O'Brien had also been in the Kennedy cabinet. Then Hughes gave Richard Nixon, Republican candidate for the presidency, a $100,000 "campaign contribution." Some thought that the contribution could be considered a "bribe." Hughes also gave Democratic candidate Hubert Humphrey a $50,000 contribution (Drosnin 1985, 250). In 1960 Hughes had given Nixon's brother a large loan that remained unpaid, and Nixon's opponents had used the loan as a major campaign issue against Nixon. In 1968, Nixon was elected, and he promptly removed objections to Hughes's purchases of more casinos. Hughes gave up his desire to purchase the Stardust, but he did finalize the purchase of the Landmark. In 1972 Nixon declared himself to be a candidate for re-election, except there was a little bug in his plans. Larry O'Brien was now the chairman of the Democratic National Committee. Nixon strongly suspected that O'Brien had information about the 1968 contribution (the alleged bribe)—as he was working for Hughes when it was made—and might use that information against Nixon. Nixon told his aides to find out what O'Brien knew and what his campaign plans were. The aides began to gather information from many sources. They decided to break into O'Brien's office in the Watergate Hotel in Washington, D.C. The irony is that O'Brien could not raise the issue of the money, because Democratic candidate Humphrey had accepted a similar contribution. But Nixon did not know that—in time. Hughes had brought down a president.

It has been suggested that Hughes purchased the hotels he did because they surrounded the Desert Inn, and he wished to own every hotel he could see from his tenth-floor suite. Maheu suggests that the casinos purchased were on a list of casinos that Robert Kennedy suspected of being Mob establishments. The practical effect of the purchases was to give the United States the impression that Las Vegas was being cleaned up and that the organized crime elements were leaving town. That was not exactly true. A major change was in order, however. Even though Hughes had brought capital to the Las Vegas Strip, he had invested in existing properties; he did not build new ones, nor did he remodel and improve those he purchased. The Strip needed infusions of new cap-ital for new casinos. The activity of Hughes had given the legitimate investment community a new perspective on Las Vegas. It could be a good place. Before Hughes left town for the Bahamas with his entourage on 5 November 1970 (firing Maheu in the process), the state of Nevada had passed (in 1969) the Corporate Gaming Act, which allowed publicly traded corporations to have Nevada subsidiaries that could be licensed for casino ownership in the name of the principal stockholders—not all of the stockholders. As Hughes exited the state, Hilton came in—what Hughes started, others would finish. As Hughes was an absentee owner while living in his secluded tenth-floor suite, he was the same while he was in the Bahamas and elsewhere. His sanity was severely questioned, as he remained in seclusion for the rest of his life. Only once did he agree to meet with Nevada officials. That was in 1972 when rumors of his death caused concern. He agreed to meet the governor—Mike O'Callaghan—in London for a very brief session just to verify that he was alive. That he was, but not really very alive. He was in miserable physical shape; nonetheless his life continued until he was defeated by kidney failure in April 1976.

Sources: Drosnin, Michael. 1985. *Citizen Hughes.* New York: Holt, Rinehart, and Winston; Garrison, Omar. 1970. *Howard Hughes in Las Vegas.* New York: Lyle Stuart; Hopkins, A. D., and K. J. Evans. 1999. *The First 100: Portraits of the Men and Women Who Shaped Las Vegas.* Las Vegas: Huntington Press, 203–205; Lalli, Sergio. 1997. "Howard Hughes in Las Vegas." In *The Players: The Men Who Made Las Vegas,* edited by Jack Sheehan, 133–158. Reno: University of Nevada Press; Presswood, Gary. 1992. "Howard Hughes: Alive and Well in Las Vegas." Manuscript. Las Vegas: University of Nevada, Las Vegas, Department of Public Administration; Sifakis, Carl. 1990. *Encyclopedia of Gambling.* New York: Facts on File, 159–160.

I

Idaho

Idaho was the next-to-last state (before South Carolina in 2000) having an existing form of legal gambling made illegal on a statewide basis. Through the 1930s and 1940s slot machines were permitted under state law on a local option basis. In 1948, however, the voters decided that all the machines should cease operations.

Since then, pari-mutuel gambling for thoroughbred, quarter horse, and dog races has been authorized, as has charitable gambling. A lottery began operations in 1991. Several tribes in the state offered high-stakes bingo games; however, they began serious negotiations for casino gambling in the early 1990s. The state refused to negotiate, using the 11th Amendment as a defense (the 11th Amendment bans suits against states in federal courts ex-

cept in certain circumstances). The Coeur d'Alene tribe of northern Idaho decided to try something new. They instituted a nationwide lottery using telephone lines and the Internet. Considerable litigation ensued; however, the game was not sufficiently profitable, and the tribe dropped it. The tribe has installed nearly 500 machines at their gaming facility, claiming that the machines are lottery games. The state has objected to their presence, but there has been no concerted action to remove them.

Sources: Thompson, William N. 1997. *Legalized Gambling: A Reference Handbook.* Santa Barbara, CA: ABC-CLIO, 163–166, 189; www.idaholottery.com.

Illinois

By the time the riverboat casinos of Iowa were in operation in 1991, the state of Illinois reacted to

The Hollywood Casino boats in Aurora, Illinois. (Courtesy of Phil Valdez)

Iowa and Illinois turned to riverboat casino gambling in the early 1990s when their agriculture business suffered hard times.

the notion that their citizens would be asked to cross the Mississippi River to gamble in another state. Illinois lawmakers feared that Iowa boats would simply become parasites upon the Illinois economy, taking both profits and tax moneys away from Illinois. Illinois knew gambling. Racetracks had been in operation since the days of the Depression. A lottery began selling tickets in 1972. Bingo games were very popular, especially in urban areas. Also, the state had considerable experience with illegal casino-type organizations. These forms of gambling would not be adequate to meet the marketing threat from Iowa.

The Illinois legislature legalized riverboat casinos. They acted quickly, with legislation on the governor's desk in January 1990 and the licensing process starting in February 1990. Ten licenses were authorized for the state, with each license holder being able to have two boats. Each boat would have a maximum capacity of 1,200 passengers. The boats would have to be on navigable waters; however, no boat could be inside of Cook County. This restriction was offered as a concession to the horse-racing tracks near Chicago, which is in

Cook County. The tracks feared that the boats would have an unfair competitive edge over racing. In 1998 the restriction was removed, and a boat was authorized for the community of Rosemont.

The casino operations began in April 1991, just after Iowa boats began operations. The Illinois lawmakers decided to meet the threat of Iowa competition by offering more "liberal" gaming rules. There was no $5 bet limit, nor was there a $200 loss limit per cruise. The boats were required to make cruises, unless there was bad weather. In such a case there would be "mock cruises," with players entering and leaving the dockside boat at set times. The Illinois boats did very well compared to the Iowa boats in their first years of operation. Therefore, Iowa felt the necessity of eliminating its $5 betting and $200 loss limits in 1994.

Well before the advent of riverboat casinos, there were efforts to bring legal casino gambling to Illinois. During the Prohibition and World War II eras, there were several illegal gambling halls in the state; however, their numbers and the openness of their operations declined in the 1950s and 1960s. Instead, an effort grew to legalize casinos.

In the late 1970s Mayor Jane Byrne suggested having casinos to produce extra revenues for snow removal activities in Chicago. The Navy Pier site was selected for casino gambling. The efforts were stymied by Springfield lawmakers. In 1992 Chicago mayor Richard Daley conferred with several Las Vegas operators, and together they proposed a $2 billion megaresort complex for the city. The project engendered considerable support; however, it was defeated owing to the opposition of Gov. James Edgar.

The Illinois riverboat casinos are regulated by a five-member Illinois Gaming Board appointed by the governor. The board issues licenses, collects taxes, and enforces gaming rules with inspections, hearings, and fines as necessary. The board may also revoke licenses. The boats pay license application fees of $50,000 each. After operations begin, they pay an admission tax of $2 per passenger and also pay 20 percent of their gaming win (players' losses) as a state tax. Half of the admissions tax and one-fourth of the gambling tax are returned by the state to the local city or the county where the boat is docked. Each boat has a single docking site. The ten boats have generated over $1.2 billion a year.

Sources: Cabot, Anthony N., William N. Thompson, Andrew Tottenham, and Carl Braunlich, eds. 1999. *International Casino Law.* 3d ed. Reno: Institute for the Study of Gambling, University of Nevada, Reno, 26–32; Dombrink, John D., and William N. Thompson. 1990. *The Last Resort: Success and Failure in Campaigns for Casinos.* Reno: University of Nevada Press, 129–130.

Indiana

Legalized gambling came late to Indiana. Before the state began its lottery in 1991, it had been one of only three in the United States that had no legal gambling. Although the effort to establish the lottery was ongoing, a campaign for casinos was also taking place. Following several years of lobbying efforts and studies of a variety of proposals, the state legislature passed a riverboat gaming law over the veto of Gov. Evan Bayh in 1993. The next legislative session authorized horse-race betting within the state.

The strongest motivation for approving casino gambling was provided by the fact that several casino boats in Illinois were drawing much of their revenue from Indiana residents. Four Illinois casinos were in suburban Chicago within fifty miles of the Indiana border, and another license was held by a boat in southern Illinois within a short driving time of the Evansville metropolitan area.

Indiana's new law authorized licensing of eleven casino boats for counties bordering Lake Michigan waters as well as on the Ohio River and Patoka Lake. The licenses can be granted only if the residents of the county where the boat operates approve casino gaming in a referendum vote. Most of the gaming-eligible counties held votes; some were positive and some were negative. The Patoka Lake license has not been activated, as the United States Army Corps of Engineers was determined to own the rights to control the water of the lake.

On 9 December 1994 the first two licenses were awarded, but there were legal difficulties. The federal Johnson Act prohibited gaming on the Great Lakes (*see* The Gambling Devices Acts [the Johnson Act and Amendments]). The state had claimed an exemption to the provisions of the act in the riverboat legislation, but the matter had to be clarified in Congress, with the attachment of a rider to the Coast Guard Reauthorization Act of 1996 that exempted Lake Michigan waters from the Johnson Act for purposes of gaming on Indiana-licensed casino boats. Difficulties with the Ohio River arose, as the waters of the river were within Kentucky. This was resolved by requiring boats on the river to cruise within a short distance of the shore.

The 1993 legislation created an Indiana Gaming Commission of seven members appointed by the governor. The governor also appointed the executive director of the commission. Nine casino boats were in operation by 1999. They accomplished at least some of their original purpose. Revenues for Illinois boats experienced a small decline while Indian boats surpassed Illinois revenues.

The commission has a very wide range of powers. It may make any rules necessary for carrying out to mandates of the 1993 act. Additionally, it accepts applications for licenses and conducts all investigations of applicants, including investigations into personal character. It selects the licensees and oversees their operations. It takes all disciplinary actions if rules are violated and may revoke licenses, which are granted for a five-year period. The boats must be at least 150 feet in length and have the capacity to carry 500 persons.

The first boat to begin operations was *Casino Aztar* in Evansville; it opened its doors for gaming on 8 December 1995. *Casino Aztar* is a 2,700-passenger boat with 35,000 square feet of gaming space.

Two boats started gaming on 11 June 1996. Both are docked in Gary, Indiana. Donald Barden's *Majestic Star* is a 1,500-passenger vessel with 25,000 square feet of gaming space. Donald Trump's *Trump Casino* occupies 37,000 square feet of gaming space on a 2,300-passenger boat.

On 29 June 1996, the *Empress Casino* boat began cruises in Hammond. The 2,500-passenger vessel has a gaming floor of 35,000 square feet. Hyatt's Grand Victoria Casino and Resort started cruises in *Rising Sun* on 4 October 1996. The boat was the first casino to invade the Cincinnati, Ohio, metropolitan area. It carries 2,700 passengers and has a gaming floor with 45,000 square feet.

The *Argosy Casino* began operations on the Ohio River at Lawrenceburg, also near Cincinnati, Ohio, on 13 December 1996. The 4,000-passenger yacht has a gaming floor of 74,300 square feet.

The *Showboat Mardi Gras Casino* started cruises out of East Chicago on 18 April 1997. It has gaming space of 53,000 square feet and carries 3,750 passengers. On 22 August 1997, the fifth Lake Michigan boat license was activated as the *Blue Chip Casino* opened in Michigan City. The 2,000-passenger vessel has 25,000 square feet of gaming space. The ninth boat to begin operations is at Bridgeport, across from the Louisville, Kentucky, metropolitan area. It is operated by the same company that runs the Caesars Palace casino in Las Vegas. The *City of Rome* riverboat carries 3,750 passengers and has 93,000 square feet of gaming space. Gaming began in late 1998.

The tenth license is reserved for the Ohio River area and may be granted for a boat near either the Cincinnati or the Louisville population base.

The casino boats must go out into waters for cruises, although one off Lake Michigan has a spe-

cial channel for its cruises. An amendment to the original 1993 law clarified conditions when the boats could remain docked. Basically, these include any times the boat captain would determine that safety required that the boats remain docked. In any case, the boats are required to have two-hour cruises. If the boat is docked, the cruises are mock cruises.

The casino boats pay a gross gaming tax of 20 percent of their win. Of this amount, one-quarter goes to the city where the boat is docked (or county if not in a city), and three-quarters goes to the state's general fund. There is a three-dollar admission fee, which is also shared among state and local governments.

—coauthored by Carl Braunlich

Sources: Cabot, Anthony N., William N. Thompson, Andrew Tottenham, and Carl Braunlich, eds. 1999. *International Casino Law.* 3d ed. Reno: Institute for the Study of Gambling, University of Nevada, Reno, 33–38.

Indian Gaming Regulatory Act of 1988. *See* Native American Gaming: Contemporary

Institute for the Study of Gambling and Commercial Gaming. *See* Gaming Institutes: Political and Research

Insurance and Gambling

Insurance has sometimes been compared with gambling. After all, an insurance company acts like a casino as it asks its clientele to wager on whether they will live or die, whether they will be healthy or sick, whether their house will burn down or not, whether they will be victimized by thieves, or other sad circumstances. It would seem that characteristics of insurance could meet the elements in the definition of gambling: Customers put up money (consideration), and they win a settlement (prize) depending upon a factor of chance (whether or not they become a victim). And of course, like a casino, the insurance company charges a fee for the service of offering its product, and the insurance company also sets the prize structure so that it will make a profit—the odds are in the favor of the insurance company.

These things being said, or to a degree admitted to be true, there are still major distinctions between gambling and insurance, distinctions that allow me to neglect the concept of insurance in the remainder of this encyclopedia. Paul Samuelson's seminal volume on economics points out the differences (Samuelson 1976). In his section on economic impacts of gambling, Samuelson writes that gambling serves to introduce inequalities between persons and instabilities of wealth (425; *see* The Economic Impacts of Gambling). Insurance has the directly opposite consequences. Insurance gives people the opportunity to achieve stability in the face of risks that are often inherent in the nature of things—risks of disease, of fire, of lost property. For a small sum of money, people can purchase policies that will guarantee that the costs of a disaster will not ruin their lives or their families. Gambling purposely introduces risk into a society that is stable; insurance purposely exists to avoid risks. Actually, the insurance company spreads the risks of disasters to a single person among a very large number of persons who buy insurance policies.

Insurance companies may sell policies that cover only a certain set of circumstances. The person purchasing insurance is limited to buying coverage only for "insurable interests." The insurable interest cannot be as frivolous as the turning of a card or where a ball falls on a spinning wheel. The interest must be a real concern to the policyholder. One can insure his or her own life but cannot insure the life of a total stranger. Insurance companies must limit the amount of insurance sold to values relative to the risks the insurance seeks to avoid. A house can be insured against fire, but only up to the full value of the house. Similarly, health can be insured up to the cost of treatment and collateral losses such as wage losses. The limits on insurance coverage preclude the gambler's behavior of chasing losses. If the "bad" event does not occur, and a premium payment is thus lost, the insured person cannot simply double the bet for the next period of time. The insurance company and the

insured both have disincentives for purchasing excessive policies. Insurance companies make those wishing to have large life insurance policies subject themselves to many medical examinations, including full health screenings. Newly covered persons with health insurance may not be able to receive benefits for a number of months.

By gambling, a person is seeking risks that might severely upset his or her financial stability. By buying insurance, a person is avoiding risks. On the other hand, if a person with a house, other property, or a family dependent upon him or her does not insure the house or property against destruction or himself or herself against illness or death, that person is gambling with fates that strike people often randomly, albeit with some rarity (in short periods of time), but almost certainly over large periods of time.

Gambling activity can be and often is very destructive to personal savings. Insurance, on the other hand, can be seen as an alternative means of savings—savings for a rainy day in some cases. In the case of whole life insurance, savings and investment are encompassed into the policies. Although in some respects the notions of insuring against the occurrence of certain natural events and betting on the occurrence of contrived events may appear quite similar, in actuality they are not very much alike.

Sources: Samuelson, Paul A. 1976. *Economics.* 10th ed. New York: McGraw Hill, 425.

International Gaming Institute. *See* Gaming Institutes; Research and Political

Internet Gambling

Gambling through the Internet became an established activity in the mid-1990s, causing great concern to many interests—governments as well as private parties seeing danger in easily accessible gambling.

The Internet system was developed three decades ago by the U.S. Department of Defense in order to connect computer networks of major universities and research centers with government agencies. The growth of the system into what has now become potentially the most active and most encompassing form of communication had to await the advent of the personal computer and its widespread acceptance. By the end of 1998 there were over 76 million Internet stations providing access to 147 million persons in the United States—mostly in their homes. An equal number of computers with Internet access are found in other countries.

There are an estimated 800 host computer sites that either provide gambling directly or provide information services for gamblers. Approximately sixty Internet sites, located mostly in foreign lands, accept bets on a variety of events. Most wagering is on sports events, but several sites also conduct lottery or casino game–type betting. In order to make a wager, a player with Internet access must first establish a financial account with a gambling Internet enterprise. Although the enterprise is typically located in another country, the bettor can send money to the enterprise by using a credit card, debit card, a bank transfer of funds, or personal checks. Wagers can then be made, and the account is adjusted according to wins and losses.

Internet gambling activity has not yet become a major part of the worldwide gaming industry, but it appears to be growing, and it possesses possibilities for becoming much larger than at present. The National Gambling Impact Study Commission reported that in 1998 there were nearly 15 million people wagering on the Internet from the United States, providing the Internet gaming entrepreneurs with annual revenues of from $300 million to $651 million (National Gambling Impact Study Commission 1999, 2–15, 2–16). This would represent an amount equaling about 1 percent of the legal betting in the land. Gaming analyst Sebastian Sinclair estimated that revenues could reach $7 billion in the early twenty-first century (National Gambling Impact Study Commission 1999, 2–16). If the expansion comes, it will essentially be because the Internet offers bettors a very high level of convenience for their activity, and it also offers a privacy they may especially want because of the illegal (or at best quasi-legal) nature of the activity. It is easier to sit

at home and wager on a computer than it is to drive to a casino sports book—especially when we consider that the only legal sports books are in Nevada. The computer is also quicker than bookie telephone betting services. It is also less likely to be intercepted by law enforcement officials.

There are downsides to Internet betting that may provide dampers to the wagering activity. The first issue is integrity. Although a player betting on a sports event has an assurance that he has legitimately won or lost a bet (assuming there are independent news reports on the sports event bet upon), other players wagering on lotteries or, especially, casino-type games have no firm guarantees that the results of the wagering are totally honest. To be sure, some Internet sites are licensed by governments, giving an appearance of legitimacy. The very staid government of Liechtenstein authorizes operation of an Internet lottery, and several Caribbean entities, such as Antigua, St. Kitts, and Dominica, oversee many Internet sites offering a variety of games, as well as sports betting. The oversight activities, however, consist almost entirely of collecting fees from the operators.

The Federal Wire Act of 1961 was confined to betting on races and sports events. It did not speak to casino-type games and lotteries. Hence, some betting on some computer-type games may possibly be legal, at least in the eyes of the federal government—that is, at the present time.

To address these questions with clarity, and to fill the possible gap in the 1961 law, U.S. senator Jon Kyl of Arizona has promoted legislation to amend the Federal Wire Act. His proposed amendment won approval in the U.S. Senate, but as of the end of the 2000 session, it had not come to a floor vote in the U.S. House of Representatives. The Kyl bill would make any and all gambling on the Internet illegal, and it would give the Department of Justice and the Federal Trade Commission powers to enforce the law. As the bill was moving toward passage, it was amended to allow exceptions for legal race betting and lottery organizations.

Sources: Cabot, Anthony N. 1999. *Internet Gambling Report III.* Las Vegas: Trace, 115–124; Kelly, Joseph M. 2000. "Internet Gambling Law." *William Mitchell Law Review* 26: 118–177.

Inter-Provincial Lottery Corporation. *See* Western Canadian Lottery Corporation

The Interstate Horseracing Act of 1978

During the last quarter-century of the twentieth century, participation in horserace-betting activities stagnated. Indeed, on-track betting declined considerably, although the decline was offset by a comparable increase in intertrack and offtrack betting. New York's state authorization of offtrack betting facilities run by a public corporation beginning in 1970 both threatened the viability of on-track wagering and at the same time offered somewhat of a solution to the impending revenue decline. By the mid-1970s there were 100 offtrack betting parlors in New York City alone. New York saw the parlors as a source of public revenue as well as a means to discourage patronage of illegal bookies.

Prior to 1970, only Nevada had offtrack betting activity. Now many other states were examining the New York experience with thoughts of duplicating it. Initially there were no formal provisions requiring that offtrack facilities share revenues with tracks, nor were there mechanisms for requiring that wagers be pooled. Rather, all such arrangements were ad hoc. The tracks across the country perceived major problems, and they turned to Congress for development of uniform policies to answer their concerns. Even though offtrack betting operations agreed that they were adding to the race-betting activity and were sharing some revenues, the tracks felt that their share was not sufficient to offset losses because bettors were coming to tracks in fewer and fewer numbers. A compromise measure was hammered out in Congress, resulting in the passage of the Interstate Horseracing Act of 1978.

The Interstate Horseracing Act recognizes that there are several interests involved in offtrack betting. There are horse owners who essentially realize economic gains through purses when their horses win races. There is the track, basically a private entrepreneurial venture; there is also the host racing state and its racing commission. There is the operation (public in New York but private in other places) that runs the offtrack betting parlor. And there is the state regulatory commission that oversees the offtrack betting activity. Of course, there are always the players—the bettors.

The act stipulated that the tracks and associations of horse owners would meet and agree on how they would split income from fees charged to the offtrack betting operations. The state racing commission would have to ratify the agreement. As with on-track betting revenues, it would be expected that portions of the offtrack betting wagers would go to the state as a tax, to the track owners, and to horse owners through purses. The three parties would then negotiate with the offtrack betting operators for a fee that essentially would be a portion of the money wagered on races (the "take-out").

The take-out portion going to the track, the owners, and the host state would be less than the amount taken from the track bettors, as it also had to be shared with the offtrack betting facility and the offtrack betting state. The Interstate Horseracing Act requires that the overall take-out percentage from the offtrack betting activity be the same take-out rates as charged to on-track bettors. This protects the tracks from price competition.

The act also stipulated that the offtrack betting facility cannot conduct operations without the permission of any track within sixty miles of the facility, or if there are no such tracks, then the nearest track in an adjacent state. The act did not address the subject of simulcasting race pictures between the tracks and the offtrack betting facilities.

Sources: The Interstate Horseracing Act (Public Law 95–515, signed into law 25 October 1978).

Iowa

Iowa may have the distinction of having more forms of legalized gambling than any other state. The pastoral agricultural land of the *Music Man* has more than pool halls to corrupt its youth. It has a lottery with instant tickets and massive lotto prizes via Lotto America; it has dog racing and horse racing—thoroughbred, harness, and quarter horse racing. It has bingo games and pull-tab tickets for charities, and it has casinos—on land, on rivers, on lakes, and on Native American lands. Although many of these games were in place by the end of the 1980s, Iowa led the nation in establishing riverboat gaming with legislation that was passed on 20 April 1989.

Even though the Iowa "experiment" led to a massive expansion of gambling throughout the Midwest, in a sense it was supposed to represent a small incremental change in gambling offerings—not a major change in the landscape. The proponents of casinos for Iowa were responding to a general downturn in the agribusiness economy of the state. They were quick to say they did not want Iowa to "be like Las Vegas." Indeed, during the legislative campaign for casinos, the words *casino* and *gambling* were not used. The casino gambling was supposedly just a small adjunct to riverboat cruises designed to recreate Huckleberry Finn excursions down the mighty Mississippi. Only 30 percent of the boat areas could be devoted to casino activities. Ostensibly, the operators would offer many activities on the boats in order to satisfy the recreational needs of the entire family. Originally the boats had to have actual cruises, betting was limited to five dollars a play, and no player could lose more than $200 on a cruise. These limits have been eliminated, and now boats no longer cruise. Instead, they remain docked while players gamble.

Sources: Cabot, Anthony N., William N. Thompson, Andrew Tottenham, and Carl Braunlich, eds. 1999. *International Casino Law.* 3d ed. Reno: Institute for the Study of Gambling, University of Nevada, Reno, 39–41.

J

Jai Alai

Jai alai is a game that is played on the basic principles used for handball and racquetball games. Jai alai contests are used for pari-mutuel betting in Florida, Connecticut, and Rhode Island and for almost a decade in the MGM casinos of Las Vegas and Reno, Nevada.

The game is considered the oldest ball game played today; it is also considered the fastest game played. Players either compete as individuals or in teams of two. The game is played on a very large court, 177 feet long, 55 feet wide, and 55 feet high. The playing facility is called a fronton. The ball is very hard—harder than a golf ball—and is about three-fourths the size of a baseball. The ball, called a *pelota,* is propelled by the players toward the front wall of the court. The players hold a *cesta,* which is a curved basket that extends from one of their arms. They catch the ball in the basket device and then without letting it settle, they propel it back to the front wall. They must retrieve and return the ball before it hits the floor two times. The balls may move as fast as 150 miles per hour in the games, faster than any other ball in any game.

The game of jai alai may have had ancient predecessors, as the notions behind handball have been found in many prehistoric societies. In its present form, however, the game is traced to Basque villages in the Pyrenees of France and Spain. The origins of the game may go back to the fifteenth century. Mythmakers suggest that the game may have been the invention of St. Ignatius of Loyola, who—like his compatriot St. Francis Xavier—was Basque. What is less mythical is the fact that the game was played during religious festival occasions in the Catholic region. The words *jai alai* mean "merry festival." The game has also been known as pelota vasca or Basque vall. The game is celebrated in the classic art of Spain. Fran-

cisco Goya created a tapestry called *Game of Pelota* for the Prado in Madrid. Many mythical heroic characters of Basque tradition were pelota players.

As the Basques and persons from the surrounding regions migrated to the Western Hemisphere, they brought the game with them. It came to Cuba by the beginning of the twentieth century, and it was displayed at the St. Louis World's Fair of 1904. (Castro closed down games in 1960 as he closed the Cuban casinos.) It came to Florida in 1924. Although the game enjoyed some natural popularity for its basic excitement, it did not draw large crowds until 1937, when the Florida legislature authorized pari-mutuel betting on the winners of the games.

In the jai alai game there are eight players (or eight teams of two players each). They play round robin matches. A player (team) who wins a point remains in the game; the loser is replaced with another player (team). They keep playing until one player (team) has scored seven points. In a sweep, one player could score seven straight points but would have to do so by scoring against every other team in the contest. The contests result in one winner with seven points and second- and third-place players (teams) with the next highest number of points. If there is a tie, the tying teams play off for their position. Those making wagers can bet the basic win, place, and show as in horse racing. Jai alai contests also were innovative because they created the quinella, perfecta, and exacta bets. A trifecta bet is also used.

Florida developed many frontons, but play levels pale in comparison with other betting venues such as bingo halls, horse tracks, and Native American casinos. The MGM Grand Hotels of Las Vegas and Reno had frontons until the mid-1980s. Connecticut authorized jai alai betting in the early 1970s, as did Rhode Island in 1976. Efforts to get the sport accepted elsewhere in North America for pari-mutuel wagering have not been successful.

Sources: Keever, William R. 1984. *The Gambling Times Guide to Jai Alai.* Hollywood, CA: Gambling Times; Scarne, John. 1986. *Scarne's New Complete Guide to Gambling.* New York: Simon and Schuster, 135–136; Sifakis, Carl. 1990. *Encyclopedia of Gambling.* New York: Facts on File, 167–168.

Japan and Pachinko

The Japanese are known in Las Vegas as "prized customers," "top-rated quality players," and "high rollers." Deservedly they are given first-class treatment whenever they hit the Strip. Moreover, it is well recognized that Japanese manufacturers supply some of the best gaming equipment for U.S. casinos. Japanese have even owned gambling halls in the United States. Although it is known that the Japanese people are very attached to gambling enterprise, there may be a false notion that the Japanese do not gamble very much at home. Nothing could be further from the truth. Per capita gaming in Japan far exceeds that present in the United States (Tanioka 2000, 13).

A casino bar in Japan that does not allow cash prizes.

Over the years, trade journals have given only the slightest attention to the games of Japan. International gaming charts indicate that the country has lotteries and pari-mutuel racing, but no casinos. Comments on what various countries are doing regarding gaming almost always leave Japan out. In the history of the now defunct *Gambling Times,* there was only a short article on motor boat racing in Japan and another one on amusement machines. The leading trade journal, *International Gaming and Wagering,* devoted only one short survey article to Japan gaming in 1994. It would be helpful if the literature gave more attention to this gambling-intense country, perhaps in an elaboration of the 1994 piece.

Gambling, as we would call it, or entertainment with prizes, as the Japanese police would call it, is very big in Japan. Japan has 130 million people—approximately half the population of the United States. Yet the total gambling revenue of Japan is more than equal the $35 billion gross win of U.S. casinos, lotteries, and pari-mutuel racing venues.

Part of the illusion that Japan does not gamble comes from the fact that there are no casinos in

Japan—that is, casinos in the U.S. sense of the word. But make no mistake about it, there are gambling halls in Japan—almost 20,000 of them. They offer players opportunities to win prizes by playing "skill" games on pachinko and pachi-slo machines. Even though there are elements of skill in pachinko, luck is a major factor in the game (Tanioka 2000). Thirty million people play on the 4 million machines around the country. The machines produce wins equivalent to US$21 billion each year (Tanioka 2000, 9). In other words, the entertainment machines with prizes win more money than is won by all the casinos—commercial, Indian, and charity—of the United States.

Pari-mutuel wagering is permitted both on and off track for motorboat, bicycle, and horse racing. Japan is unique in being the only place where wagering is offered for bike and boat races. Large stadium structures permanently line banks of rivers where the boat races take place. As there is "skill" in making wagers, the government denies that there is gambling involved in the enterprise. The race betting may not be "gambling," but make no mistake about it, it is big-time wagering. The Japan Derby (Imperial Cup) horse race each fall (November) produces a handle exceeding the collective handle of the Triple Crown in the United States.

Lotteries are in a growth phase. Until recent years, the games were passive weekly draws that were slow and did not permit the player much involvement in selection of numbers. Instant games have been played since the late 1980s, however, and in 1995 a numbers game in which the player selects the number was added. A national lottery run through the Dai-Ichi Kangyo Bank leads the world in sales for a single lottery.

The Pachinko Parlors of Japan

Pachinko may be a funny sounding word. Actually it is derived from the sound—"pachin-pachin"—that is made by balls as they bounce down the face of the game board toward winning or losing positions. It may be a funny-sounding game, but it produces some serious wins.

Pachinko has its origins outside of Japan. Some suggest that the game comes from Europe, but most find beginnings in the United States. The Corinthian game was played in Detroit in the early 1920s. The game was played with a board placed on an incline. Balls were shot up one side of the board and then fell downward onto circles of nails (arranged like Corinthian architecture) and bounced into winning slots or fell into a losing pool at the bottom. Players were given scores and awarded prizes for their play.

The game developed in two different directions. In the United States it graduated into the popular pinball games that were found in recreation halls across the land until computerized games replaced them in the 1960s. The Corinthian game moved to Japan, and in the 1930s parlors were developed offering play. The game board was placed upright into a vertical position to save space. Machines were also converted so that the balls could come out of the machine in increased volumes if winning placements were made.

Soon the machine was the most popular recreational game in Japan. In 1937, however, Japan commenced military action in China, and the nation assumed a wartime posture. The game was made illegal as plants making the games were converted into munition factories. The government did not want individuals to waste time at play, and many of the players were drafted for military service.

After the war the machines were made legal once again. The government now encouraged play, as the occupying armies used play as a means to distribute scarce goods to the public—cigarettes, soap, chocolate. Players "won" balls from the machine, then exchanged the balls for merchandise. No cash prizes were allowed (which is still the case). In ensuing decades the machines were refined. Shooting mechanisms enabled players to put over 100 balls a minute into play. Pachinko machines incorporated new games within the game. Slot machine–type reels were placed in the middle of the playing board. As balls went into winning areas, the reels spun, enabling greater prizes to be won if symbols could be lined up in winning combinations.

Machine operators have the opportunity to make payouts greater or smaller by moving the nails on the surface of the playing boards. Players

Only Japan allows wagering on bicycle races.

The editor plays pachinko—the favorite game in Japan.

find that when the nails are farther apart, the balls are more likely to fall into a winning position. Experienced players will look for such machines. Also, they will play on certain days when the weather may cause the nails to be loosened. Particular players may be consistent winners; however, even a very inexperienced player can achieve wins when a ball activates the slot-type reels and they end up in a jackpot position. Typically the machines pay out a maximum of balls worth about $160 for a top jackpot.

A new variation of the game called pachi-slo has been introduced. The game is essentially like the reel slot machines found in casinos all over the world. After the reels are activated, however, they may be stopped individually by the player's pushing buttons. With a special skill the player is supposed to be able to line up symbols in winning patterns. The reels spin so fast, however, that almost all winners claim their prizes through luck. Although pachinko wins are conveyed in balls from the machine, pachi-slo machined use tokens for play, and tokens come out for winners.

With both types of machines the balls and tokens are converted by a weighing machine into tickets with winning amounts written upon them. The tickets are traded for prizes at a special booth within the parlor. Prizes popularly won include cigarettes, music tapes, and compact discs.

Well over 90 percent of the winning players, however, choose to trade tickets for small plastic plaques, which ostensibly have value in and of themselves. Usually they include small pieces of gold or silver. But no player wants the little bit of precious metal. Instead, they take the plaques to a designated money exchange booth that is usually very near the pachinko parlor. There they receive cash payments. The process of converting balls or tokens into tickets into prizes into cash costs the player about 25 percent of the prize. That is, 100 balls for play will typically cost 400 yen (about $5). If a player wins back the 100 balls, the ticket will enable him to trade the win for a prize worth 400 yen retail. The plastic plaque may be traded at the money exchange for 300 yen cash. The parlor does not really care which way the player goes. After all, the retail merchandise costs the parlor only 300 yen. The exchange booth operators may take a portion of the win when they sell the plaque, as they are a separate business. Even so, the parlor owners sometimes may have close ties to the exchange businesses.

Today there are approximately 18,000 parlors in Japan. Collectively they have 4 million machines. About 80 percent of the machines are pachinkos and the rest pachi-slos. The parlors may also have rooms with other kinds of amusement machines that give prizes. Each machine wins an average of over $5,000 per year, substantially less than the slot machines of U.S. casinos. The machines cost only about $1,000 each, however, and halls choose to have an excess of machines so that experienced players as well as others can have the opportunity to select machines for play (Tanioka 2000, 57). The United States has about one slot machine for each 400 residents, but Japan has one gaming machine for each thirty residents. And that makes for a lot of gambling.

The reluctance of Japan to embrace casino-type gambling in part derives from a feeling that gambling enterprise is closely connected to bad influences—in Japan, that might mean the Yakusa, or organized crime. There is a fear that the Yakusa has ties to the pachinko industry.

Like the democracy of Pericles and the Golden Age of Athens, citizenship privileges in Japan are for the most part reserved for people of Japanese origin. Residents with Korean or Chinese family ties may be excluded from entrance to the major corporations of the land, and for some of the time after World War II, their children were not allowed into the universities. Those with entrepreneurial spirit had to "go it alone." These "foreign" (so considered even if native born) Japanese developed mom-and-pop retail businesses, and they also gravitated toward pachinko. At first most parlors were small and independently owned. Also, pachinko, although very popular, was considered somewhat unclean—perhaps like pool, pinball, and slot machines were in years past in the United States. The traditional Japanese did not want to associate with the business. Organized crime groups also moved into the industry, many with Korean ties. Today the police worry that some pachinko

parlor funds are utilized to support drug activities and gun smuggling. There is an ongoing fear that funds are skimmed and sent to North Korea where the Communist regime uses them to purchase nuclear materials.

These suspicions have led various members of the industry to band together to form an association with the goal of cleaning up the industry as well as the image of the industry. The group is hoping that the government will revise the prize structure of the games so that players can win cash prizes directly from the machines. The police are reluctant to do so, because, as one National Police director told me during an interview in Tokyo on 10 August 1995, "we don't want gambling in Japan."

—*coauthored by Shannon Bybee*

Sources: Cabot, Anthony N., William N. Thompson, Andrew Tottenham, and Carl Braunlich, eds. 1999. *International Casino Law.* 3d ed. Reno: Institute for the Study of Gambling, University of Nevada, Reno, 518–520; Tanioka, Ichiro. 2000. *Pachinko and the Japanese Society.* Osaka, Japan: Institute of Amusement Industries, Osaka University of Commerce.

Johnson Act. *See* The Gambling Devices Act

Jones, "Canada Bill"

"Canada Bill" Jones (1820–1877) was the master of three card monte in the middle years of the nineteenth century. Stories are told about characters in the gambling world, and some of the best are told about Canada Bill. When he was circulating through the South during the post–Civil War years conning people with his monte games and looking for any action, he found a poker game. As he entered the game he was warned that it was a crooked game. He responded simply, "I know, but it is the only game in town." Certainly the same story has been told about other gamblers. It was quite likely to be true about Canada Bill, however, who in his lifetime won millions of dollars on his own specialty game. He then turned around and lost the money gambling in other games, usually poker and faro games.

After his funeral in Reading, Pennsylvania, in 1877, it was reported that while two gamblers were lowering the coffin into the ground, one said, "I'll bet you my hundred against your fifty." "On what?" said the other. "I'll bet that he isn't in the coffin." He then related that Canada Bill had squeezed out of tighter boxes in his lifetime (Chafetz 1960, 103). Indeed, he had gotten out of town ahead of his victims on more than several occasions. During the 1850s he traveled the Mississippi River with his monte operation in a partnership with George Devol (*see* Devol entry in Annotated Bibliography). Devol was a fighter. But Canada Bill was only 130 pounds and afraid of a fight. He knew how to get Devol to make a defensive stand as he led the escape from the "tight" situations.

Bill Jones was born in Yorkshire, England, to a family of gypsies. He was raised among fortune-tellers and horse traders and thieves. He learned that the secret of living involved using con jobs. In his early twenties he moved to Canada, whence came his nickname. There he met his gambling mentor, Dick Cady, who taught him the sleight-of-hand operations of three-card monte, a card game that worked like the proverbial shell game. When Jones heard about the riverboats, he left the frozen tundra behind, becoming a man of the South.

After touring the river for several years, he worked his scams on the new railroads in the United States. He actually proposed to one line that he be given a monopoly concession for the train. He was denied the exclusive opportunity and had to travel with other gamblers—probably guaranteeing that he would not keep his winnings. Canada Bill was the best at three card monte, as he could almost change a card as he was throwing it down to the table. In his later years he worked county fairs and a world fair, and also racetracks. He was unlike other professional gamblers of the era, as he did not dress to impress. Quite the opposite, he always appeared as the rube, unshaven, in rumpled oversized clothes, looking like a sucker ready to be taken. He often said that "suckers had no business with money, anyway" (Chafetz 1960, 73). He was what he appeared to be. He died a pauper.

Sources: Asbury, Herbert. 1938. *Sucker's Progress: An Informal History of Gambling in America from the Colonies to Canfield.* New York: Dodd, Mead, 238–243; Chafetz, Henry. 1960. *Play the Devil: A History of Gambling in the United States from 1492 to 1955.* New York: Potter Publishers, 73, 82, 101–103; Sifakis, Carl. 1990. *Encyclopedia of Gambling.* New York: Facts on File, 170–171.

K

Kansas

The Kansas lottery began operations in 1987. It offers instant games, daily numbers games, and lotto, as well as participation in the multistate Powerball game. Three small Native American reservations—Iowa, Kickapoo, and Pottawatomie—won the right to offer casino games after a long struggle for a compact with the state of Kansas. One governor signed a compact only to have it repudiated by the legislature. A later compromise in the mid-1990s allowed limited gaming on the reservations.

Kansas City, Kansas, is within the Greater Kansas City metropolitan area, so it is directly accessible to the riverboat casinos of Missouri. The competition of the riverboats has effectively destroyed the market for Woodlands racetrack, which is located just west of Kansas City. Kansas allows pari-mutuel wagering for both dog and horse races. As a consequence, the owner of the track launched efforts to establish casino games on his property. The efforts have not been successful, but they are sure to continue.

Sources: www.klottery.com.

The Kefauver Committee

The Kefauver Committee is the popular name of the U.S. Senate Special Committee to Investigate Organized Crime in Interstate Commerce. The committee, which met in 1950 and 1951, was the first federal entity to make a comprehensive study of organized criminal activity in the United States. The investigations concentrated much attention upon gambling. The idea of a Senate investigating committee came from Estes Kefauver, a first-term senator from Tennessee. Kefauver's initiative came as a reaction to reports of several state and local crime commissions that had met in the postwar years. These local investigatory efforts had found that criminal organizations experienced great growth during the World War II years. They had moved from their Prohibition-era bootlegging activities to gambling, narcotics, and prostitution activities. They did so at a time when the nation's collective attention was focused upon world events.

The crime commissions' reports were accompanied by a widely reported series of sensational newspaper investigations and stories. It seemed to Kefauver that the national public was making a call for action. The ambitious senator had served as a member of the U.S. House of Representatives for five terms before winning election to the Senate in 1948. His election resulted from a bitter fight against a corrupt political machine that had dominated Tennessee politics for decades.

During 1949, Kefauver developed the idea that the federal government should follow the lead of the local commissions and have its own study of crime. On 5 January 1950, he introduced Senate Resolution 202 in order to create a new subcommittee of the Judiciary Committee on which he served. After jurisdictional objections from the leader of the Commerce Committee, the resolution was amended, and an independent special investigating committee was approved on 3 May 1950. Five senators were selected to be members by Vice President Alben Barkley (president of the Senate). The members included Democrats Kefauver, Herbert O'Conor (Maryland), and Lester Hunt (Wyoming) and Republicans Alexander Wiley (Wisconsin) and Charles Tobey (New Hampshire).

The committee gained widespread national attention for its televised hearings. Kefauver achieved celebrity status and soon afterwards launched a presidential campaign. He failed in attempts to get the presidential nomination of the Democratic party in 1952, but in 1956 he was nominated for the vice presidency on the unsuccessful ticket with presidential candidate Adlai Stevenson.

The committee held its hearings in a Senate office building in Washington, D.C., and in thirteen other cities, including Las Vegas, Miami, New York City, New Orleans, Kansas City, Detroit, and Los Angeles. Over 600 witnesses testified. These included federal, state, and local officials as well as many persons who participated in gambling enterprises both legal and illegal. Among these were members of the Desert Inn Group of Las Vegas, including Moe Dalitz and Wilbur Clark. Several thousands of pages of testimony were recorded.

The committee issued its report on 17 April 1951. The committee concluded that "organized criminal gangs operating in interstate commerce are firmly entrenched in our large cities in the operation of many different gambling enterprises . . . as well as other rackets . . ." (Kefauver 1951, 1). The committee found that there was a "sinister criminal organization known as the Mafia" that was operating throughout the country. Gambling profits were considered the "principal support" for the criminal gangs. The committee strongly opposed legalization of gambling, as they found that the "caliber of men who dominate the business of gambling in the state of Nevada is on par" with those operating illegal establishments (91). The committee members concluded that "as a case history of legalized gambling, Nevada speaks eloquently in the negative" (94). The committee wrote: "It seems clear to the committee that too many of the men running gambling operations in Nevada are either members of existing out-of-state gambling syndicates or have had histories of close association with the underworld characters who operate those syndicates." They criticized Nevada's licensing system for not resulting in the exclusion of undesirables but rather seeming only to give the individuals a "cloak of respectability" (94).

The committee's report included twenty-two recommendations for federal government action and seven for state and local governments. The federal recommendations included (1) the creation of a racket squad in the Justice Department; (2) the establishment of a Federal Crime Commission in the executive branch; (3) a continuing study by the committee of interstate criminal organizations and support of social studies related to crime; and (4) new legislative initiatives, to be suggested by the committee. The committee also applauded the establishment of a special fraud squad in the Bureau of Internal Revenue (now the Internal Revenue Service) to deal with taxation of illegal gamblers and other gangsters. It was recommended that casinos be required to keep daily records of wins and losses of gamblers and provide the records to the bureau. Officials of the bureau should have access to casino records at all times. The transmission of wagers and of betting information interstate by means of telephone, telegraph, or radio and television should be prohibited.

While the committee was meeting, the Johnson Act was passed. It prohibited the transportation of slot machines across state lines for illegal uses. The committee recommended that the prohibition be extended to other gambling devices such as roulette wheels and punchboards. Congress also increased the federal slot machine licensing tax to $250 for each machine. The tax had been established in 1941 and levied at an annual rate of $150.

State and local governments were urged to appoint committees to study the problem of organized crime in their jurisdictions, with special grand juries having extensive powers appointed in communities with wide-open illegal gambling. Greater cooperation among police agencies was suggested. Each jurisdiction was also asked to consider depriving businesses of licenses if illegal gambling was taking place on their premises. Several additional recommendations were urged upon both federal and state authorities in areas of criminal activity that did not involve gambling.

The committee had impacts beyond the presidential campaigns of Estes Kefauver. As a result of the hearings, many persons were charged with being guilty of committing contempt of the Senate for their misinformation. The report of the committee listed thirty-three notorious individuals who were cited for contempt and other charges as a result of the hearings. Additionally, many states followed recommendations and set up their own committees and commissions where they had not done so before. Through the 1950s many local gambling establishments across the country were closed down—in some places one by one, in other places en masse.

The effects on Nevada gaming were mixed. The efforts of other states to crack down on gambling pushed many illegal operators in other jurisdictions to Nevada. The state also experienced growth, as it became known as the singular place where many casinos could operate openly. Also, the attention of the committee influenced the state to improve its gaming regulatory structures with the creation of a specialized Gaming Control Board in 1955 and the Nevada Gaming Commission in 1959. Also influential in pushing regulatory improvements in the state were the work of the McClellan Committee and the administration of Gov. Grant Sawyer.

Sources: Kefauver, Estes. 1951. *Crime in America.* Garden City, NY: Doubleday; Moore, William Howard. 1974. *The Kefauver Committee and the Politics of Crime, 1950–1952.* Columbia: University of Missouri Press.
See also Crime and Gambling; The Gambling Devices Acts (Johnson Act and Amendments); McClellan Committees

Kennedy, Robert F.

Robert F. Kennedy was a U.S. senator and attorney general. Robert Francis Kennedy, known as Bobby, was born on 20 November 1925 in Massachusetts. He was the son of Ambassador Joseph Kennedy and the brother of Pres. John F. Kennedy and U.S. Senator Edward Kennedy. Robert Kennedy graduated from Harvard University with a B.A. in 1948 and received his legal education at the University of Virginia, earning an LL. B. degree in 1951. After graduation he worked briefly in the U.S. Department of Justice before becoming a counsel in 1953 with a Senate committee investigating internal security, chaired by Sen. Joseph McCarthy (R-Wisconsin).

After the Democratic party secured the Senate majority in 1955, Kennedy became chief counsel of the Investigations Committee under the chairmanship of Sen. John McClellan (D-Arkansas). In 1957, the committee became known as the Rackets Committee as it focused its attention on organized crime and illegal activity in labor unions. The first target of the investigations was the International Brotherhood of Teamsters (often referred to as the Teamsters' union). Union president Dave

Beck was implicated in personal corruption; he was subsequently tried, convicted, removed from office, and imprisoned. Then Kennedy went after Beck's replacement, James Riddle Hoffa. Kennedy was able to demonstrate Hoffa's interactions with organized crime figures and illicit gambling activity. Kennedy's work with the committee led eventually to the 1959 passage of the Landrum-Griffin Act, which regulated financial activities of labor unions. The committee action also established Robert Kennedy's reputation as a fighter against organized crime. That reputation was enhanced when he authored the best-selling book *The Enemy Within* (Kennedy 1960).

In 1960 Kennedy demonstrated his political expertise as he managed John F. Kennedy's successful campaign for the presidency of the United States. Bobby Kennedy's reward was his appointment to the office of attorney general in January 1961. He held the office until September 1964. He concentrated the energies of his office and his Department of Justice on civil rights issues and on organized crime. He continued his quest to bring down James Hoffa; however, he was frustrated in these endeavors. It was left to his successors to finally guide the prosecutions that resulted in the imprisonment of Hoffa.

Attorney General Kennedy established an organized crime task force, and he pursued his objectives with prosecutions as well as with an agenda of new legislation. Three major bills dealing with illegal gambling were passed into law as a result of his efforts. These included the Federal Wire Act of 1961, the Travel Act of 1961, and the 1962 amendments to the Johnson Act (Gambling Devices Act), which expanded the prohibition of transportation of slot machines across state lines to include all gambling equipment. Congress also passed the Racketeer Influenced Corrupt Organizations Act (RICO) in 1961.

Kennedy maintained his steady attacks on organized crime until late 1963 when his brother, Pres. John Kennedy, was assassinated. There has been more than one set of rumors suggesting an organized crime connection to the assassination. One account (Davis 1988) suggests that organized crime had been quite influential in the president's election and that crime figures maintained close relationships with the president and his father (who had been involved in bootlegging businesses decades before). Some feel that the attorney general's vigorous attacks on Mob activity somehow represented a double cross by the president.

After John Kennedy's assassination, Robert Kennedy turned his energies toward passage of civil rights legislation. In 1964 he resigned the office of attorney general in order to successfully run for a U.S. Senate seat from New York State. In 1968, while he was running for the presidency, Robert F. Kennedy was assassinated in Los Angeles.

Sources: Davis, John. 1988. *Mafia Kingfish: Carlos Marcellos and the Assassination of John F. Kennedy.* New York: McGraw-Hill; Hersh, Seymour. 1997. *The Darker Side of Camelot.* Boston: Little, Brown; Kennedy, Robert. 1960. *The Enemy Within.* New York: Harper; Navasky, Victor. 1971. *Kennedy Justice.* New York: Antheneum Press.; Stein, Jean. 1970. *American Journey: The Times of Robert Kennedy.* New York: Harcourt Brace Jovanovich; www.rfkmemorial.org.
See also "There's a Reason We Only Look Forward in Las Vegas" in Appendix A

Keno

Keno is a game that enjoyed great popularity in Nevada casinos in the mid-twentieth century. Its use is now waning, as serious players realize that it does not offer a good expected return. Casinos also realize that it requires much labor and also considerable security to ensure that all play is honest. The game that is now played can be traced back to Chinese games two millennia ago. The Chinese used boards with ninety (or more) characters. They brought the game to the United States as they emigrated to the West Coast for jobs on the railroads and in the mines.

Americans modified the game so that numbers replaced characters. When casinos reopened in Nevada in the 1930s, an 80-number game became standard, and it is still in use. The player is given a sheet of paper with ten columns and eight rows of numbers. He or she may bet on from 1 to 15 numbers. Numbered balls (or a computer number generator) are then retrieved from a randomizer, and 20 numbers are called. Hence, for a one-number pick, there is a one in four chance to have it called.

The payoff is even money. In addition to picking one set of numbers (up to 15 of them), the player may use his card for making several combination bets. After marking the card, the player gives it to a casino official (or keno runner) who verifies it and gives him a receipt.

The convenient feature of keno in a casino is that players can wager and play the game while dining, watching entertainers, or playing other games. The winning numbers are posted on boards throughout the casino facility. Games are separated by fifteen or twenty minutes, and winners usually have several hours to turn in cards for payoffs. The house edge is determined by payoff schedules. Typical Nevada payoffs to players range from about 75 percent to about 65 percent (a house edge of 35 percent) depending upon how many numbers are bet. When more than three numbers are bet, there are prizes for having some of the numbers (but not all) called.

Although the game is considered by most experts to be a "sucker's bet," many persons like the fantasy of being able to play a one-dollar game and win $25,000 or $50,000 for hitting fourteen of fifteen numbers. The casino, however, guards itself from extraordinary risks by limiting all prizes on a game to an arbitrary figure, such as $50,000. If there are multiple big winners on the game, they have to divide the prize.

Sources: Lemmel, Maurice. 1966. *Gambling Nevada Style.* Garden City, NY: Dolphin Books, 95–104; Miller, Len. 1983. *Gambling Times Guide to Casino Games.* Secaucus, NY: Lyle Stuart, 75–95; Scarne, John. 1986. *Scarne's New Complete Guide to Gambling.* New York: Simon and Schuster, 490–499; Sifakis, Carl. 1990. *Encyclopedia of Gambling.* New York: Facts on File, 173–174.

Kentucky

Kentucky is the home of horse racing. More racehorses are born and bred in Kentucky than in any other state. The Kentucky Derby is the most famous horse race in The United States. In 1988, 61 percent of the Kentucky voters said they wanted a lottery, and the next year one was established that offers instant games, lotto games, and numbers games as well as Powerball interstate lottery tickets. Charitable games are also permitted.

A horse farm in the famous "Bluegrass" country of Kentucky.

The fact that many states bordering or near Kentucky—Indiana, Illinois, Missouri, Mississippi—offer casino gambling pressured state leaders into making plans for casino gambling. In 1999, the governor recommended that as many as fourteen casinos be authorized for the state. The notion of casinos in Kentucky is not too far out of bounds for most residents, as Kentuckians remember that the middle decades of the twentieth century found many wide-open but illegal casinos operating along the Ohio border. The seven tracks of Kentucky are supporters of the idea of having casinos, as long as they are located at the tracks and operated by the tracks. The idea of casinos has not received much support in the state legislature, however.

Sources: www.kylottery.com.
See also Horse Racing

Kerkorian, Kirk

Three times one man built the largest hotel in the world. First it was the 1,512-room International Hotel on Paradise Road in Las Vegas in 1969. This is now the Las Vegas Hilton. Next it was the 2,084- room MGM Grand on Flamingo Road at the Las Vegas Strip in 1973. This is now Bally's, which is also part of the Hilton Casino Group—also known as Park Place Casinos. Then in 1993 it was the second Las Vegas MGM Grand Hotel and casino—with theme park. This facility at Tropicana and the Strip, with 5,009 rooms, was the first billion-dollar casino project in Las Vegas. These projects alone would merit the mention of that man—Kirk Kerkorian—in any encyclopedia of gambling or gamblers, but his story is more interesting than simply being a builder. Parts of his story make him sound like Howard Hughes, part like Steve Wynn, but he was really neither. He is unique in the annals of casino personalities.

Kirk Kerkorian was born in Fresno, California, on 6 June 1917. His family moved to Los Angeles, where he had to contribute to their finances by selling newspapers at the age of nine and performing whatever other work he could find. He had spoken only the Armenian language of his forefathers until he reached the streets of Los Angeles. Los Angeles taught him that life was to be a struggle, and he willing jumped into the flow of the activity. He drove trucks to carry produce from the

San Joaquin Valley, he worked with logging opera-tions in Sequoia National Park, and he was an am-ateur boxer who won twenty-nine of his thirty-three fights.

In 1939 he fell in love with flying, and within two years he had a commercial pilot's license. He soon became a flight instructor, and then at the first chance he joined the British Royal Air Force. He ferried bombers from Canada to England in one very dangerous mission after another. In one flight he set a speed record for his aircraft. After the war, his interest remained in the air. In 1945 he visited Las Vegas, bought a single-engine Cessna, and went into the charter business. He would fly into Las Vegas almost daily. In 1947 he purchased the Los Angeles Air Service. Soon he went into the business of refurbishing planes and reselling them. He renamed his company Trans Interna-tional Airlines and went into the passenger service business in 1959. His business continued to ex-pand, and he would spend much of his free time in Las Vegas at the casinos.

Kerkorian always kept his eyes open for deals. In 1962 he was able to purchase the eighty acres across from the Flamingo on the Las Vegas Strip. By consolidating other pieces of land, he was able to create the parcel of property that Jay Sarno pur-chased in order to build Caesars Palace. Kerkorian also bought eighty-two acres of land on Paradise Road in 1967. The same year he was able to pur-chase the Flamingo Hotel for $12.5 million. In 1968 he sold Trans International Airlines for $104 million. He had the resources for his first major project, the International. He invested $16.6 mil-lion of his own money in the $80 million facility. He took the properties public in 1969 when the In-ternational opened, featuring performers such as Barbra Streisand, Ike and Tina Turner, and Elvis Presley. Yet the Securities and Exchange Commis-sion did not allow him to sell sufficient shares of stock to pay off debts on this and other projects in which he was involved. He felt that he had to sell the Flamingo and International in order to satisfy his business obligations. Hilton took over the two hotel casinos in 1970 and 1971, but Kerkorian was not out of town for long.

He started out by buying a controlling interest in Western Airlines, and he began buying stock in

Kirk Kerkorian standing in front of the construction site of the International Hotel, now the Las Vegas Hilton. (UNLV Special Collections)

a failing movie company called MGM Grand. He pushed the company toward diversifying into re-sort hotels. Their first project was the MGM Grand Hotel Casino in Las Vegas, named after the 1932 film *Grand Hotel.* The hotel opened on 5 July 1973, with a 1,200-seat showroom, a shopping arcade, a movie theater featuring classic MGM films, and a jai alai fronton. In 1976, Kerkorian sold a large block of Western Airlines stock and began a new hotel-casino in Reno. In 1978 the $131 million MGM Grand–Reno opened with the largest casino floor in the world and a 2,000-room tower—mak-ing it Reno's largest hotel.

Disaster struck the MGM Grand in Las Vegas on 20 November 1980. A fire that started in an electrical panel in a kitchen quickly shot through the casino area, killing a score of players and em-ployees. When the fire reached the hotel lobby area it was knocked down by the sprinkler system. A massive smoke cloud was able to rise up stairwell and elevator shafts, however, before it was trapped on the upper floors. There the smoke penetrated guest rooms, killing dozens more. In all, eighty-seven persons perished. Although the tragedy was devastating, Kerkorian quickly decided he would rebuild. By the end of 1981, the MGM was operating at full force. In 1986, however, Kerkorian walked away from his two properties, the Las Vegas MGM and the Reno MGM, selling them to Bally's for $594 million. Subsequently Bally's Reno was sold to Hilton, and in turn Hilton bought all of Bally's, so both properties—like the International before—have become part of Park Place Gaming.

Kirk Kerkorian could not stay away from Las Vegas gambling for long. Once again, he began to plan. One plan to take control of Chrysler Corporation fell short of its goal, although Kerkorian became the largest stockholder in the automotive giant. His other plan led to the creation of the largest hotel and casino floor (at the time) in the world. His 5,009-room colossus, also called MGM Grand (he had held on to the right to the name), featured a 330-acre theme park, a health club, eight restaurants, and a 15,000-seat arena where boxer Mike Tyson has performed on many occasions (some notable, some infamous). Barbra Streisand came out of a twenty-year moratorium on personal concerts to perform there as well for the grand opening in 1993.

When Kerkorian opened the International, he included a youth hostel in the facility. Later the Hilton had a youth recreation area in the facility. His 1993 MGM Grand was heralded as a casino for families with children. It had a Dorothy and the Wizard of Oz theme with an Emerald City and a Yellow Brick Road. The word went out that Las Vegas was a place to bring children. Within a very short time, Kerkorian and the MGM management realized that children want two things from their parents—time and money. Both ways the casino loses. Kerkorian has backed off the "family" theme, and so has Las Vegas. The theme park at the MGM Grand has been consistently downsized, and plans have been made for expanding convention space and also for developing more rooms for prosperous gambling patrons. Kerkorian, in the meantime, keeps moving forward, always seeking new business deals. In 2000 he failed in an effort to take over Chrysler Motors, but he did succeed in a takeover of Steve Wynn's Mirage Resorts.

Sources: Hopkins, A. D., and K. J. Evans. 1999. *The First 100: Portraits of the Men and Women Who Shaped Las Vegas.* Las Vegas: Huntington Press, 178–180; Palermo, Dave. 1997. "Kerkorian: The Reticent Billionaire." In *The Players: The Men Who Made Las Vegas,* edited by Jack Sheehan, 159–167. Reno: University of Nevada Press.

The Knapp Commission (1970–1972)

The Knapp Commission (officially known as the Commission to Investigate Allegations of Police Corruption and the City's Anti-Corruption Procedures) consisted of five leading citizens of New York City. The commission was instituted by an executive order of Mayor John V. Lindsay on 21 May 1970. Lindsay appointed Whitman Knapp as chairman. Joseph Monserrat, Arnold Bauman (later replaced by John E. Sprizzo), Franklin A. Thomas, and Cyrus Vance (later secretary of state in the Carter administration) were commission members. The commission met for two years and issued its final report on 26 December 1972.

The creation of the commission was not driven by policy considerations of Mayor Lindsay. Quite to the contrary—city officials, as well as top police administrators, were said to be quite content to allow a persistence of on-street corruption of policy activity through bribery in exchange for having a police force that could basically ensure publicly acceptable levels of social control and criminal activity. Their priorities were often directed toward overlooking certain illegal activities by police if strict enforcement would negatively impact police morale.

Allegations of police corruption have dogged the police force of New York City since its creation in 1844. Investigations have been conducted on a periodic basis. A New York state senate committee (known as the Lexow Committee) looked at police extortion of houses of prostitution and gambling operations in 1894. In 1911 the city council appointed a committee led by Henry Curran to look into police involvement in the murder of a gambler in Times Square. The gambler had revealed to city newspapers a pattern of bribes that he had paid to the police. In 1932 the state legislature again sponsored an investigation under the leadership of

Samuel Seabury. It examined cases of bribes paid to police by bootleggers and gamblers. In 1950 and 1951 the district attorney again held grand jury hearings into bribery tied to gambling. Harry Gross, the head of one of the largest gambling syndicates in the city, agreed to testify. Twenty-one policemen were indicted, but charges were withdrawn when Gross ceased to cooperate in the hearings.

In the mid-1960s, it could be expected that the issue would somehow resurface again. This time the catalyst for investigations was a policeman whose quest was to be an "honest cop." His name was Frank Serpico. Serpico's story was the subject of a popular book by Peter Maas (Maas 1973) and a widely acclaimed movie, *Serpico,* released in 1973, starring Al Pacino in the role of Frank Serpico. Shortly after joining the police force, Serpico became aware that officers were taking bribes from persons involved in numbers betting and illegal sports betting. Soon he discovered the depth of a network of bribes tied to protection given to various games. Operators of different kinds of games would pay different levels of bribes depending upon the volume of their activity and the public exposure given their activities. Open gambling games would require higher bribes. All the police of a precinct would participate in the police bribes, with varying shares given to uniformed officers, plainclothes officers, detectives, and higher administrators.

At first Serpico simply refused to accept his share of the bribe money. But as he could not escape personal involvement with the situation on a day-by-day basis, he confided his displeasure to higher police officials. Although he was very reluctant to name any fellow officers in his discussions, he was eager that an investigation follow so that the practices would cease. He found little satisfaction within the police hierarchy and instead was severely ostracized. Even contacts with the mayor's office were futile. The highest politicians in the city were more concerned that police morale be high, as race riots were anticipated and general social "peace" in the streets was their priority. Serpico's persistent actions led to internal proceedings that resulted in individual convictions of lower-level policemen. He saw little action at top

levels where general reform had to start, although a higher-level investigation was initiated. In frustration and fear for his personal safety, Serpico and two supportive fellow officers decided to go on record and make their story public.

On 25 April 1972, the *New York Times* reported Frank Serpico's story on the front page "above the fold." The cat was out of the bag, and Mayor Lindsay could no longer hide behind bureaucratic values. He immediately appointed an interdepartmental committee to recommend action. The committee asked for public complaints that would back up the *New York Times* story. They received 375 complaints within a couple of weeks. They told the mayor that as regular city employees they did not have time to follow up with an investigation. They urged that the mayor create what became the Knapp Commission (Knapp Commission 1972, 35).

The city council approved a budget for the commission and also gave it subpoena power. Additional funds were received for the work through the U.S. Law Enforcement Assistance Administration. An investigating staff was formed, and several inquiries into illegal activity were made in the field. The commission also held two sets of hearings. Five days were spent with Frank Serpico and his fellow confidants. The commission also invited public complaints, and they received 1,325 in addition to those sent to the mayor's earlier committee. In addition to the Knapp Commission's report, their work led to the indictments of over fifty police officers. Over 100 were immediately transferred after the hearing began.

The commission spent considerable time discussing what is known as "the rotten apple theory," specifically that corruption is not pervasive but rather the result of a few "rotten apples" that somehow get into every barrel. They rejected that supposition, as their report began with the words, "We found corruption to be widespread" (12). In one precinct they found that twenty-four of twenty-five plainclothes policemen were involved in receiving bribes from illegal gamblers. Although group norms motivated police to participate in networks of bribery, so did their realization that the enforcement of gambling laws was not taken seriously by the judicial system. The commission reported that between 1967 and 1970 there were 9,456 felony arrests for gambling offenses. These resulted in only 921 indictments and 61 convictions. Of these, only a very few received jail sentences, and the sentences were "nominal."

Although the commission's report dealt with a wide range of corrupting activities, a special focus was upon gambling and the bribes gamblers paid to the police in their part of the city. The activity was found in all parts of the city. Ghetto neighborhoods were especially susceptible to this police activity. One witness indicated: "You can't work numbers in Harlem unless you pay. If you don't pay, you go to jail. You go to jail on a frame if you don't pay" (71).

The commission found that the "most obvious" result of the gambling corruption was that gambling was able to operate openly throughout the city. Although those with no moral opposition to gambling were not upset, they realized that the pattern of bribery in this area opened the police up to other corruption—looking the other way during drug activity, during certain Mob larcenies, and during other Mob activity. The commission saw a definite link between Mob organizations and gambling activity. The bribery pattern also taught the public that the police were not to be respected. This was especially harmful for children.

An additional danger to police corruption was that the police neglected their specific law enforcement duties as they concentrated on collecting their bribes and protecting gamblers. One remark from Serpico was telling. In effect, he said that all the crime in New York City could be ended if the police were not so busy seeking payoffs (76–77). The police responded to the commission by indicating that they were no longer concentrating on small gambling operatives but rather would focus on leaders in gambling operations. The commission felt that this might be admirable, but that it was not sufficient. They believed that "gambling is traditional and entrenched in many neighborhoods, and it has broad public support" (90). Such being their belief, they recommended that numbers, bookmaking, and other gambling should be legalized. Moreover, the regulation of such legalized gambling should be by civil agents and not by the police (18).

As the commission rejected the "rotten apple" theory, so did the Commission on the Review of the National Policy toward Gambling. They reported that a Pennsylvania Crime Commission that began its study in 1972 also found bribes from gamblers to be pervasive in Philadelphia, and the same was also found in other large cities.

Sources: Commission on the Review of the National Policy toward Gambling. 1976. *Gambling in America: Final Report.* Washington, DC: Government Printing Office; Knapp Commission. 1972. *The Knapp Commission Report on Police Corruption.* New York: George Braziller; Maas, Peter. 1973. *Serpico.* New York: Viking Press.

L

Lansky, Meyer

In 1902 Meyer Lansky was born Meyer Suchowljansky in Grodno, a small city in a region that has been—at different times—in Russia, Poland, and Germany. The mostly Jewish community was confronted by pogroms conducted by Czarist Russia. Meyer's father fled to the United States in 1909. When Meyer was about ten years old, he came to the United States with the rest of his family. They all settled in a low-rent neighborhood in Brooklyn, New York. From these humble beginnings in the tenements, Meyer Lansky rose to become the "godfather" of a national crime syndicate, a principal in an organization called "Murder, Incorporated," and the person recognized as the financial director of Mob activity in the Western Hemisphere.

Much of the financial activity conducted by Lansky concerned money used for the establishment of casinos—both legal and illegal—and also money taken out of the profits of these casinos. Meyer and his brother, Jake, who became involved in many of Meyer's activities, learned about crime on the streets of Brooklyn. Lansky was also an excellent student with a mind finely tuned for mathematical skills. He took a liking to the gambling rackets he observed on his neighborhood streets, because the games and scams conducted by various sharps and gangsters had a certain mathematical quality at their core. He also learned about the psychology of gambling and how the activity could prey upon the gullibility of players. Lansky also learned that street life had its violent side. While still a teenager, he intervened to stop another boy he had never met from shooting a fellow craps player. The aggressive boy was Benjamin Siegel. There on the streets, in the middle of what could have been a violent episode that could have ended what became a violent career anyway, Lansky and Siegel (later to be known as "Bugsy") became very close friends. They became partners in crime until the end—that is, to Siegel's end. Lansky was able to control Siegel's temper as no one else could, and he was also able to direct Siegel's penchant for violence. The two shared a similar background on the streets. When Prohibition began in 1921, they were prepared to be business partners.

Together Lansky and Siegel operated bootlegging activities. Bootlegging also brought Lansky into contact with Charlie "Lucky" Luciano. As their imbibing customers also craved gambling, their businesses were expanded. Liquor, betting, and wagering went together. With regard to gambling, Lansky was different from other mobsters running gambling joints. The others had proclivities to cheat customers, but Lansky knew the nature of the games. You did not have to cheat to make money. The odds favored the house, and all the operator needed was to have a certain volume of activity and to make sure that players were not cheating the house. Lansky could handle the numbers of customers he needed, and the numbers involved in determining the odds of each game. His mind was a calculator that allowed him to play it straight with the customers—and with his partners. But his operations also had rivals, and he cooperated with Luciano, Siegel, and others in consolidating control over their business enterprises by using violence.

When Prohibition ended on 5 December 1933, gambling became the major business interest for Lansky and many of his associates. Lansky became involved with gambling facilities in Saratoga Springs, New York; New York City; New Orleans; Omaha; and Miami. He also formed alliances with operations in Arkansas and Texas. In 1938, Cuban dictator Fulgencio Batista begged Lansky to come to the island and establish some honesty in their gambling casinos. The dealers were cheating the customers, and they were also robbing the dictator blind. He wanted his share. Lansky agreed to give him $3 million plus 50 percent of the profits the casino made. True to his word, Lansky cleaned up the operations. Later he took his skills for running an "honest" game for illicit operators to Haiti, the Bahamas, and London's Colony Club.

Perhaps Meyer Lansky's greatest legacy in gaming was found in Las Vegas. There he established the Mob's reputation for running honest games—albeit on behalf of mobsters. Lansky became a silent partner in the El Cortez in 1945. Soon his syndicate sold the property for a profit (they demonstrated it could make a profit), and they reinvested the money in the construction of the Flamingo Hotel and Casino in the Las Vegas Strip, six miles from the established casino area in downtown Las Vegas on Fremont Street. Bugsy Siegel was given the primary responsibilities for finishing the project. Siegel completed the job on time but not on budget. When the Flamingo opened in December 1946, it began to lose money. Lansky and his partners felt that Siegel had siphoned off much of the construction overruns as well as the operating revenues and put them into his own pockets—or into Swiss bank accounts. In June 1947 Siegel was murdered (by person or persons unknown) in the Beverly Hills apartment of his girlfriend. Soon afterwards the Flamingo was returning good profits under the operating hands of other Lansky associates.

Lansky's presence in Las Vegas persisted through the 1960s, as he was a silent partner in many gambling houses. It was said that he developed and perfected the art of skimming in order to get his share of the profits into his own pockets. A typical skimming device was to give large amounts of credit to players on gambling junkets. The players would then repay their loans to Lansky's associates, and not the casino, which would write them off as "bad debts." It was alleged that Meyer Lansky skimmed $36 million from the Flamingo over an eight-year period. He was also alleged to have taken portions of the profits from the Sands, Fremont, Horseshoe, Desert Inn, and Stardust through similar skimming scams. Lansky

also availed himself of large sums of money by taking a finder's fee when the Flamingo Casino Hotel was sold to Kirk Kerkorian in 1968.

In 1970 Lansky started an abortive campaign to legalize casinos in Miami Beach, where he had a residence. The year was not a good one for Lansky, as he was charged with tax evasion in federal court. He escaped prosecution by fleeing to Israel. There he sought citizenship under the Law of Return, which offered asylum to any person with a Jewish mother. As a result of considerable international as well as domestic pressure, he was denied Israeli citizenship and was exiled from Israel in November 1972. Back in the United States, he had to face tax charges and skimming charges, as well as contempt of court charges for fleeing prosecution. He dodged these charges at first because the court recognized he was in ailing health. Then in 1974, after he had undergone heart surgery, his case was brought before federal judge Roger Foley in Las Vegas. Foley dismissed all charges. The U.S. Justice Department appealed the judge's action but could not get it overturned.

Lansky was free and in the United States. But he was old and in ill health, and his family was in considerable turmoil. Although some sources suggested that he was a wealthy man—with resources between $100 and $300 million—he was not. His resources were depleted as he lived out his last years alone and with very few assets. He was estranged from his daughter, and one handicapped son died in abject poverty. Perhaps the longest reign of an American "godfather" ended with little notice when he died in 1983.

Sources: Hotaling, Edward. 1995. *They're Off! Horse Racing at Saratoga.* Syracuse, NY: Syracuse University Press, 217; Lacey, Robert. 1991. *Little Man: Meyer Lansky and the Gangster Life.* Boston: Little, Brown; Messick, Hank. 1971. *Lansky.* New York: Berkeley Medallion.

Las Vegas

From its earliest days, Las Vegas catered to travelers. Its springs watered not only the crops of local Indians but also the meadows (*las vegas* is Spanish for "the meadows") that in the 1830s supported an oasis for whites traveling the Old Spanish Trail between New Mexico and southern California. In

The Las Vegas Strip. Here on one street are eighteen of the twenty largest hotels in the world. Note the critical position of McCarran Airport at the foot of the Strip.

1855, Mormons built a fort and mission there, which also acted as a hostel for those plying the route between Utah and the church's colony in San Bernardino, California. Following the Civil War, several farm-ranches occupied the valley until 1905, when Sen. William Clark, principal owner of the newly created San Pedro, Los Angeles and Salt Lake Railroad, purchased Helen Stewart's ranch for $55,000. On this tract he platted his Las Vegas Townsite, a division town complete with yards, roundhouse, and repair shops. In addition, he used the ranch's water rights to supply his town and the thirsty boilers of his steam locomotives.

The little whistlestop struggled along into the 1930s, experimenting with commercial agriculture and other small industries to supplement its transportation economy, but without success. The first seeds of change came in 1928 when Congress appropriated funds for building Hoover Dam. Construction began in 1931, the same year that the state legislature re-legalized gambling and liberalized the waiting period for divorce to six weeks. The dam was an immediate tourist attraction, drawing 300,000 tourists a year. But even with these visitors and the 5,000-plus men who toiled on the project, gambling remained a minor part of Las Vegas's economy. When construction ended in 1936 and the dam workers left, the city experienced a mild recession. By decade's end, the town's population numbered only 8,400.

The real trigger for casino gambling was World War II. The sprawling Desert Warfare Center south of Nevada's boundary with Arizona and California, along with Twentynine Palms, Camp Pendleton, Las Vegas's own army gunnery school, and other military bases, provided thousands of weekend visitors who patronized the casinos. Supplementing these groups were thousands more defense workers from nearby Basic Magnesium and from southern California's defense plants.

This sudden surge in business sparked a furious casino boom, helped by reform mayor Fletcher Bowron's campaign to drive professional gamblers out of Los Angeles. Beginning in 1938, they began fleeing to Las Vegas, bringing their valuable expertise with them. Former vice officer and gambler Guy McAfee opened the Pioneer Club downtown and the Pair-O-Dice on the Los Angeles Highway (later the Strip) before unveiling his classy Golden Nugget (with partners) in 1946. Las Vegas also drew the attention of organized crime figures. Bugsy Siegel and associate Moe Sedway

The name Las Vegas is famous worldwide; here it is on a store front in Montevideo, Uruguay.

came to town in 1941 at the behest of eastern gangsters who were anxious to capture control of local race wires, the telephone linking system for taking bets on horse races.

Fremont Street grew, as older establishments bordering its sidewalks yielded to modern-looking successors. But a more significant trend in the 1940s was the Strip's development. The first major resort was the El Rancho Vegas, which revolutionized casino gambling. The brainchild of Thomas Hull, the hotel exemplified the formula he developed for the Strip's success. In 1940, he amazed everyone by rejecting a downtown location for more spacious county lands in the desert just south of the city. In the old West, gambling had always been confined to riverboats and small hotels near some railroad or stagecoach station. With his El Rancho Vegas Hotel, Hull liberated gambling from its historic confines and placed it in a spacious resort hotel, complete with a pool, lush lawns and gardens, a showroom, an arcade of stores, and most important, parking for 400 cars. It was Hull, the southern Californian, who recognized that the highway (with its cars, trucks, and buses) rather

than the railroad was the transportation wave of the future and that in the age of electric power, a downtown location was no longer superior to a suburban one.

For the most part, the El Rancho's successors in the 1940s, such as the Hotel Last Frontier, the Flamingo, and Thunderbird, followed Hull's model although with a larger and more plush format. The Flamingo, built by Bugsy Siegel and the *Hollywood Reporter*'s Billy Wilkerson, freed Las Vegas from the traditional Western motif slavishly followed by resorts such as the El Rancho and El Cortez downtown. With its Miami Beach–Monte Carlo ambience, the Flamingo opened a new world of thematic options for future resorts such as Caesars Palace and the Mirage.

The Strip assumed its familiar shape in the 1950s with the addition of eleven new resorts. Contributing to this growth was the liberalization of the nation's tax laws, which now permitted substantial deductions for business travel for professional improvement or the exhibition of goods. Anxious to fill their hotel rooms during the week, Las Vegas and Clark County officials formed a convention and visitors board in 1955 and built the Las Vegas Convention Center behind the Riviera Hotel on land donated by Horseshoe Club owner Joe W. Brown. Beginning in 1959, this new meeting hall, with its proximity to the Strip, tended to divert delegates away from Fremont Street. The construction of a new airport in 1947–1948 south of what became the Tropicana Hotel and its enlargement into a modern jetport in 1962–1963 only intensified the trend away from downtown. Construction of Interstate 15 in the 1960s along the resort corridor's west side, with five strategic exits compared to just one for downtown, contributed further to the flow of traffic to the emerging Strip.

In the 1960s, funding of the Southern Nevada Water project by Pres. Lyndon Johnson awarded the metropolitan area enough Lake Mead water to support a city of 2 million people, a vital prerequisite for the city's future growth. In addition, passage of Gov. Paul Laxalt's corporate gaming proposal in 1969 promoted the city's future development by ending the traditional requirement that every stockholder be investigated. The new law limiting the licensing procedure to only "key executives" permitted the entry of Hilton, Hyatt, MGM, and other corporate giants into the state. Only these entities, with their access to large pools of capital, could afford the billions necessary to build the megaresorts that characterize Las Vegas today.

In the 1950s and 1960s, a number of new technological advances and social trends reinforced the city's growth, leading to construction of spectacular newcomers such as Caesars Palace. Chief among these trends was the so-called middle-classification of the United States. In the postwar era, with more Americans graduating from high school and even college and with the postindustrial economy creating more high-paying white-collar jobs, both disposable and discretionary income—crucial to the budgets of gamblers and vacationers—soared. Moreover, income in California increased by more than the national average. Even blue-collar workers enjoyed substantial income gains. Las Vegas also benefited from the growth in automation and generous union contracts that gave workers more vacation and holi-

The Paris Casino on the Las Vegas Strip: The ultimate themed casino.

day time for leisure pursuits. In addition, the introduction of the credit card by Diner's Club in 1950 and arrival of the first commercial passenger jets in 1957 not only expanded Las Vegas's market zone to the East Coast, Europe, and Asia, but also eliminated the need to travel with large amounts of cash. These innovations, along with automated teller machines, debit card, and computers, all made long-distance travel easier, liberating Las Vegas from its dependence upon southern California.

Following a brief recession occasioned by the debut of Atlantic City, which temporarily siphoned off some of Las Vegas's East Coast market, the city rebounded in the 1980s and 1990s. In what has been Las Vegas's most spectacular round of expansion, a new generation of casino executives epitomized by Steve Wynn joined an older group led by Kirk Kerkorian to transform the casino city into a major resort destination. Several factors contributed to the metropolitan area's mercurial

Table 1 Casinos Listed by Date Opened and Motif

Property	Date	Motif	Comments
El Rancho Vegas	1941	Western	Across from Sahara front entrance; 1st hotel on Strip
El Cortez	1941	Mexican	First large hotel downtown
Hotel Last Frontier	1942	Western	Later site of New Frontier, 1955; Frontier, 1966
Golden Nugget	1946	Alaska-Western	Later added hotel rooms; 1st corporately owned hotel
The Flamingo	1946	Florida-Monte Carlo	Bought by Hilton from Kirk Kerkorian in 1970
Thunderbird	1948	American Indian	Later called the Silverbird, El Rancho
Desert Inn	1950	Arizona Resort-Spa	First hotel with golf course, 1952
Horseshoe	1951	Western	Remodeled version of the 1931 Apache Hotel
Sands	1952	Arizona Resort-Spa	Imploded for Venetian in 1996
Sahara	1952	Africa	
Showboat	1954	Mississippi Riverboat	
Dunes	1955	Sultan-Turkey Mideast	Imploded in 1993 for Bellagio
Riviera	1955	French	First Las Vegas high-rise hotel
Royal Nevada	1955		Just north of the Stardust; demolished in 1970s
Moulin Rouge	1955	Parisian Club	Near the Westside (first interracial hotel)
Hacienda	1956	Mexican	
Fremont	1956	Western	First downtown high-rise
Tropicana	1957	Cuba-Caribbean	
Stardust	1958	Disney-like	Disneyland in Anaheim opened in 1955
Mint	1962		Today the Horseshoe's hotel high-rise
Castaways	1963		Formerly Sans Souci—in today's Mirage Front Driveway
Aladdin	1966	Arabian Nights	Opened as Tally-Ho; high-rise, 1976; imploded, 1998; open 2000
Caesars Palace	1966	Greco-Roman	
Four Queens	1966		
International	1969	Cosmopolitan Cultures	Became Las Vegas Hilton, 1971, after Kirk Kerkorian sold it
Landmark	1969	Cape Canaveral Missile Gantry	Imploded 1995—across from convention center entrance
Plaza	1971	Railroad Station	Formerly Union Plaza on site of old railroad station
Circus Circus	1971	Circus	The casino opened in 1968
1st MGM Grand (Ballys)	1973	Hollywood; New Year's Eve	Burned in November 1980 and rebuilt by Kirk Kerkorian
Harrahs	1974	Riverboat, now Carnival	Formerly Holiday Inn–Center Strip until 1992
Marina	1974	Nautical	Today part of new MGM Grand
Palace Station	1976	Railroad	Opened as Bingo Palace
Maxim	1977		Closed 1999
Imperial Palace	1979	Japanese-Chinese	
Sam's Town	1979	Western	
Barbary Coast	1979	San Francisco	
Vegas World-Stratosphere	1979	Outer Space; now World's Fair	Reopened as Stratosphere Tower, 1996

(continues)

Table 1 *(continued)*

Property	Date	Motif	Comments
Fitzgeralds	1980	Irish	
Gold Coast	1986	Alaska Gold Rush	
Arizona Charlies	1988	California Gold Rush	
The Mirage	1989	South Seas	
Rio Suites Hotel	1990	Brazil	
Excalibur	1990	Medieval Europe	
Santa Fe	1991	Santa Fe	
Luxor	1993	Ancient Egypt	
Treasure Island	1993	Pirates-Buccaneers	
2nd MGM Grand	1993	Wizard of OZ; now City of Entertainment	1st hotel with a theme park
Boulder Station	1994	Railroad	
Hard Rock Hotel	1995	Rock 'n' Roll	
Texas Station	1995	Texas and Railroad	
Monte Carlo	1996	Monte Carlo	
The Orleans	1996	New Orleans	
New York-New York	1997	New York	
Sunset Station	1997	Spain and Railroad	
Reserve Hotel	1998	African Jungle	
Bellagio	1998	Tuscan Village	Replaced Dunes Hotel
Mandalay Bay	1999	Tropical Paradise	Replaced Hacienda Hotel
Paris	1999	Paris	
The Venetian	1999	Venice	Replaced Sands Hotel
The Regent Las Vegas	1999		First resort in Summerlin
Hyatt Regency–Lake Las Vegas	1999	Mediterranean	First resort at Lake Mead
The (new) Aladdin	2000	Arabian Nights	Replaced old Aladdin

Source: Prepared by Dr. Eugene Moehring, Department of History, UNLV.

growth. First was the construction of several lavish new hotels. The $630 million Mirage set a record for cost when it opened in 1989 and instantly became the state's leading tourist attraction, usurping the title held by Hoover Dam for over five decades. Quickly eclipsing the Mirage's price tag was Kirk Kerkorian's 1993 MGM Grand Hotel and Theme Park, which at nearly $1 billion was the most expensive hotel ever built. Steve Wynn, however, upped the ante almost immediately by imploding the Dunes Hotel and replacing it with the $1.6 billion Bellagio. At the same time, former COMDEX Convention mogul Sheldon Adelson took over the venerable Sands Hotel and demolished it to make way for the Venetian, a $1.5 billion Renaissance successor. These and other city-themed resorts such as New York–New York and Hilton's Paris combined with Circus Circus's up-scaled properties embodied by Luxor and Mandalay Bay to transform the Strip into an even greater tourist Mecca.

The second factor went beyond the money, the new restaurants, and bigger and grander casinos. Wynn helped pioneer a new approach to luring additional visitors to Las Vegas when he introduced the concept of offering special attractions both inside and outside his casino. The Mirage initiated the idea in 1989 with its erupting volcano, white tigers, and bottlenosed dolphins; Wynn continued the trend with his outdoor pirate battle at Treasure Island and Bellagio's "dancing fountains." MGM's theme park, Paris's Eiffel Tower, the Stratosphere, and the Las Vegas Hilton's Star Trek Experience only added to the fare.

A number of other themes have also characterized Las Vegas's efforts to broaden its market, among which has been an appeal to families. This trend actually dates from the 1950s when the Hacienda's Warren and Judy Bayley pursued the niche by offering guests multiple swimming pools and a quarter-midget go-cart track. In the 1970s, new Circus Circus proprietors William Bennett and William Pennington took their casino's clown theme and applied it to families rather than to high rollers as the original owner had tried to do. They added a carnival midway of games, candy stands, and toy shops and later supplemented it with a domed, indoor amusement park packed with thrill rides. Circus Circus repeated this success in the 1990s with its Excalibur Hotel, a dazzling medieval castle priced to attract the low-end family market. But despite these and other efforts to soften Las Vegas's image nationally, families have consistently represented no more than 8 percent of the town's visitors.

A third factor was that in the 1980s and 1990s, Las Vegas gamers also acquired a substantial home market as the metropolitan area's population skyrocketed from 273,000 in 1970 to more 1.3 million by century's end. The first major neighborhood casinos catering primarily to locals came in the 1970s when Palace Station (1976) and Sam's Town (1979) began operations. Reinforcing this market was the development of a new sector in the Las Vegas economy, the retirement industry. Following the deaths of gaming figures Del Webb (1973) and Howard Hughes (1976), their two companies joined forces to build what eventually became Sun City Summerlin. Since Hughes had purchased most of the outlying lands west of the city in the 1940s and Del Webb possessed the construction expertise to build homes, the companies formed a partnership and began work on Sun City in the mid-1980s. This project, along with its satellite communities, will ultimately contain more than 30,000 homes. Already, thousands of retirees have moved to Sun City and other small projects around the city. Las Vegas is the only place where they can not only "go to the malls" and engage in the traditional forms of leisure offered by Miami and Phoenix but also gamble on horses, sports, and cards.

In addition to these new flourishes, the casinos have pushed the addition of high-end retailing centers, such as the Forum Shops at Caesars Palace and its clones at the Venetian and elsewhere. The results have been nothing less than dramatic. As the twentieth-first century dawned, more spectacular resorts, world-class shopping, and special attractions had combined with the growing national and global popularity of casino gambling to make Las Vegas the leading tourist center in the United States—surpassing its nearest rival, Orlando.

—written by Eugene Moehring

Sources: Elliott, Gary. 1999. *The New Western Frontier: An Illustrated History of Las Vegas.* Carlsbad, CA: Heritage Media Corp.; Findlay, John M. 1986. *People of Chance: Frontiers of Gambling from Jamestown to Las Vegas.* New York: Oxford University Press; Moehring, Eugene. 2000 *Resort City in the Sunset: Las Vegas 1930–2000.* 2d ed. Reno: University of Nevada.

Las Vegas Nights. *See* Casino Nights (Las Vegas Nights)

Laughlin, Don

The post office said if he wanted delivery service he had to give a name to the town. And so in 1970, Laughlin, Nevada, was added to the map. Don Laughlin had moved to the "community," if it could be called that, four years before. He had been looking for a place to put a gambling hall, and he found a patch of land at the extreme south end of the state, near Davis Dam and across the Colorado River from a small town called Bullhead City, Arizona. Laughlin had run a small casino called the 101 Club in North Las Vegas for five years before he sold it in 1964 for $165,000. That was his stake as he entered the barren desert 100 miles south of Las Vegas.

Don Laughlin did not come to Nevada as an amateur in the gambling business. He was born and raised in Owatonna, Minnesota, in the 1930s and 1940s. There he saw gambling machines and other paraphernalia and instantly found them fascinating. As a teenager just beginning high school, he somehow ordered a slot machine from a mail-order catalog and was able to place it in a local club. Using profits from the machine, he bought more machines, and soon he ran a route of ma-

Don Laughlin. (UNLV Special Collections)

Laughlin was gambling's boomtown of the 1980s as Harrah's, the Hilton, Circus Circus, Ramada (Tropicana), and the Golden Nugget all built there. In the 1990s business fell off as Native American casinos in both California and Arizona picked off customers on their way to the river resort. Laughlin has also been hurt by large casinos in Las Vegas and by the fact that commercial air travel to the town is very limited. The essential market for the town is drive-in traffic from southern California and the Phoenix area as well as a steady stream of senior citizens from all over the United States and Canada. Laughlin features many RV parks near all of its resorts as well as the most inexpensive hotel rooms in a gambling resort in North America. Don Laughlin continues to be a booster for the gambling town, seeking to have events that will attract both younger and older patrons. Country music artists and motorcycle rallies are always part of the fare.

Sources: Hopkins, A. D., and K. J. Evans. 1999. *The First 100: Portraits of the Men and Women Who Shaped Las Vegas.* Las Vegas: Huntington Press, 240–241.

chines, punchboards, and pull tabs. Of course, all of this was illegal. He was forced to leave school because of his activity, but he did not mind, as he was making very good money for the time. It was not until 1952, following the work of the Kefauver Committee, that Minnesota cracked down on this illegal activity. With the passage of the Gambling Devices Act of 1951 (the Johnson Act), manufacturers could not easily ship gambling machines into the state. Laughlin knew there had to be better places to ply his trade. He vacationed in Las Vegas and quickly repeated the words of Brigham Young, "This is the place." In his twenties he worked in casinos and bars and then purchased his own beer and wine house. He added slot machines. His modest success allowed him to have funds to buy the 101 Club.

In Laughlin, Don Laughlin acquired an eight-room motel, which became the basis for expansion. He called his resort the Riverside. By 1972 it had forty-eight rooms and a casino. Eventually the Riverside grew to 1,400 rooms and a recreational vehicle (RV) park with 800 spaces.

Today the Riverside is but one of ten casino hotels in a community having 11,000 rooms. Certainly

Laws of Gambling on the High Seas. *See* Gambling on the High Seas, the Laws of

Let It Ride. *See* Poker

Lionel, Sawyer, and Collins. *See* Gaming Institutions: Research and Political

Lotteries
The drawing of lots probably constitutes the oldest form of gambling, and in modern times these games are the most prevalent form of gambling. Public opinion polls also show that the public approves of legalization of lotteries more than any other form of gambling.

History and Development
There is evidence that lottery games were played in ancient China, India, and Greece. The "drawing of lots" constitutes most of the references to "gam-

An elderly man sells lottery tickets in Santiago de Compostela, Spain. Outside of North America lotteries are major institutions for employing the poor, the handicapped, and the elderly. In the United States and Canada large corporations sell most of the tickets in their stores.

bling" in the Holy Bible. The technical elements of gambling may not necessarily have been present, however, in all the biblical situations, as lots were used mostly for decision making.

Lotteries were part of Roman celebrations. They were used at Roman parties to present gifts to guests, much as door prizes are given at parties and events today. Lotteries were also found in the Middle Ages, as merchants used drawings to dispose of items that could not otherwise be sold.

The first lottery game based upon purchases of tickets and awards of money prizes was instituted in the Italian city-state of Florence in 1530. Word of its success spread quickly, as France had a lottery drawing in 1533. The English monarch authorized a lottery that began operations in 1569. The English lotteries were licensed by the crown, but they were operated by private interests. One of the first lotteries held was for the benefit of the struggling Virginia Colony in North America. The 1612 drawing was held in London. Lotteries were soon being conducted in Virginia and the other colonies, however. It cannot be known for certain when the first lottery occurred in North America, as Spanish royalty had also approved of lotteries and may have held drawings in their colonial possessions. And, of course, Native Americans had games which encompassed the attributes of lotteries.

Lotteries were very popular throughout the seventeenth and eighteenth centuries in North America, and they were utilized both by governments and private parties. As in the Middle Ages, merchants used lotteries to empty shelves of undesired or very high priced goods. Individuals would do the same when they wished to sell estates, and no persons had sufficient capital to purchase large holdings. Institutions used lotteries to fund many building projects—for both public and private use. Canals, bridges, and roads were funded through lotteries, as banking institutions and bonding mechanisms were not yet developed in the colonies.

The reconstruction of Boston's Faneuil Hall in 1762 was accomplished through the sale of lottery tickets. So, too, were construction projects for many colleges, including Harvard, Yale, Princeton, Dartmouth, Brown, and William and Mary. Colonial churches were not universally opposed to lotteries, as they also used ticket sales to build structures. Only the early Puritans and the Quakers voiced opposition.

Generally, governments did not use lotteries except for specific building projects. They did, however, institute laws to license as well as govern operations of lotteries; many lotteries were outside of government supervision. Most uses of lotteries had a noble or charitable purpose. Several entities, first as colonies and then as states used lotteries for the support of military activities during both the French and Indian Wars of the 1750s and the Revolutionary War two decades later. The Continental Congress authorized four lotteries in support of George Washington's troops.

As the new nation began and a new century opened, lotteries remained very popular. Thomas

Jefferson, who had earlier (in 1810) indicated that he would never participate in a lottery "however laudable or desirable its object may be" (Clotfelter and Cook 1989, 299), changed his outlook in 1826, as he was financially short and desperately needed money to manage his estate. He asked the Virginia legislature to allow him to operate a lottery. In his later years he had mellowed on the subject of lotteries, as he described the lottery as a "painless tax, paid only by the willing" (quoted in Clotfelter and Cook 1989, 298; Thompson 1997, 8–9).

Lotteries proliferated in the early decades of the nineteenth century. In 1832 there were 420 drawings in the United States. The price of all the tickets combined constituted 3 percent of the national income and exceeded by several times the federal government budget. Soon the lottery was on a downhill slide, however, as the reform movement led by Pres. Andrew Jackson coalesced opposition to the drawings. Loose regulations and controls had permitted many scandals to surround the games. In one case a bogus lottery sold $400,000 worth of tickets but awarded no prizes. A Maine lottery director was discovered to have personally kept $10 million as expenses for a lottery that sold $16 million of tickets. In 1833 states started passing laws abolishing lotteries. First, Pennsylvania, Massachusetts, and New York prohibited the games, then all other states followed suit. As new states wrote their constitutions, the prohibitions were locked into basic laws. By the start of the Civil War only the border states of Delaware, Missouri, and Kentucky allowed lotteries. At the end of the war there were no lotteries.

The Civil War brought devastation to the American South, and several states looked toward lotteries for help. Most of the attempts to raise money with this kind of gambling were short-lived, however. Only the notorious Louisiana Lottery persisted into the 1890s. The Louisiana Lottery was conducted by private parties under a license from the state. Considerable corruption and bribery generated by the operation led the citizens of the state to ban the lottery in a public referendum. Legal lotteries ceased to exist in the United States until New Hampshire authorized a state-run sweepstakes in 1963.

Although legal lotteries remained dormant for nearly seven decades, illegal operations flourished in many parts of the country. In the nineteenth century, side lotteries had developed, as private syndicates, for a few pennies, would allow a person to "insure" that a number would not be selected. This game became known as policy, and was the forerunner of the numbers game. By the early decades of the twentieth century, the numbers game was well entrenched as an organized crime enterprise.

Lotteries returned to the legal scene with the passage of the New Hampshire Sweepstakes Law in 1963. Ticket sales began days after local communities approved their sale. Each cost three dollars, and buyers registered their names and addresses. The new lottery was based upon results of a horse race. First, forty-eight winning tickets were picked and each assigned to a horse in a special race. Depending on how the horse ran, the winners received from $200 to $100,000. The results were not an overwhelming success, but they generated substantial interest in the lottery idea. In 1967 New York State instituted a state-run lottery with monthly drawings. Tickets were purchased at banks where the buyers registered their names as in New Hampshire. In 1969 New Jersey followed. New Jersey was the first state to achieve desired levels of sales, as they used a weekly game and attracted customers with mass-marketing techniques. New Jersey also appealed to customers by selling tickets for fifty cents each, and players did not have to declare their names. New Jersey also utilized computers to track sales.

New Hampshire, New York, and New Jersey were not the first North American or Caribbean jurisdictions to have lotteries in the twentieth century. Mexico had established a game in the 1770s while it was still governed from Madrid, and the game persisted as the country gained its independence. Puerto Rico started its lottery in 1932. Canada, however, was influenced by the activity in the United States, as the national Parliament approved lottery schemes under provincial control in 1969. The first provincial lotteries appeared in Quebec in 1970. The spread of lotteries was quite rapid after the 1970s. All Canadian provinces as well as the Yukon Territory and Northwest Territo-

A Megabucks slot machine offers jackpots up to $20 million as a way to compete with lotteries.

ries instituted games, as did most of the states. By the end of the century lotteries were in thirty-seven states plus the District of Columbia. Politically, the lotteries have commanded public favor, as many states adopted lotteries through popular referenda votes that amended state constitutions. Of all the states only two, North Dakota and Alabama, have ever rejected lottery propositions.

Lottery revenues constitute over one-third of all the gambling revenues in North America. State and provincial governments have come to rely on the revenue, although in most cases it constitutes 3 percent or less of the budgets of the jurisdiction. The revenues fluctuate from year to year, but over the past several decades they have provided a constant steady flow of money to public treasuries. The certainty of that steady flow is dependent upon governments' adjusting to changing market desires of players and to advertising efforts. Game formats have changed considerably since New Hampshire first used its horse-race sweepstakes drawings. When one state offered an innovation—as New

Jersey did in 1969—other lottery states and provinces often followed with imitations. In 1974 Massachusetts began an instant lottery game using a scratch-off ticket that is preprogrammed to be a winner or loser. In 1975 New Jersey started a numbers game with the specific goal of competing with (and hopefully destroying) the prevalent illegal numbers game. New Jersey also installed an online system for tracking numbers at the same time.

Massachusetts tried a lotto game temporarily in 1977; then Ontario instituted the first permanent lotto game in 1978. Players choose six numbers from one to forty, and if no player has all six winning numbers, part of the money played is carried over into a future drawing with new sales of fresh tickets and a new drawing of winning numbers. Massachusetts allowed telephone accounts for lottery sales in 1980. South Dakota introduced the video lottery in 1989 with state-owned gambling machines that operate not unlike slot machines—albeit winning players receive tickets they must redeem for cash. The state of Oregon introduced its sports lottery also in 1989. Players pick four teams on a parlay card and if all the teams win, they receive a prize awarded on a pari-mutuel basis. In the 1970s Delaware had tried a sports lottery based upon individual National Football League games, but dropped the experiment after it suffered significant financial losses. Sports lotteries did not spread to other states, as Congress passed a law banning sports betting in all but Nevada, Oregon, Delaware, and Montana. Canadian provinces have sports lotteries.

With the beginnings of lotto games, lottery operations all went online; all the gaming sales outlets in the jurisdiction were linked together with a computer network. The next stage of lottery gaming could consist of games linked to individual home computers. Several European jurisdictions and Australian states offer these games. The Coeur d'Alene Indian tribe of Idaho had such a game for a brief time. Political opposition to Internet gambling, as well as attempts to enforce existing laws against transmitting bets over state lines, have precluded lotteries from venturing more into Internet gambling.

Several small states have banded together in order to offer bigger prizes and thereby compete with the bigger states. The first multistate lottery began in 1985 and involved New Hampshire, Maine, and Vermont. This was but a precursor of the Powerball game that started in the mid-1990s with the participation of twenty-one state lotteries. Another latter-day innovation for lotteries has been the use of instant ticket vending machines. It is estimated that there are 30,000 of the machines in operation in thirty states today.

Definition

In a generic sense, the word *lottery* can cover almost any form of gambling. The word has been applied to any game that offers prizes on the basis of an element of luck or chance in exchange for consideration, that is, something of value. In Canada, the term *lottery scheme* has come to include all casino games. The term as used in Wisconsin law similarly encompassed casino games, and as a result Native Americans were permitted to have casinos because the state had a lottery.

Thomas Clark's definition in *The Dictionary of Gambling and Gaming* is typical (Clark 1987). On the one hand, he views a lottery as "a scheme for raising money by selling lots or chances, to share in the distribution of prizes, now usually money, through numbered tickets selected as winners. . . ." On the other hand, he then adds, "in cards, a game in which prizes are obtained by the holders of certain cards" (122).

The Variety of Games

Passive Games

The first lottery games set up in the 1960s and 1970 were what are called passive games, in which the buyer is given a ticket with a number preprinted on it. At a later date—perhaps as much as a week (but originally even months)—the lottery organization selects the winning number in some random manner. Usually the organization will use a Ping-Pong ball machine that is mechanical and can be easily observed by viewers. Computers might do a better job in the selection process, but ticket buyers seem to like to see the process of numbers being selected. The ordinary games involved numbers with three, four, five, six, or more digits. Passive games have been operated on monthly, weekly, biweekly, or even daily sched-

ules. These games are described as passive because the player's role is limited to buying a ticket; the player does not select the number on the ticket. Also, the player must wait for a drawing; the player cannot affect the timing of the drawing.

Instant Games

In the case of instant tickets, a finite number of tickets are sold. The state contracts to have all the tickets printed. A number or symbol indicates that the player wins or loses. The symbol is covered by a substance that can be rubbed off by the player; however, the substance guarantees that the symbol cannot be viewed in any way before it is rubbed off. If all of a batch are sold, the lottery is like a bingo organization, as it merely managers the players' money, shifting it from losers to winners and taking out a fee. The lottery organization is the winner. Unlike passive games, in instant games the player determines the speed of the game; the player activates the game at any time by rubbing off the covering substance.

Numbers Games

In numbers games, players are permitted to actively select their own numbers, which are then matched against numbers selected by the lottery at some later time. Many numbers games are played on a daily cycle. Usually the lottery will have a three-digit number game and a four-digit number game. A pick-three game allows the player to pick three digits, which may be bet as a single three-digit number or in other combination of ways. A machine may also pick the number or digits for the player. However the number is picked and bet, the player is guaranteed a fixed prize if the number is a winning number. For instance, if it is bet as a single number such as 234, and number 234 is selected by a randomizer as the winning number, the player receives a fixed prize of $500 for a one-dollar play. For a pick-four game the prize typically would be $5,000 for a winning number bet "straight-up."

In these games, there can be no doubt but that the lottery organization is a player betting against the ticket purchaser. These are in effect house-banked games. Some states have sought to improve their odds (even though their payoffs give

In early national history the United States had lotteries that supported building projects. Fanneuil Hall in Boston was rebuilt after a fire with the proceeds of lottery ticket sales.

them a theoretical 50 percent edge over the player) by limiting play on certain numbers or by seeking to adjust the prize according to how many winners there are for the number picked.

Lotto Games

There is a variety of lotto games. In Texas there is a pick-six game. The lotto player selects six numbers or lets a computer pick six numbers from a field of numbers one through fifty. A ticket costs one dollar. A random generator picks six winning numbers. A fourth prize guarantees the ticket holder $3 for having three numbers. A pool amount for third prize is divided among players who have four numbers selected. A second-place pool is divided among players who have five numbers, and a grand prize pool is reserved for players with all six winning numbers. If no player has six winning numbers, the grand prize pool is placed into the grand prize pool for a subsequent game played at a later time. The lotto games gain great attention owing to superprizes that often exceed $100 million—the biggest prize was over twice that much. On 26 April 1989 the Pennsylvania lot-

tery gave a prize in excess of $100 million for the first time (NBC's *Today Show,* 26 April 1989). In the early 1990s a multistate lottery awarded a prize of about $250 million.

Video Lottery Terminals

Video lottery terminals are played very much like slot machines. They are authorized to be run by lotteries in several states, including South Dakota, Oregon, and Montana, in bars and taverns. In Louisiana the machines also are permitted but are operated by the state police. Racetracks operate machines under government control in Iowa, West Virginia, New Mexico, Delaware, Louisiana, and Rhode Island. Seven of the Canadian provinces have lottery-controlled machines in bars. They are also at racetracks in Alberta, Saskatchewan, Manitoba, and Ontario. Where the machines are operating in large numbers, they usually dwarf other revenues of the lottery.

Lottery Revenues

An overview of lotteries shows that in 1998 traditional (nonlottery machine) ticket sales amounted to $33.9 billion. Of this amount, $18.8 billion (55.4 percent) was returned to players as prizes, and $15.1 billion (44.6 percent) was winnings for the lottery. Each resident in the lottery states spent an average of $149.52 on tickets. This represented 0.6 percent of the personal income in the states. Governments retained $11.4 billion (33.7 percent) of the money spent on tickets after all expenses were paid. A study of lottery efficiency by *International Gaming and Wagering Business* magazine showed that overall it cost $0.3439 for each dollar raised for government programs by the lotteries (Christiansen 1999). The efficiency of raising money ranged from New Jersey, where it cost $0.2020 cents, to South Dakota and Montana, where it cost over one dollar in expenses to raise the dollar for government programs via lotteries.

Criticisms

Criticisms of lotteries come from several sources. With information such as that in the preceding section, many have suggested that lotteries are an inefficient way to raise money for government. Lotteries are also open to the charge of being regressive taxes, albeit "voluntary" ones, as Thomas Jefferson suggested. The National Gambling Impact Study Commission reserved many of its harshest criticisms for state lotteries. It should be added that lottery organizations were not represented in the membership of the commission. The commission was strong in protesting against lottery advertising both for being misleading and for encouraging people to participate in irresponsible gambling. The commission also concluded that lotteries did not produce good jobs (National Gambling Impact Study Commission 1999, 3–4, 3–5). Special criticism was reserved for convenience gambling involving lotteries, as the commission recommended that instant tickets be banned and that machine gaming outside of casinos— such as video lottery terminals at racetracks—be abolished (3–18).

Some also criticize lotteries as inappropriate enterprises that redistribute income by taking money from the poor and making millionaires, suggesting that some of these new millionaires are unprepared for their wealth and do not use it responsibly. This criticism is dealt with at length in H. Roy Kaplan's *Lottery Winners* (1978), discussed in the Annotated Bibliography.

Sources: Christiansen, Eugene Martin. 1999. "The 1998 Gross Annual Wager." *International Gaming and Wagering Business,* August, 20ff; Clark, Thomas L. 1987. *The Dictionary of Gambling and Gaming.* Cold Spring, NY: Lexik House Publishers, 122–123; Clotfelter, Charles T., and Philip J. Cook. 1989. *Selling Hope: State Lotteries in America.* Cambridge: Harvard University Press; Kaplan, H. Roy. 1978. *Lottery Winners.* New York: Harper and Row; Karcher, Alan. 1989. *Lotteries.* New Brunswick, NJ: Transaction Publishers; National Gambling Impact Study Commission [NGISC]. 1999. *Final Report.* Washington, DC: NGISC; Thompson, William N. 1997. *Legalized Gambling: A Reference Handbook.* 2d ed. Santa Barbara, CA: ABC-CLIO; Weinstein, David, and Lillian Deitch. 1974. *The Impact of Legalized Gambling. The Socioeconomic Consequences of Lotteries and Off-Track Betting.* New York: Praeger.
See also Economics and Gambling; Louisiana Lottery Company

Lottery Laws, Federal. *See* Federal Lottery Laws

Lotto Games. *See* Lotteries

Louisiana

Louisiana has both a long historical attachment to gambling enterprise and a recent one as well. Louisiana was a critical part of early gambling history in the United States, as New Orleans was the site of many clandestine dens of games when Andrew Jackson led the national military forces against the British redcoats in the battle named for the Crescent City in 1815. In 1828, John Davis opened what has been considered the first real casino in the United States at the corner of Bourbon and Orleans Streets. Following the Civil War, a well-bribed state legislature authorized the infamous Louisiana Lottery Company. The company began to sell tickets throughout the United States. It continued operations until 1895, after federal laws prohibited its use of the mail system. In the early 1900s all gambling was technically illegal, but gambling continued. Slot machines were openly played through the 1930s. Gambling clubs

Slot machines carry many popular themes. This "Elvis" machine is in the New Orleans Harrah's Casino.

kept operating even as Sen. Estes Kefauver's Senate committee on organized crime targeted the state for enforcement activities. In the meantime gambling on horse races had been legalized.

The modern era of legalized Louisiana gambling began in 1990 when the legislature gave the green light for the start of a new state lottery. In 1990 an act was also passed that opened the door for Native American casinos. In 1991 riverboat casino gambling was approved along with video poker machines for truck stops, race courses, restaurants, and taverns. The next year authorization was granted for a single land-based casino in New Orleans.

There are now multitudes of gambling sites in the state. Lottery tickets and charitable bingo games are in each parish. Video gaming machines are widely dispersed throughout the state. In 1966, however, the voters of each parish were empowered to vote on whether there would be machine gaming in their parish—at casinos, tracks, truck

stops, or restaurants. About half of the parishes said "take out the machines," although none of the casino parishes voted against the machines. One parish with a track said no to the machines. Machines were removed from the parishes objecting to them in 1999.

Louisiana has three Native American casinos. The largest, at Marksville (Tunica-Biloxi tribe) and Kinder (Alabama-Coushatta tribe), were originally constructed and operated by Grand Casinos. The third casino is near Charenton and is run by the Chitamacha tribe. Fifteen riverboat casino licenses have been granted, as has the license for the New Orleans casino. The New Orleans casino project opened in a temporary facility, however, and failed to generate sufficient revenue flows. The project for a permanent casino was put on hold for three years as the operators sought the protection of the bankruptcy court. The permanent facility was opened at the end of 1999. Several of the riverboats operations have also experienced failure and have seen licenses withdrawn and given to new vessels.

Louisiana has suffered from having considerable competition for its gambling patronage. Louisiana does not exist in a vacuum. Many gaming opportunities are available to residents in adjacent jurisdictions. Texas offers lottery sales and racetrack betting and also has had machine gaming in truck stops—although prizes were awarded in the form of merchandise, not cash. Mississippi has a wide array of casinos. A major Native American casino is in the central part of the state. Several casinos are located in Tunica, a northern Mississippi county near Memphis, Tennessee. Others are located in cities on the Mississippi River. The largest casinos are found on the Gulf Coast within a hundred miles of New Orleans. A considerable portion of the patronage of Mississippi casinos comes from Louisiana.

But patronage and revenue do not constitute the major problem with Louisiana gambling. Patterns of public corruption that seem endemic in the state's history came to the fore once again as licensing of gaming facilities and distribution of gaming equipment began. One governor, Edwin Edwards, was linked to a system of bribery involving several casino license holders. He was convicted and in 2001 is awaiting a prison term while appealing his case. Also, an organized crime ring was tied to persons distributing slot machines around the state.

Sources: Cabot, Anthony N., William N. Thompson, Andrew Tottenham, and Carl Braunlich, eds. 1999. *International Casino Law.* 3d ed. Reno: Institute for the Study of Gambling, University of Nevada, Reno, 42–63; Dombrink, John P., and William N. Thompson. 1990. *The Last Resort: Success and Failure in Campaigns for Casinos.* Reno: University of Nevada Press, 167–170.

Louisiana Lottery Company

Most lottery activity was banned by law before the advent of the Civil War. All but three states had constitutional or statutory prohibitions on the activity. In the 1860s the federal government began to consider legislation to keep lottery schemes from using the mail system (*see* Federal Lottery Laws). Amid these efforts to discourage lotteries, Louisiana lawmakers were persuaded in 1868 to charter a private company to run a lottery for twenty-five years. Other Southern states had also established lotteries as means of creating revenues during a period of governmental impoverishment brought on by the aftermath of war, defeat, and reconstruction. The Louisiana lottery was clearly the largest, and within ten years the other states ended their lottery experiments, leaving Louisiana's lottery in a monopoly position in the entire country.

The twenty-five-year charter was won for an annual fee of $40,000 that was promised by the promoters—a New York syndicate including John Morris and John Morrisey as well as New Orleans front men. A nationwide promotion campaign popularized drawings, which were conducted with much fanfare by two retired Confederate generals. Tickets cost from two dollars to forty dollars. Ninety percent of the sales of tickets were to persons living outside of Louisiana, and they used the mails to purchase tickets. Monthly prizes were as high as $600,000. Annual profits for the lottery company reached as much as $13 million. When the lottery charter was about to end, Morris sought a renewal for a fee of $1 million a year.

Considerable opposition to the lottery arose from many sectors. The lottery's operators were accused of corruption as well as extensive bribery. The federal government passed many acts seeking to stop the sale of tickets outside of Louisiana, but there was little effort to enforce the laws. An 1890 statute seemed to be more effective, and the promoters were cut off from the use of the mail. Efforts to win support for a renewal of the lottery were unsuccessful, and in 1893 the state joined all the others in the country and banned all lotteries. The syndicate that operated the lottery moved its operations to Honduras and shipped tickets into the United States through Florida. Congress plugged the loophole discovered in the law, however, and passed a very definitive prohibition against the importation and interstate transportation of lottery materials. The effective end of the Louisiana Lottery in 1895 marked the end of this form of gambling until New Hampshire began its state-run sweepstakes sixty-nine years later in 1964.

Sources: Commission on the Review of the National Policy toward Gambling. 1976. *Gambling in America: Final Report.* Washington, DC: Government Printing Office, Appendix 1.

M

Macao

The fate of the gambling operations in Macao passed into the hands of the officials of the People's Republic of China when the sovereignty of the Portuguese enclave in the South China Sea was transferred to the Chinese in 1999. Macao is a small peninsula and two tiny islands totaling only six square miles of land lying forty miles from Hong Kong by water.

As an enclave beyond the reach of the Chinese government, Macao became the site of many so-called sin activities. Gambling was illegal but operated openly until 1934, when the Tai King Company was given a concession to develop casinos and hotels. The company was led by Fu Tak Yam until his death in 1962. After that, operations were taken over by Stanley Ho, a Macao native. Ironically, Ho went on to purchase the largest casino in Portugal at Estorial.

There are now five large casino-hotel operations, as well as a floating casino docked in Macao. Additionally there are two machine-only casinos. A greyhound racetrack has one of these casinos. The casinos offer Western games such as roulette, baccarat, and blackjack, as well as slot machines of every variety. They also offer a wide assortment of Asian games such as fan tan, pacapio, tai-sai, pai gow, and mah jongg. Macao has been called both "the Monte Carlo of the Orient" and "the Las Vegas of the Orient." The Portuguese authorities over the enclave were glad to offer the sins of Macao to the Hong Kong community. Now that both entities are under the sovereignty of China, it remains to be seen how long the enclave will remain the regional "sin city."

Sources: Cabot, Anthony N., William N. Thompson, Andrew Tottenham, and Carl Braunlich, eds. 1999. *International Casino Law.* 3d ed. Reno: Institute for the Study of Gambling, University of Nevada, Reno, 523–525; Tegtmeier, Ralph. 1989. *Casinos.* New York: Vendome Press, 164–175.

Machine Gambling. *See* Slot Machines and Machine Gambling

Maine

In 1980 Congress passed the Maine Indian Claims Act, granting a financial settlement of $81.5 million to the Passamaquoddy, Penobscot, and Maliseet tribes. Part of the funds were used to purchase 300,000 acres of land that was put into trust for the tribes. The act specifically gave the state of Maine jurisdiction over civil and criminal law matters on any lands put into trust for the tribes as a result of such purchases from the settlement. After Congress passed the Indian Gaming Regulatory Act of 1988, however, the tribes sought negotiations so that they could have gambling that would be controlled by the federal government or by the provisions of a compact. The Penobscots held bingo games that violated state rules. Subsequent court actions upheld the state's power to control the gaming. Nonetheless, the state has tolerated bingo games that may extend beyond limits approved for other charity games in Maine.

Since 1973 the state has offered several lottery games, including instant tickets, lotto, and a daily numbers game. In the 1980s, Maine was a member of the Tri-State Lotto game with New Hampshire and Vermont. There are also charitable raffles and bingo, and harness racing is conducted on three tracks.

Sources: www.janus.state.me.us/agriculture/racing; www.mainelottery.com.

Manitoba

Manitoba quickly jumped into the gambling business after the Penal Code was amended in 1969. The Manitoba Centennial Lottery Act was passed in January 1970. In 1971 the province included large jackpot sweepstakes games among their product mix, and the tickets were sold locally as well as in other provinces. Soon the other provinces adjusted to meet the competition, and Manitoba decided it was better to work in tandem with other jurisdictions as it helped form the Western Canadian Lottery Corporation in 1974. Manitoba maintained a provincial lottery organization, however, that sold tickets to benefit charities and also licensed the selling of pull-tab tickets (called Nevada tickets) and the conducting of bingo events to benefit the charities. Casino events were also licensed, but soon the government found that they generated a wide range of control problems. There were three violent incidents concerning casino suppliers in the early 1980s. Accordingly, the Manitoba Lottery Foundation was created in 1984 in order to centralize all the char-

ity casinos into one operating organization. For most of the year the casino activity was conducted out of the Convention Centre in Winnipeg; in the summer, casinos were operated on the road by the government. Only table games were permitted, although the casinos had a slot machine with two dice faces on the reels—it was used to simulate craps games.

The government brought all the charities together and formed umbrella organizations that would distribute the profits to many good causes in the community. Among the recipients of the lottery and casino revenues was the municipally owned Winnipeg Blue Bombers football team.

The Casino at the Centre was closed in 1988, as the government decided to open a year-round casino. The Crystal Casino in Winnipeg was created as the first permanent government-owned casino in the Western Hemisphere. The Manitoba Lottery Foundation leased the seventh floor of the historic Fort Garry Hotel, a landmark railroad hotel built in 1913. The casino opened in 1990. In 1993 the foundation built two new gaming centers

A Canadian charity casino uses a slot machine to simulate dice rolls as dice were not allowed for many years. Scene from the Casino at the Centre in Winnipeg, 1988.

that served to replace bingo halls that they had been operating. The McPhillips Street Station and the Club Regent offered bingo and also video gaming. Later the casinos added table games, and on 22 May 1997, when the government closed its Crystal Casino, the two facilities absorbed all casino operations.

The government gaming agency also played a role in the establishment of First Nations gaming. Agreements have been undertaken between the government and twenty-six reservations for the conduct of bingo and casino-type games on their lands. The province also began a program for video lottery terminal gaming in 1991. By the end of the decade there were 4,500 machines operating in 580 commercial locations in the province. Additionally, the province authorizes all forms of pari-mutuel wagering both on and off track.

—coauthored by Garry Smith

Sources: Cabot, Anthony N., William N. Thompson, Andrew Tottenham, and Carl Braunlich, eds. 1999. *International Casino Law.* 3d ed. Reno: Institute for the Study of Gambling, University of Nevada, Reno, 180–185; Manness, Garth. 1989. "Views from the Regulators: Manitoba Situation." In *Gambling in Canada: Golden Goose or Trojan Horse?* edited by Colin Campbell and John Lowman, 69–76. Burnaby, BC: Simon Fraser University.

Martinique

Martinique is a Caribbean island that is governed as a department of France. It has a population of 350,000 on 425 square miles of land. It has two casinos, which are in the capital city of Fort de France: the 200-room Hotel Casino La Bateliere and the 300-room Meridien Martinique.

Sources: Cabot, Anthony N., William N. Thompson, Andrew Tottenham, and Carl Braunlich, eds. 1999. *International Casino Law.* 3d ed. Reno: Institute for the Study of Gambling, University of Nevada, Reno, 234–235.

Maryland

In 1973 Maryland began a state lottery. The state's gambling products include instant games, a lotto, a daily numbers game, and keno. It also participates in the six-state Big Game lotto. In 1974 Maryland authorized an "interest-only" lottery, based upon Great Britain's premium bonds. In Great Britain a player purchases a bond and remains a player in a monthly lottery as long as he or she holds the bond. The bonds draw no interest. Instead, funds equal to part of the interest are put into a prize pool. At any time the player may redeem the bond for the full price paid for it. In other places, such as Cuba and the former Soviet Union, these are called "lottery savings bonds." Many people buy such bonds for a couple when they are married or when a child is born. The former Soviet Union used these bonds in the 1920s, and Castro tried to institute this form of lottery in Cuba to replace the traditional lottery that had been operating before the revolution of 1959. After much planning, Maryland dropped its plans for the "interest-only" lottery, as the game could not promise the flows of revenue the state could gain from the other lottery games.

Maryland has had its share of active casino proponents, but their efforts have never gotten too far off the ground. Instead, nonprofit service clubs and organizations have won the right to have slot machine gaming at locations in counties that border the ocean. The state has also had an active horse racing industry for hundreds of years. There are six tracks as well as five offtrack betting facilities.

Since 1870, the Preakness, one leg of thoroughbred racing's Triple Crown, has been run at the Pimlico track in Baltimore. Pimilico is located on the edge of Baltimore. The track was also the site of one of the most notable match races in U.S. history, when in 1938 Seabiscuit defeated War Admiral, a Triple Crown winner.

Sources: Clotfelter, Charles T., and Philip J. Cook. 1989. *Selling Hope: State Lotteries in America.* Cambridge: Harvard University Press; Thompson, William N. 1997. *Legalized Gambling: A Reference Handbook.* 2d ed. Santa Barbara, CA: ABC-CLIO.

See also Horse Racing

Massachusetts

Gambling (European-style) came to Massachusetts with the Pilgrims. In fact, the gambling activity must have been pervasive, because the leaders of the colony saw fit to ban all gambling in 1621 in the Plymouth settlement's second year. Similar prohibitions were instituted by the Puritan groups that settled the Massachusetts Bay Colony. The political leaders knew at the beginning what they surely know now, that residents of Massachusetts love to gamble. The state lottery begun in 1972 now has sales of more than $3 billion a year, trailing only New York in sales. The state has instant games, lotto, and daily numbers games and also sells tickets in the multistate Big Game lotto. Massachusetts introduced the first instant lottery game in the United States in 1974. Massachusetts has also had a strong charitable gambling establishment, as well as pari-mutuel gambling for five dog and horse tracks.

Massachusetts has attracted much interest from casino gambling entrepreneurs. In 1978 a major campaign was initiated to win permission to place commercial casinos in the towns of Hull and Adams. The MGM Grand casino company was a major promoter of the idea. Local residents voted in favor of having casinos; however, efforts in the legislature that lasted more than three years only resulted in rejection. The state has one Native American tribe, the Wamponoags. The tribe has a small reservation on the exclusive resort island of Martha's Vineyard. Residents of the island have adamantly opposed the notion of having a casino near their expensive homes. The tribe agreed and made a deal to purchase land and create a new portion of their reservation near New Bedford, a declining city on the main coast. The governor negotiated the first stages of a compact for a casino. The proposed casino has confronted a series of roadblocks, however, and has not been opened as of early 2001. In the meantime casino ships began to operate three miles off Gloucester in the international waters of the Atlantic Ocean.

Sources: Dombrink, John D., and William N. Thompson. 1990. *The Last Resort: Success and Failure in Campaigns for Casinos.* Reno: University of Nevada Press, 108–114; Thompson, William N. 1997. *Legalized Gambling: A Reference Handbook.* 2d ed. Santa Barbara, CA: ABC-CLIO, 90, 165.

McClellan Committees

In January 1955, Democratic senator John McClellan of Arkansas became chairman of the Senate's Permanent Subcommittee on Investigations. Previously Sen. Joseph McCarthy (R-Wisconsin) had used the chair position to conduct his discredited investigations into the Communist influences in the national government. McClellan turned the committee toward other topics. Initially he looked at corruption in government contracts and trade with Communist China. He selected a young attorney named Robert Francis Kennedy to be the chief counsel and chief investigator for the committee. Kennedy sensed a presence of the International Brotherhood of Teamsters (the Teamsters' union) in certain contract abuses, and he began to probe Teamsters' activity. During 1956, he stumbled upon evidence of corruption by Teamsters' president David Beck. Kennedy was influential in having McClellan's committee transformed into a Select Committee on Labor Corruption. The eight-member bipartisan committee met for two years, during which Robert Kennedy's efforts were directed first at Beck, who was forced to resign his union position after a conviction for stealing from the union, and then at Beck's successor, James Riddle Hoffa. The investigations of Hoffa revealed a widespread involvement of Teamsters' union funding of casinos in Nevada, as well as other connections of union officials and organized crime figures; in turn, union activity was linked to illegal gambling. The committee reiterated the conclusions of the Kefauver Committee that there was indeed an organized crime association known as the Mafia and that its major illegal activity concerned gambling.

Following the 1960 elections, McClellan was appointed to be the chair of a newly organized crime committee while Kennedy became the attorney general in the presidential administration of his brother John F. Kennedy. The crime committee met for three years.

Kennedy created a crime task force within his office and pursued gamblers and their activity whether it was legal or illegal. He also pursued Jimmy Hoffa, seeking to expose him as a thief and gangster within the union. Kennedy and McClellan often worked in tandem, especially in the legislative field. Their joint efforts led to the passage of two major pieces of legislation in 1961 that grew out of the Kefauver Committee report. One law banned the use of interstate commerce for any illegal gambling equipment—hence expanding the thrust of the Johnson Act. The other prohibited the use of any interstate communication devices (wire services) in order to transmit information used for wagering activities.

Sources: U.S. Senate Committee on Government Operations. 1962. *Gambling and Organized Crime—Report.* Washington, DC: U.S. Government Printing Office.

See also The Federal Wire Act of 1961; The Gambling Devices Acts; Hoffa, Jimmy; The Kefauver Committee; Kennedy, Robert F.

Mexico

With a population approaching 100 million and an active tourist industry, Mexico could expect to be a lucrative market for casino gambling. Actually, for many decades in the early twentieth century, it was. Casinos performed well in cities bordering the United States, drawing in gamers from their northern neighbor. The casinos were associated with corruption, however, and following the election of reform president Lazaro Cardenas, they were closed down in 1938. The casinos of Tijuana and Mexicali had been very popular with Americans, and hopes have remained over the past six decades that they could reopen.

Indeed, discussions for reopening casinos have had the appearance of being quite serious. In the 1990s the discussions had an increasing measure of urgency, especially as economic troubles in Mexico increased. In 1996 the final draft of legislation for legalization was prepared for the National Congress. The plan called for ten casinos, one each to be located in a tourist city or border town. Sites selected included Tijuana, Juarez, Mexico City, Acapulco, Cancun, Cabo San Lucas, Cozemal, Monterrey, Puerto Vallarta, and Reynosa. Many U.S. companies rushed their representatives to Mexico City to offer governmental officials their proposals. The Mexican Tourism Agency studied the issue of casino gambling and concluded that the gambling would benefit the tourist economy.

As with every proposal before, however, just when action was about to be taken, forces of resistance intervened. Governmental corruption again was exposed, as was an increasing drug trade and involvement of organized crime operatives close to the government. Fears were expressed by leading politicians that casinos could be dangerous and that they could aid drug dealers with money-laundering services. In 1997 the proposal was set aside. The talk continues.

Mexico, while reluctant to embrace casinos, has embraced many other forms of gambling. The lottery has been active all throughout the nation's history, even in its colonial era. There are dog races and horse races and sports betting opportunities on international soccer as well as on all major U.S. sports events, both professional and collegiate.

Sources: Cabot, Anthony N., William N. Thompson, Andrew Tottenham, and Carl Braunlich, eds. 1999. *International Casino Law.* 3d ed. Reno: Institute for the Study of Gambling, University of Nevada, Reno, 217.

Michigan

In November 1996, Michigan voters passed Proposition E, which allows Detroit to develop three un-

Sign in Detroit casino promotes major league baseball to players.

The Motor City Casino in Detroit.

limited stakes, Las Vegas–type casinos. Although the victory for casino proponents was relatively narrow (51.8 percent to 48.2 percent), it was unexpected in most quarters. In the 1996 elections, voters in Ohio and Arkansas turned down casino proposals by wide margins. Detroit voters had rejected casinos in advisory votes in 1976, 1981, 1988, and 1993 before voting yes in advisory votes in 1994 and 1995. The Michigan vote was the first statewide victory for unlimited casino gambling since the 1976 New Jersey vote. Detroit has become the largest city in the Western Hemisphere with casinos located within its boundaries.

Michigan passed supplemental legislation to enable the licensing process to begin. The process involved recommendation from the city government and final action by a new state casino gaming commission. Proposition E actually designated two of the companies that would receive licensing. It was stipulated that preference had to be given for two licenses to organizations that had sponsored the successful Detroit advisory vote in favor of casinos in 1995. Those two companies were Greektown and Atwater groups. The Greektown Group of investors took on as partners a Chippewa

Native American tribe that runs several casinos in Michigan's Upper Peninsula. The Atwater Group teamed with the Circus Circus (now Mandalay Resort) Company for its proposals. These two winning proposals joined a successful proposal for the MGM Grand Company of Las Vegas. As a part of the licensing, the casinos won the right to have temporary facilities. The first temporary facility was opened by the MGM in the summer of 1999, and the other two followed in the fall.

In addition to many fees, the casinos must pay a tax of 18 percent of their gambling winnings. Of this amount, 55 percent goes to the city of Detroit and 45 percent goes to the state government's public education fund. Originally it was estimated that the casinos would have revenues approaching $1.5 billion a year. In the first year, two casinos had more than $700 million each.

The voters in Michigan were not strangers to casino gambling and other forms of gambling. In fact, the election victory on Proposition E could be credited to the existence of the Windsor, Ontario, casinos. The first Windsor casino had opened in 1994. A second riverboat casino opened two years later. Approximately 80 percent of the business in the casino came from the United States, and most of those gamblers were from the Detroit region. It was claimed that the Detroit economy was losing around $1 million dollars a day as Detroiters crossed over the Ambassador Bridge and through the Detroit-Windsor tunnel.

The state had its own casinos, which were operated by Native American tribes under agreements made in 1993. A state lottery was established in 1972 after voters removed a ban on this form of gambling. The removal of the ban also enabled the establishment of casino gambling for the Native Americans, as did a 1975 law that authorized charitable gambling, including charitable casino gambling. Pari-mutuel horse-race betting began in the state in 1933 in an effort to garner public revenues amid the Depression economy.

The billion-dollar Native American casino industry of Michigan is anchored by the Soaring Eagle Casino in Mt. Pleasant on the lands of the Saginaw-Chippewa tribe. The casino is the second largest Native casino in the country, having a gaming floor of 150,000 square feet, over a hundred tables, and 4,000 slot machines. Other large casinos are located in Pshawbetown near Traverse City, in Sault St. Marie, and in Baraga near Marquette. Fourteen other casinos are scattered across the state in Brimley, Watersmeet, Wilson, Petoskey, Athens, Manistique, Manistee, St. Ignace, and New Buffalo. The Native casinos had agreed to pay the state 10 percent of their machine revenues (with 2 percent going to local governments) as long as there was no other machine gaming in the state. After Detroit casinos were licensed, the state dropped its 8 percent share of the tax, but the tribes agreed to continue the 2 percent tax to the local governments.

—*coauthored by R. Fred Wacker*

Sources: Cabot, Anthony N., William N. Thompson, Andrew Tottenham, and Carl Braunlich, eds. 1999. *International Casino Law.* 3d ed. Reno: Institute for the Study of Gambling, University of Nevada, Reno, 64–71; Dombrink, John D., and William N. Thompson. 1990. *The Last Resort: Success and Failure in Campaigns for Casinos.* Reno: University of Nevada Press, 114–119; Wacker, R. F., and Thompson, W. N. 1997. "The Michigan Question: A Legal Quandry." *Gaming Law Review* 1 (Winter): 501–510.
See also Ontario

Minnesota

Minnesota has been a very active gambling state, as I observed during a tour of the state in 1996. Shortly after the state lottery began in 1989, the governor signed agreements so that Native tribes could have casino gaming. The agreement (which could only allow such gaming as was permitted others in the sate) was based upon the fact that Minnesota also allowed private social card games and machine games that could give replays as prizes.

The eleven tribes in Minnesota now run nineteen gambling halls with bingo, blackjack, and machine games. The largest casino is Mystic Lake, which is run by a Sioux tribe and located within the Minneapolis metropolitan area. The facility has 2,500 slots and 100 table games. With a monopoly facility serving several million people, the casino grosses several hundred million dollars in net profits each year. Each of the 300 tribal members has received annual per capita bonuses of more than $700,000 because of the casino profits. Other large casinos include the Treasure Island in Red Wing; the two Grand Casinos in Hinckley and Onamia; and casinos in Duluth, Carleton, Granite Falls, Mahnomen, and Morton.

The state also has pari-mutuel racing. Canterbury Downs, the largest track, was closed, however, shortly after the Mystic Lake Casino opened. Since that time there have been repeated efforts to allow the track to have machine gaming as a tool to restore live racing and also to gain revenues for a new stadium in downtown Minneapolis. The efforts have failed. The facility remains open as an intertrack horse race-betting parlor.

Charitable gaming prospers, as Minnesota sells more pull-tab tickets than any other jurisdiction. Charities win over $200 million a year from the sale of the tickets, ten times as much as they win at bingo games.

Sources: Minnesota State Lottery. 1994. *Gambling in Minnesota.* Roseville: Minnesota State Lottery.

Mississippi

The state of Mississippi has the third-largest volume of casino gambling of any venue in North America. Approximately thirty casino boats gener-

The Las Vegas Casino boat in Mississippi.

The Cotton Club Casino near Greenville, Mississippi.

The Lady Luck Casino in northern Mississippi near the famous "Jazz Highway" from Greenville to Memphis.

ate nearly $2 billion in gambling wins each year. The state also has one of the largest Native American casinos—the Silver Star run by the Las Vegas Boyd Group on behalf of the Mississippi Choctaw tribe. The casino, near Philadelphia, has almost 100 tables and 3,000 machines. The state has no other legal gambling activity—no lottery gambling or charity games.

Mississippi did not set out a deliberate course for casino gambling. Instead, the state seemed to just let it happen. Casino-style gambling arrived in Mississippi aboard the cruise ship *Europa Star* on 19 December 1987. The 157-foot ship with a Panamanian registration docked at Biloxi and began a series of "cruises to nowhere." Gambling activities on the ship included roulette, bingo, and slot machines. Short round-trip cruises were made three miles offshore of Biloxi but within the boundaries of a series of barrier islands. The ship operators claimed they were in international waters. The state attorney general sought to end the gambling by claiming the ship was in state-controlled waters until it was three miles outside the barrier islands.

Before the matter was resolved in court, the legislature took up the issue. At first legislators sided with the attorney general. In March 1989, however, a law was passed allowing large ships—at least 300 feet long—to conduct gaming in the waters inside the islands. One ship, the *Pride of Mississippi,* operated under provisions of the law for one season; however, it could not operate at a profit. Nonetheless, businesses along the Gulf Coast pleaded to the legislature for more open gambling rules, as the ship had generated significant tourist revenue for them. The legislature now had the Iowa model for riverboat gambling and decided to duplicate it—to an extent.

On 23 March 1990, the governor signed into law an act permitting casino gambling on riverboats. The boats had to be at least 150 feet long and located in navigable tributaries and in oxbow lakes in counties bordering the Mississippi River or on the Gulf Coast. The counties were given the option of having elections banning the boats from their waters. A measure describing a regulatory framework almost identical to that in Nevada was enacted into law in the summer of 1990.

The Mississippi law is distinguished from other riverboat laws in that there was never an expectation that the riverboats would have to leave shore. There was no cruising requirement. Eventually the facilities lost all pretense of being navigable operations. Instead, barges were moved into the permissible waters; gambling structures were constructed on top of the vessels, and hotel and restaurant facilities were constructed around the barges. The barges included flotation mechanisms so they could rise and fall as water levels changed during flood seasons. Most gamblers cannot perceive that they are over water when they are gambling. In addition to fees, the boats pay taxes of 8 percent on their gambling wins to the state and additional taxes of 10 percent of the state amount to local governments. The casinos are open twenty-four hours a day and unlike the situation in other riverboat states, players may enter and leave gambling areas whenever they wish to do so.

Most of the boats are located in several distinct areas of the state. The Gulf Coast (Biloxi and Gulfport) has a dozen casino boats; Tunica County near Memphis, Tennessee, has about ten boats; there are four boats in the Greenville area and four boats in the Vicksburg area. The largest casino is Steve Wynn's Beau Rivage, which opened in Biloxi in 1999 with 1,000 hotel rooms.

Sources: Cabot, Anthony N., William N. Thompson, Andrew Tottenham, and Carl Braunlich, eds. 1999. *International Casino Law.* 3d ed. Reno: Institute for the Study of Gambling, University of Nevada, Reno, 72–91.

Missouri

Missouri started a state lottery in 1986. The state also permits charity gaming, and in June 1987 pari-mutuel racing began. The most noticeable form of gambling in the state is found on fourteen riverboats that started operations in the mid-1990s, during a very confusing series of court battles and voter referenda.

The initial vote to approve riverboat gambling came on 3 November 1992. The legislative initiative authorized casino boats for the Mississippi and Missouri Rivers. The boats had to take two-hour cruises, and players could not lose more than $500

during the cruise. After the referendum, seven companies applied for licenses. Before the boats could cruise with full-scale casino gambling, however, the state was hit with a lawsuit challenging the right to operate casino games. The state constitution banned lotteries. The initial court ruling was that most casino games were lottery games. The boats that were operating had to close down their machines, roulette wheels, and baccarat games, as these were considered lotteries. They were permitted to have live poker and blackjack games. A few did for a short time. (The state could have a lottery because the voters in 1986 had amended the constitution to permit a state-run lottery only.)

The casinos got together and put a new constitutional initiative on the ballot in April 1994. This time the voters said no, to their games. The casinos immediately started another petition campaign, however, and finally the voters approved the required constitutional amendment in November 1994. Fourteen casino boats were then approved for the state's waters. The boats pay fees and a tax of 20 percent on their gambling win, which is shared between the state and the local community. They have enjoyed a mixed success, as they face considerable competition—among themselves and with boats in Iowa, Illinois, and Mississippi. Since the beginning the boats have sought to have the $500 betting loss cap eliminated, but they have failed in these efforts.

They have also sought to remove the requirement that they have to cruise in the rivers and be docked within the channels of the rivers. This ridiculous requirement was revealed for its stupidity when a commercial barge hit one of the boats in its dockside position at a time when there were 2,500 players aboard. A major catastrophe was narrowly avoided. Several companies began to put boats in artificial channels cut into the river. The gaming commission approved this move; however, the state supreme court ruled that this violated the requirement that the boats be in the river. Again the casinos went to the voters, and in 1998, the voters said the boats could be in artificial "moats" and that actual cruises were no longer necessary. The boats must still have "mock" cruises of two hours, however, during which the gamblers cannot lose more than $500.

Sources: Cabot, Anthony N., William N. Thompson, Andrew Tottenham, and Carl Braunlich, eds. 1999. *International Casino Law.* 3d ed. Reno: Institute for the Study of Gambling, University of Nevada, Reno, 92–97.

Monaco

For a century and a half Monaco, with its Monte Carlo Casino, has been the essence of classical gambling elegance. The casino, or casino complex, has been the leading European gambling facility until recent times. It was the most prominent casino property in the world until the advent of the Las Vegas megacasinos. Monaco itself is a historical throwback, a city-state of less than one mile square on the French Riviera coast of the Mediterranean. It is surrounded by water on one side and by France on the other three sides. The state began as a semi-autonomous political entity in the thirteenth century when an exiled clan called the Grimaldis established their independence from the Republic of

Monaco: An entire country built its economy around a casino.

Genoa on the then-barren seacoast spot. The geographical isolation and seemingly worthlessness of the land helped preserve its independence. That independence has over the centuries become the reason for existence of the state of Monaco. Survival has come through isolation, treaties and diplomacy, and trade concessions, but mostly through the establishment of an economic base by means of the creation of the casino resort complex.

The gambling industry of Monaco developed mostly because its neighbors turned puritanical regarding the world of risky games in the nineteenth century. France closed its casinos in the 1830s, and soon afterward so did the states of Italy and Germany. An early effort to build casinos in 1861 failed in Monaco owing to the lack of capital resources. Soon Louis and Francis Blanc came to the rescue. The two brothers had been very successful in a casino venture at Bad Homburg near Frankfurt. That property had been closed under pressure from the Prussian government. Francis survived Louis, and he contracted with the prince of Monaco to set up a company—Societe des Bains de Mer (SBM)—to build and operate a casino. The SBM promised to improve the harbor and to finance the building of a road to Nice. Local opposition to casino gambling was overcome when the SBM persuaded the prince to suspend all taxes on local residents. The residents were also denied access to the casinos except as employees. This restriction applies to the 25,000 citizens of Monaco, but not to the alien residents of the tax haven.

Unlike other European casinos today, Monaco is a very democratic place that welcomes all visitors. It sets forth a philosophy of operations similar to that found on the Las Vegas Strip—gambling is considered an exported tourist product.

Francis Blanc was succeeded by his son, Camille, in 1889. Working with Monaco's Prince Albert, the SBM under Camille's leadership helped finance a ballet, as well as an oceanographic museum and research center. World War I greatly hurt business, but Sir Basil Zaharoff, a Turkish-born financier of Greek ancestry, came to the rescue. He helped Albert negotiate a new treaty for autonomy from France and generated new capital resources for the casino. Zaharoff took over the property in 1923 (Jackson 1975, 124).

The casino was able to remain prosperous through the Depression years and also through World War II as Monaco maintained a posture of neutrality. After the war, however, there was a major business downturn. While the SBM was nearly bankrupt, its control was taken over by Aristotle Onassis in 1951. Through the 1950s, Onassis worked closely with Monaco's Prince Rainier to build up the facilities. The two had a major falling out in the early 1960s, and Rainier seized the reins of control over the SBM. The prince directed the completion of a railroad tunnel that took tracks away from the seafront, and he added a new beach area, as well as developing new casino facilities. One of the facilities was an American Room that featured slot machines. Rainier also invited the Loews Hotel Corporation of New York to build a new casino complex that today represents the closest one can come to a Las Vegas–style casino in Europe. There are no door fees and no dress codes, and slot machines are adjacent to the table games.

The Monaco casinos now produce wins approaching $200 million a year, and they still provide the basis for a tourist atmosphere and for the economic support for the small city-state of Monaco.

Sources: Cabot, Anthony N., William N. Thompson, Andrew Tottenham, and Carl Braunlich, eds. 1999. *International Casino Law.* 3d ed. Reno: Institute for the Study of Gambling, University of Nevada, Reno, 441–445; Jackson, Stanley. 1975. *Inside Monte Carlo.* New York: Stein and Day.

See also The European Casino

Money Laundering. *See* Cash Transaction Reports and Money Laundering

Money Laundering Act of 1986. *See* Cash Transaction Reports and Money Laundering

Money Laundering Suppression Act of 1994. *See* Cash Transaction Reports and Money Laundering

Montana

Montana has more gambling sites than any other state with the exception of Nevada, and perhaps South Carolina. There are well over 1,700 age-restricted locations offering over 19,000 machine games of poker, keno, and slot simulations. The "casinos," which have twenty machines each, may also allow poker-like games on premises. Additionally the operators may sell raffle and pull-tab tickets. Montana is also one of four states that is permitted to have sports betting. Taverns are allowed to let players participate in pools on events such as football games and World Series games.

The state permits wagering on quarter horse races and participates in the sale of tickets for Lotto America. The bulk of the Montana gaming is at the "casino" sites, 93 percent of which are places that sell alcoholic beverages.

Gambling operations came to Montana more as a result of legal decisions than of deliberately studied policy. The voters legalized gambling in 1972, and two years later the legislature authorized sports pools, bingo games, raffles, and live card games. In 1976 the state supreme court ruled that video keno games were "live" keno games. Tavern owners across the state began installing not only video keno games but also other machines for gambling. In 1984 the Montana Supreme Court said these did not satisfy the "live games" designation. Therefore, the legislature was called into action by the tavern owners. First they approved the placement of five machines in a tavern. Subsequently, the number of machines was changed, and it now rests at twenty per liquor license. As some taverns hold multiple licenses, they actually operate forty or sixty machines.

The "casinos" pay a state tax of 15 percent on their machine winnings, as well as a fee of $250 to $500 for (really) live tables. The state receives approximately $20 million in gaming taxes each year.

Four Native American tribes also operate machine and poker gambling casinos in the towns of Box Elder, Crow Agency, Lame Deer, and Wolf Point.

Sources: Cabot, Anthony N., William N. Thompson, Andrew Tottenham, and Carl Braunlich, eds. 1999. *International Casino Law.* 3d ed. Reno: Institute for the Study of Gambling, University of Nevada, Reno, 98–100.

Morrisey, Jack

Jack Morrisey (1831–1878) was born in Ireland. His family moved to Troy, New York, when he was a boy of three. It was not long before the small boy became a man larger than life. In Troy he was a gang fighter. He gained the nickname "Old Smoke" from a barroom brawl in which he and his adversary knocked over a stove. They finished their "match" on the floor among burning coals. When Morrissey rose up as the winner, his hair and clothing were on fire. Soon afterward, "Old Smoke" was fighting according to the rules of professional boxing.

Morrisey sought a fortune by joining the Gold Rush West. The nuggets he got, however, were the result of an arranged prizefight. He performed so well that he was recruited back East, where he participated in and won a heavyweight championship match. There is no record of a defense, so he probably retired as the undefeated champ. He was only twenty-two at the time, but there was real money to be made, in politics, in the saloon business, and in gambling. He opened a dancing and gambling joint in 1852, and he used it as a staging point for political activity.

He became an important player in the Tammany political machine, as the organization needed tough characters to monitor their ballot-stuffing activities and to keep opponents at bay. Although an Irishman, Morrisey was their man, and he often led fights against immigrant opponents—often other Irishmen. Through his aliances in politics, Morrisey won two terms in the U.S. House of Representatives. He is the only heavyweight champion of boxing to have served in the United States Congress. While not exactly a legislative leader, he would occasionally make a fiery speech on the House floor. There he would rant and rave and challenge any ten of his political opponents to fight him at a single time.

In the meantime, Morrisey was attracted to the racing scene. He organized the first thoroughbred races at Saratoga, New York, and he also built the track that is still in use today. Morrisey wanted the high social status he saw in Saratoga, and he went after it. He upgraded the quality of gambling action at the resort by building the Saratoga Club House, then the most plush casino in the United States. He had only two rules for his house: no residents of Saratoga could gamble, and no women were permitted in the gambling saloons. Women, however, could come to the restaurants and the other entertainment areas. It is reported that over 25,000 women came into the Saratoga Club House each season (Chafetz 1960, 285–286). For a dozen years the Saratoga Club House was the national champion casino. Through it all Morrissey smoked twenty cigars a day and led a very fast life and a tough life to the end. By the age of forty-seven in 1878 he had worn his body out, and when he was hit by a heavy cold, the champ was out for the count.

Sources: Asbury, Herbert. 1938. *Sucker's Progress: An Informal History of Gambling in America from the Colonies to Canfield.* New York: Dodd, Mead, 358–418; Chafetz, Henry. 1960. *Play the Devil: A History of Gambling in the United States from 1492 to 1955.* New York: Potter Publishers, 271–296; Hotaling, Edward. 1995. *They're Off! Horse Racing at Saratoga.* Syracuse NY: Syracuse University Press, 30–40, 78–85; Longstreet, Stephen. 1977. *Win or Lose: A Social History of Gambling.* Indianapolis, IN: Bobbs-Merrill, 61–64.

Moss, Johnny

Johnny Moss, superb gamester and gambler and world champion of poker, was born in 1907 in a poor Texas town. Eventually his family drifted into Dallas when their economic condition did not improve much. At eight years old Johnny quit school and began selling newspapers. He also met his lifelong friend, Benny Binion. Together they learned games, and they began their life careers as players. By the time Johnny Moss was fifteen, he was making a living at dice.

Soon he was wandering around Texas playing games and learning games. In West Texas he also worked on a ranch. There one day he rode his horse by a golf course and saw two hackers betting as they played. He figured, "What folks are betting on, you learn to play, that's all." So he learned to play golf. He learned so well that he much later played a round of golf at the Desert Inn for a $100,000 stake. He beat 80, shooting 79, with irons only. At an earlier time, he won a $5,000 bet that he could shoot 9 below 45 with only a four iron. Johnny also learned to bowl. But these were really the side games. Following an automobile accident he could no longer compete in physical activities at the level that a hustler must compete in order to win. He turned to his real game—poker.

But still there were physical dangers. "To be a professional gambler," he related, not only means "you have to know how to play the games, [but also] you have to keep your eyes open for two dangers, the hijackers and the law" (Bradshaw 1975, 165). But that was before the big action moved to Las Vegas and was held under the big tops of the legal casinos. In 1949, Nick the Greek Dandolos came to Las Vegas looking for a game. Benny Binion, of the Horseshoe casino, called his friend Johnny Moss in Texas and suggested they have a one-on-one match in his casino. It was the first world championship poker match, and it lasted five months before Nick the Greek threw in his cards and walked away.

Twenty-one years later, the formal World Series of Poker began. Johnny Moss won it three times in the 1970s. Moss won the first tournament and played in every one until 1995. In his later years he played regularly, but not for the big stakes that had previously driven him. For a while, he was the poker room manager at the Aladdin Hotel. But mostly he traveled back and forth between Las Vegas and his home in Odessa, Texas. He died there at the age of eighty-eight, in 1995.

Sources: Alvarez, A. Alfred. 1983. *The Biggest Game in Town.* Boston: Houghton Mifflin, 17–27; Bradshaw, Joe. 1975. *Fast Company.* New York: Harper Magazine Press, 145–196; Konik, Michael. 1996. "The Grand Old Man." *Poker World* (February): 447.

N

National Center for Responsible Gaming. *See* Gaming Institutes: Research and Political

National Coalition against Legalized Gambling. *See* Gaming Institutes: Research and Political

The National Gambling Impact Study Commission (1997–1999)

The National Gambling Impact Study Commission met from June 1997 through June 1999. It produced a report recommending seventy-six changes in public policy toward gambling activity. The commission was the creation of a new set of political forces in U.S. politics.

As casino-style gambling rapidly spread across the United States in the early 1990s, forces in the debate on gambling turned their attention to the national policymaking arena. Under the leadership of Tom Grey, a United Methodist minister and Vietnam War veteran from Galena, Illinois, the National Coalition against Legalized Gambling emerged to fight gambling wherever the issue arose as an issue of public policy. The coalition also urged politicians in Washington, D.C., to examine gambling and to consider regulation and taxation of gambling activity. In 1994, President Clinton sought to increase the federal budget by $1 billion dollars after Congress had established spending caps for the year. To do this, he would have had to either reduce other spending by a billion dollars or find a new source for the money. He suggested a new source: a 4 percent tax on all gambling profits in the United States. As his real target was the commercial casino industry, casinos reacted. Major Las Vegas and Atlantic City properties quickly came together and formed the American Gaming Association (AGA). The association selected Frank Fahrenkopf, formerly the chairman of the Republican National Committee, to be its spokesman and executive director. The tax measure was silently killed, but national politics were changed forever, as the gaming industry moved onto the stage as a major political campaign contributor for both parties.

The forces were joined in battle in 1995 when Congressman Frank Wolf (R-Virginia) introduced H.R. 497, a bipartisan bill to create a national study commission to examine gambling in the United States. Senators Paul Simon (D-Illinois) and Richard Lugar (R-Indiana) cosponsored companion legislation in the Senate. The AGA immediately feared that Grey and Wolf had their sights set on destroying big casino gaming with a "witch hunt" that would lead to recommendations for national taxation and regulation of gambling, as well as restrictions on the spread of legalized gambling. The AGA was outmaneuvered in committee hearings on the bill, as Grey and others emphasized the many negative consequences of gambling and the fact that political leaders did not have a full knowledge of the impacts of gambling. The AGA had to back off of its effort to simply kill the bill. Instead it used its power base—its campaign funding potential as well as congressional voices from gaming states—to make the bill less offensive to its interests. The bill to create the commission was substantially changed from the bill Wolf wanted. The commission was charged with investigating impacts of all gaming, whereas Wolf had wished to target casino gaming only. The AGA knew it could deflect much of the criticism of casino gaming by having investigators look at lotteries, charities, and Indian gaming. The commission was denied wide-ranging subpoena powers, whereas Wolf had desired that the commission be able to subpoena casino files and data on players.

The casino interests also negotiated a selection process that allowed them to have a strong voice on the panel. It appeared that Congress wished to satisfy conservatives by establishing the commission, but members of Congress were also quite aware that casinos were a major source of campaign funds. Unfortunately for the state lotteries, they were not able to make campaign contributions. They were not given an "inside voice" in the membership on the commission. The amended bill was quickly passed by each house, and on 3 August 1996 it became Public Law 104–169 as it was signed by President Clinton.

Three of the nine members of the National Gambling Impact Study Commission were appointed by the president, three by the Speaker of the House, and three by the majority leader of the Senate. The two congressional leaders each allowed minority party leaders in their chambers to select one of the three respective appointments. The commission ended up as a bipartisan group with both vocal antigambling advocates and commissioners who were close to the casino industry.

Two strong voices against gambling won appointment. James Dobson serves as the president of a religious-right organization, and Kay James has been a dean at religious-based Regent University in Virginia. On the other side, one major casino executive—Terrence Lanni of the MGM Grand—was selected, as was the head of the largest labor union in Nevada's casino industry, John Wilhelm, and the head of the Nevada Gaming Control Board, Bill Bible. A Native American from a nongaming Alaska tribe was selected—Robert Loescher. He turned out to be very much an advocate not only for Native American gaming but also for the industry as a whole.

Three "neutrals" seemed to hold the balance of power. One was radiologist Paul Moore, a close friend of Senate majority leader Trent Lott. (Lott became the target of a public interest group as it was revealed in the commission's last days that he had received an exorbitant amount of campaign funding through the casino interests.) Also considered in the center were Leo McCarthy, former

lieutenant governor of California, and Richard Leone, a former New Jersey state official.

The commission selected Kay James to be its chair. She set an antigambling tone to the proceedings from the very start, and it appeared that it would be very difficult for the commission ever to come together for a final report. Nonetheless, many hearings were held across the country, and although there was much verbal acrimony, the commission did unite to make a final report. The commission operated on a budget of $5 million. It engaged in a wide variety of activities. Public hearings were held in Washington, D.C.; Atlantic City; Boston; Chicago; San Diego; Tempe, Arizona; Biloxi, Mississippi; New Orleans; and Las Vegas. Several hundred citizens, public officials, industry officials, and academic experts offered testimony. Information was also gathered from over a thousand documents examined by the commission staff. The National Opinion Research Center of the University of Chicago was contracted to conduct a survey of compulsive gambling. It surveyed 2,417 adults and 534 adolescents by telephone and 530 other adults in gambling facilities. The center's study also involved making case studies of 100 communities that were located near gambling facilities. As a result of the work, the center concluded that approximately 1.8 million adults were currently "pathological gamblers" and another 4 million were currently "problem gamblers." Thirteen percent of patrons at the gambling facilities indicated attributes of either pathological or problem gambling at some time in their lives (National Gambling Impact Study Commission 1999, 4–5). All the information resources were utilized in making recommendations, which appeared in the final report.

The report had many antigambling messages in it, but on most substantive matters, the casino industry of Nevada came out on the winning side. The gaming industry was bothered by an initial recommendation that states and tribal governments accept a moratorium on new legalizations of gambling activities. That recommendation was passed over in the final report that was issued on 18 June 1999. Instead, the commission urged that the jurisdictions make comprehensive socioeconomic impact statements before they endorsed new legalizations. Other recommendations gave great comfort to the casino industry. Their fears were completely defused with the initial recommendation of the panel. The initial findings of the National Gambling Impact Study Commission included a definitive statement that gambling policy should remain a matter for state governments to control. With two exceptions—Native American gaming and Internet gaming—the commission felt that the federal government should stay out of gaming. There should be no special federal taxes on gaming, and there should be no direct regulation of the gaming industry by the federal government. The policy arena for making laws and rules about the casinos and the other gaming venues of Nevada should be in the hands of state leaders and in the counties and cities of the states.

The commission followed its first recommendation with a full set of suggestions for changes to be made at state and local levels. Many of these were quite critical of current gaming operations around the country. Nevada casino operators had been criticized before—this was not new. But the criticisms were much easier to take from sources that recognized that they should have no power over the choices that the state makes regarding gaming.

The commission recommended that the minimum age for gambling be twenty-one in all jurisdictions. They also recommended that children not be permitted to linger or loiter in gambling facilities. Gambling "cruises to nowhere"—that is, ships that dock in a nongaming state then go beyond the international waters boundary, allow gambling, and then return to docks—should not be allowed unless the nongaming state specifically approved of their activity. The commission also suggested that gaming interests not be allowed to make campaign contributions. Convenience gambling, such as slot machines or other gaming machines in grocery stores, was condemned.

The national commission opposed money machines in gaming areas. They claimed that "the easy availability of ATMs and credit machines encourages some gamblers to wager more than they intended" (National Gambling Impact Study Commission 1999, 7–30). Therefore, they recommend that "states, Tribal governments, and pari-mutuel facilities ban credit card cash advance machines and other devices activated by debit or credit cards from the immediate area where gambling takes place" (7–30).

The commission took a slap at sports betting by recommending that no betting be allowed on college or amateur contests. There was also a recommendation against the sale of instant tickets by lotteries and the use of machine gaming by lotteries. Lotteries were also chastised for excessive and false advertising. Pari-mutuel racing facilities were urged not to have slot machine–type gambling.

All gambling arenas were requested to have warning signs telling players about the dangers of compulsive gambling. States were encouraged to devote funds from gaming taxes to programs for research, prevention, education, and treatment programs for problem gamblers.

The commission urged that Congress pass legislation making all Internet gambling illegal. Moreover, it indicated a desire for legislation to make credit card debts incurred for Internet gambling unrecoverable in courts. The commission also recommended that Indian gaming be subjected to more stringent reporting requirements and that the federal government fully enforce the provisions of the Indian Gaming Regulatory Act.

The commission lamented that even with its extensive study, too many gaps remained in our knowledge of gambling. They recommended an extensive program of continued research.

Generally, the gambling industry was happy with the *Final Report*. It had feared a more severe condemnation of casino gambling. Nonetheless the opponents of gambling received encouragement from the *Final Report* as well. They used the study effectively in a campaign in the fall of 1999 to defeat a proposed lottery in Alabama and to win a court decision ending machine gambling in South Carolina.

Sources: National Gambling Impact Study Commission [NGISC]. 1999. *Final Report.* Washington, DC: NGISC.

National Indian Gaming Association. *See* Gaming Institutes: Research and Political

Native American Gaming: Contemporary

The U.S. government recognizes 558 Native American tribes. In 1990 there were almost 2 million Native Americans. An equivalent number of First Nation bands is found in Canada. Of the tribes in the United States, 198 had some kind of gambling operation in 1999. The operations included bingo games, which are considered Class II games, and various kinds of casino-type games, or Class III games (classifications found in the Indian Gaming Regulatory Act of 1988). The Class III operations are found in twenty-four states. As described in this entry, these games are conducted in accordance with agreements made between the tribes and the state governments.

Since 1990 Native American gambling has been the fastest-growing sector of casino gambling in the United States. Tens of billions of dollars are gambled at the Native American bingo halls and casinos each year. As a result, tribes take in approximately 15 percent of all the gambling revenues in the United States. In 1999, the gambling facilities had wins of $8.26 billion. The revenues support over 200,000 employees as well as critically needed social programs for many Native Americans who have collectively been the most economically deprived subpopulation in the United States. Gambling monies have also been vitally important for economic development projects, making many tribes self-sufficient. Gambling has not been a panacea for all, however, as a majority of the revenues go to only twenty-two casino operations out of more than 150 casinos (*see* Native American Gaming: Data). Some of the largest tribes have no gambling operations.

One of the tribes, the small Mashantucket Pequot tribe of Connecticut, has the largest casino in the world. The 300 members of this community control a casino that wins over $1 billion a year, or about 12 percent of the Native gambling money. Their casino, Foxwoods, is located in Ledyard, Connecticut, near the interstate highway that links New York City with Boston. For most of the 1990s, the casino was the only casino in all of New England. The facility has more than 250,000 square feet of gambling space, with a casino with more than 5,500 machines, 200 table games, and a bingo hall. The gaming resort complex also has two hotels, several theaters, amusement game rooms, and a sports arena. The facility is larger than any casino in Las Vegas, and it earns twice the revenues of the largest Las Vegas casino. Except for the state government itself, the casino is the largest employer in Connecticut.

Other leading Native American casinos are found on Oneida reservations in both Oneida, New York, and Green Bay, Wisconsin; on Chippewa reservations at Sault St. Marie and Mount Pleasant, Michigan, and Mille Lacs, Minnesota; on a Dakota Sioux reservation at Shakopee, Minnesota; on the Choctaw reservation near Philadelphia, Mississippi; and on the Ft. McDowell Apache reservation north of Phoenix, Arizona. Any of these gaming facilities could be transplanted to the Las Vegas Strip, and customers would be hard-pressed to notice the difference in gambling operations, although their markets all tend to be contained within areas of a one-day car drive, and few have large hotels.

Historical Development

In the 1970s many Native American tribes began to participate in charity gambling in accordance with state rules regarding how the games would be played and the types of prizes that could be offered. In 1979, the Seminole Nation decided to do something different for the bingo hall on its reservation in Hollywood, Florida. Faced with considerable competition from other charities, the tribe threw aside the state's prize limits and began a high-stakes game with prizes in the thousands of dollars. The Broward County sheriff filed criminal charges and sought to close down the Seminole bingo game. His actions led to a series of law cases, culminating in the 1981 approval of the games without state limits by a federal court of appeals (*Seminole Tribe* v. *Butterworth,* 658 F. 2d. 310). In 1982 the U.S. Supreme Court refused to review the ruling (455 U.S. 1020). In a very similar case in 1982, another federal court of appeals permitted a California tribe to conduct bingo games and other card games in manners that violated state rules (*Barona* v. *Duffy,* 694 F. 2d 1185). Key to the cases was the fact that in both Florida and California the games themselves were legal and could be played. The tribes were only violating the manner in which the games were played. The courts of appeals ruled that states did not have regulatory authority over Native nations' activities unless the activities were totally prohibited by the states as a matter of public policy.

Tribes across the United States took notice of the very successful gambling activities of the tribes and especially of the legal cases, which seemed to affirm the special status the tribes enjoyed in this realm of economic enterprise. During the early years of the 1980s, gambling began to appear on most of the reservations of the United States. Except for internal tribal regulations, there was almost no oversight for the gambling activities. As the activities involved larger and larger sums of money, there were both perceived and real problems. There were cases of non-Native managers setting up games and then taking the bulk of the revenues. Evidence of cheating emerged. Members of organized crime families made their presence felt on some reservations. There were also some unscrupulous tribal members who used gaming for personal advantages in ways adverse to their tribes' interests. Organized commercial casino interests, especially those in Nevada and New Jersey, expressed fears that corruption and organized crime activity on the reservations could result in a popular backlash against all casinos along with calls for federal regulation of commercial casinos. Of course, they also had concerns about the competitive positions held by unregulated casinos in monopoly-like markets. Congress began to explore the manner in which the Native gambling could be regulated.

Congressional action was held back, however, as the U.S. Supreme Court had not ruled on the legality of Native gambling, and many state governments sought to have the highest court overrule the previous decisions of lower federal courts. This did not happen. In 1987 the U.S. Supreme Court upheld the earlier rulings by a six to three vote in *California v. Cabazon Band of Mission Indians.* Moreover, the Court endorsed Native gambling as being consistent with federal policies designed to promote self-sufficiency for tribes. The Court pointed out that the Bureau of Indian Affairs had actually given grants for construction of some of the gambling facilities, that gambling revenues were accomplishing goals for federal policy, and that gambling revenues "provide the sole source of revenues for the operation of tribal governments, and the provision of tribal services. They are also major sources of employment on the reservations." The Court added, "Self-determination and economic development are not within reach if the Tribes cannot raise revenues and provide employment for their members. The Tribes' interests obviously parallel the federal interests" (*California v. Cabazon Band of Mission Indians* [480 U.S. 202]).

The Court added that state regulation or any other regulation by a nontribal entity could take place only if there were a specific act of Congress authorizing the regulation. Now the states besieged members of Congress to act. Conversely, the tribal interests were less inclined to endorse congressional action, as the status quo was quite acceptable to their desires. A compromise was reached with the passage of the Indian Gaming Regulatory Act of 1988, signed into law by President Reagan on 7 October 1988.

The Indian Gaming Regulatory Act of 1988

The 1988 Indian Gaming Regulatory Act (IGRA) established a three-member National Indian Gaming Commission. Two of the three members must be enrolled members of Native tribes. The chairman is appointed by the president and the two other members by the secretary of the interior. The commission is given some direct regulatory authority over bingo-type gaming. It is also empowered to make general rules for gambling operations. The chairman has subpoena powers, and the commission may assess fines against tribal gambling operations and even close them if it feels they are not sufficiently abiding by the rules. The commission approves all agreements outside operators make with Native gambling establishments and conducts background checks on gambling personnel.

Casino-type gambling was to be regulated in accordance with rules established in negotiations between the tribes and the state governments. These negotiated compacts would be given the force of law by the secretary of the interior. If the states refused to negotiate compacts in good faith, tribes could sue the states, and the states could be mandated by federal courts to negotiate. On 27 March 1996, in a five to four vote (*Seminole Tribe* v. *Florida*), the U.S. Supreme Court ruled that the provision of the act that allowed tribes to sue states in federal courts over the lack of good faith negotiations was unconstitutional because of the 11th Amendment. The amendment implies that states are sovereign units and generally cannot be sued in federal courts.

The Court did not rule the entire act unconstitutional, nor did the Court address how negotiations impasses would be resolved in the future—whether states could simply say no to tribes, or whether tribes could seek relief from the secretary of the interior. In 1999, the secretary of the interior issued guidelines for tribes to take appeals to the secretary's office when states refused to negotiate compacts.

The act defined three classes of gambling. Class I gambling consists of small prize games between tribal members. It also consists of games traditionally played by tribes in ceremonies or celebrations. These activities are regulated entirely by the tribes. No issues have arisen over Class I games since the passage of the act.

Class II gaming encompasses bingo in its various forms as well as pull-tab cards, punch boards, and tip jars (jars filled with a fixed number of pull tabs, hence guaranteeing a predetermined number of winners). Certain card games such as poker are also included as long as the games are nonbanking, that is, do not involve bets between the casino and the player instead of bets among players. Tribes can conduct Class II gaming as long as the game involved is permitted in the state to be played "for any purpose, by any person, organization or entity." The tribe must pass an ordinance in order to offer Class II games. The ordinance is then approved by the National Indian Gaming Commission chairman. The commission conducts background investigations on the gambling facility and its employees.

The Commission then regulates the gambling for a period of three years, after which the tribe can apply for permission to self-regulate the Class II games. Most tribes have successfully won permission for self-regulation. The permission can be revoked if the commission feels that the self-regulation efforts are inadequate. Although the commission regulates the gambling, the commission may assess the tribes a fee for the cost of regulation.

Class III gaming consists of all forms of gambling not covered by Class I and Class II definitions. Basically, the Class III category covers all casino-banked games including blackjack, baccarat, roulette, craps, and all slot machines. Class III also includes lottery games as conducted by state governments and pari-mutuel racing wagers. As with Class II games, the Class III games may be played only if the tribe has an ordinance permitting them and if the games are permitted "for any purpose, by any person, organization or entity" in the state where the tribal facility is located. Additionally, for Class III gambling to be permitted, the tribe must enter into a compact with the state. The compact will provide a detailed provision on games allowed in the facility, the manner of offering the games, and the regulatory structures for oversight of the games.

The Class III negotiated compacts may provide very specific authority for tribal and nontribal (be they county, city, or state) law enforcement agencies to supervise and enforce provisions of the gaming agreements. Without such specific authority being granted to nontribal authorities, all enforcement activities regarding gaming on Indian lands remain in the hands of the tribal government and the federal government. In other words, if there is no compact, and tribes are permitting games the state believes to be Class III games, the state cannot enforce the law. The state must wait for federal district attorneys and marshals to make all enforcement actions. As these officials operate under direction of the U.S. attorney general, the basic enforcement activity is on the shoulders of one federal officer.

State governments may not tax the Native gaming facilities. The state may charge the tribes sums of money to cover the actual costs of state regulation of the facilities, however. In fact, many tribes have acquiesced in state requests for special fees in order to finalize negotiations. The secretary of the interior willingly closes his eyes to the legal violation and accepts that the fees are somehow quid pro quos for some mysterious services the state or local governments might give the gambling facilities.

All net revenues from gambling must be allotted as the law provides. They must be used for tribal purposes. If the tribe shows that it is meeting its obligations to provide for the social welfare of its members, however, the tribe may authorize up to 40 percent to go to individual members in a per capita distribution. Some tribes have done so; others have not. In 1999 there were forty-seven tribal governments that gave per capita payments from gambling revenue to their members. Some have given the full 40 percent in per capita distributions; others have given smaller proportions. In the case of one Minnesota tribe with a small membership, the per capita distribution of funds was in excess of $800,000 per individual member for one year. Some other tribes have allocations exceeding $100,000 per member per year; however, most of the per capita payments are not so large.

The National Indian Gaming Commission also regulates non-Native persons who wish to work with the gambling facilities on reservations. Moreover, arrangements for outside management of games are regulated, with the outside managers being limited to agreements for no more than 30 percent of the net revenue of the facility going to them in exchange for their services. Agreements may not last for more than five years. Under special cases managers may receive 40 percent of net revenues for seven years if they also provide financing for the Native casino facilities.

The IGRA anticipated that tribal leaders and other entrepreneurs would see opportunities in creating new tribes in order to place gambling facilities in certain locations with outstanding market possibilities. The law provided that new lands designated as Indian lands by Congress or the Department of the Interior could have gambling only if such was approved by the secretary after some (unspecified) consultations with local residents of the area as well as rival gambling tribes in the vicinity. Moreover, the governor of the state would have to specifically approve the gambling, and of course there would have to be a compact. Plans for new tribes and new tribal lands proliferated, and many applications were made to Congress, the In-

terior Department, and governors. As of the beginning of 2001, however, only about a dozen tribes had been given new recognition by federal authorities, and only one of these had a casino operating. Only two existing tribes had been given authorization for gambling on new lands not adjacent to their existing reservations.

Selected Developments

Every state with organized and recognized Native populations has had a special history with its tribes over gambling, with one exception—Utah. As that state has no legal gambling, the federal law is clear that the tribes in the state may not have any Class II or Class III gambling operations. Tennessee and Hawaii, also states without any non-Native gambling (except a provision for pari-mutuel betting in Tennessee), have no Native lands. Certain state situations deserve extra attention.

Negotiations in Connecticut took many unusual turns on the way to creating the largest casino in the world, Foxwoods. Originally, the Mashantucket Pequot tribe sought a compact so that they could have table games only, as the state did permit charities to use table games in their fund-raising events Gov. Lowell Weickert refused to negotiate, however, claiming that the games were commercially illegal in the state. The tribe won a court mandate ordering the governor to negotiate. He refused. A mediator was appointed, to whom the tribe and the governor both submitted proposed compacts. The governor's proposal actually included provisions for allowing the games. The mediator selected the governor's proposal. The state then appealed the selection, asking the secretary of the interior to reject its own proposal. The secretary instead signed the proposal, which became the compact. The state lost its further court appeals.

It was clear that the state did not permit anyone—charities or commercial operators—to have slot machines. Also, the IGRA clearly says states cannot tax tribal gaming. Nonetheless, in 1993 the state and its governor reached a "side agreement" with the tribe to allow them to have as many slot machines as they wanted, providing they paid the state 25 percent of the revenue for the machines.

The agreement was never approved by the secretary of the interior (it could not be; it was patently illegal), but the casino offers 5,500 slot machines for its customers. The 25 percent tax was called a monopoly fee that would go to the state only as long as the Mashantucket Pequots had a monopoly on the machines (which could not be possible, as the law would allow machines only if they were permitted for others). The monopoly ended in 1996 when a second tribe opened a casino, and the 25 percent share was renegotiated with the governor's office, without the approval of federal authorities. The state of Connecticut receives nearly $200 million a year as its share of the tribes' slot revenues. The state certainly has not sought to appeal the slot agreement. While of dubious legitimacy, the gambling situation in Connecticut has widespread support.

The most protracted battles over Native American gambling have occurred in California, one of the states to pioneer Native American gambling. After the federal court rulings in the Seminole and Barona cases in the early 1980s, gambling expanded on California Native lands. The tribes went beyond bingo and player-banked games and started offering games that appeared to have the qualities of Class III games. After 1988, California governors George Deukmejian and Pete Wilson declined to negotiate compact agreements to allow tribes to have Las Vegas–style slot machines and house-banked casino games, however, claiming that casino-type gambling was unconstitutional in California. As all enforcement of gambling laws on tribal lands was placed into the hands of the federal government, the governors could not demand closure of tribal casinos. An impasse ensued for several years during which the tribes expanded machine operations, operating as many as 15,000 of them outside the boundaries of the federal law.

Eventually the tribes turned to the ballot to win their compacts. In 1998 they sponsored Proposition 5, and in 2000 they sponsored Proposition 1A. Governor Wilson opposed Proposition 5; Gov. Grey Davis helped design Proposition 1A, and he supported it. Both passed, but a court ruling held that a 1984 constitutional ban on casinos precluded enforcement of Proposition 5. Hence, Proposition 1A was initiated as a constitutional amendment.

The measure allows individual tribes to have casinos with up to 2,000 slot machines in each, with an overall state limit of approximately 43,000 machines. This represents a doubling of the number of existing machines in the state.

The 1998 Proposition 5 in California presented the greatest threat to Nevada casinos since the Kefauver hearings of the 1950s. The Native Americans in California wanted a compact and felt they were being stonewalled by Governor Wilson. But in their proposition they did not stop at merely asking for a compact. They asked for wide-open unlimited casino gambling on all 100-plus reservations in the state. The Native interests put almost $70 million into the campaign—one tribe in San Bernardino contributed $26 million of the amount. Nevada casinos responded with $25 million in opposition. Money won the contest, as the voters gave the proposition over 60 percent approval. Unfortunately the proposition was in the form of a legislative initiative, and the courts found it to be constitutionally defective. Nevada paid for the court challenge. The tribes quickly gathered and lobbied the California governor for support of a constitutional initiative to grant them compacts. The new compact (Proposition 1A) limited the numbers of slot machines that the tribes could have and provided for more definitive regulations—including the possibility of having labor unions for employees. Nevada interests had been stung by the amount of money that the Natives were willing to spend on the campaign in 1998. They were happy with the Proposition 1A compromises, and they were happy that they did not have to advance money against casinos again—a position that makes them feel somewhat hypocritical—but a position they had to take. It is possible that 1A will now allow the casinos of Nevada and the Nevada political establishment to build important bridges to California tribes.

A Canadian Note

The situation in Canada has some parallels to that in the United States. Native peoples (or First Nations) in Canada are the poorest residents of the country. They want to have gambling operations to help them deal with problems arising from their impoverished situations. There is no national

Slot machines in a Native American casino, North Dakota.

Canadian law on Native gambling, unlike the situation in the United States.

It had been well established that all relationships between Native bands (tribes) and non-Native peoples must be conducted with the federal government in Ottawa. In 1985, however, the federal government delegated all authority over gambling to the provinces. Since then the Native bands have felt like political footballs, as provinces say "go talk to Ottawa," and Ottawa says "go talk to the provinces." In the mid-1990s, however, several provinces entered into agreements somewhat similar to compacts in the southern U.S. states. Tribal casinos are operating in Alberta, Saskatchewan, Manitoba, and Ontario. Disagreements persist between bands and provincial authorities in several of the other provinces.

A unique arrangement was negotiated in Ontario, as one band (Rama) was permitted to have a casino at Orilla, as long as it shared revenues with other bands in the province. Another casino in Ontario, the Blue Heron Casino in Port Perry, has also been authorized to operate under the control of a Native band. The tribes in the United States have generously shared their revenues with many charities in many communities. No tribe, however, has willingly allowed any other tribe to have a precise share of its gaming revenues.

In 2000, the Alberta government provided guidelines for Native casino operations. At the same time, the Manitoba government held hearings and took advice from people throughout the province before designating five communities as sites for Native casinos. In one case there was no band in the community, and arrangements had to be made to create First Nation land for the casino. Saskatchewan created four Native casinos when it established its own provincial casino in Regina. All participate in revenue-sharing provisions.

Sources: Ponting, J. Rick. 1994. "The Paradox of On Reserve Casino Gambling: Musings of a Nervous Sociologist." In *Gambling in Canada: The Bottomline*, edited by Colin Campbell, 57–68. Burnaby, BC: Simon Fraser University; Thompson, William N. 1996. *Native American Issues: A Reference Handbook*. Santa Barbara, CA: ABC-CLIO; Thompson, William N., and Diana R. Dever. 1994a. "A Sovereignty Check on Indian Gaming." *Indian Gaming* 4 (April): 5–7; Thompson, William N., and Diana R. Dever. 1994b. "The Sovereign Games of North America: An Exploratory Study of First Nations' Gambling." In *Gambling in Canada: The Bottomline*, edited by Colin

Campbell, 27–55. Burnaby, BC: Simon Fraser
University. Thompson 1996b; Thompson 1996.

Native American Gaming: Data

As mentioned in Native American Gaming: Contemporary, the twenty-two tribal casinos produce over half of the revenue in Native American gambling. The question of how many Native Americans win by having gambling facilities can be examined more closely by looking at the twenty largest Native casinos and the twenty largest

tribes. Although it is obvious that some tribes have been helped immeasurably in many good ways because of gambling, have all Native Americans been helped? The 1990 Census reported that there were 1,959,234 Native Americans and that 437,079 of these lived on reservation lands. Of those living on reservations, 47.3 percent were living below the poverty line. Their median family incomes were $12,459, with a mean income of $17,459. The median national family income was $32,225, and less than 10 percent were below the poverty line. Table 1 lists the twenty largest tribal casino operations

Table 1 The Twenty Largest Tribes and Gambling

Tribe	Gaming Square Footage	Employees	Tables	Machines	Native Population*	Household Income Median	% Below Poverty
Navajo AZ, NM	0	0	0	0	143,000	9,769	54.20
Pine Ridge SD	30,000	129	8	113	11,181	10,633	75.00
Ft. Apache AZ	5,300	700	5	299	9,823	12,403	49.90
Gila River AZ (2)	68,000	1,200	40	771	9,113	12,744	62.80
Tohono O'Odham	48,000	750	28	500	8,476	8,552	62.80
Rosebud SD	0	0	0	0	8,041	10,887	54.40
San Carlos AZ	65,000	350	10	500	7,106	8,360	59.80
Zuni NM	0	0	0	0	7,073	15,536	47.40
Hopi AZ	0	0	0	0	7,059	13,418	47.70
Blackfeet MT	0	0	0	0	7,025	13,315	45.70
Turtle Mt ND	22,800	323	10	0	6,770	11,033	51.90
Yakima WA	0	0	0	0	6,165	14,807	42.50
Ft. Peck MT	0	0	0	0	5,782	13,822	41.80
Wind River WY	0	0	0	0	3,674	13,463	47.80
Cherokee NC	25,000	180	0	874	5,387	16,330	30.00
Flathead	0	0	0	0	5,110	14,898	31.80
Cheyenne River	0	0	0	0	5,100	9,885	57.20
Standing Rock ND	42,000	400	12	470	4,866	9,493	54.90
Crow Mt	20,000	70	0	100	4,724	14,031	45.50
Mississippi, Choctaw	90,000	2,000	96	2,800	3,932	16,702	37.60
Total of Larger Reservations	415,300	6,489	204	6,432	271,400		
Percentage of All	6.90%	6.70%	4%	7.20%	62.10%		
All Native America	6,037,223	96,584	5,044	88,892	437,079	13,570***	
Average	20,765	324	10	322	6,758	—	—
Median	0	0	0	0	6,898	13,030	49

*On reservation only. This collectively represents approximately 35% of enrolled memberships.
**Tribal District Statistical Area.
***Larger figure is for 20 reservations; small figure is for 19 reservations, excluding Navajo.
Source: Based on information in June 1997 *Casino Executive* magazine, 1990 Census, and other research.

as of 1997. Table 2 lists the twenty largest reservation populations (1990 census). Only one of the largest casinos is located on one of the largest reservations. The Mississippi Choctaw, the twentieth-largest tribe, has the fifteenth-largest casino.

Using data from the July 1997 issue of *Casino Executive Magazine,* I discovered that there were 6,037,223 square feet in gambling space in all Native American casinos. The casinos employed 96,584 persons. They had collectively 5,044 tables and 88,892 gambling machines.

The twenty largest reservations in terms of population do not have the largest casinos. Only eight have casinos. Averaging the casino attributes among the twenty, we find gambling floors averaging less than 21,000 square feet and employee numbers averaging 334 persons.

The tribes average ten tables and 322 machines at the casinos. Although the twenty largest tribes had 62 percent of the Native American population living on reservations, they had only 6.9 percent of the gambling space, 6.7 percent of the casino em-

Table 2 Tribes with the Twenty Largest Casinos

Tribe	Gaming Square Footage	Employees	Tables	Machines	Native Population*	Household Income Median	% Below Poverty
Mashantucket Pequot, CT	284,236	10,687	312	4,585	55	41,667	
Saginaw Chippewa, MI	205,000	2,500	80	3,600	735	15,083	39.80
Mohegan, CT	150,000	5,600	180	3,000	**219	23,611	46.20
Ft. McDowell, AZ	150,000	1,400	0	475	560	15,982	23.70
Mille Lacs (2), MN	270,000	2,334	87	2,875	428	6,796	84.00
Viejas, CA	120,000	1,600	73	1,132	227	18,170	26.00
Barona, CA	115,000	1,100	32	1,000	373	25,625	25.00
St. Ste Marie (5), MI	97,507	2,183	96	2,284	315	21,875	46.80
St. Croix (2), WI	95,000	1,112	44	1,270	459	9,287	44.60
Oneida, WI	95,908	1,520	80	2,500	2,447	19,133	27.50
Cabazon, CA	94,000	550	10	800	20	27,500	50.00
San Manual, CA	92,000	1,400	50	1,000	56	11,250	81.80
Shakopee Mdewakanton, MN	90,000	4,000	120	2,500	153	62,661	5.80
White Earth, MN	90,000	1,000	32	850	2,759	11,867	46.40
Choctaw, MS	90,000	2,000	96	2,800	3,932	16,702	37.60
Prairie Island Mdewakanton, MN	80,000	1,400	60	1,500	56	5,714	71.40
Morongo, CA	80,000	800	49	1,627	527	18,929	30.10
Coushatta, LA	71,000	2,100	60	2,010	33	7,111	61.50
Sycuan, CA	70,000	1,100	72	444	0	—	
Oneida, NY	68,000	2,000	148	1,000	37	16,250	
Total of Larger Casinos	2,407,660	46,380	1,680	37,260	13,120		
Percentage of All	39.90%	48.00%	33.30%	41.90%	3.00%		
All Native Americans	6,037,223	96,584	5,044	88,892	437,079		
Average	120,383	2,319	84%	1,863	656	—	
Median	94,954	1,560	72.50%	1,564	315	16,702	40%

*On reservation only. This collectively represents approximately 35% of enrolled memberships.
**Tribal District Statistical Area.
Source: Based on information in June 1997 *Casino Executive* magazine, 1990 Census, and other research.

ployees, 40 percent of the gambling tables, and 7.2 percent of the gambling machines.

On the other hand, the tribes with the twenty largest casinos employed an average of 2,319 in gambling, whereas their reservation populations averaged one-third of that number. The large casinos had average floor spaces of 120,383 square feet, with 83 tables and 1,863 machines each. The tribes owning the casinos had 3 percent of the 1990 reservation populations, but they had 39.9 percent of the gambling space, 48.0 percent of the casino employees, 33.3 percent of the gambling tables, and 41.9 percent of the casino machines. It can be suggested that these big facilities produced about half of all the gambling revenues generated in Native American facilities.

Although there is little doubt that gambling has been the best economic development tool available to Native Americans since the occupation of their lands by European settlers, the tool has not reached its potential for helping large numbers of the economically poorest people in the United States. Some attention should be given to mechanisms such as those utilized in Canada for spreading this wealth and the opportunities it can engender to more Native peoples.

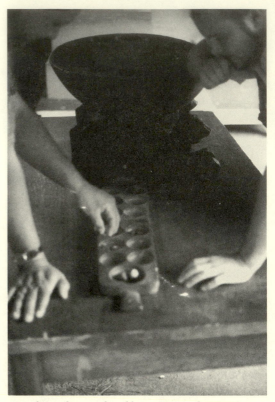

A traditional game played by native peoples.

Sources: Thompson, William N. 1998. Testimony presented to the National Gambling Impact Study Commission, Tempe, Arizona, 30 July; Thompson, William N. 1996. *Native American Issues: A Reference Handbook.* Santa Barbara, CA: ABC-CLIO.

Native American Gaming: Traditional

Long before the ships of Columbus brought playing cards to North America, the indigenous peoples engaged in gambling activities. The Native populations of the Western Hemisphere have been no different than other populations since the beginning of time. They have had games and have wagered valuable possessions on the outcomes of the games.

Stewart Culin's *Games of the North American Indians* (Culin 1907) classifies hundreds of Native games into categories of (1) games of chance, including dice games and guessing games, and (2) games of dexterity, encompassing archery, javelin and darts, shooting, ball games, and racing games. All categories were found among all North American tribes at the time of contact with the European intruders upon the continent.

Guessing games usually involved sticks that one person would hold in his or her hands behind the back. Another person would seek to determine which hand held the most sticks or held a stick with a particular marking. Other guessing games would involve having to find a hidden object such as a stone or a ball that might be placed into one of several moccasins or in some place in a room.

The most prevalent game of chance involved objects that had characteristics of today's dice. Tribes of every linguistic group had dice games. Most often the dice were stones with two distinguishable sides. They were tossed by hand into baskets or bowls, and counting systems were used to keep score for two individuals or two groups competing with one another.

All tribes in North America had some game involving throwing or shooting an arrow, spear, or dart through a hoop placed at a distance. A variety of other targets would be used as well. Also, some contests involved keeping arrows in the air for a long time or achieving great distances with shooting. Ring and pin games were also quite popular. A ring (the target) was tied to a stick by a string. The string was then used to swing the stick into the air with the object of having the stick go through the ring.

Although most arrow-type games and running games were based upon individual skills, Native Americans also had a wide range of team games involving kicking balls or moving balls toward goals by means of rackets or clubs. Europeans learned the game of la crosse from the indigenous populations of the North American continent. In addition, all tribes had varieties of running games involving individual runners as well as teams of relay runners.

Wherever there was a game or a contest, schemes existed to place wagers on the results. In most of the skill games the participants in the games were men; however, those making wagers would often include both men and women, and the betting activity could become rather excessive.

Culin relates some harmful effects of tribal gaming, citing an account of a bowl and stick-dice game among the Assiniboin of the northern plains: "Most of the leisure time, either by night or by day, among all these nations is devoted to gambling in various ways, and such is their infatuation that it is the cause of much distress and poverty in families" (Culin 1907, 173–174). He suggests that if a young man gained a reputation for being a heavy gambler that this would be an obstacle in the way of gaining a wife. Many arguments ensued among the people because of gambling. Culin writes, "We are well acquainted with an Indian who a few years since killed another because after winning all he had he refused to put up his wife to be played for" (174).

According to Culin, among the Assiniboin women could become as addicted to gaming as the men; however, as they usually did not control property resources as much as men, their losses were not as "distressing" (174).

Other accounts of Native American games have been more positive. Burt and Ethel Aginsky found that among the Pomo of California, gamblers were a highly honored group and that a family would happily welcome an apprentice gambler as a son-in-law. The gaming was also sanctioned by tribal religion, and the full society participated in games that involved wagers. Tribal members, however, were cautioned against winning too many possessions from one another as this would cause "hard feelings" (Aginsky and Aginsky 1950, 109–110).

Henry Lesieur and Robert Custer reviewed several studies of Native American gaming and found patterns of activity that mitigated the possibilities of the development of pathological gambling behaviors: (1) Games were formalized rituals with many spectators, (2) players could not go into debt as a result of the games—they could wager only those possessions they brought with them to the games, and (3) individuals had to have permission of their family in order to make wagers (Lesieur and Custer 1984, 149).

Although the modern era has seen a massive expansion of Native gaming facilities in North America, today's Native games are patterned almost exclusively upon games developed by Asian and European newcomers to the continent. Similarly, while the new Americans very early established contact with Native peoples and also incorporated gambling practices into the life of their new communities, there is very little evidence that they borrowed games from Native peoples, la crosse being one exception.

The lack of a general cross-fertilization of game development among tribes and settlers of European origin is evidenced in the almost complete lack of mitigating controls over pathological gaming, such as those identified by Lesieur and Custer, in modern Native American casinos. Today's Native American gaming is simply an outgrowth of emerging patterns of non-Native gaming.

Sources: Aginsky, Burt W., and Ethel G. Aginsky. 1950. "The Pomo: A Profile of Gambling among Indians." In *Gambling* (special volume of *The Annals of the Academy of Political and Social Science*), edited by Morris Ploscowe and Edwin J. Lukas, 108–113. Philadelphia: The American Academy of Political and Social Science; Culin, Stewart. 1907. *Games of the North American Indians.* Washington, DC: Government Printing Office; Desmond, Gerald D. 1952. "Gambling among the Yakima." Ph.D. diss.,

Catholic University of America; Devereux, George.
1950. "Psychodynamics of Mohave Gambling."
American Imago 7: 55–65; Flannery, Regina, and John
M. Cooper. 1946. "Social Mechanisms in Gros Ventre
Gambling." *Southwestern Journal of Anthropology* 2:
391–419; Lesieur, Henry, and Robert L. Custer. 1984.
"Pathological Gambling: Roots, Phases, and
Treatment." In *Gambling: Views from the Social
Sciences* (special volume of *The Annals of the
American Academy of Political and Social Science*),
edited by James H. Frey and William R. Eadington,
146–156. Beverly Hills, CA: Sage.

Nebraska

Nebraskans voted for a lottery in 1993. The state
has also permitted live keno gaming statewide. As
a result of these decisions, the Santee Sioux, Win-
nebago, and Omaha tribes have won the right to
have casino table gambling on their small reservations. I visited Omaha in December 1995 and
toured local gaming facilities.

For many years Omaha was the site of the very
successful Aksarben thoroughbred racing track.
Competition from a dog track in nearby Council
Bluffs, Iowa, as well as from Iowa riverboats destroyed the prospects for profits at the track. Efforts for full casino gambling at the track failed
(although it has been the site of a keno game). The
track is permanently closed.

Sources: Thompson, William N. 1997. *Legalized Gambling:
A Reference Handbook.* 2d ed. Santa Barbara, CA:
ABC-CLIO, 165.

Netherlands Antilles
(Sint Maarten, Curaçao,
and Bonaire)

The Netherlands Antilles consist of two of the
three "ABC" islands (Aruba, Curaçao, and Bonaire)
of the southern Caribbean and the Dutch half of
the island of St. Martin/Sint Maarten. These islands are autonomous in their domestic affairs,
but they report to the government at The Hague in
matters involving international affairs. Casino
policy is in the latter category. St. Martin/Sint
Maarten is an island of thirty-seven square miles;
sixteen square miles (Sint Maarten) are on the
Dutch side, and twenty-one square miles (St. Martin) are controlled from Paris as a subperfecture of

Guadeloupe. The casinos on the French side have
not been developed to attract large numbers of
tourists; on the other hand, the Dutch casinos operate within large resort hotels. The seven Dutch
casinos have gambling junkets and offer credit for
high-stakes gamblers.

Bonaire and Curaçao were governed jointly
with Aruba until that island won independent national status in 1986. Bonaire has two casinos, one
of which—the Flamingo Beach Casino—is the
only casino in the world where players may be
barefoot. The dealers too may be barefoot, but they
always wear black ties. Curaçao has six casinos, all
of which are in resort hotels and are located on
beaches or next to the harbor.

Sources: Cabot, Anthony N., William N. Thompson,
Andrew Tottenham, and Carl Braunlich, eds. 1999.
International Casino Law. 3d ed. Reno: Institute for
the Study of Gambling, University of Nevada, Reno,
234–235.

Nevada

The state of Nevada is clearly the primary gambling state in the United States. For almost half of
the twentieth century it was the only state to permit casino gambling. Even today, nearly one-third
of the casino gambling activity in the United
States occurs in Nevada. The state has over 300 unrestricted casino license holders offering both
table games and machine gaming, and 235 of
these have gaming wins in excess of $1 million
dollars per year. Another 2,000 restricted locations
each have fifteen or fewer gaming machines. The
casinos are found in each of the seventeen counties of the state and in every city of the state except
for Boulder City—which was a federal enclave
until the 1950s. No other North American jurisdiction allows such widespread locations for casinos;
instead, most confine casinos to specific communities. The casinos produce revenues of approximately $8 billion per year from gambling and $6
billion more from other sources. The casinos employ nearly 200,000 persons, representing one-
third of the employment in the state. The taxes
from gambling and other aspects of casino enterprises constitute approximately half of the public
revenues of the state and its local governments. No

In Nevada gambling is found everywhere. Here are slot machines in McCarran Airport in Las Vegas.

other jurisdiction in the world receives as large a share of its public budgets from gambling taxes.

Although casino gambling is found in all but one jurisdiction in the state, there are certain important concentrations of casinos in the state. Of course, the primary gaming center is the Las Vegas Strip, a four-mile-long section of Las Vegas Boulevard, which has 19 of the 20 largest hotels in the world—all with casinos. Downtown Las Vegas has a dozen large properties located around Fremont Street. The town of Laughlin on the Colorado River at the southern tip of the state has 10 casinos. In the northern part of the state, the traditional gaming city of Reno (and its suburb, Sparks) has 35 major casinos, and the Lake Tahoe resort area has 5.

History of Gaming in Nevada

Nevada became "the" gambling state by a series of historical accidents as well as by deliberate policies. As late as the 1840s, Nevada was basically an unexplored region of barren desert and mountains. Paiute, Washoe, and Shoshone Indian tribes had traversed parts of the state and established

some communities, but their numbers were small, and their lifestyle was often nomadic, as they would live in the climatically comfortable mountains during the summer and then descend to the desert floor in winter months. The climate and terrain made the area one that most people moving westward sought to avoid or to cross in great haste. Mark Twain described the journey with humorous detail in *Roughing It* (Twain 1872).

One critical aspect of Nevada's geography that is pertinent to its economic development is its proximity to California. (Even today one-third of the state's gambling customers come from California.) The two states have the longest land border of any two states in the United States. People rushed to California in the late 1840s as gold was discovered. The new state of California was populated by all sorts of prospectors and other independent get-rich-quick entrepreneurs during the 1850s. The area that became Nevada was made part of Utah Territory in 1850. The volume of gold strikes in California began to wane in the late 1850s just as the great Comstock Lode was discovered near Virginia City, Nevada, in 1859. A mad silver rush par-

Slot machines are found throughout the state in bars, taverns, restaurants, convenience stores, and grocery stores.

alleled the earlier California gold rush, except this time the fortune hunters came to Nevada from California. The first waves of population left an indelible mark upon the character and outlook of politics in the state. The influx of the new population was accompanied by desires to cut off political relationships with Utah Territory and its religiously oriented government. President Buchanan signed a bill on 2 March 1861, just two days before he left office, which established Nevada Territory out of the western one-third of Utah Territory. Buchanan had been rather hostile to the nature of Utah society throughout his presidency, and the new status for Nevada was his parting shot against a community that seemed almost diametrically opposite to that found in Nevada.

The issue of gambling was quickly placed on the public agenda of the new state. President Lincoln appointed New Yorker James Nye to be territorial governor. Nye was not a prospector, and Nye did not care for gambling. He recoiled at the prevalence of sin institutions when he settled down in Nevada and persuaded the new legislature to prohibit gambling. A person who operated a game

could be charged with a felony; a person who played at a game could be charged with a misdemeanor. In spite of the law, the games continued.

After statehood was achieved in 1864, the legislature reversed its thinking. In the 1867 session a law was passed legalizing casino games. It was vetoed by the first elected governor, H. G. Blasdel. Two years later, the legislature repeated its action, and when the bill was vetoed again, they overrode the veto. The new law barred local governments from passing ordinances against gambling. Any person was able to get a license to operate a game from the county sheriff for a fee ranging from $1,000 to $1,600 (depending upon the population of the county). The fee was split equally between the state and county treasuries.

By the turn of the twentieth century, the Populist movement was gaining strength across the United States and in the Silver State. In concert with temperance organizations, civil leaders attacked the local sin industries. A ballot initiative sponsored by such groups sought to make both gaming and prostitution illegal in Reno. When the voters turned down the measure in 1909, the sponsors approached the state legislature. There they were successful, and gaming ceased to be legal on 30 September 1910. Another way of saying the same thing was that illegal gambling began on 1 October 1910.

By 1911, the legislature had second (and third) thoughts. Certain card games were legalized, only to be made illegal again in 1913. In 1915 limited gaming was permitted again. Enforcement of the gaming limits was sporadic at best and nonexistent as a rule. In lieu of fees when gaming was legal, operators now paid bribes to local officials, who pretended that gaming did not take place.

A move to legalize gambling was revived in 1931 when state assemblyman Phil Tobin of Humboldt County introduced the legislative measure. Although opposition was voiced by religious groups, Tobin's bill passed the assembly on a 24–11 vote, and the state senate on a 13–3 vote. On 19 March 1931, Governor Balzar signed both the six-week divorce law and the measure to legalize casino gambling. A second law passed later in 1931 permitted local governments to regulate gambling and fixed fees for gaming statewide. The fees were shared, with 75 percent going to local governments and 25 percent to the state. Licenses were granted by county commissions, and all regulations were enforced by the sheriffs.

In 1945, the state legislature decided that state control was necessary, as several outside operators were planning larger and larger casino projects. The state Tax Commission was given the authority to license casinos, which had previously received licenses from county boards. Subsequently the process became one of dual licensing. The state also imposed a 1 percent tax on the gross gaming wins of the casinos. The Tax Commission was empowered to collect the tax. Two years later the state attorney general ruled that the Tax Commission could deny a license based upon its assessment of the character of the applicant. In 1949 the requirement that applicants must be of good character was written into the law. The Tax Commission was given a staff for casino regulation for the first time.

Emergence of the Gaming Regulatory Structure

During the early 1950s considerable negative attention was cast upon the casino industry as a re-

sult of the national Kefauver Committee hearings on organized crime. The state responded with regulatory reforms. Legislation in 1955 established a specialized three-member full-time Gaming Control Board, which was administratively located with the Tax Commission. In 1959 the Tax Commission was eliminated from the state's casino regulatory picture. A five-member Nevada Gaming Commission was created. This part-time group serves as the final voice for the state on gaming matters. In a sense it is the "supreme court" for gaming.

As a result of these changes, Nevada now has a two-tier structure for regulating gambling. The Gaming Control Board acts essentially like a policeman and a tax collector for the casino industry; the Nevada Gaming Commission makes final decisions on licensing casinos and formulating regulations as well as handling disputes that cannot be resolved by actions of the Gaming Control Board.

The three board members are appointed by the governor for four-year terms. One member is designated as chair by the governor. He or she must have five years of experience in public or private administration. A second member must be a certified public accountant or have expertise in finance or economics. The remaining member must have law enforcement experience. Board members may not be engaged in any partisan political activity during their term of service. They may not have any financial ties to casinos, nor may they be employed by any casino for one year following their board service.

The board oversees the work of a staff of over 400 individuals, who are organized into several divisions. The investigations division checks into the backgrounds of persons who wish to have gambling licenses. The cost of this background check process is paid by the license applicant. An enforcement division works in the casinos to ensure that all the games are honest and that all gaming laws and regulations are being obeyed. An audit division checks accounting procedures in the casinos and makes sure that all flows of money are accurately recorded and reported for purposes of taxation. A tax, license, and administration division collects gambling taxes and publishes reports on casino activity in the state. There is also a corporate securities division that monitors the financial condition of casinos that are owned by publicly traded corporations. An electronic laboratory investigates all gaming devices to ensure their integrity.

The five members of the Nevada Gaming Commission are also appointed by the governor for four-year terms. They, too, must not have an interest in any casinos, nor may they be involved in partisan politics. The commission has no staff. It gives final passage to rules and regulations and makes final decisions regarding disciplinary action against any gaming interest—action that can also include revocation of a license. In 1969, the legislature created a seven-member Gaming Policy Board headed by the governor. The board was charged with making recommendations to the legislature for reforms in the gaming law. It has met only occasionally over the past thirty years.

Although the state's gaming regulatory structure is considered one of the finest arrangements for regulating gaming in the world, local governments (counties or cities) are still involved in the process. They must also license casinos, and they collect fees separately from the state fees and taxes. The state gaming tax has risen to 6.25 percent of the gross gaming win, and casinos must also pay a variety of fees based upon the number of tables and machines in the facility.

Sources: Cabot, Anthony N. 1999. *Federal Gambling Law.* Las Vegas: Trace; Cabot, Anthony N., William N. Thompson, Andrew Tottenham, and Carl Braunlich, eds. 1999. *International Casino Law.* 3d ed. Reno: Institute for the Study of Gambling, University of Nevada, Reno, 101–120; Hulse, James. 1997. "Nevada and the Twenty-First Century." In *Towards 2000: Public Policy in Nevada,* edited by Dennis L. Soden and Eric Herzik, 1–14. Dubuque, IA: Kendall-Hunt; Skolnick, James. 1978. *House of Cards: Legalization and Control of Casino Gambling.* Boston: Little, Brown; Twain, Mark. 1872. *Roughing It.* Hartford, CT: American Publishing.

See also Boulder City, Nevada: Nongambling Oasis; The Kefauver Committee; Las Vegas; Reno

New Hampshire

New Hampshire has prided itself on being a low-taxation state. It is one of a very few states that has never had a state income tax or sales tax. In the 1950s and 1960s, however, the costs of government were going up, and because the state was familiar with gaming—it had legalized both horse-race and dog-race wagering decades before, and charitable bingo games were popular—political leaders felt that there was a better way of raising revenues than raising taxes. In 1963 the legislature came up with a novel idea: sell sweepstakes tickets in the manner used with the Irish Sweepstakes. The state was close to large population concentrations in Massachusetts, Connecticut, and New York. A rationale behind the idea was that the state could gain public revenues from nonresident gamblers. Tickets cost three dollars each, and persons purchasing them had to register their names and addresses for drawings. Winners would have horses assigned to them, and the grand prize winners would be those whose horse came in first. There was considerable interest in the sweepstakes, but the ticket sales fell far below expectations. The state was quick to change the lottery format after New York adopted a more direct lottery ticket sales procedure in 1966, and then after New Jersey revolutionized ticket distribution methods as it began its lottery in 1970.

As New Hampshire modernized its lottery in the 1970s, sales picked up, and revenues became an important part of funding for education in the state. New Hampshire formed a partnership with Maine and Vermont to offer the Tri-State Lotto game. Subsequently, they became part of the Powerball consortium. The state had become a winner through a process of imitation.

The legalization of casino gambling for Atlantic City seemed also to call for imitation in the minds of many. After the momentum for casinos gained speed in the early 1980s, Gov. Hugh J. Gallen appointed a Commission for Gambling in 1982. The commission studied jai alai betting, offtrack betting, and casinos. The commission came out against all three forms of gambling. Its strongest criticisms were aimed at the casino industry, stating, "for the little promise it holds out as a source of state revenue, [the casino industry] will bring with it serous disadvantages. It will burden the state government and local communities with the cost of policing its operations and providing municipal services for the mass of patrons needed to make it run on a paying basis. It will devastate the existing family-oriented vacation industry" (Dombrink and Thompson 1990, 127). A bill to establish casinos was defeated in the legislature. Since 1982, there has been no serious push to legalize casino gambling.

Sources: Dombrink, John D., and William N. Thompson. 1990. *The Last Resort: Success and Failure in Campaigns for Casinos.* Reno: University of Nevada Press, 126–127; Thompson, William N. 1997. *Legalized Gambling: A Reference Handbook.* 2d ed. Santa Barbara, CA: ABC-CLIO.

New Jersey (and Atlantic City Casinos)

After Nevada, New Jersey is the nation's leading gambling jurisdiction. The state has one of the nation's premier lottery organizations, it has an active horseracing business, and of course, it has the casinos of Atlantic City.

In 1969, New Jersey became only the third state to institute a government-run lottery. The state's operations were different than those in New Hampshire and New York, the pioneer lottery states. Both of these jurisdictions had fallen short of their desired revenue goals because their games were slow and relatively expensive. New Jersey set its revenue targets, and lottery organizers went after the targets aggressively. They advertised the lottery to wide markets. They reduced the price of tickets to fifty cents each, and they held weekly drawings. Using a new style of ticket distribution, they witnessed unparalleled success. New Jersey became a model for other new lottery states—a model that suggested significant sums of money could be raised through the lottery. The state were widely imitated.

The major reason that New Jersey is a leader in gambling revenues is the fact that the state has authorized land-based casino gambling for Atlantic City. It now has twelve very large casinos, which generate gambling win revenues exceeding $4 billion a year.

The casinos of the city draw over 30 million visitors a year to the gambling halls, with over 1 million square feet of gambling space, 35,000 slot machines, and 1,450 tables for games. The hotels also have nearly 12,000 rooms.

For most of a century, New Jersey and urban political corruption seemed to go together like the proverbial horse and carriage, whether it was Jersey City's Boss Frank "I am the law" Hague, or mobsters in control of activities in Newark, or the Republican political machine of Atlantic City. That machine meant Louis Kinley, "Nucky" Johnson, and "Hap" Farley. Scandal surrounded the southern New Jersey beach city that had been known as "the queen of American resorts."

Atlantic City had developed as the premier summer resort after a railroad connected Philadelphia with the seaside in the 1850s. A permanent two-mile-long plank boardwalk along the ocean became a community symbol. Dozens of resort hotels, some being the most luxurious in the country, sprang up near the beach area. A pier was constructed, and carnival rides, pitchmen, and shows featuring palm readers, snake charmers, and freak displays appealed to the masses while other accommodations sought to reach out to the most affluent. By the beginning of the twentieth century, over 700,000 visitors a year were crowding into Atlantic City. The community also attracted the new gangsters who flourished during the Prohibition era, and these individuals had their hand in many illegal activities, including prostitution and gambling. But mainly Atlantic City was known for its entertainment. The Miss America show was created there in 1921, and in 1929 it moved into a new convention center.

The bosses kept illegal activities alive, but the community itself began to undergo a slow death during the Depression years and World War II. Postwar prosperity did not turn the town around, as its infrastructure—its many old hotels—no longer had the amenities that summer visitors demanded. Moreover, better transportation—faster trains and air service—could take vacationers to Florida just as easily as to Atlantic City.

The city fathers had to react, or the community would be totally lost. Kinley and Johnson ended their careers with criminal convictions; Farley looked for a better conclusion for his reign. He was instrumental in winning the Democratic National Convention for the resort in 1964. This exposure only showed the resort for what it was, a decaying relic from the past. Out of that public relations dis-

Atlantic City casinos stand out on the famous "Boardwalk."

aster emerged a concerted effort to bring casino gaming to Atlantic City. In 1970, Farley used his political power and his position as a state senator to seek state legislation to authorize a vote on casinos. He was unsuccessful and was soundly defeated for reelection as his political corruption was exposed. Others picked up the casino campaign, however. In 1972 a commission was authorized to study casino gambling. The notion that legalized gambling could help eliminate illegal gambling was voiced as well as concerns that casinos would bring in more organized crime. The report recommended that the voters of the state decide the question.

A 1974 referendum was placed upon the ballot by the legislature. It called for state-owned casinos in communities desiring them. Opposition led by religious groups used the notion that casinos would be in every city—"in your backyard"—of the state and also that the state would be at risk if it were the owner of the casinos. The measure failed by a 60 percent to 40 percent margin.

City fathers were devastated, but in 1976 they reorganized for another battle, making sure the power structure of the state was fully organized on behalf of casinos. Legislative leaders sponsored the bill that put the casino proposition on the ballot. This time the casino proposals called for casinos only in Atlantic City, specified that taxes from casinos would go to aid seniors and the handicapped, and specified that casinos were to be committed to urban redevelopment projects for decaying Atlantic City. The bill also called for casinos that would be private rather than state sponsored. That last provision was important, as the casino advocates found a company that was operating casinos in the Bahamas—Resorts International Casino of Freeport—that stepped forward to finance most of the campaign. Resorts put more than $1 million into the campaign. The casino proponents included the governor, the legislature, seniors groups, and local leaders throughout the state; opposition was again confined to religious groups. This time the measure passed by a 56 percent to 44 percent margin. Resorts and the other proponents of casinos had spent $1.5 million on the campaign; the church groups opposed to casinos had spent $22,000.

New Jersey casinos are big, but they have not solved all the economic problems of Atlantic City.

The state legislature passed enabling legislation for the regulation of casinos in 1977, and on 2 June of that year Gov. Brendan Byrne traveled to Atlantic City to sign the bill into law. Governor Byrne promised that the people of Atlantic City would be helped by the casinos and not hurt by them. The casinos were to be the most strictly regulated casinos in the world—a claim heard in every jurisdiction that opens gambling halls. The state of New Jersey was going to keep its vigilance at the highest levels to ensure that there would be no wrongdoing. Byrne ended his signing ceremony with these words, "I've said it before and I will repeat it again to organized crime. Keep your filthy hands off Atlantic City. Keep the hell out of our State" (quoted in Mahon 1980, 136).

To accomplish the task he set before the state—to revitalize an economically depressed community with classy casinos run with integrity—the 1977 act created two bodies: the Casino Control Commission (CCC) and the Division of Gaming Enforcement (DGE). The CCC was an independent body of five full-time members appointed by the governor. It had its own staff. The DGE was part of the state attorney general's office. The DGE investigated license applicants, and also it took initial ac-

tion against license holders if they violated regulations. Its actions were in the form of nonbinding recommendations to the CCC, however (Lehne 1986; Demaris 1986; Mahon 1980). The casinos were required to give the state 8 percent of their gambling gross profits to be used for the designated purposes and also additional funds (up to 2.5 percent of gross profits) to be used by a Casino Reinvestment Redevelopment Authority for projects in Atlantic City. Casinos had to be in facilities with 500 hotel rooms each. They would be allowed to have 50,000 square feet of gambling space with 500 rooms, and more space if they had more rooms. There were very strict limits placed over advertising activity. At first the casinos had to close each evening, but after a decade, they were allowed to remain open twenty-four hours every day. The notion of strict regulation was supported by the placement of state inspectors on the gambling floors at all times, as over 1,000 regulators were available to monitor the action of the casinos, which eventually numbered twelve.

From the onset, it may be suggested that the whole process was compromised. Only one company sought a license at the beginning, and the state was exceedingly interested in gaining revenues from gambling so that it could start fulfilling the many promises made. The first applicant was Resorts International, a company that had developed casinos in the Bahamas. In doing so, the company had developed many ties with questionable characters and had also been involved in giving many gratuities and favors to government officials. The DGE advised that a license not be granted. The CCC after much soul searching agreed to grant a temporary license. In the duration of the temporary license period, the casino realized net profits almost equal to its $75 million capital investment. At the end of the time, it was again investigated by the DGE. The DGE not only reasserted its past reservations about the activity of Resorts in the Bahamas but also pointed out many violations of New Jersey regulations by Resorts during the temporary license period. Again the DGE recommended that no license be given. As there were as yet no other casinos in operation, however, the CCC overruled the DGE and a permanent license was granted (Mahon 1980; Demaris 1986).

The first casino, Resorts International, had started its operations with the temporary license on Memorial Day weekend in 1978. The success of the opening was dramatic, reflecting a strong pent-up demand for legalized gambling on the East Coast. Most players then, as today, came to Atlantic City by roads, with a good share on bus tours. They were not typical tourists in that they stayed only an average of four to six hours each and spent about fifty dollars each visit.

As the 1980s developed, many operators rushed into Atlantic City to set up shop. The Golden Nugget, Showboat, Harrah's, and the Tropicana came in from Nevada, and Bally's slot machine company set up its first casino shop in Atlantic City, as did Donald Trump. Some of the casinos experienced substantial success, but for others a reality of flat revenues and slow growth set in. In the early years of casino gambling, the crime rates in the community soared and charges of organized crime involvement were heard. Yet some researchers claim that the criminal activity was more related to the fact that so many visitors came to town than to the fact that they came to town to visit casinos.

By the time Donald Trump built the largest Atlantic City property, the Taj Mahal, in the late 1980s, the era of growth was put on hold. The casinos were supposed to be a catalyst to cause a rebuilding of the decayed resort city, but this had not happened. Properties near the casinos were boarded up, the city's population declined (although the area population grew), and unemployment levels remained high. The casinos had done their job—they made revenues, and they certainly paid enough in tax revenues to rebuild several Atlantic City–sized cities. There was simply something missing from the political formula. It did not work. On the other hand, the casino owners remain optimistic that true success is right around the corner.

Sources: Demaris, Ovid. 1986. *Boardwalk Jungle: How Greed, Corruption and the Mafia Turned Atlantic City into the Boardwalk Jungle.* New York: Bantam Books; Dombrink, John D., and William N. Thompson. 1990. *The Last Resort: Success and Failure in Campaigns for Casinos.* Reno: University of Nevada Press, 25–41; Johnston, David. 1992. *Temples of Chance: How America Inc. Bought Out Murder Inc. to Win Control of the Casino Business.* New York: Doubleday; Lehne, Richard. 1986. *Casino Policy.* New Brunswick, NJ: Rutgers University Press; Mahon, Gigi. 1980. *The Company That Bought the Boardwalk.* New York: Random House; Morrison, Robert S. 1994. *High Stakes to High Risk: The Strange Story of Resorts International and the Taj Mahal.* Ashtabula, OH: Lake Erie Press; Sternlieb, George, and James W. Hughes. 1983. *The Atlantic City Gamble: A Twentieth Century Fund Report.* Cambridge: Harvard University Press.
See also Casino; Crime and Gambling

New Mexico

New Mexico has many forms of gambling. Horse racing as well as charitable gambling operations have been in existence for many decades. In 1996 a state lottery began operations. Fourteen Native American tribes have been able to negotiate the right to offer casino gambling.

With the expanding gambling establishments, the horse tracks of New Mexico were heavily hit by competition during the 1990s. Over the years the tracks in the state sought relief from the state legislature. Finally, in 1997, the tracks were authorized to have slot machines. The state agreed to let tracks have 300 machines each as long as they could all be tied together in a slot information network. The tracks give 25 percent of the revenue directly to the state and give 20 percent to horsemen through race purses. The tracks keep 55 percent. Machines are permitted to run twelve hours a day, every day—as long as the track offers some racing products.

On 4 May 1999, Ruidoso Downs, less than a half an hour away from the large Native American casino of the Mescalero Apache tribe, was permitted to start operating its machines. The track also has simulcast racing each day of the year so the slot machines are available to players 365 days. Live thoroughbred and quarter horse racing occurs four days a week from Memorial Day to Labor Day. The nation's leading quarter horse race—the All American Futurity—is run on Labor Day. The track is beginning to turn around several years of losses (it never stopped racing), but it would like to be able to stay open longer hours and also have more machines in order to compete more equitably with the Mescalero casino.

Nonprofit clubs are also permitted to have fifteen gambling machines each.

Sources: www.nmlottery.com; www.nmracing.com.
See also Horse Racing; The Racino

New York

New York has been of great historical importance to gambling. New York being the first state to greet most of the immigrants to the country, New Yorkers saw those immigrants as customers for gambling products. In turn the immigrants became employees and then the entrepreneurs of gambling. Figures such as Jack Morrisey and Richard Canfield developed casinos that became models for later operators. The first horse racetrack in the New World was on Long Island. Racing has continued to be a major gambling activity throughout the state's history.

When gambling moved westward, it moved with New Yorkers. The Louisiana Lottery was run out of New York City. The early founders of the Las Vegas Strip were from New York; prominent latter-day casino developers in both Las Vegas and Atlantic City have New York roots. New York was the second state to create a lottery (1966), the first state to authorize offtrack betting (1971), and the first state to utilize a lotto (progressive jackpot) lottery game (1978).

New York remains an important state for gambling. Although campaigns for commercial casinos have failed repeatedly, the state has excelled in other gambling activity. New York leads the nation in both lottery revenues and revenues from parimutuel wagering. The state is the venue supporting several of the nation's major race tracks—Belmont, Aqueduct, and Saratoga. The state receives more public revenue in terms of actual dollars from gambling than any other state. Historically, and in contemporary times, New York has also led the nation in illegal gambling activity.

Given this history, New York officials were very aware of the activity in Atlantic City after 26 May 1978 when the first legal casino gambling began on the boardwalk. Coincidentally, New York was suffering an economic downturn at the time. Not only did the Atlantic City experience look like one New York could duplicate, but the New Yorkers feared that competition from Atlantic City could have a drastic effect on hotel trade and other tourism in New York City. It was not long before there was a concerted effort to get casinos into the Empire State. There were two big barriers to the campaign for casinos. First, such gambling authorization would require an amendment to the state constitution. That would take a supermajority in two consecutive legislatures, followed by a vote of the people. Second, interests from around the state wanted casinos in their vicinities. Buffalo and Niagara Falls wanted casinos; the Catskills wanted the casinos; so did the Adirondack resort area; and so did several rival locations in the New York City area—the Rockaways, Coney Island, and Manhattan. Legislative representatives could not decide among the communities. Therefore, in 1980 they decided to pass eight different casino amendment bills. Before they could act in 1981, Atty. Gen. Robert Abrams wrote a devastating report on Atlantic City, calling it a failure from every possible angle—crime, social consequences, and economic development. The bills did not get out of committees in 1981. Since 1981 bills have been introduced, and there has been lots of talk about casinos and slot machines here and there. Even with the opening of a Niagara Falls, Ontario, casino, which gained over half of its revenues from New York residents, New York officials have not been able to build a consensus in favor of any casino proposal.

But this does not mean New York has no casinos. The existence of a wide variety of charity gambling, including Las Vegas Nights, meant that the state was required to negotiate with Native American tribes for gambling facilities. The Oneida tribe in the central part of the state actually opened a bingo hall in the early 1970s, before the Seminoles in Florida did so. The Seminoles had the resources to take the controversy over Native gambling through the courts, so they get credit for being the Native gambling pioneers. The Oneidas continued bingo through the 1980s until they negotiated for casino gaming. At first their Turning Stone Casino offered only table games, but now they have over 1,000 machines in the 120,000-square-foot facility. Two other tribes, the Senecas and Mohawks, had bingo games, but there was no other casino until the Mohawks entered into a compact with New York State for a facility in northern New York near the Canadian border. In the early 1990s, the Mohawk site near Massena was the scene of deadly violence as pro- and antigambling factions among the tribe contested gambling decisions, and law enforcement officials from Quebec and New York intervened. They have maintained a sometimes shakey but nevertheless effective peace since then. Plans to open a casino are ongoing in 2001.

Sources: Dombrink, John D., and William N. Thompson. 1990. *The Last Resort: Success and Failure in Campaigns for Casinos.* Reno: University of Nevada Press, 98–108.

North Carolina

North Carolina permits limited stakes bingo games offering maximum prizes of ten dollars per game. Charities in the state achieve benefits of less than $10 million a year as a result of the games. According to my personal interview with tribal member Earl Dixon in Las Vegas on 13 February 2001, the Eastern Tribe of Cherokee Indians has utilized North Carolina's charitable gambling

statutes in order to negotiate a casino compact under the provisions of the Indian Gaming Regulatory Act of 1988. In conjunction with Harrah's Gaming Company, the tribe operates a large casino with over a thousand video gambling machines.

North Dakota

The state of North Dakota has perhaps the widest-ranging charity gaming operations based upon casino games in the United States.

Residents of the state had played many games of chance ever since statehood was achieved in 1889. Although the games were illegal, authorities were very tolerant of their existence, especially when the beneficiaries of the games were local charities. In the 1970s the operators of the games began to advertise openly, and it was clear that they were making no pretense about flouting the law.

The attorney general of the state decided to enforce the law. As he did so, he told complaining citizens that they should change the state constitution that banned all gambling. The citizens petitioned the legislature to propose an enabling amendment that would permit the legislature to govern gambling. Such an amendment became part of the state constitution with widespread citizen approval in 1976. Then a law was passed legalizing bingo, tip jars (jars filled with a fixed number of pull tabs), pull tabs, and raffles. In 1981 a law was enacted permitting charity blackjack games and poker games. Next the citizens who opposed gambling petitioned to have a vote repealing the law. They got the vote, but not the results they wanted. In 1982 a majority of 63 percent of the voters cast ballots in favor of blackjack.

The blackjack and poker games must be played in sites approved by local governments. The games must be conducted by nonprofit charity organizations certified by the attorney general of the state as qualifying under federal Internal Revenue Service code Section 501c criteria. Individual wagers are limited to five dollars per hand. The games are usually held in bars or restaurants, and those enterprises cannot participate in any way in running the games. They must rent their facilities to the charities at a fixed rate that does not depend upon

The Prairie Knights Casino: A Native American casino in North Dakota.

Pickle jars and pull tabs for sale in a North Dakota blackjack casino.

the revenue of the gambling. The establishments may not give any food or beverages to the players, but the latter may purchase such items. The state imposes a tax ranging from 5 percent to 20 percent (depending upon the amount) on the charities' gambling returns.

The charity gambling provides the most important supporting revenues for major cultural organizations such as public television, the Plains Art Museum in Fargo, and local humanity councils. The leading recipient of funds has been the North Dakota Association of the Disabled.

Until Alabama defeated the lottery in 1999, North Dakota was the only state in the twentieth century that experienced voter disapproval of a specific lottery proposal. The voters defeated lotteries three times. The leaders in the campaigns have been the charities running blackjack games.

The state does permit some pari-mutuel gaming; however, there are no major facilities in operation. There are four major Native American casinos offering machine and table games. They are at Spirit Lake, Fort Yates, New Town, and Belcourt.

Sources: Cabot, Anthony N., William N. Thompson, Andrew Tottenham, and Carl Braunlich, eds. 1999. *International Casino Law.* 3d ed. Reno: Institute for the Study of Gambling, University of Nevada, Reno, 135–136.

Nova Scotia

The idea to introduce casino gaming in Nova Scotia in order to stimulate tourism first surfaced in the early 1970s when a study of the experience with gaming in the United States and Europe was commissioned. It took another twenty years before the issue of casino gaming emerged again. Other forms of commercial gaming have been big business in Nova Scotia for a long time. Lotteries, bingo, betting on horse tracks, and, more recently, video lottery terminals (VLTs) registered a total wager of approximately $500 million in 1993.

It is somewhat ironic that the momentum for casino gaming started at a time when public sentiment was divided, if not outright hostile, toward gaming. In fact, sparks literally flew in the wake of the government's decision to remove VLTs from non-age-controlled premises such as convenience stores, laundromats, and bowling alleys in February 1993. Store owners were justifiably incensed about the unexpected loss of revenue, whereas the vocal opponents of VLTs argued that this step was necessary to keep minors away from gaming. The government was somewhat caught in the middle, and it responded with a review of the gaming laws. A subsequent report struck a cautious note with a recommendation not to expand gaming in Nova Scotia until the residents had a chance to express their views on this matter. In the meantime, the Nova Scotia Lotteries Commission conducted an independent study on gaming with specific reference to VLTs, casinos, and bingo. After carefully weighing the pros and cons of casino gaming and taking account of a survey that found that 59 percent of the respondents were not in favor of introducing casino gaming to Nova Scotia, the study group made an interesting recommendation. Two casino pilot projects should be granted—one in the Halifax-Dartmouth Metro Area and the other one in Cape Breton—for a one-year trial period in order to monitor and assess the impact of casino gaming and its acceptance by the residents.

The interest in operating casinos was enormous: The study group received no less than thirteen proposals to do so, and among them were fairly detailed project descriptions by Hilton and Grand Casinos. The Hilton proposal suggested building a casino in a Halifax landmark hotel, the 1928 Hotel Nova Scotian, which was being operated by Hilton Hotels after a complete renovation in 1988. This proposal was endorsed by the Halifax Board of Trade.

Grand Casinos suggested a large hotel–casino–resort complex in the Ragged Lake Industrial Park Area outside Halifax; no surprise here that this proposal was supported by the Halifax Industrial Commission. What was surprising was the entire fanfare and promotion of these two proposals, and particularly the one of Grand Casinos, since it must be remembered that the introduction of casinos was not even on the drawing board.

All of this and the report itself became history with a change in government. But the casino issue did not fade into oblivion. After only four months in office, the new government resurrected the thorny issue of gaming in Nova Scotia and empowered the House Committee on Community Services to conduct hearings all over the province on the issues of whether casino gaming should be introduced and whether VLTs should be brought back to convenience stores. In its report, the committee recommended (1) that casino gaming should not be introduced in Nova Scotia or, more specifically, that it should not yet be introduced because too little was known about the socioeconomic impact of gaming, and (2) that in view of the potential harmful effect on Nova Scotia's reputation as a nature-oriented and peaceful tourist attraction, VLTs should be in age-controlled premises only.

To everyone's surprise, the government did not follow the committee's line of thinking. In a complete turnaround, it was announced that casino gaming would be introduced, and the sooner the better because of its beneficial impact for the province. This meant a fast tracking period for casino gaming. The reasons for this move lie in the dire situation of provincial coffers: Nova Scotia has one of the highest ratios of public debt per capita in Canada, and it suffers from persistent double-digit unemployment. Casino gaming as a very labor-intensive business was simply seen as an opportunity that could not and should not be missed.

The Casino Campaign

After the announcement that casino gaming would be coming to Nova Scotia, the government appointed a Casino Project Committee to (1) draft a request for proposals (RFP) for bidders and (2) select and recommend a proponent to the government for the license to operate the two casinos. The RFP was designed in a record time of four weeks. Its most important aspects and requirements were as follows:

- The two casinos would be publicly owned and operated.
- A gaming commission would be established to regulate and monitor gaming.
- A gaming corporation would be established to operate and manage the two casinos. The day-to-day operations of both casinos would be conducted by a private

company on behalf of the gaming corporation; this agent would be determined through the bidding process.
- The tax on gaming revenue (win tax) was set at 20 percent; in addition, 70 percent of the net income of the Halifax casino would go to public coffers; the remaining 30 percent would go to the private company. The Sydney casino would be a charitable casino operation, and the casino operator would receive a management fee plus a negotiated percentage of the net income.
- Two interim casinos would have to be in operation within sixty days of acceptance of a proposal.

At the time of the announcement of the short list, the names of the six initial bidders were officially disclosed. They were ITT Sheraton Canada, Casinos Austria, Harrah's, Aztar, Grand Casinos, and Crystal Casinos. With the exception of Harrah's, all casino companies had entered into partnerships with local interests in order to enhance their chances. The first three bidders made the short list, and ITT Sheraton Canada eventually got the nod. Since the proposals of other bidders were not made public, one can only speculate about the reasons why it was ITT Sheraton Canada. Most likely, ITT's guarantee of a payment of C$100 million for the first four years, which ended on 31 July 1999, may have tilted the balance in its favor. These payments ensured that total provincial revenue from gaming would not be less than C$25 million in each of the first four years. In return, ITT received the license to be the sole casino operator in Nova Scotia for twenty years, after which time the casino assets along with the customer database would become property of the province for a symbolic amount of one dollar.

In order to enhance its chances to become the operator of the two casinos, ITT Sheraton Canada had formed a partnership with a Halifax-based company, Purdy's Wharf Development Ltd., on a 90 percent to 10 percent basis. This partnership would operate the casinos under the name Sheraton Casinos Nova Scotia (SCNS). SCNS became part of Park Place Entertainment Inc. (PPE) in 1999 when PPE acquired the gaming assets of

Starwood Enterprises, which, in turn, had acquired ITT in 1997; subsequently, SCNS changed its name to Casino Nova Scotia.

An Economic Assessment

Nova Scotia is one of the four Atlantic provinces of Canada. The province has an area of 21,425 square miles and a population of 935,000 (1998). The two casino cities—Halifax, the capital of the province, and Sydney—have populations of 350,000 and 85,000 in the respective metro areas.

In a province with high unemployment and a suffocating debt load, any new business investment that creates jobs is a welcome option. Casino gaming is such an option, and the government was wise to pick this option. Casino gaming not only creates jobs just as other business investments do, it creates many jobs and many secure jobs. In fact, casino gaming is perhaps the most labor intensive of all entertainment industries. In addition to the direct employment effect there is the indirect employment effect through the casinos' purchases of goods and services. Furthermore, there would be a direct and indirect employment effect during the construction period of the casinos. Altogether, this would create an employment effect of substantial proportions.

Next in line is the tourism imperative. Tourism is a very important industry for Nova Scotia, and the government and casino proponents eagerly emphasized the enhancement of tourism through casinos. A note of caution is in order, however. Nova Scotia is known for its beautiful nature and tranquility, and that will remain the premier cause for tourists to come and see such attractions as Peggy's Cove and the Cabot Trail. It would appear very unlikely that "gaming tourists" can be attracted in the sense of tourists who did not have Nova Scotia on their map previously and excluding visitors from the other three Atlantic provinces. Nevertheless, there can be no doubt that casino gaming will represent an additional incentive for tourists. This well-to-do category of gaming patrons is a premier target group for casinos in general and for the two Nova Scotia casinos in particular. Take, for instance, cruise passengers. The number of cruise ships coming to Halifax has risen considerably in recent years, and this increase has been fueled mainly by the New Atlantic Frontier consortium of sixteen East Coast ports. Cruise passengers will come to the casino, and they come in droves since the Halifax casino is only a leisurely twenty-minute walk away from the cruise terminal at Pier 21.

Finally, there is the monopoly aspect for the operator, which is perhaps the most powerful incentive and a lifeline for sustained profit performance in a sparsely populated province. The twenty-year contract with the government provided SCNS/Casino Nova Scotia with the franchise to be the sole casino operator in Nova Scotia. In fact, the monopoly extends to all of Atlantic Canada, at least for the foreseeable future, since there are no active casino-initiatives in New Brunswick, Prince Edward Island, and Newfoundland. This means a monopoly in a territory the size of France, with a population of 2.4 million people. It should also be noted that the Halifax and Cape Breton gaming markets can be viewed as separate markets, since they do not intersect at the 0–100-mile range. Consequently, the likelihood of cannibalism is very low.

After the announcement that casino gaming would come to Nova Scotia, some bands of the Mikmaq Indians indicated plans to establish casinos on Native land. Consequently, the government started negotiations with the Indian bands in order to preserve the monopoly status of the two casinos. In February 1995, an agreement was reached with the Eskasoni Band Council in Cape Breton regarding gaming activity on the reserve and profit sharing from the proceeds of the Sydney Casino. Specifically, under the terms of the agreement, the band would regulate and monitor gaming activity on the reserve, which would include VLTs and charitable gaming but not a casino. Furthermore, 50 percent of the profits of the Sydney Casino would be earmarked to go to the entire Mikmaq Community in Nova Scotia.

The Legal Framework

According to the Nova Scotia Gaming Control Act, casino gaming is under the auspices of the Nova Scotia Liquor and Gaming Authority and the Nova Scotia Gaming Corporation. The authority is in charge of the regulation and control of all legalized gaming in the province. The corporation, in turn, conducts and manages all legalized forms of gaming in the province. For casino gaming, the corporation entered into a contractual arrangement with Sheraton Casinos Nova Scotia to operate the two casinos as the sole appointed agent on behalf of the corporation for a period of twenty years.

Games of chance permitted to be played in Nova Scotia casinos are roulette, baccarat, mini-baccarat, blackjack, slot machines, keno, video poker, video keno, video blackjack, pai gow, pai gow poker, big six, craps, and poker and its variations. For slot machines, the payout must not be less than 86 percent.

Nova Scotia casinos are open all days of the year with the exception of Good Friday, Easter Sunday, Remembrance Day (11 November), and Christmas Day. The casinos can operate on a twenty-four-hour basis, but only the Halifax Casino does so for seven days a week; as an economy measure, the Sydney casino operates twenty-four hours a day on Fridays and Saturdays and from noon to 4 A.M. on Sundays through Thursdays.

In accordance with the strict liquor regulations in Nova Scotia, the Gaming Control Act does not permit the provision of complimentary alcoholic beverages in casinos. From day one, Sheraton Casinos Nova Scotia made numerous attempts to have this rule changed. These efforts were successful to the extent that the operator will be able to provide free alcoholic beverages to high-end players in the designated area (Crown Club area) of the Halifax Casino Nova Scotia. In addition, high-end players from outside of the province will be able to receive credit on demand in this casino.

The Halifax Casino Nova Scotia has a gaming floor space of 34,900 square feet with 40 table games and 688 slot machines. The Sydney Casino Nova Scotia has 20 table games and 350 slot machines on 15,400 square feet of gaming floor space.

—written by Christian Marfels

Sources: Cabot, Anthony N., William N. Thompson, Andrew Tottenham, and Carl Braunlich, eds. 1999. *International Casino Law.* 3d ed. Reno: Institute for the Study of Gambling, University of Nevada, Reno, 186–191.

Numbers Games. *See Lotteries*

O

Ohio

In 1973 Ohioans voted for legalized lottery gambling with a 64 percent majority vote. The active games generate over $2 billion in sales. Net revenues are dedicated to educational programs. Since the 1930s most forms of horseracing (thoroughbred, harness, and quarter horse) have had pari-mutuel betting. Telephone wagering and intertrack simulcast race wagering are permitted and are operational; offtrack betting has been approved. Ohio also has a very active charitable gaming operation with both bingo games and Las Vegas nights.

Ohio citizens have been a strong market for many gambling operations over history. The Ohio River attracted riverboat gamblers during the nineteenth century, and illegal numbers games and sports betting flourished during the twentieth century. Ohio residents have been the primary player base for illegal casinos in Steubenville and also for northern Kentucky locations such as Newport and Covington. The Mayfield Road Gang ran illegal liquor operations during Prohibition and also established gaming outlets for the Cleveland and Toledo populations. Gang leader Moe Dalitz eventually became one of the founding fathers of the Las Vegas Strip, as he became an owner of the Desert Inn and Stardust in the 1950s.

In the 1990s Ohio became surrounded by new gaming facilities in nearby states and in Canada. Indiana had riverboat casinos just outside of Cincinnati, Casino Windsor and the new Detroit casinos were but an hour's drive from Toledo, Casino Niagara was within a day's trip of Cleveland, and West Virginia racetracks had machine gaming within miles of the Ohio border. Ohio also furnished hundreds of thousands of gamblers for Las Vegas and Atlantic City casinos each year.

The encroaching competition for Ohio gaming dollars generated two concerted campaigns for casinos in the Buckeye State during the 1990s. Both campaigns were led by the Spitzer family, who owned a shipyard in Lorain, just twenty miles outside of Cleveland on the shores of Lake Erie. In 1990 they sponsored a petition drive and statewide election to place a casino boat on their lands. They called the casino a pilot project, suggesting that five years later casinos could be placed in other locations. In the 1990 election, 58 percent of the voters rejected the proposals. In 1996 the Spitzers sponsored a petition drive for five casinos, with two on Lake Erie and three on the Ohio River. That year nearly 52 percent of the Michigan voters said yes to Detroit casinos, but in Ohio 62 percent of the voters rejected casinos. As more casinos come to rely on Ohio for gambling patrons in the twenty-first century, Ohio interests will no doubt continue to push plans to legalize casinos within their own borders.

Sources: Thompson, William N., and Ricardo Gazel. 1995. "The Last Resort Revisited." *Journal of Gambling Studies* 12, no. 3 (Fall): 335–339; Wacker, R. F., and W. N. Thompson. 1997. "The Michigan Question: A Legal Quandary." *Gaming Law Review* 1 (Winter): 501–510.

See also Dalitz, Morris

Oklahoma

Pari-mutuel wagering was authorized by a 58 percent vote of the Oklahoma citizens in 1982. One major thoroughbred track was established, but it ceased operations for financial reasons. Several quarterhorse tracks continue to operate.

The state has no lottery; however, charity bingo games are permitted. Several Native American tribes have sought compacts so that they could offer full casino gambling, but the state has refused to negotiate. The tribes have compacts for offtrack betting facilities. Also, Oklahoma tribes pioneered the establishment of a multistate, multi-tribal satellite bingo gambling operation that has offered prizes up to a million dollars.

Sources: Dombrink, John D., and William N. Thompson. 1990. *The Last Resort: Success and Failure in Campaigns for Casinos.* Reno: University of Nevada Press.

Ontario

Ontario is the most populated province of Canada, with nearly 9 million people. It also produces the largest share of gaming revenues of any province. The three commercial casinos of the province generate 55 percent of all the casino revenues in Canada, and the leading racetracks of Canada are also located in Ontario. Nearly 65 percent of the racing handled in Canada is wagered in Ontario. The Woodbine track in Toronto hosted North America's premium racing card, the Breeders' Cup, in 1997. The tracks also have the most successful gaming machine operations in Canada. Ontario also has the most profitable lottery operation in Canada.

Ontario is clearly a leader in gaming volume today, but the province trailed others in initiating gaming operations. The lottery did not start until 1975, and lotto games were not in place until five years later. Instant tickets were not sold before 1982. The Ontario Lottery Corporation was responsible for overseeing charity gaming; however, until the mid-1990s charities could only sell raffle tickets and break-open tickets (similar to pull tabs) and conduct bingo games.

The Ontario Lottery Corporation may have hesitated a bit, but in the 1990s it went into high gear. In 1993 it made a decision to have major casinos. To "test the waters" it authorized a pilot project for Windsor. Windsor was chosen for an obvious reason that provincial leaders made no attempt to conceal. Quite to the contrary, they boasted that the Windsor casino would market its gaming products to residents of the United States, more specifically residents of the Detroit metropolitan area. Only a one-mile waterway—the Detroit River—separated Windsor from Detroit, and

there were two border crossing stations—a bridge and a tunnel. It was projected that 80 percent of the casino's revenues would come from the United States. The Ontario Lottery Corporation secured a remodeled museum and art gallery building for a temporary casino. The government owned the casino, but it contracted with a consortium consisting of Caesars, Hilton, and Circus Circus companies to run the casino. The casino opened in May 1994, with greater than anticipated success. Seventy table games and 1,700 slot machines collected more revenue per square foot than had ever been collected in any casinos anywhere. Continuous crowds led the province to purchase a riverboat (the *Northern Belle*) and open it as a second Windsor casino. No longer was Windsor a pilot project. In 1998, a permanent facility was opened in a 1.2-million-square-foot facility on the riverfront. The facility included all the amenities of a Las Vegas casino—a hotel of 400 rooms, showrooms, multiple restaurants, and of course a gaming area of 100,000 square feet with 3,000 slot machines and 130 table games. The two temporary casinos closed.

Success is measured in many ways. One thing the success of Windsor's casinos generated was a massive concern in the Detroit area over revenues leaving not only the city but also the country. Detroit retaliated by voting in 1995 to approve a nonbinding resolution supporting casinos. Then in 1996, the voters of the state of Michigan made it binding as they voted for a new state law permitting three casinos for the city of Detroit. The first one opened in 1999.

While things were happening in southwestern Ontario, the Ontario Lottery Corporation decided that more casinos should be located elsewhere. In 1996 temporary casinos were opened in Niagara Falls and also in Orilla. Although a temporary facility, the provincially owned Niagara Falls casino was managed by the Navagante Group—led by several former casino executives from Las Vegas. Soon the revenues at the Niagara Falls facility came to surpass those in Windsor. In November 1998, the corporation entered into an agreement with Hyatt Hotels for the construction of a permanent casino facility, which was to have a 350-room hotel, convention center, arts center, and cinema

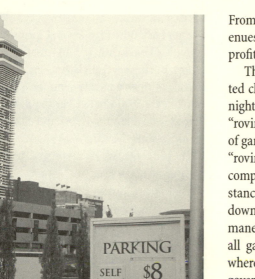

Parking can be costly when casinos have a monopoly.
The Niagara Falls Casino in Ontario.

complex, along with show rooms, restaurants, and a 100,000-square-foot casino. The province also planned to place casino gaming in the popular Skylon tower that oversees the falls. Hyatt was to manage the new facilities in conjunction with a new management group of Americans. The facility is under construction as of 2001.

A new project is also slated for the Casino Rama in Orilla. As would be expected, this gaming hall has exceeded expectations. It is only one hour north of the Toronto metropolitan area. Casino Rama is owned by a Chippewa Band of First Nations peoples. The casino is operated by Carnival Cruise Lines' casino division.

The three commercial casinos give 20 percent of their revenues directly to the Ontario provincial treasury; however, in the case of Casino Rama, the revenues are placed into a fund to benefit all the First Nations' peoples of the province. The operators also take a 5 percent share of the gaming win.

From the remaining 75 percent of the gaming revenues, all expenses are deducted. The residual net profits go to the province.

The Ontario Lottery Corporation also permitted charity casinos in the early 1990s. The casino nights featured table gaming only. These had to be "roving" casinos because no more than one night of gaming could be in one location per month. The "roving" games were operated by management companies, and many problems surfaced. For instance, with all the moving, equipment broke down frequently, and also there could be no permanent security systems installed to ensure that all gaming was honest and that all funds went where they were supposed to go. So in 1997, the government announced that it would create forty-four charity gaming sites in the province. How funds would be distributed was not clearly addressed, although most of the funds would go to the Ontario Lottery Corporation. (This presented a legal challenge, as the charity gaming laws require that most of the net revenues must go to the charity). The casinos would each be allowed forty tables and 150 machines. Most of the communities selected for the casino sites expressed displeasure with the idea, as citizens propelled round after round of protest at the government. In 1998 the province backed down and decreed that there would only be four "pilot" charity casinos, to be located in Thunder Bay, Sault Ste. Marie, Point Edward (adjacent to Sarnia), and Brantford. These cities were the only ones that had voted in favor of having charity casinos. Sault Ste. Marie and Point Edward were especially desirable sites as they bordered Michigan cities. One of these cities, Sault St. Marie, Michigan, boasted a very large Native American casino (the Kewadin Chippewa casino) that had been drawing most of its revenue from Canadians. Only Brantford did not have direct highway access to the United States and to potential American customers. Additional charity casinos were permitted for First Nations' reserve lands. One is in operation near Port Erie. The four pilot casinos were allotted 450 gaming machines and eighty tables for players. All are now in operation and drawing good business from players.

The Ontario Lottery Corporation was also dissuaded from another plan owing to the protests of the citizens. The government announced that it would authorize 20,000 video machines for bars, taverns, and racetracks in the province. In 1998 the corporation abandoned the overall plan but instead finalized plans to place up to 20,000 machines in eighteen provincial racetracks, with as many as 2,000 at a single track. The operation of the machine gaming began in 1999 with 800 machines being installed at Windsor Raceway. Other tracks now have machines.

—coauthored by Garry Smith

Sources: Alfieri, Donald. 1994. "The Ontario Casino Project: A Case Study." In *Gambling in Canada: The Bottomline,* edited by Colin Campbell, 85–92. Burnaby, BC: Simon Fraser University; Cabot, Anthony N., William N. Thompson, Andrew Tottenham, and Carl Braunlich, eds. 1999. *International Casino Law.* 3d ed. Reno: Institute for the Study of Gambling, University of Nevada, Reno, 192–204; Prowse, Peter. 1994. "An Operator's View." In *Gambling in Canada: The Bottomline,* edited by Colin Campbell, 105–110. Burnaby, BC: Simon Fraser University; Tomovic, Shirley M., casino studies coordinator, Niagara College. Interview by author. Niagara Falls, Ontario, 2 April 2001.

See also The Racino

Oregon

Oregon has authorized several forms of gambling activities. I have gathered information on these activities during several visits to the state, including participation in a faculty seminar, "Oregon Games: Don't Leave It to Chance," at the School of Urban Studies and Planning, Portland State University, on 14 November 1997.

In 1984 the voters approved a lottery by a margin of 66 percent to 34 percent. The lottery started operations in 1985. The lottery was conducted with traditional lottery games at first. In 1989 the lottery was then modified to include betting on sports events through parlay cards, and it was later modified for making wagers at video lottery terminals. The state of Oregon is one of only four states that is permitted to have sports betting. All bets are made on parlay cards, which require the player to pick winners of at least four games. Point spreads are indicated on the cards for football and basketball games. The winnings are paid on a pari-mutuel basis. Proceeds from the sports betting are dedicated to university athletic programs.

The Chinook Winds Casino in Lincoln City, Oregon.

The state has also permitted card games with financial prizes to be played among players in bars, restaurants, and fraternal clubs (the various establishments may not be participants in the game) and bingo games to be conducted by charitable organizations. Oregon also has had horseracing with pari-mutuel betting for several decades.

These gaming authorizations provided the legal foundation for Native American tribes in Oregon to negotiate agreements with the state so that they could offer casino-type games. The authority for Native American gaming is granted in accordance with the Indian Gaming Regulatory Act of 1988. Seven tribes started casinos with machine gaming and bingo in their facilities. Agreements were amended to allow blackjack games. The casinos are operated by the Grande Ronde Indian Community (Grande Ronde), Umatilla Indian Reservation (Pendleton), Warm Springs Reservation (Warm Springs), Klamath Tribes (Chiloquin), Coquille Indian Tribe (North Bend), Cow Creek Band of Umpqua Indians (Canyonville), and Siletz Indians (Lincoln City).

Two of the tribes have negotiated agreements that permit them to offer all games that are authorized by the Nevada Gaming Control Board for Nevada commercial casinos. These are the Grand Ronde and the Cow Creek. In exchange for this privilege to have all games, the tribal organizations agreed to provide a community assistance fund equal to 6 percent of the gaming revenues for local areas. The other tribes are positioned to negotiate for such agreements if they wish to do so.

All the tribes pay the state fees to cover the costs of regulating the games.

Organized Crime Control Act of 1970

Pres. Richard Nixon signed the Organized Crime Control Act of 1970 into law on 15 October. The act was in reality a long list of ideas rather than a comprehensive coherent package of tools with which to deal with organized crime. Some called it "a smorgasbord of legal odds and ends" and a series of "nuts and bolts" for dealing with crime.

Among the matters of concern in the act was gambling. The act provided federal tools for enforcing state provisions on gambling under certain conditions. Penalties were provided for persons who financed, owned, managed, supervised, or directed an illegal gambling enterprise. The illegal enterprises had to involve five or more persons who acted contrary to state and local law to participate in gambling over a period of thirty days or more with revenues involved exceeding $2,000 for a single day. If two people conspired to break a state law on gambling and one was a public official, the federal government was also empowered to take action against the offenders. The act also authorized the appointment of the Commission on the Review of National Policy toward Gambling, which was appointed in 1974 and made a report of its findings in 1976.

Sources: New York Times, 18 October 1970, IV-9; Organized Crime Control Act of 1970 (Public Law 91–452, 84 Stat. 922, signed into law 15 October 1970).

See also Commission on the Review of National Policy toward Gambling (1974–1976)

P

Pachinko. *See* Japan and Pachinko

Pachi-slo. *See* Japan and Pachinko

Pai Gow Poker. *See* Poker

Panama

Panama has had a national lottery and casino gambling during most of its history as a nation. The Republic of Panama gained its independent status in 1903 following a separatist revolution from Colombia, which was supported by the United States. The United States then negotiated for rights to dig the Panama Canal and control its operations. A Canal Zone area was put under the American flag, and U.S. military bases were located in the zone. The U.S. presence as well as canal activities has brought people from all over the world to Panama, and the country looked to these people to support casino activities. The lottery, however, has been marketed to local residents, and it has served a social welfare function—first, by giving jobs to many persons who sell tickets and administer operations, and second, by dedicating its profits to programs to help the poor.

The U.S. military left the Canal Zone and invaded the governmental center in Panama City in

Not only in Las Vegas. Panama City Airport also has slot machines in its lobbies.

The headquarters for the Panama National Lottery. The goal of the lottery is to provide employment and benefits for the poor people of the country.

1989 in order to capture Pres. Manual Noriega because of his involvement in the drug trade. That invasion involved a major firefight and the loss of hundreds of lives. Along with the invasion, the United States imposed an embargo on Panama. The hostile policies had the effect of killing any tourist-type activity for many years. On 1 January 2000, the United States gave up control over the operations of the Panama Canal and by that time had withdrawn almost all its military from Panama. The withdrawal removed much of the market that had existed for casino gaming in the earlier years. Panama has readjusted with new government initiatives for redeveloping a new tourism opportunities. Casino gaming has returned to the tourist package, and the government has authorized new casinos with private ownership.

The first casinos in Panama were also under private control. Several gaming rooms were opened in the Old Balboa Gardens region of Panama City. They offered dice, roulette, and blackjack games. In the early 1940s, several gaming establishments came to the Plaza Cinco de Mayo in Panama City and to the city of Colon, where the canal meets the Caribbean Sea. After a government change in 1945, all casinos were placed under central ownership of three Panamanians who won a government concession for the activity. In the early 1950s the government permitted several casino gaming activities to be held for the benefit of the Red Cross and other charities. The private and charity gaming ventures came to an end in 1956 when the national government took over the casinos.

A national casino administration was established within the Ministry of Finance and Treasury. Its goal was to enhance tourism and to generate greater revenue from tourists as well as from Americans stationed in Panama and other businesspersons coming to the country. The national policy was directed at the placement of casinos in hotels. In the late 1950s casino activity began in the El Panama, Continental, Granada, and Siesta hotels. In 1965 a new national law reorganized the casinos, permitting their location in hotels located in cities over 200,000 population with a capital value of $1.5 million. The law also authorized slot machine–only casinos in other locations. At the time of the U.S. invasion, the government operated ten full-scale casinos in six Panama City hotels, two in Colon hotels, and one each in the city of David and on Contradora Island (which was exempt from the population requirement.) Six Panama City hotels had slot machine–only casinos as did three shopping centers, three airport locations, a bar, bowling alley, and five smaller cities. The full casinos offered blackjack, roulette, craps, and poker games, as well as slot machines.

According to my interview with gaming board officials in Panama City on 27 December 1998, in 1997 the government shifted its policies, realizing that its casino administration did not have the resources to fully develop the industry for tourism. Privatization was authorized. Bids were accepted from thirteen prequalified companies to run the casinos. Three companies were granted licenses to run casinos for twenty years. At that time licenses may be renewed. The casino facilities must be located in new five-star (and old four-star) hotels that have 300 rooms. The facilities may be open twenty-four hours a day. They must have security cameras, and new slot machines must be centrally linked together on computer systems. The casinos must advertise the tourist aspects of their facilities. In addition to annual licensing fees, the casinos pay a tax equaling 20 percent of their win. Slot machine–only casinos pay a tax of 25 percent.

Today, Crown Casinos runs casinos at the Granada, Continental (slot machines only), and Caesars Park hotels in Panama City. The Thunderbird, a Vancouver, British Columbia–based company, has casinos at the El Panama and Solon hotels in Panama City, as well as the Washington hotels in Colon and David. A third corporation runs separate slot machine parlors and has slot machines in the Panama City airport.

Sources: Cabot, Anthony N., William N. Thompson, Andrew Tottenham, and Carl Braunlich, eds. 1999. *International Casino Law.* 3d ed. Reno: Institute for the Study of Gambling, University of Nevada, Reno, 303–305.

Paraguay

Paraguay, perhaps the most remote country in South America, is a landlocked country surrounded by Argentina, Bolivia, and Brazil. It is a founding member of the Southern Cone Common Market (MERCOSUR). The other members of MERCOSUR are Argentina, Brazil, and Uruguay. The four countries of MERCOSUR have eliminated import tariffs and have a free exchange of goods, services, capital, and labor. Paraguay has about 5.5 million inhabitants residing in an area of about 157 thousand square miles.

Paraguay permits almost all forms of gambling, including horse racing, lotteries, cockfighting, bingo games, and casinos. Casinos have been located in all the major urban areas of the country: Asunción, Ciudad del Este, and Pedro Juan Caballero (Greater Asunción area). Paraguay also has small gaming casinos operated by local owners holding government licenses. With the exception of the operations in Asunción, the capital of Paraguay, the casinos are very small. The Ita Ra-

mada was the leading facility prior to the overthrow of Pres. Alfredo Stroessner in 1989. Soon afterward it became overshadowed by the casino at the Asunción Yacht Club.

Casino gambling began under the regulation of the national government in 1943 when a casino opened in a hotel in downtown Asuncion. The casino owner, Sr. Valentino, formed a corporation that later developed the Ita Enramada Hotel and Casino resort complex on the Paraguay River in suburban Asunción. The casino relocated to the Ita Enramada facility in 1975.

The Asunción casino operated under a long-term concession granted by the government of President Stroessner. Valentino's wife, Dora Valentino, maintained operations after his death. She also owned the casino at Ciudad Puerto Presidente Stroessner (now Ciudad del Este), the Paraguayan border city near Iguazu Falls, the Brazilian city of Iguazu Falls, and the Argentinian city of Port Iguazu (which has a casino). The Valentino company also held concessions to operate a weekly national lottery game, a quinela game, and bingo in Asunción. The Catholic University has operated the sports pool (PROBE), and horse-race betting has been under the control of other private operators. Small casinos in other communities have been operated by local owners holding government concessions.

The Valentino company's monopoly over major gaming activities received a serious setback after President Stroessner was deposed in February 1989. Dora Valentino's concession for the casino at the Hotel Acaray in Ciudad del Este expired. Unexpectedly, it was not renewed, and the concession was awarded to a group of Brazilian businessmen. They moved the casino to the Club Rio Del Este in downtown Ciudad del Este. That casino closed. The Acaray Palace Hotel and Casino is again open, but under new owners who also operate the Amambay Suites Hotel across the street from the Acaray.

Dora Valentino began constructing a $30 million, 250-room resort hotel just north of the city near a proposed major international airport. The foundation and shell of what could have become the largest hotel in the nation was built. Intentions were to move the casino to the facility. Construc-

The Ita Enramada Casino in Asuncion Paraguay.

tion halted, however, when casino plans stalled. The government had given only one casino concession for each region. Obtaining another concession in Ciudad del Este proved a difficult process. As the new hotel is technically outside the city and within the Hernandez region, Dora Valentino has claimed that the area is eligible for a second casino.

While the Valentino company argued for a second casino in the Ciudad del Este area its competitors won the right to have a second and third casino (besides the Ita Enramada Casino) in Asunción. Another casino is at the Asunción Yacht Club (the Paraguayan Hotel and Casino and Yacht and Golf Club). The Asunción Yacht Club Casino has outclassed the Ita Enramada Casino. The Ita Enramada Casino is eight miles downriver from downtown Asunción on the Paraguyan River. The Asunción Yacht Club Casino is also on the Paraguyan River about four miles downriver from downtown Asunción. Concessions for the casinos were extended in 1995.

Besides the casinos at Asunción and Ciudad del Este, the cities of San Bernardino and Pedro Juan

Caballero have casinos. The San Bernardino Hotel and Casino is in San Bernardino on Lake Ypacarai. The La Siesta Hotel and Casino is in Pedro Juan Caballero, a city on the Brazilian border, opposite the City of Ponta Pora, Brazil. The Amambay Casino is on the outskirts of Pedro Juan Caballero, and the La Siesta Casino is in the downtown area of the city. In addition, there is a bingo casino in the city of Encarnación, which is in southern Paraguay on the Argentina border, opposite Posadas, Argentina.

—coauthored by Larry Dandurand

Sources: Cabot, Anthony N., William N. Thompson, Andrew Tottenham, and Carl Braunlich, eds. 1999. *International Casino Law.* 3d ed. Reno: Institute for the Study of Gambling, University of Nevada, Reno, 306–312.

Pari-mutuel Wagering Systems

Pari-mutuel wagering systems are used for almost all horse-race and dog-race betting, as well as for betting on jai alai games in the United States. The system allows for player-banked betting with all

Boat racing in Japan with pari-mutuel betting system.

bets pooled and prizes awarded from the pool. Winning bets on other racing events are also determined on a pari-mutuel basis. In Japan, the system is used to award prizes to winners of wagers on motorboat and bicycle races. In Oregon, sports betting card bets are distributed to winners on this basis also. The state permits players to pick four winners of football games on a single card. The state takes 50 percent of all the money played and then divides the remainder among those who picked four winners. The California lottery actually uses a pari-mutuel system for its pick-three numbers game in order to avoid exposure to high risks because many players' favorite numbers are the same favorite numbers. Whenever there is a pari-mutuel system, the organization running the system takes a percentage of the pool before bets are redistributed from the losers to the winners.

Although the pari-mutuel system is built on quite a simple concept, it was not a part of the betting fabric until late in the nineteenth century. It

was invented in Paris, France, by Pierre Oller in 1865. Scarne's *Guide to Casino Gambling* (Scarne 1978) suggests that Oller acted in response to a bookie who quoted odds on each horse before a race, but was not very good at his trade and therefore often suffered losses because too many bettors placed their wagers on the winning horses. The bookie asked Oller if he could figure out a way in which the bookie could take bets without ever having to suffer losses—the gambler's eternal dream. Oller found a way: take bets but announce odds only after all bets were taken. Oller invented what became known as a totalizator. His tallying machine would add up all the bets on each horse, compare them, and then determine odds. All the odds could then be cut a set percentage to ensure a profit for the bookie. Soon a ticket machine was added to a totalizator device, and with the passing of time, more advanced machines made the bet-taking process more efficient and allowed tracks to consider changing their betting structures to the pari-mutuel system. As they did so, the tracks themselves became the operators of the betting on horse racing.

It is suggested that the system became known as pari-mutuel as a shorter reference to Paris Mutuel. The totalizator was first used at North American tracks in 1933; as horse-race betting was revived in more and more jurisdictions during the 1930s and afterwards, the pari-mutuel system totally displaced other betting systems.

A simple example of how a pari-mutuel wager works might find that all bettors wagered $100,000 on a race. Horse Surething attracted $30,000 of the bets in the eight-horse field. The track calculated all bets, totaled them, and then subtracted 18 percent as its fee. Actually this 18 percent, or $18,000, was divided three ways— $6,000 to the government as a tax, $6,000 to the track owners, and $6,000 as a prize for the winning horse. Sure enough it was Surething. All the people who bet on Surething were winners. Together they shared the $82,000 that was left in the pool of betting money. For example, if 500 people bet $100,000 on the race, and of these 50 bet on Surething to win, the 50 would share the $82,000 prize. They would share it in proportion to the amount they had bet. If collectively the 50 persons had bet $50,000 on Surething to win, each $1 they had bet would be rewarded with a prize of $1.64. A typical $2 bet would receive a return of $3.28, and a person who made a $1,000 bet would receive $1,640 in return. In actuality the $2 bettor would receive $3.20, because the track always rounds down to the nearest ten cents. The eight cents is called the breakage. Money from breakage is usually assigned to some party that takes money from the 18 percent (the track, horse owners, government).

In racing there are many kinds of bets (*see* Horse Racing). There are the straight bets—betting that the horse will come in first (win), first or second (place), or first, second, or third (show). There are also exotic bets, such as the daily double (winners of the first two races) or the exacta (picking the first-place and second-place winners in a race). For each kind of bet—show, exacta, daily double—there is a separate pool, and winners are paid from that pool alone. The betting arrangements can get very complicated, but modern computers can calculate results instantaneously, whereas in the past, several minutes would pass before a winner would know how much the winning prize was.

In the past, offtrack betting houses—such as the casinos in Las Vegas—would not participate in the pari-mutuel pools. Rather, they would simply pay the track odds and keep the takeout percentage (18 percent). In doing so they would put themselves at risk, as they were running a banking game. Now all participate with the tracks in the pari-mutuel system, as the offtrack bets are thrown into the same pool as the track bets. In exchange for being able to avoid the risk of being a house banker, however, the offtrack facility, such as the Las Vegas casino, gets to receive only a very small portion of the action wagered at their facility—5 or 6 percent rather than the theoretical 18 percent they would have received if their bettors made wagers in the same proportion as those at the track.

Sources: Scarne, John. 1978. *Scarne's Guide to Casino Gambling.* New York: Simon and Schuster; Thompson, William N. 1997. *Legalized Gambling: A Reference Handbook.* 2d ed. Santa Barbara, CA: ABC-CLIO.
See also Horse Racing; House-banked Games; Player-banked Games

Pathological Gambling. *See* Gambling, Pathological

Pendleton, Edward

Edward Pendleton was a nineteenth-century gambling service provider for the nation's leaders. To get an idea of what he provided, just suppose that the mid-1990s proposal for a legalized casino within the jurisdiction of the District of Columbia had passed. Imagine that congressmen, cabinet members, Supreme Court justices, maybe the president himself, could come to the casino and be wined and dined, then offered credit for gambling at the tables. Imagine lobbyists circulating within the facility the day before a major vote in Congress or a major decision by the court. Imagine the opportunities to buy favors, to line the pockets of the mighty in exchange for policy outcomes.

Well, it is not necessary to imagine. You need only read a history of Edward Pendleton and his Palace of Fortune located within walking distance of the houses of government in the District of Columbia through the 1830s, 1840s, and 1850s. The facility at 14th and Pennsylvania Avenue, two blocks from the White House, became the favorite of the ruling classes. The president of the United States, James Buchanan, was a regular at the faro bank. The nation's most important policymakers would wager at Pendleton's faro bank and inevitably lose. They would then become indebted to the casino owner. He, of course, was a lobbyist. Actually, win or lose, he came out ahead. It is reported that in the twenty-six years that Pendleton ran the Palace of Fortune he was responsible for the passage of hundreds of bills, most of which were private bills providing favors for selected citizens. The casino was extremely luxurious, as the owner became a very rich man.

The casino was also the meeting place where abolitionists and slave-owning senators could come together on neutral ground. Many of the compromises that kept the Civil War from erupting until 1861 may have been reached over the tables of the Palace.

Pendleton married the daughter of one of the leading city architects of the District of Columbia. The couple became a dominant part of the social scene, well respected, as many other gamblers were not in other venues. When Edward Pendleton died in 1858 at the age of sixty-eight, his funeral was attended by the president and most leaders of Congress.

Sources: Asbury, Herbert. 1938. *Sucker's Progress: An Informal History of Gambling in America from the Colonies to Canfield.* New York: Dodd, Mead, 140–146; Chafetz, Henry. 1960. *Play the Devil: A History of Gambling in the United States from 1492 to 1955.* New York: Potter Publishers, 180–181; Longstreet, Stephen. 1977. *Win or Lose: A Social History of Gambling.* Indianapolis, IN: Bobbs-Merrill, 37–38; Sifakis, Carl. 1990. *Encyclopedia of Gambling.* New York: Facts on File, 224.

Pennsylvania

Pennsylvania has had a wide variety of legalized gambling activities for many decades. But even before wagering on harness racing and thoroughbred racing was authorized in the 1930s, there was an established illegal network of numbers games and casino games. A lottery was established in 1971, and charity bingo was given the stamp of approval by government in 1981. Illegal numbers gambling persisted. This was evidenced by the "666" scandal that touched the state's legal lottery in 1979. A Pittsburgh television station that announced lottery results controlled the Ping-Pong balls used for the state lottery's numbers game. A dishonest person approached the television announcer and made an offer that should have been refused. But instead the television announcer allowed the dishonest person access to the lottery balls; that person then applied weights (using a paint substance) to all but the fours and sixes. A network of confederates then traversed the state making bets on all three-number combinations of fours and sixes. There were eight such combinations. Unfortunately, 666 came up. This is a very popular number for bettors in that it has biblical significance. Not only the network of dishonest people but also the general population bet heavily on the number. But the population bet on the numbers with illegal gamblers as well; and the illegal gamblers used the state-selected number as their winning number. The state and the illegal game lost more money to winners on that day than they had ever lost before or since that time. The illegal gamblers became suspicious, as there were rumors that people were betting heavily on certain numbers in certain locations. In a case of good and evil working together to protect the integrity of the game, the illegal numbers organization launched its own investigation, tracked down people in the network, and then informed the state police, who in turn were led to the television announcer. He and the others received prison sentences for their involvement. There were two consequences of the "666" scandal that merit consideration. First, there was no state oversight of the rigged game; after all the state ran the game. After cheating was discovered, there was no attempt to close down the game. The numbers game continued without any interruption. Second, the state made no attempt to reimburse the losing players who were cheated in the scandal.

From the moment legal casinos opened in Atlantic City, Pennsylvania could feel the dollars flowing out of the state. Entrepreneurs found it easy to convince many government officials that Pennsylvania had to legalize casinos in order to keep gambling revenues in the state. There were several campaigns for casinos in the 1980s and 1990s. The first major effort focused upon establishing casinos in three Pocono Mountains resort area.

Caesars World was a campaign sponsor, as they had purchased four resort properties in the area. Wayne Newton also owned a Pocono property. Several polls and advisory votes were taken in the region, and in all cases the residents rejected the idea. The governor also offered his opposition. Legislative bills for casino failed in 1981, 1982, and 1983. In the early 1990s, following Iowa's lead, several bills were introduced to permit riverboat casinos. One plan had 20 boats in the state, with from 5 to 10 in Philadelphia, 5 in Pittsburgh, 2 in Erie, and others in the northeast part of the state. The plan failed to get a floor vote in either house of the legislature. In 1999 the boat plan was attached to a plan for slot machines in bars and taverns and at tracks. The governor said he would approve the bills if the legislature called for a popular referendum. Three bills appeared headed for passage, calling for three separate statewide votes. Opponents, however, maneuvered votes to defeat the measure, and Pennsylvania exited the century with no casinos or machine gaming.

Sources: Dombrink, John D., and William N. Thompson. 1990. *The Last Resort: Success and Failure in Campaigns for Casinos.* Reno: University of Nevada Press, 119–126; Thompson, William N. 1997. *Legalized Gambling: A Reference Handbook.* 2d ed. Santa Barbara, CA: ABC-CLIO.

Peru

A variety of gambling activities is permitted in Peru, including horse racing, cockfighting, lotteries, and casinos—the last becoming legal only in 1992. At that time the country of nearly 25 million persons was in the midst of a violent struggle with revolutionary guerrillas. The economy was on the edge of collapse with unmanageable inflation.

Things turned around in the past decade. What was once a hostile atmosphere for casino operations is now a strong market in a stable political and economic situation under the leadership of former president Alberto Fujimori.

The Peru casino law requires that full casinos must be located in one of ten tourist zones. They receive ten-year renewable licenses, and they pay taxes of 20 percent on their gross gaming wins.

The capital city of Lima has about 80 percent of the casino action in the country. The city has eight full casinos, and another forty are located around the country. Most of them are privately owned, although the government owns some. There are also separate slot machine parlors. In all there are over 5,500 total machines in Lima, including a Megabucks system linking 300 machines and offering prizes in excess of $100,000.

Whereas an overall political and economic stability helps the gaming industry in general, continuing disputes over whether the national or the local law applies to the slot machine parlors has caused much confusion. In 1996 the national government set forth new rules that resulted in the closings of over half of the slot parlors. The rules required casinos to have at least 120 machines each and to guarantee 85 percent payouts; they were not allowed to have machines over five years old. Many parlors could not comply and closed. Others went to court and got injunctions against enforcement of the new national rules. They continue to operate while others seek to follow the rules, and the market continues to be in disarray.

Growth of the Peruvian casino industry is unlikely, as the markets are near saturation at the moment. It is estimated that over 90 percent of the play comes from local residents and not from tourists, a situation that does not allow for casinos to contribute to the economic development of a country.

Sources: Cabot, Anthony N., William N. Thompson, Andrew Tottenham, and Carl Braunlich, eds. 1999. *International Casino Law.* 3d ed. Reno: Institute for the Study of Gambling, University of Nevada, Reno, 313.

Player-banked Games

In a player-banked game, the money wagered by the players is either put against the funds of one other single player who acts as "the bank" (much as in a house-banked game), or it is put into a common pool of funds that is then distributed to the winner (or winners) when the game (hand) is over. Player-banked games include many variations of live poker games, special variations of blackjack such as California Aces, and pari-mutuel games in which wagers are placed on results of horse or dog races and jai alai games in the United States and Canada.

In poker games that are played socially—probably the most prevalent social game in North America—players usually make an ante bet, that is, a wager before any cards are dealt. The ante is thrown into the middle of the table area. Then either as successive cards are dealt or as individual players are asked to state what they are willing to risk if the game continues, extra money is thrown into the center area by all players wishing to remain in the game. When the betting is done (according to the rules of the game), the winner is determined, and all the money is given to the winner.

When such games are played in casinos or poker rooms (as in California), the house provides a neutral dealer who oversees and monitors the game to ensure that it is honest and that specific rules of the game and rules on betting procedures (antes, raises, limits) are followed. For this service, the house charges either a per-hand price to each player in the game, a fee based upon the time the player is at the table (usually collected each half hour, as in California), or a percentage of the money that is played in the game (the practice in Las Vegas casinos).

The players in the player-banked game are seeking to win money from each other and not from the casino or the poker room organization. In traditional baccara, players rotate the bank, holding it as long as the "bank" position in the game is a winner, then when losing passing it on to an adjacent player. The bank therefore passes around the table as if it were a train moving on a track. The game is also known as chemin de fer, a French expression meaning *railroad*. In charitable bingo games, the organization running the game sells cards for play. After all cards are sold, the organization totals up the sales (money that comes from the players), takes out its share (usually 20 percent

to 40 percent), and then announces the amount of money that will be given to the winner(s).

Several Native American tribal casinos use player-banked systems for games that are normally house banked. For instance, in both California and Texas, tribal casinos offer a standard blackjack game with extra opportunities for player wins. The casino still wins money from the actual game, however. This money is then placed into a pool, and players are given chances to win the pooled money by spinning a wheel or playing another chance game. In this way, 100 percent of the money played is returned to the players, so in a very real sense, their play is merely a redistribution of money among themselves. Another player-banked version of blackjack is called California Aces. Cards are dealt in a standard fashion, but there is no dealer hand. Also there is no busting (losing) for going over 21. Actually 22 is the best hand, and other hands are ranked according to how close to 22 they are, with lower numbers being superior to numbers over 22. (For example, the order of best to worst hands is 22, 21, 23, 20, 24, 19, 25, 18, and so on.) All money played goes to the player with the best hand. The casino does not collect any money from the game; however, the players in all these games pays the casino a fee for each hand they play. (After Proposition 1A passed in California in 2000, the Native American casinos there made compacts that allow them to offer house-banked games.)

Sources: Thompson, William N. 1997. *Legalized Gambling: A Reference Handbook.* 2d ed. Santa Barbara, CA: ABC-CLIO.

See also California; House-banked Games; Pari-mutuel Wagering Systems

Players, Demographic Categories of. *See* Demographic Categories of Players

Poker

Poker is the most widely known card game. In one or another of its many formats, it is played more often than any other game. Live poker games are typically player-banked games that involve not

In Pai Gow Poker the player makes bets on two hands made from seven cards. The game has become a popular casino attraction for Asian players.

only the luck of drawing certain cards but also much skill in determining how the cards should be played in order to defeat the hands held by other players. Some forms of the game, typically those played with machines (video poker), are house-banked games in which the player seeks to achieve hands of certain values in isolation of any other hand, whether held by a person or by a machine. (As the preponderance of poker players are male, in this entry I will use male gender forms to refer to players.)

The Poker Hand

All poker games are based upon the value of a five-card hand. The ten best hands are listed here in descending order. (1) A royal flush consists of an ace, king, queen, jack, and 10, all of the same suit (e.g., all hearts or all spades). (2) The straight flush also consists of five cards in the same suit and also in order. Next to the royal flush, the best straight flush would be king, queen, jack, 10, and 9 of the same suit. (3) Four of a kind consists of four aces, four kings, four 2s, and so on. (4) A full house con-

sists of three of a kind and two of a kind (a pair). The highest-ranking full houses have the top three of a kind (three aces and another pair). (5) A flush consists of five cards all of the same suit but not necessarily in any order or sequence. (6) A straight is a consecutive sequence of cards that are not necessarily of the same suit, for instance, a 3, 4, 5, 6, and 7 of varying suits. (7) In a three of a kind, the cards are of the same rank (three 4s, etc.), along with any two other cards. (8) Next is the combination of two pairs of cards and one other card. The highest pair would decide the value of the hands if two players had two pairs each. (9) The next combination is one pair. (10) Last is a hand valued by the highest card in a hand without at least a pair. (In pai gow and pai gow poker, two card hands are ranked according to the highest pair [the best hand is two aces] or the highest card if there is no pair.)

Draw and Stud Poker

Two styles of poker games are draw poker and stud poker. In draw poker, the several players are each dealt (in turn) five cards. They may then request up to three new cards (more in some games) and throw away up to three cards. In the other form, stud poker, there is no draw. The player must utilize the cards that are dealt the first time. Stud poker games may involve more than five cards. In seven-card stud, the player is asked to make the best five-card hand possible from the seven cards.

The sequence of betting is tied to the rules of particular games. For two examples, consider five-card draw and a seven-card stud game called hold 'em, a game popular in Las Vegas. In a five-card draw game, all players at a table make an initial bet (called an ante). Then five cards are dealt to each player, all face down only, for the one player to see. Usually there must be at least one player with a minimum hand (for instance, a pair of jacks or better) in order to start the next round of betting. Such a player may open with another bet, and other players decide to either stay in the game and match the bet or drop out. Other players also may raise the bet, requiring all others to meet the raise or drop out. (Rules of the particular game put limits on the amount of bets and raises. If there are no limits, a person is entitled to stay in a game by placing all his money into the game pot. His winnings are confined to moneys equal to his bet from each other player. If he loses he is out of the game.) The players then throw away cards they do not want and draw new replacement cards. They then engage in another round of bets and raises according to rules (some games limit the number of raises to three). The final player to call or raise then must show his cards; others may drop out without showing cards. Of course the player who wins must show his cards. All cards are secret until the final play is made.

In variations of stud poker, cards are dealt face up as well as face down, so that all players can know partial values of their opponents' hands. In seven-card hold 'em, there is an ante bet, and then initially two cards are dealt face down to each player. There is then another round of betting that is followed by a dealing of an additional three face-up cards that are placed in the center of the table. These are common cards. Each player now can make a five-card hand. Then another round of betting ensues in which players match each others'

bets or drop out. A fourth common card (one that may be used by any or all players in their hands) is dealt for all to see, and there is a final round of betting. Finally, the fifth common card is placed upon the table, and each remaining player puts forth his best five-card hand using his own two cards and three of the five cards from the common pool of cards on the table.

Each of these poker games involves many calculations of which cards are likely to be dealt from the remainder of the single deck that is used for the games, as do the many variations, including low ball, in which bettors seek to have the lowest hand at the table. There are also great psychological skills used to seek how to discover signs that will reveal what an opponent may be holding. The main questions asked about the heavy bettor in a game are, "Is he bluffing?" "Does he really have a good hand, or is he just trying to scare others out of the game?" If all others drop out, he can win without having to show his hand. As suggested by Kenny Rogers's famous gambling song, each hand can win, and each hand can lose, depending upon how it is played and on how the player is able to "read" other players. Even a royal flush can be misplayed in such a way that the one holding it can really be a "loser." If the player cannot conceal his joy at such a good hand, the other players will drop out, and all he will win is their ante. If played properly, the hand can be used to draw out big bets from the other players. Players seek to find characteristics called "tells" that will reveal an opponent's holdings.

The live-card poker game among players is extremely exciting. The game is one that, more than any other, attracts professional players. Some of them actually make a living with their skills, although there are not many examples of biographies revealing players who kept their fortunes well into old age.

Caribbean Stud Poker

Other forms of poker games do not have the suspense and psychology of the live player-banked game, but they do involve the poker hand. In Caribbean stud poker (a house-banked game), the player puts his five-card stud hand against a dealer's hand.

First the player makes an ante bet. Then the dealer gives him five cards and also takes five cards. Four of the dealer's cards are down, and one is up for the player to see. The player looks at his cards and then either drops out or bets an amount double his ante. The dealer does not look at his cards until the players' bets are finished. When he looks at them, he determines if he has a "qualifying hand." The qualifying hand has at least an ace and king cards high or one pair. If the hand does not qualify, the dealer folds and pays the remaining players a win equal only to their ante bet. The second bet they made is simply returned.

If the dealer's hand is qualified, however, the player either loses or wins an amount equal to the ante and the second bet. He also is eligible to win a bonus depending upon the value of his hand. For instance, a straight gets a 4-to-1 bonus (on the second bet amount); a flush, 5-to-1; four of a kind, 20-to-1; and a royal flush, 100-to-1.

There is also another side bet that the player makes at the beginning. He may bet one dollar on the value of his hand, and he can win a special payoff if he stays in the betting, even if the dealer's hand is not qualified. The casino will have a progressive jackpot for this bet. A flush will get $50, a full house $100, a straight flush 10 percent of the progressive jackpot, and a royal flush the full jackpot. The progressive meter displayed above the Caribbean stud tables attracts players with the notion that they can win six figures on a one-dollar bet. Experts who study the game find that this extra one-dollar bet favors the house until the progressive jackpot grows beyond $200,000, which is rather rare.

Let It Ride

The game of let it ride poker was introduced to Las Vegas casinos in 1993 and has gained some popularity with casinos in many jurisdictions. Like Caribbean stud, it is a five-card stud poker game that is house banked. In this game the player hopes to get a hand with a good value. There is no dealer's hand. The player lays three equal bets on the table. Each player then receives three cards face down. At that time he may let his first bet stay on the table, or he may withdraw it. A fourth community card is dealt (to be used by all players), and he

then can make another decision to withdraw his second bet, or "let it ride." His third bet must stay. Then a final card, also a community card, is revealed. He now has his hand. The hand is paid off according to a schedule. If the player does not have at least a pair of tens, he loses. The one pair of tens gets the bettor's wagers returned to him. Two pairs give him a 2-to-1 return; a flush, 8-to-1; a royal flush, 1,000-to-1. Like Caribbean stud, there is also an opportunity to make a one-dollar bonus bet that pays off $20,000 for a royal flush and less for other good hands. On this bonus bet payoff, the expected return to the player is less than 80 percent, whereas the basic game pays back over 96 percent.

Pai Gow Poker

Pai gow poker is a house-banked even-payout game. The player is given seven cards, as is the dealer. Each then makes his best two-card and best five-card hand. If both of the player's hands are better than the dealer's two hands, the player wins but pays a 5 percent commission on the winnings. If both of the dealer's hands are better, the dealer wins; if one is and one is not, it is a tie. One fifty-two-card deck is used along with a joker, which may be used as an ace or as a card to complete a straight or a flush. The best possible hand is five aces.

Sources: Jensen, Martin. 2000. *Secrets of the New Casinos Games.* New York: Cardoza, 14–105; Miller, Len. 1983. *Gambling Times Guide to Casino Games.* Secaucus, NJ: Lyle Stuart, 97–108; Scarne, John. 1986. *Scarne's New Complete Guide to Gambling.* New York: Simon and Schuster, 670–671; Sifakis, Carl. 1990. *Encyclopedia of Gambling.* New York: Facts on File, 233–237; Silberstang, Edwin. 1972. *Playboy's Book of Games.* Chicago: Playboy Press, 25–97.

Political Culture and Nevada: Reassessing the Theory

How can the culture of a people be related to policies regarding gambling? A political culture is a collective set of beliefs and values that can define how a people orient themselves toward government in general and what their feelings are about their own political jurisdiction, political participation and rules of participation, their obligations as citizens, their attitudes toward their fellow citizens, and their attitudes toward their leaders. The late Daniel Elazar, a renowned political scientist, postulated that although there was a dominant type of political culture for the United States reflecting our national heritage and our national system, there were major subtypes of political cultures in different parts of the United States. He identified three such subtypes: the (I)ndividualistic, (M)oralistic, and (T)raditionalistic (Elazar 1971, 79–94).

The I culture envisions a democratic order expressed through a marketplace of issues. Government does not exist to create "a good society" but rather to respond to demands of citizens on economic and other issues. Mass political participation is not encouraged, as politics is an activity reserved for "professionals," not amateurs. Policymaking is transactional, a bargaining process between self-interested groups and individuals. People who seek political office do so as a means of controlling the distribution of rewards of government, not of pursuing programs and/or ideology. Politics is like horse trading.

The M culture was brought to the New World by the Pilgrims and then the Puritans who set up a series of religious colonies in New England. The M culture emphasizes the commonwealth as the basis for democratic government. Politics is considered a lofty pursuit in humankind's search for the "good society." Although politics is a struggle for power, it is also an attempt to exercise that power for the betterment of the commonwealth. Government is a positive instrument to promote the general welfare, which is more than a balance of or the sum of individual interests. Citizen participation is an essential ingredient in the M culture. Politics is the concern of every citizen. Thus it is the citizens' duty to participate. Those who serve in government and politics assume high moral obligations.

The T political culture had its roots in British royalty. It persisted past the revolutionary years within the United States in the plantation South, where citizens were seeking economic opportunity through their agricultural system. That system relied to some degree upon the institution of slavery. According to Elazar, the T culture is based upon an ambivalent attitude toward the marketplace coupled with an elitist conception of society. The T political culture reflects an older, precommercial attitude that accepts a largely hierarchical society and expects those at the top of the social order to take a special and dominant role in government. That role is defined as keeping the existing social order. Government functions to continue to confine real political power to a comparatively small and self-perpetuating elite who often inherit their "right" to govern through family or social ties. Those who do not have a definitive role to play in the political system are not expected to become active in politics.

Elazar seeks to categorize each state as well as regions within states with one of the three subtypes, or with a combination of the subtypes of political cultures. Elazar placed Nevada clearly under the I culture category, although he did not specifically discuss Nevada politics. Nevada historian James Hulse offers a commentary. He correctly reads Elazar's description of I culture, saying that it "assumes that the function of the marketplace is given top priority" by the government. He goes on to indicate, "Nevada as a society has been relaxed, permissive and at times even reckless in its receptivity to the *individualistic* prospector and promoter. The contemporary gamblers on both sides of the betting tables belong in that category" (Hulse 1997).

Furthermore, the position that Nevada is an I culture is espoused by state senator Dina Titus, Democratic leader of the Senate and also a professor of political science at the University of Nevada, Las Vegas. She offers that Nevadans are notoriously antigovernment, indicating that their greatest antipathy is directed toward Washington and that they resent any mandates imposed from "inside the Beltway." Indeed, in support of the argument, both the Sagebrush Rebellion (an effort to have the federal government return lands to state control) and a County Supremacy Movement originated in Nevada. Closer to home, Nevadans' suspicions of government are reflected in the maintenance of a "citizen legislature" that meets for only 120 days every other year and is hamstrung by such constitutional restrictions as a requirement for a two-thirds majority vote on any new tax levy and also a term limit of twelve years service. There are also provisions for extensive direct democracy via recall and initiative procedures. Although Nevadans do cherish their ability to keep government at a minimum, Titus relates that they seldom exercise the power they have, which is also consistent with the I culture identified in Elazar's model.

Senator Titus also points out the fact that the state has very low voter registration and turnout. In addition, partisanship is extremely weak, as many if not most voters split their tickets frequently. Pragmatic politics prevails over ideology, and libertarian values are espoused by both major parties. Finally, Titus, as did Hulse, emphasizes that Nevada's independent attitude is reflected in a myriad of "anything goes" policies adopted over the years. Protecting personal freedoms is a priority, as she points out in policies such as the prohibition against one-party wire taps, the legalization of medical marijuana, and the existence of lawful prostitution in parts of the state. Nevada also prides itself on being the "Delaware of the West" when it comes to corporation statutes, moreover, the state has promulgated fewer environmental regulations on business than most states. "Individualism?" she asks. Where else, for example, can you build a roller coaster atop a 115-story tower next door to a wedding chapel with a drive-through window and a mechanical arm that throws rice on your windshield? Where else can you breastfeed your baby in public while carrying not one but as many concealed weapons as you desire?

The arguments that Nevada has essentially an I culture may be many, but are they necessarily conclusive?

A Reassessment of the Categorization of Nevada as an I Culture

My research leads me to offer a dissent to the distinguished trio, claiming instead that Nevada represents a prototypical example of the T culture. Indeed, I suggest that Nevada may be the only pure example of a state T culture in the United States today. The states identified by Elazar as T states included most of those in the Old South (former Confederate states). They, of course, were isolated in their defense of slavery, and then after emancipation, in their defense of states' rights policies de-

signed to support an apartheid posture to life. Isolation of the South grew during the civil rights era of the 1950s and 1960s, and as the racist separation policies fell under the force of national edicts for change, a wave of change ensued throughout the South. Nevada had also been isolated, with its adherence to gambling policies, and a national political establishment also demanded change—an elimination of Mob-controlled casino gambling—in the same decades as the civil rights era. While Nevada was resisting that change, gambling enterprise entered into the economic and political fabric of many other states. Gambling spread first with horse racing, then with government-operated lotteries, and finally with casino gambling that in the form of games was quite similar to that found in Nevada. On the one hand, the T culture of the Old South was overwhelmed with national opposition; the T culture of Nevada, on the other hand, survived to a point where the rest of the nation came to accept the critical element of the Nevada political establishment—the defense of a casino industry.

To a large degree, communities in both California and Nevada began in a similar way. People were attracted to the possibilities of "getting rich quick." John A. Sutter, a pioneer settler in California, discovered gold on his land near Sacramento in 1848. Word quickly spread. Between 1848 and 1860 the population of California went from less than 30,000 to nearly 400,000. Statehood came in 1850, and California entered the union as a wild and sinful place. Nevada's society developed around the discovery of the Comstock Lode of silver in 1859. Populations rushed in from both the East and the West (California prospectors), creating a society that mirrored that of its wild neighbor to the west. Nevada statehood came not as a natural response to the growth of an American population but as a response to political needs in Washington, D.C. Abraham Lincoln had political struggles. Congress had proposed the 13th amendment abolishing slavery, but states (even some northern states) had been reluctant to ratify the amendment. Lincoln needed another vote, and Nevada's ratification vote was the one necessary for the 13th amendment to take effect. The state's birth thus can be associated with freedom. Lincoln also wanted congressional support for the proposed 14th and 15th amendments, and Nevada gave that support—especially in the Senate, where it had two votes just as did the biggest states. And, of course, Lincoln also wanted to be reelected, and Lincoln thought his 1864 opponent Gen. John McClelland would have a strong campaign. Nevada gave Lincoln its three electoral votes—just in time. Statehood was granted on 31 October 1864, just one week before the presidential election. (The timing was perfect, as today Nevada is the only venue of the union that makes Halloween an official state holiday!)

After the initial wave of miners, Nevada's population development slowed. The second wave of family population that hit California completely missed Nevada in the nineteenth century. When mining resources dwindled, Nevada communities became ghost towns. The state's population fell from a peak of almost 63,000 to less than 50,000 in 1890. There were actually discussions in the nineteenth century and even later that pondered the notion of revoking statehood status because of depopulation. It also can be noted that in 1922 the Methodist church removed "district status" from the state and designated Nevada as a "mission." Early-on, sin represented a style of life as well as economic opportunity for part of the population; and when mining collapsed, there were no serious efforts to interfere with the jobs provided by alcohol, gambling, and prostitution, albeit a prohibition and antigambling crusade was played out to formal success, then totally ignored.

Early in the state's history a defense against the outside world was necessitated by the declining mining industry. Control of politics was in hands of railroad giants. The Big Four (Leland Stanford, Mark Hopkins, Colis Huntington, and Charles Crocker) who controlled California also controlled Nevada. Nevada was in a sense their colony. Gilman Ostrander has chronicled the era in his book *Nevada: The Great Rotten Borough 1859–1964.* One force kept Nevada's neighbor California supporting Nevada's existence as a state— its two votes in the U.S. Senate. The California railroad interests wanted the votes to support their interests, but also the seats represented desirable commodities for social reasons. During the latter

decades of the nineteenth century, on at least five occasions California-based Senate candidates made overt purchases of elections from the Nevada legislature. In Washington they did not distinguish themselves in any way, and the representation they gave to Nevada interests was minimal—beyond resisting attempts to place the issue of rescinding statehood on the national agenda.

The system of boss selection of senators changed little as the state embraced popular election of senators along with the rest of the nation. By the time the 17th amendment took force, Nevada had a political boss—George Wingfield— who effectively controlled both parties. Personality battles over offices manifested themselves, but the contestants made little noise on policy matters that counted.

At the turn of the twentieth century, Francis Newlands, one of the senators who purchased his seat, emerged as a national leader of Progressives. He was the son-in-law of another Nevada senator who had purchased his U. S. Senate seat—William Sharon. Newlands distinguished himself in the field of conservation. In that role he served Nevada well, as he advocated a national involvement in projects that could reclaim lands for farming and provide water for western communities. The progressive Newlands Reclamation Act of 1902 bears his name. Although Newlands believed that the national government should be a positive force in people's lives, and such notions may have been against fears Nevadans had of federal control of their activities, a pattern was being established. Nevadans then and even now show a tremendous tolerance for its national leaders' pursuing a variety of causes—liberal, conservative, moderate— as long as they adhere to the central cause of protecting the state's economic base and its right to pursue its economic future as it pleases.

Nevadans survived threats to statehood, but they still had to make their own way economically. In the nineteenth century, many individual Nevadans felt that "making their own way" meant they had to leave the state, and many did. Those who stayed tried many things. They always fought to make mining work, but it could not do so in a reliable way over generations. The state occupied space and took advantage of that simple fact. The state sought to become a center for business incorporation in the way that Delaware was in the East. This effort was short lived, as California refused to recognize Nevada corporations unless they met California standards. The state allowed boxing matches when California refused to; the Jeffries versus Jackson "Great White Hope" match of 1910 in Reno was the most famous one until the modern era. The state permitted prostitution to remain legal in registered brothels; even today this activity continues in several of the state's counties. Nevada sought to become the divorce capital of the country, as it had very lax rules on exactly who was a resident of the state—it being necessary that one party of a divorce be a resident. The state also sought tax revenues from commerce moving across its borders to and from California. Additionally, the state became a warehousing center by eliminating inventory taxes. In all these things, Nevada was somewhat different or even exceedingly different from other states. The first duty of the political establishment was to protect the economic life of the state, and often this meant protecting the ability of the state to be different. Populism was acceptable when it accomplished the essential goals, progressivism was acceptable when it accomplished the essential goals, and so too were activities that seemed to be of an I, M, or T culture.

The Twentieth Century—Prelude to the New Gambling Era

While California was establishing itself as the Golden State, Nevada was sinking constantly into disrepute. In that disrepute, however, Nevada found the final solution to its economic conundrum—Nevada found wide-open mass-marketed casino gambling. Before that discovery in the 1940s and 1950s, the state had built in its style of political power. During the Progressive era and through the 1920s, 1930s, and 1940s, the state had essentially abolished a notion of competitive two-party politics. As alluded to earlier, George Wingfield was the "boss" of both parties early in the century. Wingfield's office was in room 201 of the Reno National Bank Building, and that room was considered the "real capital of Nevada." Wingfield was the head of the state Republican party. Anyone

who wished to speak to the head of the Democratic party did not have to seek out a different address, however. The party chairman was in the same office—he was Wingfield's junior law partner. They shared the same telephone number, 4111. The bipartisan Wingfield machine purposely sought to send one Democrat and one Republican senator to Washington.

This pattern allowed the state to have two members on the same committee in the Senate—the committee of choice was the one with power over mining issues. The pattern also allowed the state to have a Senate delegation with considerable seniority. Two "key" Democrats gained control of important committees where they could trade favors and votes in manners that could benefit the state in different ways. The incurable alcoholic Key Pittman became the chair of the Senate's Foreign Relations Committee during Pres. Franklin D. Roosevelt's difficult years prior to World War II. Pittman's considerable embarrassments were overlooked; he died in 1940 before he could ruin U.S. international relations during the war years. Toward the middle decades, Wingfield's role was absorbed by the jingoist senator Patrick McCarran (for whom, ironically, the Las Vegas McCarran International Airport was named). Senator McCarran used his seniority to join hands with U.S. senator Joseph McCarthy (R-WI) in his witch-hunts against real and imagined communists. He sponsored very restrictive immigration legislation as well. McCarran was a force in putting boundaries around the anticasino work of Sen. Estes Kefauver of Tennessee. And both McCarran and Pittman managed to get considerable "pork" for the state in the form of military facilities as well as that plum of all plums—the Nevada Test Site, the facility for atmospheric atomic bomb testing. Fortunately (for Nevadans), most "downwinders" lived in Utah.

State leaders measured their performance in political office in very mundane terms, and most were judged on their personalities. Although individual leaders were permitted to pursue progressive or populist causes on a wide range of issues, they pursued one general protection on all essential issues: They did what was necessary to guarantee that the state's primary industry was protected. There were no noticeable differences in defending gambling policies whether the governor was civil libertarian Grant Sawyer, arch conservative Paul Laxalt, education reformer and labor advocate Mike O'Callahan, Republicans Bob List or Kenny Guinn, or Democrats Richard Bryan or Bob Miller. The public showed a great willingness to elect to the Senate extreme conservatives such as Laxalt and Chic Hecht (who called Jesse Helms "my liberal friend"), or liberal activists such as Harry Reid and Howard Cannon. All were "free" to pursue any national policies they wished to pursue. They had to be united, however, on defending gambling and on funding state military projects, including nuclear testing. More recently they have had to staunchly oppose the storage of nuclear waste in the state.

Nevada Gambling

Gambling activities persisted in early Nevada, although casinos were made illegal for a brief time after statehood was granted. By the turn of the twentieth century, however, the Progressive movement was gaining strength across the United States and in the Silver State. In concert with temperance organizations, civil leaders attacked the local sin industries. They approached the state legislature and gained passage of a bill that closed the casinos on 30 September 1910 (Skolnick 1978, 106).

By 1911, the legislature had second (and third) thoughts. Certain card games were legalized, only to be made illegal again in 1913. In 1915 limited gaming was permitted again. Enforcement of the gaming limits was sporadic at the best and nonexistent as a rule. In lieu of fees when gaming was legal, operators now paid bribes to local officials who pretended that gaming did not take place (Skolnick 1978, 107).

A move to legalize gambling was revived in 1931 when Nevada assemblyman Phil Tobin of Humboldt County introduced the legislative measure. Although opposition was voiced by religious groups, Tobin's bill passed the assembly on a 24 to 11 vote and the state senate by 13 to 3. On 19 March 1931, Gov. Fred Balzar signed the measure to legalize casino gambling. A second law passed later in 1931 permitted local governments to regulate gambling and fixed fees for the gaming statewide. The fees were shared, with 75 percent going to local governments and 25 percent to the state. Licenses were granted by county commissions, and all regulations were enforced by the sheriff.

State regulation began in the 1940s as larger gambling operations were established, and casino gambling began to emerge as the state's dominant industry. In 1950 the state weathered the first concerted national attack on its casino industry. The U.S. Senate Special Committee to Investigate Organized Crime in Interstate Commerce (the Kefauver Committee) targeted Nevada. The state resisted the attack through the efforts of its congressional delegation and also by means of the adoption of new rules for licensing and controlling casinos. In 1955 a full-time Gambling Control Board was established. In 1959, the state responded to continuing attacks that now came from the McClelland Committee, which included Sen. John F. Kennedy (D-MA) and had his brother, Robert, as its special counsel, by adding the Nevada Gaming Commission to strengthen its regulatory framework. During the 1960s more federal attacks ensued, and governors Grant Sawyer and Paul Laxalt coordinated the state's response by inviting Howard Hughes to the state in 1966 to become a major player by buying out casinos tied to Mob interests.

In 1969 the state authorized publicly traded companies to own casinos, hence welcoming a type of federal control over big operators—through the Securities and Exchange Commission. The state also strengthened its control over casino operators by banning licensees from having gambling operations in other jurisdictions. This ruling was later modified in 1977 to allow licensees to go into New Jersey. This change was effectuated after Nevada reviewed New Jersey regulatory structures to assure that they would adequately oversee casino operations in such a way that no federal authorities would challenge their industry.

The Las Vegas casino interests had not taken a role in the New Jersey casino campaigns of 1974 and 1976 (when the vote was successful). The competition from the East blindsided Nevada. Coupled with a general national economic slump, in the early 1980s Nevada casinos had their only three-year period (since statistics were gathered) when gambling revenues fell in terms of constant-value dollars. Nonetheless, the casinos stood by silently during the 1984 California lottery campaign. Nevada was very much aware of the possibilities of harm that could be done to its industry by Indian gambling, however, seeing the harm in terms of unregulated gambling that would draw organized crime and consequently discredit all casinos. Native Americans saw it differently. They saw Nevada as only fearing the competition they would give. In any event, the Nevada congressional delegation came forth with the proposals for a national law to regulate the Native American gambling after the U. S. Supreme Court in the *Cabazon* case of 1987 said states could not regulate the gambling without an act of Congress. After the Indian Gaming Regulatory Act was passed, Nevada interests provided research help for state attorneys general throughout the nation who stood in opposition to Native American gambling. In most cases the Nevada interests and state attorneys general lost their battles.

During the 1990s, Nevada interests, with the support of Nevada political leaders, continued to fight for the gambling industry. Nevada participated in a congressional initiative to limit sports betting to Nevada and three other states where it already existed—although not in the open way it exists in Nevada. In 1993, the Nevada legislature abolished its rule precluding Nevada licensees from participating in gambling elsewhere. Other states had succumbed to the inevitability of Native American casinos, and eventually nine additional states permitted commercialized casino gambling. The Nevada casino industry was quite eager to be able to cash in on opportunities to manage Native American casinos or to have their own gambling halls in other states.

A new threat to the gambling industry came in 1994 when Pres. Bill Clinton proposed a 4 percent surtax on all gambling winnings in the United States. As lotteries and Native casinos were exempted, it was clear that the impact of the tax would fall upon the casinos of Nevada. The state (which cast majorities for Clinton in both 1992 and 1996) rallied together in opposition. While the congressional delegation did its job in Washington the casinos formed a new national lobbying bloc—the American Gaming Association (AGA).

The AGA read Clinton's message well, and campaign funds started to flow. Ironically, the Clinton election team was probably the biggest beneficiary of this money spigot. In 1996 the AGA and Nevada forces sought to prohibit the creation of the National Gambling Impact Study Commission. Failing in this endeavor, they succeeded in limiting the powers of the commission, and they gained control over several of its appointments. The venom of the commission—which was led by a decidedly antigambling chairwoman—was deflected away from commercial casinos and onto targets such as Native American casinos, lotteries, and Internet gambling. Betting on college games also attracted commission opposition, leading to proposed legislation to effectuate a ban. Again the Nevada political forces closed ranks in defense of the status quo monopoly the state's gaming industry has over this form of gambling.

The 1998 approval of Proposition 5 in California presented the greatest threat to Nevada casinos since the Kefauver hearings of the 1950s. After it was set aside by California courts, Nevada interests were content to accept the compromises of the new Proposition 1A. It is possible that Proposition 1A will now allow the casinos of Nevada and the Nevada political establishment to build important bridges to California and its power structure (*See* Native American Gaming: Contemporary).

Which Culture Is Nevada's?
These events suggest a misread of the I culture that may also have been implicit in Elazar's placement of Nevada in the I complex. The culture is not the activity of private individuals. That Nevada has many "free spirits" and "gamblers" does not mean that the government is also a "free spirit" for sale to the highest bidder. Rather, Hulse seems to offer more poignant words in support of the notion that Nevada has been a traditionalistic (T) state, quite like the states of the South that seemed the only major bastions of T culture in Elazar's study.

James Hulse writes, "Nevada as a political and social entity has from the beginning been especially vulnerable to [an] ambitious and wealthy oligarchy ... largely because of its inherently weak and impoverished economic situation"

(Hulse 1997, 6). He goes on to suggest that the pattern has survived to this day, with the state being "exceptionally receptive to those with large amounts of money" (6) He then singles out persons of the gambling industry: William Harrah, Howard Hughes, Kirk Kerkorian, and Steve Wynn. Hulse even indicates that the state was exceedingly warm to mobsters who were essential in the expansion of the casino industry. Then he adds that "gambling control agencies were designed not only to regulate [gambling] but also to protect it from those elements that might . . . endanger its prosperity. Likewise, Nevada's Senators and Representatives in Washington and the elected state officials have assumed the position of feudal knights protecting their domain from challengers" (7). The leaders were not merely brokers giving government favors to the winners in some marketplace of policymaking.

A new population influx has made Nevada what California was just a few decades ago—the fastest-growing state in the Union. Great population influxes changed California's collective political orientations, as illustrated by Peter Schrag's *Paradise Lost* (1998). The state moved away from an M culture as a lower-income population both grew and demanded more services at the expense of older Californians. So too did population changes make the Old South different in the latter decades of the past century. The population growth of Nevada, however, has not made noticeable changes in the orientation of politics in the Silver State. Of course such growth could have an influence if it continues. Many of the newcomers, however, are drawn to the state because of its low-cost and high-employment environment. In both cases, these attractive attributes are tied to the state's reliance upon domination by a single industry. Quite frankly, although the state's business climate regularly ranks at the top or in the top two or three places in *Inc. Magazine* rankings, the state does not attract nongambling enterprises in numbers sufficient to absorb employment demands of new residents. Newcomers also appreciate the very low state taxes, which are among the lowest in the nation. This is especially the case with senior citizens attracted to the several new Sun Cities of the Las Vegas area.

Nevertheless, there is a crisis of public services much like that witnessed in California. The school population is growing, and the Clark County school district does not have the tax resources to hire sufficient teachers or to build new school buildings fast enough. The state is also facing crises in transportation and the environment.

The casino industry is quite willing to let the politicians have a "free vote" on school issues or almost any other issue that does not directly affect their interests. They closely keep their eyes on tax policies, however. Here they are like residents—they appreciate low taxes. There have been calls for incremental tax increases from some and for monumental increases in gambling taxes by others. In the latter case, one state senator has called for a doubling of the gambling tax rate. In the 1998 gubernatorial primary, he also advocated higher gambling taxes. This was a unique stand, as all legislators in the state have taken campaign funds from the gambling industry. But the word *unique* is not a word to crave when seeking votes. The good senator won 15 per cent of the vote. That 15 percent probably represents a reasonable number for a subculture of Nevada that wants the casinos to pay much higher taxes.

In 1994, a feature story in *Time* magazine called Las Vegas "America's City" and indicated that the city was not becoming like the rest of the nation but that rather the rest of the nation was becoming like Las Vegas (Andersen 1994). Perhaps the rest of the nation finds the "free spirit" life of Las Vegas inviting. The other states have embraced the gambling industry, and by doing so, they have allowed Nevada to have allies in its fights against federal interference with casinos. No other state has fallen into a posture of allowing gambling interests to completely dominate its politics, however. In the other states, such as California, the gambling interests have to fight out their battles against other interests that are already organized. The welcoming of gambling is an indicator that these states in many cases may have abandoned Elazar's M culture. It is not an indicator that I cultures have fallen.

Nevada has played its politics game within the tenets of the T culture. In the past, Nevada felt it had to fight competition from other states that might have desired to have casinos. But now gambling has spread to all corners of the nation, and the game on gambling issues need not be played in a way that precludes compromises with competing states. The fear that a national political establishment will now ban all gambling, once a major fear for Nevadans, no longer grips the state. Unlike the Old South, which embraced a T culture when it was opposed by all the other regions of the nation, Nevada has seen much of the nation become as it is—gambling territory. Nevada now has allies in every region, something the South never had on race issues.

Contemporary Cultures and Interstate Cooperation on Gambling Issues

California voices are occasionally heard calling for wide-open casino gambling in order to check the outflow of money that its citizens take to Nevada casinos. Internal fights among various components of California's gambling interests—tracks, card clubs, Native Americans, the lottery—will probably preclude this real threat to Nevada gambling from occurring within the foreseeable future. The compromise of Proposition 1A has also made California Native American gaming acceptable to Nevada—not only acceptable but also an opportunity for Nevada industry investment. Moreover, Nevada's failure to attract manufacturers that can provide a large portion of supplies to the casinos means that the Silver State's main industry will continue to support California's industries with purchasing activities that will largely offset the Golden State's citizens' losses in the green-felt jungles of Glitter Gulch.

—*coauthored by Carl Lutrin and Dina Titus*

Sources: Andersen, Kurt. 1994. "Las Vegas: The New All American City." *Time* 143 (10 January): 42–51; Cabot, Anthony N., William N. Thompson, Andrew Tottenham, and Carl Braunlich, eds. 1999. *International Casino Law.* 3d ed. Reno: Institute for the Study of Gambling, University of Nevada, Reno, 101–120; Elazar, Daniel. 1972. *American Federalism: A View from the States.* 2d ed. New York: Crowell; Hulse, James W. 1991. *The Silver State.* Reno: University of Nevada Press; Hulse, James W. 1997. "Nevada and the Twenty-First Century." In *Towards 2000: Public Policy in Nevada,* edited by Dennis L. Soden and Erick Herzik, 1–14. Dubuque, IA: Kendall-Hunt; Ostrander, Gilman. 1966. *Nevada: The Great Rotten Borough 1859–1964.* New York: Alfred A. Knopf; Schrag, Peter. 1998. *Paradise Lost: California's Experience, America's Future.* New York: New Press; Skolnick, Jerome H. 1978. *House of Cards: Legalization and Control of Casino Gambling.* Boston: Little, Brown.

The Positive Case for Gambling: One Person's View

[Author's Note: At my invitation, in this entry Felicia Campbell presents her interesting analysis concerning the positive aspects of gambling.]

My doctoral dissertation, "The Gambling Mystique: Mythologies and Typologies," is the first major study of the positive effects of gambling for the nonproblem gambler. (Campbell 1973). Until 1973, the literature dealing with gambling behavior had been overwhelmingly negative and focused almost entirely on compulsive gamblers. Wire service coverage and an article, "The Future of Gambling" in the *Futurist* magazine (Campbell 1976), gave me more than my fifteen minutes of fame, and I must admit that it was rewarding to pick up the newspaper and find Dr. Joyce Brothers citing my saying that "casinos don't cause compulsive gambling any more than soap causes compulsive handwashing." It was even rather entertaining to walk into a session at a gaming conference in Montreal and hear my words in slightly altered form supposedly coming from the mouths of other gamblers.

It is my view that gambling represents a preservative rather than a destructive impulse. When I began writing about gambling, a prevailing view was that all gamblers were masochistic and had a profound desire to lose. Leading the attack was Edmund Bergler, who saw gambling as an attack on bourgeois values, reducing them to absurdity, and the gambler as a "private rebel" who attacks societal norms with dice, stocks, and chips rather than guns or ballots. One wonders what he would think of today's trading revolution (Bergler 1957).

Although I have continued to take an essentially phenomenological approach to gambling, viewing the gambler as part of the entire context in which he or she exists, today's context is wildly different from that of twenty-five years ago. The twenty-first century has arrived with a vengeance in all of its cyber and virtual glory. In a world of cybersex, daytrading, extreme sports, and robot technology rivaling anything in science fiction, the casino gambler no longer stands out as one of Bergler's social rebels, although I believe the rebel still gambles for the same reasons—an altered state of consciousness that offers hope, opportunities for decision making, possible peak experience, and a respite from the day's cares, a minivacation, if you will. Note that I am speaking here of normal gamblers, not desperation gamblers.

For its adherents, gambling is a form of adventure and sometimes of therapy. As far back as the sixteenth century, universal genius and gambler Girolamo Cardano prescribed gambling to alleviate melancholy, noting that "play may be beneficial in times of grief and the law permits it to the sick and those in prison and those condemned to death" (Cardano 1961). Although the altered state of gambling provides part of the therapy in the action, it is the wins, few as they may be, that count. As a young friend of mine who prefers casinos to tranquilizers after a hard day teaching high school says, "It's ecstasy, it's Paris, France that is. I've been to Paris on a handful of quarters. On my income by the time I saved enough I would be too old to go. Oh, the casino is a wonderful place."

Today's adventurer gamblers can enhance their experience by prowling the alternate reality of their choice, the Las Vegas Strip obligingly having turned into a form of virtual reality. Almost as quickly as you can change channels on your television set, you can move from Mandalay Bay to Egypt or Rome or a horde of other destinations. You pay your money and walk into the fantasy of your choice, which may be one of the reasons that the Wizard of Oz theme failed at the MGM. Although the casino is definitely not Kansas, it seems to me unlikely that many people revving up for an evening at the tables or machines want to identify with Dorothy or the Tin Woodman. The casino gambler may have isolated himself or herself from nature, but not from a need for sensate experience, an experience that for good or ill moves ever closer to virtual reality, a concrete fantasy that provides escape from the mundane.

Casinos even present a kind of in-house camaraderie. A fellow feeling exists among card players that may not always be present in the real world. At the blackjack table, players all face the same odds whether they are betting five or 500 dollars and have a common adversary in the dealer. Here cultural and racial differences and biases disappear during the action, often, sadly, to be replaced after the players leave the tables and reality returns.

Even machines take on personalities in these palaces of escape. I have always been fascinated by relationship between machine gamblers and their adversaries. In my early research I cited an elderly woman who said that she played because she was lonely, and the machines seemed friendly and acknowledged her existence. To her the ringing bells and flashing lights of even a small payoff said, "I like you."

To see that this feeling is not isolated, one need only observe the give-and-take that goes on between player and machine. I have created a brief typology that illustrates some of the major behaviors. Except where noted, these behaviors are common to both genders. There is the Lover, whose hands move softly over the machine or gently slide up and down the handle, when such exists, as though it were a beloved other, caressing it, trying to lure it into spewing its riches into his hands. Not for nothing is gambling parlance studded with sexual terms such as betting "the come" or the "don't come." The Patter, a variation on the Lover, softly pats the sides of the machine, all the while talking to it. More violent, Thumpers beat a rhythmic tattoo on the side of the machine, while Ragers, almost always male, literally pound the machines with their fists and both cajole and threaten them in language fine for television but probably not appropriate for this entry, seeming to believe that they can bully the machines into submission. In contrast, the Pleader maintains a constant dialogue with the machine, usually referring to it as "baby" as he begs for its favors. Players sit silently in front of their idols, lips constantly moving.

Perhaps the most annoying to other players are Singers, usually out of tune, and Whistlers, totally oblivious to those around them (at least I hope they are) and seemingly less in communication with the machine than the others I have mentioned. All, however, regardless of their annoyance factor, are totally absorbed in "the action" within the world of the machine, largely unaware of anything going on around them and often of their own behaviors. They have for the moment escaped. You have probably noticed as have I an uncanny resemblance to the relationships between hackers and their machines, which also carry their users to alternate realities.

Clearly everything about casinos is designed to assist gamblers in slipping the perceptual boundaries of their worlds. Linear time and space are smashed. Themed casinos representing diverse historical eras and geographical settings help to destroy the concept of an orderly, linear time line and traditional geography. I think we need note that theming is not confined to businesses but has become a part of home decor and planned communities everywhere.

In the twenty-first century, we no longer collectively believe in a linear universe of simple cause and effect. We now know that we dance on a web of intersecting realities, where the effect of the flapping of a butterfly's wing in Hong Kong can escalate to create a dust storm in Las Vegas. In essence, as chaos theory explains, everything influences everything else.

Greed is not the primary motive for these new beliefs. The motive is the slipping of ordinary perceptual bounds and moving into the intensity of another reality.

—by Felicia Campbell

Sources: Bergler, Edmund. 1957. The Psychology of Gambling. New York: Hill and Wang. Reprint 1985. New York: International Universities Press; Campbell, Felicia. 1973. "The Gambling Mystique: Mythologies and Typologies." Ph.D. diss., Department of English, United States International University; Campbell, Felicia. 1976. "The Future of Gambling." The Futurist, 1 April, 84–90; Campbell, Felicia. 1976. "The Positive View of Gambling." In Gambling and Society: Interdisciplinary Studies on the Subject of Gambling, 219–228. Springfield, IL: Thomas; Cardano, Girolamo. 1961. The Book on Games of Chance. Translated by Sydney Henry Gould. New York: Holt, Rinehart, Winston.

President's Commission on Law Enforcement and Administration of Justice

On 23 July 1965, Pres. Lyndon Baines Johnson issued Executive Order 11236, establishing the Commission on Law Enforcement and Administration of Justice. Atty. Gen. Nicholas Katzenbach was asked to chair a nineteen-member commission whose numbers included former attorney general William P. Rogers; American Bar Association and later Supreme Court justice Lewis F. Powell; Julia Stuart, president of the League of Women Voters; New York City mayor Robert Wagner; Yale University president Kingman Brewster; Los Angeles Times publisher Otis Chandler; San Francisco police chief Thomas Cahill; California attorney general Thomas Lynch; director of the Urban League, Whitney M. Young; federal judges Luther Youngdahl, James Parsons, Charles Breitel, and future Watergate prosecutor Leon Jaworski; and several leading law professors and attorneys. This blue ribbon panel worked for two years with 63 staff members and 175 consultants to produce its report, entitled The Challenge of Crime in a Free Society (President's Commission on Law Enforcement and Administration of Justice 1967). The report, issued in February 1967, made over 200 recommendations. A new focus of this effort was placed upon victimization, as the commission conducted a survey of 10,000 households regarding their experiences with crime. A secondary focus was given to organized crime activity. Although gambling did not receive much attention, the report offered some strong words about the activity:

> Law enforcement officials agree almost unanimously that gambling is the greatest source of revenue for organized crime. . . . In large cities where organized crime groups exist, very few of the gambling operators are independent of a large organization. Anyone whose independent operation becomes successful is likely to receive a visit from an organization representative who convinces the independent, through fear or promise of greater profit, to share his revenue with the organization. (188)

The report suggested that gross revenues from gambling in the United States resulted in profits of $6 to $7 billion for organized criminals each year.

The recommendations did not include any that focused specifically upon gambling crimes; however, new weapons for dealing with organized criminals were advanced, including a clarified statute on the use of wiretapping, witness immunity and protection programs, special grand juries, and extended prison terms for criminals involved in illegal businesses (that is, gambling enterprise). Every law enforcement organization from the federal government down to the municipal level was urged to have an organized crime section, and citizens and business groups were urged to create permanent community crime commissions.

Sources: President's Commission on Law Enforcement and Administration of Justice. 1967. *The Challenge of Crime in a Free Society.* Washington, DC: U.S. Government Printing Office.

President's Commission on Organized Crime

On 28 July 1983, Pres. Ronald Reagan issued Executive Order 12435, creating the President's Commission on Organized Crime under the auspices of the Federal Advisory Committee Act. The commission was given the charge to make a "full and complete national and region by region analysis of organized crime; define the nature of traditional organized crime, as well as emerging organized crime groups, the sources and amounts of organized crime's income . . . ; develop in-depth information on the participants in organized crime networks; and evaluate Federal laws pertinent to the effort to combat organized crime." The commission was to have up to twenty members.

The president appointed U.S. Court of Appeals judge Irving Kaufman to chair the three-year work of the panel. Kaufman was certainly one of the most prominent federal jurists on any bench. As a federal district judge, he had presided over the trial of Julius and Ethel Rosenberg. The two were executed in 1950 for being spies for the Soviet Union, stealing atomic secrets. Kaufman had also been the judge during the trials arising from the raid on the organized crime meeting at Apalachin, New York, in 1957. The commission membership also included U.S. Supreme Court Associate Justice Potter Stewart, U.S. Senator Strom Thurmond (R-South Carolina), U.S. Representative Peter W. Rodino (D-New Jersey), Louisiana State Attorney

General William J. Guste, associate Watergate prosecutor Thomas McBride, and law professor Charles Rogovin of Temple University. The other members included the sheriff and district attorney for San Diego County, a former U.S. attorney, members of congressional investigating staffs, police officials, private attorneys, and the editor of *Reader's Digest* magazine.

The commission had an overall budget of $5 million. Its staff of thirty-six included sixteen investigators and seven lawyers. The commission met in a series of hearings on selected topics over a three-year period. Hundreds of subpoenas were issued by the commission. Major topics examined included money laundering by organized crime, Asian gang activity in the Unites States, labor union violence, involvement of legitimate business with organized crime, illicit drugs, and gambling. The commission issued reports on the separate topics during the course of its work; however, it limited the scope of its recommendations to only a few topics.

Special importance was given to money laundering. Forty-one banks were investigated. One in Boston was shown to have "knowingly and willfully" allowed $1.22 billion in cash transfers with Swiss banks on behalf of clients who were not asked why they were bringing in large sums of money in paper grocery bags. In a court action the bank was fined $500,000 for failing to abide by provisions of the Bank Secrecy Act of 1970. That was not enough. In October 1984, the commission recommended that a new law be passed making money-laundering activities more clearly illegal under federal law. A first offense could be punished by fines of up to $250,000 or twice the value of the laundered money and imprisonment up to five years. Illegal gambling was seen as a problem area in money laundering, and legal casinos were viewed as agents of potential money laundering. In 1985, regulations of the Treasury Department were amended so that casinos with revenues in excess of $1 million a year were to be considered banks for purposes of the Bank Secrecy Act of 1970. In 1986 Congress passed the Money Laundering Act of 1986, which made money laundering illegal for the first time. The new law indicated in excess of 100 specific activities that would constitute illegal sources of moneys restricted from exchanges by banks and casinos. Illegal drug sales and illegal gambling proceeds were included.

Hearings on Asian gangs found a high level of involvement in gambling operations that were both legal and illegal. Gang members were involved in running Chinese games such as mah jongg in legal poker rooms in California, and they also attempted to use a front business to buy a casino in Las Vegas. It was feared that Asian organized criminals such as the Japanese-based Yakuza and the Bamboo gang of Taiwan could grow into an influence that would exceed that of the Mafia.

The commission focused its investigatory energies on the misuse of labor unions in order to achieve the goals of organized crime interests. The commission recommended more rigorous implementation of provisions of the antiracketeering statutes already on the books. They sought to have such involvement by labor considered as "unfair labor practices" under provisions of the National Labor Relations Act.

Hearings on gambling activity looked closely at Cuban-American racketeers who were discovered to be operating a $45-million-a-year gambling syndicate in New York City. This activity was a major component of organized crime's control over $1.5 billion in the New York metropolitan area. There were also hearings on gambling and its effect on professional and amateur sports activity.

A study made by Wharton Econometric Forecasting of Philadelphia for the commission concluded that organized crime activity exceeded $100 million a year in drug trade alone. Overall organized crime activity cost Americans 414,000 jobs each year and $6.5 billion in lost tax revenues.

The commission ended its work somewhat in disarray. A final report recommended that bar associations take steps to self-police lawyers who would work for Mob groups. The commission also endorsed wiretapping to discover illicit practices by lawyers. Moreover it sought expanded drug testing in the workplace. Nine of eighteen commission members refused to endorse the final recommendations. The commission was criticized for having too many hearings and not enough meetings to discuss the substance of its investigations.

The topic of gambling pervaded all the investigations. The commission did not issue a separate report on gambling, however. Although commission chairman Irving Kaufman hinted that illegal gambling was a major source of income for organized crime, the commission chose to allow the transcripts of its hearings to suffice to cover the area. The federal administration did not consider organized crime to be a major factor in legal casinos in the United States. The silence was a statement (*New York Times* 1986, I-1).

The commission did not conduct any original research into gambling activities, but it did contract for a consultants' report on policy options. The report was written by professors John Dombrink of the University of California–Irvine and William N. Thompson of the University of Nevada–Las Vegas. The report lamented that a wave of legalizations of gambling across North America had not been accompanied by serious research and thoughtful consequences of legal gambling for society. A program of federally supported research was recommended. It was especially important that the extent and impacts of compulsive gambling be known before more gambling was legalized, making it advisable to have a moratorium on new legalizations for a time during which research could take place. Also during the time of a moratorium (three years was suggested), state officials, industry personnel, and other interested parties should be brought together by the U.S. Department of Justice to create a set of minimum standards for gambling activity to ensure a uniform integrity and to ensure that organized criminals would be excluded from operations. The minimum standards could then be enforced by state governments or, alternatively, by the Department of Justice if the states chose to ignore the standards. States could be given incentives to follow the standards through law enforcement grants. The consultant's report rejected the notion that the federal government should be involved in either direct regulation or taxation of gambling operations. There is no evidence that the commission used the consultant's report. Later in 1996, however, a bill to regulate Native American gambling was introduced in Congress. The bill included a moratorium provision such as the one in the report.

—coauthored by John D. Dombrink

Sources: Dombrink, John, and William N. Thompson. 1986. "The Report of the 1986 Commission on Organized Crime and Its Implications for Commercial Gaming in America." *Nevada Public Affairs Review* 1986 (2): 70–75; *New York Times,* 2 April 1986, I-1.
See also Cash Transaction Reports and Money Laundering

Problem Gambling. *See* Gambling, Pathological

Professional and Amateur Sports Protection Act of 1992

Betting on professional sports and college sports games is very popular in the United States. There can be little doubt that tens of billions of dollars are wagered on these games each year. Most of the betting action is illegal. Only Nevada permits wagers on individual games, and the Oregon lottery allows players to wager on sports cards that require them to bet on at least four games on a single card—meaning they have to pick all four winners in order to have a winning bet. Delaware had authorized a similar system for betting on national football for several years starting in 1976. Montana permits private sports pools to be operated in taverns. The tavern organizes the pool, but all betting is among the players, who retain all of the prizes.

Several public officials expressed concern over a rising level of sports betting in the United States during the 1980s and early 1990s. The concern was attached to the fact that over a dozen states were entertaining prospects of legalizing the betting on games. One concerned official was U.S. senator Bill Bradley (D-New Jersey), who had been a star player in the National Basketball Association on the world championship New York Knickerbockers team. He deplored sports gambling, fearing that it would draw children into gambling activity as younger people were more attracted to games. He also saw the wagering as harmful to the honesty of the games, as sports betting could lead to attempts to bribe players to try to alter the results of games in ways favorable to certain bettors. The public confidence in the integrity of the games was in jeopardy.

In February 1991, legislation was introduced in the U.S. Senate to block the expansion of publicly authorized sports betting. The bill was signed into law as the Professional and Amateur Sports Protection Act by Pres. George Bush on 28 October 1992 (Public Law 102–559).

The law provides that no government entity may sponsor or authorize or otherwise promote any lottery or gambling scheme based in any way upon the results of one or more competitive games in which amateur or professional athletes participate. The four states with existing authorizations for sports betting—Nevada, Delaware, Oregon, and Montana—were exempt from the act's provision. Also, New Jersey's standing as the second state with large casinos was recognized, and the state was given until the end of 1993 to legalize sports betting in Atlantic City casinos if it desired to do so. When 1 January 1994 came, New Jersey had not legalized sports betting for the casinos, so the law's effect is to prohibit sports betting in forty-six states. The act does not apply to horse-race or dog-race betting or to as pari-mutuel betting on games of jai alai.

Sources: Professional and Amateur Sports Protection Act (Public Law 102–559, signed into law 28 October 1992).

Puerto Rico

There are approximately fifteen casinos in Puerto Rico. The largest and most successful are in San Juan near the Condado Beach area. The casinos are all contained within hotels. Hours are restricted to afternoons and evenings. There is no live entertainment within the casinos. Casinos are restricted in size, with most offering less than 10,000 square feet of gaming space.

Table games, blackjack, baccarat, and craps are operated by the private casinos, and slot machines are operated by the Puerto Rican Tourism Company, a government agency that regulates the casinos. The government takes the revenue from the slots and returns a portion to the casinos. The number of slots is limited by a formula based upon the actual number of players at table games.

The most prominent casinos are the Condado Plaza, the El San Juan, the Sands, and the Hilton.

Caribe Hilton, the first modern casino in Puerto Rico.

These properties draw tourists from the United States. The very high cost of hotel rooms and high occupancy rates limit opportunities for extensive gambling junketing, however. Local residents are permitted to gamble, although the casinos cannot direct advertising to the local market.

It is difficult to determine the rate of taxation on the casinos. Changes in the rates were made in 1989. As the casinos yield considerable potential revenue by not controlling the slots, it may be estimated that the tax rate in reality is about 20 percent of the gross win.

The Puerto Rican casinos have potential marketing advantages over other regional casinos, as San Juan is a major airport hub for the Caribbean, easily accessible to other American cities, and as Puerto Rico is a U.S. jurisdiction with no currency restrictions for Americans. Disadvantages, however, include high room costs and U.S. taxation reporting requirements.

Several of the casinos in Puerto Rico have been suffering financial trouble. These problems are attributed to heavy taxation and to mismanagement, especially in the area of credit policies. Nevertheless, there have been several applications for new casino licenses in recent years, and new casinos have opened.

Sources: Cabot, Anthony N., William N. Thompson, Andrew Tottenham, and Carl Braunlich, eds. 1999. *International Casino Law.* 3d ed. Reno: Institute for the Study of Gambling, University of Nevada, Reno, 240–260; Thompson, William N. 1989. "Puerto Rico: Heavy Taxes, Regs Burden Casinos." *Gaming and Wagering Business,* 15 September, 73–76.

Q

Quebec

Public officials in Quebec in a sense "jumped the gun" when a lottery was introduced in Montreal in 1968 as a device to generate revenue for the municipal government. Judicial officials in Quebec took exception to the gaming operation, as they held it to be in violation of the Canadian Penal Code of 1892. Action did not stop for long. After the Penal Code was amended, the Quebec government created Loto Quebec in 1969, and the next year Quebec became the first province in Canada to establish a lottery. A separate agency licensed a wide range of games for charities and also to support agricultural fairs: bingo games, raffles, and limited-time casino events. The agency also regulated pari-mutuel horse-race wagering.

As the lottery grew along with private charity-oriented gaming, the province initiated studies of casinos' gaming. The studies persisted from 1978 into the early 1990s. Part of the motivation guiding a conclusion that tourist-oriented casinos should be authorized was the revelation that illegal gambling and particularly illegal slot machines were quite prevalent in Quebec. In 1993 the province opened Casino du Montreal in a facility that was the French Pavilion at the Montreal World's Expo of 1967. The casino has a 90,000-square-foot gaming floor, the largest in Canada until a permanent casino was built in Windsor, Ontario. The province also authorized government-owned casinos for Charlevoix, sixty miles north of the city of Quebec, and for Hull,

Casino du Montreal was built into the structure of the French Pavilion from the 1967 Montreal World's Fair. This is a fully government-owned and -operated casino.

across the Ottawa River from the national capital city.

The three casinos welcome 10 million visitors a year, 20 percent of whom are tourists. Most of the revenue (67 percent) is derived from slot machine gaming; tables generate 31 percent, and keno games 2 percent. The casinos have a combined 200 table games and approximately 4,000 slot machines. The casinos do not offer credit to players; however, they do have automated teller machines. Casino du Montreal actually has a branch of a major bank located on its premises.

The mid-1990s also brought another new policy to the province. Video lottery terminals are now permitted in restaurants, bars, and taverns. The province has placed over 15,000 machines in 4,400 locations.

Sources: Cabot, Anthony N., William N. Thompson, Andrew Tottenham, and Carl Braunlich, eds. 1999. *International Casino Law.* 3d ed. Reno: Institute for the Study of Gambling, University of Nevada, Reno, 205–207.

R

Racing. *See* Dog Racing; Horse Racing

The Racino

The racino is a facility that mixes dog or horse track activity with casino-type activities.

For myriad reasons racetrack entertainment has experienced a steady decline over the past several decades. There have been many efforts to stem the ongoing decline. For the most part, however, these efforts have not achieved desired goals. During the 1990s a new solution received considerable support from track interests as well as political leaders in many jurisdictions. They recommended that tracks become venues for other forms of gambling, specifically gaming machines—video poker and slot machines. The policy recommendations have become manifest in several states and provinces. Six states (Iowa, Louisiana, West Virginia, Rhode Island, Delaware, and New Mexico) and four provinces (Alberta, Saskatchewan, Manitoba, and Ontario) have permitted gaming machines to be installed at racetrack facilities. In addition California's Hollywood Park has a very large card room casino. A racetrack in Omaha offered keno games; however, racing activity ceased after the keno operations began.

The tracks have particular advantages as casino-type venues. They have large parking areas, they are separated from the core urban populations by natural land barriers, and they have space that is underutilized. On the other hand, critics suggest that the facilities may prey too much on local habitual gamblers, as very few racinos are geared to attract tourists. Additionally there is debate over whether the casino-type gambling can add to the profitability of racing activity or whether it merely offers more competition, hence hastening the doom of the racing events.

Richard Thalheimer conducted an in-depth economic analysis of market demand forces, a type of investigation he has followed also in analyses of other innovations such as simulcasting, off-track betting, and exotic betting as well as impacts of lottery and casino gaming on track operations. He found that the introduction of machine gambling results in decreased pari-mutuel wagering and decreased pari-mutuel revenues. But overall, revenues at the tracks increased as the machines more than made up for the deficit in pari-mutuel activity. He concluded that the issue of importance that must be addressed is just what share of the machine profits are assigned to the track and to horsemen either in purses or through other means. Thalheimer found that the regular horse players at the tracks did play the machines; on the contrary, however, those attracted to the track to play the machines did not tend to make wagers on horse races. His data are confined to Mountaineer Park in West Virginia (Thalheimer 1998).

Track dynamics are such that pari-mutuel gambling is not fully compatible with machine gambling. Seasoned horse players are renowned as cerebral, educated calculators of odds and probabilities that particular horses may win a race. For them, information is critical. Their activity requires a considerable amount of entry knowledge. Learning is a long process. One gaming executive commented that "betting on horse races is a game of skill, unlike the mindless tapping of a slot machine button, and our philosophy is that the customer must be gently educated on how to study form before he places his bets" (Learmont 1998, S-13).

Features of the style of horse-race betting can be found in some other games. For instance, persons betting on other sports events often use great amounts of information in calculating their betting activity. The same is true in the live casino game of poker. Most casino games, however, require almost no skill. Wheel games and dice games require no skill, as the result of the game is determined fully by chance. Machines call for almost no skill in play.

Wherever machine gaming is introduced, it seems to dominate other gambling products. Inside Las Vegas's most plush casinos, machine revenues now exceed revenues from tables that cater to high rollers. The Oregon Lottery introduced video lottery terminals (VLTs). According to information in *International Gaming and Wagering Business* in June 1994, revenues from the machines quickly dwarfed figures from traditional lottery products. Machines have brought in 90 percent of the lottery revenues in South Dakota. Governments seem to enjoy the opportunities to expand budgets as a result of machine gaming.

Racino Jurisdictions

West Virginia

The West Virginia legislature authorized an experimental installation of video gaming machines—keno machines, poker machines, and machines with symbols—at Mountaineer horse-racing track beginning on 9 June 1990. At first only seventy machines were installed. During the experimental time the number grew to 400 in 1994. Most were keno machines. The first machines had payouts of 88.6 percent. During a three-year experimental period, the lottery agreed not to put machines in other locations. Now machines are at other tracks. According to information in *International Gaming and Wagering Business* in June 1994, the track was able to keep 70 percent of the revenues, and 30 percent went to the state.

Rhode Island

The second state to have machines was Rhode Island. The machines were authorized for Lincoln Greyhound Park and a jai alai fronton. Operations started in September 1992. The greyhound facility soon dropped the word *greyhound* from its name and directed most of its advertising toward machine-playing customers. By mid-1994 there were 1,281 machines at the track. They were video machines, which in initial years won profits of $31,912 per machine per year. At first, 33 percent went to the track and 10 percent went to purses for the dog races, according to information in *International Gaming and Wagering Business* in January 1995. Later the state took 33 percent, the track took 60 percent, and 7 percent went to purses.

In late 1993 Rhode Island added "reel" machines to the mix, as it was felt that the players should have the same variety of machines that was offered by a casino in nearby Connecticut.

"The introduction of VLTs stopped the bleeding," according to Dan Bucci, vice president and general manager of the track. In July 1994, he commented in *International Gaming and Wagering Business* that "we're living proof it can help. But I'm not sure gaming machines are a panacea. If there's a magic bullet out there for all of racing's problems, I don't know what it is." He commented that "it's a lot harder to create new pari-mutuel patrons than it is to create new machine patrons."

Louisiana

Although Louisiana has a long history of gaming, legal gaming machines appeared only in the 1990s. Pari-mutuel racing was well established when a state lottery was authorized in 1989. Tracks were affected by the new competition, and they immediately began to lobby for machines. VLTs were authorized for truck stops, restaurants and bars, and racetracks in 1992. Tracks were allowed to have an unlimited number of machines. The advantage of having machines was short lived, as tracks had to compete with fifteen newly licensed casino boats.

One track with machines was Louisiana Downs near Shreveport. The general manager of the track, Ray Tromba, commented that "it [the installation of 700 machines] was hopefully a way to help the race track be more of an entertainment facility; for the first two years it worked extremely well." Attendance at the track went up. Purses were raised and used to attract better horses for races. The patrons enjoyed the better races. Eighteen percent of the machine revenue was authorized for purses. Tromba maintained that "pari-mutuel can stand on its own if it's a good enough product that people will want to wager on it, it's as simple as that. This is not rocket science" (McQueen 1998, 59).

Delaware

Delaware authorized all types of slot machines and other gaming machines for its tracks in 1995 (McQueen 1996). Delaware Park offered the machines first, but according to information in *International Gaming and Wagering Business* in October 1996, that track was soon followed by Harrington Raceway and Midway. Delaware Park pursued a strategy somewhat different from that elsewhere (Rhode Island, Iowa), as it sought to make a strong separation between the machine gaming and the track wagering. According to marketing director Steven Kallens, track efforts to bring slot players to the track windows were simply unsuccessful. "People got too confused. It was clear we had a pretty dedicated group of slot players with no interest in racing." But perhaps the situation was made to be that way. An unused 60,000-square-foot section of the grandstand was converted to slots. No racing monitors were placed in the room, and players had to go to another room to make racing wagers (McQueen 1996).

Iowa

Like Delaware, Iowa authorized slot machines (as well as VLTs) for its tracks right from the start of racino operations. Local approvals were given for the operations. The Prairie Meadows horse track in Altoona near Des Moines was the first to open in 1995. Machines are also at two dog tracks, the biggest one in Council Bluffs. Prairie Meadows has 1,164 machines. Without a doubt, they have turned the finances of the facility around.

The Prairie Meadows racetrack opened in 1989, but the opening preceded the state's approval of riverboat casinos by only months. In 1991, as the boats opened, the last races were held, and the track entered bankruptcy protection. There were no races in 1992. In 1993 a short calendar with a mixture of thoroughbreds and quarter horses was held, but it was not successful. By then a large Native American casino had opened its doors only sixty miles away in Tama. Machines made all the difference. With their installation, racing began anew in 1995, but it was machines that led the way.

The 1995 revenues consisted of $118 million from the machines, $4.9 million from on-track race betting, and $25.8 million from simulcasting (McQueen 1996).

Iowa's Prairie Meadows has tried very hard to involve the machine players in track wagering, although the track racing has not become a self-supporting cost center. Machines have horse racing themes. One block of quarter machines is called Quarter Horses. The slot players can see track events from the slot area. Staff members circulate among slot players promoting racing and answering questions about race wagering. The players can also make bets to the staff directly while sitting at their machine locations. According to media director Steve Berry, slot players are also able to win free pari-mutuel tickets (McQueen 1996).

Of the retained revenues, $14 million is put into purses for horse races. Purses were only $1 million in 1994 prior to the introduction of slots. As a result of the increased purses, the quality of racing is improving, and simulcast revenues are up 4–5 percent. Attendance is approximately 10,000 a day, and handle has increased 16 percent. No other horse track in the Midwest has done as well as Prairie Meadows.

New Mexico

In 1998, the state of New Mexico agreed to let tracks have machines as long as they could all be tied together in a slot information network. The track gives 25 percent of the revenue directly to the state and gives 20 percent to horsemen through race purses. The track keeps 55 percent. Machines are permitted to run twelve hours a day, every day—as long as the track offers some racing products.

There are four tracks in the state with machines. On 4 May 1999, Ruidoso Downs, less than half an hour away from the large Native American casino of the Mescalero Apache tribe, was permitted to start operating 300 machines. Of the machines, 70 percent are traditional reel-type slot machines, and 30 percent are video gaming devices. The machines are played with coins, and they distribute coins to winners. The track has simulcast racing each day of the year, so the slot machines are available to players 365 days. Live racing—thoroughbred and quarter horse—occurs four days a week from Memorial Day to Labor Day. The nation's leading quarter horse race—the All American Futurity—is run on Labor Day. According to a telephone interview on 8 June 1999 with Keith Henson, the track is beginning to turn around several years of losses (it never stopped racing), but it would like to be able to stay open longer hours and also have more machines in order to compete more equitably with the Mescalero casino.

Canada

In 1998 a decision was made to allow eighteen racing tracks in Ontario to have slot machines under the direction of the provincial lottery corporation (McQueen 1998). Windsor Raceway, a track just a few miles away from the very successful Windsor Casino, was the first to start operations. In December 1998, 712 machines were set into action. The lottery corporation receives 15 percent of the revenues; 10 percent goes to the track and 10 percent to horsemen through purses and other awards. The remaining revenues go to the provincial treasury in Toronto (McQueen 1999).

According to John Millson, president of the raceway, "When the first coin went in, I knew there would be no turning back. it was music to my ears." He was also very supportive of the fact that the lottery corporation ran the machines. "It's a government agency, and quality and proper perception is extremely important, so they do it right." He also commented, "It means a tremendous opportunity for us to market our facility as a gaming and entertainment facility"(McQueen 1999).

The track-machine situation was mixed in other parts of the province. The major track in Toronto—Woodbine—was stymied in its early efforts to get machines, as the city council refused to grant a zoning variance for the activity. That action was appealed by the lottery corporation. Overall, it was expected that twelve of the eighteen tracks in the province would have machines by the end of 1999.

The earliest province to embrace gaming on tracks was Saskatchewan. There a full casino was placed into operation underneath the stands of the Regina Exhibition Park's racing facility. Revenues from the casino were earmarked for Exhibition ac-

tivities. The casino at the track discontinued operations a year after the provincial government began a major casino in downtown Regina. When the new casino opened, track handle decreased 23 percent. The new casino agreed to give a share of its revenues to the Exhibition, according to an interview with Kathy Maher-Wolbaum, Casino Regina, on 15 September 1998.

Racinos are also found at the tracks in Alberta and Manitoba.

Mexico

The Agua Caliente track in Tijuana developed a sports betting complex to supplement dog racing and horse racing activities, but the horses have stopped running at the tracks. An operation in Juarez also offers dogs and sports betting.

Sources: Doocey, Paul. 1994. "Taking the Weakening Pulse of the Greyhound Industry." *International Gaming and Wagering Business* (July): 44–47, 60; Learmont, Tom. 1998. "Racing's Rebirth." *International Gaming and Wagering Business* (June): S-13; McQueen, Patricia. 1996. "Not Just for Racing Anymore." *International Gaming and Wagering Business* (August): 98; McQueen, Patricia. 1998. "Reeling Them In." *International Gaming and Wagering Business* (May): 59; McQueen, Patricia. 1999. "Slots Debut at Windsor Raceway." *International Gaming and Wagering Business* (February): 45; Thalheimer, Richard. 1998. "Pari-mutuel Wagering and Video Gaming: A Racetrack Portfolio." *Applied Economics* 30: 531–544 (this article was first presented at the 9th International Conference of Gambling and Risk Taking, Montreal, June 1997, and published in the proceedings of the conference); Thompson, William N. 1999. "Racinos and the Public Interest." *Gaming Law Review* 3 (December): 283–286.

Red Dog

Red Dog is a casino card game (as well as a private game) in which the player is dealt a total of three cards from a standard deck. The player makes an opening bet, and then the first two cards are dealt face up. The player may then double the bet or let stand the original bet. The player wagers that the third card, which is then dealt, will fall between the first two cards. (An ace is considered the highest card). If the first two cards are consecutive (e.g., a 6 and a 7), the play is considered a draw, and no

Red Dog is a simple game with great odds favoring the casino.

third card is given. If both cards are the same (e.g., a 3 and a 3), a third card is given to the player. If it is the same (another 3), the player wins an eleven-to-one payoff. If it is different, the game is a draw. For other cards the player wins if the third card falls between the first two. The payoff is even money if the first two cards have at least a four-card spread between them. If the spread is three cards in between, and the third card comes between the first two, the payoff is two-to-one; if the spread is only two cards, and the player wins, the payoff is four-to one; but if there is only one card in between the first two, and that card is played for the player, the payoff is five-to-one.

Red Dog is a very simple game to understand, as the table indicates all play and payoff possibilities, and as such it has some popularity. It is not found in many U.S. casinos, however, as it provides the house a substantial advantage of nearly 10 percent.

Sources: Jensen, Marten. 2000. *Secrets of the New Casino Games.* New York: Cardoza Publishing, 125–126; Sifakis, Carl. 1990. *Encyclopedia of Gambling.* New York: Facts on File, 249.

Religion and Gambling

Las Vegas and religion have a strange but enduring relationship. For many years local boosters would proudly proclaim that Las Vegas had more churches per person than any other city in the country. Perhaps that was because the population used to be small, and the boosters probably counted all the wedding chapels as churches.

Actually Las Vegas is pretty well "churched," but not more than any other large city today. What is true even today is this: Las Vegas has more prayers per person than any other city in the country. It is said that there are no atheists in a foxhole, and the same can be said about the people standing around a high-stakes craps table. There just possibly may be a difference between the prayers heard near a casino craps table and the ones mumbled in a church on a Sunday morning—the prayers in the casino may be more serious.

As the casino entertainment industry became entrenched in Las Vegas, various ministries would make their appearances on the Las Vegas Strip. In the 1970s, the Southern Baptist Convention as-

Religion and gambling: Is the water holy? Does it absolve gamblers of sin? In many states such as Mississippi, casino rooms must be built above water.

signed a young minister to the Strip to establish a ministry among the employees, entertainers, and players in the casinos. More recently, the Riviera Casino put a clergyman on its own staff. He is available to counsel other staff as well as tourist guests who experience immediate personal and family needs while they are in Las Vegas. He also conducts services in the casino facility.

Religious and gambling institutions need not be incompatible, although leaders in each are found at loggerheads with one another. The primary leader of the opposition to gambling in the United States at the beginning of the twenty-first century is Tom Grey, a Methodist clergyman. Churches have been prominent in campaigns against gambling, as documented in John Dombrink and William Thompson's *The Last Resort: Success and Failure in Campaigns for Casinos* (Dombrink and Thompson 1990). On the other hand, casinos, wary of political opposition from religious groups, have often extended financial support to church groups. The famous casino at Baden, Germany, actually constructed both the Catholic and the Protestant church buildings of its town. The Berkeley Casino Company of Glasgow, Scotland, aided a local Presbyterian church body by purchasing its old building in order to utilize it as a casino. The pews were removed, but the religious aura seems to hang over the roulette wheels and blackjack tables. On the other hand, the Guardian Angel Church on the Las Vegas Strip features a large stained glass window that depicts scenes of several nearby casinos. Of course, many churches have also used bingo games and raffles for fund-raising reasons.

The relationship of gambling and religion goes back to the dawn of human time. Was the snake tempting Adam and Eve with a gamble when he suggested that they disobey God and eat of the fruit of the tree of knowledge? Could they have known where that quest of knowledge would lead them? Could they have contemplated the nature of life had they not searched for something different?

Moral and religious views on gambling are probably as old as gambling activities themselves. Prehistoric and primitive societies have engaged in exercises to try to make sense of their universe and control their environment by appealing to the supernatural, forces often expressed as gods or God—that is, powers beyond their world. David Levinson's *Religion: A Cross-Cultural Encyclopedia* describes religion as a "relationship between human beings and the supernatural world" (Levinson 1996, vii). The exercises involving appeals to chance would be part and parcel of a people's religion.

For instance, in all societies from the prehistoric to even modern times, the notion of divination has been present. Divination involves beliefs and practices of human beings that enable them to communicate with gods (or God) in order to tell the future. In divining the future, leaders might throw sticks or stones into the air and watch where they fall in order to gain the answers. It was as if they were throwing dice or rolling a gambling wheel. Religious leaders might also hold long sticks that would somehow point them in a direction that their people should follow on a journey, perhaps in quest of water or food. A large part of early religions may have involved the use of gambling instruments (Levinson 1996, 53–54, 182–183). The origins of many games played among traditional Native American tribes may have had religious connotations. The following discussion, however, concentrates on early experiences in the Judeo-Christian heritage as well as established Eastern world religions.

The Hebrews were probably carrying on prehistoric traditions as their leaders sought ways to find the "truth" about the future or about the proper decisions they should make. They would throw stones that were in essence two-sided dice called Urim and Thummim in order to choose between two alternatives. They would also draw lots in situations calling for choices. There are many references in the Old Testament regarding the use of these gambling devices for decision making. Urim and Thummim are mentioned in the following eight cases. Aaron was made to carry Urim and Thummim upon himself as he came before the Lord, as the objects would tell him the judgment of the people of Israel. (Exodus 28:30). The Lord commanded that Moses place the Urim and Thummim on Aaron (Leviticus 8:08). In Numbers 27:21, Moses chooses Joshua to lead the people, and he is given Urim and Thummim to help him find the right answers in his leadership. Similarly, Levi is given the objects in order to make choices (Deuteronomy 33:08). As Saul was preparing for war with the Philistines, he was bothered when the Lord did not urge him forward. He thought it perhaps was because of his sins, his son's sins, or those of his peoples. Urim and Thummim told him the sins were not his people's. Then he threw the stones again, and he was told they were sins of his son Jonathan. His son confessed that he had broken the laws. When Saul determined that his son would have to die, the people intervened, and Saul was forced to walk away from battle (I Samuel 14:41). Later Saul threw the stones again in order to get directions he should take in another battle with the Philistines (I Samuel 28:6). Solomon (Ezra 2:63) and Nehemiah (Nehemiah 7:65) both used Urim and Thummim to determine which of the people who came to the temple were clean—in the sense of having the proper family heritage—and could enter the priesthood and partake of holy food.

The Old Testament also records more than a dozen references to the use of lots or lotteries. The first was when Aaron used lots to decide which of two goats were to be sacrificed to the Lord as a sin offering (Leviticus 16:08). Joshua divided the land of Israel into seven portions and awarded them to families through a casting of lots (Joshua 17:6). Moses used lotteries to divide the lands of Israel among families (Numbers 33:54). Soldiers were selected for battle by lottery (Judges 20:9). Saul was chosen to be king by the process of a drawing (l Samuel 10:20–21). David was told which way to go in order to assume command of his troops (2 Samuel 2:1).

Leaders of the Israel church community were chosen by lots (1 Chronicles 24:31ff.), and the music was organized for the temple by using lots to assign duties to individuals (1 Chronicles 25:8–31). Specific duties such as controlling gates and roads, as well as storehouses, were also given by lots (1 Chronicles 26:13–14). In Nehemiah (10:34) it is reported that lots were cast to decide which families would bring wood offerings into the house of God. One-tenth of the people were allowed to live in Jerusalem; the others lived in smaller villages. Those who were allowed into the city were chosen by lotteries (Nehemiah 11:1). Job (6:27) has a reference to one remonstrating with God, saying "you would even cast lots over the fatherless and bargain over your friend." In a passage that must have been in anticipation of the crucifixion, the Cry of Anguish in the Psalms (22:18) talks of one dying and of dogs who "divide my garments among them, and for my raiment they cast lots."

Joel spoke the word of the Lord condemning the nations that had scattered the Jews, claiming that they "cast lots for my people and traded boys for prostitutes" (Joel 3:03). In Obadiah (1:11) the Lord condemned the people of Edom for allowing foreigners to cast lots for Jerusalem, looking down on your brother "in the day of his misfortune." Jonah (1:07) offers the story of a ship that has been disabled by a storm. The crew believes it is because a sinner is on board, and they cast lots to find that it is Jonah. Nahum records the Lord's anger at Nineveh as he spoke of people casting lots for her nobles and putting her great men in chains (Nahum 3:10).

In Isaiah (36:08) it is reported that Judah is asked to make a wager with the king of Assyria in which he can win 2,000 horses for Israel if he is able to put riders upon them. The story is repeated in 2 Kings (18:23).

These references to lots, throwing of dicelike objects, and wagering are not at all judgmental (collectively) regarding the desirability of gambling or the acceptability of gambling. The same may be said for New Testament references that include the use of lots (some think dice) by Roman soldiers to decide which centurion would receive the clothing of the crucified Christ (Matthew 27:35; Mark 15:24; Luke 23:24; Acts 1:26). Certainly this is a negative light in which gambling is classed. But contemporary with that event was the use of lots to select a replacement for Judas in the group of twelve disciples (Act 1:21–26).

Because the Bible contains no direct condemnation of gambling (not even in the Ten Commandments), different religious groups among Christians and Jews interpret its writings in various ways. Some point to the many uses of gambling devices in decision situations, essentially as objects for divination, as a justification of gambling. Others say that the use of lots to determine God's will is substantially different from using gambling for personal gain. Other biblical passages suggest that there might be evil in gambling. The writers of Isaiah (65:11–12) state, "But you who forsake the lord who set a table for fortune and fill the cups of mixed wine for destiny, I will destine you to the sword, and all of you shall bow down to slaughter." Proverbs (13:11) suggests that winnings from gambling are only temporary: "Wealth hastily gotten will dwindle, but he who gathers little by little will increase it." Other Old Testament references suggest that gambling represents covetousness or stealing, which is condemned (Exodus 20:15–17). The New Testament admonition to give up possessions and follow the Lord suggests that the quest for wealth through gambling is not appropriate. Tom Watson, in *Don't Bet on It,* feels that a further commandment against gambling beyond the Ten Commandments would have been somewhat redundant. "If God didn't get our attention with his laws about stealing and coveting, He probably felt any reference to gambling would be ignored as well" (Watson 1987, 63).

Judaism

The issue of gambling for religious groups from Judaism through the most modern Christian sects has been addressed, but not at all times and certainly not always in the same way. In Judaism, rabbis and other scholars meticulously analyze historical evidence regarding activities. Jewish law changes and grows with interpretations. The interpretations have differed considerably at times; however, there is a general position of tolerance couched in considerations of the situation of the gambling activity.

Occasional gambling in social situations has been moderately acceptable. Indeed, because an enemy king had once rolled the dice to determine when to attack Israel armies, and he attacked at the wrong time losing the battle, the Jewish people have come to celebrate a day called Purim. Games even involving gambling are played on Purim, a time also known as the Feast of Lots. The winner of money at such a game, however, is supposed to make an offering to the synagogue (Wigoder 1989, 576).

Hanukkah celebrates the miracle of the lamps. As a "lucky day" for the Jewish people, it has also been known as "the New Year's Day for Gamblers."

A person who gambled either professionally, as a means of personal support, or habitually was shunned, despite these other examples. The professional gambler was considered a thief, not earning his money through honest labor, and the habitual gambler as one who harmed society. A gambler was "a parasite engaged in useless endeavor and contributing nothing to the world" (Werblowsky and Wigoder 1966, 152). Time spent in gambling games has been viewed as time away from study and productivity. Jewish courts traditionally will not honor gambling debts. And gamblers could not have weddings or funerals in synagogues, nor could they be witnesses in court, as their word was not considered truthful (Bell 1976, 217).

There have been divided interpretations regarding the use of gambling for charitable and fund-raising purposes. Some synagogues have allowed bingo games on their premises, but an association of synagogues condemned the process. Some scholars have interpreted tragic events suffered by the Jewish people at different times in history as being punishments for sins such as gambling. Leaders in the faith have actively opposed legalization of gambling at certain times, although not taking positions or allowing passive support at other times (Jacobs 1973, 151–153).

Christianity

Theologian H. Richard Niebuhr postulates that Christians look at the involvement of Christ in the culture of worldly activity in five basic ways. (1) They see Christ *against* the culture of the world. Here one must choose the sin of this world or a heavenly world that is totally separate. (2) A second approach is that Christ is *of and in* the world. God is the force that directs culture toward its greatest (human) achievements. (3) Christ is *above* the culture. People may live lives directed toward a good, but to achieve the highest human aspirations they must make a supernatural leap to the higher power. (4) Christ *and* culture are forces with dual power over people. As subjects we render unto both God and Caesar, seeking to keep religious and civil authority separate yet together. (5) Christ is seen *as the transforming agent* to remold the culture. People undergo a conversion while they are in the culture (Niebuhr 1951).

Christian views on gambling can be guided by these approaches. Absolutist views—always negative views—toward gambling are found among groups adhering to the first view. For instance, Jehovah's Witnesses seek not to let the materialism of this world become dominant forces in their lives, and accordingly, they disdain all gambling. The Jehovah's Witnesses do not lobby governments or campaign for or against any gambling questions. Members do not vote. Although they show respect for authority, they see governments as worldly, secular institutions, which should not be encouraged, albeit the edicts of government will be obeyed. Their spokespersons make it clear that their members do not participate in or support gambling. The *Watchtower*, the official journal of the faith, regularly reports on gambling, calling it an activity of "greed" and "covetness" stimulating "selfishness and lack of concern for others." Gambling "degrades" people and "entraps them in false worship" (1 October 1974, 9).

The Salvation Army also rejects gambling in its entirety; however, it subscribes more to the second approach of Christ and culture, that Christ is of the world, that he came and walked among the sinners and gave them the light by which to transform their lives and lift up the culture. With this approach the church does not actively campaign against proposals for gambling, but rather like Gamblers Anonymous groups concentrates its efforts on reforming the individual suffering from the influences of gambling.

The third and fourth approaches that churches take toward the role of Christ in culture seem to accept the status quo with regard to public policy. Many of the churches do not oppose gambling outright but look at it in its full context. Churches such as the Methodists (United), Southern Baptist, and Latter-day Saints condemn all gambling by members in all circumstances while they adhere to the fifth notion that Christ is the transforming agent sent to earth to remold the culture by converting individuals within the culture.

The Book of Discipline of the United Methodist Church, for instance, proclaims:

> Gambling is a menace to society, deadly to the best interests of moral, social, economic, and spiritual life, and destructive of good government. As an act of faith and love, Christians should abstain from gambling and should strive to minister to those victimized by the practice. Community standards and personal lifestyles should be such as would make unnecessary and undesirable the resort to commercial gambling, including public lotteries, as a recreation, as an escape, or as a means of producing public revenue or funds for support of charities or government. (General Conference of the United Methodist Church 1984, 98–99)

The Southern Baptist Convention is the largest non-Catholic denomination in the United States. Their director of family and moral concerns, Harry Hollis, told the Commission on the Review of the National Policy on Gambling much the same story:

> In all its resolutions, the Southern Baptist Convention has rejected gambling. Obviously, some

A Presbyterian church was remodeled and is now the Berkeley Casino of Edinburgh, Scotland.

forms of gambling are more serious than others, but all forms have been consistently rejected in Southern Baptist statements and resolutions. The use of gambling profits for worthy activities has not led Southern Baptists to endorse gambling. . . . The availability of gambling tempts both the reformed gambler and the potential gambler to destruction. For the entire community, gambling is disruptive and harmful. Thus, concerned citizens should work for laws to control and eliminate gambling. (Bell 1976, 172–173)

The Church of Jesus Christ of Latter-day Saints (Mormons) has been equally vehement in maintaining that gambling is always wrong. In 1982 Spencer Kimball, the twelfth president of the church wrote:

From the beginning we have been advised against gambling of every sort. The deterioration and damage come to the person, whether he wins or loses, to get something for nothing, something without effort, something without paying the full price. Profiting from others' weaknesses displeases God. Clean money is that compensation received for a full day's honest work. It is that reasonable pay for faithful service. It is that fair profit from the sale of goods, commodities, or service. It is that income received from transactions where all parties profit. (Kimball 1982, 355–356. *See also* Ludlow 1992, 533)

An interesting side issue arose recently over temple privileges. A member of the Church of Latter-day Saints (Mormon) must be in good standing in order to enter a temple. In the past if a Mormon worked in a gambling establishment or in a gambling-related job, especially if the job was on the "frontline" of providing gambling service such as being a dealer, he or she might be denied good-standing status. When the church decided to build a temple in Las Vegas (about 10 percent of the local population are Mormons), many members who held jobs in casinos wished to have temple privileges. Casinos provide the largest number of jobs in the Las Vegas community, so many members of the Mormon faith do work in casinos. The church stand against casino employment was reviewed, and it was decided that casino workers who did not personally gamble and did not overtly encourage others to gamble could have good standing if they met other church and community obligations.

Churches that accept gambling in some circumstances generally view Christ's role in culture in the third or fourth way as advanced by H. Richard Niebuhr. L. M. Starkey writes in *Money, Mania, and Morals* that "[A]ll Catholic moralists are agreed that gambling and betting may lead to grave abuse and sin, especially when they are prompted by mere gain. The gambler usually frequents bad company, wastes much valuable time, becomes adverse to work, is strongly tempted to be dishonest when luck is against him, and often brings financial ruin upon himself and those dependent upon him" (Starkey 1964, 90–91). Nonetheless the Catholic Church reconciles gambling with the fact that Christ must have been of the world as God had given people personal freedom that led them into certain activity. *The New Catholic Encyclopedia* relates, "A person is entitled to dispose of his own property as he wills . . . so long as in doing so he does not render himself incapable of fulfilling duties incumbent upon him by reason of justice or charity. Gambling, therefore, though a luxury, is not considered sinful except when the indulgence in it is inconsistent with duty" (*The New Catholic Encyclopedia* 1967, 276).

The Catholic Church believes that it is sinful for a person to gamble if the money gambled does not belong to him or if the money is necessary for the support of others. The Church also condemns gambling behavior when it becomes compulsive and disruptive to family and social relationships. Moreover, the freedom to gamble implies a knowing freedom to enter into a fair and honest contract for play. Cheating at gambling is considered wrong, as are all dishonest games.

The Church also looks at the end result of the activity. If through gambling good consequences may follow, the gambling activity may even be considered good and may be promoted by the Church. Hence, a limited-stakes bingo game conducted honestly by Church members within a church building in order to raise funds for a school or hospital is not bad.

On questions of legalization of gambling, Catholic Church leaders ask if the particular form of gambling puts poor people at disadvantages, if it causes people to become pathological gamblers, and if the gambling will be adequately monitored to ensure that it is honest and fair. Church leaders have opposed some public referenda while they have supported others.

The Church of England and its U.S. offspring, the American Episcopal Church, both essentially reformed Catholic organizations, accept the same approach toward gambling as is taken by the Catholic Church. The National Convention of the church has no stated position on gambling. Individual church organizations have used gambling events to raise funds; others have prohibited the use of gambling within church facilities. Basically the issue of gambling is a low-priority ethical issue. Individuals are left to develop their own attitudes on the subject.

Eastern Religions

Middle Eastern and Asian countries usually ban gambling. For the most part Arab states, India, China, Japan, and other Asian countries have no casinos. Regional religions such as Islam, Hinduism, Buddhism, and Shintoism—which are also practiced by many Americans—generally account for the legal prohibitions.

It is written in the Koran—the holy scriptures of the Islamic faith—"Only would Satan sow hatred and strife among you, by wine and games of chance, and turn you aside from the remembrance of God, and from prayer; will ye not, therefore, abstain from them?" Islamic law therefore condemns gambling as being contrary to the word. The activity is viewed as "unjustified enrichment" and "receiving a monetary advantage without giving a countervalue" (Survah V, verses 90–91). The evidence of a gambler is not admissible in an Islamic court. Anyone receiving gambling winnings is obligated to give the money to the poor. There are, however, two exceptions to the general prohibition on gambling: Wagers are permitted for horse racing, as such betting was an incentive for training necessary for the holy wars; also, prizes may be given for winners of competitions involving knowledge about Islamic law.

Under Hindu law, gamblers are also disqualified as witnesses. Because of their "depravity," they are considered, as are "thieves and assassins," to be people in whom "no truth can be found." The Hindu law books indicate that gambling—among the most serious of vices—makes a person impure and that "the wealth obtained by gambling is tainted" (Eliade 1987, 5:472). The devout Buddhist considers gambling wrong. In the Parabhava Sutta, the Buddha includes addiction to women, strong drink, and dice as one of eleven combinations of means whereby men are brought to loss. The one path to victory is loving the "dhamma"—the Buddha's teaching. Monks are warned that games and spectacles—including fights between elephants, horses, buffalo, bulls, goats, rams, and cocks; also, various board games, chariot races, and dice games—are detrimental to their virtue.

Buddha saw that the world was suffering because of desire. Desires could not be satisfied, and therefore we had frustration. When we achieved our wants we only wanted more, and then we became obsessed with fears that others would take away what we had. In rejecting desires, we had to seek the ten "perfections" in generosity, self-sacrifice, morality, renunciation, energy, forbearance, truthfulness, loving, kindness, and equanimity. These perfections come with a rejection of worldly passions including those aroused by gambling activity (Eliade 1987, 5:472).

The Shinto faith of Japan emerged after centuries of contact with Buddhism. It became a national religion in the nineteenth century, incorporating many Buddhist beliefs. It extols the virtue of industriousness and strong willpower. Hence, gambling is accorded the status of an evil activity, as it diverts one from the path to virtue and righteousness.

Marxism has replaced religion to a major extent in China and North Korea, although remnants of religious practices can be witnessed. The notions of Marxism are consistent with the prohibitions of gambling found within the major regional religions. Marxist and socialist thought views gambling as an activity that takes people away from productive pursuits, and in an organized sense, gambling is another capitalist activity that exploits the working classes.

The force of Marxism and religious doctrines of Islam, Hinduism, Buddhism, and Shintoism upon the laws of most Middle Eastern and Asian countries has been pronounced. Nonetheless, the affluent among the populations of the region have always found gambling outlets available for their play. Middle Eastern and Asian gambling enclaves thrive in places such as Macao, Beirut, Cairo, Manila, and Kathmandu. And Las Vegas casinos include nationals from the Eastern and Middle Eastern countries, which forbid gambling, high on the lists of their most exclusive high-rolling players. Religions in the East as well as the West do impact upon attitudes people have toward the legalization of gambling, but the force of beliefs as a determinant over whether people will personally gamble or not may be less pervasive.

—*coauthored by James Dallas*

Sources: Bell, Raymond. 1976. "Moral Views on Gambling Promulgated by Major American Religious Bodies." In *Gambling in America,* Appendix I. Washington, DC: National Commission on the Policy of Gambling; Dombrink, John D., and William N. Thompson. 1990. *The Last Resort: Success and Failure in Campaigns for Casinos.* Reno: University of Nevada Press; Eliade, Mircea, ed. 1987. *The Encyclopedia of Religion.* 16 vols. New York: Macmillan; General Conference of the United Methodist Church. 1984. *The Book of Discipline.* Nashville, TN: United Methodist Publishing House; Jacobs, Louis. 1973. *What Does Judaism Say about . . .?* Jerusalem: Keter Publishing; Kimball, Spencer, ed. 1982. *The Teachings of Spencer W. Kimball.* Salt Lake City, UT: Deseret Book Company; Levinson, David. 1996. *Religion: A Cross-Cultural Encyclopedia.* Santa Barbara, CA: ABC-CLIO; Ludlow, Daniel H. 1992. *Encyclopedia of Mormonism.* New York: Macmillan; *The New Catholic Encyclopedia.* 1967. 17 vols. New York: McGraw-Hill; Niebuhr, H. Richard. 1951. *Christ and Culture.* New York: Harper and Row; Schacht, Joseph. 1964. *An Introduction to Islamic Law.* Oxford: Clarendon Press; Starkey, L. M. 1964. *Money, Mania, and Morals.* New York: Abington Press; Thompson, William N. 1997. *Legalized Gambling: A Reference Book.* 2d ed. Santa Barbara, CA: ABC-CLIO; Wagner, Walter. 1972. *To Gamble, or Not to Gamble.* New York: World Publishing; Watson, Tom. 1987. *Don't Bet on It.* Ventura, CA: Regal Books; Werblowsky, R. J. Z., and Geoffrey Wigoder, eds. 1966. *The Encyclopedia of the Jewish Religion.* New York: Holt, Rinehart, Winston; Wigoder, Geoffrey. 1989. *The Encyclopedia of Judaism.* New York: Macmillan.
See also "The Best Gamblers in the World" in Appendix A

Reno

The Biggest Little City in the World—Reno, Nevada—was settled in 1868 as a community planned around a railroad center serving the Comstock mining area of Virginia City. The city grew sufficiently during its early years to allow its survival after silver-mining interests waned. Nonetheless, the city had to turn to other activities to remain economically viable. Reno and Nevada accepted certain behaviors and activities not allowed elsewhere. The city did not ban the prostitution that became part of the scene in the early mining years. The city held the Jeffries-Jackson boxing match in 1910 when other states banned the sport. In the early decades of the twentieth century, Reno established its reputation as a place where divorces could be easily obtained. Gambling was permitted from the beginning without interruption. From 1910 to 1931, however, the gambling activity was illegal, even though openly tolerated.

When Nevada's legislature passed the wide-open casino bill of 1931, Reno became the premier casino city of the United States. It maintained that

Virginia Street in Reno: Biggest Little City in the World.

status until Las Vegas accelerated its development in the 1950s.

The first legal casinos of the 1930s were merely the same bars, taverns, and restaurants that had operated gambling over the previous two decades in their back rooms. The largest was the Bank Club, which had conducted games in its basement. Within a month of the new law, a renovated and enlarged facility was opened on the ground floor. It had the first electric bingo board in a casino. Other facilities proliferated with small-scale gambling.

The operations of Bill Harrah and the Smith family redefined the nature of Reno and of casino gambling generally in the later years of the decade. When they developed their properties, Reno became much more than just an outlaw town with quickie divorces. It was a destination resort.

The Smiths came from Vermont, where Raymond I. "Pappy" Smith had run carnival games. In the early 1930s he migrated to a beach location near San Francisco, where he began to take the "suckers'" dollars. In 1935 California attorney general Earl Warren began an antigambling crusade. "Pappy" and his two sons, Raymond A. and Harold, decided

that the legal air of Reno would be better for their health. They started a bingo hall on Virginia Street in the red-lined area where gambling was permitted by the city council. They called their place Harolds Club. The other clubs and casinos acted like carnival operators and tried to take all the players' money as fast as they could, but the Smiths tried a new approach in their facility. They viewed their customers as their ultimate "bread and butter" only if they were nurtured, well respected, and well treated. Every day Pappy Smith would walk the floor, joke with players, and give "donations" to players who lost all their money. Every player always had a meal and enough money for a bus ride home.

The Smiths were also promoters. For a short time they had a game called mouse roulette. A mouse would be released into a cage having a circular board with numbered holes. The mouse would eventually go into one of the holes, and the number on the hole would be the winning number in the game. Players discovered, however, that they could make noises, causing the mouse to quickly run into the nearest hole. The game had to be taken out as it lost too much money for the casino.

The Smiths launched casino gambling's first national (and world) advertising campaign. They placed 2,300 billboards on major highways throughout the country. The billboards featured a covered wagon and the words Harolds Club or Bust. The signs soon appeared in countries on every continent. The world knew that there was a Reno and that Reno had casinos. The Smiths also opened their doors to women players by being the first casino to hire women as dealers. In 1970 Harolds Club was sold to Howard Hughes. It was Hughes's only northern Nevada property.

Bill Harrah and his father were also encouraged by authorities to close down their "bingo" games in California. Bill had grown up in luxury, but unfortunately his father's fortune fell apart during the Depression, and he had to leave college to help run his father's remaining business venture, a bingo game at Venice Beach. When Bill visited Reno he was generally disgusted with the "sawdust" nature of the low-class joints he found. He thought the city could do a lot better. After several tries he was finally able to set up operations on Virginia Street. He gave his players the feel of luxury—carpets, draperies, good furniture, comfortable restaurants. He was the first Reno operator to bring big-time entertainers to a casino. He also drew customers by creating the largest automobile collection in the world. Harrah is also credited for developing internal casino security by installing the skywalk, also known as the "eye in the sky."

Harrah also developed a casino at South Lake Tahoe, bringing his ideas of luxury surroundings to gambling properties there. While developing marketing strategies there, he instituted bus tours for players out of the San Francisco area and other parts of California.

Harrah's was the first casino organization with publicly traded stocks. Nevada passed its legislation enabling public stock ownership for casino in 1969, and Harrah's went public in 1971. In 1973, the stock was traded on the New York Stock Exchange. After Bill Harrah's death in 1978, the company was sold to Holiday Inn. Today it is among the giants of the corporate casino industry, having revenues second only to the Park Place conglomerate.

Reno grew with other new properties and with expansions. In the 1950s, the red-line casino district was eliminated, and casinos could be placed in other commercial areas. The 1950s saw gaming grow with the Mapes and Riverside Hotels on lower Virginia Street; John Ascauga started the Nugget in suburban Sparks. Competition from Las Vegas dampened expansion in the 1960s, but the 1970s brought a building revival. Several major properties were opened. The Eldorado started games in 1973, and the Comstock, Sahara (now the Reno Flamingo Hilton), and Circus Circus opened in 1978. The same year Kirk Kerkorian constructed the MGM Grand with over 1,000 rooms—later expanded to 2,000. The MGM Grand had the largest casino floor in the world when it opened—over 100,000 square feet of gaming space. The MGM Grand was later sold to Bally's, and subsequently to Hilton.

Until 1995, there was no more casino construction in Reno. The market essentially went flat. In 1995, however, the Eldorado and Circus Circus combined to build the largest downtown casino—the Silver Legacy. Today Reno seeks to "hold its own" against competition from Native American casinos in California and the aura of Las Vegas to the south. The city has developed marketing around a series of events throughout the year. The National Bowling Center was built downtown, and it features many tournaments. The city also hosts the world-class Reno Hot Air Balloon Races each year. There is also a multitude of music, ethnic, and nationalities festivals. Canada Days is especially popular with a key market segment—tours from the country to the north.

The forty-five casinos of the Reno-Sparks area (Washoe County), with approximately 15,000 rooms, produce gambling revenues of approximately $1 billion a year, or 12 percent of the state's revenue and 2 percent of the national gambling revenue. The casinos are not as able to appeal to "high rollers" as are the Las Vegas properties. Las Vegas casinos win about 40 percent of their revenues from table games, whereas Reno properties win less than 30 percent from tables. Next to Las Vegas, Reno will continue to be number two, and they will have to "try harder" just to stay in place.

Sources: Kling, Dwayne. 2000. *The Rise of the Biggest Little City: An Encyclopedia History of Reno Gaming, 1931–1981.* Reno: University of Nevada Press; Land,

Barbara, and Myrick Land. 1995. *A Short History of Reno.* Reno: University of Nevada Press; Rowley, William D. 1984. *Reno: Hub of Washoe County.* Woodland Hills, CA: Windsor Publications.
See also Harrah, William F.

Sources: Dombrink, John D., and William N. Thompson. 1990. *The Last Resort: Success and Failure in Campaigns for Casinos.* Reno: University of Nevada Press, 130–131.
See also The Racino

Rhode Island

Rhode Island from its inception has been a community marching to its own drummer. In its first era of European settlements it was a place for persons who rejected the rules of other colonies and migrated. In the modern era immigrants have also left their mark on the character of Rhode Island life. These populations have very willingly become patrons of gambling activity, whether the activities were conducted by illegal mobsters or by legitimate authority. The state has been only one of four states to permit betting on jai alai games. Pari-mutuel betting is also authorized for dog and horse tracks. A lottery started in 1974 offers instant games, keno, daily numbers, lotto tickets, and tickets for the Powerball games.

There was an effort to introduce casino gambling into the resort city of Newport in 1980. An advisory vote showed that 81 percent of the residents did not want casinos. State officials took heed and the effort died. In the late 1990s the Narragansett Native American tribe won a compact to offer casino-type games; however, no casino was opened by the end of the century.

In 1992, Rhode Island became the second state to have machine gaming at racetracks. The machines were authorized for Lincoln Greyhound Park and a jai alai fronton. The greyhound facility soon dropped "greyhound" from its name and directed most of its advertising toward machine-playing customers. By mid-1994 there were 1,281 machines at the track. At first, 33 percent of the machine revenue went to the track and 10 percent went to purses for the dog races. Later the state took 33 percent, the track took 60 percent, and 7 percent went to purses.

In late 1993, traditional "reel" slot machines were added to the mix, as it was felt that the players should have the same variety of machines offered by a casino in nearby Connecticut. Machines were positioned so that their players could watch the races and had easy access to betting windows.

Rothstein, Arnold

Arnold Rothstein (1882–1928) represents a great transitional mark in gambling life in the United States. He took gambling enterprise from being an entrepreneurial activity of individuals operating at the edge of the law toward becoming a major industry centrally controlled by criminal elements. In the process he established a reputation for being a man of his word and a dominant high-stakes player. He defeated Nick the Greek Dandolos in a dice game with stakes of $600,000. Rothstein owned several casinos, and he was the financial linchpin who held together the ring that fixed the 1919 World Series. He also developed the layoff system for bookies across the country. His transitional role coincided with the coming of national Prohibition, which, of course, provided great incentives for centralized Mob activities.

Arnold Rothstein was born in 1882, the son of Arthur Rothstein. His father was a successful merchant. Although he wanted Arnold to follow in his footsteps, it was not to be. Arnold loved games, and he also loved to play. In 1909, Arnold was married at Saratoga during the racing season. He actually used his ring and his wife's jewelry as collateral for his bets on his wedding night. Compulsive gamblers say that gambling is the most powerful of life's urges, and whatever is in second place cannot even compete. Rothstein coveted the lifestyle he found at Saratoga, and he vowed (some vows are taken seriously) that he would come back in a role other than a tourist player.

Rothstein started playing harder and harder in New York City and also on ocean liners. Then he ran the games. Before he was thirty he had gambling halls in the city, and soon he was planning his return to Saratoga.

In Saratoga he created and opened the Brook, a nightclub with gambling. He began to restore an aura that Richard Canfield had established in the first decade of the century. Rothstein later acquired the Spa casino, and he invited Meyer Lansky and Lucky Luciano to be operators of his games. Other figures who emerged as leading mobsters and propelled the Mob's gambling activity toward the Las Vegas Strip were his friends—Frank Costello, Dutch Schultz, Waxey Gordon, and Jack "Legs" Diamond.

Rothstein had a stable of horses, and he became very active in bookmaking—for races and sports events. At a casual meeting of other bookies, one remarked that he had passed up a lot of action recently because too many bets were on one side of the proposition, and he had to control his risks. Rothstein told him if that happened again to call him, and he would cover the action and thereby help the bookie balance his books—for a small percentage. Rothstein's headquarters suddenly became the center of sports and race betting for the United States. Layoffs came from Rothstein. (Layoffs occur when the clients of minor bookies bet too heavily in favor of one team. The minor bookies seek out major players, such as the Rothsteins, in order to spread out their risk—that is, lay off some of their bets with a bigger bookie.) The central headquarters also became the source of odds for sports gambling.

From such a position of power and influence in sports betting, Rothstein became involved in the most notorious sports scandal of the twentieth century. A Boston bookie called him because some players on the Chicago White Sox had requested $80,000 to throw the World Series in which they were playing the underdog Cincinnati Reds. Definitive facts do not exist to say for sure if Rothstein provided all or part of the $80,000. Many writers think he did. For sure he gambled heavily that the Cincinnati team would win. He took hundreds of thousands of dollars in gambling wins on the series. The fix held. Revelations of the fix were not made public for a year. The subsequent response was for major leagues (especially the baseball leagues) to establish strict rules governing betting by players. Owners were treated differently. Neither players nor owners, however, were ever to bet on games involving their own teams. Rape, drug sales, and even murder were lesser crimes compared to this serious matter. Players involved in the 1919 scandal were banned forever from baseball, just as Pete Rose has been for his alleged bets

that his team would win games in the 1980s. The name of the greatest hitter in the history of the sport is not found in the Hall of Fame because of transgressions that violate the rules that arose from the 1919 scandal.

Rothstein's days as a leading hitter came early in his life. Actually, there were not many days later in his life. Although he had been considered a man of integrity, he welshed on gambling debts stemming from a game in 1928 in which he lost $340,000. He indicated a refusal to pay because he thought the game was rigged. A few weeks after refusing to pay, he was found with a bullet in his side. He knew enough of the code of honor not to squeal on his assailant in the day or so he lingered before he died. He was only forty-six.

Sources: Chafetz, Henry. 1960. *Play the Devil: A History of Gambling in the United States from 1492 to 1955.* New York: Potter Publishers, 442–432; Hotaling, Edmund. 1995. *They're Off! Horse Racing at Saratoga.* Syracuse, NY: Syracuse University Press, 216–221; Longstreet, Stephen. 1977. *Win or Lose: A Social History of Gambling.* Indianapolis, IN: Bobbs-Merrill, 166–172; Moldea, Dan E. 1989. *Interference: How Organized Crime Influences Professional Football.* New York: William Morrow, 42–46; Sifakis, Carl. 1990. *Encyclopedia of Gambling.* New York: Facts on File, 252.

Roulette and Wheels of Fortune

The notion that fortune is tied to cycles and turning of wheels is buried in deep antiquity. The wheel itself was developed about 5,000 years ago. During the time of Christ, the Roman emperor Caesar Augustus had a rotating horizontal chariot wheel fixed with numbers around its circumference and used it in games of chance. The Zodiac wheel was also conceived of more than 2,000 years ago and forms the basis for horoscopes that predict a person's fortune based upon cycles of movements of the stars and planets. Wheels or other objects were spun in various ways for games in primitive societies. Despite this long history, the origins of the wheels used in casinos today came much later in European history.

Hoca and E-O

Carl Sifakis suggests that today's roulette wheel may have had its origins in wheels called E-O and

Wheel of fortune in the Royal Haitian Casino in Port-au-Prince.

hoca that appeared in the early 1600s in central Europe. E-O stands for even-odd. A circular table had 40 gouges or pockets carved into it around the edge. Twenty pockets were marked as even and 20 as odd. Two (1 odd and 1 even) had X's marked on them as well. The game paid even money to a winner. If a player bet on even, and an even number received the ball that was rolled around the table, the player won. If the ball fell into an even pocket marked with an X, it was a tie. If the ball fell in any of the 20 odd pockets, the player lost. This gave the house a 2.5 percent advantage. The game of hoca also had the table with 40 pockets, but 3 were marked with zeros, and the even money payouts gave the house an advantage of 7.5 percent. These games ceased operation with the appearance of the French roulette wheel.

The French wheel was purportedly developed by French mathematician Blaise Pascal, who lived from 1623 to 1662. In his mathematics work he expounded at length on probability theory. His wheel was useful for explaining his theories. Legend has it that Pascal conceived of the wheel during a re-

treat at a religious monastery. Others perfected the wheel that is used in French roulette (also called European roulette) today. Given the early origins of the game, it can be suggested that roulette is the oldest casino game still in active play.

French (European) and American Roulette

There are two basic styles of roulette games—French (European) roulette and American roulette. There are other variations of games with different sets of numbers, including the big wheel, boule, golden ten, and *espherodromo.* which are discussed later in this entry.

Both the French and American wheels have numbers from one to thirty-six on parts of the inner circle, each separated by frets. The French wheel also includes a zero, and the American wheel has a zero and a double zero. The croupiers rotate the wheel, and as it spins in one direction, he or she rolls the ball (plastic or ivory) in the opposite direction in a circular groove at the top of the wheel. Soon the ball slows down and falls toward the numbers in the inner circle. As it does, it hits small metal bumps on the surface of the wheel that cause the ball to bounce in ways making its path random as it finds its number or the zero or double zero. This number is the winner.

The player makes bets on a layout showing the thirty-six numbers in three columns and twelve rows. At the top of the columns the zero (and double zero) are placed. On the sides of the columns are places for bets on odd or even numbers, red or black, and low or high numbers.

The French wheel has a different distribution of numbers around the wheel than does the American wheel. On both, red and black numbers alternate, but not even-odd or high and low numbers. The logic of the number arrangement seeks to enhance making the number selection random.

The French game is worked by several dealers who are called croupiers. The main croupier controls the wheel. Others help by making bets for players by placing their chips on the layout. The players all use casino value chips, so it is important that the croupiers keep a close track on just who is making each bet, as all the chips are the same. Another croupier places a marker on the winning number and separates the winning bet chips from other chips that he rakes in. All bets are paid out with wins that allow the casino to have a 2.70 percent edge. The bets on the individual numbers are paid at 35 to 1 even though the true odds are 36 to 1. Even payouts are given for odd-even, red-black, and high-low, and the chance of each bet winning is 18 in 37. Bets may also be made on columns, rows, adjacent numbers on the layout, four numbers on the layout, and special combinations of numbers that appear near other numbers. A *voisins* bet (meaning "neighbors") is placed on the four numbers that surround the last winning number. A *les voisins du zero* bet covers the numbers surrounding the zero. A finals bet can be placed on all numbers ending in the same digit (for example, 6, 16, 26, and 36), and *les tiers* is a bet covering one-third of the wheel. *Les orphelins* is a bet covering numbers not in *les tiers* or *les voisins du zero*.

As the croupiers place bets for the players and deliver payouts for players, and all the chips look the same, the playing process is slow. Each game involving the spinning of the wheel takes two minutes or more if there are several players. This contrasts with the American wheel game where a play usually occurs more than once a minute, and even as many as 100 times an hour.

The American game offers worse odds for the player, as the wheel has two zeros along with the thirty-six numbers. The odds against the player hitting a single number are therefore 37 to 1, but the payoff is the same as with the French game, 35 to 1. This gives the house an edge of 5.26 percent. Red-black, even-odd, high-low bets are paid even money, but the player's chances of success are 18 in 38 for the same 5.26 percent house advantage. The player could do worse yet. He or she could bet on a series of five numbers at the end of the table—the 0, 00, 1, 2, and 3, with a payoff possibility of 6 to 1, whereas the true chances are 33 to 1, for a house advantage of 7.89 percent. In some casinos with American roulette (e.g., Atlantic City casinos), a bettor on even payout bets (odd-even, red-black, high-low) loses only half of his or her bet if the zero or double zero comes up. This rule, called *en prison* (because half of the bet remains on the table unless it is withdrawn), reduces the house edge to 2.70 percent on this bet.

In American roulette, only one dealer is needed to spin the wheel and to handle all wagers. The players purchase (with cash or casino value chips) individual colored chips that are distinguished from those of all the other players. The players place their own chips. All the dealer must do is make sure there are no bets placed after the ball descends into the winning number's space.

The English variation of roulette offers the player the best odds. A French wheel is used with its single zero, but players have their individualized American chips. The house edge of 2.7 percent is in contrast to French roulette because of another difference. In French roulette the player is obligated to tip the dealer with each win. If the player wins thirty-five chips, he or she "must" pay one to the croupiers as a tip. *Must* is a strong word, but if the tip is not paid, the croupier just might lose track of that player's future bets if they are winners (after all, the chips are all the same for all the players). In England this is not a major problem—first, because the players have individualized chips, and second, because tipping of dealers

A game of roulette at the Apache Casino in Las Vegas, ca. 1940. (UNLV Special Collections)

is prohibited in the casinos. Hence in effect, the true edge in England is 2.7 percent, whereas, in reality, in France it is closer to the American edge of 5.26 percent.

Because of the odds disadvantage, the game of American roulette is not popular. Indeed, roulette action in Las Vegas casinos is close to zero, certainly less than 1 percent of the action. Yet the game of roulette has qualities that should be attractive worldwide. Actually, roulette is the premier table game of most European casinos. Roulette is a simple game that is easily understood even by the most novice gambler. Also with but a few exceptions (the en prison rule and the five-series bet in American roulette), all bets on the roulette table have the same expected payout—94.74 percent for American roulette and 97.3 percent for French roulette—whether the player bets on one number, two, a column, or odds or even, red or black, or high or low numbers. It is a democratic game; all the players, amateur and professional, get the same chances. Unlike blackjack or craps, there is no "stupid" bet—that is, once one decides to start playing.

Roulette is also a game that permits players to try a wide variety of systems. Many casinos encourage systems by keeping boards that display the last twenty numbers that have come up on the wheel. Also some casinos publish books showing the actual numbers that came up on individual wheels over weeks, months, and even years. Whatever system a player may conjure up, the player can pretest it by applying it to real numbers and sequences of numbers that have come up on actual wheels.

Boule

Boule is quite similar to roulette. A stationary rounded table has eighteen pockets, two for each number from one to nine. A ball is rolled into the table, which is essentially a cone in shape. The ball bounces around and falls into one of the numbers—the winning number. Players betting on the number are paid off at 7 to 1, although true chances are 8 to 1, for a house advantage of 11.11 percent. Players can also bet on red and black, odds or evens, high or low, for an even payoff. They lose on even bets when a five appears, making the true chances of winning only 4 of 9, for the same house advantage of 11.11 percent. The game was very popular in France prior to the introduction of slot machines in the late 1980s. Slot rooms and boule rooms in France do not have admission charges. The game was also played at the Crystal Casino in Winnipeg, Manitoba, through the 1990s. Until recently, it was the only game allowed in Switzerland, where the payout was only 6 to 1 for a single-number play, for a house edge of 22.22 percent.

Big Wheel (Wheel of Fortune or Big Six)

A big vertical wheel of fortune is a common sight at carnivals and charity casino events. The wheel of fortune is also popular in U.S. casinos but less prevalent in casinos of other jurisdictions. The mechanical wheel is spun by a dealer who also supervises betting activity on a table in front of the wheel. The wheel's simplicity and exposure to a gambling crowd makes it susceptible to cheating, so it would be advisable not to play the game except in a regulated atmosphere. Casinos must be vigilant to ensure that the wheel is not compromised by players.

The wheel is about five feet across from top to bottom. It has fifty-four equally spaced sections that are separated by nails that are near the rim of the wheel. A strap of leather is mounted above the wheel, and it hits the nails as the wheel spins around. The friction of contact slows the wheel, and it stops with the leather strap settling on one of the fifty-four spaces—the winning space.

The spaces are designated by denominations of dollar bills. Twenty-three sections are marked with a $1 bill, 15 with $2 bills, 8 with $5 bills, 4 with $10 bills, and two with $20 bills. Two others are marked with a joker and a flag marking. The player bets on the category of bill he or she expects the wheel to hit. He or she receives an even money payout for a successful bet on the $1 bill, although the chances of success are only 23 of 54. This gives the house a 14.8 percent edge. A bet on $5 pays 2 to 1 for a casino advantage of 16.6 percent; other bets give the house an edge of from 14.8 percent to 22.2 percent. A bet on the joker or the flag is paid at 45 to 1. These odds advantages for the house make the big wheel a bad bet for the player. The simple

nature of the activity and the symbolism of the wheel of fortune have sustained a modicum of popularity of the wheel among amateur players.

Espherodromo

Legal restrictions on gambling are not often followed to the letter. In addition to those who would confront the law with blatant illegality, there are those who seek to find nonconfrontational ways around the law. The roulette form of gambling is quite popular, so where roulette is in itself illegal, there are those who will seek to find other games like roulette that might survive legal challenges. Two of those games are espherodromo and golden ten. Espherodromo appeared in the city of Bogota, Colombia, where casinos were always on the edge of the law. Therefore entrepreneurs came up with a game that certainly did not look like roulette, but in format was a roulette-style game. (*See* description of the game in entry for Colombia.)

Golden Ten

The golden ten game was offered to players in nonauthorized settings; however, its operators were quite successful in avoiding prosecution on the basis that their game was not a gambling game. The golden ten wheel game was instead advanced as a skill game. The game gained an especially viable hold in the Netherlands in the 1980s after the government tried a crackdown on patently illegal casino gaming. Operators came up with this new game, although some suggest it was invented by Germans. The game is called golden ten because it uses a wheel with numbers in the center around a circle; one of the numbers is marked zero, and the other is marked with a big golden X. There are twenty-four numbers on the wheel, so if it were a random-ordered game, the house would have an advantage of about 8 percent, as payoffs on single numbers are 23 to 1, whereas the expectation should require a payoff of 25 to 1. But those running the wheel claimed that the numbers, although falling randomly, could be predicted by the players. Indeed, the game was also called observation roulette.

The circular bowl for the game is stationary. A ball rolled into the smooth metal bowl makes slow, descending spirals downward until it hits the center area, where it bounces into one of the numbered areas or the area marked zero or X. The metal bowl contains two concentric circles on its sides, about one-third and two-thirds of the way down the sides. The circles are simply markings on the bowl that do not affect the roll of the ball. The player makes his or her bet after the ball has passed the first circle but before it crosses the lower circle. The player can watch the ball come out of the dealer's hand and watch it cross the first circle line. By observing the rolls over and over, the player is supposed to be in a good position to "predict" where the ball will likely land. With successful predictions, the player becomes a skillful winner, not a gambler at all. Gambling demands that chance be a material part of the play on at least a meaningful part of the play. The casinos with golden tens provided lists of rules requiring players to make many observations before they tried playing. They wanted the players to be skillful. When legal authorities claimed it was a gambling game, the defenders of the game asked the government to prove that players were not using skill. One judge suggested that prosecuting officials would have to show that the players did not do better, or could not do better, than achieving the 92 percent expected payout. As the golden ten games closed down whenever police or government officials came into the premises, it was difficult to achieve such proofs.

For over a dozen years the court officials allowed the game to be played and not harassed by the law. In the mid-1990s, judicial policies allowed a more effective enforcement of the law, and most of the games closed down permanently.

Was golden ten a skill game? When I interviewed one operator in Rotterdam on 20 July 1986, I asked whether indeed a skillful player could "beat the casino." I was assured that one could. Truly, one could use skill and predict where the ball would fall. So I asked what would happen if a player came in and did predict over and over where the ball would fall. The operator paused a bit before replying slowly, "Well, we would have to throw him out." (An option always open to illegal casinos). In truth they never had to do so, because no player could pick a winner by any other force than the force of luck.

Sources: Cabot, Anthony N., William N. Thompson, Andrew Tottenham, and Carl Braunlich, eds. 1999. *International Casino Law.* 3d ed. Reno: Institute for the Study of Gambling, University of Nevada, Reno, 446–451; Miller, Len. 1983. *Gambling Times Guide to Casino Games.* Secaucus, NJ: Lyle Stuart, 65–74; Sifakis, Carl. 1990. *Encyclopedia of Gambling.* New York: Facts on File, 30, 44–45, 252–256; Silberstang, Edwin. 1980. *Playboy's Guide to Casino Gambling.* Chicago: Playboy Press, 245–348; Thompson, William N., and J. Kent Pinney. 1990. "The Mismarketing of Dutch Casinos." *Journal of Gambling Behavior* 6: 205–221.

S

St. Kitts–Nevis

St. Kitts and Nevis are two islands in the North Leeward Islands of the West Indies. Together they constitute one of the smallest countries in the world. Its population of 48,000 occupies 100 square miles of land. The Jack Tar Village Resort in the capital city of Basseterre has its only casino. Other casino licenses may be granted by the Minister of Finance to any bona fide person owning a tourist hotel of over 100 rooms.

Sources: Cabot, Anthony N., William N. Thompson, Andrew Tottenham, and Carl Braunlich, eds. 1999. *International Casino Law.* 3d ed. Reno: Institute for the Study of Gambling, University of Nevada, Reno, 238–239.

St. Martin

St. Martin is an island in the North Leeward Islands of the West Indies. The area is a shared dependency of France and the Netherlands, with the Dutch referring to their holding as Sint Maarten. Along with other tropical amenities the island offers casinos on both national sides. Most of the casino gaming, however, occurs on the Dutch side. Casinos are found in the town of Philipsburg at the Cupecoy Beach Resort, the Holland House Bay Beach Hotel, and the Maho Beach Hotel. The largest casino is at the Mullet Bay Beach Hotel. Renovated in 1984, it offers 9,000 square feet of gaming space. The other casinos each have approximately 5,000 square feet per casino.

During the season the Mullet Bay facility is extremely crowded. Players often have to wait in line in order to get a seat at one of the 26 tables (19 blackjack, 3 craps, 3 roulette, and 1 big six wheel). Additionally, there are 265 slots in the facility, which is patterned after a Las Vegas–style casino. Junket activity to St. Martin's is restricted, as opera-

tors seem not to have the capital necessary to accommodate big high rollers. Limits are too low. Attempts to entice the high rollers with appeals suggesting that they could avoid tax-reporting requirements on the island were not too successful. The majority of gamers remain hotel guests on both sides of the island. Local residents are allowed to gamble but not on a regular basis. The gaming tax is a fixed sum paid to the government annually.

Sources: Cabot, Anthony N., William N. Thompson, Andrew Tottenham, and Carl Braunlich, eds. 1999. *International Casino Law.* 3d ed. Reno: Institute for the Study of Gambling, University of Nevada, Reno, 234–235.

St. Vincent

The independent nation of St. Vincent is in the Windward Islands of the West Indies. It has 120,000 residents on an island of 120 square miles. It offers casino gaming at the Emerald Isle Casino, about 30 miles outside of the capital city of Kingstown.

Sources: Cabot, Anthony N., William N. Thompson, Andrew Tottenham, and Carl Braunlich, eds. 1999. *International Casino Law.* 3d ed. Reno: Institute for the Study of Gambling, University of Nevada, Reno, 234–235.

Saskatchewan Gaming Corporation

The Saskatchewan Gaming Corporation (SGC) was established under the Saskatchewan Gaming Corporation Act of 1994. The corporation consists of seven persons appointed by the lieutenant governor of the province. Three of the persons are nominated by the Federation of Saskatchewan Indian Nations. The SGC operates four casinos.

On 26 January 1996, Saskatchewan opened its first permanent casino—Casino Regina. The

The railroad station was converted into a casino in Regina Saskatchewan.

casino facility is located within the historic Union Station railroad building in downtown Regina. The casino provides 25,000 square feet of gaming space and entertainment space, with 500 slot machines and forty-one table games, a poker room, restaurant, lounge area, and bar.

The province added three additional casinos on lands of First Nations peoples later in 1996. The Gold Eagle Casino opened on 1 March in North Battleford. It has 8,800 square feet for gaming with 159 machines and 14 tables. The Northern Lights Casino opened on 6 March in Prince Albert. It is an 8,000 square-foot-facility with 229 machines and 15 tables. The Painted Hand Casino is in Yorktown. Its 1,500-square-foot facility with 108 slots and 16 tables opened on 14 December. The three First Nations casinos employ 414 persons. They are operated by the Saskatchewan Indian Gaming Authority under an agreement with the provincial government.

Casino Regina has generated many positive economic benefits for the province. A report prepared by the Saskatchewan Tourism Authority and released in January 1997 (the most recent statistics available) found that on an annualized basis, the casino generated C$54.3 million in gross output, with 1,112 full-time and part-time positions and $21.5 million in wages. The impact of the casino has been equivalent to the hosting of two Grey Cup Canadian professional football championship games. The report suggested that the casino attracted 101,000 nonlocal visitors who came to Regina specifically to gamble at the casino. While visiting the casino, each one spent an average of $167. Also non-Saskatchewan visitors spent an average of three nights in Regina and spent $41 each night for lodging (Saskatchewan Tourism Authority 1996).

In all there were 1,426,000 casino visits, with only 37 percent of these coming from Regina residents and another 17 percent from other residents of Saskatchewan. Neighboring provinces of Manitoba and Alberta produced 42 percent of the visitors. Fewer than 2 percent of the visits were by persons from the United States or overseas (Saskatchewan Tourism Authority 1996).

When the casino was planned an agreement was negotiated with the province's charity casinos to allow them to have slot machines. The Regina charity casino had been operating at the Exposition Park. It was first known as Buffalo Buck's and later as the Silver Sage. It agreed to have machines and give 37 percent of the revenue from the machines to Casino Regina and the Saskatchewan Gaming Corporation. In 1997 the Regina charity casino agreed to close its doors in exchange for a share of the profits of Casino Regina. Also, when Casino Regina opened its doors, the SGC made an agreement with Holland Casinos, a Netherlands government corporation, for that entity to train the staff and oversee the opening of operations. Holland Casinos received part of the casino revenues as well as a fixed fee for its services.

Sources: Cabot, Anthony N., William N. Thompson, Andrew Tottenham, and Carl Braunlich, eds. 1999. *International Casino Law.* 3d ed. Reno: Institute for the Study of Gambling, University of Nevada, Reno, 208–215; Saskatchewan Tourism Authority [STA]. 1996. *Report on Casino Gambling.* Regina: STA.

Sawyer, Grant

Grant Sawyer came to the governorship of the state of Nevada somewhat accidentally, but once in office he set about his job with defined purpose. During his eight years in office, Sawyer directed the restructuring of gambling regulation in the state, defended the sovereignty of the state against an abusive federal Justice Department, championed integration of gambling casinos, and championed civil liberties for Nevada citizens.

On 14 December 1918, Grant Sawyer was born in Twin Falls, Idaho. His parents were doctors, but they were divorced when he was very young. He remained with his mother and a stepfather in Idaho. The home was staunchly Baptist, and young Grant was encouraged to go to Linfield College in Oregon. At the Baptist college he gained a love for history and political science. He felt that the social rules imposed by the school were too much for his tastes, however, so he moved to Nevada where he could be near his father (who had moved to Fallon) and attend the University of Nevada campus at Reno. In Reno he became plugged into Nevada politics. After graduation he won the sponsorship of U.S. senator Pat McCarran and went to Washington, D.C., with a job in the U.S. Capitol. He also attained a spot in the student body at the George Washington University Law School. His stint in law school was interrupted by World War II service in the Pacific. He finished legal studies at Georgetown Law School and then returned to Nevada and politics.

Although he was certainly expected to be a McCarran loyalist, McCarran's very conservative politics did not suit Sawyer—just as a Baptist college that banned dancing had not suited him. McCarran was allied with Senator Joseph McCarthy in his Communist witch hunts, and Sawyer simply disagreed with those politics. But national policy was not that important to his first political jobs. He moved to Elko, Nevada, where political opportunities were open. He became active in the Democratic party and was elected to the post of district attorney. In 1956 he sought a post on the University of Nevada Board of Regents. Although he was not successful in the election, he received an appointment when the size of the board was increased. In 1958 he decided to seek statewide office. His father urged him to seek the attorney general post, as the position was being vacated by the incumbent so that he could run for governor. That man was the very conservative Harvey Dickerson, a protégé of the late senator McCarran. On an impulse, however, Sawyer filed to be a candidate for governor. His political sense was right. The Democratic party in the state had turned away from McCarran conservatism, and Sawyer was a much more dynamic candidate than Dickerson could hope to be. Sawyer won the primary and then faced the very popular Republican governor Charles Russell. Russell was finishing his second term in office, however, and Nevada had never elected a governor to serve three terms. Besides, 1958 was a good year for Democrats everywhere. Sawyer was elected governor by a small margin.

Sawyer immediately put together a legislative package for reforms in gambling. His bill called for the creation of a Nevada Gaming Commission to replace the state taxation commission as the "supreme" gaming regulatory agency. The Gaming Control Board would then report to the commission. Members of both the commission and the board had to be nonpartisan and not involved in any politics. The legislation passed. At Sawyer's direction the commission created a black book, officially called the Book of Excluded Persons. Sawyer was very aware of the work of the McClellan Senate Committee and its attacks on racketeering in gambling. He knew that federal officials were looking at Nevada, and he wanted to make sure that the federal government knew that state officials did not want organized crime interests to play an active role in casino gambling. The black book included a list of notorious persons who would not be allowed to set foot in any casino property in the state.

Sawyer was a strong supporter of Sen. Jack Kennedy in the nomination campaign and in the presidential election of 1960. He was excited to see Kennedy inaugurated and was happy to see Robert (Bobby) Kennedy selected as attorney general. Sawyer had reason to believe that they understood Nevada and that they would support his efforts to keep the state's gambling industry clean. It was not very long, however, before Robert Kennedy put Nevada in his sights and aimed to destroy gambling. Robert Kennedy revealed to the state attorney general a plan to deputize all fifty-six assistant attorneys general in Nevada as federal assistant attorneys general. Then Kennedy was going to conduct a simultaneous raid on the cages of all the casinos in the state. Sawyer's civil liberties inclinations enraged him, and he was on the next plane to Washington, D.C., as soon as the Nevada attorney general reported the plan to him. There Sawyer confronted a Bobby Kennedy at his office in socks and a tennis sweater. He found Bobby to be condescending and extremely arrogant. There was no resolution of anything, and Grant Sawyer simply went to the White House and demanded an audience with the president. The president listened seriously, promised nothing, but Sawyer felt he had made his point. In a symbolic gesture one Nevada assistant attorney general was deputized by Bobby Kennedy, and there was no raid.

Sawyer did not contend that all was well with Nevada gambling. He knew that the commission and the board would have to be tough. He backed them to the hilt when they disciplined casinos for improper activities. He supported them when they revoked Frank Sinatra's casino license because he had hosted a member of the black book at his casino and then refused to cooperate with the board when he was called to appear to be disciplined.

Nevada was selectively segregated all through its early casino era. Sawyer recognized that this was wrong, bad for business, and certainly adverse to the interests of the gambling industry in Washington, D.C. In 1963 he supported civil rights leaders in their effort to integrate the casinos. He brokered the deal that precluded a march on the casinos by African American activists, in return for the immediate opening of all casino resort facilities to persons of all races without discrimination. When it appeared that there might be race riots in Las Vegas two years later, Sawyer personally drove into the west-side neighborhoods of Las Vegas and met the residents one on one. The residents knew where he stood on civil rights matters, and they supported him in keeping the community peaceful during a troubled time.

Sawyer was also instrumental in beginning the interstate cooperation with California that led to growth limits and environmental protection policies for the Lake Tahoe Basin.

During Sawyer's second four-year term in office, the state had a popular new lieutenant governor named Paul Laxalt. When Sawyer sought a third term in 1966, he had several disadvantages: He was running against Laxalt, and he had made important enemies due to tough policies on civil rights, gambling, and other issues. Ironically, his opposition to Bobby Kennedy spilled over into opposition to J. Edgar Hoover and the Federal Bureau of Investigation's attempt to tap telephone lines in the casinos searching for evidence of organized crime involvement. After Sawyer condemned the actions, Hoover let key people in the state know that Sawyer was being soft on criminals. Laxalt won a close victory.

Sawyer retired from public office. He founded the world's largest law firm specializing in gambling law—Lionel, Sawyer, and Collins—in Las Vegas. He also became the chair of the Nevada chapter of the American Civil Liberties Union. Sawyer died in Las Vegas on 24 February 1996.

Sources: Hopkins, A. D., and K. J. Evans. 1999. *The First 100: Portraits of the Men and Women Who Shaped Las Vegas.* Las Vegas: Huntington Press, 148–150; King, R.

T., ed. 1993. *Hang Tough! Grant Sawyer, An Activist in the Governor's Mansion.* Reno: University of Nevada Oral History Program.

Senate Special Committee to Investigate Organized Crime in Interstate Commerce. *See* The Kefauver Committee

Sex and Gambling in Nevada

Public opinion changes on a daily basis in the United States. Perception can slowly shift until practices that were once illegal, or at least taboo, become acceptable and even commonplace. This trend can be illustrated by the recent nationwide explosion of gaming and sexually oriented businesses. Like gambling, a formerly marginal activity now epitomized by glamorous and family-oriented resort casinos, segments of the sex industry have transformed themselves from seedy operations operating without license to socially acceptable and upscale operations that cater to members of both sexes. Nowhere is this transition more evident than in Las Vegas, where the nexus between the casino gamer and the "new" sex industry has replaced the nexus between the miner or military recruit and prostitution of the late 1800s.

Brothels operated openly throughout Nevada from its earliest existence. In 1881 county commissioners were given the authority to regulate and tax or prohibit brothels, and 1907 city councils were given the same authority. In 1971, the state legislature banned prostitution in any county with a population of 200,000 or more. At the time, this law applied only to Clark County, where Las Vegas is located. Actually most of the brothels had been effectively closed because of military orders first issued in 1942 from nearby Nellis Air Force Base declaring the brothels off-limits.

Historical records suggest that the law banning prostitution in Clark County was the result of two major influences. First was the potential involvement in the Las Vegas area of Joe Conforte, the notorious owner of Nevada's largest brothel, who was opposed by the Las Vegas area gaming community. Second was the belief that maintaining a "good image" was essential for gambling and the exploding convention and tourism industries. In effect, prostitution had to give way as a perceived threat to dominant business interests.

The sex industry is openly advertised on Las Vegas taxicabs.

Several, but not all, small counties throughout the state continued to allow prostitution. The economic realities of sparse tax revenues and the notion that prostitution depressurizes things—that is, takes the pressure off of wives and daughters in rural communities—helped maintain a status quo that accepted brothels in rural Nevada. In larger communities, Nevada's brothels were simply not as powerful as the industry's gaming community. Any conflict of interest between another Nevada industry and gaming would invariably be resolved in favor of gaming.

Legal prostitution has not grown much in the last thirty years. For example, there were thirty-three brothels open in Nevada in 1971. Today there are thirty-six brothel licenses, although three are only open part time. Most of the brothels are relatively small, and there are only a few hundred licensed prostitutes within the whole state.

When most people think about the sex industry, they usually think about prostitutes and perhaps individuals involved in the adult entertainment or pornography businesses. The scope of the sex industry is much broader, however, than a stereotypical prostitute.

The adult entertainment segment of the sex industry is nationally an $8-billion institution that is becoming a significant part of popular U.S. culture. Like gambling, the adult entertainment industry has changed dramatically over the last three decades. Technological advances such as cable television, videocassettes, and DVDs have allowed individuals access to a wide variety of adult entertainment in the privacy of their homes. Expenditures on adult entertainment are larger than those on Hollywood movies and larger than the revenues for recorded popular music. "Strip clubs" in the United States have seen even greater growth. The number of female exotic dancers grew from fewer than 15,000 in 1980 to more than 300,000 in 2000. It is apparent that the industry's growth is linked to a changing popular culture that tolerates, if not embraces, traditional vices such as gambling and divergent sexual activities. There is no doubt that sex is being used throughout the United States to sell many consumer items and to promote television ratings.

Sex also sells in Las Vegas. Topless reviews are still common at major strip casinos, but more eco-nomically significant are "gentleman's clubs" and high-priced outcall and escort services. Las Vegas has maintained its reputation as Sin City. This reputation is based, in part, on a belief that the community has a diverse and extensive sex industry. There is no doubt that the Las Vegas sex industry substantially contributes to the local economy. There are approximately 1,500 to 2,000 illegal prostitutes and between 2,000 and 2,200 active exotic dancers who work and live in the metropolitan area. These numbers often swell on key convention and prize-fight weekends to nearly 3,000 illegal prostitutes and nearly 3,500 exotic dancers.

Prostitution did not disappear from Las Vegas (when it was legislatively banned) in 1971. Illegal prostitution still flourishes despite efforts by local police departments to keep it under control, particularly in the Las Vegas Strip area. The county has implemented an "order out" ordinance that strongly discourages prostitutes from working in or near the Strip casinos. This ordinance has forced low- to medium-level prostitutes who had traditionally worked the Strip's bars and streets into walking high crime areas elsewhere.

It is estimated that street prostitutes in Las Vegas each make between $25,000 and $60,000 per year. Outcall entertainers average between $65,000 and $100,000 per year, depending upon skill and work schedule. (The local Sprint *July 2000 Yellow Pages* carries 104 pages of "entertainers." Only lawyers have more pages in the book—138). Most outcall entertainers work up to four evenings per week. Most do not stay in the business for more than three years. High-priced prostitutes average between $100 and $500 per client interaction. Private referral escorts cost between $500 and $10,000 per day depending upon the individual entertainer and client. The casinos often arrange the services of these women. There is evidence of one woman who was paid in excess of $250,000 for one weekend's work by a high roller at a major casino.

The largest segment of the sex industry in Las Vegas is the gentlemen's clubs that employ exotic dancers, commonly known as strippers. The number of gentlemen's clubs in the United States roughly doubled between 1987 and 1992. There are now nearly 3,000 clubs in the United States

Brothels are a part of the history of Nevada.

employing between 250,000 and 300,000 women. The Las Vegas area has over 30 gentlemen's clubs. Their annual revenues range from $500,000 to more than $10,000,000. These clubs span the gamut from old run-down operations to up-scale full-service operations that include food and gambling.

The growth of the local clubs has been fueled by four major developments. First is the rapid growth of convention business. This growth has created a substantive increase in the visitation of professional males aged twenty-five to fifty-four. Second has been the substantial investments made by local operators to upgrade their establishments in line with other major cities throughout the nation. Only in the last decade did the major operators make facility investments and physical changes to reflect the national trends in upscale clubs. Third, there has been a growing acceptance of upscale gentlemen's clubs by a larger segment of the nation's business community. Last, the relationship between the casinos and the clubs has improved, and a codependence has developed to form a variation of the network prostitution system of the pre-1980s. This relationship recognizes that these clubs provide an entertainment venue that is sought after by many of the casinos' key customers. The clubs provide a safe outlet for many of these important casino customers. For legal prostitution, casino customers can easily take the one-hour cab ride to visit a Pahrump brothel (outside of Clark County). Nevertheless, many casino customers believe they can procure sex at local gentlemen's clubs. As such, casino hosts have developed relationships with individual gentlemen's club managers to enable them to provide their customers with the services desired.

The upper tier of Las Vegas–area gentlemen's clubs independently contract with women for their services. The dancers pay to dance at the local establishments. The fees vary significantly depending on the club's policies and the time of day and the day of the week. Weekend nights (8:00 P.M. to 4:00 A.M.) are generally the most expensive times for dancers to work. Additionally, high-traffic conventions such as COMDEX (a computer dealers' exposition) increase the rates that clubs charge dancers. The typical dancer is paid between $35 and $75 per night plus tips and fees to work, but at top clubs a good dancer will make between $300 and $1,200. The number of dancers increases by over 40 percent on most weekends in

Las Vegas. The majority of this weekend increase in dancers is a result of out-of-state dancers who work only the weekends. The traditional economic concept of supply and demand is clearly at work in the Las Vegas community. These services exist to satisfy the demand.

The major difference between the prostitution network today and that of 1981 is that the managers of the gentlemen's clubs have replaced the prostitutes in the network. Additionally, these establishments have substantially more power than in the past. This is not to suggest that all exotic dancers are prostitutes. Yet, like gambling, the gentlemen's club is about an illusion of winning. Sure, sometimes gamblers win, but mostly they lose. The dancers understand this illusion concept as well. Some dancers will perform a sex act for money, but others will not.

The casinos recognize that it is in their interest to have high-class prostitutes and escorts available—inconspicuously—for their customers. Publicly, casinos denounce the evils of prostitution; privately, they recognize its importance to their customer base and support its continued existence. Nevada's economy was built upon the legalization of activities that were considered vices by the rest of the United States. As the nation becomes more like Las Vegas, Las Vegas becomes more like the nation, and what once were vices are now only minor variances on the norm.

—*written by Robert Schmidt*

Sources: Frey, James, Loren Reichert, and Kenneth Russell. 1981. "*Prostitution, Business, and Police: The Maintenance of an Illegal Economy.*" Paper presented to the Pacific Sociological Association, July 10 1981, Portland, Oregon, 239–249; Schlosser, Eric. 1997. "The Business of Pornography: Who's Making the Money?" *U.S. News and World Report* 22 (10 February): 42–50; Schmidt, Robert. Forthcoming. *Illusions of Sex: Lap Dancing in Las Vegas.*

Sic Bo. *See* Craps and Other Dice Games

Siegel, Benjamin

It has been said that it is an ill wind that blows no good. When I heard of such an occasion on a visit to Puerto Rico, it reminded me of a similar situation in Las Vegas. I visited Puerto Rico a year or so after a tragic fire had killed scores of patrons at the Du Pont Plaza Hotel and Casino on New Year's Eve 1986. I asked a manager of another hotel about the effects of the disaster on casino business in San Juan, expecting to hear that revenues had gone down. To my surprise, he said, "I can't say this too

Benjamin "Bugsy" Siegel. (UNLV Special Collections)

loudly, but you know, that fire really helped our business." I was somewhat stunned, but he added, "Before the disaster nobody knew that Puerto Rico had casinos; now the story about one of our casinos was on the front page of every newspaper in the world." I was reminded that years before that tragedy in Puerto Rico, Las Vegas had been just a cowboy town with a few casino joints, hardly in the minds of anyone far away. Then on 20 June 1947 a bullet rushed through the handsome head of Benjamin Siegel, a mobster who had orchestrated the construction and the opening of the most glamorous casino of the day. The next day his murder was headline material for newspapers everywhere. Part of the story focused upon the property he had developed and the many glamorous people—mainly movie stars—who frequented his Flamingo Hotel Casino resort. Las Vegas was on the map!

In death, Benjamin Siegel, also known as "Bugsy" (although no one dared to call him that), became an indelible part of the history of Las Vegas, credited in large part for developing the Las Vegas Strip. The reality diverges somewhat from the myth. Siegel did not start the Strip, he did not own the Flamingo, and his role as the manager-builder of the property was secondary to his image as a handsome but nonetheless ruthless mobster who controlled rackets on the West Coast mainly through intimidation. But his death certainly was a bit of marketing genius for Las Vegas, although it can be certain that city promoters were not responsible for pulling the trigger on the Army carbine that did the trick.

Benjamin Siegel was born in 1905 in Brooklyn. As a youngster he became a friend of Meyer Lansky, and the two drifted into rackets, including bootlegging and illegal gambling. The engendered fear that Siegel cast upon others as he walked through his shortened life was a product of the fact that the "Bugsy and Meyer" gang gained a reputation for doing contract work for other organized crime interests. But all need not have feared. As Siegel told builder Del Webb, who was constructing the Flamingo, "We only kill each other." Lansky and the other New York Mob leaders chose Siegel to be the chief of their West Coast operations, specifically the wire services that carried information on horse and dog races. In California, Siegel befriended the Hollywood movie crowd, and himself became somewhat of a celebrity. He pushed himself into most local rackets. He took a piece of the action from gambling boats operating off the Pacific shore, he controlled action at dog tracks, and he had a piece of the Agua Caliente track and casino in Tijuana. Siegel also bought into several Las Vegas casinos, including the Golden Nugget and Frontier.

In 1945, Meyer Lansky and Siegel drove to Las Vegas together to check on their interests there—the casinos and the wire services—and they discussed the notion of having a new resort that could attract a real tourist crowd as opposed to the existing "sawdust" joints that throve on local and drive-in trade. They found the Flamingo. It had been the dream of Billy Wilkerson, an owner of a nightclub in Hollywood. Wilkerson shared lots of friends with Lansky and Siegel, but he did not have access to their money. His dream was stymied by a lack of financial resources. Siegel and Lansky saw an opportunity, and they took over the project. The organized crime elements in New York and Chicago invested $1.5 million into the venture. Siegel was given the task of getting it done and opening the doors.

Siegel, like Wilkerson, had financial problems with the property. World War II was ending, and materials were scarce. He paid Del Webb's construction firm top dollar for overtime to rush the construction schedule. Many suppliers found that Siegel did not have a business sense that allowed him to keep track of inventories, and they effectively cheated him out of many dollars worth of goods. Cost overruns followed cost overruns. At the same time, Siegel was carrying on a relationship with Hollywood actress Virginia Hill. That tempestuous affair caused him to neglect work duties as well. As the mobsters back East were being hit for more and more money for construction, they became suspicious that Siegel himself was stealing from the project. They became convinced when Virginia Hill started making trips to Europe and visited Swiss banks. By the end of the project, the price tag had risen from $1 million to $6 million, and the conversations about changing management via assassination had arisen.

The Flamingo Casino on the Las Vegas Strip started by Bugsy Siegel in 1946 is now a corporate monster with over 4,000 rooms.

Siegel was allowed to survive to open the property, and he did so on 26 December 1946. The opening was another financial disaster, however. The hotel's rooms were not finished, so guests stayed elsewhere. Bad weather precluded many celebrities from flying in from Los Angeles for the opening. And the players had a run of luck beating the house. To stop the financial hemorrhaging, Siegel closed the Flamingo. He reopened it in March 1947 when the rooms were done and the weather was better. His luck was better, too, and soon the Flamingo was turning a profit. Unfortunately, it was not soon enough for Siegel. His mobster partners had entered the contract for his life. Virginia Hill was in Europe in June, but Bugsy decided that a trip to her apartment in Beverly Hills would beat staying in the Las Vegas heat. He was sitting in her living room reading the *Los Angeles Times* when three bullets flew into the window and changed the mythology and probably also the history of Las Vegas. The identity of the killer was never discovered.

Sources: Hopkins, A. D., and K. J. Evans. 1999. *The First 100: Portraits of the Men and Women Who Shaped Las Vegas.* Las Vegas: Huntington Press, 108–110; Sifakis, Carl. 1990. *Encyclopedia of Gambling.* New York: Facts

on File, 118; Smith, John L. 1997. "The Ghost of Ben Siegel." In *The Players: The Men Who Made Las Vegas,* edited by Jack Sheehan, 81–91. Reno: University of Nevada Press.

Slot Machines and Machine Gambling
A Personal Story

Let me tell you about my introduction to slot machines, an introduction that taught me about beginner's luck. That is what I had the first time I went to a casino in Las Vegas. I was on my job interview at the University of Nevada, Las Vegas, in 1980. The department chairman recruiting me suggested that we go to the Hilton. There I saw bank after bank of slot machines and tables. I indicated a hesitation to play the table games, as I did not know the rules, and they seemed somewhat complicated. Moreover, the games moved very fast, and the players at the tables really looked as if they knew what they were doing. Like other slot machine players, I felt "intimidated" by the table play. So we found some empty machines. I thought I would just have to put in the coins, so I "bought" ten dollars worth of quarters. The machine asked me a question, however: Did I want to play one, two, or three coins? I had to think about that for a while (something a player cannot do when he sits down at a table—take a little time to think things over). The machine indicated that with one coin I could win only with cherries; with two, I could win with cherries and other fruit and bells; with three coins, I could win any time the machine showed a winning combination—cherries, fruit, bells, and the jackpot bars. Well, we were educated, smart people (we both had Ph.D.s, and those are not easy to come by). So we figured the jackpot ($100) was just a bit too much to hope for, too much of a "long shot." I would play two coins. I played the two coins the first time and lost. I played two coins again, the reels spun, and what do you know, one, two, then three bars—jackpot! Bells and whistles, lights, the $100 jackpot sign flashed. The trouble was that no money flowed from the machine. I had not won the jackpot that the machines so proudly proclaimed for the world to see, because I had only put two coins into the machines. That was bad enough, but soon other people around me were telling me, "Why, you didn't win because you have to put three coins in for a jackpot." I was quite aware of what had happened (Ph.D.s have some intelligence). Then someone else would tell me the same thing. I also heard side comments about that "stupid tourist" who does not know you always put in the maximum number of coins. I had most of my roll of quarters left, so I played on, but with very little enthusiasm. When the coins were gone, I left as quietly as I could.

Beginner's luck? Some might not think so. I certainly did not feel "lucky" at the moment. After I began to study gambling, however, I became quite convinced that that is precisely what I had experienced—beginner's luck.

Just think, within five minutes of my first exposure to slot machines, I had learned that machines were not easy things that could be played without some thought. Indeed, since 1980 the slots have increased in variety and in complexity. I learned that the gambling devices were smarter than I was and that that might have something to do with the fact that they seemed to be taking over the casinos and winning so much money from the players. I also learned the best lesson any new resident of Las

Vegas can ever learn—that the player has to be a loser, or to put it in personal terms, this player (I) was a loser. The lesson has not stopped me from gambling, but it sure has slowed me down. Imagine my potential gambling history had I won $100 after playing one dollar and fifty cents. I shudder to think about it. I have to live in Las Vegas, a city with nearly 200,000 slot machines, and they are everywhere—on the Strip, in locals' casinos, in bars and taverns, restaurants, car washes, liquor stores, convenience stores, drug stores, and supermarkets.

The Value of the Machines

Slot machines are very attractive. They are the devices that usually get amateurs started gambling. They move very fast and they can be quite "captivating." This can be quite all right if the gambling is responsible. Certainly, machines add a lot to the entertainment value of many lives. They also shift revenues to employees, as well as to government coffers. Individual slot machines make considerable sums of money for their owners, ranging from about $50 a day ($18,000 plus a year) to over ten times that much ($200,000 plus a year) *each*, depending on where they are found. Yet each machine usually represents an investment of less than $3,000 or $4,000 a year. A machine and related equipment cost from $5,000 to $10,000, and labor and energy costs to operate the machine are minimal, perhaps an equal amount of dollars (supervisors can watch ten to twenty machines, and a service person can handle 100 machines). These are lifetime costs. The costs can then be divided by a three- to five-year annual cycle. For example, the typical Las Vegas casino machine might cost the operator $4,000 a year to maintain (including all overhead), whereas it produces $35,000 in revenue—that is, it takes $35,000 a year away from the players (even the "smart" ones who know they should put in the maximum three coins each time they play).

In the early days of Las Vegas casinos (the 1930s into the 1970s), slot machines were an extra among the gambling products. The really serious gambling was at the tables, and the machines produced only a small part of the house revenues. Casino owners would say such things as, "They

These Wheel of fortune slot machines play the theme of the television show when a player wins.

pay the electric bills," or in a sexist phrase, "They keep the women busy while their men are doing the real gambling at the tables." Now this casual attitude about machines is gone. One discussion of Las Vegas games published in the 1960s told how machines made about 15 percent of the revenues of the big Strip casinos. Now many Nevada casinos, especially those such as Texas Station that serve local residents or casinos appealing to drive-in gamblers from Phoenix or southern California (e.g., those in Laughlin), bring in over 80 percent of their revenues from machines. Over the past two decades, the machines have also become much more generous to the players, often giving respectable returns of over 95 percent—a gamble as good as that offered at many table games. The higher returns are essential for the success of the machines, as the players of machines are now much more sophisticated—in terms of searching for best payout schedules.

The value of slot machines for the casinos is reflected in the fact that almost all the casino properties in any competitive jurisdiction will give free services (complimentaries) to slot machine players, something they did only for table high rollers

in the recent past. Since the mid-1980s, the casinos have instituted "slot clubs," and through magnetic cards they record the amount of play an individual has, then award extra prizes—free meals, free casino stays, free shows, merchandise, and even cash bonuses—based on the player's patronage. In the Harrah's chain of casinos (over twenty properties) there is a single slot club, and players can use their card in any of the casinos to accumulate points for prizes.

If there is a Gresham's law in gambling, it would simply be that slot (and other) machines for gambling will, where permitted, eventually drive out all other forms of gambling. I have studied the intricacies of European casino gambling over the past fifteen years. Country after country seriously deliberated over issues such as whether the casinos could serve drinks on their gambling floors; whether local residents could enter the casinos; whether casinos could advertise and have signage; whether the casinos could cash patron's personal checks. Although public officials oversaw such earthshaking measures in order to properly protect the public from this "sin" industry, the same governments with very little deliberation decided that slot machines could go almost anywhere—in taverns, in children's arcades, in seaside recreation halls. Even though Spanish casinos were being "taxed to death" (they pay a gross win tax averaging over 50 percent), over 500,000 slots filled Spanish restaurants and bars, paying scant taxes. British authorities delayed for years a decision to allow casinos to expand their offerings of two machines to four, while at the same time giving no attention to the fact that gambling halls throughout the urban areas and recreational communities were able to have hundreds of machines. The issue in European gambling is no longer how to apply intricate detailed regulation to casinos, but just how wide open noncasino machine gambling can become. Or in the case of France, the issue is to what extent will machine gambling be allowed to go within casinos that were prohibited from having them until the late 1980s. In several U.S., Canadian, and other Western Hemisphere jurisdictions, lotteries are finding that their best revenues come from slot machines dispersed throughout their territories and called video lottery terminals. In many of these places, horse- and dog-race tracks have turned to machines to boost their revenues and have found that slot machines have become their essential business product. More and more, all over the world, the expansion of gambling has become essentially an expansion of machine gambling.

The era of machine gambling seems to have arrived with the twenty-first century, but the ride of machine gambling from the latest years of the nineteenth century has been an uneven and rocky journey.

The History of Slot Machines

The notion of using a machine for gambling bounced around in many inventors' heads during the last decade of the nineteenth century. It was the era of inventions, after all. Gambling contraptions of one sort or another proliferated around San Francisco. There, in 1893, Gustav Frederick Wilhelm Schultze registered a patent for a wheel machine. This gave the inspiration for Charles August Fey to make a machine with spinning reels. Three years later he put together his final version of a machine that bears a resemblance to today's machine. Fey called his machine the Lib-

erty Bell. It had three reels with bells, hearts, diamonds, spades, and horseshoes. Three bells paid off ten-for-one in drinks. Schultze challenged Fey's and others' rights to make machines, but he was unsuccessful in having his patent stand up in court, as the validity of gambling machines was questionable.

Fey did not seek to win a patent for his machine. Instead, he sought to guard it by maintaining ownership over each unit he produced. He arranged to place the machines in establishments around San Francisco and other nearby areas with an arrangement that he would take 50 percent of the revenues from the machine and let the owner of the premises have 50 percent. The process was effective for several years, but according to Fey's grandson, Marshall Fey, in 1905 someone from the Mill's Novelty Company of Chicago secured a machine through unauthorized means and used it as a model for their own machine (Fey 1983). Soon the Mill's company was making a wide line of machines. In 1906 it developed the first machine that stood upright on its own and did not have to be placed on a stand. This machine, "the Kalamazoo," and all others came under the scrutiny of legal enforcement against gambling.

Back in San Francisco, the police chief arrested several premise owners. One was fined but appealed. He won the appeal in the Superior Court, which ruled that the machine games were not lotteries. Police actions were also frustrated by defense allegations that enforcement was hypocritical in that California permitted poker card clubs. Nonetheless, the machine makers were wary of legal crackdowns, and they made several adjustments to try to defend their products. Some adjustments and subterfuges used by the manufacturers over the early days of machines included the following (many of these ruses are still attempted in various places):

1. Machines indicated that prizes were paid off as cigars or drinks or other merchandise rather than cash.
2. Signs on machines indicated that the machines were *not* gambling machines.
3. The machines played music as the coins entered them, and they had signs saying

that any coins coming out had to be reinserted to play more music.

4. Buttons were placed on the machines, and reels could be stopped from spinning when the buttons were pushed. In this way a skillful player could always win, hence the element of chance was removed and the machines were not gambling machines.

5. The machines portrayed game symbols from games that were legal. For instance, they used poker hands in California.

6. One of most ingenuous attempts at seeking to avoid the tag of being a "gambling" machine came early, as machines were developed that would tell the player *exactly* what they would win when they put the next coin in. There was no chance. Of course, what the player was seeking was a chance to play in order to find out what would come after that. Courts wrestled with definitions of gambling on these kinds of machines for many decades.

7. Machines also were configured so that a player would actually get a piece of gum or some other novelty prize with each play, under the ruse that they were buying merchandise from the machine.

Through the twentieth century, cat-and-mouse games were played among machine owners, operators, police, and the courts. But these games were often quite secondary to the fact that machines were illegal and yet were operating. Public acceptance along with patterns of public bribery and lax law enforcement allowed the machines to proliferate in most locales of the United States. During the years of national prohibition of alcoholic beverages, mobsters gained control over the placement of many machines, and accordingly, the machines became associated with organized crime in the minds of many law enforcement people. As gambling became legalized in many forms, such an association caused policymakers to leave machines out of the mix of legalized gambling products. Even down to the current day, the biggest battles over the scope of Native American gambling permitted under the Indian Gaming Regulatory Act of 1988 has focused upon whether a state has to allow a tribe to have slot machines (or other gambling machines).

Over the years since Fey's first Liberty Bell, down to the 1980s, the machines did not change much in basic appearance. Although their facades contained many variations, they all had the spinning reels. Growth in the numbers of machines was constant into mid-century. In 1931, a new company in Chicago developed the Ballyhoo pin ball machine. Bally's placed over 50,000 of such "skill" machines in bars and restaurants during their first year of operation. The machines allowed players to win more games but not money. In fact, winners could be paid for the number of games they won. Bally's concentrated on these "novelty" machines as its corporate strength grew.

In 1951 the federal government passed the Johnson Act in an attempt to stop illegal gambling machines. The law exempted machines from prosecution if they were in legal jurisdictions, and as a result, many operators moved their businesses to Nevada. The law also caused Bally's to lobby Illinois for permission to make machines. In 1963 Illinois repealed the state prohibition on manufacturing machines. At this time the Mill's company and two others (including Jennings, a spin-off from Mill's), dominated the gambling machine business. This was soon to change, as Bally's entered the field with a new knowledge base about recreational machines and their players. Within twenty years Bally's took over three-quarters of the machine business in the United States.

The Era of Bally's, IGT, and Their Competitors

Bally's was the worldwide innovator. It moved machines from being mere mechanical devices activated by pulling a handle to being electromechanical devices. The handle pull was now just an alternative way to push a button to make the machine run. Bally's first machine was the Money Honey, which contained a much larger capacity to store coins, making bigger payoffs more possible. In 1964, Bally's developed a progressive machine, which permitted a jackpot amount to grow each time the player made a losing play. The possibility of winning thousands of dollars on machine play was opened up. Also, the machines could accumulate jackpots large enough that the expected payoff return for a player could become positive (over 100 percent). Soon the company made multipliers, that is, machines that accepted up to five coins; with each additional coin put in, the prizes would multiply. Bally's added reels to some models. In 1968 it marketed a machine that had three play lines on it. In the late 1970s it developed low-boy machines that had flat horizontal playing surfaces, over which the player could lean. Eventually, this style of machine was adjusted to be operational on a bar surface. Bally's also developed the popular Big Bertha, an extremely large machine (six to eight feet across) that would dominate a casino floor, drawing attention to slot machine play. In 1980 Bally's engineered another breakthrough. It linked machines together so that several could offer one very big progressive jackpot. The Hilton casinos of Las Vegas used these networks of machines to offer million-dollar guaranteed Pot of Gold jackpots.

The 1980s were not kind to Bally's. It entered the casino business as an owner of an Atlantic City casino and then several casinos in Nevada. Other casinos became somewhat reluctant to buy Bally's products and thereby display the name of a competitor of their gambling floors. But more importantly, the computer age had descended, and Bally's was hesitant to make the leap. One of Bally's sales executives, Si Redd, worked on the development of a video gambling device with a cathode-ray tube. Poker could be played on his device. He wanted Bally's to market the machine and give him the appropriate credit. Bally's higher executives, however, did not want to stray from their "winning formula" of the 1960s and 1970s. They struck a deal: Si Redd would leave the company and promise not to make any machines that would compete with the Bally's models nor to use knowledge he had gained at Bally's. In turn, Redd would be given a five-year exclusive right to develop his poker machine. Redd became instrumental in starting International Gaming Technologies (IGT), which manufactured and sold video poker machines. Five years was all he needed. By the mid-1980s, IGT surpassed Bally's in machine sales, and after IGT won the right to make reel machines as well, it thoroughly dominated the market, with over 75 percent of the sales of machines

in the United States and Canada. IGT now stands as perhaps the largest slot machine company in the world, sharing that world market stage with Aristocrat and Sigma.

The computer technologies and cathode-ray tube video screens have changed the look and operations of machines in many ways. When California authorized a state lottery in 1984, Nevada casinos worried. They could not compete with a multi-million-dollar jackpot; IGT came to the rescue. The company developed Mega-Bucks, a statewide network of machines offering one progressive jackpot. Although the jackpot has never risen to the levels of some lottery jackpots, it has gone over $10 million several times, and it keeps many Nevada regulars from running to the state line to buy California tickets—at least until the California jackpots get really high. The Mega-Bucks network includes upward of 1,000 machines. Within casinos there are many other linked networks of machines.

Modern machines developed by IGT, Sigma, Bally's, Anchor, Mikohn, and other companies have also incorporated other features. One machine has holograms in its displays. One blackjack machine features a three-dimensional dealer who appears to actually deal out cards as he talks to the players, wishing them good luck, congratulating them on wins, consoling them on losses, and urging them to try again. Sigma has simulated a racetrack and horse races. The games have also taken on names of popular nongambling games. Mikohn has a Yatzee machine. Anchor developed a Wheel of Fortune game involving reel play; when a certain winning combination appears, a wheel above the machine spins for the superjackpot as noises from the television *Wheel of Fortune* game are heard. There is also a monopoly game. Several casinos have banks of Elvis machines. Although all the machines offer gambling games, with their variety has come a variety of rules, making the machines much more sophisticated than the ones that just asked the player to pull a handle—or decide how many coins to play and then pull a handle.

Characteristics of Machine Gambling

Machine gambling is essentially a house-banked gambling operation. Certainly the player is wagering against a machine. As many states have lotteries or allow only games such as bingo that are played among players, the states have sought to keep Native American tribes from having slot machines of the type that are found in casinos. For instance, in California, the state spent a decade fighting the tribes, insisting that the tribes had to have only machines that were linked together so that players had to electronically pool their money, from which 95 percent—or some percent—could be awarded as prizes. Only the voters who passed Proposition 1A in March 2000 were able to change the situation, and now by popular approval, the tribes have slot machines. In the state of Washington many tribes agreed to have these pooled arrangements for their machines. Although the state may seek to find some legal technicality that makes pools acceptable and regular slot play unacceptable, the players will have a hard time telling the difference. Moreover, the state is doing a major disservice to the notion that the player should be given an equal chance to make the big win on every play as he is in Las Vegas, rather than having a list of winning prizes that diminishes every time a player takes a win. In Las Vegas and other places with regular slot machines, the machines have random number generators that are activated with each play. The player has the same chance of winning a jackpot, a line of bells, bars, or other prizes with every single pull, and the casinos could conceivably lose on every single pull. It is called gambling, after all.

The reality is, however, that the law of large numbers applies to slot machine play, and the payout rates are very consistent over time. Table 1 shows the rates of returns for each of the casinos in New Jersey, Illinois, Indiana, and Iowa over each month of 1999. Even if the state mandated a specific return, as it does for a lottery or for a bingo game, the returns could not be much more consistent. Note that some states and casinos have better returns than others—actually Las Vegas casinos offer the best returns—consistently over 95 percent. In no way does the different return amount come from any manipulation of the computer randomizer chip in the machines. Quite simply, it comes from the payoff schedule. Two machines can have exactly the same play dimensions, but payout percentage returns to the player can differ greatly simply by setting the win for a certain configuration (say three bells) at 18 rather than 20, or on a poker machine making the wins for flush and full house 5 and 8 instead of 6 and 9. Sophisticated players know the machines, and they can discern the best payout machines by simply looking at the prizes listed on the front of the machines. For obvious reasons, payoffs are better at the higher-denomination machines. A five-cents machine may cost as much to buy as a dollar machine; therefore the casino expects that it needs to hold a higher percentage of the money played on the nickel machines. Actually today all the big casinos have very high denomination machines; indeed, several have machines that take $500 tokens in play—and to win the best prizes on these machines, the player has to play three coins a pull—you would not want to make my mistake on a $500 machine.

Machines have appeal to both the player and the operator. In most cases they can be played alone. The player can study the machine before playing it. It is rare that a player will criticize the way another one plays (I enjoyed one of those rare moments), and with a little study the machine playing is easy to learn. Operators like machines because they do not involve much labor, they are very secure (although cheating has been a historical problem), and they can be left alone to do their job without complaining.

Machine play is the bread and butter for most casinos around the world. Machine gambling offers opportunities pursued by many lotteries and offers the golden hope (or silver bullet) that many feel can save the racing industry. Machines have also crawled into Nevada convenience and grocery stores, and if policymakers allow them, they will be in bars and taverns across the country, all across the globe. It could easily be predicted that machine gambling is the wave of gambling in the future, but now the Internet has come onto the scene, and perhaps it is that machine that will soon be the most lucrative and alluring gambling device.

—The assistance of William Holmes
in providing resources and advice
on this section is appreciated

Table 1 Machine Gaming Revenue 1999 (hold %)

	Jan	Feb	Mar	April	May	June	July	Aug	Sept	Oct	Nov	Dec	Ave	Medn	Std Dev
Illinois															
Alton Belle	5.31	5.43	5.48	5.49	5.39	5.66	5.52	5.43	5.16	5.39	5.39	5.25	5.41	5.41	0.13
Par-A-Dice	6.51	6.60	6.49	6.61	6.54	6.61	6.55	6.31	6.79	6.60	6.44	6.24	6.52	6.55	0.15
Rock Island	7.44	7.24	7.46	6.98	6.81	6.84	6.40	6.68	6.22	6.36	6.25	6.65	6.78	6.75	0.44
Empress Joliet	5.60	5.74	6.01	6.12	5.85	5.84	6.04	5.84	5.90	5.75	5.59	5.59	5.82	5.84	0.18
Harrah's Joliet	5.72	5.99	5.77	5.88	5.83	5.80	5.73	5.86	5.97	5.77	5.94	5.91	5.85	5.85	0.09
Players Metropolis	6.77	6.69	6.70	6.25	6.44	6.34	5.85	5.70	5.95	5.96	6.06	6.00	6.23	6.16	0.36
Hollywood Casino	5.50	5.77	5.77	5.70	5.94	5.85	5.89	5.69	5.94	5.86	5.79	5.90	5.80	5.82	0.13
Casino Queen	4.98	4.89	5.01	4.82	4.85	4.82	5.29	5.08	5.19	5.11	5.04	5.03	5.01	5.02	0.15
Grand Victoria	5.22	5.30	5.42	5.46	5.18	5.26	5.29	5.26	5.17	5.30	5.46	5.12	5.29	5.28	0.11
*Total ave. for Illinois	5.89	5.96	6.01	5.92	5.87	5.89	5.84	5.76	5.81	5.79	5.77	5.74	5.86	5.85	0.19
Indiana															
Casino Aztar	8.10	8.60	7.90	7.70	8.04	8.38	8.14	8.00	8.59	8.00	8.00	7.99	8.12	8.02	0.27
Empress Hammond	6.74	6.80	6.90	6.80	6.83	6.80	6.92	6.70	6.74	6.96	6.96	7.13	6.86	6.82	0.12
Grand Victoria	6.01	6.30	6.60	6.20	6.49	6.30	6.58	6.20	6.21	6.46	6.46	6.55	6.36	6.38	0.19
Majestic Star	7.07	7.30	7.00	7.00	6.58	7.10	6.71	6.90	6.91	7.12	7.12	7.08	6.99	7.04	0.19
Trump Casino	6.00	6.30	6.20	6.50	6.65	6.60	6.78	6.60	6.82	6.58	6.58	6.36	6.50	6.58	0.24
Argosy Casino	6.21	6.10	6.00	5.90	6.07	6.00	5.97	5.90	6.01	5.71	5.71	5.64	5.94	5.99	0.17
Blue Chip Casino	5.99	6.20	6.30	6.10	6.25	6.20	6.43	6.30	6.12	6.24	6.24	6.11	6.21	6.22	0.12
Caesars	6.32	6.60	6.80	7.00	6.90	6.60	7.10	6.90	6.96	6.97	5.97	6.79	6.74	6.85	0.33
Harrah's	6.37	6.60	6.70	6.10	6.40	7.00	6.95	6.90	6.83	6.97	5.97	6.70	6.62	6.70	0.35
*Total ave. for Indiana	6.53	6.76	6.71	6.59	6.69	6.78	6.84	6.71	6.80	6.78	6.56	6.71	6.70	6.73	0.22
Iowa															
Ameristar Casino	5.33	5.69	5.60	5.87	5.90	6.12	6.43	6.45	6.10	5.90	5.85	5.79	5.92	5.89	0.32
Catfish Bend	7.68	7.67	7.60	7.53	7.68	7.84	8.06	7.63	7.62	7.37	7.95	6.78	7.62	7.65	0.32
Dubuque Diamond Jo	6.40	6.72	6.40	6.64	6.10	6.24	6.25	6.47	6.25	6.03	6.11	6.41	6.34	6.33	0.21
Harvey's Iowa	5.86	5.80	5.74	5.84	5.72	5.88	5.99	5.61	5.76	5.86	5.84	5.98	5.82	5.84	0.11
Lady Luck Casino	6.11	6.31	6.23	6.21	5.95	6.19	6.21	6.19	6.25	6.17	6.26	6.06	6.18	6.20	0.10
Miss Marquette	6.32	6.84	6.89	6.64	5.74	5.86	6.59	6.35	6.76	6.53	6.53	6.41	6.46	6.53	0.36

(continues)

Table 1 *(continued)*

	Jan	Feb	Mar	April	May	June	July	Aug	Sept	Oct	Nov	Dec	Ave	Medn	Std Dev
Mississippi Belle 2	7.03	7.33	7.07	6.76	7.12	6.95	7.21	7.21	7.40	7.01	7.19	7.32	7.13	7.16	0.18
President Casino	6.38	6.60	6.56	6.34	6.46	6.47	6.62	6.17	6.32	6.38	6.51	6.07	6.41	6.42	0.17
Belle of Sioux City	6.83	7.50	7.10	7.27	6.34	6.84	6.94	6.80	6.84	6.78	6.51	6.91	6.89	6.84	0.31
*Total ave. for Iowa	6.44	6.72	6.58	6.57	6.33	6.49	6.70	6.54	6.59	6.45	6.53	6.41	6.53	6.54	0.23
New Jersey															
Hilton	7.60	7.70	8.20	8.10	8.10	8.40	8.40	8.10	8.10	8.70	8.30	8.00	8.14	8.10	0.30
Park Place	8.30	8.50	8.40	8.50	8.20	8.10	8.10	8.00	8.30	8.20	8.10	7.90	8.22	8.20	0.19
Caesars Casino	7.80	8.20	8.00	7.80	8.50	8.40	8.00	8.50	8.30	7.90	7.90	8.80	8.18	8.10	0.33
Claridge Casino	8.70	8.70	9.20	8.50	8.00	9.70	8.00	9.20	9.80	10.00	8.60	8.50	8.91	8.70	0.67
Harrah's Casino	7.40	7.50	7.40	7.90	7.30	7.70	7.50	7.70	7.70	7.60	7.70	7.60	7.58	7.60	0.17
Resorts Casino	9.20	9.40	9.60	10.01	9.70	9.60	9.30	9.30	9.30	9.20	8.90	8.60	9.34	9.30	0.37
Sands Casino	8.00	8.30	8.10	8.40	8.20	7.90	8.20	8.80	7.90	8.00	8.00	7.90	8.14	8.05	0.26
Showboat Casino	9.00	8.90	8.80	8.80	8.90	9.00	9.10	9.30	9.20	9.20	9.10	8.70	9.00	9.00	0.19
Tropicana Casino	7.30	7.60	8.10	8.10	8.00	8.10	8.00	7.90	7.80	7.90	8.00	7.80	7.88	7.95	0.24
Trump Plaza	7.80	8.10	8.10	8.20	8.10	8.00	8.20	8.10	7.90	8.00	7.90	7.70	8.01	8.05	0.16
Taj Mahal Casino	7.90	8.30	8.20	8.30	8.40	8.30	8.10	8.60	8.50	8.20	8.10	8.00	8.24	8.25	0.20
Trump Marina	n/a	8.50	8.30	8.20	7.90	7.90	7.90	8.00	8.00	7.80	8.00	8.00	8.05	8.00	0.21
*Total ave. for New Jersey	8.09	8.31	8.37	8.40	8.28	8.43	8.23	8.46	8.40	8.39	8.22	8.13	8.31	8.28	0.27
Averages four states	6.74	6.94	6.92	6.87	6.79	6.89	6.90	6.87	6.90	6.85	6.77	6.75	6.85	6.85	0.23**

*These are averages of the monthly average for each casino.

**The standard deviation represents 3.35% of the total averages.

Source: Based on information in various issues of *Casino Journal.*

Sources: Fey, Marshall. 1983. *Slot Machines: An Illustrated History of America's Most Popular Coin-Operated Device.* Las Vegas: Nevada Publications; Holmes, William L. 1987. "Effect of Gambling Device Laws: Foreign and United States." Paper presented to the Seventh International Conference on Gambling and Risk Taking, 23 August, Reno, Nevada; Scarne, John. 1986. *Scarne's New Complete Guide to Gambling.* New York: Simon and Schuster, 430–458; Sifakis, Carl. 1990. *Encyclopedia of Gambling.* New York: Facts on File, 276–281.

South Carolina

During the 1990s, South Carolina became the land of gambling loopholes. During the 1970s and 1980s video game machines began to appear in many South Carolina locations. Cash prizes were given to players who accumulated points representing winning scores at the games. No cash was dispensed by the machines; instead, the owners of establishments with the machines paid the players. Although the arrangements seemed on the surface to violate antigambling laws, they survived legal challenges. In 1991 the state supreme court bought into a loophole that the operators offered in their defense. The operators argued that the machines were not gambling machines as long as the prizes were not given out by the machines directly. The court agreed, and so naturally a gaming machine industry began to blossom throughout the state (Thompson 1999).

Operators "seen their opportunity," as the famous turn-of-the-last-century political philosopher George Washington Plunkitt of Tammany Hall would say, "and they took 'em." As the gaming revenues flowed in, the operators formed a very strong political lobby to defend their status quo. The legislature addressed the issue of machine gaming, but it could only offer a set of weak rules that have not been rigorously enforced. Legislation provided that gaming payouts for machine wins were supposed to be capped at $125 a day for each player. Advertising was prohibited. There could be no machines where alcoholic beverages were sold, operators could not offer any incentives to get persons to play the machines, and there could be only five machines per establishment. Machines were also licensed and taxed by the state at a rate of $2,000 per year. (Of the tax, $200 is now given to an out-of-state firm to install a linked information system.)

The rules have not been followed in their totality. Establishments have linked several rooms, each having five machines. As many as 100 machines have appeared under a single roof. Progressive machines offer prizes into the thousands of dollars. Operators claim they pay each player only $125 of the prize each day. In some cases, they award the full amount of the prize and have the player sign a "legal" statement affirming that the player will not spend more than $125 of the prize in a single day. Advertisements of machine gaming appear on large signs by many establishments. Bars and taverns have machines.

There have been thousands of citations against establishments, and fines have been levied. In 1997 and 1998, there were $429,000 in fines in a nine-month period. The practices did not end, however (Palermo 1998, 1, 18).

Several interests in the state did not care for gambling. They persuaded the legislature to authorize a statewide vote on banning the machines. According to the legislation authorizing the elections, votes were to be counted by counties. If a majority of the voters in a county said they did not want the machines, the machines would be removed from that county. In 1996, twelve of forty-six counties said they did not want the machines. Before they could be removed, however, the operators won a ruling from the state supreme court saying that the vote was unconstitutional. The court reasoned that South Carolina criminal law (banning the machines) could not be enforced unequally across the state. Equal protection of the law ruled supreme in the Palmetto State.

Over the last years of the 1990s, the legislature and state regulators continued to wrestle with issues surrounding machine gaming. One effort to have all the machines declared lotteries and banned in accordance with a state constitutional prohibition on lotteries failed, as the supreme court held by a single-vote majority that the gaming on the machines did not constitute lottery gaming. The 1998 gubernatorial election seemed to turn on gambling issues, as supporters of machine gaming and lotteries gave large donations to the winning candidate. The new governor has sought to win wide support by initiating new "more effective" regulations, but these have not yet won consensus support in the legislature. One new proposed regulation would allow machines to have individual prizes of up to $500 that could be won on a single play. Another proposal would set up a new state regulatory mechanism for machine gaming.

In the meantime, machine gaming flourishes. At the beginning of 1999 there were over 31,000 machines in operation. They attracted over $2.1 billion in wagers, and operators paid out prizes of $1.5 billion. Machine owners and operators realized gross gaming profits of $610 million—approximately $20,000 per machine per year. Almost all of the machines were made outside of the state. Over half were Pot o' Gold machines made in Norcross, Georgia. These cost $7,500 each. Most of the operators share revenues with owners of slot machine routes. There has been no mandatory auditing of machine performance, although the state authorized the installation of a slot information system.

In 1999 the voters were authorized by the legislature to decide if the machines should stay or be removed. If the voters did not determine the machines could stay, they had to be taken out. But in a surprise decision, the state supreme court ruled the referendum vote unconstitutional and ordered that the machines be removed by 30 June 2000. In November 2000, the voters removed a constitutional ban on lotteries. A lottery will begin in 2001.
—*coauthored by Frank Quinn*

Sources: Cabot, Anthony N., William N. Thompson, Andrew Tottenham, and Carl Braunlich, ed., 1999. *International Casino Law.* 3d ed. Reno: Institute for the Study of Gambling, University of Nevada, Reno, 137; Palermo, David. 1998. "The Secret Slot Market." *International Gaming and Wagering Business* (December): 1, 18–22; Thompson, William N. 1999. "The South Carolina Battlefield." *Gaming Law Review* 3, no. 1 (February): 5–8; Thompson, William N., and Frank Quinn. 2000. "South Carolina Sage: Death Comes to Video Machine Gambling: An Impact Analysis." Paper presented to National Conference on Problem Gambling, 6 October, Philadelphia, Pennsylvania.

South Dakota

The voters of South Dakota made the state the nation's third commercial casino jurisdiction at the

Convenience-style casinos like this one in South Dakota were opposed in a report of national gambling study.

ballot box in November 1988. The voters in effect amended the state constitution to permit limited stakes gambling, but only in the town of Deadwood. In 1989 the legislature passed an enabling act, and the voters of Deadwood ratified the decision to have casinos in their town. Several casinos opened in November 1989, and there are now over sixty casinos in Deadwood. The ostensible purpose of casino gaming was to generate revenues for tourist promotion and for historical preservation projects in Deadwood. Wild Bill Hickok had been shot in the back while playing poker in Deadwood in 1876, but the town was a decaying relic from that time. The town's main block of buildings had burned in the mid-1980s.

Prior to casino gaming, the state had permitted dog- and horse-race wagering. The state had instituted a lottery in 1987, and in 1989 the lottery had also began operation of video lottery terminals in age-restricted locations. Each location was allowed twenty machines that awarded,

Casinos can be found everywhere in South Dakota.

on average, 80 percent of the money played as prizes given back to the players. In the 1990s, nine Native American casinos compacted with the state to operate facilities. The casinos are located at Sisseton, Hankinson, Watertown, Wagner, Lower Brule, Mobridge, Fort Thompson, Pine Ridge, and Flandreau.

The commercial casinos in Deadwood were originally allowed to have thirty games (machines or tables), but as facilities were built together, the state changed the limitation to ninety games each for a single retail location. In addition to machines, which guaranteed prizes equaling 90 percent of the money played, the only games permitted were blackjack and poker. Bets were limited to five dollars per play. In the poker games the casino could rake-off as much as 10 percent of the money wagered. The casinos pay 8 percent of their winnings to the state in taxes; of this, 40 percent goes to tourist promotions, 10 percent to the local government, and 50 percent to the state for regulatory purposes. If regulatory costs fall below this amount, the remaining money is dedicated to historical preservation projects.

In 1989, the lottery began using video machines located in restaurants and bars around the state. In 2000, antigambling interests made attempts to stop the lottery machines, but according to the *New York Times* of 9 November 2000 (B-10), the voters decided to keep them.

Sources: Cabot, Anthony N., William N. Thompson, Andrew Tottenham, and Carl Braunlich, eds. 1999. *International Casino Law.* 3d ed. Reno: Institute for the Study of Gambling, University of Nevada, Reno, 138–153.

Sports Betting

Sports betting occurs when gamblers make wagers on the results of games and contests played by other persons. The results of the games and contests are completely independent from the wagering activity of the gamblers. In other words, the gamblers have no control over the outcome of the games—that is, as long as the wagering is honest. Whether it is legal or not is another matter.

There are sports betting opportunities with a wide variety of games and contests. Although in a generic sense sports betting includes wagers made on the results of horse races and dog races, these games (contests) are usually considered to be different than other contests. In this encyclopedia,

Sports-betting shop in England.

they are discussed separately, as are jai alai contests and betting on dog fights (pit bull fights) and cockfighting.

Sports betting in North America involves many kinds of games. It may be suggested that making wagers on the results of games is the most popular form of gambling in North America. It is certainly the most popular form of illegal betting in the United States.

In Nevada, there are 142 places, almost all within casinos, that accept bets on professional and amateur sports contests. Nearly $2.3 billion was wagered in these sports books in 1998. The casinos kept $77.4 million of this money; that is, they "held" 3.3 percent of the wagers, owing to the fact that the players bet on the wrong team and also that the casino structures odds in its favor. The sports wagers constituted just over 1 percent of all the betting in the Nevada casinos. About two-thirds of the wagers were on professional games and the rest on college games (National Gambling Impact Study Commission 1999, 2–14).

Although the profits casinos realize directly from sports bets seem to be low, sports betting is very important in Las Vegas and Reno. The major gamblers like to follow sports, and the wagering possibilities draw them to the casinos. Also, the casinos sponsor championship boxing matches and give the best seats to their favorite gamblers. Superbowl weekend is the biggest gambling weekend in Las Vegas each year, as the casinos have special parties, usually inviting sports celebrities (retired) as well as other noted personalities to come and mingle with their gamblers. Of course, many of these invited celebrities turn out to also be heavy gamblers.

In 1998, the Oregon sports lottery sold $8.5 million worth of parlay cards on professional football and basketball games, and the state retained over $4.2 million (50 percent) as its win. This is less than 1 percent of total lottery winnings, but 4 percent of the winnings on non–video lottery terminal lottery games. The sports lottery is structured to produce a return of 50 percent to the players on a pari-mutuel basis (Christiansen 1999).

The National Gambling Impact Study Commission suggested in its 1999 *Final Report* that illegal gambling activities draw wagers of several hundreds of billions of dollars each year, perhaps as much as $380 billion (National Gambling Impact Study Commission 1999, 2–14). It is likely that the operators of these games hold 3 to 5 percent of the wagers as profits. The illegal sector commands considerably more activity than the few legal outlets for sports gambling in the United States.

Betting has developed rapidly in recent decades. In 1982, the Nevada sports books attracted $415.2 million in wagers and kept only $7.7 million (less than a 2 percent hold). The hold increased an average of 16.6 percent every year until 1998, after which it leveled off. Only California card rooms and Native American gambling operations had greater annual increases. In comparison, casinos increased 10.4 percent each year and lotteries 13.5 percent (Christiansen 1999). The added interest in sports betting has been affected by an added interest in sports in the United States. Although individual sports have different experiences with their growth, one factor that has affected all sports has been television access to games and news media on odds and points spreads. Most Nevada sports betting was confined to small parlors outside of the major casinos until the late 1970s. The gambling activity was discouraged by the fact that the federal government imposed a 10 percent tax on each sports wager; however, this was lowered to 2 percent by 1975. In that year, the amount wagered in Nevada quadrupled. The state of Nevada changed laws in 1976, making it easier for casinos to have sports books. Then, a final breakthrough came in 1982 when Congress lowered the federal betting tax on sports contests to 0.25 percent, which is where it is today. Major sports betting areas were constructed in many casinos, the largest books (in physical size) being found today in the Las Vegas Hilton and Caesars Palace.

Ironically, given the widespread nature of sports betting, the gambling is also very controversial. Popular opinion on betting is very mixed, and indeed, opinion is more strongly against legalizing this particular form of gambling than are negative factors on any other type of gambling. The survey taken for the Commission on the Review of the National Policy toward Gambling in 1974 found majority acceptance of several forms of gambling—bingo, horse racing, lotteries—whereas fewer than half of the respondents supported legalization of casinos (40 percent) and offtrack betting (38 percent), and the fewest supported legalized sports betting (32 percent) (Commission on the Review of the National Policy toward Gambling 1976, App. II). A 1982 Gallup poll found majority support for all other forms of gambling but only 48 percent approval for betting on professional sports events (Klein and Selesner 1982). Opponents of sports betting suggest that the activity may have a tendency to corrupt the integrity of games, as those making wagers could try to influence the activity of the players in the contests.

Sports betting is authorized in Canada, Mexico, and other parts of Central America and the Caribbean region; however, sports betting is very limited in the United States. Actually only in Nevada can a gambler legally make a wager on an individual contest or game. In Oregon the lottery runs a sports game in which the player must select several professional teams playing basketball or football on the same day or weekend. Nonetheless, sports betting is very pervasive in the United States, as bets on almost all sports events take place among friends or fellow workers or among social acquaintances in private settings. Almost all of these wagers, as already discussed, are illegal, as are wagers made through betting agents known as bookies. The appearance of the Internet and the worldwide web, which provide services in a form available to most residents, has led to a substantial increase in the amount of sports betting by Americans, most of which is also clearly illegal. There is some debate, however, as to whether Internet gambling, which is controlled by an operator in a jurisdiction where it is licensed and legal, is always illegal if the player is in another jurisdiction.

The greatest amount of sports betting—both legal and illegal—in the United States consists of wagers made on American football games. The National Football League (professional) games attract the most action, with the championship game (the Superbowl) being the initial attraction, the most wagering "action." The Superbowl attracts wagers approaching $100 million in the casinos of Nevada, and perhaps fifty times that amount or more is gambled on the game illegally. Most of the illegal gambling on the Superbowl consists of private bets among close friends or participation in office "pools" in which the participants pick squares representing the last digit of scores for each of the two teams. Following the Superbowl in importance for the gambling public are the college basketball championship series, the World Series for professional baseball, and the National Basketball Association (NBA) championship series.

Each kind of game has different structures for gambling. Basically, wagers are made on an odds basis, on a basis involving handicapped points for or against one of the contestants (teams), or on a combination of odds and handicapped points.

Sports Betting in Las Vegas Casinos

The structure of betting in Las Vegas casinos is discussed for football, basketball, baseball, hockey, and boxing.

Football

Football did not carry much interest among bettors until the National Football League gained tel-

A typical parlay card from the Horseshoe Casino in Las Vegas.

evision contracts and displayed its special kind of action for the public. A critical event was the climax of the championship playoffs of 1957, as the Baltimore Colts defeated the New York Giants in a sudden-death overtime game viewed by the largest television audience for a sports event up to the time. The game marked a critical point at which national interest in football exceeded interest in baseball, a game that did not translate well to the public over television, as it had too many breaks in action.

Football sports betting received an extra boost as a new professional league began operations in the 1960s and then merged with the National Football League, bringing teams and games to each major city in the United States.

The Point Spread. The growing interest in football was tied to betting on the games. Betting increased considerably among bookies when a handicap system of point spreads was developed. Prior to the use of point spreads for football wagering, the bookies only offered odds on winners and losers of games. As many games were predictable, odds became very long. Players realized

that they had little chance to win with the underdog, but at the same time, the bookies did not want to accept bets of sure-thing favorite teams, and they were reluctant to accept the possibilities of an underdog winning with odds of twenty to one or more. Therefore, many games simply were not available for the betting public. There is a dispute over just who invented the point spread. A Chicago stock market adviser, Charles McNeil, was credited by some for inventing the spread in the 1930s; two other bookies, Ed Curd of Lexington, Kentucky, and Bill Hecht of Minneapolis, are also cited for creating the spread decades later.

Bookies and the few legal sports books in operation in the 1950s and 1960s loved the spread for football and certain other games, as it greatly reduced their risks. Bookies do not want risks. They are businesspeople who want stability in their investments. The essential feature of the point spread was a guaranteed profit for the bookies—if the books could be balanced. Points are set for games with the goal of having an equal (nearly equal) amount of money bet on either side.

The point spread is called the line. The point spread refers to the betting handicap or extra point given to those persons making wagers on the underdog in a contest. Those betting on the favorite to win must subtract points from their team before the contest begins. The point spread is used most often for bets on basketball or football games. As an example, the New York Giants may be a seven-point underdog against the Green Bay Packers. Thus the line is Green Bay minus seven. Those betting on Green Bay will lost their bets unless Green Bay wins by more than seven points. Those betting on the New York Giants will win unless the Giants lose by more than seven points. The bet is a tie (called a push) if Green Bay wins by exactly seven points (Thompson 1997, 279).

In 1969 the New York Jets were double digit underdogs against the Baltimore Colts in the Superbowl football game. The point spread was as high as eighteen points. Yet New York, under the guiding leadership of quarterback Joe Namath, defeated the Colts sixteen to seven. Although some considered that the point setters failed miserably on that game, they did anything but fail at all. Money books were balanced, and the bookies won their transaction fees. Although players bet on one side of the line, they must put up $11 in order to win $10. This means that if the books are perfectly balanced, with $11,000 bet on one side, and $11,000 bet on another, the bookie pays back $21,000 to the winning bettor, and keeps $1,000 out of the $22,000 that has been bet—for a 4.55 percent advantage over the bettors.

In actuality, this theoretical advantage is seldom realized. Bettors do not line up evenly on either side of the point spread, and some bettors have knowledge about the games superior to that of the point setters, taking advantage of the spread numbers. The bookies often find that they have to adjust lines in order to get more even betting on each side. In certain cases, a line may move two or three points, resulting in a situation called "middling," whereby bettors on both sides—early bettors on one side, later bettors on the other side—can be winners. This happened with betting on the Superbowl in 1989. The three-point line, with San Francisco favored over Cincinnati, was moved to five or more points, as the bettors clearly favored the San Francisco 49ers (they were not only a California team—that is, near Las Vegas—but also they had won the Superbowl twice in the previous seven years). The game finished with a four-point San Francisco victory. Early San Francisco bettors won; later Cincinnati bettors won. Many of the bettors won both ways. The bettor gets the point spread that is listed at the time the bet is made, unlike the pari-mutuel situation in which odds are based upon the cumulative bets of the players.

Then there is the case in which the point setters do what some might consider their "job" perfectly. In the 1997 Superbowl game between Green Bay and New England, the Green Bay Packers were favored by fourteen points. The point setters were on target; they were perfect. The Packers won with a fourteen-point margin. The bookies and legal sportsbooks won exactly 0 percent on the game. They had to give all the money bet back to the bettors. The bets were a tie, a "wash." Because ties on point spreads are bad for the sports books, there is a tendency to use half points in spreads, although these are moved when betting behavior demands that the points be changed. Also, bookies realize that certain spreads will lead to ties more often than others will. More games end with a three-point victory than any other specific point margin. Moving points up or down around the three-point margin is also dangerous because of the "middling" factor.

The Structure of Football Bets.   The standard bet on football results has a player wagering that a favored team will either win by so many points or, conversely, that an underdog team will either win or will not lose by more than a determined number of points. If a game is considered to be an even match, no points are given either way. Such an even-match bet, with no points either way, is called a "pick-'em" by bettors. If the point spread is expressed as a full number, and the favorite team wins by that many points (or an even match ends in a tie), the bet is considered a tie (or "wash"), and the money wagered is returned to the player. There is no bet.

There are many betting opportunities other than a straight-up bet on which team will win and whether it will win by so many points. A very popular bet made on professional football games and many college games as well is the over-under. Here the point setters indicate a score that is simply the total number of points scored in the game. Bettors wager $11 to win $10 that the total score of the game will be more or less than the set number. There are also teaser bets that may be used either with one game or usually with bets on several teams. The bettor is given extra points for a game in exchange for having the odds on the bet changed against him.

Parlay bets are combination bets whereby the bettor wagers that several games (with point spreads) will be won or lost. For instance, on a two-team parlay, a bettor wagering $10 will win $26 (for a payback of $36) if both picks are correct. At even odds, the player should receive 3 to 1 for such a bet, or a return of $40. This means that the house edge on the bet is theoretically 10 percent—again assuming that bets on all sides of the parlay action are even amounts of money. A three-team parlay pays 6 to 1, and the even odds of such a parlay would be 7 to 1. The theoretical edge in favor of the sports book would be 12.5 percent. There are two kinds of parlay bets: ones made based upon the point spreads of the moment, and others made on a card where the point spread is fixed until the game is played. The latter type of cards may have a theoretical edge as high as 25 percent or more. For a three-bet parlay, cards usually payoff at a 5 to 1 rate. Sometimes cards allow tie bets to be winners; other times they are figured as "no-bets"; some cards may treat ties as losers.

There is also a wide array of proposition bets that are usually reserved for special occasions. Bettors may wager on many situations for the Superbowl game each year. For instance, the bettor is allowed to wager on which team will win the coin toss, have the most passes completed, score first; on how the first score will be made (touchdown, field goal, etc.); on which player will score first, how many fumbles there will be in the game, which team will lead at halftime, and many other situations. In the 1986 Superbowl, a Las Vegas casino offered a wager on whether Chicago Bear William "the Refrigerator" Perry—a 300-plus-pound offensive lineman would score a touchdown in the game against New England. He had been used as a back on gimmick plays during the season. The betting started with odds at thirteen to one but quickly came down as the betting public wagered that Perry would score a touchdown. Late in the game, which had become a rout (Chicago won forty-six to ten), coach Mike Ditka called Perry's number. He lined up in the backfield and was given the ball. He scored a Superbowl touchdown.

There are possibilities for odds betting for some football games, although the sports books put the players at a considerable disadvantage for any games where the point spread betting exceeds seven points. One can wager on the "sure thing" but only at considerable risk. For instance, on an even, no-points, "pick-'em" game, players betting either side advance $11 in order to win $10. With a three-point spread, those wagering on the favorite bet $15 to win $10, and those wagering on the underdog wager $10 to win $13. For a 7.5 point game, those betting on the favorite might be asked to wager $40 to win $10, while those betting on the underdog would wager $10 to win $30. The theoretical house edge thereby moves from 4.55 percent for the even game, to 8 percent for the three-

point spread game, to 20 percent for the 7.5-point game.

The biggest bet on a football game was made by maverick casino owner Bob Stupak, the owner of Vegas World and the creator of and an initial investor in the Stratosphere Tower. In 1995 he bet more than $1 million on a Superbowl game. He wagered $1,100,000 to win $1,000,000. And he won. It was great publicity all the way around. The Little Caesar's Casino and Sports Book basked in the glow of publicity as it happily paid the $2,100,000 check (for winnings and original bet) to Stupak. He basked in the light of publicity, as he was seen as the ultimate "macho-man." He put it all on the line for his team, and he had won.

One newspaperman was rather suspicious about the deal, as it seemed too good to be true for both the casino and the bettor. The newspaperman made an official inquiry of the Nevada Gaming Commission as to the veracity of the bet. The commission confirmed that Stupak had bet $1,100,000 on the game and that his win was legitimate. The commission reported no fact other than it was a legitimate bet. Sometime later, news media personnel uncovered "the rest of the story." Stupak may have bet on both teams. He may have been a $100,000 loser for the day—but it was worth it to gain the desired publicity, if he had won $1 million on one bet and lost $1.1 million on the other. The Nevada Gaming Commission has absolutely no obligation to report information on losing bets—indeed, that information is rightfully considered to be very private. Publicly, that information certainly would harm the industry, as Las Vegas seeks to portray itself as a place where "winners" play. There was nothing illegal about playing both sides of a sports bet.

Basketball

Basketball betting for both professional and college games follows the general structure of football betting, with straight bets utilizing a point spread and with bets on total scores also being popular. Parlay bets with and without cards are also wagered quite often. As margins of victory vary considerably and do not come together on specific numbers—such as three in football—the threat of middling is less for the sports book. Most sports books also offer teaser bets.

The general condition of basketball betting would seem to suggest that theoretical hold percentages would be more likely achieved than with football games; however, another factor makes this achievement more difficult. There are many more basketball games than football games, and the results of basketball games are much more dependent upon individual players. One player or two can dominate a team's performance much more than in football—with the general exception of the quarterback. There is a need for greater information about players in order to more accurately predict the outcomes of games. Yet with the number of games all over the country, bettors may have more information than the sports books—information about players' health, emotional disposition, disputes within teams with accuracy, distractions based upon player life circumstances (perhaps examination schedules and class performance for college players). The college basketball betting public is also the most sophisticated of those making sports wagers. The most sports betting scandals have hit the college basketball ranks. Professional gamblers sense that they can compromise players who can more easily affect the points of victory (shave points) in college basketball. Many major league professional players make $1 million or more per season and hence are not vulnerable to offers of money or other favors to shave points. It must be noted, however, that the sports books (and illegal bookies as well) will probably be very cooperative with authorities in exposing players or teams that may be willing to compromise their point spread lines, because as the line is compromised, the sports books not only lose customers who feel that games are not honest but also find it more difficult to balance their books, hence realizing their theoretical profit margins. Dishonest games hurt the bookies and sports book the most—in a financial sense, anyway.

Baseball
Baseball is bet on an odds basis. For instance, a bet on a game between the Detroit Tigers and the Chicago White Sox may be listed as Tigers plus 110 and White Sox minus 120. This means that the person making the wager who bets on Detroit puts up $10 and wins $11 (collects $21) if Detroit is victorious. One betting on Chicago wagers $12 for the chance to win $10 (and collect $22). This "dime" line (so called in recognition that there would be a dime difference if bets were expressed as single dollar amounts rather than in terms of 100) produces the theoretical win of $10 per $220 wagered or 4.55 percent. As the bet odds increase, more money is bet, but the house edge remains at $10, hence the percentage edge falls. If the favored team demands a $200 wager to win $100, and the underdog a $100 bet to win $190, the house theoretically wins $10 on action of $590 (both player and house money), for a win of only 1.7 percent. For this reason casinos will abandon the dime line and move to fifteen-cents or twenty-cents lines on longer odds games. Hence, a bet may read Detroit plus 150, Chicago minus 170.

It is rare for the game to have a run differential—that is, a point spread,—but if the casino feels such is necessary, it awards 1.5 runs or more to one side, and then keeps the odds line (dime, twenty cents, etc.) the same.

Most baseball bets are made with pitchers for both teams listed on the betting proposition. The pitchers are usually listed a few days before a game. If by circumstances, a pitcher is withdrawn, and the pitcher listed was part of the bet, there is no action and all money is returned. For the bet to be effective, the listed pitchers must each make at least one pitch in the game as a starter.

Bettors are also able to bet on total runs, usually with a plus 110 and minus 120 edge. If the total runs are expressed in whole numbers, and the number is the actual game result, the bets are returned. Extra innings do not affect bet results.

Parlay bets are figured on the basis of the lines offered, with payoffs of each game multiplied.

Hockey
In hockey contests, both goals and odds are used in the betting. In some cases there is a split line, with one team receiving 1.5 goals and the other team giving up 2 goals. Such a bet will be started at even odds. The house would be guaranteed a win of half the money bet if the game ended on the whole goal total—the plus–2 bettor would have

his or her money returned, and the minus 1.5-bettor would lose his or her wager.

Most hockey betting does not use the split line approach. Rather an advantage of 1.5, 2.5, or 3.5 goals (or more in very rare cases) is assigned to one team, and on top of this there is a money line—usually set as a forty-cents line.

Parlay bets are figured the same way as in baseball. The hockey games also offer over and under bets on total goals scored.

Boxing

Boxing matches are bet in many different ways. The simple win-loss bet carries a money line (odds) that features a large spread. For instance, one favored fighter may be bet at minus 400 ($400 must be bet to win $100), and the underdog is bet at plus 300 ($100 wagered to win $300). Fight bets are usually returned if the fight is canceled or postponed for more than a few days. Casinos and bookies also offer odds on whether there will be a victory by knockout or decision and on the round in which a knockout will be scored.

Futures

In futures contests, the sportsbook or bookie offers odds on future results of contests—such as who will win next year's Superbowl, World Series, the Stanley Cup for professional hockey, the NBA basketball championship, or the National Collegiate Athletic Association basketball championship playoffs. Most of these odds are offered as inducements for players to put a wager on their favorite or home team. The futures betting produces little serious wagering action.

Noncontests

Boxing is one of the few sporting contests bet upon in which judges of performance may determine the results. The Nevada Gaming Commission does not otherwise permit bets on noncontests in which victory is not determined in some arena or field of action. Although sports books in England often list political election contests (even election contests in the United States), this is not permitted in Nevada casinos and sportsbooks. Las Vegas bettors are not allowed to wager on Academy Award winners, winners of contests such as the Miss

America pageant, or *Time* magazine's Person of the Year. A decade ago a famous television series ended its run with a revelation about who shot the star of the series ("Who Shot J. R."). One casino put odds up on the list of television characters that might have done the terrible deed, but the odds were listed only in jest—or as a publicity stunt. No bets were taken.

Five years ago, however, the Palace Station casino did post odds and took bets at the beginning of a baseball season on just who would be named the most valuable player in each league. One bettor, Howard Schwartz, who just happens to run the Gambler's Book Club in downtown Las Vegas—the largest gambling specialty bookstore in the world—decided he liked the twenty-five to one odds on Andre Dawson, a player with the Chicago Cubs. Schwartz wagered a modest ten dollars. When at the end of the season Dawson was named as the most valuable player; Schwartz retrieved his "winning" ticket and marched to the Palace Station. There he was cheerfully greeted and handed back ten dollars. He was told that the Nevada Gaming Commission had heard about the contest (it was advertised in the local newspapers); the commission had determined that the contest violated gaming rules, and it ordered the casino to stop the contest—to close it down. It was, of course, a stupid move on the part of the commission. They could have warned the casino never to do it again and fined it a sufficient amount of money to assure it they would never do it again and that others similarly inclined to have such contests would never do it again. Had they known the names of all persons who entered the contests, they could have returned all the entry money. But such names were not known, as bets (unless over $10,000 in cash) are made anonymously. Instead, they voided bets already taken. Schwartz was, to say the least, irate. Schwartz had a bona fide bet. He had put his money at risk. He had won. When told he could have his money back, he inquired if the casino had a plan to return money to all players including losers—including losers who quite naturally would not come to the casino expecting to cash in their tickets. They had no plan outside of some minimal signage. All the casinos were put on notice not to be put into such a position in the future, as Schwartz used his critically central location among serious bettors—his bookstore, as well as all the talk radio shows of Las Vegas—to inform the public that one casino would not pay off its winners. Of course, the Palace Station would have liked to pay off the winning ticket, but the gaming commission told it that it could not do so. Considerable public relations damage was done to the casino and all sports books in Las Vegas over the incident, but the point was made clear—it must be a legitimate sporting event determined on the field of play, or no bets can be taken.

Issue: The Integrity of the Game

Baylor, the home team, had fought hard, sometimes uphill, but now it had the game in the proverbial bag. Five points ahead. Just kneel down, and it is over. Baylor had the ball on the opponent's eight-yard line. Second and goal. Ten seconds remaining in the game. University of Nevada, Las Vegas, (UNLV) had no time outs. But wait, the Baylor quarterback takes the snap and hands it off, the runner swings to the outside, but he bobbles the ball. A UNLV linebacker somehow grabs the ball in the air, and ninety-five yards later, with no time left on the clock, the linebacker runs into the Baylor end zone. UNLV wins. This incident really happened in the fall of the 1999 season. It cannot be explained. Or could it be explained? Could a coach or quarterback be so foolish as to try to score points after the game is all wrapped up in their favor? Players take intelligence tests to assure that they are qualified to be students at the college they are attending. Could the coach or player that made the call have been able to pass a simple intelligence test? Should such tests be given to coaches? Perhaps the following could have happened. Could a point spread of nine or ten points with Baylor being favored represent a motivation to try to score not just a victory, but a victory of eleven or twelve points—not five points? Could a team risk victory in order to win by a big enough margin to satisfy all their fans that might have bet on the game?

That is precisely the kind of rationale that is used by the National Collegiate Athletic Association (NCAA) as well as professional sports leagues when they urge that there be no legalized betting on their games. More worrisome to the leagues is the notion that players could try to manipulate the score (called shaving points) so that professional gamblers could be assured of winning their bets while at the same time the players' team could still win the game.

Scandals have followed sports throughout the past century. The scandals are single episodes, but they are also ongoing; they date back to the first decade of the twentieth century, and they occurred in the last century of the twentieth century. The scandals have in almost all cases involved betting and wagering on contests—usually illegal wagering.

Early boxing matches of the twentieth century were held in Nevada towns such as Goldfield, as the contests were illegal in most states. The matches were used to draw players to casinos, but betting was also very heavy on the contests. Boxing promoters such as Tex Rickard had close ties with members of organized crime, and it was generally accepted that matches were often rigged in order to favor certain gamblers. At the end of the century, the reputation of the sport had not been fully cleansed, as promoters such as Don King and fighters such as Mike Tyson have records of legal problems.

Early baseball leagues also had problems with gambling. The National League began in 1876, and attempts to control bribery and gambling passed to team owners. The owners instituted the "reserve clause" that prohibited players from freely leaving one team and negotiating to play for another team. In turn, the owners lowered salaries for players and made many working conditions intolerable. Players responded by selling favors to gamblers—favors including fixing game results. There were attempts to fix the World Series games in 1903 and 1904, and rumors spread that the 1912 and 1914 series were "thrown" by the losing teams. The game was put into major disrepute when it was revealed in 1920 that eight members of the Chicago White Sox team had accepted bribes that were passed by professional gambler Arnold Rothstein (who controlled bookies in many major cities) through an intermediary and had purposely lost the championship to the Cincinnati Reds. Their purported motivation was a salary dispute with an owner reputed to be

Casinos like sports stars. New Orleans Harrah's Casino uses stars to attract gamblers.

"one of baseball's biggest skinflints," Charles Comiskey (Sifakis 1990, 32–33).

As a reaction to the "Black Sox" scandal of 1919, the eight players implicated were banned for life from the sport, although no legal action was ever taken against Rothstein and his organized crime cohorts. A new commissioner of baseball was appointed and given extreme powers to clean up the image of baseball. He was a federal judge named Kenesaw Mountain Landis. Landis proclaimed that "no player that throws a game, no player that entertains proposals or promises to throw a game, no player that sits in a conference with a bunch of crooks where the ways and means of throwing games are discussed, and does not promptly tell his club about it, will ever play professional baseball" (quoted in Moldea 1979, 43).

Landis came down hard on players who were accused of fixing games, but he was not so strict with others who merely gambled on games. Gambling and baseball were never far apart. In the

1940s Brooklyn Dodger manager Leo Durocher was a close friend of gambling gangster Bugsy Seigel and was perhaps a compulsive gambler. Durocher was suspended from the game for the 1947 season for activities related to his gambling. As late as 1969, there were suggestions that he may have manipulated games, as he was the manager of the league leading the Chicago Cubs while they let an almost sure championship slip out of their hands with a end-of-the-season losing streak. The next year, a leading pitcher, Dennis McClain, who had led the Detroit Tigers to a championship in 1968, was suspended from the league for his own gambling activities and associations with mobsters. Contemporaneously, two of the most outstanding players of the century—Mickey Mantle and Willy Mays—were banned from having official associations with baseball for a period of time in the late 1970s because of their employment by Atlantic City casinos in public relations positions. The ban was lifted when the stars ended their casino employment.

One of the most notable sports gambling scandals became public in 1989 and its effects have carried over into the twenty-first century. Pete Rose, one of the greatest players of all time, was accused of betting on his own team while he served as the manager of the Cincinnati Reds. As a player, Rose had set the major league all-time hits record. He led the league in hitting three times, and he held the longest hitting streak in the National League history—forty-four games. He had been an All Star team member over a dozen times, and he wore a World Series championship ring. Rose admitted that he had been a relatively heavy gambler, but he also insisted that he had never bet on baseball games. The Rose episode was exposed when he and some compadres won a pick-six race ticket at Turfway track in northern Kentucky. His gambling habit was exposed, although the proof of his betting on baseball, especially betting on his own team, was not definitively revealed in a public way to the satisfaction of all observers—but certainly to some. Even his harshest critics have never in one single case accused him of betting against his team or in any specific way changing his coaching strategy in order to favor bets that he made. I noted earlier that baseball is bet on an odds bases and not on a handicapped runs (point spread) method. Rose acquiesced in a commissioner decision that he be banned from baseball for life, with the status of the ban open to review after one year. Because Rose had many of his winning bets recorded, but did not keep recorded proof of his losing, the Internal Revenue Bureau made a claim that he had not paid sufficient income taxes. He was without a defense, and because of his losses, he was without the funds necessary to pay the back taxes, penalties, and fines. He was sentenced to prison and served six months because of these tax problems. Rose's lifetime suspension has not been fully reviewed by league officials. He has been banned from consideration for membership in the Hall of Fame, a body filled with many old-time players and managers who regularly gambled—even on their own teams.

Basketball scandals have touched college basketball and professional basketball; however, the latter cases have not received close public attention. Professional basketball did not have a widespread public following until race barriers were broken down and the tempo of the games increased to make them more exciting. Professional league expansion and television exposures have also increased support. Very high salaries have made the prospects of bribing players unlikely. On the other hand, many players have succumbed to temptations of illicit drug use. College players often have financial needs. Bribes are always available to key major teams if they leave themselves open to the possibility—if they do not purposely decide to avoid certain contacts. In 1951, everything "hit the fan" with revelations that thirty-three players on seven top national college teams had "shaved" points in exchange for money from gamblers. It was suggested that eighty-six games had been influenced—and that in some, players threw victories. Colleges such as Columbia, City College of New York, Manhattan, and Long Island University were never able to regain their reputations as nationally competitive teams. Kentucky fans did not give up, and that team has remained solid. In the 1980s, a hint that difficulties existed returned, as a former Boston College player admitted to taking bribes, and a Tulane player revealed that he had traded point-shaving activities for cocaine.

In December 1999, a former defensive back on Northwestern University's football team pleaded guilty to lying to a grand jury about his role in betting on college games. Ten other players on both the football and basketball teams had already been charged, and all had pleaded guilty to offenses related to betting and point-shaving activities. The century was ending with a cloud over sports activity—much as the century had begun.

Early football games must have been important for someone beyond local supporters or campuses, as games became very violent, and quite often "ringers" (noneligible players) were put into lineups. The initial owners of professional football teams had ties to organized crime confidants. George Hallas, founder of the Chicago Bears, was backed by a "crony" of Al Capone. Art Rooney was a prominent Pittsburgh gambler before he was owner of the Steelers. So was Baltimore Colt (and later Los Angeles Rams) owner Carroll Rosenbloom, also a very high stakes gambler in the 1950s. In fact, he was close to Mob leader Meyer Lansky and others who owned Havana and later Bahamas casinos. In contemporary times, Philadelphia Eagles owner Leonard Tose lost the team because of his compulsive gambling activity.

Players were in a different situation. Two New York Giant players were approached by gamblers prior to the 1946 championship game and offered a bribe to shave points. They refused; however, because they did not disclose the bribe offer, they were suspended. They went to play in the Canadian Football League. One of the players, Frank Filchok, was later the head coach of the Denver Broncos. In 1963, Detroit Lions star Alex Karras and Green Bay Packer Paul Hornung were forced to sit out a year because they had bet on their own teams (Moldea 1979, 58–59, 98, 124–125).

The famous 1958 championship game was celebrated for making football the number-one spectator sport in the United States, but the game was never officially investigated for obvious manipulations. Baltimore Colts owner Carroll Rosenbloom reportedly had made a very large wager on his own team—the Colts. In fact, his betting caused the original line (Colts favored by 3.5) to move up two points (Colts favored by 5.5 points). The game ended with a tie score of seventeen to seventeen and was decided in a sudden-death overtime period. After holding the Giants on their first series, the Colts marched eighty yards down the field toward the Giants' goal line. They reached the eight-yard line with a second down. They did not try a "sure thing" field goal. Rather they passed the ball. They were lucky; the ball was caught and run to the one-yard line. On third down, they did not try a field goal. Instead, halfback Alan Ameche ran the ball over the goal line. It was a risky way to win the game, but then it was the best strategy to follow *if* you had to win by more than 3.5 or 5.5 points and cover the owner's bets. Moldea reported that rumors circulated around the National Football League that the Colts were playing to make sure they covered the point spread (Moldea 1979, 89).

There was a league investigation of Leonard Tose's gambling problem. Officials found that as long as he had the money to make his wagers, there was no problem. The problem was that he was a compulsive gambler, and he did not have enough money to cover his losses. He supposedly would bet as much as $70,000 a hand at blackjack. The league had a rule against owners' borrowing money from each other, but Tose was allowed to break the rule. The owner of the Tampa Bay Buccaneers loaned him $400,000 so he could pay off casino debts. Then Tose turned to William Clay Ford (of the Ford Motor Company family), who owned the Detroit Lions. Ford arranged for a bank he controlled to make more loans to Tose. The league's commissioner Pete Rozelle, commented that he would be "a hell of a lot more concerned if he knew that a player had bet at the casinos . . ." (Moldea 1979, 370).

There is a reason why the league had a rule against inside financial deals among owners. One of the consequences of the Ford-arranged loan to Tose was that Tose—who had a winning personality, a common trait among many compulsive gamblers—lobbied hard among all the owners to have the 1985 Superbowl game played in January 1985 in the frozen tundra of Pontiac, Michigan—albeit inside the Silverdome stadium.

Rules Today—NCAA

The National Collegiate Athletic Association, along with the professional leagues, has been a critic of betting on sports games. The NCAA is currently lobbying Congress for a national law that would ban all legal betting on college sports contests. Bills were introduced in Congress in both 2000 and 2001 to effectuate the ban. The college sports regulatory group cautions that gambling activities are now widespread on campuses throughout the country. Cedric Dempsey, who serves as the executive director of the NCAA, asserted that "every campus has student bookies. We are also seeing an increase in the involvement of organized crime on sports wagering" (National Gambling Impact Study Commission 1999, 2–15).

Gambling rings were exposed in recent years at many colleges, including Michigan State University, Boston College, and the universities of Maine and Rhode Island (National Gambling Impact Study Commission 1999, 2–15). The betting did not have to be confined to local bookies, as college students have ready access to Internet services. There are over 400 sports betting services on the web. Most are operating illegally, but some are sanctioned and licensed by foreign governments.

A University of Michigan study reported by the National Gambling Impact Study Commission indicated that 45 percent of male college athletes admitted to betting on sports events. Five percent indicated that they furnished information about team activities to others for gambling purposes and also may have gambled on games in which they participated (National Gambling Impact Study Commission 1999, 3–10).

During the late 1990s, a series of scandals involving student athletes' altering their performance in games in exchange for bribes from gamblers rocked college sports. The scandals involved basketball players at high profile schools such as Northwestern University and Arizona State and football players at Boston College. All of the college scandals involved illegal gambling, but in some cases, college gambling rings used Las Vegas sports books for lay-off services when they found that their student gamblers were betting too heavily for one team against another. Las Vegas casinos helped the Federal Bureau of Investigation (FBI) and the NCAA in exposing the sports betting scandals as they discovered unusual betting patterns that prompted investigations.

The NCAA bylaw 10.3 prohibits any student athlete from sports gambling involving any team, professional or collegiate. The organization's literature explains:

> In clear, simple language, here's what the rule means: You may not place any bet of any sort on any college or professional sports event. You may not give information to anyone who does place bets on college or professional sports. That means . . . NO wagers . . . even those that don't involve your college. NO sports "pools," . . . NO Internet gambling on sports events . . . NO sports wagering using "800" numbers. NO exchange of information about your team with ANYONE who gambles. In other words, no information about injuries, new plays, team morale, discipline problems, or anything else. (National Collegiate Athletic Association 1999, 1–2)

The penalty for violations of the rule was put bluntly: "You are declared ineligible to compete in college sports. You are off the team" (National Collegiate Athletic Association 1999, 2).

U.S. senator Bill Bradley, himself a former professional basketball player, commented on the need to ban legalized betting on sports. "Based upon what I know about the dangers of sports betting, I am not prepared to risk the values that sports instill in youth just to add a few more dollars to state coffers . . . sports gambling raises people's suspicions about point-shaving and game fixing" (National Gambling Impact Study Commission 1999, 3–8).

Spokesmen of the American Gaming Association, representing Nevada casinos and sportsbooks, accept that the integrity of games is extremely important. Indeed, they realize that without honest games, the sports book function of the casino would collapse. For this reason, they point out that the Las Vegas casinos work closely with the NCAA, the professional leagues, and the FBI in any investigation of corruption of sports by gamblers or gambling. In fact, they have been the source of much information that has led to investigations. On the other hand, they can easily point out that almost all of the situations mentioned above involved gambling that was illegal. They

question whether making sports gambling in Las Vegas illegal would markedly improve the integrity of games. It would take the eyes of the Las Vegas establishment—including those of the Nevada Gaming Commission—off the intricacies of play inside each game covered on the boards of the casinos. There was no Las Vegas betting on the UNLV-Baylor football game. There was no central betting place where wagers could be monitored to observe if the play on the field was just "stupid" play or if it was motivated by something else.

When the professional leagues oppose legal betting on games, questions have to be raised about possible hypocrisy, as almost every league allows gambling behaviors by owners and also works with media that spread betting information to the public. Every league also recognizes that public betting adds to the television interest and revenues that come to the team owners through television contracts.

Sources: Christiansen, Eugene Martin. 1999. "The 1998 Gross Annual Wager." *International Gaming and Wagering Business* (August): 20ff; Commission on the Review of the National Policy toward Gambling. 1976. *Gambling in America: Final Report.* Washington, DC: Government Printing Office; Klein, Howard J., and Gary Selesner. 1982. "Results of the First Gallup Organization Study of Public Attitudes toward Legalized Gambling." *Gaming Business Magazine* (November): 5–7, 48–49; Moldea, Dan E. 1979. *Interference: How Organized Crime Influences Professional Football.* New York: William Morrow; National Collegiate Athletic Association [NCAA]. 1999. *Don't Bet on It: Don't Gamble on Your Future.* Indianapolis, IN: NCAA; National Gambling Impact Study Commission [NGISC]. 1999. *Final Report.* Washington, DC: NGISC; O'Brien, Timothy L. 1998. *Bad Bet: The Inside Story of the Glamour, Glitz, and Danger of America's Gambling Industry.* New York: Random House, 212–257; Rombola, Ferde. 1984. *The Book on Bookmaking.* Hollywood, CA: Romford Press; Rose, Pete, and Roger Kahn, 1989. *Pete Rose: My Story.* New York: Macmillan; Roxborough, Michael (Roxy), and Mike Rhoden. 1989. *Race and Sports Book Management.* Las Vegas: Gambler's Book Club; Sifakis, Carl. 1990. *The Encyclopedia of Gambling.* New York: Facts on File; Sugar, Bert Randolph. 1992. *Caesars Palace Sports Book of Betting.* New York: St. Martin's Press; Thompson, William N. 1997. *legalized Gambling: A Reference Handbook.* 2d ed. Santa Barbara, CA: ABC-CLIO.
See also Cockfighting; Dog Racing; Horse Racing; Jai Alai; Pari-mutuel Wagering Systems; Rothstein, Arnold

The Stock Market

Proponents of legalized gambling of one form or another are wont to call "the law" a hypocrite by pointing to the fact that governments that proscribe gambling in casinos, at racetracks, or in private homes are the same governments that endorse the existence of the stock markets. Indeed, they are the same governments that invest pension funds in the markets, the same governments that go to the markets for bonds to use for various public projects. If it is good enough for the government, why will the government not allow others to play games of chance as well?

There can be little debate about whether stock market and bond market trading (stocks and bonds are referred to as securities) involves some of the elements of gambling. Persons put up something of value for consideration; that is, they advance money into the market. They do so with the hopes of achieving a prize; that is, a financial gain. And, as with gambling, there is some risk involved. Yet although all of these elements of gambling may be found in the market, and although some people who enter the market do so with the same inclinations as people who wager on the green felt tables of Las Vegas, there are material differences between betting at a casino, at a race track, or on a lottery, on the one hand, and putting your money down on a commodity—bond or stock—in the market, on the other hand. The differences are so substantial in a material way that I choose not to give any in-depth treatment to stock markets. Nonetheless, I feel that a clear delineation between market investments and wagers at games of chance should be offered.

Those who would think that Wall Street is a casino must also think that any business venture is gambling. Yet stock investments, bond investments, and other commodity transactions are vehicles for the creation of wealth. By investing, the stock-purchasing public is saying it has confidence that certain products and services will be desired by others and will serve to meet demands of a public. A bond purchase or the purchase of an initial public offering (IPO; the first sale of a stock by a company) does indeed transfer money from individuals to entrepreneurs. Most stock purchases, however, are on a secondary market, such as the New York Stock Exchange; that is, people buy and sell stocks, and money is transferred back and forth between the buyer and seller without any money going to the company. Nonetheless, if the stock performs well it benefits the entrepreneurs in many ways. First of all, such a performance creates an incentive for recruiting talent, as the companies invariably give stock options to top managers and perhaps to all other employees as well. The company takes some stock and holds it in reserve, putting a current price on it as of the time it was put into the reserves. The company then tell the employees that if they stay with the company for some period of time, they may buy the stock from the company at that predetermined price. If the value of the stock goes up, the employees of the company gain wealth, and their loyalty to the company is enhanced. New employees can more easily be recruited if the stock values are rising. A second benefit of a successful stock, in terms of its market price, is that it makes it much easier for a company to issue new shares, through an IPO and hence recruit more capital for corporate projects.

But let us go back to the individual investor. The investor may or may not give close study and scrutiny to the purchase of a stock. After all, not all of us have the time, energy, or financial acumen to make the best choices on the market. For a fee, however, we can find persons with expertise. On the other hand, we may want to play a hunch. Or we may just wish to take a dart and throw it at the New York Stock Exchange or National Association of Securities Dealers Automated Quotations (NASDAQ) listings in the *Wall Street Journal*. Is this not just like going to Las Vegas and betting on a red seven on the roulette wheel? The answer is "No, it is not." The roulette wheel, the craps table, the blackjack game, the lottery, and the horse race are all zero-sum games. For each set of winning numbers there is more than that number of losing numbers. Indeed, the casino game is not a zero-sum game, but by necessity must be a negative-sum game that casts the players as a collective into a losing position over any period of time except a very short run.

Although the stock player going through a broker must give a commission for a sale, that commission can be considerably less than 1 percent of the value of the purchase. This compares favorably to the best odds one can get at a craps table and is substantially better than the casino's brokerage fee of 2 to 20 percent on other games. It is far better than the predetermined house edge of 20 percent on the typical horse or dog race and even much better than the 40 percent to 50 percent commission the lottery player pays the government for the right to enter that market. The casino games are rigged against the players as a whole, and this can be justified only on the basis that they are selling an entertainment value for the play experience. Wall Street does not exist to sell entertainment value in trading.

The stock market can very well be a positive-sum game in which every player can be a winner. Indeed, through the 1990s the substantial majority—perhaps 90 percent or more—of the investors were winners. They did not take their wins away from anyone; they did not win against other stock owners; they did not win against the companies in which they invested. They won because the companies in which they invested created wealth through their entrepreneurial activities. They made products out of raw materials and labor and ingenuity, and when the products were sold, the public bought them at a price considerably higher than that of the sum of the input investments into the products. In turn, this gave greater value to their shares. Ah! But it is true that everyone can also lose. Witness the sad days of October 1929, or October 1987, or more recently April 2000. Here then is another difference between the casino and Wall Street. In the casino the roulette wheel stops, the dice stop, the reels of the slot machine stop, the Ping-Pong balls of the bingo or lottery game quit floating to the surface, and the horses cross the finish line. The game in terms of time is finite. It ends, and someone has to pay the piper right then and there. But until a company goes fully bankrupt—the bankruptcy laws, with their chapters 9 and 11 and in the worst cases chapter 7, use the lucky numbers of gambling to indicate the status of a company that has failed—the stockholder can hold on and wait for a better day. The stock market may be a game, but if it is, the game is continuous, and it need end

only when the investor decides to make his or her final sale. It hurt to receive my portfolio statement in May 2000. As I am for the most part a passive investor, however—I have a broker, and I have a pension fund that handles my investments—I just sat still with a small frown. A smart investor could have grabbed at the opportunity—because just as in poker, every day is a winner and every day is a loser on the market, but I just sat still. My pension fund was back on target by the end of the summer of 2000, and my other investments were beginning to approach their March 2000 levels—at least they were way ahead of the 1998 and 1999 levels at which I had made my purchases.

Who knows what tomorrow may bring? If we look at history, we can see only good results. The cumulative stock exchange has never gone downward for a full decade. Indeed, for a ten-year span, the stock market since its beginnings in the nineteenth century has never moved upward less than 10.5 percent. That was the gain during the Depression years of 1929 to 1939. There is no secret to success on the market. To be on the safe side, however, one could suggest that investors purchase index funds that go up and down with the full market—for instance, a fund consisting of all the stocks on the New York Stock Exchange or one of the 500 funds—or the thirty leading stocks upon which the Dow Jones average is based. There is a fund (with the symbol QQQ fund) that includes the top 100 NASDAQ stocks (newer stocks that have become identified with technologies of the computer age).

If one gets in the mood to throw darts and really feels like taking a risk, however, one can buy options. These are purchases of the right to buy or sell a stock at a certain value at a time 30, 60, or 90 days in the future. Here, unlike other stock investments, there is a time certain when a transaction must be completed, and although the options may promise great rewards, they also carry risks of great losses—such as the loss of the total investment, a risk that is very rare for a stock purchase. Even more risky is a practice that has become more popular in recent years as computers have allowed investors to have immediate information on the movement of prices of stock. It is called day trading.

Day trading is the act of quickly buying and selling stocks and bonds throughout the day. At the end of the day, the day trader usually owns no securities. Indeed, when he or she places an order to buy, there is a period of time (usually three business days if he or she has an account with the broker) to complete the purchase by providing funds for the security, during which time the investor eagerly seeks to make a sale of the security, because it is unlikely that he or she has the actual funds to cover the initial purchase. The day trader is not a professional and typically has little or no formal training in the financial markets. He or she is an amateur, usually working without any supervision and using his or her own money to buy and sell the stocks, futures, and options. The day trader may sit in front of a computer screen, watching the price movements of the stocks he or she is trading, hoping to make a quick "killing" with the slightest movement upward of the stock during the day.

As an example, consider that AT&T is selling for $60 a share. The trader places an order for 1,000 shares, hoping to sell it for $60.125 (60 and one-eighth) if it moves. This very small movement is the smallest movement publicly listed on the exchange, which measures prices in eighths (although an exchange can be at the 1/32th of a dollar value). The smallest movement is soon to be changed from eighths to tenths. If the investor sells the stock, the quick profit is $125. By making similar moves throughout the day, the day trader can achieve some very nice gains.

Several factors work against repeated success on these ventures, however, and make day trading quite similar to gambling. For one thing, there are commissions that must be paid when purchases and sales of stock are executed. Even at a low rate of $8.95 from a broker who will handle the transaction without offering advice, the buy and sell will cost $17.90. This commission is paid, win or lose, whether the stock goes up, stays at sixty, or descends in value. For each dollar the stock goes down, the trader loses $1,000 plus the commission. Another psychological factor against repeated success is that the trader has to hold his or her breath waiting to see whether he or she makes a sale before the payment is due—it is unlikely the day trader actually has the $60,000 for the purchase.

Another cost to day traders, who may gather at a broker's office, is a fee to use computers there. Also, under the arrangement, the broker is not selling advice but rather only a space to work. A broker who works with an ordinary investor seeks to find value in the market, because he or she too will be receiving a commission—a little higher than the $8.95 charged by the passive broker—and wants a lot of repeat business. The broker has an incentive for performing well. On the other hand, a day trader and a gambler are both alone with their money and the roll of the dice on the computer screen. Each day the gambler trader must prove his worth by successfully trading to make a profit or by getting out of the deal with as little a loss as possible.

Often if losses begin to accumulate, the day trader's money reserve begins to dwindle. Possessing some of the same traits as a pathological gambler, the losing day trader will seek funds from every possible source for his games. A brokerage firm, like a casino, may actually loan the day trader money for transactions and, in a sense, help him or her string out the losing experience. The loans have to be secured with the day trader's stock account assets. Losing these, the trader turns to his or her home mortgage and other hard assets to bail himself or herself out. Often day traders do not get out in time, and they start downward on the same slippery slope as the problem gambler.

Over the course of time, the stock market performs quite rationally. Long-term trends have been solid. In the short run, the market can do many irrational things. Stocks of established companies could be expected to increase in the long run if the company has a record of successful performance and has value behind the price of the stock. In the short-run, however, prices can take quick dips and rises that may be totally unexpected. The inability to live with these wild short-term swings in price has ruined many a day trader. The market can be beaten, but it takes patience, and actually there is no one to beat—as there is with the casino.

Spurred on by greed and promises of great riches, day trading has become the modern-day California gold rush. Unfortunately, very few day traders make money—or perhaps this is fortunate, because day traders are not playing the game the way it is supposed to be played. They are not investors. Still, no one really likes to lose money, and fewer accept losses when they realize that their own bad judgment caused them. Consequently, day traders have been known to irrationally blame others for losses. This happened in Atlanta, Georgia, during the summer of 1999. A day trader faced with losing everything, including his business and his house, blamed the manager of a brokerage house where he did his trading. He felt that the manager of the firm that specialized in giving services to day traders should have warned him to be more vigilant. He also was angry with other day traders for not sympathizing with his plight. He went to the firm's office and began shooting people. After a murdering rampage, he committed suicide.

A long-term, patient investor should be secure in feeling that the stock market will be kind to him or her. A short-term day trader may make a killing, but it is just like the pathological gambler's first big win. Losses are sure to catch up and overtake wins, if he or she does not get out quickly. There is only one difference between day trading and gambling: In Las Vegas the gamblers get free drinks.

—coauthored by Bonnie Galloway

Sources: Know, Harvey A. 1969. *Stock Market Behavior.* New York: Random House; Mallios, William S. 2000. *Modeling Parallels between Sports Gambling and Financial Markets.* Boston: Kluwer Academic Publishers; Mayer, Martin. 1988. *Markets: Who Plays, Who Risks, Who Gains, Who Loses.* New York: W. W. Norton; Shelton, Ronald B. 1997. *Gaming the Market.* New York: Wiley and Sons.

Stud Poker. *See* Poker

Suriname

The Republic of Suriname, the former Dutch Guyana, is located on the northeast coast of South America. There are an estimated 450,000 inhabitants; more than 300,000 of these persons live in and around the capital, Paramaribo. Paramaribo is on the coastal plain of the country and is by far the largest and most developed city. Because of the early importation of slave labor from Africa and contract labor from Asia, the society is one of the most ethnically diverse in the world. The main language is Dutch, but English is widely spoken. Owing to the multicultural environment, additional languages commonly heard include Spanish, Hindi, Chinese, and Portuguese as well as the local language, called Sranan.

Suriname has been claimed at various times by England, France, and the Netherlands. It remained a dependency of the Netherlands from 1815 until 1954, when it obtained a parliamentary form of government and the right of local constitutional revision. Suriname became independent from the Netherlands in 1975. In 1980, the country experienced its first military revolution, and during the next fifteen years there were at least three attempted coups. A newly elected democratic government was formed in 1996.

Suriname has the lowest market share of tourism receipts and tourist arrivals of any of the countries in the Americas. Gambling is not a tourist attraction. There is a lottery, which serves as a distraction for local citizens seeking to forget the grueling trials of daily life. Bingo may also take up their time.

In 1962, while still under Dutch authority, casino gambling was legalized by a government corporation, the Landsverordening Hazardspelen. In 1962 the Hotel Maatschappij Torarica opened the first legal casino. Shortly after that the Palace Hotel opened its casino, but it closed in the late 1970s owing to high maintenance and refurbishing costs. Tararica, the only legal casino currently operating, has seventy-four slot machines, four blackjack tables, and four roulette tables. The slots are very popular, with a minimum bet of US$0.25. Blackjack has an average wager of US$10 and roulette US$125. The casino currently enjoys a loyal enthusiastic clientele.

In 1996, the Wild Forest Hotel Resort and Casino and two additional hotel companies were issued casino licenses. The Wild Forest Casino and one other are located in Paramaribo, and the third is two hours' driving distance from Paramaribo.

Gaming is a privileged industry. Ownership and employment in the casino are limited by the Gambling Act. The district commissioner is authorized to provide permits in compliance with the Ministry of Justice and Police. The district commissioner must approve casino employees with supervisory responsibilities.

The licensee is required to refuse entry to or evict any individual who is believed likely to disrupt the normal operation of the casino. The licensee is required to ensure against alcohol abuse. Patrons who are intoxicated are not to be allowed entry to the casino. Patrons who become intoxicated while in the casino are to be evicted from the casino. Any incidences of disturbances or eviction due to intoxication are required to be reported to the police.

—coauthored by Sergio Buth and Patricia A. Maguire

Sources: Cabot, Anthony N., William N. Thompson, Andrew Tottenham, and Carl Braunlich, eds. 1999. *International Casino Law.* 3d ed. Reno: Institute for the Study of Gambling, University of Nevada, Reno, 314–316.

Systems, Gambling. *See* Gambling Systems

T

Taxes, Gambling

A primary rationale for the legalization of almost any form of gambling has been the anticipation of government revenues derived from special taxation on the gambling activities. Proponents of gambling often argue that "since people gamble anyway," the activity should be legalized so that it can be taxed. Persons opposed to gambling might dispute the premise that there is "gambling anyway," and they claim that even where there is legalization, the amount of tax revenue gained is in most cases only a small part of a government's budget. It is also argued that the legalization efforts will result in increased gambling, as government actors will begin to rely upon gambling revenues, whatever their amount, and they will therefore encourage the activity. This is especially the case where the gambling is conducted as a government enterprise (e.g., state and provincial lotteries). Increased gambling can have a depressing effect upon other tax revenues when the gambling products are substitute purchases replacing the sale of other goods, which would also be taxed. Mindful of these arguments, when Great Britain legalized commercial casinos in 1968, the nation purposely provided that there would be no special casino taxes. The government simply did not want government officials to have an incentive for allowing the activity to increase.

Additional issues concerning the taxation of gambling revolve around the "fairness" of the taxes. Critics ask: Do the taxes fall most heavily upon poor people, or upon people who can afford to pay more taxes? Of course, proponents of gambling emphasize that taxation in this case is "voluntary."

Rates of Taxation
Lotteries
A typical lottery ticket may sell for $1. Of this amount, half may be designated for prizes to be returned to players. Fifteen percent of the ticket price is often directed toward expenses (advertising, ticket distribution and sales commissions, printing tickets, managing funds). About 35 percent is reserved for government treasuries, either for a specific use or for general uses. If we consider that a ticket purchase results in a value of $0.50 going to the player, we can assume that the player has purchased a product worth $0.50. At the point of purchase, however, the price was $1, or $0.50 more. If the lottery purchase was considered to be the purchase of any other product, we could say that it carried a 100 percent sales tax. If we see the extra $0.50 as a profit margin, we could say that the seller was paying a tax of 70 percent on the gross profit—that is, $0.35 on $0.50. Or we might simply say that the government tax is 35 percent of the gross sales, and all other costs are costs of doing business. However we conceive the rate of taxation, we can see that lottery operations carry the highest taxation rates of any gambling products. Also it can be claimed that the use of a lottery to raise money for government activities is very expensive. It costs $0.15 in expenses to raise $0.35 for government use.

Pari-mutuel Racing
In pari-mutuel wagering, players typically make all their bets, and these are placed into a common pool (e.g., $1,000). A set amount of the pool is then given back to the winning players (about $800). As a sales tax, we can say that the tax on the player is 25 percent ($20 on $80). Expenses and shares given to the track and animal owners constitute most of the $200, however. The government would typically keep only $60 or $70. It might then be said that the government tax is 30 percent or 35 percent of the profits from the wagering, or 6 percent or 7 percent of the gross sale price of the bet-

ting tickets. As the government incurs only a very small part of the cost of race-betting operations (having a state racing commission), the cost of raising the $60 or $70 is very small, perhaps less than 10 percent of the amount raised.

Casinos

Casinos typically pay many kinds of fees as well as taxes on their gambling winnings. Fees are charged for licensing activities and also for having individual numbers of machines or gambling tables. Taxes on the winnings are assessed on the gross gambling win—that is, the amount of money the casino retains after all prizes are given to the players. The rates of the casino win taxes vary considerably among the commercial casino jurisdictions of the United States. Nevada has the lowest rate—6.25 percent of the win—followed by a rate of 8 percent in New Jersey, Mississippi, and South Dakota. In Michigan, the state tax on wins is 18 percent, and Louisiana has an 18.5 percent win tax. Several states have taxes of 20 percent (Iowa, Indiana, and Missouri). The highest rate is found in Illinois, where a graduated tax climbs to as high as 35 percent of the casino win. These taxes are generally more efficient than those for lotteries and pari-mutuel racing. The government collection costs are consumed by state regulatory commissions and are normally less than 5 percent of the revenues collected.

Tax Incidence and Equity

The questions of who pays the gambling tax and its impacts upon society are important policy questions. The answer is that the gambler pays the taxes, as the gambler is the source of the tax money—no matter how many hands it is processed through before it reaches a state treasury. When gambling opponents proclaim that we should "tax the casinos" more or that the "casinos must pay their fair share," false notions are being generated. All taxes come from people, and that is especially the case with gambling taxes. The proper question to ask is, "which people?" For sure they are volunteer gamblers. But are they local residents, or are they tourist visitors who would not otherwise be spending money in the community? More important, are they affluent people who can afford the recreational activity of gambling, or are they poor people who must divert funds from family needs in order to gamble?

Studies of lotteries have suggested that the burden of taxation from sales of tickets falls most heavily upon poorer people. Their purchases of tickets constitute a higher proportion of their income and resources than do purchases of tickets made by more affluent persons. Moreover, many have suggested with empirical studies that governments purposely put lottery ticket sales outlets in poorer residential areas in higher proportion than they do in other neighborhoods. They also direct their advertisement messages toward poorer people. These people are considered their best potential customers in terms of volumes of sales. The National Gambling Impact Study Commission was very critical of lottery advertising. Lottery taxes are considered to be regressive (National Gambling Impact Study Commission 1999, 3–17).

Pari-mutuel racing locations are such that betting on races is not as convenient as buying lottery tickets. Hence, fewer numbers of poor people are attracted to this kind of gambling. Also, the process of selecting probable winners of races is much more difficult than buying a lottery ticket. Nonetheless, many of the regular race-track bettors are poorer people—perhaps because they are regular bettors.

Casino taxes may be regressive or progressive. Casino betting may be convenient, or it may require such major investments of time, energy, and travel money that poorer persons avoid the gambling. For instance, in Las Vegas, taxes on casino gambling can be considered both regressive and progressive. Slot machines are permitted in bars, convenience stores, and grocery stores within walking distance of almost all the residents of Las Vegas. Tourists do not play at these machines. Nor do affluent persons. Many of the bars and 7–11–type stores are established for the primary purpose of offering machine gambling. The grocery stores of Las Vegas stay open twenty-four hours a day in order to service gamblers. A high proportion of the grocery store and 7–11 players are probably problem gamblers. Taxation of the gambling exploits the conditions of these players and must be considered regressive (Thompson 1998, 459–461).

On the other hand, the Las Vegas Strip casinos attract tourists. Over half of the casino visitors arrive in Las Vegas by air. They stay at the hotels for an average of four days, but they gamble only four hours each day. Their gambling dollars are from their recreational budgets. They can afford to gamble; hence, taxes on their activity tend to be progressive taxes (Las Vegas Convention and Visitors Authority 1999).

Volume of Gambling Taxation

Special gambling taxes provide large amounts of revenues to many of the jurisdictions with legalized gambling. In the state of Nevada, casino taxes provide the largest share of public revenues from any tax source. In 1997, more than $586 million was generated by the 6.25 percent gross win tax, plus various fees on licensing, machines, and table games. Additional revenues go to local governments in the form of fees as well as property taxes. That year more than 40 percent of the state's internal source funding came from the casino sector of the economy. More revenues flow to the state treasury as a result of the nongambling activities of tourists who are drawn to the state because of its casinos. These taxes take the form of room taxes, entertainment taxes, and general sales taxes. No other state or provincial jurisdiction in North America receives as high a proportion of its revenues through gambling activities.

In a recent year the state of Mississippi receives $262 million, or about 10 percent of its internally generated revenues from casino taxes. No other state receives as much as 4 percent of its revenues from casino taxes. Lotteries yield low portions of state budgets as well. At the low end, New Mexico's lottery gives the state only 0.4 percent of its budget; at the high end, Georgia receives 4.1 percent of its state revenues from its lottery (Christiansen 1999).

Although Nevada is the state that is most dependent upon gambling revenues, many other states receive more dollars from gambling sources. Nevada ranks only thirteenth among the states in taxes and other gambling revenues. New York leads the list. Governments of the Empire State, Texas, and Massachusetts each receive over $1 billion a year from lottery operations. Illinois and New Jersey each receive approximately $900 million from a combination of lottery revenues and casino taxes. Ohio, Florida, and California receive between $700 million and $800 million from lotteries. Lottery receipts in Pennsylvania and Georgia exceed Nevada gambling tax revenues, as do the combined lottery revenues and casino taxes of Indiana and Michigan. Quebec and Ontario, the two largest Canadian provinces, also receive more government funds from gambling sources than does the state of Nevada. Both provinces have large lotteries. Quebec has three government-owned casinos, which provide all their profits to the government. In Ontario, the government is the casino owner, but there are private operators. The operators pay a 20 percent gross win tax, then they take 5 percent as their share of the profits. After other casino expenses are paid, the province is given the remainder of the revenues.

Earmarking Gambling Taxes

Many jurisdictions with gambling operations earmark tax revenues for certain functions. In Canada, governments devote some gambling revenues to private charities, and in the United States, a variety of activities are selected to be beneficiaries of revenues. Most of the thirty-nine lotteries (thirty-eight states plus the District of Columbia) earmark some funds to specific functions of government. Most of the funds are designated for educational activities; others send funds to senior citizen programs, parks and recreation programs, or public safety. Casino taxes are often earmarked as well. Special slot machine taxes in Nevada are designated for education, as are parts of the casino taxes in Illinois, Michigan, Mississippi, and Missouri. Colorado and South Dakota use casino taxes for tourism and historical preservation. Indiana uses casino taxes for economic development, Iowa for infrastructure and local governments, Missouri for public safety, and New Jersey for senior citizens and urban redevelopment.

Earmarking is not necessarily the most efficient way to distribute public funds. The process removes a certain amount of flexibility from legislators who may be trying to set priorities for the state on the basis of current needs. By designating a specific function to receive gambling taxes, however, proponents of casinos, lotteries, or other forms of gambling can win critical support from important groups in their campaigns for legalization. Proponents of the lottery in Georgia won such critical support by offering lottery money for college scholarships for all Georgia high school graduates who received B averages.

After a form of gambling operations begins, the objectives of the earmarking process are often difficult to maintain. If the functions supported by earmarking are old activities, legislators are prone to reduce previous funding of the activities from other taxes and merely replace the funding with gambling revenues. The activity receives the same funding as it did before. Also, when earmarking provisions are established, legislators seek to broaden definitions of the activities. As mentioned, Nevada uses special slot machine taxes to fund education. One year the state wished to build a basketball arena for the Running Rebel basketball team of the University of Nevada, Las Vegas, and the state was short of general fund monies for the project. With some minor redesign, the basketball facility ended up with some meeting rooms, which were sometimes scheduled to hold classes. Hence, the basketball arena became an educational facility.

Federal Gambling Excise Taxes

The first federal excise tax on gambling devices was passed as part of the Revenue Act of 1941. A stamp act of ten dollars was levied on pinball and similar amusement machines and fifty dollars on slot machines—meaning machines that operate by means of insertion of a coin or token and that "by application of the element of chance may deliver . . . cash premiums, merchandise or tokens." Ordinary vending machines were excluded from the tax.

The Revenue Act of 1951 raised the stamp act to $250 for slot machines. The amusement machine and slot taxes were repealed in 1978. The state of Nevada took over the tax, however, and has dedicated the receipts to educational programs. The 1951 Revenue Act also imposed a 10-percent fee on the amount of money wagered on a sports

event or on a lottery conducted for private profit. This tax was lowered to 2 percent in the 1970s and to 0.25 percent in 1982. (The tax remains at 2 percent if the gambling is illegal.) In addition, the 1951 law created an occupational tax of $50 for each person working for a gambling establishment. Later the tax was raised to $500. Today it remains $500 for illegal gamblers but is only $50 for those engaged in legal wagering. Those involved with lotteries, pari-mutuel gambling, slot machine games, and casino table games (not considered wagering) are exempt from the occupational tax.

In 1994, President Clinton proposed a 4 percent tax for all gambling profits realized by commercial operations. The proposal died in Congress among a flurry of opposition from casino interests.

The federal gambling taxes have produced only a minuscule amount of revenue for the national budget. The real purpose of the taxes seemed to be to discourage gambling and also to delineate a separate criminal offense for persons not paying the taxes. Illegal gamblers were obligated to pay the tax, and of course, most did not. In 1968, however, the U.S. Supreme Court ruled that the government could not require illegal operations to pay the taxes, as such payment would constitute a forced self-incrimination in violation of the 5th Amendment of the U.S. Constitution.

Sources: Christiansen, Eugene Martin. 1999. "The 1998 Gross Annual Wager." *International Gaming and Wagering Business* (August): 20ff; Las Vegas Convention and Visitors Authority [LVCVA]. 1999. *Las Vegas Visitors Profile.* Las Vegas: LVCVA; National Gambling Impact Study Commission [NGISC]. 1999. *Final Report.* Washington, DC: NGISC; Thompson, William N. 1994. *Taxation and Casino Gambling.* Las Vegas: Mirage; Thompson, William N. 1998. "Not Exactly the Best Gaming Venue: The Nevada Grocery Store Casino." *Gaming Law Review* 2, no. 5 (October): 459–461; Revenue Act of 1941 (Public Law 77–250, signed into law 20 September 1941); Revenue Act of 1951 (Public Law 82–183, signed into law 20 October 1951).

See also Casino; Economics and Gambling; The Economic Impacts of Gambling; Lotteries; Pari-mutuel Wagering Systems

Tennessee

When Tennessee received statehood in 1796 as the fifteenth state, it was a land on the frontier filled with individualists. Leaders such as Andrew Jackson were very active gamblers, playing many kinds of card games and also wagering on horse races. The heritage of wide-open community life did not last into the twentieth century. In the modern era, horse-race betting was legalized; however, tracks were not economically viable, and all of them closed before the 1990s. Charitable gambling is not permitted, although it has taken several police crackdowns to stop many of the games. The state has no lottery, nor does it permit any other gambling. In 2000, Tennessee was one of only three states without any active form of legalized gambling.

Sources: Thompson, William N. 1997. *Legalized Gambling: A Reference Handbook.* 2d ed. Santa Barbara, CA: ABC-CLIO, 163–166,176.

Texas

Texas has been the home to gamblers since its inception as a political entity. Whether the Texans were on the frontier in gambling saloons, in illegal Galveston or Dallas casinos, or off in Las Vegas (or in recent years Shreveport, Louisiana), they have loved the "action." The attorney general of the state, Will Wilson, cracked down on illegal casinos in Galveston in 1957, prompting an effort to legalize the gambling. The efforts were aborted after local voters expressed a dislike for the casinos in advisory votes. Periodically there have been weak attempts to gain support for casinos, but these have all been unsuccessful. In the meantime, charitable gambling operations have been established in the state. Also, "gray" machines offering winners coupons for merchandise have existed openly in truck stops across the state, although their legality has been questioned.

In 1992, the state launched a lottery, which quickly became one of the most successful in the United States, trailing only New York in sales for some years. The lottery offered instant games, lotto, and daily numbers games. Horse-track racing experienced ups and downs in attempts at legislation over seven decades, but finally in the 1990s licensing for tracks began. There are now eight tracks, the biggest being the Lone Star Park near Dallas–Fort Worth.

A lottery ticket machine in a Texas grocery store.

The state has only three Native American reservations. One—the Alabama Coushatta—is near Livingston, seventy miles north of Houston. The tribal members once voted against casinos, as they believe that outside gamblers would disturb their quality of life. They are also strongly religious. Another vote in 1999, however, indicated that they were destined to have a casino. Two other tribes, the Kickapoos in Eagle Pass and the Tiguas in El Paso, have started gambling operations with bingo games, card games, and machines. The state has refused to negotiate compacts with the two tribes, and legal controversies surround the gambling.

Sources: Dombrink, John D., and William N. Thompson. 1990. *The Last Resort: Success and Failure in Campaigns for Casinos.* Reno: University of Nevada Press, 138–144.

Thompson, "Titanic"
(Alvin Clarence Thomas)

Alvin Clarence Thomas was one of the great gambling hustlers of the modern era. He was born in the Ozarks near Monnet, Missouri, on 30 November 1892. There are several different stories about why he was called "Titantic." Some refer to the notion that he was unsinkable, unlike the ship. Others suggest that when he won a lot of money, he was on the top of the world, but that he would often sink rapidly if he continued to play. For many years he was "Titanic Thomas," but once a newspaper mistakenly called him "Titanic Thompson," and he did not bother to make a correction, perhaps liking the sound of the name better. After all, he was not fond of being called Alvin Clarence either—why not change it all. Titanic was renowned for the proposition bet. He loved all games, and he loved to participate in physical games as well as to turn cards or roll dice. As a teenager, he trained his dog to dive into a fifteen-foot-deep pond to retrieve rocks he threw. One day he "chanced" upon a fisherman who had a modern rod and reel that the teenager coveted. He engaged in conversation with the fisherman, who said he sure liked the dog. Thompson made a wager—"I'll bet my dog against your rod and reel that my dog can fetch this small pebble from the bottom of the pool if I throw it in." The bet was made, and to ensure that all was on the up and up, Titanic marked the pebble with an X. He threw it in, the dog jumped after it, dived to the bottom of the pool, and brought up a pebble in his mouth. The pebble was marked with an X. Thompson won his first proposition. He neglected to tell the fisherman that he had spent the previous day marking pebbles with X's and lining the pool with them.

His talents as an athlete were renowned. Al Capone once wagered that Thompson could not throw an orange over a five-story building. Titanic extracted a good odds advantage and then indicated that he needed a harder orange. He returned from a fruit stand and threw the "orange" over the building. In fact, with sleight of hand he had changed the orange for a harder and smaller lemon. Capone just laughed and paid him off, not knowing he had been tricked.

Titanic Thompson was an accomplished golf player, and he hustled millions of dollars on various wagers on the golf courses. He often won money from professional players from whom he would negotiate a handicap advantage—although he was capable of winning straight up. He was very adept at determining the changing odds as a poker game progressed. Had blackjack been popular, he would have been able to execute the card-counting strategies of Edward Thorpe with the best of them. Thompson could also work magic with his hands, dealing any card from the bottom or middle of a deck of cards. He could substitute crooked dice into a craps game. With his crowd and such advantage he could achieve what was always considered "fair game." The loser had only two options, pay up and play again, or pay up and not play again.

Titantic Thompson did not have a formal education, and he could not read or write for his entire life. But he could count, he could figure out numbers quickly in his head, and he could memorize words. He achieved great wealth during the course of his hustling days, and he used all the trappings of wealth in his games. He had a fine home in Beverly Hills, he drove the best cars, and he wore elaborate clothes. He also had beautiful wives—five of them at different times.

Thompson played with the most renowned gamblers of his time, from Al Capone to Johnny Moss. He also played with Arthur Rothstein. In

1928 he was in Rothstein's last card game. Rothstein, like other gamblers, had his favorite games, but there were also games where he was a sucker. In poker, Rothstein was a sucker. Leading players from all over the country descended upon his New York City apartment when he put out the word that he wanted to play. He liked games with no limit, and he had a reputation of paying off. In this game, he lost hundreds of thousands of dollars to Thompson and others, and he gave his word that he would make his payoff later. He word was accepted, but he welshed on his promise. After several weeks passed, and he kept avoiding his obligation, he declared that the game was rigged and would not pay. He was found in a hotel lobby with a bullet wound in his side. He refused to talk from his hospital bed, where he died a day later. Thompson was arrested along with the other players in the big game. He testified in the murder trial to the integrity of his co-players, and the charges were dropped for lack of evidence. Thompson was never considered the triggerman, although in his hustling career he had killed at least five men in "self-defense" situations.

Titanic Thompson was in his heyday through the 1950s when the big players discovered Las Vegas and routinized their play. They sought regular games with rules. The big gambling scene for hustlers was over. He suffered a major downfall when he was jailed for several months in 1962 after a big party at his Phoenix home. It was found that one of the "playmates" in his crowd of friends was underage. He dropped from the scene, although for his remaining days he kept trying to hustle—efforts that led to losses as often as wins. In May 1974, at the age of eighty-one, he died of a stroke in a rest home near Dallas. He was broke and broken.

Sources: Bradshaw, Jon. 1975. *Fast Company.* New York: Harper Magazine Press, 197–239; Chafetz, Henry. 1960. *Play the Devil: A History of Gambling in the United States from 1492 to 1955.* New York: Potter Publishers, 425; Stowers, Carlton. 1982. *The Unsinkable Titanic Thompson.* Burnet, TX: Eakin Press.

See also Rothstein, Arnold

The Travel Act of 1961

The Travel Act of 1961 was designed to target members of organized crime. It was part of Attorney General Robert F. Kennedy's crime package of legislation. The law was written in very general terms and could be applied to myriad situations involving individuals or criminal groups. A person could be punished with a fine of $10,000 or a prison sentence of five years for traveling "in interstate commerce" or using any facility of interstate commerce (including the mail) with an intent to commit a "crime of violence" or to "otherwise promote, manage, establish," or carry out any unlawful activity." "Any unlawful activity" included gambling.

In the broad sweep of the language in the act, it could apply to a wide variety of methods of "transportation," possibly even the Internet, and credit card machines. Courts have even held that intrastate mails are covered by the act, as they are part of an interstate mail system.

Sources: The Travel Act of 1961 (Public Law 87–228, signed 13 September 1961).

Trente et Quarante (30 and 40)

Trente et quarante has been a very popular game in Continental European casinos, especially in France, where the game was developed. It is a simple luck game that gives the player a very good expected return of more than 98 percent. All the bets are even-money bets. The dealer uses a six-deck shoe. Cards are given their number value; aces count as one, and face cards count as ten. The dealer deals out two rows of cards. The first row is called *noir* (black); the second row is called *rouge* (red). Cards are dealt until each row has a collective card value between 31 and 40. For instance, the dealer deals a 6 of hearts, 10, queen, 3, and 8 for a total of 37 for the first (noir) row. Then he or she deals a 9, jack, ace, five, and seven for a total of 32 on the second (rouge) row. The row with the lower number (closest to 31) wins. In this example, the rouge row wins. Players betting on rouge win even money; for example. $100 on a $100 bet. The players may also make an even-money bet on whether or not the first card dealt (the 6 of hearts) has the same color as the winning line (rouge). As the heart is red, and the winning line is red, those betting "color" (yes) win. Those betting "inverse" (no) lose that bet. If the two lines tie, there is no bet, unless there is a tie on the number 31. Then the house takes half of all bets, giving the house a small edge of about 1.1 percent.

A side bet of 1 percent of the original stake (ergo, $1) may be made to insure that the 31 tie situation does not arise. If this insurance bet is placed and there is a 31 tie, the player does not lose half of his or her bet and keeps his or her insurance bet. If there is no 31 tie, the player loses the insurance bet, but the other bets are paid as if there were no insurance side bet. The insurance bet reduces the house edge to 0.9 percent. (If the casino requires an insurance bet in excess of 1 percent, it increases its edge, and players are wise to avoid the bet). There is a 2.19 percent chance that there will be a 31 tie.

Being a simple game with easily tracked results, trente et quarante attracts system bettors. The low house edge also makes the game very desirable for high rollers. It is also a fast game, making the table one of the most exciting places in the staid European casino halls.

Sources: Scarne, John. 1986. *Scarne's New Complete Guide to Gambling.* New York: Simon and Schuster, 515–518; Sifakis, Carl. 1990. *Encyclopedia of Gambling.* New York: Facts on File, 295–296.

Trump, Donald John

Donald John Trump emerged as the dominant personality of Atlantic City in the 1980s as he developed three casinos in the East Coast gambling center. He was not yet in his forties when he won a license in 1982, along with his younger brother, Robert, to build and operate the Trump Plaza. Soon he negotiated a merger for the ownership of the property with Holiday Inn. The finished property opened in 1984 as the Harrah's at Trump Plaza. In 1986, Trump bought out his Holiday Inn partners and also purchased a casino, which was being constructed by the Hilton Corporation, after Hilton was denied a license. The project became known as the Trump Castle. In 1988 he acquired rights to the Taj Mahal casino in a financial struggle with Resorts International and directed the completion of Atlantic City's largest property, which at the time featured the largest casino floor in the world. By the time the Taj Mahal opened in 1989, it carried a price tag of $1 billion, the highest

price for any casino project in the world up to the time. High prices come at a cost, and in the early 1990s, the property went through a bankruptcy action in order to survive. But as the economy began to improve in the mid-1990s, Trump's properties made money again, or at least could satisfy their creditors. That is, he did well enough to be able to sell equity shares in his properties and keep everything afloat. Out of the debts he arose again as the champion of the Boardwalk. He also reached out to the Midwest by opening a large riverboat in Indiana on the shores of Lake Michigan. The self-proclaimed master of "the deal" even allowed his sights to scan the political landscape, as he publicly pondered a run for the presidency in year 2000 on the Reform party ticket.

Donald Trump was raised in wealth. His father, Fred Trump, was a builder who parlayed construction of individual housing beginning in the 1920s into development of tracts and building of large apartment complexes, often with government subsidies. His father learned all about political connections and how they were necessary in his line of work. Donald was born in 1946 in the Jamaica Estates in Queens, a borough of New York City. His family lived in a twenty-three-room mansion. As a youth, the younger Trump gained a taste for fancy cars, tailored clothes, and fancy women—what he would consider to be the most important things in life—possessions. He also showed a proclivity to follow in his father's footsteps as a builder.

He was sent to the New York Military Academy in Cornwell on the Hudson. He was a good student, and he demonstrated leadership qualities. After military academy Trump attended Fordham University and the Wharton School at the University of Pennsylvania. He graduated with a B.A. in economics in 1968. Trump expressed disappointment that the real estate courses at Penn emphasized single-family dwellings because he desired to build big things. Soon he was working with his father building bigger things. And soon after that, he left to go on his own because his father did not want to build big enough things. His father was somewhat content to be rich building in the neighborhoods, but Donald Trump wanted Manhattan.

Trump saw his first big opportunity come when the Penn Central Railroad declared bankruptcy. He took options on some of their land alongside the Hudson River, and he also took an option on the fifty-nine-year-old Commodore Hotel. He persuaded the city to purchase the riverfront land for a major convention center. Trump cut a deal with the Hyatt Corporation to construct the Grand Hyatt on the Commodore location; the new hotel, with 1,400 rooms, was finished in 1990. Almost simultaneously, Trump started other hotel projects and also a high-rise apartment building called Trump Towers. He visited Atlantic City often and pondered casinos. He never gave them serious thought, however, until he saw reports saying how Hilton's two Las Vegas hotel casinos made almost half the income of all Hilton properties in the United States. Suddenly he realized that even a mediocre hotel with a casino could be much more profitable that the most luxurious hotels of the world.

Trump took a long look at Atlantic City before jumping into that market. He wanted land near the center of the Boardwalk area. In 1980, some land investors came to him with a plan by which he could gain control over what he considered the most prime land in the city. In his book *The Art of the Deal,* Trump describes the intricacies of how to put many separately owned parcels of land together (Trump and Schwartz 1987). Every offer he made for a purchase was contingent upon all parcels being purchased. He also determined that he would not start to build a casino until he was fully licensed. In 1982 he and his younger brother, Robert, won casino licenses. After he began to construct his casino, he went into a partnership with Holiday Inn. When the casino hotel was finished in 1984, it was called Harrah's at Trump Plaza. He bought out his partner in March 1986 and installed his brother as its manager. Later Steve Hyde took over control of the casino aspects of the operation. The property became the Trump Plaza. By then, Trump had taken over the Hilton's 614-room hotel casino complex in a deal that was necessitated by the fact that the New Jersey gambling authorities had denied Hilton a license in 1985.

When the complicated deal was completed, Trump chose his wife, Ivana, to be the property manager of the new Trump Castle. Ivana had absolutely no experience in gaming—for a fact, nei-

ther did Trump. She saw the Castle as a place of glamour that could attract high rollers, whereas Hilton had intended to have a slot-intensive facility that would cater to the masses. The Plaza was a place for high rollers. Rather than working with a strategy that tied the two properties together, Trump encouraged Hyde and Ivana to operate as competitors. Soon internal corporate battles turned vicious. Also, Trump had found a girlfriend named Marla Maples. In order to conceal his affair with Maples, Trump allied himself with Hyde in the battle between Hyde and Ivana. His tryst flowered in the Plaza. Finally, Trump felt it was necessary to remove Ivana from the Castle and get her out of town. He publicly humiliated her as he moved her into management of one of his New York City properties. An inevitable divorce was followed by a short marriage to Marla Maples.

The next casino opportunity came for Trump when Resorts International president James Crosby died on 10 April 1986 at the premature age of fifty-eight. In 1984 he had revealed plans for the largest casino attached to a hotel in the United States. The Taj Mahal was to have over 120,000 feet of gambling space and over 1,000 rooms—the largest number in Atlantic City. Resorts won all the approvals for construction, and the process of building began. The death of Crosby plunged Resorts into a fiscal crisis, however, and Trump made a move to buy out the company and hence acquire the rights to the "largest casino in America." As the New Jersey law provided that a casino owner could have only three properties, Trump indicated that he would close the Resorts Casino as soon as the Taj Mahal opened. Trump did win a controlling position in Resorts with his stock purchases. He found, however, that he lacked the capital to finish the Taj Mahal. Television entertainer Merv Griffin, in a sense, bailed Trump out by purchasing all Resorts property except the Taj Mahal from Trump in 1988. In 1989, the project was completed. Trump, however, did not have the funds to properly open the facility. Legal troubles flowing from his divorce further complicated his already complex financial affairs. The property was also beset with a tragedy, as Steve Hyde, who was to become its manager, and two other top executives were killed in a helicopter accident on 10 October 1989. Only recourse to bankruptcy proceedings in 1992 and transfers of equity in the property to bond holders and other creditors saved the property.

In 1995, Trump completed an initial public offering on the New York Stock Exchange to sell more than $300 million of common stock and senior secured notes backed by his casino revenue flow. That same year he was named to be a member of the World Gaming Congress Hall of Fame. When his rival, Stephen Wynn, heard this, he asked the congress to remove his name from the Hall of Fame. A rivalry persists, but Trump is the one who can say he "turned things around." Showing that he has something like the proverbial nine lives of a cat, Trump has survived to go into riverboat gambling (actually lakeside) and set his visions on a run for political office. He remains a man in search of a big deal, wherever that deal might be found.

Sources: Johnston, David. 1992. *Temples of Chance: How America Inc. Bought out Murder Inc. to Win Control of the Casino Business.* New York: Doubleday; Morrison, Robert S. 1994. *High Stakes to High Risk: The Strange Story of Resorts International and the Taj Mahal.* Ashtabula, OH: Lake Erie Press; Trump, Donald, and Tony Schwartz. 1987. *Trump: The Art of the Deal.* New York: Random House.

Two Up

Two up is a popular game in Australia. It was played briefly at the Main Street Station casino in downtown Las Vegas during the 1990s. It is quite a simple game that involves tossing two coins in the air and watching them make their random falls to the floor. Its social setting provides the action in the game. A group of players surrounds the one who is selected to toss the coins using a special stick. Players can bet that two heads or two tails will come up. If the two coins are different—odds—there is no decision, and they are tossed again. When two heads or two tails are the correct bet, the payoff is even money. If five odds come up in a row, however, all players lose. All persons in the circle around the coin tosser may make bets. The players may bet that heads or tails will come up three times in a row, and if they do, players are paid off at 7.5 to 1 for a 6.25 percent house advantage (odds are ignored in the sequence).

U

Uruguay

Uruguay is a small country with an area of only 63,000 square miles (the size of Missouri) and a population of about 3,200,000. It is between the two largest countries of South America: Argentina and Brazil. These countries, with their restrictions on casino gambling (nearby Buenos Aires does not have casino gambling), provide tourist market customers, especially for Uruguayan facilities along the Atlantic Coast beaches. Uruguay has a free economy, and the flow of foreign currency in and out of the country is unrestricted. There is no discrimination between nationals and foreigners, and for that reason there has been an inflow of casino investment dollars.

Private casinos existed in Uruguay more than 100 years ago. The first gaming law passed in 1856.

Legend has it that French immigrants started casinos to conduct their tradition roulette games. The government took over the casinos early in the twentieth century, and up until the 1990s, governments owned all casinos. Two municipally owned casinos were in the capital city of Montevideo, and the national government owned a series of small facilities along the ocean and in interior cities bordering Brazil and Argentina. Then the government authorized the building of a private five-star hotel with a casino in Punta del Este. The facility, which opened on 1 January 1997, is operated by Conrad International.

In Montevideo, the earnings of the two municipal casinos—the Parque Hotel and Hotel Casino Carrasco—go to the city government. In the rest of the country, Dirección Nacional de Casinos del

The municipally owned Carrasco Casino in Montevideo, Uruguay.

Parque Casino of Montevideo, Uruguay

Estado (an entity of the central government) owns and operates the casinos. Forty percent of its earnings go to the municipality in which the casino is established, 20 percent to the Ministry of Tourism, 10 percent to the National Food Institute, and the last 10 percent to a special fund for the preservation of the casinos. In 1995 a national casino was opened in the Hotel Victoria Plaza in Montevideo.

Uruguay also has facilities for horse racing and bingo games, and the government also operates a lottery.

Sources: Cabot, Anthony N., William N. Thompson, Andrew Tottenham, and Carl Braunlich, eds. 1999. *International Casino Law.* 3d ed. Reno: Institute for the Study of Gambling, University of Nevada, Reno, 317–319.

Utah

Utah is one of two states to enter the twenty-first century with no legally authorized form of gambling (the other is Hawaii). In 1992, the voters de-feated an effort to establish pari-mutuel betting on horse racing. Horse races are conducted at fairs, but no betting is permitted. Throughout the state there are small charity games, but these are operating contrary to the law. Utah residents are not totally adverse to casino betting, however, as Nevada casino entrepreneurs have set up facilities near state lines in order to capture their patronage. Several casinos in Mesquite, Nevada (in Clark County thirty miles from St. George), and Wendover, Nevada (in White Pine County 100 miles from Salt Lake City), market their products to Utah gamblers. Periodically, supporters of casino gambling in Utah try to start campaigns for casinos by pointing out how gambling money is leaving the state. The political leaders of what is probably the most church-oriented state in the union do not, however, give much attention to the advocates of any form of gambling.

Sources: Thompson, William N. 1997. *Legalized Gambling: A Reference Handbook.* 2d ed. Santa Barbara, CA: ABC-CLIO, 162–167.

V

Venezuela

Some gambling activity is quite legal in Venezuela, but other activity operates on the edge of the law. Bingo parlors, horse and dog racing, and government lotteries are authorized; however, casinos are in some sort of limbo. In recent years, many casinos have operated on Margarita Island—a tourist resort area—and other locations under authorizations from local governments. The country of 15 million avoided resolving many regulatory issues, however, as there was no national law on casinos. Finally in 1996 a national law was passed. National authorities sought to preempt all local authorization of casino gaming. Under the law, casinos were permitted in five-star hotels with 200 rooms if they were located in tourist zones. Margarita Island was one such zone. The casinos were to be given ten-year renewable licenses. They were taxed at a rate of 20 percent of their gross gaming wins. Most of the casinos closed because they could not meet requirements for licensing, and only one received a license. That casino, the Grand Casino Margarita, is located in the Margarita Hilton Hotel. It is run by CIRSA, a Spanish gaming company. The government has approved eight other zones for casinos, but no licenses are pending.

Sources: Cabot, Anthony N., William N. Thompson, Andrew Tottenham, and Carl Braunlich, eds. 1999. *International Casino Law.* 3d ed. Reno: Institute for the Study of Gambling, University of Nevada, Reno, 320.

Vermont

Vermont ranks forty-sixth in gambling revenues among the forty-seven states that have some form of legalized gambling. Only Alaska has less gambling. Vermont created a state lottery in 1978. Of the thirty-eight lottery jurisdictions in the United States (thirty-seven states plus the District of Columbia), only Montana sells fewer tickets. Although Vermont is a very small state, it has not joined the Powerball multistate lottery that was designed so that small states could generate sales through offering large jackpot prizes. Previously, the state joined with New Hampshire and Maine in the Tri-State lotto game.

Although horse-race betting is permitted at Vermont tracks, there were no such tracks as the state entered the twenty-first century. There is a short dog-racing season at the Green Mountain racetrack.

The closest the state has come to considering casino gambling has been the effort of the Abeniki Native Americans to have lands in the state declared to be reservation lands. It is assumed that if they ever get federal recognition, they will seek also to gain a compact for gambling.

Sources: www.vt.lottery.com.

Video Lottery Terminals. *See* Lotteries

Virgin Islands

The Virgin Islands lie off the eastern edge of Puerto Rico. The islands are controlled by the governments of the United States and Great Britain. The U.S. Virgin Islands (USVI) consist of fifty small islands. The most populated of the USVI are St. Croix, St. Thomas, and St. John. Together the USVI have just over 100,000 residents. In 1989, Hurricane Hugo devastated the tourist islands. Many properties were destroyed, as was much of the islands' infrastructure. A depression ensued during which many of the air flights to the islands ceased. In 1995 the two leading employers—Hess Oil and Virgin Island Alumina—cut production and downsized by 650 employees. Casino gambling, an idea that had been rejected several times before, suddenly became popular. A referendum was authorized, and the voters endorsed casinos by a narrow margin. On 3 November 1995, the Virgin Islands' representative assembly followed the popular will by passing legislation authorizing casino licenses. The law was amended on 6 March 1997.

The legislation provides for up to six casinos in hotels on St. Croix island. The first of the six opened in 2000 at the Divi Carina Bay Resort. The resort now has only 126 rooms, twenty villas, and a convention center. The licenses are issued by a board of commissioners appointed by the governor. Of the six licenses, one must go to a company that is obligated to build a 1,500-room hotel and have a gaming area of 20,000 square feet or more in the facility, along with convention and banquet facilities. Two licenses go to hotels with at least 300 rooms and a casino of 10,000 square feet or more, while another two go to hotels of at least 200 rooms located in two historic districts of the island. A smaller casino may be licensed in another hotel with at least 150 rooms. The Divi Carina barely qualifies. Licensing fees are related to the size of the casino. The taxation formula for the casinos is an 8-percent win tax for their first two years, then 10 percent for the next two years, and 12 percent thereafter. The taxation formula was derived from the laws of New Jersey. As in New Jersey, the casinos must also make investments of 1.25 percent of their gross revenues in development projects on the island. The casinos are also subject to the U.S. cash transaction reporting rules and the reporting rules of the Internal Revenue Service.

Many of the details of the New Jersey gaming law were incorporated into the legislation, as the lawmakers felt that the "strict" regulatory model of New Jersey would best suit the Virgin Islands' needs for high integrity. The needs may indeed have been met in their entirety. No one can challenge the integrity of casino gaming in the Virgin Islands.

Sources: Cabot, Anthony N., William N. Thompson, Andrew Tottenham, and Carl Braunlich, eds. 1999. *International Casino Law.* 3d ed. Reno: Institute for the Study of Gambling, University of Nevada, Reno, 261–272; www.carinabay.com.

Virginia

Virginia established a lottery in 1988 after many false starts over the previous fifteen years. Fifty-six percent of the voters supported the lottery proposition. Virginia participates in the multistate Big Game lotto, as well as selling its own lotto tickets, numbers games, and instant tickets. The revenues of the lottery are earmarked for educational purposes. Charitable gaming is also permitted, and there are facilities for offtrack race betting. There is no casino gambling, as the state has successfully fought off efforts of ocean cruise ships to dock at ports in the state.

Although Virginia has come to gambling authorizations only recently in the modern era, the state certainly has had a history of gambling. Within the first five years of its existence as an English colony, Virginia became the beneficiary of a lottery authorized by King James. In 1620, twenty mares were shipped from England to Virginia Colony, and horse racing with private wagering became a regular activity for the settlers. In later colonial days, lotteries were prevalent. George Washington and Thomas Jefferson participated in most forms of gambling—they played cards, raced horses, and were involved in lotteries. Jefferson conducted a lottery in 1826 in an effort to dispense of his property so that he could pay all his debts prior to his death. Unfortunately, he died before this result could be realized.

Sources: Thompson, William N. 1997. *Legalized Gambling: A Reference Handbook.* 2d ed. Santa Barbara, CA: ABC-CLIO, 7–9, 89–90.

The Wagering Paraphernalia Act of 1961

The Wagering Paraphernalia Act of 1961 was part of Atty. Gen. Robert F. Kennedy's crime-fighting legislation package. The act authorized fines up to $10,000 and prison sentences up to five years for any person who "knowingly carries or sends" in any interstate commerce any information that is conveyed as writing, paper, token, slip, bills, certificates, tickets, record, paraphernalia, or "devices used" for the purpose of "bookmaking," "wagering pools with respect to a sporting event," or lotteries and numbers games. The law did not apply where the wagers were legal in the state to which they were sent.

The purpose of the act seemed to be to cut off supplies to illegal gamers, especially those in numbers games and illegal lotteries that were dependent upon paper products. The act did not apply to materials carried by common carriers as a normal part of their business, to pari-mutuel materials sent to tracks where wagering was legal, to newspaper publications, or to materials used in legal lotteries.

In 1993, the penalty provisions were amended to authorize fines from $3,000 to $30,000, with maximum prison time remaining at five years.

Sources: The Wagering Paraphernalia Act of 1961 (Public Law 87–218, signed into law 13 September 1961).

Wagering Systems, Pari-mutuel. *See* Pari-mutuel Wagering Systems

Washington

The state of Washington has had legalized gambling for most of a century. Pari-mutuel horse-race betting was established with the opening of the Longacres course in 1933. The state now has five tracks. The Longacres facility was purchased by Boeing Aircraft Company for plant use.

The state also has a government-operated lottery under control of the Washington State Lottery Commission. The lottery was authorized in 1982. The state's most popular games are instant tickets. It also offers lotto and daily numbers games. Additionally, gambling games may be conducted by charities, by amusement centers for children, and by commercial establishments in the form of casino table games; pull tabs, including video pull-tab machines; and punch boards. The machines, which may also include a daily keno game, are under the supervision of the lottery.

There are sixteen Native American casinos operating under state-negotiated compacts, pursuant to the Indian Gaming Regulatory Act. Table games have been authorized through compacts; however, machines have not been, although the tribes utilize machines that appear to be slot machines anyway, and they have operated them while the state was unsuccessful in winning federal support to stop their play.

In 1996, the voters of the state were asked to approve slot machines for the tribes. Only 44 percent were in favor of the machines. The state also authorizes instant video ticket machines (IVTMs) to dispense instant lottery tickets (scratch-off tickets) directly to a buying public that inserts currency into the machine for tickets. These machines can be placed in any location in the state and dispense tickets twenty-four hours a day, 365 days a year.

Bingo games are conducted for charities and at Native American facilities as live games. Bingo is also conducted through satellite operations connecting Native American casinos in Washington to ones in other states. Additionally, bingo is conducted through electronic machines.

A bank of pull tabs, an instant lottery-type game, in a Washington state casino.

Washington authorized commercial public card rooms in 1976. Initially, the games were basically player-banked games—poker and blackjack in which the deal rotated among players—until the legislature approved house-banked card games in 1997. The commission first approved a two-year test project, which allowed these commercial card rooms to essentially be full-scale casinos. They were allowed to have fifteen table games. The commercial minicasinos also could have banks of state-owned pull-tab machines and large boxes of pull tabs for sale. There was no limit on the number of machines. During the first six months of the test, the minicasinos had twenty-five-dollar limits per play; however, afterward the limits were raised to $100 for each play. The pilot project for having commercial (mini) casinos was ended in March 2000. The state deemed it a success, or so it must have done, for the project was made permanent. There are now approximately sixty such casinos. I toured casinos as a consultant for the Colville tribe in April 2000.

These minicasinos are not small facilities, as they offer players up to fifteen live casino games that operate almost identically to the casino table games found in Las Vegas. They certainly have the form and appearance of table games in Las Vegas. Considering the world of gambling, it may be suggested that fifteen tables represent not a minicasino, but rather an average-sized casino. Off the Las Vegas Strip, fifteen tables would be considered average or even a large casino facility. The minicasinos call themselves casinos.

Revenues from legalized gambling in Washington are substantial. In 1997, players gambled over $1.5 billion in legal facilities in the state, in non–Native American facilities. The players lost over $460 million of this amount. The addition of commercial minicasinos and expanded compacted Native American casinos and machine gaming makes the amount of gambling money much higher today—probably well over double the amount.

Sources: Christiansen, Eugene Martin. 1999. "The 1998 Gross Annual Wager." *International Gaming and Wagering Business* (August): 20 ff; "North American Gaming Report 1998." 1998. *International Gaming and Wagering Business* (July): S27–S28.

Native American casino run by the Tulalip Tribe of Maryville, Washington.

West Virginia

West Virginia launched a state lottery in 1986. By that date, horse-race wagering was firmly in place, having won legislative authorization in 1933. Charitable bingo games were also popular. The appearance of the lottery gave the tracks of the state a hook with which they sought to win the right to have machine gambling, and they were successful.

The West Virginia legislature authorized an experimental installation of video gaming machines—keno machines, poker machines, and machines with symbols—at Mountaineer horse-racing track beginning on 9 June 1990. At first, only seventy machines were installed. During the experimental time the number grew to 400 in 1994, most of them being keno machines. The first machines had payouts of 88.6 percent. During a three-year experimental period the lottery agreed not to put machines in other locations. Now machines are at the three other tracks as well. The track keeps 70 percent of the revenues, and 30 percent goes to the state.

The machines were operated by the state lottery. Lottery director Butch Bryan said, "We developed VLTs [video lottery terminals] to save our horse racing industry. We think it is doing what we designed it for. It has been very beneficial to the horse track. It may not cure their problems in the long run, but it will certainly prolong their life. We believe the entertainment aspect of VLTs is good for the horse racing industry" (LaFleur 1992, 65). In 1993, Bryan was convicted of insider trading, bid rigging, and lying to a grand jury in the state's purchase of the machines. According to a news story in *International Gaming and Wagering Business* November-December 1993, he owned stock in the major company that won the supply contract.

Sources: La Fleur, Terri. 1992. "Charting the Growth of Video Lottery." *International Gaming and Wagering Business* (August-September): 1, 62, 64–65; Thompson, William N. 1999. "Racinos and the Public Interest." *Gaming Law Review* 3(5–6): 283–286.

See also The Racino

Western Canadian Lottery Corporation

The Western Canadian Lottery Corporation (WCLC) was formed in 1974 by an agreement among the governments of British Columbia, Alberta, Saskatchewan, and Manitoba. The Yukon and Northwest territories have joined the WCLC as associate members, and the products of the corporation are sold in the territories. The products include instant tickets, weekly draws, and lotto games. In 1976, the WCLC governments entered into an agreement with Ontario to run nationwide lotto games. The Inter-Provincial Lottery Corporation is now an organization encompassing all provinces and territories. Sales of the WCLC are recorded by each province, and revenues are distributed accordingly. The profits are distributed within the jurisdictions in a manner designated by the individual province or territory. In 1985, British Columbia withdrew from the WCLC, and it now conducts its own lottery games.

Sources: Cabot, Anthony N., William N. Thompson, Andrew Tottenham, and Carl Braunlich, eds. 1999. *International Casino Law.* 3d ed. Reno: Institute for the Study of Gambling, University of Nevada, Reno, 154–157.

Wheels of Fortune. *See* Roulette and Wheels of Fortune

Wisconsin

The primary form of gambling in Wisconsin is found in the seventeen casinos on eleven Native American reservations. The casino gambling was legally authorized in compacts between the tribes and the state, first negotiated in 1992 and then renewed in 1998.

The 1998 compacts permit machine gaming and blackjack table games as well as bingo, and the tribes agree to pay the state 3 percent of the revenues they win.

The largest gaming complex in the state is on the Oneida reservation near Green Bay. The complex, which includes a full-service Radisson Inn Hotel, a new casino, and a bingo hall as well as satellite gaming areas, has over 4,000 machines and 120 blackjack tables.

The development of casino gambling in Wisconsin fits the general scheme in the United States. It did not happen "on purpose." It started in 1973 with a public referendum vote that approved a state constitutional amendment to allow bingo games for charities. In 1975, the legislature implemented the action of the voters by designing rules for charity bingo games. Using the status of a charity, the Oneidas offered a bingo game in September 1975. The voters also approved an amendment authorizing raffles in 1977.

For several years, Wisconsin tribes ran games according to the state's legislated rules. Like other tribes with severe economic needs, however, they took notice when in 1978 a Seminole reservation in Hollywood, Florida, decided to gain an edge on its bingo non–Native American competition. The tribe began offering very large prizes, which violated the state's rules. The large prizes immediately attracted large droves of customers, and profits increased. As with the Seminoles, the Wisconsin tribe's actions were upheld as being legal.

During the 1980s, Wisconsin tribes experimented with a variety of games. The Menominees used a Ping Pong ball device to generate numbers for roulette games and also to indicate cards for blackjack games. But the real casino games came

The Hudson Dog Track in Wisconsin: Scene of a political battle over Native American casino gambling.

in 1987, following the U.S. Supreme Court's *Cabazon* ruling, handed down in February 1987.

In March 1987, the Menominees decided to offer regular blackjack games at their gaming facility. In April 1987, just two months after the *Cabazon* ruling, the voters were asked to amend the state constitution to remove the ban on lotteries and to authorize pari-mutuel betting on dog races. The legislature had put the question on the ballot. The public wanted a lottery to compete with lottery games in Illinois and Michigan and passed the measure by a 70 percent to 30 percent margin.

Based upon the lottery amendment, in 1989 the state Department of Justice indicated that the state could negotiate agreements (under provisions of the Indian Gaming Regulatory Act) with the reservations permitting them to have casino games. Yet when the state did not follow through on negotiations, the tribes took the matter to federal courts, where they won a ruling forcing the state to negotiate. Soon after, the governor signed compacts.

In 1992, after the governor had concluded casino compacts for the other reservations, the Forest Potawatomis asked the governor if they could have casino games in Milwaukee. The governor and the tribe compromised on a plan that allows 200 machines at the bingo facility. At a later date, they were allowed to have 1,000 machines.

As the new century began, the tribes' casinos were winning over a billion dollars a year, according to my investigations for several tribes. Several tribes were seeking new locations for casinos. The four dog tracks of the state were considered to be good casino sites. Some smaller tribes were denied the opportunity to complete a deal for a dog track in Hudson, Wisconsin, because of a decision made by the U.S. secretary of the interior, Bruce Babbitt. A federal special prosecutor then investigated Babbitt, as his political party (the Democrats) had taken large contributions from larger rival tribes that did not want competition from a new casino at the track. He was cleared of any wrongdoing.

Wisconsin represents not only a strong Native American casino venue, but also one in which rivalries among the tribal gambling operations are quite open and obvious.

Sources: Thompson, William N., Ricardo Gazel, and Dan Rickman. 1995. *The Social Costs of Gambling in Wisconsin.* Mequon, WI: Wisconsin Policy Research Institute.

Wynn, Stephen Alan

Stephen Alan Wynn may be considered a modern day "savior" for Las Vegas. Even though the Las Vegas Strip had not exactly died in the 1980s, it was not healthy. Wynn may not have raised a Lazarus from the grave, but he certainly performed the role of "healer" for a moribund casino industry. He "healed" with the medicine the community vitally needed—a good dose of entrepreneurial risk-taking and an infusion of new capital investment. Revenues for the Strip were flat in the 1980s. No new Las Vegas property had been constructed since the completion of the MGM Grand (now Bally's) in 1973.

Other investors had shunned the town. New Jersey casino magnate Donald Trump had rejected Las Vegas. Wynn, however, turned away from his Atlantic City ventures and came back to the city of his corporate beginnings, Las Vegas. He "put it all on the line," and he "rolled a seven" as he developed what was truly the first mega-resort for the Strip, the Mirage.

In its sixty-five-year history in Las Vegas, the casino industry has many times had to call on individuals to rescue it from pending crashes into oblivion. A post–World War II economic letdown threatened to suspend a flow of tourist dollars as well as local dollars that could go into casino coffers. Bugsy Siegel appeared on the scene with his vision of world-class tourist-destination casinos; he built the Flamingo, and the Las Vegas Strip was in business. In the 1960s, federal investigative authorities focused attention on organized crime with investments in Las Vegas casinos. Mob-run properties went into decay as their owners sought anonymity. Almost like a miracle, Howard Hughes, a "legitimate" multi-multi-millionaire, came to Las Vegas and began buying properties and giving the Strip a cleaner image. Steve Wynn established himself as "the" entrepreneurial personality of Las Vegas with the opening of the Mirage in November 1989. This bright star was then only forty-seven years old, but he had already accumulated many years of valuable experience in the gambling industry and even before that many years near the industry.

Several antecedent events might have suggested that Stephen Alan Wynn was going to be a strong individual, a leader with personal magnetism. He was born in Utica, New York, on 27 January 1942. His nuclear family was critical in his development. Stephen Alan Wynn was the grandson of a traveling vaudeville performer and the son of gambling entrepreneur Mike Wynn, who, due to the times, was required to operate on the margins of the law, if not the margins of society. Steve Wynn's mother, Zelma, commented, "If you ran a bingo parlor, some people looked at you as if you were a bookie" (Smith 1995, 36). (Evidently being a "bookie" was not a good thing in her eyes.) Steve Wynn's inheritance from his grandfather and father suggests that the excitement of entertaining and gaming may have been ingrained in his genetic makeup. Wynn's tie to gaming was more than just genetic, however. He was also exposed to bingo facilities, other gaming, and the personalities of a marginal gaming industry early in his life.

1952 was a time of importance that appears to be noted in many profiles of Wynn. Steve Wynn has also verbalized it in several personal interviews. When he was just ten years old, his father, Mike, brought him to Las Vegas. There the father attempted to become established as a bingo operator in the gambling Mecca of the United States. Steve saw the desert and the mountains, and he rode horses. But most important, as a preteenager he saw the action of Las Vegas, and seemingly it left an indelible imprint. While in college at the University of Pennsylvania he studied chemistry, gave serious thoughts to becoming a doctor, graduated with a degree in English literature, and even briefly pursued legal studies. Yet Steve was destined to seek a career in gaming.

Although Steve may have found his dream, his father did not have a winning experience in Las Vegas. His bingo establishment within the Silver Slipper Casino lost out to competition from the better-heeled Last Frontier next door. Mike Wynn also lost his gaming profits through personal gambling activity. (Steve told one reporter, "My father made a nice living from bingo, but he'd lose all his money playing gin or betting on baseball. And God forbid if there was a crap game in the vicinity.") Mike was given further negative news when the Nevada Gaming Board denied him a gaming license in April 1953 (Karlen 1990, 397).

Michael Wynn's personal drive for the golden ring ended prematurely. Heart failure led to his death on an operating table in 1963, at the age of fifty-five. A business opportunity, or perhaps necessity, was placed into the hands and on the shoulders of the twenty-one-year-old Ivy League college graduate, Steve. The weight of necessity was heavier, too, as Wynn married Elaine Pascal two months after his father died. Someone had to manage a string of bingo halls. But more than an opportunity or a necessity, a rekindled dream was placed directly in front of Steve Wynn. He was not destined to be a chemist, a doctor, a literature teacher, or a lawyer. He was destined to chase his childhood dream and achieve a success that eluded his father. Perhaps now the mission was clear and dominant in his mind. He was going to go to Las Vegas. And he would not only make it in Las Vegas, he would make it big in Las Vegas.

Steve Wynn has been able to achieve his triumphs while somewhat confined in mobility by an incurable eye disease called retinitis pigmentosa. He is unable to drive a car by himself, as his range of vision is limited. The disease may progress, but it has not been accepted as a burden by Wynn. He does consciously seek to conceal its limiting effects from the public, and in some ways it might propel his desires to achieve. He certainly expresses a desire for visual perfection with his personal appearance and his properties. He is always impeccably dressed (even when purposely informal), and his properties rate kudos from architectural analysts and public alike for their good taste and detailed fixtures and furnishings. Paint lines are exact in corners, and brass railings are always polished. Wynn is noted for having a temper, and invariably the story is told that he expresses loud verbal displeasure when he observes that one light bulb is burned out in a sign with perhaps hundreds of lights. As a blind person is often credited with having a sixth sense, Steve Wynn's limited range of vision seems to give him a heightened sense of detailed vision. The physical limitations

Siegfried and Roy's white tigers at the Mirage Casino, a facility developed by entrepreneur Steve Wynn.

of his eye disease are outwardly considered to be but an inconvenience.

Wynn brought his family—wife, Elaine, and daughter Kevin (born in 1966; a second daughter, Gillian, was born in 1969)—to Las Vegas in 1967. Through contacts gained by work in his father's bingo halls, Wynn was given an opportunity to make a 3 percent investment in the Frontier Hotel and Casino. Subsequent investments brought that to 5 percent. The opportunity must have been especially sweet considering his father's sour experiences in 1952. With the investment came a job as a slot manager. His new associates, however, were not the best people in gaming. They were exposed in a cheating scheme and later subjected to a federal criminal indictment. As a result, the property was sold to the Hughes organization, and Wynn, untainted by the activities of his associates, had to move on.

But Wynn needed help. He found it with two very important friends, who played extremely critical roles in his commercial activities: E. Parry Thomas, president of Valley Bank of Nevada, and investment mogul Michael Milkin. Thomas helped Wynn win a liquor distributorship after he left the Frontier. More important, Thomas helped Wynn make a critical connection with Howard Hughes, also a client of Valley Bank. Thomas found that Hughes was paying a high rent for a piece of property next to his Landmark Hotel and Casino. The property was used for parking space for Landmark patrons. Hughes owned a strip of property next to Caesars, however, and he was collecting a lower rate of rent from Caesars so that it too could be used for parking. Caesars had attempted unsuccessfully to buy it from Hughes for about $1 million. Wynn found the owner of the Landmark parking lot and executed an option to buy the land for about a million dollars. Wynn then approached the Hughes organization and suggested a land swap. Hughes went for the deal. The financing for Wynn's purchase was arranged by Thomas. Wynn then started to play high-stakes poker. He turned down a cash offer from Caesars to buy the land that would have given him a modest profit. Instead, he initiated a process to win a license for a newly constructed casino that would abut Caesars. He filled out all the application materials and went through the full planning process to obtain all necessary building permits. He even had a contractor break ground, before he extracted the price he wanted for the land—over $2 million. Wynn's personal profit was in excess of $700,000. This money was then used to buy shares of the Golden Nugget Casino.

In 1971, Wynn purchased a large block of Golden Nugget stock, won a place on the corporate board, and in 1973 emerged as the new chief executive of the downtown Las Vegas property. He constructed a new hotel tower and transformed an ordinary property into the most fashionable downtown casino. From his position as chief executive officer of the Golden Nugget, he masterminded the construction and operations of the Golden Nugget in Atlantic City; by all measures the most successful casino on the East Coast. But Wynn was constrained by resource limitations. Then in 1986 he was given a golden opportunity, as Bally's perceived that the only way it could defend itself from a hostile takeover move by Donald Trump (owner of two Atlantic City casinos) was to purchase a second casino of its own. (Atlantic City restricts owners to holding only three licenses, so Trump could not complete the hostile takeover if Bally's had two licenses rather than one.) Bally's wanted the Golden Nugget and wanted it quickly. The company agreed to pay Wynn an exorbitant sum for the property—well above its appraised value—and did so.

Steve Wynn was then free to make his defining Las Vegas move. The move, of course, was the creation of his dream property—the Mirage. It was the first new casino property built in Las Vegas in sixteen years when it opened in 1989. Almost instantly, the Las Vegas community was transformed in its self-image. Development money was flowing into the Strip, not only for a big new property (Circus was building the Excalibur, but that was just a bigger Circus Circus), but also for the world's premier gambling entertainment center. The Mirage brought a new popular (but still high-roller) casino into Las Vegas along with the world's top magic team—Siegfried and Roy—in a new production considered the greatest stage extravaganza in entertainment history. The front exterior of the Mirage featured a waterfall with an "erupting volcano" shooting flames fifty feet into the air all hours of the evening. The back exterior included a dolphin tank and arena. Inside, behind the front desk there was a shark tank. The interior also featured a tiger cage adjacent to a shopping mall, along with top-grade restaurants and state-of-the-art convention facilities. A new standard was set for the Strip; a new psychology of pride and growth took over the town. Others jumped up to follow. The Flamingo expanded, Circus Circus grew some more, and Kirk Kerkorian set his sights on creating the world's largest hotel-casino complex. The new MGM Grand opened with 5,000 rooms, and, of course, Wynn followed with his own Treasure Island (which opened in 1993) and his next dream property, the Bellagio (which opened in 1999). The 1990s became a decade of growth, but the decade would not have happened without its catalyst—Steve Wynn.

The year 2000 brought many surprises, as Kirk Kerkorian of the MGM Grand launched a successful bid to buy a majority of the shares of the Mirage Company. He was thus able to secure control of Steve Wynn's empire in a $6-billion transaction. Undaunted, Wynn took his share of the proceeds—about $600 million—and looked over the landscape for his next move. For less than half that amount, he was able to take over 100 percent of the ownership of the classic Desert Inn property, the famous location of Hughes's campaign to control Las Vegas. Wynn now had one of the historically best high-roller properties, and the only golf course on the Las Vegas Strip—a wonderful launching pad for a fresh start (Smith 2000, 331–354).

Other industrial towns have found their economies transformed from ones of entrepreneurial dominance to ones of corporate dominance with the passing of generations. But in Las Vegas (and Nevada), until 1963 the law precluded public corporations from operating casinos. Although corporations have now built very large casinos, private groups still have a major presence in the industry—Binions, Engelstadt, the Boyd Group. Also, corporations within the industry are still open to personal leadership, as open competition still welcomes imagination even if Wall Street investors shy away from it. Nevertheless, the first wave of corporate leadership in the casino industry did seem to stifle that imagination by trying to impose values of Wall Street and the Harvard Business School onto the gambling floor. At first, the traditional thinking held gambling back from creativity. Wynn suggests that this made his task as an emerging leader so much easier. "There was this sameness . . . on the Strip. Las Vegas was like the portrait of Dorian Gray. The world had been moving by for twenty years, but everything here stayed the same. You didn't have to be a genius to be a top dog; all you had to do was walk into the present" (Karlen 1990, 395).

Sources: Hopkins, A. D., and K. J. Evans. 1999. *The First 100: Portraits of the Men and Women Who Shaped Las Vegas.* Las Vegas: Huntington Press, 255–257; Karlen, Neal. 1990. "Mr. Lucky." *Gentleman's Quarterly.* (September): 393–397; Seal, Mark. 1997. "Steve Wynn: King of Wow." In *The Players: The Men Who Made Las Vegas,* edited by Jack Sheehan, 168–182. Reno: University of Nevada Press; Smith, John L. 1995. *Running Scared: The Life and Treacherous Times of Steven Wynn.* New York: Barricade Books; Smith, John L. 2001. *Running Scared: The Life and Treacherous Times of Steven Wynn,* 2d. New York: Four Walls Eight Windows; Thompson, William N. 1999. "Steve Wynn: I Got the Message." In *The Maverick Spirit: Building the New Nevada,* edited by Richard O. Davies, 194–210. Reno: University of Nevada Press.
See also Hughes, Howard; Siegel, Benjamin; Trump, Donald John

Wyoming

Wyoming has a quarter horse racing circuit that draws betting action to tracks at Evanston, Gillette, and Rock Springs. There are also charity bingo games and bingo games operated by the Wind River Reservation. Wyoming residents are within the marketing areas for the low-stakes casinos of both Colorado and Deadwood, South Dakota. The state also borders Montana, with its policies for machine gambling. For this reason, there have been several attempts by Wyoming business groups and by some political leaders to authorize machine gambling in taverns as well as low-stakes card games. These efforts have never received serious consideration.

Sources: www.gamblingmagazine.com (Wyoming and Gambling); www.ohwy.com/al/gambling

Y

Yukon Territory

The first Canadian casino was not in a province, but in the Yukon Territory. Its operation received little notice. The casino is a special exception for this remote northern location and has not spawned attempts to duplicate it elsewhere. Still, the casino operates under the guidelines of the 1969 Criminal Code amendments.

The Yukon Territory had considerable gambling activity during the Klondike gold rush days of the Gay Nineties. Gaming halls offered a wide range of gambling opportunities along Dawson City streets. After the gold fever subsided, Canada annexed the territory in 1898 and began enforcing the Criminal Code. Gaming activity declined.

Under the 1969 amendments, the territory granted a special gaming license to the Klondike Visitor's Association, a division of the Yukon territorial government. The license permits casino gaming from mid-spring through the summer months at a location known as Diamond Tooth Gerties (Diamond Tooth was the name of a renowned Klondike personality). The 9,000-square-foot gaming facility offers twenty-six games of blackjack, roulette, wheels of fortune, and poker as well as fifty-two machines. Maximum bets are as high as $100 per hand. The casino has a professional manager and gaming staff. The casino is open from 7:00 P.M. to 2:00 A.M. during the spring and summer seasons. Patrons pay an entrance fee of three dollars. Annual passes are available for ten dollars. Alcoholic beverages and snacks are available, but there is no restaurant. Live productions in the style of the gold rush days entertain the patrons. A regular feature is the Ballad of Sam Magee Show. Although designed to attract tourist play, the casino draws the most play from Dawson City residents. The casino attracts annual play of about $1 million. Gross wins approach $400,000. The Canadian government under the 1994 Lottery Licensing Act and Regulations receives 25 percent of the gross win. Remaining profits minus payroll expenses go to promote tourism and preserve historical buildings. A deputy minister within the territorial Ministry of Justice regulates the casino.

Sources: Cabot, Anthony N., William N. Thompson, Andrew Tottenham, and Carl Braunlich, eds. 1999. *International Casino Law.* 3d ed. Reno: Institute for the Study of Gambling, University of Nevada, Reno, 216.

APPENDIX A: ARTICLES

The Best Gamblers in the World

Almost all of Asia is closed to casino gambling, yet from my study of gambling, ironically enough I have found that Asians are the world's "best" gamblers. They gamble more, they are high rollers, and they enjoy gambling more than others. Casinos around the world rely upon the patronage they receive from Asian players. Over half of the money gambled in Britain's 120 casinos comes from Chinese players. Las Vegas markets its high-stakes products to Japan, Taiwan, and Hong Kong. The card rooms in California are filled with Asian Americans.

Asians gamble the most, but why? In my travels to gaming establishments in Asia, Europe, North America, Central America, and South America, I have found some explanations that seem plausible.

I have not seen many Asians among the "homeless" or "street people" of the large cities. Poor Asians do not have to live on the streets. Asians have strong families, they have family businesses, and they work very hard. Asian people are active, their heads are raised upward, and they exude self-confidence. I even saw these qualities when I visited mainland China. Fifty years of Communist efforts to change human nature did not stymie energy inside the people. This may have relevance for gambling behavior.

You cannot be a "good gambler" unless you have a bankroll. You cannot afford to win unless you can afford to lose. A player needs staying power. When a player knows he or she can lose, he or she can play, and play to the limit. Many an Asian knows that if he or she loses enough to no longer own a house, there will still be a roof over his or her head. The extended family will take the gambler in and provide food and a job in a family business—perhaps a laboring job, but one he or she will be willing to do. The gambler knows that by working hard he or she can get ahead. Quite likely, the wealthy gambler was once a poor person, and through personal effort worked to the top. That can be done again, and the gambler's confidence is not broken by gambling losses.

The manager of a London casino told me the story of a Chinese player who saw his fortune disappear with heavy gambling. Being totally broke, he was soon working in the kitchen of a cousin's restaurant. A year later, he was managing the restaurant, and the next year he owned two restaurants. And he was back in the casino gambling high stakes. The downside of the equation is that the safety-net formula of family and self-confidence provides no inhibitions to stop forces that lead players into compulsive gambling.

Asians often gamble in groups, and they exude excitement in play. They believe the best thing is to win. The second best thing is to lose. The worst thing is not playing. Often at a roulette table they will shout loudly when one of the group wins. They will also shout loudly when the ball falls on a number that is next to the one played. Coming close is cause for cheering.

The players will come and leave in groups, and casino managers must be aware of this. The lesson was learned by one British casino manager confronted with a loud Asian player one night. After seeing that the player was annoying more staid "European" players, the manager tried to gently tell the player to be a little less excited during play. He noticed that the player was young and had had too much to drink. He told the bartender to serve him no more. After several increasingly less subtle warnings, the manager gave up and asked the bouncer to escort the player out of the premises. No sooner had this happened than a crowd of twenty players at six tables gathered their chips and went to the cage, cashed in, and left. Many were regulars, who were not seen for over a month. When the manager threw one of their group out, he threw the entire group out. The next time an incident occurred, the manager found an older gentleman among the group and told him that the casino would like the "loud" player to come back another evening to play, but in the meantime would like to buy the young man and his immediate party (of four) dinner in the adjacent restaurant. The older gentleman made all the arrangements and laughingly accompanied the young man to a very private corner booth in the restaurant. All were happy, and the Asian entourage continued their gambling merriment for several more hours—that night and the next.

Casino managers have offered additional explanations. The players may work in family businesses that operate until late hours. Because these businesses operate on a cash basis, the owner has cash receipts that can easily be brought to the casinos. Also, the owners and the employees have no other place to go (if they do not want to go straight home) at the hour they close their shops. They are like the dealers of Las Vegas with tip money in their pockets when the shift changes at 2 A.M. These people can meet their friends and enjoy camaraderie in the late hour (or 24-hour) gambling establishments.

Asian players are drawn to luck games. Eastern cultures emphasize the luck of certain numbers; persons born in certain years have lifetime luck. One who has luck is urged to act upon the luck. Numerology and horoscopes are well respected. The players gravitate to games that depend on luck. Most Asians are not found at poker tables; they are not blackjack card counters, nor do they frequent craps tables that demand detailed concentration on various combinations of odds. Their calculation is a calculation to find one's lucky number, not a calculation to minimize the house odds. Asians dominate the baccarat tables of Las Vegas. They favor pai gow and pai gow poker games and simple dice games such as sic bo.

I was astounded to find no fortune cookies during travels to central China. Most of the Chinese people with me had never heard of fortune cookies. But an older gentleman had. He told me that Chairman Mao had banned them. The people were supposed to get ahead by hard work, not by luck. The cookies were a bad influence. Mao did not want people to gamble. Everywhere I went, however, I saw people playing games. I never saw money being wagered, but I sensed the spirit was still there. Certainly their relatives around the world have the spirit.

> Sources: Adapted from William N. Thompson. 1994. "The World's Best Gamblers." *You Bet: Canada's Gaming Report* (November): 8–9; also based on author's visits to casinos and on author's classroom lectures in Public Administration 736 ("The Social Impacts of the Gambling Industry"), University of Nevada, Las Vegas, Spring 2001.

The Family That Gambles Together

"We're just here to have fun, we create excitement, it's a family experience. It pays off for Las Vegas."
——Mike Hartsell, director of entertainment, Luxor Casino (*48 Hours,* CBS television, 30 March 1995)

"The Las Vegas market is an adult destination that people can easily bring kids to."
——Alan Feldman, general manager, Treasure Island Casino, quoted in

Las Vegas Review Journal,
7 September 1993

"If there's a twelve year old in my casino, he'd better be shooting craps."
——Burton Cohen, president, Desert Inn Country Club and Casino, in talk given to International Gaming Exposition, Las Vegas, 21 March 1995.

In 1989 casinos opened in South Dakota, signaling a nationalization of the casino industry. In Las Vegas, a megaresort called the Mirage opened. That opening was followed by a new Circus Circus property, the Excalibur.

Las Vegas was getting ready for competition. Las Vegas was going after family markets. The idea of appealing to younger nongaming family members was not new. Circus Circus had had carnival games for kids since 1974. But the idea it incorporated—providing entertainment for children while parents engaged in gambling—was not made part of general marketing until the Mirage and Excalibur came into existence.

A Checklist

Is this effort to capture family vacationers going to work for Las Vegas? Is the marketing approach good for Las Vegas business enterprises? Is it good for families? For society? Let us make some checklists.

One group of considerations applies to the business dimensions. We look at business advantages, then we examine the downside. The second major grouping involves social issues. We look at societal advantages arising from marketing casinos this way; then we explore negative consequences for society.

Business Factors—The Positive

1. *Increase the Size of the Potential Market.* Since families constitute one of the largest vacation markets, the potential associated with this target is substantial. This "family" market is difficult to ignore in an increasingly competitive market.

2. *Fill Hotel Rooms.* In 1994, the hotel room occupancy for Las Vegas was 89 percent. With more hotel rooms scheduled to be completed in the next few years, the challenge to maintain high occupancy rates will be intense. Family vacationers are an obvious target to fill these rooms.

3. *Long-term Customer Pool.* In 1991, the median age of the Las Vegas visitor was 50, with 44 percent of the tourists over the age of 60. A 60-year-old provides a potential 10- to 15-year income stream. A parent, age 40, provides a potential 30- to 40-year income stream. A 40-year-old repeat visitor is worth 3 times as much as a

60-year-old. It makes good business sense to go after a younger market.

4. *Atmosphere.* There is a benefit of having a casino full of people. It makes the whole experience more enjoyable. This is true even if many of the patrons are not actually gambling.

5. *Total Revenue Dollars.* Every tourist who visits Las Vegas spends money. Those who choose not to gamble will still spend money on shopping, shows, transportation, hotel rooms, food, and other entertainment.

Negative Business Implications

1. *More Nongamblers.* As the number of families vacationing in Las Vegas increases, the number of nongamblers also increases. With visitors not gambling, the management of Las Vegas properties will change dramatically.

2. *Low Rollers.* Vacationers, especially families, are likely to spend less money gambling. Families will spend less money, and the money they do spend will be targeted toward family-related activities.

3. *Change in Way Business Is Done.* To make a less gambling oriented market profitable, casinos need a change of philosophy from generating the bulk of the property's income from gambling to finding ways to generate revenues from family activities such as entertainment, meals, amusements, shopping, and lodging. In addition, those activities considered as offensive for families may have to be eliminated.

The days of losing money on rooms and making it up in the casino will end. While it is true that not all properties will attract equal percentages of families, the impact will be felt everywhere, since families will search out room, meal, and entertainment values in all properties.

Even though most casinos do not like creating activities that reduce the number of hours that a gambler spends in the casino, the family market will demand that they do so.

4. *Changing the Experience for Current Visitors.* When firms go after new markets, they often ignore what brought them their original success. In the case of Las Vegas this is crucial. The allure of Las Vegas has always been the gambling, nightlife, and glitz. It has not been white tigers and theme parks. As Las Vegas becomes less gambling oriented, it starts to look like other resort destinations. The danger is that potential gamblers will go to other gaming locations, rather than deal with the family crowds in Las Vegas.

5. *New Costs and Liabilities.* Security problems generated by doubling the number of children in casinos is overwhelming. In addition, what will properties do when a minor is caught gambling? The altercation can only have a negative impact on the satisfaction of the family involved. The parents will either blame the casino, the child, or the town. Additional problems can arise from a large number of unescorted children roaming around in a megaresort. Abductions and accidents are examples.

Social Issues—The Positive Side of the Equation

1. *Promotes Family Solidarity.* The new marketing approach in Las Vegas supports the notion of family values, a theme that is now receiving much attention from national policy makers. Las Vegas is promoting the family vacation by offering accommodations, transportation packages, and various entertainment events at reasonable costs. Family vacations promote solidarity within a threatened institution.

2. *Marketing for All Age Groups.* The appeal of the Las Vegas excitement is one that can grip all age groups, whereas other destinations that are offered as "family" vacation spots typically appeal to separate generations or at least separate age groups.

3. *Accommodations at Reasonable Costs.* The family marketing emphasis has led to a major expansion in the number of hotel rooms in Las Vegas. This volume will act as a damper on efforts to greatly increase room prices. The average room rates in Las Vegas are now considerably lower than those at alternative family vacation destinations.

4. *Makes Children Look at Gambling with More Realism.* The new marketing approach exposes children to the reality of gambling, which is now legal in forty-eight states. Gambling has become an ordinary part of American life, yet many cling to Victorian notions that it is not only "sinful," but that anyone under the age of adulthood must be shielded from it. This total prohibition attitude can foster pent-up frustrations and desires that may not be easily discarded at a later time.

5. *Teaches Moderation and Management of Money.* Children can learn the value of money by observing the exposure of money to risk factors.

Social Issues—Downside Factors

1. *Casinos Are Attractive Nuisances.* Children are kept out of bars not just to keep kids from drinking. They are excluded because the people who go to the bars may reach a condition where their language or physical behavior may be offensive to other adults but would be traumatic to children. The bar is a venue where children could be easily hurt. Casinos are no different.

2. *Children Are Drawn into the Gambling Environment.* The placement of rides and attractions makes

it impossible for children to avoid gaming areas of casinos.

3. *Children Imitate Other Children.* Young people drawn to Las Vegas can be expected to emulate the behaviors of young people living in Las Vegas. The emphasis on families in casinos has led many local kids to believe this is a place for them as well. A newspaper survey of 769 Las Vegas high school students found that over 47 percent had gambled at local casinos, even though the gambling age was twenty-one.

4. *The Seeds of a Later Compulsive Gambling Problem.* Early exposure to gambling is associated with later compulsive gambling.

5. *Invites Family Discord.* Gambling activity offered in a family vacation setting may not add to family solidarity. Families budget expenses very closely on their travels so that they may experience a variety of activities. There is no room for risks of gambling.

Conclusion

Although Las Vegans might disagree, for most Americans, gambling and children do not belong together. Even though the approach has certain advantages, the family resort destination strategy appears also to have many irrational and perhaps even financially dangerous sides to it.

> *Sources:* Adapted with permission from William N. Thompson, J. Kent Pinney, and Jack Schibrowsky. 1996. "The Family that Gambles Together: Business and Social Concerns." *Journal of Travel Research* 34, no. 3 (Winter): 70–75.

Sovereignty Checklist for Gambling

The Indian Gaming Regulatory Act of 1988 was passed to promote tribal "economic development, self-sufficiency, and strong tribal governments." The Act was passed to enhance a renewal of sovereignty for Native American tribes. Has the Act been successful? The following sovereignty checklist serves as a guide to answer that question.

Consider the positive:

1. Gambling money means tribal survival. If the people of a nation cannot survive, they cannot be sovereign. Survival means food, housing, and medical care. Money from gambling activities has been placed into programs meeting basic needs. Survival is threatened by substance abuse—drugs, alcohol. Gambling revenues are used for treatment and prevention programs.

2. Gambling money means economic opportunity. Without jobs in their homelands, peoples gave up their nationalism by leaving. Gambling has brought jobs to Native lands. Jobs have given members of Na-

tions an incentive to return home and renew native nationalism.

3. Gambling revenue is invested in other enterprises to gain a diversity of employment and secure a stable economic basis for the future.

4. Revenue allows tribes to choose the direction of economic development. Before gambling, many felt pressured to accept any economic opportunity. They allowed lands to be strip-mined, grazed, or timbered in nonecological ways, polluted with garbage and industrial wastes. One tribe explored the prospects of having a brothel.

5. Gambling money gives educational opportunities. Tribes use funds for books, computers, new desks, new roofs, remodeled halls, and plumbing for schools. Schools serve tribes with both cultural and vocational education.

6. Revenues allow tribes to make efforts to reestablish original land bases. They hire archaeologists to identify traditional lands. Lost lands must be the most vital symbol of lost sovereignty, and now through gambling, a measure of sovereignty is being returned.

7. Reservation gambling focuses upon cultural restoration activities. Money is spent on museum buildings that chronicle Native history. Tribes are turning funds to educational programs to reestablish their languages.

8. Sovereignty is political. The money of gambling allows tribes to assert all manner of legal issues in courts and in front of other policy makers. Gambling has also provided a catalyst for the creation of the National Indian Gaming Association in 1983. The Association has participated as a serious lobbying group within the American political system.

9. Economic power is directed at state and local government treasuries. Tribes bring several economic benefits to local and state governments. Gambling employment has resulted in reduced welfare rolls. Gambling tribes give state and local governments payments in lieu of taxes for services they would otherwise receive at no cost. This money is important, and the payments give the tribes a new measure of influence in relationships with these governments.

10. The Indian Gaming Regulatory Act has lent itself to an expansion of Native American sovereignty by requiring American state governments to deal one-on-one with tribes on an equal footing basis.

In gambling, however, there is a danger to the renewal of Native sovereignty. Consider these items:

1. Native gambling presents opportunities for exploitation of tribes. If nonnative peoples are not closely watched, they can become a force that will seize the gam-

ing opportunity for sovereignty right out of the hands of Native peoples. There have been several accounts of "White Man's greed" in Native gambling enterprise.

2. Native Americans must also be critically aware that any gambling enterprise can be a magnet for scam artists and thieves of all sorts. Although the overall record of Native gambling is good, there is some evidence that thievery has occurred at gaming facilities.

3. Gambling operations can mean less sovereignty if tribes in quest of economic resources willingly yield authority to nonnative governments.

4. Gambling has torn some tribes apart. It can be a divisive issue, as many Native Americans oppose gambling for a variety of reasons—economic, social, cultural. One tribe found that members who lived in an area close to major highway access points tried to separate and form a new reservations because they could reap a greater share of the casino benefits. The collective good was being set aside, because gambling had placed a dollar sign in front of them.

5. Internal divisiveness regarding tribal gambling comes over the issue of how to distribute the gaming profits. Where tribes neglect collective concerns—education, health, housing, substance abuse—and instead direct the bulk of the revenues to per capita distribution programs, they may not be building sovereignty.

6. Gambling can tear apart Native cultures. Several tribes resisted having gaming operations because gambling itself violates religious beliefs, and operations would be seen as desecrations of lands. Others share those attitudes but allow the gambling because they desire economic rewards. Gambling opens up lands to outsiders. They come in buses and automobiles that cause congestion and pollution. They bring drinking and drug abuse behaviors. They engage in gambling. These behaviors serve as model behaviors for members of tribes, especially the young.

7. Gambling jobs may not be the best building blocks for sovereignty. Many of the jobs do not require intensive training—which may be good; however, the skills may not be transferable. Unless revenues are utilized to develop a diversified economic base, the concentration on gambling jobs may only create trained incapacities.

8. Sovereignty for tribes is diminished if the definition of what is a Native American can be so inclusive as to remove the unique qualities of the tribes' political position. The quest for gambling opportunities has brought many strange folks out of the woodwork, claiming that they constitute a Native nation.

9. Native gambling can invite a backlash. Non-Natives have a five-century track record of taking any benefit they see in the hands of Native Americans away from them.

10. Sovereignty comes with international recognition and open diplomatic relationships. Gambling presents an ultimate danger to sovereignty if gambling Native nations see in their new economic power a weapon for dominating their neighbors rather than a new opportunity to build cooperative relations on an international basis.

—*coauthored by Diana Dever*

Sources: Adapted from William N. Thompson and Diana Dever. 1994. "A Sovereignty Checklist for Indian Gaming." Parts 1 and 2. *Indian Gaming* 4 (April): 5–7; 4 (May): 8–9.

Supermarket Casinos

There are questions surrounding how the products of the gaming industry should be marketed. Which products should be legal? Where should gaming product distribution places be located?

The Nevada Gaming Commission is focusing upon locations of restricted license locations. These are places permitted to have fifteen or fewer gaming machines. The Commission should seek to analyze policy for restricted licenses guided by an overriding concern for the public interest of the citizens of Nevada.

Some gambling operations should be encouraged by state policy; others should be strongly discouraged; still others should be outright banned.

Both opponents and proponents should agree that some gaming can be in the interest of some communities and society—even if individuals find the activity to be offensive in all its forms. Both opponents and proponents should agree that some forms of gambling are offensive to the community and to society. The opponents should not waste energy condemning all gaming, but rather should seek out the most offensive forms and concentrate attacks on those forms. The proponents should not take the position that all gambling no matter the form is good for society. Instead, the proponents should seek out forms that offer benefits to society and make their defense around those forms.

I endorse the religious theology that accepts some gambling. If the game is honest, if the players are not habitual, if the players can meet their other social obligations, and if the bottom line helps the community in pursuit of good things, the activity may be permissible. An occasional game is played at low stakes, honestly, and the beneficiary is the local parish, school, hospital, etc. Permissible. The same can be said of other charity gambling, some Native American gaming, and maybe also of the Las Vegas Strip. Gamblers are recreational tourists, games are honest, and the end result is a growing economy that provides lots of entry-level jobs for persons who otherwise would not be employed.

There are better targets than the casinos of the Las Vegas Strip. My target—the slot machines of the grocery stores of the Las Vegas Valley. The machines of the grocery stores, while honest, attract habitual players whose activity reduces their ability to meet obligations to family and community, and in doing so the machines hurt the community. There is no redeeming value achieved to offset the harm.

The appropriate policy is obvious: take the machines out of the grocery stores. Consider these questions:

1. Who plays these machines? Is the money being played being brought into Las Vegas? Are the players tourists? How many are tourists? I think the percentage would be somewhere near zero. Are the players young or old, male or female? I think we would find most are upper-age females. What is their economic situation? Are they lower-income persons? How many purchase their food with food stamps, before (at least I hope) they play?

2. How many of the patrons of supermarket video slot machines are compulsive gamblers? How many of the players at 3 A.M. are compulsives? How many of the players who stay at the machines for ten hours in a row are compulsives? I think many.

3. Who is exposed to gambling in the supermarkets of Las Vegas? Everyone. Everyone is not exposed to the Strip gambling. We do not have to go to casinos. But we have to eat; we do not have a choice about going to the market. Children are exposed to this gambling. Teenagers, too, whereas Strip casinos throw out the teenagers. Recovering addicted gamblers have to have this gambling thrown into their faces when they shop for food. People who want absolutely nothing to do with gambling must be exposed. People are not forced to witness drinking and intoxicated people; they are forced to witness gambling and gambling-crazed people—in grocery stores.

4. Do I receive a better price for food, because of the gambling in grocery stores? When I go to a casino, I can enjoy a low-cost meal, because the casino forfeits profits on the meal in order to get me into the facility, because I might just drop a roll of quarters into a machine. Is my grocery bill less because of the slot machines in the grocery store? After all, my supermarket is sucking out anywhere from $300,000 to $900,000 a year from my neighbors with the machines. The reality is that our grocery store prices are not lower than those in surrounding states.

5. How much money do the machines make? Are the fifteen machines (the limit for grocery stores) making an average $30,000 a year (the average for the Strip), or maybe $40,000, or as is the case of one bar, $60,000 per machine? Are the machines taxed (they pay a flat fee) an amount more or less than paid by casinos for their slot machines? There is a $2,000 annual flat tax for grocery store machines, and a $1,000 annual flat tax plus 6.25 percent winnings tax for casino machines.

6. Where does the money go from the profits on the grocery store machines? To employees? Some. To local slot route companies? Some. Most goes to outside corporations that own the grocery stores. Each owner is an out-of-state company.

7. Would the Commission support putting slot machines in bank lobbies? That would be ridiculous. Guess what, each Las Vegas supermarket chain has an over-the-counter branch bank in its lobby along with the gambling machines. Not only do we have the issue about ATMs nearby (also in every lobby), but banks. My ATM will only give me $500 a day—the bank that owns the ATM wants to make sure I spend my money responsibly. But here I am with my bank account; the cash is only a few steps away—junior's college fund.

8. Machine play in restricted locations is supposed to be "incidental" to other business. Can the markets say that from 12 midnight to 6 A.M. the machines are incidental? Would it be more accurate to say that the sole purpose of keeping the grocery stores open at those hours is to serve the cravings of habitual gamblers?

Sources: Thompson, William N. 1998. Comments made in presentation to Special Hearing on Restricted Gambling Licenses, Nevada Gaming Commission, Carson City, Nevada, 22 February.

Casinos without Crime: Is It Possible?

Any criminological theory that emphasizes the factor of "opportunity" would have to assess the casino industry—an industry where the essential product in money itself—as one which by its nature is a magnet for criminal activity.

Other studies establish that casinos in the United States have attracted criminal activity. There may be limits to the generalization offered, however. There may be casinos that do not manifest an aura of criminality. In my study tour of 140 European casinos, in 1986 and 1987, I gathered a distinct impression that these casinos were not magnets for crime.

The reaction of the casino industry and its regulators to crime is varied on the European side of the Atlantic. American regulators are defensive about crime. The American reactive posture can be contrasted with the massive roundup of public officials and casino operators following a simultaneous raid by the central

Italian government on the country's four casinos in 1983. The casinos were closed and only reopened with a supervisor from Rome placed in each. In 1958 Bavarian officials discovered skimming in the private casinos of the region; they were all closed. Subsequently, the state took over both ownership and control of the casinos. The Golden Horseshoe casino of London won a license over the objections of its neighbors on Queensway Road. The casino agreed, however, that its patrons would not drive on nearby streets. In the first year of operation, the casino permanently banned 167 players, many of them good customers, because they parked cars on adjacent streets. Such a ban can be contrasted with the difficulties the American casinos have in excluding the most notorious criminals from their premises, the legal challenges to the Nevada black book being a case in point. Why the difference? Let us look at a mix of factors distinguishing European casino environments from American environments.

In the United States, most casinos are concentrated in a few locations. There are megacasino groupings in Atlantic City, on the Las Vegas Strip, and in downtown Las Vegas and Reno. European casinos, on the other hand, can be found throughout the continent. In all, there are nearly 300 casinos in Europe.

The European casinos are not concentrated in any immediate location. This pattern of dispersal yields very much of a local clientele for each casino. Typically the player is a regular who goes to only one or two casinos and is personally known to casino managers. Managers are aware when new players come to gamble. With the presence of strangers, they are alerted to the need for greater surveillance.

The monopolistic position of each casino relieves competitive drives that cause American casinos to use psychological traps to entice the maximum play from each gamer.

American casinos traditionally have been red, loud, and action filled. European casinos come in every color, but a calming blue is typical. Art objects purposely draw players away from games in order to break action and emphasize an ambience of relaxation. Windows present vistas—forests, sunsets, seashores, valleys, mountains—and also inform the player that time is passing and that time must be enjoyed. Drinks are not allowed on the gaming floors. The free drink is reserved for the special player only, and it is given to the player when he or she desires to take a break.

The American casino seeks to attract the best players—the biggest losers. This leads to policies of granting credit. European casinos do not have credit gaming. The registration desk is a major attribute of the European casino that distinguishes it from the American counterpart. Every player must register before being allowed to enter. The player must identify himself or herself and show a passport if from another country. The player must show his or her age and often occupation as well. The players are required to pay an admission fee. Great Britain's casinos require membership.

The registration desk weeds out nongamers and hangers-on. Such people who wander through Las Vegas houses pose a constant threat as purse snatchers, pickpockets, and petty thieves. Prostitutes, once identified, can be permanently banned from the European casinos.

The traditions of European gaming are very definitely rural, and most casinos are still in rural communities. Additionally, the casinos of Europe are small in comparison to American casinos. A typical European casino might have ten tables and a separate slot machine room with 50 low-denomination machines. The average casino would attract 300 gamers per night during the week and 500 on weekend evenings. By contrast, the open entrance, big crowds, and multiple game offerings in the United States make it difficult to spot much criminal activity—gaming cheats, machine manipulators, gamers trying to launder money at tables, and gamers perpetrating scams upon one another. It is also more difficult to spot dealers who cheat. Being outside of strong bottom-line competitive pressures, the European casinos do not really want compulsive gamblers. These gamers are especially persona non grata if there is reason to believe that they might be gambling with other's money. The casinos honor requests by family members to exclude relatives who might have gambling problems. The casinos observe the occupational status of players, and they can inquire about the nature of the player's job. Belgium excludes lawyers, bankers, and civil servant from casinos. It is felt that these professionals are trusted to handle other people's moneys, and the trust could be broken if they gambled heavily or were observed gambling at all.

The governments of Europe do not have a high financial stake in the casino gaining, yet they make their presence felt at the casinos. Inspectors are always present in most European casinos. They open tables, close tables, and participate in counts. In many they collect taxes on the spot each evening. Gaming tax rates are extremely high, as high as 80 percent of gross win. Yet even with the very high rates, the governmental units do not receive a large share of their revenues from casinos. It is typical for casino taxes to be less than one-tenth of 1 percent of tax revenues. The government—

except at the local town level—has almost no stake in casino operations. Therefore, the government exhibits little reluctance in closing casinos if they engage in improper practices.

Another factor that limits criminality in European casinos is the career nature of gaming employment. Dealers are not salaried. Rather they are paid from a collective tip pool. They can more easily accept the notion that they benefit by giving service rather than just working for a check. They know that their success is tied to the success of the casino. Hence they have a greater loyalty to the casino. The loyalty is enhanced by the knowledge that all position promotions are from within and that they have only rare opportunities to gain employment with other casinos. Dealers think in terms of having long-range careers. The bottom line is that it is a good job, it is a career, and it must be pursued in one casino only. Most European casino dealers have a lot to lose if they participate in scams. Skimming and cheating are not worth the risk.

Sources: Adapted from William N. Thompson. 1998. "Criminal Enterprise in American and European Casinos: A Comparative Analysis." Paper presented to the Western Society of Criminology, Annual Meeting, 23 February, Monterey, California.

Word-of-Mouth Advertising:
The Win Win Game in Las Vegas

I had lived in Las Vegas only six months, and we were entertaining our first guests from our old home town—Kalamazoo. It was Joe's first trip to Vegas and he was anxious to get to the Strip and "get it on," as he said. "Where should I go? Which casino?" he pleaded. I asked, "What do you want to do?" "Play some slots and maybe some blackjack," he offered. "Ok," I replied, "you should go to the Holiday Inn Center Strip casino (it is now Harrah's), and play the one dollar, stand-alone, slots. Put in the maximum of three coins—three dollars—on each pull of the handle." I told him to stay away from the progressive machines that offer very enormous jackpots, but very bad odds. I was only repeating the local wisdom that a new resident quickly picks up upon moving to Las Vegas. The stand-alone dollar machines at this one casino purportedly offered the best pay-back odds—over 97 percent—of any place in town. Joe told me he had a bankroll of $200. I emphasized to him that he must leave all his credit cards in his suitcase when he went to the Strip. "If you lose it, just quit!" I told him.

Joe went to the Strip at 8 P.M. He returned to my door at midnight. He looked "high." He was "high." His eyes were glazed over, and he was almost jumping up and down. He said (that is, he yelled), "How can you stay at home at night; why aren't you down on the Strip? This is the greatest place on Earth." I offered that I had a job, I had classes to teach in the morning, and I enjoyed reading and watching the news and Carson on television at night. He shouted, "My God, get your coat on, let's go back to the Strip right now." I offered that I was thinking more about going to sleep. Then he yelled out, "$1,200, this is the greatest place on Earth. I won two jackpots, $1,200." Again he begged me to go to the Strip. Then he ran to the telephone and began dialing. He said, "Don't worry, I got my telephone card. I gotta call Jack." I asked, "Jack back in Kalamazoo, Joe! It's 3 A.M. in Michigan." Joe said that did not matter. I heard him say, "Jack, I'm in Vegas, this is the greatest place on Earth, I hit two jackpots, $1,200. You gotta come to Vegas. Oh? Ok. Bye." Joe hung up the phone. "Well?" I asked. Joe said Jack was a little upset being called at 3 A.M. Then he added, "He'll thank me for telling him about Las Vegas." Again he begged me to go down to the Strip. I said, "O.K., tomorrow we'll go to the Strip, and by the way, why don't you treat us to a show while we're there." (Shows were only $20 back in the early 1980s).

He paused in silence for the first time. He asked, "Why do you think I should take you to a show?" "Well, you do have $1,200." He was silent. "Don't you?" I asked. "Oh, well, I put it all back in." "What about your $200 bankroll?" "Oh, well, I put that in too."

Joe's behavior is one of the primary reasons that Las Vegas has grown to be the number one overnight tourist destination in the world. In 2000, Las Vegas had 35.8 million visitors, more than even Mecca. Mecca gets 35 million visitors each year, because a Muslim must (if he or she possibly can) make at least one pilgrimage to Mecca in a lifetime, if he or she wishes to get to heaven. Many of the visitors to Las Vegas make repeat visits, and I do not think they are making the visits in order to get to a religious heaven.

Las Vegas has succeeded in selling its gambling products through word-of-mouth advertising. As we say in Las Vegas "winners talk and losers walk." With almost any other product—automobiles, appliances, clothing, restaurant meals—those who believe they have received bad results talk. Bad customer stories are repeated to many people; one survey found that one in five people will repeat a bad results story to twenty people or more. Good stories are repeated to three to five others (Thompson and Comeau 1992, 26). This is not the case with gambling stories. Winners spread the word, and losers stay quiet. It goes even so far as Joe's story. Losers tell stories about their winning experiences and neglect to balance them with stories of the negative bottom line. A winner in Las Vegas is exhilarated and desires congratulations and admiration from others. Others see them as worthy and brave. But if a person would tell another that he lost money gambling, the reaction would be quite different. From a spouse: "You lost that much gambling! How could you, we need that money for (a) our retirement, (b) our car repairs, (c) the kids' summer camp, (d) the kids' college educations" (pick the poison). A friend might shake his or her head and mumble something about the loser being stupid. A boss might shift his eyes to the cash register and enter a mental note to watch the loser closely. A client or customer might think, "Hmm! So that's why the costs are so high." From a macho to a zero. Just one word difference, "I won"; "I lost." Losers may indeed be stupid, but they are not so stupid that they let the world know about it.

In our customer service book, Michele Comeau and I emphasize the need to keep what we call the Win Win game. Casinos will lose this edge on all other businesses if they ever let customers feel that the games are somehow dishonest (the customers know the odds favor the house, but they expect an honest game). The customer edge is lost through exploitation—for instance, if casinos aggressively pursue compulsive players or young players. And the edge is lost when the casino does not offer good customer service to players.

There is a reason gambling is the fastest-growing industry in America.

Sources: Thompson, William N., and Michele Comeau. 1992. *Casino Customer Service = The WIN WIN Game.* New York: Gaming and Wagering Business; also based upon author's classroom lectures in Public Administration 736 ("The Social Impacts of the Gambling Industry"), University of Nevada, Las Vegas, Spring 2001.

Will Nevada Become Another Detroit?
Probably Not

The automotive industry came to Detroit by accident. The industry could have been located elsewhere. But Henry Ford set up shop in Detroit. There he applied ideas of mass assembly and economies of large scale to the construction and distribution of automobiles. Detroit was centrally located with railroad lines and Great Lakes transportation. It attracted the best labor from populations swelling with European immigrants. Ford's successes attracted other industry innovators and leaders. With his leadership, Detroit came to hold undisputed leadership in the auto industry that lasted into the 1960s.

Today when we think of quality, however, we do not think of the American automakers. We look to the Japanese, who have cornered a third of our domestic market. Although just twenty years ago Detroit was on a roll, that ended. Similarly, for sixty years, when people thought of casinos, they thought of Nevada. Now there is competition. Will Nevada share the same fate as Detroit?

In 1931 Nevada legalized casino gambling. In the 1940s gaming personalities such as Bugsy Siegel, Meyer Lansky, and Moe Dalitz played roles similar to those played by Henry Ford: They made their product accessible to ordinary people. In the world market, at the same time, the effects of war kept other countries from embracing mass-produced gambling. Now, however, there is casino gambling in many areas of the North American continent and in a preponderance of countries of the world.

Let us look at the factors that led to the downfall of Detroit and ask if they will have the same impact upon Nevada.

1. Groupthink. Detroit was "blindsided" as the forces of groupthink led automakers to believe that their success would last forever.

Is groupthink present in Nevada? Casino managers may feel they "know it all." Yet in order to maintain a dominant market position, they must accept new ideas whatever their source. Yet this is not the case. Nevada's larger and more fluid casino leadership group reaches out for new knowledge. Casino projects need new financing, and the financing necessarily comes from the outside. With the outside money comes new ideas.

2. Innovations in marketing. Henry Ford achieved profits by marketing a basic product to the masses. The notion of making a few models to realize economies of scale became part of management thinking. Year-to-year model changes were essentially cosmetic. When customers wanted real variety, Detroit did not give it. Japan did. The Japanese manufacturers demonstrated an ability to introduce new models by taking only three years to produce a new product. Detroit took five years.

In the gaming field, Nevada may view production as a mass operation allowing for cosmetic changes only. The new operators on the rivers and on the reservations, however, many of whom are Nevadans, are showing that they can put new approaches into place quickly, aimed at completely different markets.

3. Customer demand. Detroit would not listen to the customer. The "Big Three"—General Motors, Ford, and Chrysler—kept making big cars. They were the last to hear the cry for quality. "Recall" became the industry byword. Competitors came to understand that problems with cars were customer problems.

Customers coming to Las Vegas have many demands, and sometimes Nevada has been slow to listen.

Customers want more than just a gambling table. One group of foreign casino tourists asked for a tour of Death Valley. Management balked. They were a gambling house. They refused to help find a means to take the group to Death Valley, hoping, of course, that the group would decide to remain in Las Vegas. The group located a bus company that would transport them. They were given a very complete tour, and they returned to Las Vegas with one thought on their minds—sleep. If the casino had catered to these guests, they could have organized a more relaxing four-hour tour of Death Valley that included slot play beforehand and afterwards, a dinner show, linking gambling and tourism together.

Casino management must capitalize on the tourism value of Nevada by working closely with customers. Managers need to work a lot more on listening skills if they hope to avoid a Detroit-like fate in the future.

4. An easily replicated industry? The automobile industry symbolized America's world economic dominance. Dominance continued as long as other nations lacked capital resources to duplicate factories. As soon as others found resources to invest in manufacturing, they replicated our auto industries. They realized that they could make cars as efficiently as we did and that they could meet the needs of American consumers as well.

Although a car factory can be rather easily replicated, a gaming environment such as Nevada's cannot. Its industry is built upon an infrastructure of variety, entertainment choice, inexpensive hotel accommodations, an ambience of good weather, and constant offerings of many special events.

5. Multiplier factors. Automobile manufacturing is desirable because the factory jobs involved have a high multiplier effect. As many as six residents can be supported from the activity of one autoworker. As autoworkers are laid off, other jobs are also lost. The demise of the Detroit auto industry has been quickened by this negative multiplier.

The multiplier effect in the casino industry is less pervasive. It is greatly influenced by the residence of its gamers. In Nevada, most are outsiders. In new gaming jurisdictions, most players are local residents. If these jurisdictions cannot offer gaming to patrons who come from outside the region, economic growth will be elusive. As future experiences are analyzed, there will be less pressure on other jurisdictions to seek to replicate the Nevada gaming scene.

6. Expertise. Japanese car manufacturers demonstrated an ability to quickly learn the American market and to deliver products that met demands of Americans. They were good competitors. The same cannot be said for several non-Nevada gaming operators. Las Vegas has witnessed the experiences of four Japanese-owned casino operations. Only one was successful.

Also, in foreign arenas, casino gaming is not conducted in a manner that will lure Nevada customers away. Nevada need not fear foreign operators, either within or outside the United States, The experts are in Nevada.

7. Economic incentives. Labor costs and other provisions provided disincentives for automobile manufacturers to remain in Michigan.

The Nevada casino scene is quite different. Gaming employees are not unionized, and wages are standardized at lower levels. Most other casino jurisdictions have higher wages, and dealers are organized.

8. Taxation. Government taxation—both national and local—has driven the cost of automobile production to uncompetitive levels for Detroit automakers. The taxation situation has been a major incentive for auto plants to relocate.

Gaming operations will not relocate outside Nevada for taxation reasons. Nevada casino taxation is the lowest of any jurisdiction—just over 6 percent. New Jersey has a gross tax approaching 12 percent, and most European casinos assess taxes of 50 percent or more on gambling wins.

Conclusion
The factors that brought decay to the Detroit automobile industry appear not to be major concerns for the Nevada gambling industry.

> Sources: Adapted with permission from William N. Thompson. 1992. "Is Las Vegas Doomed to Become Another Detroit?" *Las Vegas Metropolitan Economic Indicators* 5 (Spring): 1–4; previously presented as a speech to the Governor's conference on Tourism, 9 December 1991, South Lake Tahoe, Nevada.

Machismo and the Latin American Casino
The casino is a social institution encompassing an array of interactions that focus upon patterned financial risk taking-gambling. Gambling is an activity that reflects the cultural values of a society. Indeed, the casino may be a microcosm of all society, sometimes an institution for social escape, sometimes an alternative social support system, sometimes an extension of a society. Accordingly we can find that the Latin American casinos reflect a dominant value in society— *machismo.*

In 1989, I witnessed casino managers setting up a cockfighting ring in the casino showroom of Casino del

Caribe in Cartegena, Colombia. Locals were invited to bring in their prize birds for matched fights to the death. Actually the casino did not participate in betting on the fights, but it did permit its patrons to do so. The holding of a cockfight in a Latin American casino is doubly symbolic of the main cultural value extant in the society.

Anthropologist Clifford Gertz, in his "Deep Play: Notes on the Balinese Cockfight," offers the arena of the cockfight as a metaphor for life on a South Seas island. He writes, "As much of America surfaces in a ball park, on a golf links, at a race track, or around a poker table, much of Bali surfaces in a cock ring . . . only apparently cocks that are fighting there. Actually, it is men" (Gertz 1972, 5). He continues, "In the cockfight, man and beast, good and evil, ego and id, the creative power of aroused masculinity and the destructive power of loosened animality fuse in a bloody drama of hatred, cruelty, violence, and death" (5). Gertz related that the owner of the winning cock takes the losing bird home to eat, but in doing so engenders feelings of embarrassment mixed with "moral satisfaction, aesthetic disgust, and cannibal joy" (7).

Actually, as a legally recognized event, the cockfight is usually confined to Latin American countries. It is in these countries that the set of ideas called machismo is most blatantly recognized and accepted as a guiding course of conduct for many members of society.

What is machismo? What does it mean, and where does it come from? Machismo has been called a "system of ideas," a "worldview," an "attitude," a "style," and a "personality constellation."

Macho is a term dating back to at least the thirteenth century. The central value among the qualities of macho is maleness. Webster's *New World Dictionary* (1975) defines *macho* as "strong or assertive masculinity," and Webster's *New Collegiate Dictionary* (1984) defines *macho* as "aggressively virile." One achieves the ideal of maleness by displaying fearless courage and valor, welcoming challenges of danger and even death with daring. Positive values of pride, courage, honor, charisma, and loyalty are accompanied with negative values of recklessness and aggressiveness carried to extremes of violence. The macho man is quick to take insult, and he refuses to back away from fights. In sexual relations machismo is associated with chauvinistic behaviors. The woman is in all ways a subordinate partner in relationships.

Economic theories focus on the lack of employment, poverty, and the need of the male to migrate to other locations for economic sustenance—for opportunities to support his family. These are seen as forces taking the male away from the home and placing the young male child under the yoke of his mother. The child aggressively seeks to assert a male role in behavior designed to show an independence from his mother.

The ideas of machismo also are derived from a societal need for hero worship. El Cid, Don Juan, Pancho Villa—these and others stand up to the forces that subjugate the males of the society. They are revered for their charismatic appeal. The macho society becomes a society willing to follow, and the strongman ruler is idealized.

Machismo is manifested in myriad ways in the Latin American casino.

Charismatic Authority Structures

The forces of machismo have left a heavy measure of charismatic authority upon Latin American political entities. The *caudillo*—or "man on horseback"—gains power through battles where mystical leadership traits may be displayed. As a ruler, these traits allow him to win support for his decisions. Respect is only diluted if he relinquishes authority to subordinates. He certainly is very reluctant to permit alternative authority structures such as legislative assemblies to share real power with him.

The Latin casino industry is too often dependent upon the whims of leaders, and it often suffers dislocations when leadership changes hands. Many jurisdictions operate according to presidential decrees rather than deliberative legislative policy.

Violence: Suppressed but Ever Present

The machismo syndrome includes a glorification of violence and a measure of reverence for tools of violence. As suggested above, the macho man believes that the knife and gun, phallic symbols as they are, nevertheless are integral to feelings of manliness. The beliefs would be quite compatible with those of the board of directors of the National Rifle Association.

I asked the manager of the Royal Casino in Tegucigalpa, Honduras, if the sign was serious. He assured me that it was. The sign greeted visitors as they entered the casino door. It read (in both Spanish and English): "For everyone's security, no weapons are permitted in the casino. Thank you." When the casino first opened, the management installed twelve lockers to hold patrons' guns. On the first day the lockers were completely full. Quickly the casino ordered an additional dozen lockers. These are now regularly full of weapons.

The casino managers interviewed in this study denied that violence ever erupted in their casinos. Several establishments, however, most notably those operated by governments, kept medical doctors on premises at all times when the gaming rooms were open. The casinos were certainly mindful of the stress associated with gaming wins and losses and were in a state of readiness in case of strokes or heart attacks.

Creditors, Debtors, and the Sense of Honor

A manifestation of machismo is witnessed in the ability to gain access to money. The macho can successfully borrow money. The true machismo finds ways not to pay it back. This kind of attitude can be dangerous for a casino organization.

Casinos in Latin America, especially ones managed by Americans, have been "stung" by local machos. They learned that it is easy to make loans to local players, but it is very difficult to get repayment. When they tried to collect, they found they were "insulting" the borrower by suggesting that he was indebted to them. Some casinos will make loans only through local agents or if guaranteed by a local businessperson.

National Integrity

The sign on the side of the mountain hovers over the national capital. It is brightly illuminated in the evening, seeming to almost be the symbol of Tegucigalpa, capital city for a "sovereign" nation. The sign simply reads, Coca Cola. One of the driving forces of machismo is the notion that the male must personally compensate for feelings of inferiority derived from the subjugation of local populations by foreign interests, colonial masters from Europe, or economic masters from north of the Rio Grande. For this reason, most of the countries with casinos insist that gaming work forces consist of local citizens only.

Gender Roles in the Casinos

The casinos of Latin America exhibit employment discrimination against women. Several casinos do have women dealers. These invariably are gaming halls controlled by Americans or foreign nationals and those in Puerto Rico. In Vina Del Mar, Chile, women are permitted to work only on low-stakes games or games not considered to be games for serious players.

Discrimination against women is defended with phrases such as "We would like to have women dealers someday. But we are not ready for that now." In one casino I was told that it would not be good. "It is the Latin blood, you know." Part of the message was that male players did not feel comfortable having women controlling their fate by turning cards or spinning the wheels. The casinos felt that the male players would harass the women dealers and seek to compromise their integrity at the games. The casino operators know that the macho man is just too much; the women inevitably submit.

The Games Machos Play

The macho man is favored by supernatural forces. If he is brave, he will keep the favor of his gods. Bravery is really more important than cleverness or rationality. Games such as craps and blackjack offer very good odds to the player, but the good odds can be exploited only by educated play, which involves a long-term commitment to the gaming activity. The machos favor casino games of roulette and baccarat, games based upon the luck factor. In roulette the macho challenges fate by going for the single number.

When playing blackjack, strategy play is rarely seen, and card counters are almost nonexistent. Players would often split tens, and then they hit 18s and 19s. It seemed that a successful hit on a 19 was evidence of daring and a display of manliness.

Adapted with permission from William N. Thompson. 1991. "Machismo: Manifestations of a Cultural Value in the Latin American Casino." *Journal of Gambling Studies* 7, no. 2 (Summer): 143–164; Gertz, Clifford. 1972. "Deep Play: Notes on the Balinese Cockfight." *Daedalus* 10: 1–37.

There's a Reason We Only Look Forward in Las Vegas

Las Vegas, Nevada, is a very unlikely place to find American history. After all, in this city people worship the future as they always look to the next pull of the handle, roll of the dice, or turn of the card. Also, they make a point out of forgetting that last loss. Just as a gambler would choose to "blow up" (figuratively) all past failures in the casinos, local entrepreneurs choose to "blow-up" (literally) the evidence of the city's seamy past. Las Vegas implodes casinos. The city blows-up its history.

First, the Dunes fell in 1993, then the Landmark was imploded in 1995, and in 1996, the Sands bit the desert dust. The Dunes was pushed aside to make way for the new Bellagio Resort, the Landmark made way for a convention center parking lot, and the Sands (once the building was removed) became the site of the $2 billion Venetian Casino Hotel. Two of the implosions were used as footage for Hollywood movies. So there were economic and commercial reasons for taking these three icons away from our sight. But perhaps there were other motives in getting these venerable locations out of our minds. We do not have even a single plaque to recognize the significance of the locations, but if we did? Maybe one would simply say "Hoffa," another might say "Watergate," and the third just possibly might say "Prelude to Dallas, 1963."

The Landmark was where Watergate began, because it was the reason behind Howard Hughes's loan to Pres. Richard Nixon—and it is generally believed that it was not a loan, it was a bribe given so that when Nixon was elected, he would remove an antitrust action so that Hughes could buy the Landmark. Democratic Party chairman Larry O'Brien was working for Howard Hughes when the bribe went thorough, and it was information about that bribe that Nixon's people were trying to get out of O'Brien's Watergate office. I personally talked to Howard Hughes's guy Robert Maheu, and Maheu said absolutely, the Watergate break-in was to get information about the bribe on the Landmark (Drosnin 1985, 434–447).

The Dunes just may have provided the motivation for the murder of Jimmy Hoffa. It was money from the International Brotherhood of Teamsters (the Teamsters' union) that went to finance the Dunes—and Teamsters' money was spread around Las Vegas—but the Dunes was the main place. The Teamsters' loans had all sorts of crooked things around them. There were invitations to skim, and Hoffa got kickbacks on the loans. Hoffa's successor Frank Fitzsimmons kept the loans going after Hoffa was in prison and then he kept them going after Hoffa was pardoned, but Hoffa could not run for union office.

Hoffa wanted to ingratiate himself with the Nixon administration. The federal government passed a new law in 1974 called the Employee Retirement Income Security Act, giving the Department of Labor and the Federal Bureau of Investigation special powers to investigate and prosecute union pension funds that were being misused. I worked for the new pension administration in 1976 and 1977, and the story was still in the rumor mill. In 1974, Hoffa starts singing to the government in exchange for a change in his pardon so he could run for union office, and he was murdered. And what was he singing about before he was murdered? The Dunes. He was telling the government how Fitzsimmons was skimming money out at the Dunes much as he had done. Hoffa told about the Teamsters' loan structure for constructing the property.

Ah! But the historical possibilities that lurked in the hallways of the Sands, at one time the most famous of all the resorts on the Las Vegas Strip. Denton and Morris (2001) tell many of the seedy stories that came out of the Sands. This was the home of Frank Sinatra and his "Rat Pack" This is where he held a secret ownership and where he solidified his alliances with Chicago mobster Sam Giancana. I always pointed to the Sands and

said, well, in my mind it's as good as the theory that Lee Harvey Osward acted alone. The theory that there was a plot to assassinate the president. If there was, it may have started at the Sands. It was not just the Rat Pack. The Sands was John F. Kennedy's casino; that is where he met Judy Campbell Exner, through Peter Lawford (Rat Pack member and Kennedy brother-in-law) and Frank Sinatra. She was also the girlfriend of Sam Giancana, who was working with Salvatore Traficante to kill Fidel Castro. One scenario was that killing Kennedy was Castro's revenge, because Kennedy was going with the girlfriend and must know about the Mob plot to kill Castro. Another scenario was that the Mob was compromising Kennedy and that they had the fix in that Kennedy would back off of Mob activities, but his brother Bobby Kennedy was a wild card and would not stop, and sort of screwed everything up, and the assassination was to get at Bobby Kennedy. But where did it start? The Sands (see Davis 1989).

I think it's beautiful—the triple. Of course, I am happy to repeat the myths. It is a lot of history. Maybe now we will be more sterilized, part of the "we're-a-clean-wonderful-town" thing. But it takes a little bit of the glamour away from Las Vegas.

Sources: Brill, Steven. 1978. *The Teamsters.* New York: Simon and Schuster; Burbank, Jeff. 1996. "Vegas History Shifts with the Sands." *International Gaming and Wagering Business,* (August): 63; Davis, John. 1988. *Mafia Kingfish: Carlos Marceloo and the Assassination of John F. Kennedy.* New York: McGraw Hill; Denton, Sally, and Roger Morris. 2001. *The Money and the Power: The Making of Las Vegas and Its Hold on America.* New York: Knopf; Drosnin, Michael. *Citizen Hughes: In His Own Words—How Howard Hughes Tried to Buy America.* New York: Holt, Rinehart, and Winston.

If Gambling Entrepreneurs Took Their Product to the Food and Drug Administration

On 10 December 1984, Thomas R. O'Brien, director of the New Jersey Division of Gaming Enforcement, spoke to a meeting of the Sixth National Conference on Gambling and Risk Taking at Bally's Casino Hotel in Atlantic City. He commented:

It seems to some of us, such a long time ago, that New Jersey undertook to establish this new industry as a "unique tool of urban redevelopment," the success of which is based upon how successfully that industry marketed its only product. That product is not entertainment or recreation or leisure—it's really Adrenalin—a biological substance capable of producing excitement—highs and generated usually by anticipation or expectation of a future event especially when the outcome of that event is in doubt.

I think most of us here today who have had experience with gambling will agree that no form of risk taking or risk acceptance generates the intensity or can produce the amount of Adrenalin in the shortest period of time than a roll of the dice, spin of the wheel or turning of a card, and interestingly enough, the level of excitement is not in proportion to the amount of money riding on the event but depends to a large extent upon the subjective psychological approach to the game by the player. (O'Brien 1985, 122)

Thus the product of legalized gambling, according to a top regulator, was an internally generated chemical substance that moved to the brain and could thereby affect mental activity, that is, produce excitement.

Let us ask if we would really legalize gambling or new forms of gambling if all policymakers accepted this view. If government officials accepted that gambling was in essence a mind-altering drug—as Thomas O'Brien clearly suggested it was—would it be legalized? Consider that legislators might have a hard time making such a decision. After all, how many legislators are biochemists? How many are pharmacologists? How many are medical researchers? None—or at least very very few. As collective bodies, Congress and state legislatures simply lack the required expertise to make good decisions in the area of legalizing new drugs. Rather than flying blind, or simply refusing to make any legalizations of new drugs, Congress has established another procedure. Congress delegates decision-making authority in this realm to the Food and Drug Administration (FDA). The FDA has the required expertise.

So now we can ask: If the FDA were given the mind-altering "gambling drug" to analyze, would it legalize the drug? The answer is not easy. But the process the agency would follow in making a decision is clear. They would first authorize extensive tests—initially on animals (perhaps Canadian mice), but then on selected human beings. What would the tests tell them? The results might be similar to those in our Wisconsin survey (Thompson, Gazel, and Rickman 1996) in which we asked questions about serious problem gambling symptoms (the criteria in the *Diagnostic and Statistical Manual of Mental Disorders*-IV). In that survey, 12.9 percent of all persons questioned—but 19.8 percent of the gamblers—answered yes to any of the symptoms. Perhaps the gambling drug is completely safe for 80.2 percent of those taking it. But 19.8 percent show one or

more side effects that suggest the use of the "drug" might possibly be troublesome under the wrong conditions. Almost 1 percent of the population and 1.4% of the users (in the Wisconsin study) exhibited serious side effects. These side effects could potentially be life threatening, as this drug leads to widespread urges to commit suicide and to perform socially unacceptable activities—stealing, writing bad checks, cheating on insurance matters, missing work regularly. Nonetheless, many of the 80.2 percent might believe (accurately) that the drug helps them relax, allows them to get away from daily work or home problems, and gives them a measure of excitement lacking in other phases of their lives. They believe the drug (gambling) improves their lives, and it may. Moreover, there may be economic advantages for promoting the commerce entailed in merchandising the drug. Drug manufacturers (casinos, lotteries, racetracks, and so on) provide jobs to society, and drug sales people pay good taxes. There is also evidence that some people will use the drug (gamble) even if it is not legalized, and if they do, the government will not receive any taxes, nor will the government have the opportunity to control facets of how the drug is used.

So should such a drug be legalized? Perhaps. But before certifying a drug as safe enough to be legalized, the FDA would insist that certain controls alluded to be exercised over its use. First, the FDA might recognize the drug as an adult drug. They could stipulate that the drug could not be taken by children. It would be sold only in select locations, and the dosages sold would be regulated. The buyers, moreover, would have to receive the prior approval of an outside expert (a doctor, perhaps, or a financial adviser) before they could make a purchase. And experts (again, doctors, or financial advisers) would have to monitor the drug use and certify that the individual taking the drug was not having serious side effects. When the side effects became noticeable, the person would be weaned off the drug or in serious cases taken off the drug immediately and completely, lest the drug become addictive.

The FDA has established elaborate controls for the dispensing of drugs. Government policymakers might be wise to follow FDA-type procedures as they establish additional controls over gambling in order to ensure that serious problem gamblers do not succumb to the bad side effects of what might otherwise be a good drug for many people.

Sources: Adapted from William N. Thompson, Ricardo Gazel, and Dan Rickman. 1996. *The Social Costs of Gambling in Wisconsin*. Mequon, WI: Wisconsin Policy Research Institute, 26–27; O'Brien, Thomas.

1985. "Perspectives on the Regulation of Casino Gaming in Atlantic City, New Jersey." In *The Gambling Studies,* edited by William R. Eadington, vol. 1: 121–127. Reno: Bureau of Business and Economic Research, University of Nevada, Reno.

French Casinos—Saved by the Slots

The attitude of the authorities in France has always been ambivalent as far as casinos are concerned. The French penal code outlaws gambling, but then special exceptions are allowed. For a long time, French casinos were the most splendid in Europe, but by 1987 they were becoming decrepit and were unable to modernize because of very strict regulations. Until that year they were not permitted to have machine gambling. They were doomed to go under. The French casinos' contribution to total earnings from gambling (2 percent) was derisory compared to that of German casinos (9 percent). France took first place in Europe in terms of its total number of casinos, but only sixth place in casino revenues. Casino earnings per resident were less than one-half the earnings of casinos in the Netherlands, three times less than in Germany and the United Kingdom, and six times less than in Spain. While casino revenues in all other European countries were doubling in the early years of the decade the revenues in French casinos were falling. The other countries permitted casinos to have slot machines.

The discussions in the National Assembly in 1987 were quite animated, but in the end economic interests won the day, given that around 10,000 jobs in casinos were at stake, as well as considerable tax revenues both for the state and, more important still, for those municipalities that possessed a casino. Among the political parties, those on the right voted for the authorization of slot machines, and the interior minister, Charles Pasqua, signed the decree in 1987, just before leaving the government. Pierre Jox, who took over from him in a government of the left, imposed a limit of sixteen, however, on the number of casinos that were permitted to have machines. There were 138 casinos.

The appearance of the machines marked a decisive turnaround point for these casinos. It gave them a new lease on life. The changes were profound for the manner in which the casinos operated and for their clientele. Although the machines were confined to only a small number of the casinos, the overall casino revenues increased almost 60 percent in one year. Pressure on the government mounted accordingly, and in 1991 all the other casinos—then only 83 in number—were allowed machines. Today there are 150 casinos.

Numerous changes have taken place in the world of the casino since the advent of machines. The decor of the casinos has changed as have opening hours, the ages of players, the amounts of money wagered, and the winnings. The access to the slot machine rooms in the casinos is free, whereas the traditional games areas required admission charges, typically fifty French francs. The slot areas may be entered without showing identification cards, except to demonstrate that one is at least eighteen years old. Some casinos had operated only seasonally before; now all are open around the year, and they are now open for extended hours. Dress codes have changed, and in some cases they have been eliminated. The gambling rooms no longer require that players remain subdued and quiet even when engaged in large winning or losing experiences. Neon lights have invaded the gambling space as well, along with the sounds of changing coins. Slot rooms have even introduced rock music.

As a result the French casinos are pulling in more people than they used to. At peak periods players have to wait to get at the machines. Players can engage in activity with a minimum of resources—one franc for a play—compared to high minimum bets at table games. The possibilities of big wins are more apparent as well, as machines have linked jackpots. The socioeconomic makeup of players has changed, as casinos are no longer the private reserve of the affluent. Casinos have become increasingly popular, with the largest ones receiving as many as 10,000 people a week, where before a crowd of several hundred on any evening would be considered large. The new clientele is not only more numerous but also more representative of the society as a whole. Women have also begun to make their appearance in the casinos, providing 30 percent of the business, whereas before 1987, they were a minuscule portion of the patronage. Immigrants now flock to the casinos as well, as do older people.

In the final analysis the casino operators have been quite pleased at seeing large numbers of small stakes players instead of small numbers of high rollers. The machines represent over 80 percent of the casino play, and the casino establishments are realizing profits unimagined but a dozen years ago.

(In 1986, before the introduction of the slot machines, coauthor William Thompson visited the Trouville Casino on the Normandy Coast on a Thursday evening in July—tourist season. There I was told that I could not be shown to the gambling room, as on this evening there were no players in the house. The casino association records showed that this was the ninth most prosperous casino in France at the time.)

—*coauthored by Elisabeth Vercher*

APPENDIX B: MAJOR CASES

1. *California v. Cabazon Band of Mission Indians,* 480 U.S. 202, 94 L.Ed.2d 244, 107 S.Ct. 1083 (1987). The United States Supreme Court reaffirmed the right of tribes to offer any form of gambling permitted by the state where their land is located. Congress responded by enacting the Indian Gaming Regulatory Act (IGRA). Congress may have thought it was legalizing high-stakes bingo. But what it got was coast-to-coast casinos.

2. *Seminole Tribe of Florida v. Florida,* 517 U.S. 44 (1996). The Indian Gaming Regulatory Act allows tribes to operate Class III gaming—the most serious forms of gambling (that is, gambling with heavy action), including casino games, slot machines, and lotteries—only if the state and tribe enter into a compact. The United States Supreme Court declared states cannot be sued in federal court without their consent, throwing out the provision in the IGRA that allowed tribes to sue states that did not negotiate in good faith. The Court refused to say what is left: Is the rest of IGRA unconstitutional? Do tribes have a right without a remedy if the state refuses to cooperate, as the Ninth Circuit has indicated? See, *Spokane Tribe of Indians v. Washington State,* 28 F.3d 991, 997 (9th Cir. 1994), cert. granted and judgment vacated on different grounds 517 U.S. 1129 (1996), dismissed 91 F.3d 1350 (9th Cir. 1996). Or does IGRA allow the secretary of the interior to make casino regulations over the opposition of the state, as the Eleventh Circuit has held? *Seminole Tribe of Florida v. Florida,* 11 F.3d 1016 (11th Cir. 1994), cert. denied 517 U.S. 1133 (1996).

3. *Greater New Orleans Broadcasting Assoc. v. United States,* 527 U.S. 173 (1999). The United States Supreme Court held federal restrictions on broadcasting of casino commercials were unconstitutional, at least in states that had legal casinos. The Court felt that the law had too many loopholes—for example, allowing tribal casinos to advertise—and that it made an irrational distinction based on who happened to own a casino. The federal Department of Justice has announced that it will not enforce the federal law against any casino commercial. The Supreme Court did not overturn its earlier decision in *Edge Broadcasting,* 509 U.S. 418, 113 S.Ct. 2696, 125 L.Ed.2d 345 (1993), however, in which it held that the same federal law was constitutional in denying state lotteries the right to broadcast commercials from radio and television stations in states that did not have state lotteries; a distinction based on geographic location is valid. The case rejected the standard the Court had laid down in *Posadas de Puerto Rico Assoc. v. Tourism Co.,* 478 U.S. 328, 92 L.Ed.2d 266, 106 S.Ct. 2968 (1986), which had given state and federal governments *carte blanche* in regulating casinos. It is unclear what impact the *Greater New Orleans* decision will have on state laws that prohibit advertising of legal gambling.

4. The *Lottery* case, official name *Champion v. Ames,* 188 U.S. 321 (1903). This is one of the most important decisions ever handed down by the United States Supreme Court, not just for legal gambling but for the country. States were being swamped by Louisiana Lottery tickets, and they asked the federal government for help. Congress responded by passing a statute, still on the books, making it a federal crime to send lottery tickets across state lines. For the first time, the high court held that the federal government had power over a legal product, simply because it was involved in interstate commerce. This created the modern, massively powerful federal government, since virtually everything involves interstate commerce.

5. *Federal Communications Commission v. American Broadcasting Co.,* 347 U.S. 284 (1954). The leading United States Supreme Court case on the antilottery statutes, 18 U.S.C. Sections 1301–1307, and what is "consideration" under federal law. The statutes were originally part of the U.S. postal laws but have been expanded significantly to include radio, television, and federally insured financial institutions, such as banks. The Federal Communications Commission went after television game shows. The Supreme Court held that the statutes, being penal in nature, must be construed strictly. Although the Court defined lottery as being anything with consideration, chance, and prize, the Court requires players to expend cash, not just time and effort, for there to be "consideration."

6. *Yellow-Stone Kit* v. *State,* 88 Ala. 196, 7 So. 338 (1890). In this landmark case, the Alabama Supreme Court held that a drawing was not a lottery under its state law when ticket holders were not required to purchase anything or pay an admission fee. This is the first major case to set the precedent that neither benefit to the promoter nor time and effort expended by the customers is consideration; to be a lottery the customer has to pay money for the chance to win. "No purchase necessary" sweepstakes and similar schemes are therefore not gambling.

7. *Stone* v. *Mississippi,* 101 U.S. 814, 25 L.Ed. 1079, 1080 (1880), quoting *Phalen* v. *Virginia,* 8 How. 163, 12 L.Ed. 1030 (1849). The perception of gambling as something akin to disease is illustrated by the United States Supreme Court's definition of a lottery. *Phalen* v. *Virginia* lays out the test for whether a form of gambling is a lottery under federal law: whether the scheme is a "widespread pestilence," meaning, can a player go somewhere, get a ticket, and await the outcome without having to play a game:

> Experience has shown that the common forms of gambling are comparatively innocuous when placed in contrast with the wide-spread pestilence of lotteries. The former are confined to a few persons and places, but the latter infests the whole community; it enters every dwelling; it reaches every class; it preys upon the hard earnings of the poor; and it plunders the ignorant and simple.

8. *Knight* v. *Moore,* 576 So.2d 662 (Miss. 1990); *Harris* v. *Missouri Gaming Com'n.,* 869 S.W.2d 58 (Mo. 1994); *Ex Parte Pierotti,* 43 Nev. 243, 184 P. 209 (1919). In the 1820s and 1830s great lottery scandals swept the United States. The result is that most state constitutions forbid only lotteries, not gambling. Times change. To bring in a state lottery obviously involves amending the state constitutional prohibition on lotteries. But is the same true if the state legislature wants to legalize pari-mutuel wagering on horse races or bingo or casinos? States vary widely in their definition of what is a lottery, or even who decides the question. In *Knight* the Mississippi Supreme Court ruled that the test is one of what people would consider a lottery today. Because no one would think of bingo as a lottery, the legislature could legalize charity bingo without having to have an election to amend the constitution. The next year, the legislature brought in casinos. In *Harris* the Missouri Supreme Court came out with a completely different test, ruling that under Missouri state law a lottery is a game of pure chance. A game with some skill may still be gambling, but it is not a lottery. Therefore, the legis-

lature could legalize blackjack but not slot machines. Even Nevada has a constitutional prohibition on lotteries, but in *Pierotti* the state supreme court held that slot machines were not lotteries, because players had to go to a location to participate in a game. State supreme courts have reached different conclusions on whether bingo is a lottery under their state constitutions. Compare *Secretary of State* v. *St. Augustine Church,* 766 S.W.2d 499 (Tenn. 1989) with *Greater Loretta Imp. Ass'n.* v. *State ex rel. Boone,* 234 So.2d 665 (Fla. 1970).

9. *Barry* v. *Barchi,* 443 U.S. 55, 99 S.Ct. 2642, 61 L.Ed.2d 365 (1979). A gambling license is a privilege, not a right. There is an important factor of timing. There is no property right in a mere application for a casino license, *Rosenthal* v. *Nevada,* 514 F.Supp. 907 (D.Nev. 1981). However, once a license has been issued, it cannot be taken away without first giving the licensee due process notice and hearings required by the U.S. Constitution.

10. *Petition of Soto,* 236 N.J. Super. 303, 565 A.2d 1088 (A.D. 1989), certification denied 121 N.J. 608, 583 A.2d 310, cert. denied 496 U.S. 937 (1990) and *State* v. *Rosenthal,* 93 Nev. 36, 559 P.2d 830 (1977), *appeal dismissed,* 434 U.S. 803 (1977). Regulators have tremendous power under the state's "police power," the power to protect the health, safety, and welfare of its citizens. In *Soto,* New Jersey courts held that a person involved in the state's licensed casino business has given up her right to free speech, including the right to be involved in political campaigns. In *Rosenthal* the Nevada Supreme Court issued the amazing ruling that the regulation of legal gambling is purely a state issue, with no room for federal constitutional rights. Theoretically, the state could discriminate on the basis of race. The case involved the state's denial of a license to Frank "Lefty" Rosenthal, one of the main characters in the movie *Casino,* a fictionalized account of events that actually happened, as told in Nicholas Pileggi's nonfiction book *Casino: Love and Honor in Las Vegas* (New York: Simon and Schuster, 1995). *Rosenthal*'s assertion that there are no federal civil rights with legal gambling has been rejected by other courts, for example, a federal court in Michigan in *United States* v. *Goldfarb,* 464 F.Supp. 565 (E.D.Mich. 1979). Even the Nevada Supreme Court has held that state regulators must follow their own rules and procedures and that a licensee does have a constitutional property right, once a license has been issued.

11. *Fauntleroy* v. *Lum,* 210 U.S. 230, 28 S.Ct. 641, 52 L.Ed. 1039 (1908). The United States Supreme Court held that the courts of one state must enforce a judgment of another state, even if the judgment is on an illegal gambling debt. Again, there is an important factor of

timing. States and federal courts must give full faith and credit to the final judgments of all other courts in the American system. Courts do not, however, have to open their doors to lawsuits involving foreign laws that offend their public policy. The majority of courts have held that gambling, even legal gambling, violates local public policy. But the explosion of legal gambling is forcing some courts to reexamine prior decisions. In *Caribe Hilton Hotel v. Toland,* 63 N.J. 301, 307 A.2d 85, 71 ALR 3d 171 (1973), the Supreme Court of New Jersey found that the public policy of the state had changed, with the introduction of a state lottery, even before casinos were legalized in Atlantic City. So, a Puerto Rican casino could file suit in New Jersey to collect a valid casino debt.

12. *Flamingo Resort, Inc. v. United States,* aff'd. 664 F.2d 1387 (9th Cir. 1982), 485 F.Supp. 926 (D.C.Nev. 1980). Casinos lend money by having players sign written markers, which look like counter checks and can be cashed at a player's bank. The United States District Court in Nevada ruled that a casino on an accrual-basis accounting system had to pay taxes on its outstanding markers, even though gambling debts were not collectible under Nevada law. The casinos reacted by having the Nevada legislature change the law on gambling debts, but not for everyone. In Nevada today, a casino can sue a player if the player signs a written marker that bounces. Players cannot sue casinos, however. Players can only file complaints with the state's administrative agency, the Gaming Control Board.

13. *Connecticut National Bank of Hartford v. Kommit,* 31 Mass.App.Ct. 348, 577 N.E.2d 639 (1991); *Sea Air Support, Inc. v. Herrmann,* 96 Nev. 574, 613 P.2d 413 (1980). For centuries, gambling has been against the public policy of every part of the English-speaking world, including Nevada. Legalized gambling is simply an exception to the general rule: A license is seen as more a legal protection from being arrested than as a right to engage in a legitimate business. *Kommit* involved a Massachusetts resident who used a credit card from a Connecticut bank to get a cash advance to gamble in a New Jersey casino. The Court held that he did not have to pay the credit card bill, because gambling debts are not collectible under the laws of all three states. In 1980 the Nevada Supreme Court ruled, as it has consistently ruled for almost 150 years, that gambling debts are not legally enforceable even in Nevada, and the Court will leave the parties as it finds them. The *Sea Air Support* case is significant because the Supreme Court told the state legislature to change the law, which it did. See also *Flamingo Resort, Inc. v. United States,* discussed above.

14. *Com'r. of Internal Revenue v. Groetzinger,* 480 U.S. 23, 107 S.Ct. 980, 94 L.Ed.2d 25 (1987). Most lawyers and commentators overlook *Groetzinger,* seeing it only as a tax case. But this is the first time the United States Supreme Court held that a player could be in the trade or business of gambling. Lower courts had tried to distinguish gamblers from "investors," including speculators who trade solely for their own accounts. Because gambling was seen as a morally suspect industry, courts invented legal fictions, such as reasoning that a speculator is involved in buying and selling stocks or commodities from others whereas a gambler in not involved in any business relationships unless he or she accepts bets as well as makes them. The United States Supreme Court implicitly accepted the legitimacy of legal gambling by ruling that a player could declare himself or herself in the trade or business of gambling without having to hold himself or herself out to the public as a bookie. The implications of the decision are much greater than mere tax law. Here was a case argued before the highest court of the land, where a seven-to-two majority had no trouble accepting a full-time gambler, who did nothing else but handicap horses for his own bets, as being in a respectable trade or business. Interestingly, the professional gambler in this case, Groetzinger, ended up the year losing more money than he won.

15. *Spilotro v. State, ex rel. Nevada Gaming Commission,* 661 P.2d 467 (1983). The Nevada Supreme Court upheld the state's black book, which lists individuals who may not enter casinos in the state. The case involved Anthony John ("Tony the Ant") Spilotro, reported to be in charge of organized crime in Las Vegas, another figure from the movie *Casino.* In *Marshall v. Sawyer,* 365 F.2d 105 (9th Cir. 1966) the federal court of appeals agreed and held that Nevada's black book exclusion of undesirables was constitutional.

16. *Uston v. Resorts International Hotel, Inc.,* 89 N.J. 163, 445 A.2d 370 (1982), *affirming* 179 N.J.Super. 223, 431 A.2d 173 (N.J. Super. A.D. 1981). Ken Uston, the famous and successful blackjack card counter, won the right to play in Atlantic City casinos. Commercial casinos, like other businesses, have the right to exclude customers for any reason or for no reason at all, except to the extent to which a legislature has declared there will be no discrimination on the basis of race, religion, and so on. But the Supreme Court of New Jersey held that the state had so thoroughly regulated casinos, to the point where an operator could not even use a different color of felt on a blackjack table, that only the state Casino Control Commission has the authority to set rules for licensed card games. Because the commission

had not promulgated a rule about card counters, casinos could not on their own decide that these skillful players could be excluded from play. Nevada has take exactly the opposite position, allowing casinos to kick out winning gamblers. See also *Brooks* v. *Chicago Downs Assoc., Inc.,* 791 F.2d. 512 (7th Cir. 1986), which held a racetrack could keep out winning horse bettors.

17. *Martin* v. *United States,* 389 F.2d 895 (5th Cir. 1968); *United States* v. *Fabrizio,* 385 U.S. 263, 87 S.Ct. 457, 17 L.Ed.2d 351 (1966). Two cases demonstrating the law's traditional antipathy toward legal gambling and creating a problem for advocates of Internet gambling. The defendants in *Martin* were a group of entrepreneurs: Some took bets in Texas and made phone calls to their partners in Las Vegas, who then placed the bets with licensed bookies. The court upheld convictions under 18 U.S.C. §1084 for using interstate wires for gambling, ruling Congress has the power to prevent all interstate wagers, even to Nevada where the bet would be legal. The federal statute was originally passed to help the states enforce their antigambling policies. Today Nevada has to enforce special regulations to prevent out-of-state phone bets in order to prevent violations of the federal law. In *United States* v. *Fabrizio* in the United States Supreme Court, the defendant's conviction was affirmed; his crime was that he carried legal New Hampshire sweepstakes acknowledgments across a state line into New York. There was no accusation that he was helping New Yorkers place bets on this other state's lottery. But the Court ruled that the 1961 federal Wagering Paraphernalia Act and other federal antilottery laws apply to legal as well as illegal lotteries.

18. *Ah Sin* v. *Wittman,* 198 U.S. 500 (1905). The United States Supreme Court held that a state's power to suppress gambling is practically unrestrained. It upheld a California statute increasing the penalty from misdemeanor to felony for gambling conducted in "barred or barricaded" room as a constitutional classification.

19. *Bally Mfg. Corp.* v. *N.J. Casino Control Com'n.,* 85 N.J. 325, 426 A.2d 1000 (1981). The supreme court of New Jersey upheld regulation prohibiting a casino from acquiring more than 50 percent of its slot machines from any one manufacturer. Bally, which then made 80 percent of the slot machines used in the United States, was forced to buy from its competitors for its casino, a victim of its own success.

20. *In re Boardwalk Regency Corp. Casino License,* 180 N.J.Super. 324, 434 A.2d 1111 (1981), *modified,* 90 N.J. 361, 447 A.2d 1335 (1982). The New Jersey Casino Control Commission found that a corporation was qualified to run a casino, except for the presence of two corporate executives/principal stockowners, so it issued a license, subject to the company's buying out the president and the chief executive officer. The lower court upheld this idea of corporate banishment but said the two tainted individuals could stay with the company, so long as they had no control over New Jersey subsidiaries. The New Jersey Supreme Court reinstated the original conditions requiring a cleansing of the corporation. The lower court decision contains a complete discussion of the standards a court uses in reviewing decisions by administrative agencies. The decision set a precedent that a company could be licensed, so long as it got rid of any individuals who were not licensable.

21. *Brown* v. *Hotel Employees,* 104 S.Ct. 3179, 82 L.Ed.2d 373 (1974). The United States Supreme Court upheld the right of New Jersey regulators to disqualify union officials involved in the casino service industry. Local 54 of the Hotel and Restaurant Employees and Bartenders International Union tried to get the regulators' actions under the New Jersey Casino Control Act thrown out on the grounds that federal law had preempted the field of labor law. The Supreme Court rejected that argument, but remanded the case to the district court to see whether the casino regulators could sanction the union for refusing to get rid of its disqualified officials.

22. Lottery cases. Legal gambling, including state lotteries, is merely an exception to the general public policy against gambling. Therefore gambling contracts and regulations are strictly construed. This is best illustrated in cases involving players' filing claims against state lotteries. *Karafa* v. *New Jersey State Lottery Commission,* 129 N.J. Super. 499, 324 A.2d 97 (1974). An important case in the developing body of lottery law. John Karafa had purchased a lottery ticket that won a $50,000 drawing. Unfortunately, after showing the ticket around after the drawing, he gave the ticket to his mother for safekeeping—she accidentally threw it out! No one disputed that Karafa had the winning ticket, but the Superior Court of New Jersey threw out Karafa's suit. The case stands for two important things: (1) Lottery laws must be stringently enforced; (2) unlike other writings, a lottery ticket is not merely evidence of an underlying obligation, but the winning ticket is the obligation itself. *Coleman* v. *State,* 77 Mich.App. 349, 258 N.W.2d 84 (1977). Poor Mrs. Coleman was awarded, wrongly, a $200,000 grand prize by the Michigan Bureau of State Lottery. The lottery then tried to take back the prize. The Michigan Court of Appeals held that the terms of the lottery's contract with the purchaser of a lottery ticket were clear and that there was no unilateral mistake or remission. Mrs. Coleman did not win despite the mistake of

the lottery. *Madara v. Commonwealth,* 13 Pa.C. 433, 323 A.2d 401 (1974). Another heartbreaking case in the developing law of lotteries. William Madara lost his wallet, containing a winning lottery ticket, in a flood. He found the wallet and turned in the ticket one year and two days after the drawing. The majority of the Commonwealth Court of Pennsylvania held that the lottery rules put a one-year deadline on redeeming winning tickets; since the prize money had been turned over to the state, there was no money to pay Madara's claim. Another example of the courts' requiring strict compliance with lottery rules. *Molina v. Games Management Services,* 58 N.Y.2d 523, 462 N.Y.S.2d 615, 449 N.E.2d 395 (1983). An important case in lottery law. Mary Molina claimed that she won $166,950 in the lottery, but the sales agent failed to keep a record of the purchase as required by the state lottery rules. She sued the sales agent. The highest court of New York threw her claim out, stating that the state and the sales agents were immune from liability under the law and that the lottery rules had to be strictly complied with to prevent cheating.

23. *State v. Glusman,* 98 Nev. 412, 651 P.2d 639 (1982). The Nevada Supreme Court held that state regulators could require anyone who does business on casino grounds, including clothing stores, to undergo licensing process. The court did say it was unconstitutional to require the clothing store to pay the $100,000 required to investigate itself.

24. *Marchetti v. United States,* 390 U.S. 39 (1968). An important case—the Supreme Court overturned a conviction for failure to obtain the federal occupational tax stamp to operate as a bookmaker because the requirement that an illegal gambler must file tax returns, which could then be used against him, violated the Fifth Amendment protection against self-incrimination. Companion case is *Grosso v. United States.*

25. The question of skill versus luck has come up in hundreds of cases. Unless a game is a game of chance, it does not fall under the antigambling laws. Examples of how states test for skill: *Morrow v. State,* 511 P.2d 127 (Alaska 1973). In this particular case the question involved tickets for a football pool. The Supreme Court of Alaska understood that there are two lines of cases: Older cases sometimes required that there be no skill at all, an impossibility. New cases look to see if chance is a deciding factor in determining the outcome. The court decided that Alaska should go with the more modern dominant factor test and that the burden is on the prosecution to prove at trial the factual question that chance, rather than skill, predominates. *In Re Allen,* 59 Cal.2d 5, 27 Cal.Rptr 168, 377 P.2d 280 (1962). The California Supreme Court ruled that the card game bridge is legal despite a Los Angeles city ordinance outlawing "games of chance" because bridge was held to be predominantly a game of skill and not luck. The court used the interesting test of looking at how many books had been published on bridge.

26. *Olk v. United States,* 536 F.2d 876 (9th Cir. 1976), reversing 388 F.Supp. 1108 (D.Nev. 1975). The higher court held that tips for dealers, "tokes," are taxable income and not gifts. Dealers argued that tips are merely nontaxable gifts, because dealers were not allowed under the casino's rules to help players.

—written by I. Nelson Rose

GAMBLING TERMINOLOGY—
A BASIC GLOSSARY

Bank or house (casino)   The organization that conducts gambling activity (gaming or wagering). In a house-banked game the player is gambling against the house; that is, the house is a player in the game. In a player-banked game, the players make wagers against one another, and the bank or house is a neutral observer, usually receiving a set fee regardless of which player wins the game.

Book, bookie   The taking of bets on races or sports events or on the drawing of numbers. A person who makes book, or takes the bets, is called a bookie, although that term is usually reserved for one who takes bets where gambling is illegal.

Chance   An outcome that is determined by a randomly occurring risk that can be calculated. The odds—the probabilities—of a game of chance are known, and a person makes wagers with the knowledge that a random event will determine the outcome. In pure chance games the player cannot affect the outcome with the use of any skill he or she may possess.

Drop   The amount of money that the players put into action with their play. This is the money the player brings to the game and puts at risk. For a casino it can be measured by the sale of chips from the cage and tables and also by counting cash bets made. For instance, if a gambler brings $100 with him to a blackjack table and plays for several hours (winning and losing), the drop is $100. On the other hand, the handle (q.v.) may be several multiples of $100, as the player could accumulate large wins and then keep playing them until he or she decides to leave the table.

Exotic bets   These are combination bets at horse tracks, dog tracks, and jai alai games. They include the daily double, exacta, trifecta, and quinella. In the daily double betting combination, the bettor makes a wager on which two horses (or dogs) will win the first two races of the day. Both must win for the wager to be successful. The exacta is a combination bet in a specific horse or dog race in which the bettor seeks to predict the first- and second-place finishers

in the race in exact order. In a trifecta, the bettor makes a wager on the first three finishers in order. Another combination bet is the quinella. Here the bettor picks the first two finishers, and if they are first and second or second and first, the bettor wins.

Gambling   An all-encompassing term covering activities in which a player places something of value at risk in order to win a prize of greater value should a chance (or an event determined at least in part by chance) occur. The chance events are usually determined by the outcomes of card or dice games, roulette or big wheels, contests, or the drawing of lots or raffle tickets. The legal definition of gambling contains three main elements: consideration, chance, and prize.

Gaming   Gambling activity at games in which a player (gambler) is a participant, as opposed to bets on the outcomes of contests involving other people (sports or racing) or bets on the drawing of lots or raffle tickets. The term *gaming* is the preferred term used by casino executives to describe the activities taking place in the facilities.

Grind joint   A casino or gambling facility that seeks to gain revenues from smaller gamblers by having maximum levels of play. This type of casino is the prevalent form in riverboat and Native American jurisdictions. This kind of play is found in Nevada in casinos that cater to local residents. Also, most of the play in Atlantic City is a grind-type play. The grind casino is contrasted with high-roller, tourist-oriented casinos such as Caesars Palace and the Venetian, found on the Las Vegas Strip, as well as finer European facilities such as Baden Baden and casinos in Monaco.

Handle   The total amount of money that is gambled (played) on games or contests over a period of time. For lotteries and horse races, it would include all the bets made; for machines, it would include all the coins placed into the machine, regardless of the number that came out as a result of player wins. For a casino table game, the handle is difficult to determine, as it consists of all the bets made in every game, whether by chip or by cash play.

Hit There are various uses for the term *hit*. It indicates a player's desire to have another play or, in the game of blackjack, to have another card dealt to him or her. The term is also used to designate a one-time bet of a player against another player or against the house (casino). Casinos operate on the principle known as the law of large numbers. Using this principle, they may allow high rollers to make very large bets with the understanding that such a player will continue to make the large bets over a period of time. A one-time hit is very risky for a casino, as the casino cannot use its long-term-odds advantage over the player to make up for occasions when the player will win the hit. Therefore most casinos will limit the size of single bets they allow a player to make.

Hold The amount of money that the house wins from the player over a period of time. If the player drops $100, plays for a period of time, and then leaves the table with $80, losing the rest, the casino has held $20.

Junket A junket is an excursion that is organized to bring a large number of players to a casino so that they will gamble, in most cases, a large amount of money. Quite often the casino will pay much if not all of the travel expenses of the players (such as transportation, room, food, beverage, as well as entertainment) in addition to giving a fee to a junket organizer. In exchange for the discounts or free gifts, the player will agree to gamble a certain amount of money over a specified period of time. Although mid-market and low-market casinos (often called grind joints, as they wish to grind their profits out of players) will have bus tours for daytime or weekend players, the term *junket* is usually applied to tours arranged for wealthy players by the more upscale casinos. The junkets are closely supervised by gambling regulators as well as by the casinos. Junket players are very often playing on credit lines. Junkets have been used to skim (take money illegally) from casinos. Sometimes players will use false credentials (sometimes false identities) to establish their large credit lines, and they will not play all the money advanced to them. Unscrupulous junket operators may extract fees from casinos as payoffs for illegal (unlicensed) ownership of the casino. Also junket operators may be loan sharks operating on behalf of the casinos. Where used properly, however, the junket is a very important element for marketing casino products.

Las Vegas Line The betting odds or point spreads that are offered for sports betting in Las Vegas casinos. These odds and point spreads are listed in the larger casinos first and then they are imitated by smaller casinos and also by illegal betting operations that operate throughout the country (and world) and through the internet.

Luck The experience of success following a randomly occurring event. Games of luck are tied essentially to randomness, and the risks of the successful random events are subject to laws of probability. The player cannot affect the results by his or her efforts on a single play, but the odds of attaining success are subject to calculation. (Synonymous with chance, q.v.)

Odds The advantage that one side of a wager has over the other. In house-banked games, the casino will have an odds advantage in an actual game, or it will have an advantage in the payoff structure used in the game.

Player The person making the bet, wager, or gamble. Other terms for players include *bettor, gambler, gamer, punter,* or *plunger.*

Rake A part of the pool of funds that the casino (or house) takes from a game such as poker, in which the players are competing against one another. It is essentially the same as the portion of the bets that a racetrack takes from all bets on a race.

Skill The ability of a player to affect the outcome of a game by utilizing a talent either as the result of personal qualities or of training or study. Where skill may be a major factor in determining the outcome of the game, the game is called a skill game. For game players, most athletic contests are considered skill games—i.e., a skilled football team will defeat a less-skilled team a large proportion of the time if they meet in games repeatedly. Games such as dart games are skill games. In casinos, card counters have the ability to use skills at blackjack games.

Wagering The betting or staking of money on the outcome of an event such as a sports contest, a horse race, or a dog race.

Win (casino), or gross gaming win The amount of money the casino (house) holds over a period of time. The gross gaming win is actually the amount bet minus the prizes given back to the players. This is also referred to as the casino's gaming revenue.

Sources: Clark, Thomas L. 1987. *The Dictionary of Gambling and Gaming.* Cold Spring, NY: Lexik House Publishers; Fenich, George G., and Kathryn Hashimoto. 1996. *Casino Gaming Dictionary: Terms and Language for Managers.* Dubuque, IA: Kendall-Hunt; Thompson, William N. 1977. *Legalized Gambling: A Reference Handbook.* 2d ed. Santa Barbara, CA: ABC-CLIO, 273–281.

ANNOTATED BIBLIOGRAPHY

Abt, Vicki, James F. Smith, and Eugene Martin Christiansen. 1985. *The Business of Risk: Commercial Gambling in Mainstream America.* Lawrence, KS: University Press of Kansas. 286 pp.

The Business of Risk is perhaps the most comprehensive academic treatment of the gambling industry to be published in the 1980s. The book covers a lot of ground. The authors present a historical development of gaming followed by a string of evidence of the economic power in the industry in the mid-1980s. They present a philosophical analysis of the gambling phenomenon, but more important, they realize that there are crucial differences among the variety of games that are offered for play under the rubric of commercial gambling. They offer a detailed critique of factors that describe state lotteries, casinos, and pari-mutuel betting. Thirteen factors are used for comparisons: (1) the frequency of playing opportunities, (2) prize payout intervals, (3) the range of odds, (4) the range of stakes, (5) the degree of player participation, (6) the degree of skill in the game, (7) winning probabilities, (8) addictive qualities and relationships with other addictions, (9) payout ratios, (10) credit and cash play possibilities, (11) the price of the game, (12) intrinsic interest within the game, and (13) the extent of knowledge needed to play the game.

Abt and her associates also consider the location of the play, the situations surrounding the play, the ownership of the operations, and the bottom-line public purposes of the gambling activity. A valuable contribution for readers is that the authors treat players as individuals. They do not drift into a common pattern of lumping all players together as deviants or pathological types. Instead, they give a reasoned discussion to many categories of players, including casual players, occasional players, risky (risk-seeking) players, professional gamblers, habitual gamblers, serious gamblers, and—the two categories that receive most treatment elsewhere—obsessive gamblers and compulsive gamblers. The authors clearly see that for the majority of participants, gambling is a normal phenomenon. In this respect the authors proceed to view commercial gambling as a social institution representing but an extension of other legitimate leisure activities. The acceptance of gambling is measured as part of the broader values of the culture.

In the final chapter, Abt, Smith, and Christiansen tried what few before them had tried. They sought to find a model of gambling that could fit "the public interest." "The public good should be the first and overriding consideration of gambling policy" (213). They do not address the topic with precision, nor do they offer the means for accomplishing the goals of achieving the good model. Nonetheless, they advance ideas worthy of consideration even now (more than fifteen years later). The public interest must incorporate concerns for player losses as well as for revenues gained for the industry and for government coffers. Jobs gained through gambling enterprise should be considered along with jobs gained or lost in other economic sectors as a result of the gambling activity. Close attention should be given to the relationships of legal and illegal gambling. Does the one drive the other out, or are they complementary activities? The price of legal gambling should be low enough so that players will not seek out illegal gambling competitors. Games must be run honestly, and society must seek to mitigate the harms that arise from excessive gambling by the few. The authors present ample evidence that people do want to gamble, and so the authors support legalization as a freedom of activity issue as well. It is refreshing that three authors who are interested in gambling, who support the existence of legal gambling, also express the viewpoint that gambling can have both good and bad sides and that policymakers should seek out the good side as they consider legalization and regulation.

American Gaming Association [AGA]. 1996. *The Responsible Gaming Resource Guide.* Kansas City, MO: AGA. 111 pp.

The American Gaming Association was formed in 1994 as the public relations arm of the commercial casino industry in the United States. From the onset, the organization has expressed concern about problem gambling and the need to have programs to mitigate the negative impacts of irresponsible gambling. The association has found that the industry is positioned vis-à-vis critics much as the tobacco industry and the liquor industry are. Looking at those two industries for models of reaction to criticism, the gambling industry is trying very hard to avoid the posture taken by tobacco, namely a stonewalling posture of denial of problems until there becomes no room for reasonable change. On the other hand, the liquor industry has taken a lead in admitting that drinking causes major problems in society as it seeks to work with other groups in mitigating the problems through general awareness and campaigns such as "the designated driver" program.

The association has sponsored many university research programs, including studies of the prevalence rates of problem gambling and of the effectiveness of public awareness campaigns and treatment programs. They also invited Carl Braunlich of the faculty at Purdue University and Marvin Steinberg, executive director of the Connecticut Council on Compulsive Gambling, to prepare *The Responsible Gaming Resource Guide.* The purpose of the guide is "to disseminate as widely as possible the best programs, approaches and ideas available for dealing with problem and underage gambling" (7). Dealing with problem and underage gambling has been viewed as "good business" by the industry.

The *Guide* offers sixteen chapters covering a range of related topics. It leads off with an attempt to find consensus in a definition of problem gambling; it then offers suggestions for mission statements that casinos may utilize as they approach the problem gamblers in their midst. Employee assistance programs are described, as are awareness programs. The authors point to the need for customer awareness as well, and they offer suggestions for signage. Casino credit policies are examined and analyzed as means for mitigating problem gambling. The *Guide* provides a lengthy listing of problem-gambling programs that are available in each of the fifty states plus the District of Columbia. An appendix presents the common measuring devices, such as the Gamblers Anonymous question list, the criteria of the fourth edition of the *Diagnostic and Statistical Manual of Mental Disorders,* and the South Oaks Gambling Screen. There are also bibliographic entries and a wide range of advertising posters that have been utilized by casinos to warn of the problems of gambling and to discourage youth gambling.

The *Responsible Gaming Resource Guide* is a very valuable tool for every gambling enterprise, as it gives "helpful hints" for this very important arena for public relations. The *Guide* is also valuable for policymakers and students of the gambling phenomenon.

Asbury, Herbert. 1938. *Sucker's Progress: An Informal History of Gambling in America from Colonies to Canfield.* New York: Dodd, Mead. 493 pp.

Asbury's *Sucker's Progress* stands as a classic book on gambling mainly because it offers one of the first comprehensive historical treatments of the subject from the first days of the American nation. Today other books rival and surpass it, however, in intellectual content. Asbury's book seems to just present the topic. It has no introduction, no conclusion, and no theory and little in the way of direction except for part II's chronological order of events that follow part I's chapters concerning specific games—faro, poker, craps, lotteries, and numbers. Reviews have faulted the book for lacking any moral condemnation of gambling and for taking the opposite approach and glamorizing the topic through an admiration of the scoundrels portrayed on the pages. I concur with these views.

The many many details in the book are not documented, but then, there is an extensive bibliography. Although Herbert Asbury does not really show the reader a forest, he more than makes up for that by showing trees, trees, and more trees. The chronology begins with tales of gambling in New Orleans, which he calls the Fountainhead of Gambling in this country. The story goes back to the days of the first French settlers in the area and carries through to the role played by New Orleans and the Mississippi River during the Mexican War and the later Civil War. The activities of the early gambling pioneers are featured—John Davis, Edward Pendleton, Canada Bill Jones, George Devol, and Michael Cassius McDonald. Asbury describes gambling on the Western frontier with glimpses of casino games in Kansas City, Denver, San Francisco, El Paso, and Santa Fe, as well as in the mining camps. His book ends up back in the East with major chapters on John Morrisey and Richard Canfield.

One particularly interesting facet of the perspectives offered is that they are made before Nevada emerged as the gambling capital of the world. There are no references to either Las Vegas or Reno, and the book was written only sixty-two years ago.

Barker, Thomas, and Marjie Britz. 2000. *Jokers Wild: Legalized Gambling in the Twenty-First Century.* Westport, CN: Praeger. 224 pp.

This up-to-date volume treats legalized gambling behavior as a given for society, yet as a phenomenon that has both positive and negative consequences for society. Barker and Britz present cogent descriptions of gambling and various types of gambling activity along with a history of the development of the gambling industry in the United States. Considerable attention is given to Las Vegas and how gambling in that Mecca changed from the Mob days to the corporate megaresort models of today. A full chapter entitled "The Dam Bursts" is devoted to the breakthrough in casino legalizations that accompanied the passage of the Indian Gaming Regulatory Act of 1988 and the authorization of riverboat and small-stakes casinos in Iowa, South Dakota, and Colorado.

There is an excellent descriptive chapter on state lotteries as well as an up-to-date account of the use of the Internet in wagering. The book surveys the issue of compulsive gambling and the relationship of crime and gambling as well as the economic impacts of gambling. A later chapter looks at the work of the National Gambling Impact Study Commission, and an appendix lists all of the commission's recommendations. Another appendix reviews the nature of gambling in thirty-four separate jurisdictions within the United States.

Barthelme, Frederick, and Steven Barthelme. 1999. ***Double Down: Reflections on Gambling and Loss.*** Boston: Houghton Mifflin. 198 pp.

The Barthelme brothers are college professors at the University of Southern Mississippi. They teach English, and they write. In this book, the brothers record their trials with the loss of both of their elderly parents within a short span of time and their increasing losses at the machines and tables of Gulf Coast casinos in Mississippi. Neither had developed his own nuclear family. They record the emotions of family travail that is contemporary as well as part of their psychological past, and they try to relate their gambling problems to the emotions evoked. Their text suggests that gambling activity has provided each of them with a coping mechanism. They have gone through many of the phases of pathological gambling—the big wins, the losses, and chasing behaviors. Yet they indicate that they continued to meet their daily obligations and expectations as college professors, family members, and friends. Their financial gambling losses were supported by a substantial (six figures) but not excessive inheritance. In a sense they say that the money is unearned and undeserved, and hence they give themselves an excuse for throwing much of it away at the casinos—as they are conscious about what they are doing.

They are saved (perhaps—the final sequence has not been recorded) by a casino that mysteriously overlooks its own self-interest and formally accuses them of engaging in cheating activity. The casino had exploited over a hundred thousand dollars from the brothers, yet in a totally misplaced desire for security for security's sake alone, the casino accuses them (while they are losing) of exchanging signals with a blackjack dealer, ostensibly to secure knowledge about the value of the hole card. After the brothers go through the indignity of an arrest and many months of pondering their fate as potential felons, the charges are simply dropped.

In the meantime, the brothers go through a nongambling phase, but then return to another area casino for more affordable action, their basic "fortune" having been dissipated. They go through the entire progression—which at the end does not seem to reveal a "cure"—without benefit of either therapy or Gamblers Anonymous. While they are gambling they exhibit all the emotions and rationales offered by prototypical pathological gamblers, yet at the end they portray themselves as individuals who have returned to rationality. Either they are in a deep denial of their condition, or somehow they illustrate the opportunities for recovery and learning how to gamble more responsibly that are suggested as being quite normal in the work of John Rosecrance (*see* Rosecrance, 1988, *Gambling without Guilt*).

Braidwaite, Larry. 1985. ***Gambling: A Deadly Game.*** Nashville, TN: Broadman Press. 220 pp.

Although *Gambling: A Deadly Game* is presented as if it were a neutral academic study, it is indeed a straightforward attack on gambling. For the person interested in having an overview of the arguments of the opposition to gambling, it does provide a reasonably good starting point. Such a reader would also want to look at the works of Robert Goodman, David Johnston, and Ovid Demaris that are summarized in this annotated bibliography.

Larry Braidwaite's attack on gambling is a broadside. It has a moralistic tone definitely reflecting the deontological view that this "sin" is always "sin," here, there, everywhere, then, now, and forever. Braidwaite sees modern gambling as a force that seduces conservative political leaders as it purports to offer an alternative to increased general taxation. Contemporary state lotteries are denigrated as being sources of regressive taxation. Moreover, lotteries are blamed for increases in criminal activity. In a twisted logic pattern, Braidwaite decries the expansion of horse-race gambling, saying that more racing only means that the race competition will be among second-rate horses—hence depriving the racing fans of high value by giving only low-quality racing. One wonders if there are great horse race values at county fair meets that do not have pari-mutuel betting.

Braidwaite also finds that tracks are frequented by organized crime characters who do unsavory things to influence races—for example, drugging horses. The casinos of Atlantic City receive the bulk of his criticism of that form of gambling. There the patron is seen as the elderly day tripper who arrives on a bus only to lose money that he or she cannot afford to lose. But what is worse, that customer is not given a good entertainment value for the money that is spent. The author does not speak to the entertainment values that the typical visitor to Las Vegas can receive outside of the casinos. Braidwaite also attacks widespread illegal sports betting as well as charity gambling—particularly games run by churches. He finds that these games do not further true "Christian" goals.

The information on compulsive gambling in Braidwaite's last chapter is well documented but still somewhat suspect. It is followed by a lengthy discussion of the need for Christian values in a political process encompassing changes in gambling policy. Even though the book is not always factually based, it nonetheless does make a good presentation of the antigambling case.

Brenner, Reuven, and Gabrielle A. Brenner. 1990. *Gambling and Speculation: A Theory, a History, and a Future of Some Human Decisions.* New York: Cambridge University Press. 286 pp.

The Brenners present a defense of gambling by attacking its opponents. Their general conclusion holds that the opponents are self-interested parties, such as churches, government, and commercial enterprises, who want to be protected from competition from commercial gambling enterprise. Churches and other religious groups have endorsed the use of lots for determining "God's" will in decision-making situations. They have also used games for socializing situations and even for raising money for their religious activities. Governments have commanded the time, energy, and finances of the citizenry in times of war and during other situations of public need. Commercial enterprise has also come to rely upon the energies and loyalties of a workforce. Commercial gambling has posed a threat to all three institutions—church, government, and commerce. The church has seen the use of games in order to gain money (but not money for religious activities) as an affront to the supremacy of God as the supreme decision maker. Only God should determine who is worthy and who should be rewarded. Idle chance should not. All three institutions have seen gambling as encouraging idleness and a disregard for duty. More-

over, the gambler through his activity is unable to pass his resources on to the tax collector, the collection plate, or the merchants of society. In more recent years, governments themselves have run games of chance and accordingly have seen commercial gambling as a direct competitive threat.

The arguments in this book are well supported by a multitude of examples and citations to other studies. The authors give an excellent commentary on historical and contemporary distinctions between views toward gambling, speculation, insurance, and investments. Risks are endemic in society, and the insurer and speculator provide opportunities for minimizing the risks one would otherwise have to face. The gambler, on the other hand, pursues risk and seeks to increase risk in his life. Otherwise the activities of all are the same. Risk-provoking gambling activities such as lotteries can add value to lives in terms of renewed hopes for a future that is better than the present. The commentary is valuable.

Nonetheless, the arguments are skewed to support a conclusion that has only partial validity. First of all, religious thought on gambling is very mixed, and a disservice is done when researchers see it as a unity. The moral opponents of gambling, whether they be in churches, in government, or in the commercial world, can offer opposition without being self-serving. They can be altruistic and seek a higher good for all society by opposing idleness, drinking, and obsessions with games and by opposing a diversion of societal resources away from other causes. The causes need not be their own pocketbooks. Someone who opposes gambling that leads to pathological behaviors that impose real financial burdens upon all members of society might well take that view because of being truly interested in having a good society—not just because he or she perceives the possibility of having to contribute $100 to public coffers to remedy the harms caused by gambling (this is an approximate amount U.S. citizens might be burdened with because of gambling problems in the nation). Proponents of gambling also need not be financially connected with the industry. They might well be altruistic and truly feel that personal rights and freedoms are best served if gambling choices are given to members of society. Similarly the opponents of gambling can also be purely altruistic in their motivations.

Burbank, Jeff. 2000. *License to Steal: Nevada's Gaming Control System in the Megaresort Age.* Reno: University of Nevada Press. 263 pp.

In *License to Steal,* Jeff Burbank provides readers with a well-penned book containing valuable material giving insights into the regulation of casinos in Nevada. Burbank knows the Las Vegas casino industry very well. During the 1980s and early 1990s he was a reporter specializing in gambling for both the *Las Vegas Sun* and the *Las Vegas Review Journal.* He is currently the editor of the *Las Vegas Business Press.* In *License to Steal,* he ties his knowledgeable perspectives about Nevada gambling regulation to both a historical record and contemporary case studies of regulatory decision making. He completes the text with seven profiles of recent members of the Nevada Gaming Commission and the Gambling Control Board, members who played key roles in the decisions discussed. Two appendixes present descriptions of the regulatory structures in Nevada and statistical details regarding taxation of gambling and staffing of the agencies.

Burbank presents the historical record in the initial 34 pages of his 263-page book. Although less than 15 percent of the book, the first chapter nonetheless deserves extra attention from any serious student of Nevada gambling. Burbank walks the reader through critical events guiding gambling in the nineteenth and early twentieth centuries. These events included prohibition, legalization, prohibition, and new legalizations of casino-type gambling. The events provide a cultural backdrop to the "final" legalization decision in 1931. Even though much of this history can be found in other volumes, his treatment of local government regulation in the city of Las Vegas and Clark County during the 1931–1947 period is unique. The book represents the first time an author closely examines the records of the city and county during a time when gambling law first became compromised by Mob influences. The 1931 Nevada gambling law gave cities and counties complete control over who would receive a license to conduct games, how many games they could conduct, and the rules they had to follow in the operations. As the purpose of legalization was economic, the local agencies quickly adopted a posture of friendliness toward operators.

Burbank then takes the reader through the era of state predominance in regulation that began with state licensing and taxation in 1945. He shows how the state adjusted to various outside pressures—U.S. Senate investigations in particular—by adjusting its supervision processes. Even though regulators began emphasizing the critical need to have integrity in the industry, they never abandoned an attitude of laissez faire and tolerance toward industry actors. This stance comes through in the case studies.

The next seven chapters closely examine seven interesting cases of regulatory law and regulatory politics. Burbank had covered each case closely as a reporter, and he spares neither detail nor the investigative reporter's rhetorical skills in presenting the facts. The first case involved murder—the hired killing of an employee of American Coin Machine Company. American Coin was exposed for operating gambling machines that were rigged so that large jackpots could not be won. On 1 January 1990, Larry Volk, a computer programmer for the company, was brought down by a bullet outside of his home. He had been cooperating with authorities in a criminal investigation of American Coin. The company had already lost its gambling license and suffered a civil fine of $1 million for its cheating activity. The case study then takes the reader away from the gambling regulators and into the criminal courts. The case introduces Ron Harris, a technician working for the Gaming Control Board's Electronic Services Division. Harris is the subject of another story. As a state agent, Harris examined the computer chips for new slot machines and keno game number generators. He discovered some flaws in the programming in the chips. Rather than reporting his discovery, he worked to develop new understandings of the programs and figured out a way to set the chips on certain machines and then to play the games in order to win big jackpots. Harris was caught because he used a confederate who drew suspicions of New Jersey regulators when he attempted to collect a big win at a keno game. Harris was convicted of cheating, served a few years in prison, and was also placed in the state's Book of Excluded Persons. He is banned from going into casinos. Harris expressed the notion that he was not all that guilty, albeit he knew he was "wrong." Rather he felt after years of observing casinos getting all the breaks from the Nevada Gaming Control Board, he was "the little guy against the casinos."

Ron Harris was also involved as a machine tester in the case of Universal Distributing Company, a slot manufacturer. Universal developed a machine that would select winners and losers randomly. If a computer determined, however, that a player was a loser, the machine then was programmed to display a combination of symbols that made it appear to the player that he or she had been very close to having a win. Universal's sales of machines increased considerably in the mid-1980s when the issue of "near-miss" was brought to the gaming board and commission. Rival slot machine companies presented their beliefs that the machines should not be permitted. Universal was a Japanese company; their competitors were Nevada companies. The board had approved the machines before, but after lengthy hearings, the Nevada Gaming Commission ruled four to one that Universal had to reprogram all its machines to remove the near-miss factor. Accordingly, Universal's competitive advantage disappeared and so did most of its sales.

The author took a long look at one of the most embarrassing cases in Nevada gaming history. Ralph Englestadt, owner of the Imperial Palace, was "exposed" for having held Hitler Birthday Parties in 1988 and before in the private quarters of his casino property. He also had World War II memorabilia displayed in ways that seemed to glorify Nazi Germany, at least to many observers. When the matter came to public attention, Nevada's regulators sensed that they had a problem. National news media gave it prominence. Englestadt apologized and removed many of the "offensive" materials from his "war room." Nonetheless, his critics indicated that he had brought disrepute to the state's gaming industry and that he thus violated gaming rules. The Gaming Control Board asked the state attorney general's office to formulate an appropriate complaint. The board presented the complaint to the Nevada Gaming Commission. Some voices suggested that the Imperial Palace should lose its gaming license. While hearings were progressing in front of the Nevada Gaming Commission, a "deal was struck" with Englestadt. He agreed to pay a fine of $1.5 million and to dispense with several relics such as touring cars that had belonged to Adolph Hitler. The deal was accepted by all parties.

Two other cases—those of the Royal Nevada Casino and the sport of kings—seemed to have been agonizingly long episodes during which the gaming authorities bent so far over backwards before closing the doors of the operators that one wonders if they were regulatory boards at all. The authorities were certainly seen as a political group of decision makers when the Gaming Control Board recommended that the commission not license a key figure with the Sands—another case. The key person was given a license, and casino owner Sheldon Adelson moved forward with plans that eventually resulted in the creation of the billion-dollar-plus Venetian Casino.

Cabot, Anthony N., William N. Thompson, Andrew Tottenham, and Carl Braunlich, eds. 1999. *International Casino Law.* 3d ed. Reno: Institute for the Study of Gambling, University of Nevada, Reno. 650 pp.

Casinos operate in a legalized manner in over eighty countries of the world. *International Casino Law* presents a descriptive synopsis of the regulatory provisions of the casino laws of these countries as well as many of their subdivisions (e.g., sixteen states of the

United States and seven provinces of Canada). In addition there are sections on Native American casinos, gambling on the Internet, and casinos on the high seas. The editors of the book have attempted (and succeeded in about half of the sections) to follow a common outline that is useful for making a comparative analysis of casino law. The common outline includes (1) the history of casinos, (2) their economic impacts, (3) the regulatory bodies of the jurisdiction, (4) authorized games and their rules, (5) licensing provisions, (6) accounting rules, (7) taxation, (8) equipment, and (9) operational guidelines and provisions for disciplinary actions.

Over thirty-five authors contributed sections to the book. Many of them were native to the jurisdiction they described. The editors have not utilized legal style footnotes as might be found in an ordinary legal textbook, although some bibliographic materials are included. The editors have purposely avoided giving the notion that the book is to be a sole source of legal advice. Only a trained lawyer can provide that, and such advice must be tied to particular facts in particular situations. The editors also realize that their subject matter is a fast-moving (and always expanding) target. For that reason, this book has been published in three editions over a seven-year period.

I have used *International Casino Law* as a source for much of the information on various venues of gambling discussed in this encyclopedia.

Campbell, Colin, and John Lowman, eds. 1989. *Gambling in Canada: Golden Goose or Trojan Horse?* Burnaby, B.C. Simon Fraser University. 417 pp.
Campbell, Colin, ed. 1994. *Gambling in Canada: The Bottomline.* Burnaby, B.C.: Simon Fraser University. 198 pp.

The Criminology Department of Simon Fraser University conducted two national symposia on gambling in 1988 and 1993. These two volumes contain the papers from these conferences. Collectively, they present a comprehensive picture of gambling operations in Canada as well as a considerable body of other relevant information on public policy and gambling. Each volume presents a province-by-province account of lotteries and casino operations as well as references to horse racing. There are also commentaries on the general Canadian law of gambling and First Nations gambling in Canada (and the United States) as well as pathological gambling, gambling behavior, children and gambling, the ethics of gambling, charitable games, and the economics of gambling.

The articles in the books come from academic scholars, industry operators, and government regulators. Canadian gambling is intrinsically interesting for many reasons. The model of Canadian gambling has elevated the notion of charity games to the style of Las Vegas casinos (in quality if not in quantity). The gaming is quite distinct from patterns found in the United States, yet seems to pursue the same essential goal of bottom-line profits. Many innovations in modern gambling operations have come out of Canada. Moreover, the influence of casinos located near the U.S. border has seriously affected gambling politics to the south (or to the north in the case of Windsor and Detroit). These two books show the close connections between the two countries that share the longest peaceful border in the world. The books also show the unique qualities of Canadian gambling.

Chafetz, Henry. 1960. *Play the Devil: A History of Gambling in the United States from 1492 to 1955.* New York: Potter Publishers. 475 pp.

Author Henry Chafetz, a New York book dealer, views history as a product of the gambling urge within adventurous people. He presents his story in the form of one interesting character after another, one vignette followed by another vignette. It is an informal history lacking documentation for the many facts and anecdotes presented, but including a bibliography of sources at the end. Among the stories that grab the attention of the reader are ones such as the establishment of a lottery to rebuild Boston's Faneuil Hall after it was destroyed by a fire, the fact that George Washington bought the first ticket for a national lottery in 1793, the wagers on the steamboat race between the *Natchez* and the *Robert E. Lee* in 1870, and the revelation that the Chicago fire of 1874 was not caused by Mrs. O'Leary's cow, but rather by players in a craps game in the O'Leary barn. From stories of more recent years the fact emerges that the discovery of a little black book with gambling records proved to be Al Capone's downfall, as it provided the evidence that he had evaded paying federal income taxes. Chafetz also tells us about the great "Gipper" betting on his own Notre Dame team to win—could Knute Rockne have been asking the players to cover the spread with his "Win one for the Gipper" speech? General Eisenhower apparently also made a bet that our troops would be in Germany by the end of 1944. He lost that one. Chafetz also devotes a chapter to Wall Street, calling the exchange "the Greatest Gamble."

These are all interesting stories, but they are all side bars. Nonetheless Chafetz tries to draw something out of his fun-packed book that just does not seem to ring true. He thinks all the little stories add up to a grand conclusion that gambling has moved history and that it continues to be a force in the turning of great events. There can be little doubt that leaders have always challenged obstacles with risk-taking behaviors, but to claim that it was the gamble that made the event is a big stretch. The facts in no way build to a substantiated conclusion that gambling is a determining factor in history. Still, gambling is now an important commercial enterprise, and for those who support legalized gambling it is refreshing to know that the notable figures in history did partake of wagers and game-playing activities.

Clark, Thomas L. 1987. *The Dictionary of Gambling and Gaming.* Cold Spring, NY: Lexix House Publishers. 263 pp.

Gambling has its own special language. Names and words are associated with gambling by players and others who are part of "the group" or "fraternity." The proper nouns *Canfield, Lansky, Rothstein, Siegel,* and *Hughes* conjure up notions of power and influence. *Citation* and *Cigar* are linked with winning. *Upset* was also a proper noun. It was the name of a horse that defeated Man O' War although it was a 100–1 longshot. As a gambler's word, *upset* became associated with any underdog in a contest who won. The word then was taken over as part of the general language. Other gambling words have also come into the common language of the times: *square deal, new deal, no dice,* and *full deck.*

The use of special words that are not in the vocabulary of the ordinary population gives meaning to the lives of those tied to gambling. It lets them know who is "in" and who is not "in" their fraternity. The use of words is like a secret handshake. The words can be "icebreakers" for beginning conversations or friendships, for prompting one to inquire about the location of a game, or for asking for information about a race or other event. At the time that almost all gambling was illegal, special words could be used to conceal activities from persons who might not approve. The inside vocabulary can also be used to establish one's esteem and status as a player.

In 1950, David Maurer presented a glossary of terms, "The Argot of the Dice Gambler," in an essay in Morris Ploscowe and Edwin J. Lukas's *Gambling,* a special issue of *The Annals of the American Academy of Political and Social Science.* Maurer described many of the facets of gambling terminology. Since then, however, there have been no concerted efforts to document this vocabulary. In modern times, the late Tom Clark's *Dictionary of Gambling and Gaming* stands out as a unique addition to the literature. Clearly it is the best collection of gambling vocabulary available.

Turn card, puppyfoot, snowballing, zuke, blind tiger, super george, dead spot, needle squeeze, twig, king crab: These are only some of the 5,000 or so words and phrases that appear in Clark's volume. Clark was for many years a professor of English and linguistics at the University of Nevada, Las Vegas. He applied his academic training well to the environment in which he found himself, and in doing so he produced a very valuable research resource as well as an intrinsically interesting collection of terminology. He offers the reader 255 pages of terms presented from A to Z. He indicates sources for his definitions (such as *Oxford English Dictionary* or *The Dictionary of American English on Historical Principles*), provides selected pronunciation guides, and indicates parts of speech, source languages, variations in spelling, definitions, multiple definitions, synonyms, and explanatory quotations. He also adds an extensive bibliography. The book begins with an introductory section that describes the values of words in gambling and also offers an extensive discussion of the words *gambling* and *gaming* and whether they are the same or not, a topic that is still important to many people in the "industry."

Clotfelter, Charles T., and Philip J. Cook. 1989. *Selling Hope: State Lotteries in America.* Cambridge: Harvard University Press. 323 pp.

Where David Weinstein and Lillian Deitch (*The Impact of Legalized Gambling*) assessed the status of lotteries after ten years of experience in the United States, Clotfelter and Cook present a quarter-century perspective on the phenomenon. Actually they reach farther back before lotteries came to New Hampshire in 1964 to give the reader an overview that is tied to other eras and other societies. The authors present the most comprehensive (called "exhaustive, but never exhausting") treatment of lotteries to date. The two authors, both professors at Duke University, conclude that state lotteries in the United States have all fallen into identical patterns of putting revenue generation ahead of all other values. The public permits this as they do not review policy decisions on lotteries after they acquiesce in their adoption. Actually, the majorities given to lottery referenda by the public are quite large and often surprising given the fact that key public officials occasionally lead opposition efforts. Up to 1989 only one state had ever had a popular vote against a proposal of a state-operated lottery. In many cases the campaigns are led by lottery suppliers who see adoption of lotteries in new jurisdictions as their source of continued wealth.

A case study of the influence of Scientific Games in the California campaign of 1984 is illustrative. State lot-

tery officials have free rein to pursue the one goal of achieving maximum sales. To achieve more and more sales they use the most modern applications of marketing principles, identifying customer segments and using the strongest messages possible to influence sales. The consequences of maximizing lottery revenues have led to a very regressive taxation effect. Poorer people and minorities buy tickets in disproportionate amounts, and in turn, lottery organizations direct their advertising efforts at these people. Moreover the advertisements utilized are misleading; they do not tell the truth about odds, and they paint unrealistic pictures of winners while denigrating persons who resist buying tickets.

Clotfelter and Cook lament that all the lotteries have gone in the same direction—they have become revenue lotteries. They ask the public and the political leaders in both lottery states and in states that are considering lotteries to consider two other models of lotteries: one that they call the sumptary model and another that they call the consumer model. In the sumptary model, lotteries are offered as a government product designed to meet existing demands of the people for a product that they might seek from illegal sources if there is no legal supplier. In this model the government does not market and merchandise lotteries but rather offers them in a very passive manner—even without advertising at all.

In the consumer model, the government does advertise its gambling products, but it does so in a responsible and, most of all, an honest manner. Odds are accurately presented, and players are given information about play rather than fantasies that cannot be achieved. The authors suggest that those managing lotteries today consider these two alternatives, each of which would be more directed toward the public interest than lotteries under the revenue model.

The National Gambling Impact Study Commission made some rather harsh assessments of lotteries today. Their conclusions were propelled by contracted research conducted by Charles Clotfelter and Philip Cook.

Custer, Robert, and Harry Milt. 1985. *When Luck Runs Out: Help for Compulsive Gamblers and Their Families.* New York: Facts on File. 239 pp.

Robert Custer was truly the pioneer of gambling help programs. In 1972 he started the first treatment center for compulsive gamblers at a Veterans Administration hospital in Ohio. In this book he joins with professional writer Harry Milt to share with his readers experiences in his extraordinary career. Throughout the book, readers will find case studies of problem gambling that provide real substance for the accompanying textual commentary.

Custer was an important player in the effort that led the American Psychiatric Association to designate compulsive gambling as a disease in 1980. He expands on the medical model in the book. Nonetheless, the authors made a respectable review of other theories of compulsive gambling. Indeed, they put forth their own notions that the manifestation of the disease is tied to need deprivations that may be traced to early childhood experiences. People need affection and approval, recognition and self-confidence. When these are absent, people seek to cope. One means of coping is "fantasy, illusion, and escape." When gambling opportunities are placed in front of such persons, a pathway to the disease of compulsive gambling is available. But people in such situations (and everyone is exposed to some gambling today) do not just become compulsive gamblers. First they have to play. Then there are phases on the trail to the disease: the winning phase, the losing phase, the bailout, and the desperate phase.

Custer and Milt give consideration to the families of compulsive gamblers, to the female gambler, and also to treatment possibilities. The book is written for a general audience that is interested in gambling phenomena but most especially for persons who are in trouble or who are exposed to others who are. Custer and Milt offer hope—but the hope comes when people become aware. This book helps those who need a journey to recovery.

Davis-Goff, Annabel, ed. 1996. *The Literary Companion to Gambling.* London: Sinclair-Stevenson. 246 pp.

Davis-Goff presents a classic collection of wisdom and observations on gambling throughout the ages. Her compendium of literary passages on the subject is arranged into three sections: "The Gods," "Man," and "Self." The first section leads off with the Old Testament story of Jonah, followed by entries describing the use of gambling mechanisms to determine divine will and purpose. These examples include words from Tacitus, Shirley Jackson's *The Lottery,* Bret Harte, Francis Bacon, Charles Dickens, and Robert Louis Stevenson. In these passages, man is powerless in the face of the force of the Almighty. He has no control, no will.

The writings in the second section pit man against man. Here the individual has a choice, free will, about whether to play the game and how to play the game. Many feel (whether realistically or as an illusion) that they can exercise skill and power in the games in order to best their human competitors. Davis-Goff's selections include writings from Sir Walter Scott's *A Legend*

of *Montrose,* Ben Jonson's *The Alchemist,* Herodotus's *The Histories,* and F. Scott Fitzgerald's *The Great Gatsby* as well as items from the work of Tolstoy, William Thackery, Plutarch, Damon Runyon, and Mark Twain.

In the final section, gambling is portrayed as a phenomenon that has value in and of itself for the individual. The value may be in the play, which provides a diversion from boredom of life. But also the play can be seen as a lonely pastime, one that may be consumed in personal desperation, although one of excitement for others. Some passages selected are from Lord Byron, Blaise Pascal, James Boswell, Honoré de Balzac, Fyodor Dostoyevsky, and Alexander Pope. The book is replete with many little treasures for the casual or serious student of gambling, for the casual or serious player of games.

Denton, Sally, and Roger Morris. 2001. *The Money and the Power: The Making of Las Vegas and Its Hold on America.* New York: Knopf. 479 pp.

It is déjà vu one more time, as they say: another exposé of Las Vegas. The theme of Denton and Morris's *The Money and the Power* portrays Las Vegas as even more evil than the Las Vegas found in Reid and Demaris's *The Green Felt Jungle* or Johnston's *Temples of Chance.* The authors are Las Vegas residents, so they should know. Well, perhaps yes, perhaps no. They suggest that the evil force of Las Vegas is not bounded by the geographical isolation of the desert resort city. Rather, the influence of Las Vegas extends far across the nation and indeed around the globe. A big bite to chew. Two subjects are covered here that are not found in earlier broadsides against Las Vegas. The authors suggest (with a few stories) that Las Vegas is the illicit drug center for the nation and even the hemisphere. They also indicate that the gambling industry of Las Vegas has a powerful control over the politics of the United States.

On the one hand, the stories in the book are fun—a "quick read." On the other hand, the fast-paced shoot-from-the-hip style of the book leads to my assessment that it was also a "quick write." As I am also a Las Vegas resident, I found a sufficient number of factual errors (mostly but not all of minor importance) to advise the careful reader to hesitate to accept the "forest"—that is, the grand conclusions of the authors. Errors surround their selections and portrayals of certain persons as heroes and others as "devil incarnates." Nonetheless, many of the descriptions of the "trees" do have enough of a ring of truth in them that the book deserves to be read.

The drug stories seem to me to be a bit remote. It we are infested with drug magnates, it is not noticeable to the citizens of Las Vegas or to those coming to the city for their vacations and minivacations. On the other hand, the stories of our recent presidents are fascinating in and of themselves. We knew before that the Kennedys were Las Vegas kind of guys. The depth of Joseph Kennedy's involvement in the casinos seems to be fresh material, however, as do many of the interconnections of the 1960 presidential campaign and Frank Sinatra and his friends. That Lyndon B.Johnson (and Hubert Humphrey) and Richard Nixon were involved makes more good reading. The connections of Ronald Reagan and Virginia Kelly (called Virginia Clinton) and her boy Bill are even more fascinating. The more recent emergence of Las Vegas as the center for national campaign financing deserves the print that it receives. This, however, hardly makes the city a powerful force over national policy decisions.

On the local scene, the machinations of casino finance and the influence of Salt Lake City bankers, both Mormon and gentile, deserve to be explored as the authors have done. Few before them dared to do so. The notion that the local casinos control all important facets of local life in Las Vegas seems a bit overstated. All citizens (who care about it) recognize that the politicians consider the gambling industry to be their most important constituency. That does not mean that people in Las Vegas do not exercise free will over the important activities of their own lives or that they do not have a strong voice in politics on issues of concern to themselves—where the issues do not conflict with those of the casinos. Even where they do, Las Vegas is a two (competing) daily newspaper town, and contrary to the views of the authors, those critical of the casinos and casino moguls do have their say in the press. I have personally said many critical things about the casinos and their owners, and the words have been printed. I also say nice things about casinos sometimes. People might ignore my words, but at least I know casino executives read them, because they let my phone ring when they do not like my words. The casinos do not own Las Vegas, and they do not own the political leaders.

The authors suggest that politics in Las Vegas is corrupt. They suggest further that life in the city is miserable. Yet, something belies their basic theme. More people are moving into Las Vegas each month. It is the fastest-growing community in the nation. Free-thinking American citizens making life choices are choosing Las Vegas as the community they wish to call their own.

Devol, George H. 1887. *Forty Years a Gambler on the Mississippi.* Cincinnati: Devol and Haynes. 300 pp.

Students of gambling history do not have many firsthand accounts of gambling action in centuries past.

Fyodor Dostoyevsky, in *the Gambler,* provides an autobiographical account in a fictionalized format of a bout with gambling fever. George Devol provides another firsthand account of gambling but with a very different tone. Devol does not speak to despair but rather speaks of triumph, for he is the self-proclaimed "best gambler in the world." He cites the Mississippi River in his title, but his escapades extended to the tributaries and also the shores of that great river. He was born in Marietta, Ohio, in 1829, the son of a ship carpenter. Exposed as a child to the crews of river vessels, he got the urge early on to make a life on the river. He often played hooky from school to mix and mingle with the river travelers, and at age ten he took off. He jumped aboard an Ohio River steamer and was given a job as a cabin boy.

The book is his book, and his stories. The reader must seek always to separate fact from fiction, but the reader is treated to one adventure after another. The stories are presented in chronological order, but in general they appear to be rambling accounts of winners and losers, cheaters of one type or another, and other characters that Devol passed by on his life journey. By the time he was eleven years old he was stealing cards, and he practiced until he could cheat with the best of them. He soon became involved in the games, and the games often involved thousands of dollars. By his account he had won "hundreds of thousands" of dollars while still a teenager, taking advantage of paymasters and soldiers on river jaunts during the Mexican War. George Devol was a good fighter too, as many stories are about the fights he engaged in and often the narrow escapes from mortal danger. Remarkably he survived until he was an old man who could sit and reminisce about the good ol' days.

He became a philosopher in his old age too—a philosopher of gambling. Toward the end of his tome he relates that Thomas Hobbes said that "man is the only animal that laughs." Writes Devol,

He might have appropriately added, he is the only animal that gambles. To gamble or venture on chance, his own property with the hope of winning the property of another is peculiar to him. Other animals in common with man will fight for meat, drink, and lodging, and will battle for love as fiercely as the old knights of chivalry; but there is no well authenticated account that any of the lower animals ever changed any of their property on "odd or even," or drew lots for choice of pasturage. No master has ever yet taught his dog to play with him at casino, and even the learned pig could never learn what was trumps. Hence gambling is proof of man's intellectual superiority (296–297).

Dombrink, John D., and William N. Thompson. 1990. *The Last Resort: Success and Failure in Campaigns for Casinos.* Reno: University of Nevada Press. 220 pp.

The authors make an analysis of factors influencing results of political campaigns to legalize casino gambling in almost twenty states, from 1964 through 1989. They seek to explain an anomaly. During a three-decade period lottery campaigns had been successful in almost every case where the issue arose, yet only one casino campaign—that in New Jersey in 1976—had been successful. Lottery efforts usually won with large popular majorities, whereas casino propositions were defeated by equally large margins.

After a discussion of the development of the Las Vegas casino industry and its place in the public mind, the authors present case studies of casino campaigns in New Jersey and Florida. Their analysis leads them to discern two policy models at work in gambling legalization campaigns. For the successful lottery campaigns, they find a gravity model at play. Campaign factors are weighed and if a predominance of the issues favors the adoption of a lottery, the lottery proponents are successful. Another model is at work in casino campaigns, however. The authors call it the veto model. Here—if but one major factor in the campaign is negative—the whole campaign falls to defeat. The authors identify several major veto factors: the economic climate, previous experience with gambling in a state (and reputation of gambling in the state), campaign financing and the legitimacy of campaign sponsors, the position of political elites (especially governors and attorneys general), the position of business elites, whether rival gambling interests oppose the proposition, and whether the major issue in the campaign is economics or crime (crime being the veto factor).

Next the book presents case studies from over a dozen states and nearly twenty campaigns that show the veracity of the model. The governor and the crime issue defeat casinos in several Florida campaigns; the opposition of Governor Clinton brings down a campaign in Arkansas; the lack of credibility of campaign sponsors in Michigan and California dooms campaigns; the attorney general stops a New York campaign cold in 1981.

As the book was going to the publisher, new developments showed casino gambling legalization campaigns to be successful in Iowa and Colorado. Although no veto factor emerged in Iowa, in Colorado the governor offered opposition, albeit passive opposition. Moreover, the year of publication—1990—also witnessed the beginning of an era of Native American casino establishment. Was the veto model falling into disrepute?

In a later article ("The Last Resort Revisited." *Journal of Gambling Studies* 11, no. 4 [Winter 1995]: 373–378), coauthor Thompson and Ricardo Gazel suggested that the model has remained viable, although the political process surrounding Native American casino compacts is quite different, and that campaigns for limited stakes (five-dollar betting limits) gambling are not the same as campaigns for wide-open land-based casinos. Moreover, it was suggested that a governor's opposition to casinos had to be active in order to effectuate a veto. In 1996 the Michigan governor opposed Detroit casinos but did so only mildly and without enthusiasm. The proposition passed on a very narrow vote. The book offers a history of casino campaigns and still provides some valuable guidelines for those wishing to promote or oppose casino legalizations.

Dostoyevsky, Fyodor. 1972. *The Gambler.* Translated from the 1866 Russian edition by Victor Terras. Chicago: University of Chicago Press. 164 pp.

The immortal novelist Dostoyevsky penned the most poignant portrayal of a compulsive gambler and his feelings in this 1866 work. His novel about the tortured gambler "Alexis" is considered by most observers to be an autobiographical account of a phase of Dostoyevsky's own life. The diary of his wife reveals many episodes when Fyodor would disappear to the gambling tables of Wiesbaden or Bad Homburg only to emerge in a wretched state. Often he would feel compelled to write in order to get the money to gamble or the money to pay back gambling debts.

The account of Alexis became fodder for Sigmund Freud, who read his own psychoanalytical interpretations into the passion of gambling, assigning male and female representations to the equipment of the gambling tables. The book itself is about a few short weeks in the gambling career of Alexis, but it successfully captures the feelings of the moment. It reflects feelings of inferiority and melancholy, as well as heightened arousal that offer many insights into his gambling mania. Contemporary students of compulsive or pathological (or problem) gambling have a universal case study to which they, like Freud, can assign their own theories. Indeed, several reject the Freudian interpretations outright. For instance, other theories are supported by the social notion that Alexis was trying to mimic the behaviors of others (models) to whom he paid deference. His gambling was certainly part of his relationship with his wife. He experienced the spirals that Henry Lesieur addresses in *The Chase*—he chased his losses. Yet, he clung to notions of rationality, albeit the false rationality of the gambler's fallacy that the wheel knows what it has done before and will in the short run even things out. (The law of mathematics only works in the long run—you know, when we are all dead).

The Gambler is a classic because it is open to interpretation and reinterpretation by all. It is a tabula rasa for gambling scholars. All can see something that supports their own views, and all can join in arguments about what Dostoyevsky is really saying.

Eadington, William R., ed. 1990. ***Indian Gaming and the Law.*** Reno: Institute for the Study of Gambling, University of Nevada, Reno. 298 pp.

The most rapidly expanding gambling is found on Native American reservations. The rush forward with new casinos, new casino locations, and expanded facilities goes on unabated. Native gambling represents 15 percent of the full gambling market and a third of the casino market. For that reason, it would be expected that the gambling literature would contain volumes on the subject, and gambling journals would have countless articles. Such is not the case. Indeed, at the beginning of a new century, a quarter of a century after Native gambling began, there was still only this one basic book on the subject. William R. Eadington has edited a collection of essays that were initially presented to a special conference in March 1989, just months after the passage of the Indian Gaming Regulatory Act. This of course dates the book. On the other hand, the timing gives the reader perspectives of many important policymakers who were still near the scene of the major decision making surrounding the act.

The panel of writers included U.S. senator Harry Reid of Nevada, who was happy to take credit for engineering the provision of the act (tribal-state compacts) that was the essential compromise that led to the passage of the act. Former secretary of interior Stuart Udall also made a presentation, as did several tribal leaders. Academic insights were given by I. Nelson Rose, Jerome Skolnick, and William R. Eadington among others, including myself. Two speakers were Canadian First Nations representatives.

At the time of the conference, the commercial casino industry was feeling very comfortable with the misguided notion that the act had stopped the spread of Native gambling with an effective set of controls and limits. Native leaders were bristling at the notion that they were being illegally regulated in ways disturbing their sovereignty. They were launching a legal attack upon the constitutionality of the act.

In addition to the political posturing in the presentations, many of the crucial issues facing Native gaming are illuminated. Jerome Skolnick offered the most poignant observation. With the passage of the Indian Gaming Regulatory Act, the federal government for the first time in history had (through the voice of Congress) gone on record as endorsing the use of gambling for positive good in society. This was no small matter.

Editor Eadington provides a very useful service for all gambling researchers by including a full text of the Indian Gaming Regulatory Act and also a full text of the Supreme Court's opinions in the decision of *California v. Cabazon Band of Mission Indians* (1987).

Earley, Pete. 2000. ***Super Casino: Inside the "New Las Vegas."*** New York: Bantam Books. 386 pp.

Pete Earley tells another "inside" Las Vegas story. This time it is a story of the 1990s; this time it is a story about the new monster-sized casinos. But what is "inside" is not really new at all. Much of the story, indeed most of the story, has been told before, and it will be told again, and then again. He does provide some new twists, a new writing format (sort of), interesting insights, and a good read. He was formerly a reporter with the *Washington Post,* so he knows how to write, but he writes like a reporter, without footnotes and without a list of sources. As is the case with the stories in the daily press, the essential sources are the people that he interviews.

The focus of the book is one casino organization, now called Mandalay Resorts, formerly called Circus Circus. Earley introduces the reader to the founder of Circus Circus—Jay Sarno. He then takes his story through the 1970s when the Circus property is purchased by William Bennett and William Pennington. In the 1980s, the property "goes public," with the leadership of Glenn Schaeffer; then as the 1990s unfold, the company builds its three megacasinos, or supercasinos, the Excalibur, the Luxor, and the Mandalay Bay. With the coming of the 1990s, the organization seeks to change its image as the workingman's "family" casino and become a "high-roller" organization.

Earley's story of life in the modern Las Vegas scene is told thorough several major characters who all seem to find the Luxor to be a place to play out their roles. Some are very peripheral to the casino scene. There are two tourists, a show dancer, and a prostitute. The main players are Chief Executive Schaeffer, General Manager Tony Alamo, and Security Director Keith Uptain. Each actor cycles into and out of the book through a set of vignettes that are sprinkled with sidebars featuring players, room clerks, cab drivers, and others. Not all of the vignettes are at all relevant to the coming of the new casinos. Certainly the many pages devoted to the life of a prostitute and the company she keeps and to the relationships of a show dancer add very little to an understanding of what has happened since 1990. Their stories have been told for many many decades, and they did not seem to be any different this time around—well, except for the fact that one prostitute gets AIDS, which is a relatively new wrinkle. The book does offer a good discussion of card counting and also of several cheating scams—but this activity has been around a long time too. Perhaps the major contribution of the volume is found in the first book discussions of the downfall of William Bennett. Earley certainly presents a good case study that could be used in Principles of Management 301 courses at University of Nevada, Las Vegas (a subject that I teach). Perhaps in his sequel, Earley can give the inside story of the fall of Stephen Wynn. Unfortunately, the book went to press still worshipping Wynn, the fallen spirit behind the Mirage organization.

Eisler, Kim Isaac. 2001. *Revenge of the Pequots: How a Small Native American Tribe Created the World's Most Profitable Casino.* New York: Simon and Schuster. 267 pp.

Eisler presents a well-researched history of Foxwoods casino in Ledyard, Connecticut. The facility grosses almost $1 billion in gambling revenue each year for the benefit of a few hundred Native Americans—the Mashantucket Pequots. The casino came into being as a result of a political miracle that continues. About a dozen members of a state-recognized tribe somehow won federal recognition in the 1980s. Then the tribe established a bingo parlor, Congress intervened by passing the Indian Gaming Regulatory Act of 1988, and the Pequots—whose numbers began to grow as they made money—set their eyes on casino gambling. Through a maze of court cases and strange political decisions by Connecticut politicians, the tribe was given the opportunity to have table games and slot machines. Theirs became the only casino in all of New England, located just seven miles off the major interstate highway between New York and Boston—less than two hours from each of the metropolitan areas. Then the courts intervened again with rulings that effectively stopped efforts to establish Native American casinos in other New England venues.

The story details many of the maneuvers that at times were on the devious side, but at other times seemed consistent with notions of restoring Native American sovereignty in a way that fulfilled the goals of congressional action. The tribe has used its newfound extraordinary wealth in many ways. The 175 members receive a variety of bonuses that ensure each will have a lifetime of luxurious living. The tribe supports many good causes; in fact, a significant portion of the revenue—well over a hundred million dollars—is given directly to the state of Connecticut. Many Native American cultural causes are supported, and a museum of history has been established. The book emphasizes how English colonists essentially slaughtered tribal members in the 1600s but glosses over the fact that the English had many Native American allies in their conquest of the Pequots, as the Pequots had been a rather fierce tribe themselves and not well liked by any of their neighbors. Be that as it may, there is reason enough for "white guilt" regarding Native American history. The tribe has also showered its dollars on politicians, through lobbying efforts and through direct campaign donations—soft and hard. The political donations have assured that any congressional action to change the Indian Gaming Regulatory Act will effectively be nullified for many years to come.

David versus Goliath. But one wonders just who is David and who is Goliath in the final analysis. Part of Eisler's story has readers cheering for the underdog Pequots, but part should leave the readers wondering if Native America gambling policy has been rationally thought out. Native Americans are the poorest Americans in an economic sense and in the sense of many social indicators. Gambling helps, but does it really move Native Americans closer to the standards of living enjoyed by the majority of Americans? For sure, gaming helps the 175 Pequots. The trouble is that gambling helps only small numbers of Native Americans. There were over two million Native Americans in the United States in 1990, according to the census. The majority are not being helped by casinos. Should they be? My belief is that if tribes are given casinos because Native Americans have collectively been wronged (and they have) and because collectively (but as tribes) they have sovereign rights, then all Native Americans should participate in the enjoyment of gambling revenues coming from casinos that have been established in the name of alleviating the "white man's guilt." To win permanent political favor, gambling tribes should design mechanisms by which their revenues can be shared among all Native Americans—much as my tax dollars are taken from me to help all my needy fellow citizens (in some way). The book offers great history lessons and offers great questions for future policymakers—when they get around to wanting to deal with the questions.

Farrell, Ronald A., and Carole Case. 1995. *The Black Book and the Mob: The Untold Story of the Control of Nevada's Casinos.* Madison: University of Wisconsin Press. 286 pp.

Ronald Farrell and Carole Case have produced a volume on what is a side issue in casino regulation in

Nevada, the list of excluded persons. Although the so-called black book, which names individuals not permitted to come inside any of the state's unrestricted casinos, is not an important tool in the overall regulation of gambling, it is an item that has received much notoriety since its inception in 1960. The book is linked with what the authors consider to be a notion that the Mafia hovers over the state's casinos ready to move in and take over whenever given the chance.

The authors examine every entry in the black book—forty-five individuals since 1960. They look at the circumstances surrounding their inclusion. They also examine the processes followed by the Gaming Control Board and the Gaming Commission in the decisions, and they look at the legal challenges and changes in procedures over the years. The authors see the black book as coming out of an era of federal scrutiny over Nevada casinos (the 1950s), but they see it even more as a symbolic rather than a substantive response to accusations that casinos were under Mob control. What is telling for the authors is the "fact" that a preponderance of excluded persons were of Italian heritage, whereas Mob control over casinos was tied most closely to associates of Meyer Lansky: Moe Dalitz, Morris Kleinman, Lincoln Fitzgerald, Bugsy Siegel—not your typical sons of Italy or Sicily. The regulators putting the Italians in the black book all seemed to have names associated with people commonly known as WASPS (white, Anglo-Saxon Protestants). These state regulators were seeking credibility for the casino industry by showing they had control over a group perceived to be "sinful." The authors then argue that the black book is an exercise in stereotyping.

The book is well written and in most cases well documented. The arguments presented certainly carry at least a "grain" of truth and wisdom. The black book is not an important tool in regulation, and at least twenty-eight of the forty-five have "Italian-sounding" names. (The authors used the same criterion in determining they were "Italian"—that their name "sounded" Italian.) On the other hand, the argument has a superficiality that demands somewhat more evidence than is presented in the interesting 286 pages offered.

Findlay, John M. 1986. *People of Chance: Gambling in American Society from Jamestown to Las Vegas.* New York: Oxford University Press. 272 pp.

Finally, in 1986, a scholarly author produced a history of gambling in the United States that is well written, well researched, and thoroughly documented with expansive footnotes as well as a complete bibliographic essay. Moreover, the book does not just ramble from one vignette to another or from one gambling site to another one. The book has a theme, and the author seeks to organize his text around the theme. It is a neat idea, but then, the theme does not quite work, for much is left out of the pages of the book, almost as if it is irrelevant—but perhaps because it just does not fit. The book started out as a doctoral dissertation and its good-quality documentation arises from that academic exercise.

The theme is not all that original, but it is interesting and does tie the materials together up to a point. Findlay sees Americans as "People of Chance." They are risk takers descended from risk takers. They are the people who left secure (perhaps) homes in Europe for only a promise of better things (a gamble at best). A postcard currently sold at Ellis Island has this heading: "Gambling on America." The gambling did not stop at Jamestown or at Ellis Island. Americans kept looking westward for the same things their European forebears sought—the promise of better things. And so they headed out to become pioneers on the frontier, gambling with their lives, and along the way gambling at assorted other games. If one is willing to stake one's own life on chance, why not risk money as well? A culture of gambling became pervasive on the trails west and eventually became entrenched in the lives of those who arrived in California. Then the spirit in California moved east into Nevada and Las Vegas, today's Mecca for the "People of Chance."

By concentrating on the West and on Las Vegas, the author seems to neglect the role of gambling in U.S. cities, particularly those along the East Coast. Bugsy Siegel is mentioned, but he is portrayed as a Californian, and his mentor and financier, Meyer Lansky, is left out of the story. So too are the other eastern rogues who discovered Las Vegas, not during some silver rush in the 1860s but in the 1950s after Sen. Estes Kefauver gave a spirit of the hatchet to eastern gambling establishments. Kefauver is given a mention in the book as being an agent of snobbish eastern antigambling forces. In the 1960s Fidel Castro pushed other gamers toward a safe haven in Las Vegas. Jimmy Hoffa moved eastern and midwestern Teamsters' union money into Las Vegas. Hoffa was from Michigan, not California. The new visitors to Las Vegas are seen as new frontiersmen, but they are not. They are middle-class and affluent Americans who seek out a place that is different, not a place that reflects the values of their chosen communities. Half of the book is devoted to Las Vegas; an epilogue considers Atlantic City.

This is an interesting fact-filled book. It is a wonderful resource for any gambling library. The author does a great job. Unfortunately he made quite a stretch to find a theme with which to wrap all gambling in the United States. His theme just does not stretch far enough to do the job.

Frey, James H., ed. 1998. *Gambling: Socioeconomic Impacts and Public Policy.* Special volume of *The Annals of the American Academy of Political and Social Science.* Thousand Oaks, CA: Sage. 240 pp.

James Frey took up the task of compiling thirteen new essays of gambling with an end-of-the-century perspective. By 1998 the gambling industry had emerged as "America's Newest Growth Industry" with casinos—either commercial or Native American—in as many as thirty states and lotteries in thirty-eight states plus the District of Columbia. Sixty percent of Americans gambled each year, and over 80 percent approved of gambling in some form or another. Nonetheless, there were now heightened concerns about the impacts gambling was having on the social and economic fabric of the country. As the special issue was being put together, a new National Gambling Impact Study Commission was examining public policy and gambling.

This third volume of *The Annals* devoted to gambling starts with William Thompson's essay on gambling throughout the world, suggesting that the Las Vegas pattern of wide-open casinos would dominate thinking in North America but would not be exported to European jurisdictions. Colin Campbell and Garry Smith present an overview of policy issues in Canadian gambling, revealing the paradox of having governments play the roles of both regulator and protector of the public interest at the same time they are operators of gambling establishments. Editor Frey presents an updated survey of federal involvement in gambling regulation. Gene Christiansen explores the role of gambling in the U.S. economy, seeing it as one of the "fastest growing sectors" and accounting for 10 percent of all leisure expenditures in the society. William Eadington examines different styles of casino gambling, suggesting their varying impacts upon local communities. He is critical of widespread placement of gambling devices in locations accessible to masses of people.

Ricardo Gazel outlines the features of an input-output model of assessing the economic impacts on communities. He concludes that it is essential to look at both the positive and negative impacts of gambling in order to gain a picture of the net value of the enterprise for communities. John Warren Kindt examines the political influence of the gambling industry and its lobbying activities. He traces campaign contributions from the industry and expresses a fear that gambling entre-

preneurs could be gaining unhealthy political power in our society. Gary Anders views the very positive contributions of gambling to the development of Native American societies, but he also considers negative influences brought to Native peoples as a result of gambling in their midst. He also laments that Native gambling operations are on smaller urban-area reservations, thereby "exacerbating inequalities" among tribes throughout the country. Audie Blevins and Katherine Jensen conclude that the introduction of casinos in Colorado mountain towns resulted in substantial economic revival for the towns but at a cost of "cannibalized" retail businesses and extra traffic and law enforcement problems. William Miller and Martin Schwartz found a lack of common ground among studies of casino gambling and street crime. They call for additional research on specific questions tied to more clearly identified theories and hypotheses.

The final three essays of the volume examine pathological gambling. Henry Lesieur explores the costs of treatment as well as the societal costs of pathological gambling; Randy Stinchfield and Ken Winters look at problem gambling among youth. Today's youth are the first generation raised in an atmosphere of pervasive gambling that has been supported by both governments and other institutions including some churches. They call for more research, as findings are incomplete—except for a "robust" finding that young males are much more involved with gambling than are young females and thereby more likely to become problem gamblers. Las Vegas scholars Fred Preston, Bo Bernhard, Robert Hunter, and Shannon Bybee view the changing nature of the stigmas society places upon gambling behavior and consequences for public policy.

Frey, James H,. and William R. Eadington, eds. 1984. *Gambling: Views from the Social Sciences.* Special volume of *The Annals of the American Academy of Political and Social Science.* Beverly Hills, CA: Sage. July. 233 pp.

The second special edition of *The Annals* devoted to gambling examines the many changes that have involved the gambling experience since 1950. The volume offers perceptions into factors that led to the widespread expansion of gambling, most notably in the area of lotteries as well as Atlantic City casinos. Many policy dilemmas are identified as the writers accept that notion that gambling will continue to expand, yet collectively they point to a need for considerable government involvement to control potential negative attributes of gambling. Law professor G. Robert Blakey leads off with a discussion of legal events surrounding gambling since 1950. He discusses the Kefauver Commission, Robert Kennedy's program on organized crime, and the Organized Crime Control Act of 1970 as key milestones for generating federal laws on gambling. He also examines state efforts to control legalized gambling while calling for continued federal efforts to develop coherent policies on illegal gambling in the United States.

William R. Eadington follows with an essay on development of Nevada regulatory law from a time when control was essentially local in the 1940s to the comprehensive state oversight that remains in place today. He suggests that further controls will be necessary as the casino industry continues to expand. These controls may be focused upon credit policy and betting limits in order to protect problem gamblers and on advertising controls. He offers the experience taken with strict controls over casinos in England as a model for consideration. Peter Reuter explores the difficulties facing law enforcement as a result of the existence of illegal gambling. He sees public opinion as drifting away from support for enforcement of antigambling laws, especially in light of the need for law enforcement activities in other areas of more concern—mainly in the area of illicit drug trading and use. Jerry Skolnick, author of *House of Cards,* suggests that new casino jurisdictions can achieve the best control atmosphere if the numbers of licenses are restricted and that potential casino operators should compete openly for the licenses by making proposals that suggest how they will best operate in the public interest. Nigel Kent Lemon offers an excellent capsule description of regulation of casinos in the United Kingdom and how authorities have dealt with companies that violate rules of operation.

Joseph Rubenstein reviews the campaign to bring casinos to Atlantic City. On the one hand, he establishes that the casinos have accomplished great revenues through their operations. On the other hand, he suggests that there have been major difficulties in achieving the urban land development that was a primary purpose of legalization of casino gambling. He points to rampant land speculation along with ineffective government intervention as specific areas of difficulty. Atlantic City is viewed as a unique experiment with casinos but a more typical exercise in a politics whereby dominant concerns of casino revenues outweigh the altruistic goals of urban redevelopment. Dean Macomber's essay examines internal operations of casinos.

H. Roy Kaplan surveys the history of lotteries and their reemergence as a system to generate revenues for governments. He finds that lotteries are regressive taxes and that they have limited value in bringing funds to specific areas selected for political reasons. He is also critical of lottery advertising and concludes that such advertisements promote a no-work ethic in the United States. He finds lotteries to be moral paradoxes, as their increased levels of success are associated with an introduction of greater social problems. Editor Frey offers a cogent review of gambling from a sociological perspective. He laments that sociologists have not applied theories to the gambling phenomenon in a widespread manner, and he suggests that the theories provide a fruitful source of approaches for more understandings of gambling. Igor Kusyszyn concludes that the motives for gambling are quite complex. He suggests that scholars look at gambling as adult play and that psychological theories underlie both problem gambling and normal gambling activities.

Jim Smith and Vicki Abt also look at gambling as play activity and compare gambling games to other games. They suggest that our culture's embracing of many games in youth in effect teaches us how to gamble and play commercial games as adults. Leading scholar of pathology Henry R. Lesieur and treatment innovator Robert Custer present a categorization of pathological gambling, explore the phases of the problem gambling careers, and describe two methods of help—Gamblers Anonymous (GA) and professional counseling. They believed that by the year 2000 the medical model of pathological gambling (that it is a disease) would be fully accepted, the numbers of GA chapters would have increased dramatically, governments would be more involved in treatment, insurance companies would cover treatment that would also have government support, and there would be much more study of problem gambling. It should be noted that these predictions were not fulfilled.

David M. Hayano takes a look at people who experience gambling as their full-time profession. He presents a typology of these gamblers, their background, the games they play, their rates of success and failure. George Ignatin explores sports betting, starting with the premise that the betting has some attributes of rationality. He further looks at specific games, discusses odds and pointspreads, and addresses policy implications for the future.

Goodman, Robert. 1995. *The Luck Business: The Devastating Consequences and Broken Promises of America's Gambling Explosion.* New York: Free Press. 273 pp.

Robert Goodman is a former Boston newspaper reporter who has taken on the cause of fighting gambling in the United States. Along with Tom Grey he has become the leading spokesman in opposition to the spread of legalized gambling. In these pages Goodman presents a solid case buttressed with many documented facts, considerable notes, and an extensive bibliography. It is a point-of-view book, but then he has a strong point of view. He hits all the key points—compulsive gambling, crime and gambling, the economic drain caused by gambling operations that rely on local players, the cannibalization of local consumer dollars when gambling appears on the scene, the regressive nature of gambling taxation, the economic development failure of Atlantic City, and political manipulations by gambling operators.

Goodman expresses a view often heard: that governments have taken on attributes of compulsive gamblers as they chase after more and more tax revenues from games even when they realize that the revenue flows are hurting their economies. He also portrays the government as the predator in his discussion of lottery organizations. He concludes that "in considering future policies, it is crucial to understand that gambling expanded not because of a popular movement clamoring for more, but because of aggressive lobbying by the gambling industry" (179–180).

Goodman sees more pressure for expansion and more negative consequences in the future. He calls for a national plan to mitigate such harms. He believes that governments must authorize independent impact statements before there is new legalization and that the impact statements should be shared with the public. He called for a national study of gambling, and the force of his voice was heard by Congress the year after the book was published, as that body authorized the National Gambling Impact Study Commission. The commission's study focused upon many of the issues raised by Goodman.

Greenlees, E. Malcolm. 1988. *Casino Accounting and Financial Management.* Reno: University of Nevada Press. 378 pp.

The general literature of casino gambling does not contain many writings on accounting and financial management, yet this is the industry where money is the product. Without the flows of money in and out of gambling establishments (which have no other product), there would be no gambling industry. Amazingly, E. Malcolm Greenlees's volume is the only comprehensive book on the subject. Written in the late 1980s, the book is in need of updating in places, but the concepts discussed are still very relevant.

Greenlees burdens himself with the task of writing for too wide an audience, yet the result should be satis-

factory for most. The book is for a general public interested in casino gambling. Therefore there is an initial section examining the environment of casino gambling. The focus is upon Nevada, although Atlantic City information is included. The date of writing precluded a discussion of Native American and riverboat gambling. A chapter on taxation details the state and local obligations of casinos to the degree needed for an actual operator. The author includes a well-written description of revenue flows, and he provides critically needed definitions of basic terminology that is often misunderstood: *win, handle, hold.* The concepts are then applied to the specific operations—first to slot machines, and second to a variety of table games.

A very important chapter deals with credit accounting. Credit is the lifeblood of the major Strip casinos and other high-roller facilities, and controls in this area are vital for casino success. An auditing chapter outlines the many reports that are required from a casino accountant. Tax liabilities are also described along with several "tricky" issues, for example, treatment of markers and unpaid debts. The book ends with a general discussion of financial management: internal controls to assure there are no thefts of assets, controls to insure full reporting of revenues and revenue transactions, and data necessary for making managerial decisions on operations.

Greenlees's book is well written. It contains many amusing sidelights, and it contains solid documentation. Its value is greatest for the layman interested in casino operations and for the casino accountant who may be assigned to a casino project for the first time. Although the detail of this book might not be sufficient to give an accountant full knowledge to move into all facets of casino work, it certainly would provide that individual with an essential primer.

Hashimoto, Kathryn, Sheryl Fried Kline, and George G. Fenich, eds. 1998 *Casino Management: Past, Present, Future.* 2d ed. Dubuque, IA: Kendall-Hunt. 362 pp.

In 1974, Bill Friedman wrote *Casino Management,* a text describing gambling developments in Nevada along with basic processes of management and regulation. It was revised in 1982. Not until the mid-1990s did new volumes begin to appear on the scene expounding upon managerial aspects of casino gambling. The premier text on casino management, *Casino Management: Past, Present, Future,* is in its second edition. Author-editors Hashimoto, Kline, and Fenich collaborated with each other and also found outside writers to gather materials for a set of chapters that represent the essential topics necessary for an integrated whole.

The first two chapters look at basic information about the casino gambling industry. They include a discussion of terminology, a chronology of events, and the structure of gambling in Las Vegas and Atlantic City, on riverboats, and on Native reservations. The next set of chapters closely examines the rules of table games and slot games. A third collection of chapters offers commentary on management structures for surveillance, human resources, and financial controls. Following sections deal with marketing, hospitality, and broader social issues: economic impacts of casino gambling, casinos and crime, and children and casinos. A summary chapter looks at the future of gambling. I. Nelson Rose uses his "third wave" model to predict that gambling will be outlawed in the United States in the year 2029.

Accompanying the author-editors' text is a computer disk that explains many casino games. The disk and the text package represent a quantum leap forward from Friedman's 1974 and 1982 editions. The success of the first two editions of Hashimoto, Kline, and Fenich's book suggests that the future will find many more books devoted to the topic of casino management.

Hotaling, Edward. 1995. *They're Off: Horse Racing at Saratoga.* Syracuse, NY: Syracuse University Press. 368 pp.

They're Off takes off with George Washington, the first Saratoga Springs tourist in 1783. Soon there was a resort—the first resort in the United States, then horse racing, and more racing, and more racing. *They're Off* takes off but never really stops. Edward Hotaling has written a long descriptive account of Saratoga, New York, its racing, and many events surrounding the track—boxing matches and training camps, intercollegiate regattas, and casino gambling. The book is set out in chronological fashion, not going anywhere except through time. Within the pages of the meticulously researched effort (with extensive notes and bibliography), however, there are more than mere details of one race after another.

Within the covers of *They're Off* there is evidence, which unfortunately is not highlighted and labeled for the reader, that Saratoga may have truly been the gambling center of the United States from the Revolutionary era through World War II. The account presented by the author, who is a native of Saratoga, is sprinkled with many inside stories of the American horse racing set. In fact, the horse crowd at Saratoga helped establish the Travers Stakes and gave rise to the development of Belmont and Pimlico tracks and to the notion of an American Triple Crown. Saratoga was the scene of the first major boxing matches, and the first major betting on collegiate sports event took place there.

Four of the nation's leading casino entrepreneurs and gambling giants in history used Saratoga as a venue for their trade. John C. Morrisey won the U.S. boxing championship at Saratoga and later built the grandstands for the track. He also became the leading casino operator in Saratoga as well as in New York City while serving as a congressman and a state senator.

Morrisey was followed by Richard Canfield, who ran the nation's most elegant casino at Saratoga from 1890 to 1905. After Canfield left center stage, Arnold Rothstein came out of the wings. While overseeing the casino games at Saratoga he also manipulated the results of the 1919 World Series in the Black Sox Scandal. Rothstein became the leading bookie in the United States. But he did more while at Saratoga. He mentored Meyer Lansky and Lucky Luciano by giving them the operations of his craps games. In the 1930s Lansky then came to run the casino games of Saratoga, and he moved his dealers and took his newly developed talents from Saratoga on the road to Hallandale, Florida, and to Havana—and via Bugsy Siegel to Las Vegas. This incredible lineup of "Hall of Fame"-level gamblers ended its involvement in Saratoga, as did all other casino operators, only after the Kefauver investigations led illegal operators in the United States to abandon their venues and to go Las Vegas and elsewhere.

The long arduous story of Saratoga racing provides a perfect counterpoint to the notion in John M. Findlay's *People of Chance* that gambling in the United States was intrinsically tied to the nation's westward movement.

Hsu, Cathy H. C., ed. 1999. *Legalized Gambling in the United States: The Economic and Social Impact.* New York: Haworth Hospitality Press. 264 pp.

Prof. Cathy Hsu has collected twelve new essays, each of which analyzes the contemporary casino gambling scene in the United States. The first section addresses historical development of gambling, the second section examines the economic issue of gambling, and the third section analyzes social issues of gambling. The four essays in each of the sections take a close look at one major sector of the casino industry—the Las Vegas casinos, the Atlantic City casinos, Native American casinos, and finally riverboat and low-stakes (Colorado and South Dakota) casinos. The essays are written by a collection of academic scholars and gambling regulators who bring a variety of perspectives to the subject. Authors include William Thompson, Shannon Bybee, Patricia Stokowski, Denis Rudd, James Wortman, and the editor, Cathy H. C. Hsu.

Although the book presents a neat uniform structure for the topics presented, the individual essays do not parallel one another. For instance, the social impact entry for Las Vegas makes a community comparison of Las Vegas with four other comparably sized communities on factors such as population growth, government expenditures on social welfare, crime rates, and health care indices. The Atlantic City entry focuses upon crime and compulsive gambling in Atlantic City and its environs, and the Native American social impact essay considers tribal divisions and non-Native exploitation of casino developments, as well as traffic and ambient crime. The "other casinos" entry looks at how small towns have been changed with the introduction of casinos and the attitudes of residents toward the new enterprise. Although the original chapters do fly off in several different directions, each stands alone as a valuable contribution, making the book a worthwhile read for a person interested in casinos in the United States and their effects upon life in their midst.

Johnston, David. 1992. *Temples of Chance: How America Inc. Bought out Murder Inc. to Win Control of the Casino Business.* New York: Doubleday. 312 pp.

When Howard Hughes swept into Las Vegas and started buying casino properties from the Mob, the Nevada establishment celebrated. A savior had come to deliver the city from an impending federal crackdown. Nevada suddenly felt legitimate. When Hughes turned out to be a less than desirable recluse, worries started up again. But this time a new state law (1969) permitted public corporations to own casinos, and a more reliable Hilton Hotels came to town, followed by other respectable corporate leaders such as Ramada and Holiday Inns.

Starting in the 1970s, casino observers have claimed that the industry had cleaned up its act with major corporations and the federal Securities and Exchange Commission's oversight. Things could not possibly go awry. Wrong! The theme of David Johnston's polemical attack on Las Vegas and Atlantic City casinos is precisely that "business as usual" never left even after the Mob leaders were really bought out and left (at least the management offices of the casinos).

Johnston served as the Atlantic City bureau chief of the *Philadelphia Inquirer* for four years before writing this exposé. He is now on the staff of the *New York Times*. The new casino owners have not at all been reluctant to rub shoulders with mobsters; worse, they have engaged in a wide array of unsavory practices of their own: cheating stockholders, breaking contracts, laundering money for bad people, falsely advertising their products, and nurturing compulsive gamblers. The writer devotes full chapters to specific casinos and their sordid stories. He tells how the Tropicana cheated Mitzy Briggs out of her

share of the property, how several casinos were financed with Michael Milkin's junk bonds, how Donald Trump engaged in an art of deception with New York politicians and then New Jersey gambling authorities. The suspicious beginnings of Resorts International are examined, as is the way in which Steve Wynn won unfair advantages for his Las Vegas Strip and downtown properties.

The book makes fascinating reading whether one accepts its tenuous premise or not. Grains of truth certainly suggest that regulators should be more vigilant as they license and oversee operations. The writer can be faulted, however, for not making a conclusion setting out policies that should be followed by gambling jurisdictions. I feel also that a similar exposé treatment could probably be directed at electric utilities or automobile giants. Oh! I guess Ralph Nader has already done those exposés. Free enterprise makes us what we are, good and bad, and human.

Kaplan, H. Roy. 1978. *Lottery Winners: How They Won and How Winning Changed Their Lives.* New York: Harper and Row. 173 pp.

In his life story, Gen. Colin Powell observes how his father and an aunt won "big" by betting on a number. As a result his family was able to move out of a troubled neighborhood to a more stable community in Brooklyn. His aunt had had a vision of a certain number in a dream. When she went to church the next day, the first hymn listed above the altar carried the same number. Although, he does not mention it, one might surmise that certain family financial pressures were relieved by the win and that Powell could now focus more energy on the academic pursuits that opened up the stairs on the ladder of his success. His story is one story of the consequences of "the big win." Roy Kaplan gathers other stories, but they are not all as happy. The sociologist conceived of a study of winners in conjunction with Dr. Carlos Kruytbosch of the National Science Foundation. Their initial goal was to assess commitment to work in the United States. Kaplan learned much more.

With an incredible tenacity, Kaplan was able to interview 100 big money winners in Illinois, Maryland, New Jersey, New York, and Pennsylvania. He interviewed one-third of all million-dollar winners in the United States as of the mid-1970s. Interviews lasted an average of three hours each. Kaplan sought out all thirty-seven of these winners in New Jersey and was able to interview thirty-three of them even though most changed their addresses, phone numbers, and in some cases even names.

The interviews revealed that many of the big winners had a variety of psychic or religious premonitions prior to their wins; however, the stories were not all that persuasive, as similar premonitions accompanied losing experiences as well. There could be no conclusion but that the winners were not really "chosen" but instead were merely "lucky." Most had purchased multiple tickets over a considerable time before they hit their "big win."

The win was followed by a short period of elation, and then an incredible amount of harassment and feelings of fear. Generally the winner was not psychologically prepared for the onslaught of publicity and then the "nightmarish intrusions" of others into their lives. Many were threatened with physical harm. Telephones rang incessantly with callers begging for money or offering business deals. Winners often felt sympathy for the pathetic situations people portrayed as they asked for money, and as a result felt guilt when they had to turn people down. The calls included attempts to scam the winners. Friendships were strained and even broken. Relationships with co-workers were destroyed. In a period of high unemployment, many of the winners were made to feel guilty that they remained at their jobs—hence depriving others of work. Family life was disrupted as distant relatives expected gifts, and parents fought with children, and spouses with each other. There were some divorces that were a direct result of the win, although those marriages may have been weak ones before the win.

Most of the winners did quit their jobs, although many did not want to. Work relationships changed for the worse in most cases. The study suggested that people work for functional reasons—for survival and out of habit, and not because they derive true satisfaction from their jobs. When the people had a chance to get out of jobs they did not like, they jumped at the chance. The preponderance of winners, however, were people of lower educational attainment and lower income levels. Many lacked marketable skills and could not contemplate moves to better jobs. Moreover, they did not have life skills that permitted them to structure their free time in such a way as to generate satisfaction. Instead they exchanged the "tension and toil of their jobs for boredom and monotony in their expensive new homes" (115). When they wanted to return to work, they found that there were no "good" jobs for them. And psychologically they "could not go home again"; that is, they could not return to their old jobs.

Life transitions were easier for a group of widows that won the big prize. Nonetheless they had fear and confusion thrust into their lives and, cut off from previous personal relationships, felt an added burden of loneliness and isolation they did not have before their winning occurred. This group, however, achieved a greater sense of security and comfort as result of their "godsend"(133).

Kaplan writes, "of all the bitter pills lottery winners had to take, taxes were the hardest to swallow" (134). Players were quite often harassed and even prosecuted by the Internal Revenue Service. Many did not anticipate the extent of their taxation burdens, and they were also confused by a constant "torrent" of tax advice from friends, relatives, and strangers wishing to be their tax counselors. When some discovered their new high tax brackets (this was before the Reagan tax cuts of the 1980s), they felt that they had to quit their jobs as they were not keeping much of their wage earnings. Particularly bothersome were inheritance obligations, as the taxes had to be paid on the entire prize amount even though the winners (and winners' estates) were paid annual installments rather than lump sums. To cope with this possibility, many winners felt the necessity to take out special life insurance policies so their estate could meet tax obligations. The promise of instant wealth was not realized by most players, as taxes added to installment payments really only gave them a measure of additional wealth, but nothing close to the amount implied in the announced prizes. Unfortunately, those about them felt they now had the wealth implied in the total prize. Kaplan writes that the national study group examining gambling in the mid-1970s recommended that prizes be tax exempt; however, this recommendation was totally ignored by Congress. On the other hand, other countries (e.g., Canada) do not tax gambling winnings. A rationale for nontaxation is that all the players' money is already after-tax money.

The first purchase the winners went after was a new home, followed by furniture and amenities such as swimming pools. The result was that many became saddled with large mortgage payments before they could assess all their future costs. Although the winning of the big prize introduced many adverse circumstances into their lives, the lucky lottery players did not regret winning, and none wished to give the money back.

Kaplan made his study nearly a quarter-century ago, but there is no evidence that his conclusions would be materially different today. His energy and persistence in tracking down a bit of reality on gambling "winners" are valuable for anyone wishing to understand the impacts of the gambling industry today.

Karlins, Marvin. 1983. *Psyching Out Vegas: Winning through Psychology in the Casinos of the World.* Secaucus, NJ: Gambling Times of the Carol Publishing Group. 283 pp.

A new employee at Disneyland was starting his job as others do, using a broom and dustpan to pick up litter off the sidewalks. A customer approached him and said, "Excuse me. Could you tell me where Adventureland is?" As she spoke, she was facing a large sign above the employee. The sign said "Adventureland" and had an arrow pointing the direction. The employee, engrossed in picking up candy wrappers, gave her a "Duh"-type look and said, "Can't you read? It's down that way." New employees are closely watched, and a supervisor saw the exchange. He came up to the employee and kindly suggested that it would have been more appropriate to have put the broom and dust pan down, stood up, and said, "Why yes, it's down the sidewalk this way; would you like me to walk that way until we can see it?" And, "Enjoy Adventureland; it's one of our most popular attractions." The employee answered, "Okay, sure, but the sign was right in front of her; do we expect our customers to leave their brains in their cars?" "Yes," replied the supervisor, "now you are getting it."

Disneyland expects its customers to leave their brains behind and enter a fantasy land when they pass through the gates. So too do the casinos of Las Vegas. After all, the players are not making investments as if they are at a Wall Street broker. They are coming into a fantasy land, an "Adventureland," where their dreams have no limits. The casinos only ask that the customers leave their brains behind, or at least some of their brains.

Marvin Karlins dissents. He wants the players to use their brains to the fullest and control their emotions so that they can engage in a rational activity he calls "psyching out Vegas." Karlins explores the many psychological ploys casinos use to entice players to gamble and lose—noises, color schemes, floor layouts, lighting, no windows, no clocks, free drinks. He then sets forth his game plan for player victories. He looks at each casino game and presents clues for winning strategies. He explores the odds and gives advice on the best bets. In roulette, the player should only play at a single-zero wheel and make even money bets such as red-black and odd-even. (The trouble is that few Las Vegas casinos offer single-zero wheels). In craps, the player should only bet the basic pass-don't pass, come-don't come. And the player should bet the maximum odds bet after the first roll out. At baccarat, the player should only make "player" or "banker" bets. In blackjack, the player should use a basic strategy and only play at larger casinos with well-lighted tables in quiet areas. The game played properly demands thinking.

The players is advised to stay away from slots, keno, and the big wheel.

Most of the remainder of the text is devoted to money management schemes. The player should always be sober and rested, and he should learn to look like a loser so that the casino will not suspect he is "psyching" them out. For the serious player, Karlins is right on target. He fails, however, to give the most sage advice to his investors—find another broker because the casinos charge too high a commission fee. The casinos have the edge at every game except poker, where it is all between the players. If the player cannot rationalize the notion of playing and paying for the excitement, dreams, and entertainment—the essential Vegas experience will be lost. Of course, players should avoid behaviors that make losing inevitable. Most will lose, however, and most must lose if there is to be a Las Vegas. Still most also do have a lot of fun. When they get fun value for their money, they are not stupid; they are not leaving all their brains at home. Unfortunately a serious reading of Karlins's book may suggest that they are. The book is for serious gamblers, not for tourists.

King, R. T., ed. 1992. *Playing the Cards that Are Dealt: Mead Dixon, the Law, and Casino Gambling.* Reno: University of Nevada, Oral History Program. 276 pp.
King, R. T., ed. 1993. *Hang Tough! Grant Sawyer: An Activist in the Governor's Mansion.* Reno: University of Nevada, Oral History Program. 256 pp.
King, R. T., ed. 1994. *Always Bet on the Butcher: Warren Nelson and Casino Gaming 1930–1980.* Reno: University of Nevada, Oral History Program. 242 pp.

Before 1976 the casino gambling industry was not a matter of interest to large numbers of people. Casinos were confined to a single isolated state—Nevada. But then casinos were legalized for Atlantic City, and soon they were appearing on Native American lands in several states. Casinos were also approved for remote mining villages in South Dakota and Colorado and on riverboats in midwestern and southern states. Now half of the states in all regions of the country have forms of legalized casino gambling. But still casino gambling is considered a vice by many. When the public is given a vote in the matter, most jurisdictions decide to keep casino gambling illegal.

Before 1976, these three volumes published by the Oral History Program of the University of Nevada, Reno (UNR), would have commanded the attention of a very narrow range of readers interested mostly in "local color." With the proliferation of casinos, however, the books are "must reading" for scholars seeking to understand developments in what has become a national industry. They are also of interest to a growing number of general readers with curiosity about this unique industry.

Together the three volumes record insights into the development of the gambling industry from its clandestine illegal and quasi-legal origins to its present-day legitimate corporate status. Intervening steps on this journey included a stage dominated by personal entrepreneurship, organized crime, and Teamsters' union involvement, then the Howard Hughes interlude, as well as attempts by federal authorities to close the industry down and one state's fight to maintain its economic base by initiating a strong regulatory framework.

Ken Adams, a casino executive and consultant since 1969, conducted interviews for two of the three books. In 1991 he compiled thirty-two tapes with Mead Dixon, a member of the board of directors of several casino organizations and general counsel for Harrah's Casinos—a pioneer in northern Nevada gambling. Over 1,200 pages of transcripts were edited into the 1992 book entitled *Playing the Cards that Are Dealt: Mead Dixon, the Law, and Casino Gambling*. Adams also recorded thirty-one hours of interviews with Warren Nelson, a casino entrepreneur and investor who started his career as an employee of illegal gaming houses in Montana and California but ended up as a major legitimate owner in Reno. In 1994 the Oral History Program released the interviews in the form of a book, *Always Bet on the Butcher: Warren Nelson and Casino Gaming, 1930–1980*. Gary Elliott, a history professor at the Community College of Southern Nevada, engaged former Nevada governor Grant Sawyer in thirty-two hours of taped interviews during a nine-month period in 1991. The interviews were eventually honed into the pages of *Hang Tough! Grant Sawyer: An Activist in the Governor's Mansion*. Although the Sawyer interviews are devoted to a political career rather than to a career "in gambling," they touch upon his role as a major shaper of policy concerning regulation in the industry. He was the key state official who had to negotiate to maintain the state's autonomy as a regulator in the face of attacks from the U.S. Department of Justice. He devoted considerable energy to strengthening state regulatory structures, and he played a clandestine role in attracting Howard Hughes and his investment capital to Nevada.

The narrative for all three books was produced by R. T. King, who serves as the director of the Oral History Program at UNR. The notion of producing this type of interview in book form should receive a strong endorsement. Without such books, serious students of the gambling industry (and there is a growing number of these scholars) would have to travel to Reno or Las Vegas, just to have an awareness of their existence, let alone securing access to the original tapes and where available the verbatim transcripts. Of course, the serious scholar with a specific interest in certain events revealed in the books would seek out the transcripts to verify the context of the remarks as they appear in the book.

As a person deeply interested in the industry, I have personally read many of the unpublished transcripts produced by the Oral History Program. It is an arduous task requiring hours of plodding through minutiae and non sequiturs and seemingly incoherent ramblings in search of hidden gems of wisdom. It is of great value to have editors who have provided road maps for the interviews. All scholars need good shortcuts when they enter a new topic area where there is a great body of writing to peruse. It is additionally a great service when the editors format the writings so that they are a joy to encounter. The editor and editorial staff of the Oral History Program have thus accomplished a remarkable job in making each of the books read as if it were a novel. The stories have continuity, a logical flow, and instructional notes that provide understandable contexts for readers who might not be familiar with the course of gambling history. I hope that the Oral History Program is able to secure the needed funding to continue interviewing the aging giants of the gambling industry and then to publish the results.

There is a vital cadre of individuals who were in Nevada "at the beginning"—that is, when Reno and Las Vegas emerged as national gambling destination sites. They guided the communities through the eras of suspicion to the modern era of corporations and their posture of legitimacy. Many stories have yet to be told, and yet must be told soon or they may be lost forever.

The gambling industry is today seeking to be interpreted as "just another industry," with shares of interest traded on the stock exchanges, just the same as shares of interest in any other industry. Perhaps someday society will come to believe such rhetoric. But today, casino gambling and other forms of gambling are illegal in most places—certainly in most local jurisdictions. The fact that some form of gambling is legal in forty-eight states supports the "quest for legitimacy." The truth is, however, that there is free market entry into the gambling industry in no jurisdiction, and easy entry for competing gambling enterprises in only a very few jurisdictions. Public corporations in the United States were effectively banned from casino gambling until the 1970s. Up to that point casino organizations (because of licensing restrictions in Nevada—the only casino state) had to be controlled by individuals or tightly held partnerships and private companies. The role of the individual continues today to set the pace in this industry that has yet to reach capitalistic maturity.

Many critical notions in today's industry are still focused backward to ideas held by individual personalities who made their mark in Las Vegas or Reno a generation ago. The dominant casino companies today still rely upon management processes that emphasize the dominant role of individual leaders. The opportunities to penetrate the soul of an industry through the medium of oral history is nowhere greater than it is today with the casino gambling industry. The tension between seeking to be cleansed of a past filled with quasi-illegalities and yet to still hold to the myths of a "Wild West outlaw-type society" makes direct interviews with old-timers in gaming especially valuable at this time. Whereas just a few years ago there would have been almost a forbidding reluctance to talk, talk today can take the form of giving a romantic edge to days gone by—even when they have not really disappeared. Many of today's potential spokesmen might be willing to share their true adventures as they are no longer active license holders in gaming and as their partners in many of those adventures are now departed. The three adventurers who submitted to interviews now found in these three volumes did talk. They could have shared more, but they did open up, and the editors have revealed the potentialities of the oral history medium for gaining important insights into this unique casino gambling industry.

Warren Nelson represents that genre of operators who learned their trade in illegal or quasi-legal gaming halls of rural America. He started his gaming career as a teenager in Montana, and like many others, he started as a player. He soon figured out the way the games worked, however, and realized that players were like lambs going off to slaughter. Nelson was fond of saying that it was quite possible that a lamb could kill a butcher, but if one were a gambler, he should "always bet on the butcher." He determined early in his career that he would own the games. He would be the butcher. In Montana he became familiar with a Chinese game called keno. He refined the game, and he is credited with introducing keno to the casinos of Nevada.

As Nelson moved from the gambling halls of Montana and California (where he moonlighted as a dealer during a stint with the Marine Corps) to the more established casinos of Reno, he endeavored to put into practice certain marketing operations that today guarantee the success of gambling establishments. People marketing casino products enjoy a tremendous customer service advantage over those peddling other products. Customers consuming other products usually remain quiet if they receive good value for their money, telling good service stories to an average of three to five other people. For other products, the dissatisfied customer spreads the negative word widely. Bad service stories are told to an average of ten to fifteen others. For casinos, however, the situation is reversed. Losers remain quiet. Indeed, they even lie about their losses—to others, and to themselves. But winners tell everyone: relatives, friends, total strangers. Flights out of Las Vegas are rather strange phenomena—it seems from the conversation one hears that gamblers only win!

Casinos have a tremendous advantage with word-of-mouth advertising; however, this advantage can be reversed if certain things happen. If the casinos cheat players, if they exploit players, or if they are rude to players, the losers become very happy to tell of, and even exaggerate, their losses. Warren Nelson became aware of this basic formula, although he does not identify it in these same terms.

In Montana and California, and in early Reno (casinos were legalized in 1931), players were typically cheated or exploited. A person on a winning streak would find the house changing dealers. The new dealer would be a "mechanic" who would deal from the bottom of the deck or would put crooked dice into a craps game. Nelson also tells of houses that would have magnets in their roulette wheels so that certain numbers would come up. Gambling halls would also make odds of the games so much against the players that a condition of true exploitation would exist. Additionally, winning players would be given an excessive number of drinks to ensure a numbing of their gambling skills, while losers would be given more and more credit so that they could dig themselves a deep hole. Nelson took the lead in moving games away from being scams, and he established practices to minimize exploitation and to enhance good treatment of players. He reasoned that with the odds in the casino's favor, it was to the casino's advantage to run an honest game without exploitation or rudeness. What the casino needed more than anything else was a volume of play. He realized that with good honest treatment, one could shear a lamb for wool forever. Those who wished to skin the lamb, however, could do so only once.

Warren Nelson advocated good treatment of employees. He recounted how owners of the "clip joints" of California would mistreat dealers, only to have the dealers turn around and steal from the house. Nelson himself had participated in much of the seamy side of the industry in the early days. He shared in tip pools consisting of money stolen from the casinos, and he participated in the practices of beating up players who cheated the casinos. One interesting story concerns Nelson's request of a loan from David Beck so that he could purchase a Reno gambling house. Nelson quickly learned that the president of the International Brotherhood of Teamsters (the Teamsters' union) looked at casino loans as an opportunity for being cut in on a share of the casino's winnings. As Nelson matured, he led the industry toward maturity as well. Ever mindful that forces such as the Teamsters' union were lingering around the gambling communities of Reno and Las Vegas, Nelson welcomed the establishment of the Nevada State Gaming Control Board, and he served as a member of the state's Gaming Policy Board.

Mead Dixon's contributions to the gambling industry's quest for legitimacy came at a different level. Like Nelson, he was exposed to illegal gambling as a teenager in rural America—in his case, in Illinois. His talent was not in games, however, but in the law. After military service in World War II, he drifted to Nevada following an attempt to start a legal education. He first got a job as a surveyor on the Hoover Dam project in Boulder City. While he was there he learned that a person could become a lawyer in Nevada without having a full legal education. He was able to get a job in the Las Vegas (Clark County) courthouse, where he made contacts, and then commuted to California to finish a legal education and pass the Nevada state bar examination.

Dixon was at the right place at the right time. He first became an adviser to leading gaming properties. Then, in the late 1950s, he became counsel to Bill Harrah, an association that was to define his career. Dixon's story is a recitation of the personal idiosyncrasies of Harrah and the difficulties properties have when they fall under the control of charismatic personalities. Dixon witnessed Harrah's abilities decline along with the decline of Harrah's health, yet Harrah was unable to share leadership or to welcome change. Although he had been a giant in earlier years, as he was one of the first to actively market casino gaming, yet in the 1970s Harrah saw no need for innovation, renovation, expansion, or change. Dixon, however, was clearly the second in command when Harrah died in 1978. Realizing the opportunity and the need, it was Dixon who guided and maneuvered Harrah's into its merger with Holiday Inn. Together, the operations became Promus, Incorporated. Dixon turned an individually owned company into a true corporate giant in the gambling industry.

Grant Sawyer tells a story first about politics, but then about gambling regulation, and finally about law. Sawyer came to Nevada from Idaho in order to attend the University of Nevada in Reno. His father was a physician and a politician in Fallon, Nevada, and with this family connection, Grant Sawyer secured a job as an aide to Nevada's U.S. Senator Patrick McCarran on Capitol Hill. Nevada was then one of the few states that did not have a law school. As a result, its congressional delegation sponsored young politicos with patronage jobs they could hold while completing legal educations in the District of Columbia. All in all, it added to the good-old-boy-club quality of Nevada politics; all his life, Sawyer was a "McCarran boy."

Sawyer's own legal and political career began in Elko, where he became prosecuting attorney. In 1958 he was elected governor of the state. He served two terms. These were troubled years for the casino industry, as Atty. Gen. Robert Kennedy sought to close down casinos because of Mob connections. Sawyer had to venture to the Justice Building in Washington, D.C., to head off Robert Kennedy's plans to have state law enforcement officials deputized as Federal Bureau of Investigation agents. There he found a condescending Kennedy dressed for a tennis match. A further venture up Pennsylvania Avenue N.W. to visit the older brother was needed to end the crisis in federalism. Sawyer responded to national pressures to control the casino industry with new state efforts to control the casino industry. He engineered the legislation creating the current structures for gambling regulation in Nevada, and he depoliticized the licensing process with the appointment of "hang tough" regulators. He also created the black book listing of persons who were banned from all the casinos. The regulators stood up to unsavory forces, and they would not yield to an outraged Frank Sinatra when he was stripped of a gambling license for having entertained a leading Mob figure who was in the black book.

By the end of Sawyer's eight years in office, the industry was on the road to legitimacy. It still lacked the reputable sources of capital needed for healthy expansion, however. Then in the last two months of his term, a miracle occurred. As if dropping from heaven, the angel Howard Hughes brought his personal fortune to Las Vegas and started to buy casinos. The most critical missing element in the oral history of Sawyer is an honest discussion of Sawyer's role in bringing Hughes to Las Vegas. It was a critical event in the industry's development, Sawyer had to have been involved, and yet the event is not afforded a single word in the book. Was Sawyer the one who initiated the entrance of Hughes into the casino industry, was he a facilitator, or was he just a passive observer who allowed it to happen? The interviewer was positioned to make the inquiry. Either it was not made, or it could not be made. A refusal to speak to the topic would have merited an editorial comment.

Subsequent to Sawyer's service as governor, he moved to Las Vegas, where he became a partner in the largest gambling law firm in the world. The book ends with some rather ordinary partisan comments about personalities Sawyer met in his political travels. Truman will go down as a "great one"; Eisenhower was probably smarter than he seemed; Kennedy gave us dreams, "but we know more about him now" (194); Johnson was power hungry (197); and Nixon "was a charlatan of the first order" (190). No great insights on those pages.

Since the casino industry has grown to maturity within the adult lifetimes of many people still alive, oral history provides a fantastic vehicle for capturing the history of the industry. These three volumes are a good start.

The three reviews of King's work are reprinted with permission from William N. Thompson. 1996. "Discovering the Gambling Industry: A Review of Three Oral Histories. *Oral History Review* 23 (Summer): 41–46.

Kling, Dwayne. 2000. *The Rise of the Biggest Little City: An Encyclopedic History of Reno Gaming, 1931–1981.* Reno: University of Nevada Press. 226 pp.

Dwayne Kling has penned a thoroughly detailed account of all the properties and the leading personalities (inside and outside the industry) of Reno gambling over a fifty-year period. Kling was close to his subject. He lived it. Born in Turlock, California, in 1929, Kling started coming to Reno in 1947 and soon played baseball on a Harrah's Club team. After college and military service, Kling came back to Reno to begin a career in gambling. He was a dealer, pit boss, shift manager, casino manager, and owner. He retired in 1995 and began working with the University of Nevada on several history projects.

This volume proceeds from A to Z with minor and major facts—actually appearing almost as if they were the total facts about the Reno gambling scene. That he covers everything is the strength and perhaps the weakness of the book—the latter because the book does not reveal a sense of what is important and what is not. The book does not attempt to establish a theme or a story line. That being said, this is a document that can be referred to by any serious researcher who wants to know what happened in Reno from the time Nevada gave a new legal status to casinos in 1931 through the next fifty years—a time frame in which the city went from being the leading casino city to being eclipsed by Las

Vegas for that title. The book title is somewhat misleading as Kling does follow several properties into the 1990s. By cutting off much of his story in 1981 (e.g., having no separate entry on the Silver Legacy), however, he leaves the reader without an understanding of the city's most ardent attempts to cope with a new national gambling scene that includes California casinos.

The book's entries are documented by press accounts mostly from the *Nevada State Journal* and the *Reno Gazette Journal.* The book also includes a large collection of interesting photographs as well as street maps with locations of each property described. He also includes a glossary of universal casino gambling terms, which really have no direct connection to Reno for the most part.

Although the book is geographically limited to the direct Reno area, it chronicles many of the major initial events in the modern casino industry. These include the role of customer service and integrity in the industry and also the role of mass marketing and promotions—illustrated most clearly with entries on Bill Harrah and the Smiths (Raymond I. "Pappy" Smith, Harold Sr., and Harold Jr.). Kling also illustrates the beginning of entertainment in casino properties, as well as positive advances in race relations, gender inclusion in the industry, and unionization of resort workers. The entries that should command the reader's closest attention include "Boomtown," "Cal-Neva," "El Dorado," "Fitzgeralds," "Harolds Club," "Harrah's," "Mapes Hotel," "M.G.M. Grand," "Nevada Club," "Primadonna," and "Riverside."

Knapp, Bettina L. 2000. *Gambling, Game, and Psyche.* Albany: State University of New York Press. 308 pp.

Bettina L. Knapp explores the "universal and eternal mysteries" arising out of games of chance. She presents ten chapters, each of which "probes" varying types of gambling behavior found in major works of literature. Thus she seeks to bring out pertinent aspects of the gambling personality or the "achiever syndrome." The volume explores works of Blaise Pascal, Honoré Balzac, Edgar Allan Poe, Fyodor Dostoyevsky, Matilde Serao, Sholom Aleichem, Hermann Hesse, Yasunari Kawabata, and Zhang Xinxin. Knapp concludes that gambling is part of society's "mainstream behavior," and only at its extremes does it raise problems for individuals and society. At the same time players do become victims when habit overtakes reason. Superstitions, signs, omens, and even religious beliefs may serve to hasten the demise of reason and hence make the player vulnerable to the evil side of gambling. The book's brief introduction provides a valuable history of gambling in ancient societies of both the Eastern and Western civilizations. As Knapp begins with a universal discussion of the gambling phenomenon, so too does she develop her essays in a manner that seeks to bring out the universal qualities of gambling.

Lehne, Richard. 1986. *Casino Policy.* New Brunswick, NJ: Rutgers University Press. 268 pp.

Richard Lehne documents decision-making events in New Jersey government and politics from the first statewide campaign for casinos in 1974 until a decade later when nine casinos were in operation in Atlantic City. His focus is on legislative decisions regarding regulatory structures and philosophies, and then the establishment of operational rules by the legislature and the agencies of control. He also seeks to evaluate the effectiveness of the control mechanisms established. Lehne does not try to establish whether or not casinos in New Jersey have been successful, leaving that task to others (he cites the work of George Sternlieb and James Hughes, *The Atlantic City Gamble*); rather, he concentrates on what the effects of policy have been.

Lehne contrasts New Jersey regulatory styles to those found in Nevada and elsewhere. He expresses admiration for systems that provide multiple agencies for the regulatory process, even when the agencies often must do identical work. He finds that repetition and competition in regulation can produce positive checks and balances resulting in a public good. He leans somewhat toward endorsing the philosophy of Nevada regulation, which establishes strict licensing requirements and then permits casino license holders to self-regulate with a more passive state oversight. New Jersey on the other hand seemed lax in providing strict entrance requirements for licensing, but then sought to provide intensive constant oversight of all casino activities. The New Jersey system was much more expensive, allowed for considerable bureaucratic growth, was resented by operators, and at the bottom line did not seem to have any better results for the trouble. In fact, the system in New Jersey invited the operators to be in conflict with the regulators and hence to have to interact with regulators daily in order to resolve disputes. In the course of the constant interaction, the operators pressed their desires for more relaxed operational rules (some rules, such as those on color schemes in the casinos, had been extreme) and gradually overwhelmed the regulators with their desires for change. Hearing no countervailing voices from a general public, which lost interest in casino regulation soon after the doors of Resorts opened in 1978, the regulators soon began to think like the operators. Lehne uses the model of bureaucratic capture found in the public administration work of Marver Bernstein as a cogent point of reference (*Regulating Business by Independent Commission* [Princeton, NJ: Princeton University Press, 1955]). He then indicates ways in which the agencies in New Jersey could try to stem the tide of the casinos' hold on them.

Lehne seriously suggests that new gambling jurisdiction should reconsider the model of private ownership of casinos. He indicates why New Jersey endorsed the private model and why it probably could not be reversed. On the other hand, he feels that much of the regulatory turmoil that ensued in the Garden State could have been avoided had the casinos been public entities, or perhaps publicly owned with private operators. It would be valuable now with a decade of such public/public-private style of ownership and operations in Canada to return to his themes and find out if the country to the north has performed in the superior manner Lehne would envision.

Casino Policy is very well researched and thoroughly documented, with forty-five pages of notes and bibliography. It is an academic book, but it can be easily read and understood by nonacademics and policymakers who may face the crucial questions posed by the author.

Lesieur, Henry R. 1984 *The Chase: The Career of the Compulsive Gambler.* 2d ed. Cambridge, MA: Schenkman Publishing. 323 pp.

The first edition of *The Chase* was written by Henry Lesieur in 1977, at a time when he was a sociologist who rejected the notion that problem gamblers were "sick" people. Over a six-year period and after contact with the National Council on Compulsive (now Problem) Gambling as well as with many therapists treating problem gamblers, however, Lesieur accepted a fundamental value in the medical model of problem gambling. Whether or not the troubled gamblers were "sick" in a medical sense, if they could be convinced that they were, they could be put on to the path toward recovery, a path away from family disintegration, away from criminal acts and other social maladies related to their excessive play. Still a sociologist, Henry Lesieur in the second edition of *The Chase* sees no incompatibility between his profession and the psychologists who help the problem gamblers. He sees no problem in considering troubled gambling to be an addiction.

Henry Lesieur's book has received the highest praise from the true pioneers in the treatment field. Dr. Robert L. Custer wrote in the introduction to the second edition:

> *The Chase* is far and away the finest sociological study done on the pathological gambler. It is scientific with a disarming simplicity which gives

an informative and impressive body of knowledge for all mental health professionals and laymen. Henry R. Lesieur has written a fundamental study on pathological gambling. His perceptions, insights, and concepts are based on an open-minded scientific approach.

During the compulsive gambler's career, Lesieur sees the player becoming trapped in a chase. The player enters the career with many options, but as he bets and loses, his involvement in gambling action increases, and he finds himself in a spiral with fewer and fewer options available. The options may be expressed as sources of money for gambling: family, friends, job, banks and legitimate lending institutions, loan sharks, and then crime. The gambler is in a career, as the options disappear with his losses becoming more and more inevitable. Temporary wins help pay off immediate debts, but they do not help the gambler achieve levels of success desired. Even big wins are not stoppers, because the compulsive gambler needs action. Action is found in playing, and that action exceeds even sexual play in terms of pleasure. And so the chase goes on and on until the gambler either destroys himself—through ruined health, suicide, or legal penalties—or can be rescued by a recovery program with treatment.

The book is a product of a long process of interviewing problem gamblers, their families, friends, and therapists that began in 1971. Lesieur found interviewees wherever he could. He went to Gamblers Anonymous meetings, jails, and state and federal prisons. His hundreds of interviews and his discussions with treatment specialists helped direct him on his chase to find understandings of compulsive gambling that we may now share in reading his words. Of Lesieur's book, Professor Terry Knapp of the University of Nevada, Las Vegas, writes:

The Chase provides one of the best narratives of the life patterns of pathological gamblers, a useful model for describing and to some degree, explaining their behavior, and a provocative text for debating the use of medical versus social models. It will serve well in the classroom, and should be read by clinicians contemplating working with pathological gamblers. (Knapp 1987, 290–291).

Longstreet, Stephen. 1977. *Win or Lose: A Social History of Gambling in America.* Indianapolis, IN: Bobbs-Merrill. 268 pp.

Stephen Longstreet presents a history that is without a bias—with neither moral condemnation nor romantic illusions about gambling. Longstreet sees gambling as endemic to human nature and pervasive throughout all the layers of the social structure. The author admits to being an amateur gambler, and he enjoys his topic thoroughly. The book starts with a story of a Las Vegas weekend, with portraits of all the appropriate actors on the scene. These include high rollers and ordinary folks, bits of history of this casino and that casino, and descriptions of the games that are played. He then launches his historical journey from the days of the sailors on the *Santa Maria, Pinta,* and *Niña* through the colonial era. Paul Revere, George Washington, Ben Franklin, and Andrew Jackson all had gambling connections. The Mississippi riverboat gambler receives a special chapter, as do those who wagered in Saratoga during the racing season, led, of course by John C. Morrisey and later Richard Canfield.

The author then turns his journey westward to the mining camps of the frontier and to Kansas City, Denver, and San Francisco—the latter being the Mecca for the professional gambler at the midpoint of the nineteenth century. He ventures north to Alaska and the Yukon with Soapy Smith, and he wanders the West with Wild Bill Hickok, Calamity Jane (Martha Jane Burke), and Canada Bill Jones. Longstreet brings the reader into the twentieth century with stories of the Black Sox scandals and the emergence of Reno and then Las Vegas as the world cities of gambling. Additional chapters are focused upon pit bull fights, horse racing, bingo, numbers, and Chinese gamblers. The last chapter seems to be just thrown on. It takes a look at several compulsive gamblers. The book ends with a discussion of gambling terminology and a solid bibliography and index. Like the other panoramas of history that precede John M. Findlay's *People of Chance,* however, the book lacks documentary footnotes. Be that as it may, the book presents materials in a confident manner suggesting authority.

Mahon, Gigi. 1980. *The Company That Bought the Boardwalk.* New York: Random House. 262 pp.

This is the story of Resorts International (Casino Company) from its unlikely origins as Mary Carter Paint Company to its triumphant entrance on the Atlantic City scene as the first licensed casino on the Boardwalk. The story as told by Gigi Mahon is one of Mob connections and illicit political operations in the Bahamas and of compromise and sellouts in New Jersey.

When Fidel Castro took over Cuba in 1959, he (eventually) closed all of the Mob-infested casinos on the island. The operators of the crime-ridden facilities quickly sought other outlets for their talents. Many of the dealers and employees were "clean," so they could gravitate to Las Vegas and Reno. But most of the owners and managers could not meet the scrutiny of the Silver State's new regulatory and licensing bodies. They went elsewhere, finding havens in England (until 1968) and on many other islands, including the Bahamas.

The author was a reporter with *Barrons Magazine* assigned to discover the roots of Resorts International. She looks at one set of Cuban casino exiles and traces their steps through the Bahamas and on to Atlantic City, where they gained new respectability, or at least a lot of windfall profits. The characters in her book include Bahamian politicos Wallace Graves, Ralph Grey, Lyndell Pindling, and Huntington Hartford; a cast of wheeler dealers the likes of Bebe Rebozo, Robert Peloquin, and Eddie Cellini; a full array of New Jersey politicians and regulators on the make; and Resorts officials James Crosby and Jack Davis.

The story traces the influence of the characters in the New Jersey casino legalization campaign and in the implementation process afterwards. The experience documented by Mahon provides a solid prelude for the Abscam scandals that followed in 1980. The stage was set well for a federal sting operation. The state's leaders had been openly compromised; all the feds had to do was catch them at their game behind closed doors. When the New Jersey regulators willingly overlooked the obvious ethical problems of the Resorts operations in the Bahamas as well as in Atlantic City under a temporary license, they gave the signal that Atlantic City was open for the taking. The state had so bought into the rhetoric of the casino promoters that general economic prosperity would follow when the casinos opened their doors, that state regulators seemed not to care who was behind the doors running the games. The end justified the means, but unfortunately, in the eyes of the author, the ends were never realized.

McMillen, Jan. 1996. *Gambling Cultures: Studies in History and Interpretation.* London: Routledge. 321 pp.

Professor Jan McMillen has organized fifteen original essays around concepts that place gambling into a wide context of societal development. The essays look at the social and cultural environment of gambling in national and cross-national milieus. The editor sets forth the initial essay explaining why societies permit gambling. She emphasizes dominant values: for instance, pluralism in the United States and concentration of economic and state power in Canada and Great Britain. McMillen finds unique historical qualities determinant in most societies. Other authors include John Dombrink, David Dixon, David Miers, William Eadington, Vicki Abt, James Smith, Mark Dickerson, and Michael Walker. The essays look at gambling in Australia, The Netherlands, Great Britain, Cameroon, Senegal, and the United States.

Millman, Chad. 2001. *The Odds: One Season, Three Gamblers, and the Death of Their Las Vegas.* New York: Public Affairs. 260 pp.

Chad Millman has been a writer with *Sports Illustrated* and ESPN. In *The Odds* he looks at the lonely lives of three individuals and their gambling activity during the National Collegiate Athletic Association basketball tournament in 2000. In doing so he provides extensive background information on sports betting in the United States. He looks at history and at scandals associated with the activity. Millman offers his considerable knowledge about the processes of taking bets and setting lines and odds on games. His book is contemporary, and it gives attention to the two leading political issues on the subject: the proposal in Congress to ban betting on college sports and proposals to stop betting on the Internet.

The political force of the college sports betting ban and the meteoric rise of Internet gambling opportunities have had major impacts upon Las Vegas sports betting in casinos. The "good ol' boys" who used to be walking encyclopedias of knowledge on games are becoming passé as the sports betting exercise is made more democratic with information flowing on the Internet. Casinos are losing action to Internet competitors (400 sites take sports bets) as organizations have tied together web sites into quasi-legitimate operations that can be trusted by players. Although only 2 percent of the Las Vegas gambling revenues come from the sports books, the sports betting activity is important, as it draws gamblers on to the casino floors. It offers the casinos opportunities to promote their other activity.

The three characters of the book include one young man who dropped out of Indiana University to seek his fame and fortune with the "big boys" in Las Vegas. He had been very successful running a sports bookie operation in Bloomington. A second young man leads a two-coast life, alternating between running harness race horses in New England in the summer and living in Las Vegas in the winter in order to make basketball bets in the casino. Both lead lives of isolated desperation on the margins of survival, losing much more often than winning. A third character presents a similarly dismal picture from inside the casino's operations. He works for the sports book manager at the Stardust. He participates in setting and adjusting the lines and sweating out each big game day. Over his shoulder stand Federal

Bureau of Investigation agents who finally make a bust, as many players are laundering ill-gained money through their sports bets. His life is also a life of stress and isolation.

All the characters started their sports betting games in Las Vegas with optimism and excitement, and all ended on the margins of society. The book paints a gloomy picture of the future of sports betting in the casinos, with federal legislation seen as cutting out much of the activity, and the Internet pretty much making the rest of the activity unnecessary for the serious gambler.

Mirkovich, Thomas R., and Allison A. Cowgill. 1996. *Casino Gambling in the United States.* Landham, MD: Scarecrow Press. 432 pp.

This 432-page volume is a gold mine for gambling researchers. It includes nearly a thousand annotated entries for writings on gambling between 1985 and 1994. Besides the mere listings, the authors give the readers a social and historical context for the gambling industry. Especially helpful is the section on casinos gambling. It is arranged into categories such as Indian gaming, riverboat gaming, casinos and crime, casinos and society, casino law and regulation, and casinos and development. The book also lists gambling regulatory agencies throughout the United States, as well as private associations, organizations, and gambling consultants. Although admittedly limited in a geographic sense and a chronological sense, the book is an essential resource for the student of the gambling phenomenon.

O'Brien, Timothy L. 1998. *Bad Bet: The Inside Story of the Glamour, Glitz, and Danger of America's Gambling Industry.* New York: Random House. 339 pp.

Timothy L. O'Brien is a former reporter with the *Wall Street Journal.* He has written a critical book about the gambling industry in the United States. The book is jammed full of facts, anecdotes, and specks of interesting information. Although the words and passages do not always seem to be connected to a purpose, or even a general theme, they do make interesting reading, and at times they provide some good insights into gambling today. That being said, the book leaves me feeling that it falls short of accomplishing the implicit goal set forth in its title: *Bad Bet: The Inside Story of the Glamour, Glitz, and Danger of America's Gambling Industry.* The "bad" is simply not conclusively established. Quite the opposite, as a matter of fact. The book ends with a statement that the "social and human costs [are] not yet fully understood" (300). There is simply no "inside story"; rather the book is a collection (albeit an articu-

late collection) of old material previously published—or at least discussed publicly—supplemented with some good personal interviews (albeit interviews that did not reveal anything shocking or even unusual). The material simply does not speak about anything that sounds very glamorous—at least not anything today. To be sure, it mentions Las Vegas casino opening parties in the 1960s. But today—Internet gaming, simulcasting, compulsive gamblers, lottery tickets, mass-marketed Las Vegas Strip casinos, the Donald? Glamorous? Are you kidding? And if the industry is dangerous, the danger simply does not come out in the pages. Of course, vignettes of compulsive gamblers reveal that they get depressed, but there are no contemporary stories of bodies in the Las Vegas desert. References to the 1997 adduction and murder of a child in a casino fifty miles from Las Vegas are inappropriately assigned to irresponsible actions of a casino. Untold in the pages is the fact that security officers at the casino repeatedly found the child wandering alone and returned her to the father. The father was eventually thrown out of the casino because he neglected to watch the child. Unfortunately, he chose to sneak back to the tables and left her to be wander alone again. The other murders mentioned are in past years, and no relevance to gambling today is established.

There is material the book could have drawn upon to make the case it sets out to make, but instead the author chose to recite old stories and to add interview observations taken from an array of quite respectable authorities. Still the book did not seek to make an analytical assessment of the subject of gambling. The book could have relied upon many academic studies and treatments of the gambling but instead seemed to use the approaches taken by Ed Reid and Ovid Demaris in *The Green Felt Jungle,* Demaris in *Boardwalk Jungle,* and more recently John Smith in *Running Scared.* Like the authors of these books, O'Brien writes well, but in the final stages he can only point to smoke and leaves the reader with no fire.

At the onset of the book, O'Brien indicates that the opposition to gambling is "mounting," but then adds that the "most potent" opponents are "Christian activists" (6). If such is the case, it is a triple whammy that condemns the opposition to likely failure. First, the views of the "Christian activist" opponents to gambling—that all gambling is a vice and therefore all gambling is bad—are accepted by less than 20 percent of the population in survey after survey. Second, these Christian activist opponents do not have the resources to make their case politically viable in any way that can turn the public against the gambling that has already become legalized. The third whammy is that there is another moral view of gambling.

This other view accepts that some gambling is morally permissible. In judging whether O'Brien makes his case that gambling is a "bad bet," it might be appropriate to set forth the structure of this other moral approach to gambling. The religious view that gambling is always a sin and hence must be condemned at all times in all its forms is called the deontological view (*deo* = God; ergo, God says it is "bad"; end of argument; no debate). The other religious view is the teleological view (*teleo* = world; ergo, God knows man interacts with the world, and morality may be reconciled with the world). Many religious organizations (e.g., Catholic, Episcopal) approach gambling in a teleological manner. They generally agree that gambling in the abstract is bad, and in application may be bad most of the time. If certain conditions are present, however, gambling may be acceptable; that is, gambling may not be bad. Basically, the "ifs" are these: (1) If the gambling is honest. (2) If the gambling is operated by honorable people. (3) If the players are not habitual, but rather are only occasional recreational players. (4) If the players can afford to engage in the activity, are not using other people's money in order to gamble, and are meeting all of their social obligations (providing milk for their children, paying their taxes, and supporting their church). Finally, (5) if the bottom-line result of the gambling activity is positive for society. (See William N. Thompson. 1997. *Legalized Gambling: A Reference Handbook*. 2d ed. Santa Barbara: ABC-CLIO, 38–41).

The case of a church bingo game shows how the assessment might work—the game is honest and run by the clergy; players spend twenty dollars two times a month and socialize with friends and neighbors in the process; as a result of the game, a church school or hospital pays its bill and remains open to help the public.

O'Brien does not make a strong case that the preponderance of other gambling does not also successfully meet all the factors set forth. Nowhere in the book is there a suggestion that the games of the gambling industry today are dishonest. Remarkably, he neglected to mention the rigged lottery game in Pennsylvania in 1979. But even if he had done so, he would be hard pressed to say there is a role for cheating by operators in games today. His references to how the gaming industry uses modern marketing and advertising to capture players could be applied to almost any active retail business. Vance Packard told us about "hidden persuaders" in his book by that name a long time before there was a legal state-operated lottery and long before the megaresorts dominated Las Vegas.

O'Brien does play the game of pointing out the organized crime connections of many gaming operators. Most of his stories—and they are just that, stories—are from the past, however, or they refer only to very small operations today—e.g., the Shooting Star casino at Mahommen, Minnesota. He even concludes that if there are bad people working in Las Vegas today, they are on the fringes of the industry. They do not run the casinos.

O'Brien does not dwell on problem gamblers in his book, although he makes many references to these people. He does not review the literature of compulsive gambling, and he does not cite the many authoritative prevalence studies (e.g., those of Rachel Volberg) or cost analyses, but rather just throws around numbers that are not tied to strong research projects. He does not dispute that Las Vegas gamblers are mainly vacation tourists. His vignette on the compulsive gambler is illustrative of the existence of problems, but it does not tell us of the extent of the problems. Much of his text indicates that people want to gamble and see gambling as a recreation. I think a case can possibly be made against gambling in this area using strong research studies. O'Brien does not make the case. (Similarly, others can make the case that with reforms, the incidence of compulsive gambling can be reduced quite considerably.)

The last criterion for "good" gambling is the impact the gambling has on the community. Does gambling build schools, take care of the poor and elderly, help build economies? Here again, although the author offers broad generalizations about how gambling can harm society, he does not make a solid case that gambling cannot have positive effects on societies. Thus, he cannot balance positives and negatives in order to assess net results. He points to past and even contemporary cases of corruption and crime attached to gambling. But he does not establish that these antisocial activities are endemic with gambling. He points out that it is an illusion to believe that all gambling can help economies, and I agree. But he does not offer any solid economic studies making such a case. I have published studies of gambling in three states, and in some of these cases, the gambling had the effect of drawing money away from local communities, hence retarding opportunities for economic growth. But such was not the case everywhere. In some locations gambling was found to be a force for economic growth—it certainly is in Las Vegas.

I think O'Brien could not possibly use the teleological criteria and establish that all gambling is bad—all the time. Nonetheless, he did not seek to make the effort. Even though he could have made the case against gambling stronger, I am still unpersuaded that all gambling is a "bad bet." I think that authors who wish to analyze gambling would be more persuasive if they would accept that some gambling is not as good as (is worse than) other gambling and then concentrate upon policies that would have the effect of discouraging—or improving—the bad gambling.

The conclusions of the book are also bothersome—they just do not exist. The author does not tell us what we should do about the bad situations he does reveal in his book. He has an epilogue that tells about the National Gambling Impact Commission, but he does not offer any suggestions that can improve the situation that he suggests exist—that we are all succumbing to gambling, this "most dangerous of games." Some directional pointers would have been nice to have.

Certain aspects of the book are troublesome to me, at least in a mechanical sense. The author has chosen to name most of his chapters after cities. "Las Vegas" and "Atlantic City" are appropriate, but then he uses "San Francisco" as the title of the chapter on sports betting. He uses "Albany" for the title of the chapter on lotteries—Albany? And "Chicago" somehow is appropriate for charity gambling. "Louisville" means horse racing, and "New York" means stock market gambling; these are more reasonable, but still a justification for city names is not offered. The author also chooses to start the book with a chapter on Internet gambling. He admits that it is a small inconsequential part of the gambling industry. He suggests that the Internet "gambling" does not merit the "hand wringing" it is receiving from policymakers, as he implies that it is going nowhere. But he still thinks it deserves a front and center showcase position in a book on the gambling industry. I do not agree.

O'Brien has decided to include three case studies of gamblers. One he calls "the Poker Player"; a second, "the Veteran"; and the third, "the Compulsive." While readable and interesting, the stories add very little to his text, but worse than that they are presented in a very confusing way. Each is chopped into three parts. Then at the end of each of nine chapters he includes one of the parts of one of the case studies. The part has absolutely no relationship to the chapter preceding it. He could have placed the cases anywhere else, and at least kept them intact, and he would have had better results for the reader—the reader would not have been confused.

A final editorial mechanic that bothered me was the fact that he did not use footnotes or endnotes. Instead he left all indicators of source material out of the text. At the end of the book he listed page numbers and phrases on the pages, followed by references to sources. As I was reading the book I kept wondering if there was a source. I would then have to break my train of thought, go to the back of the book, and go through a mind-distracting process of trying to interpret where his references were. And unfortunately, many pages that were filled with factual statement totally lacked any references at the end of the book.

As mentioned above, many of the sources were to others who have also made evaluative assessments of gambling. Too few were to analytical academic studies.

The Nevada reader should know that O'Brien has made a reasonably adept restatement of the development of the casino industry in the state. Nothing really new, but it is still a good review. He does highlight the role of Moe Dalitz more strongly than other authors do.

Bad Bet seeks to be a journalist's exposé of an industry that has already had more than its share of exposés. He could have written as persuasive a book exposing wrong-doing in about almost any other big industry in the United States. He could have written about automobiles, sugar, computers, oil, agribusiness, chemical, or any similar topic.

O'Brien makes a reasonable punch as he tries to score against the gambling industry, but I am not too sure any boxing judge (even a legitimate one) could give him a victory in the match. I am quite certain he came nowhere near making a knockout punch.

Ploscowe, Morris, and Edwin J. Lukas, eds. 1950. *Gambling.* Special volume of *The Annals of the American Academy of Political and Social Science.* Philadelphia: The American Academy of Political and Social Science. 209 pp.

Morris Ploscowe and Edwin Lukas draw together articles that examine the subject of gambling at a time when public attention associated the activity with crime and just as the Kefauver Committee of the U.S. Senate was beginning its inquiry into the role of organized crime in the United States. This volume represents the first comprehensive collection of studies on the issue of gambling. It is the first of three special issues of *The Annals of the American Academy of Political and Social Science* devoted to gambling over the second half of the twentieth century. It is organized under four headings: "Legal Status of Gambling," "Various Forms of Gambling," "The Gambler," and "Gambling in Foreign Countries."

Five essential questions were asked by the editors as they assembled the articles: (1) Does gambling undermine public morals? (2) Is most gambling activity controlled by organized criminals? (3) Do profits from illegal gambling support other illicit activities? (4) Is legalization a tool that can be used to control illegal gambling? and (5) Can laws against gambling be enforced if it is not legalized? The thrust of most of the studies is to portray gambling in a negative light and argue against legalization.

Ploscowe, a New York judge, takes an overview of the law on gambling reaching back into English history and coming forward to discuss bookmaking, pinball (a "menace to the public health"; 7) and slots, and lotteries. Virgil Peterson of the Chicago Crime Commission explains why it is difficult to enforce antigambling laws, mostly in a Chicago context. Paul Deland sees that legalization leads to increased gambling "with all its attendant criminal evils" (23), and Joseph McDonald gives a good early description of casino gambling in Nevada, "a parasite here to stay" (33). Oswald Jacoby provides more descriptions of games such as punchboards, numbers, and cards—including canasta. Several entries focus on race betting and bookies, and Ernest Blanche presents a good historical overview of lotteries, followed by an essay entitled "Gambling Odds Are Gimmicked!" There are also a solid presentation of traditional Native American gambling along with a description of terms used by professional gamblers (also described in a separate article) and descriptive accounts of gambling in Latin America and Sweden. The volume contains an essay by Robert Lindner on the "Psychodynamics of Gambling." His work laments the fact that so little attention has been devoted to the psychology of "the gambler"—meaning the troubled gambler—heretofore, as he references the work of Ernst Simmel, Sigmund Freud, and Edmund Bergler. He recognizes gambling problems as a disease and also a behavior pattern tied to genetic sources. He sees the gambler as an "obsessional neurotic engaged in what might be called the making of magic" (106) The core of the essay is a case study that is analyzed in a Freudian framework.

Reid, Ed, and Ovid Demaris. 1963. *The Green Felt Jungle.* New York: Trident Press. 242 pp. Reprint, 1994. New York: Pocket Books.
Demaris, Ovid. 1986. *Boardwalk Jungle: How Greed, Corruption, and the Mafia Turned Atlantic City into the Boardwalk Jungle.* New York: Bantam Books. 436 pp.

In the modern era of gambling, Reid and Demaris stand out as the first two authors who leveled a wholesale attack on the legitimacy of "legalized" casino gambling. A consistency runs through these two volumes. The first views Las Vegas in the early 1960s, a dozen years after the Kefauver hearings, as still under the thumb of organized crime families and politicians who willingly did their bidding. The book looks at each major Strip facility and records how the mobsters essentially called the shots. The authors tie Las Vegas to the Lansky mobsters through Meyer Lansky's brother Jake, who was a secret owner of the Thunderbird Casino and in their opinion a partner with the lieutenant governor of the state of Nevada. The many stories, the many charges, were shocking to readers who were not familiar with the Las Vegas scene but not exactly earthshaking to people who had followed the news reports of all the events revealed. Reid and Demaris proved to be good collectors of stories, good writers who could turn a phrase and make an event interesting. They did not document their information, however, nor is it presented as new insights that could lead to any action. Nonetheless, coupled with Wallace Turner's *Gambler's Easy Money,* published two years later, the state knew it was in trouble, and perhaps state authorities were quite willing to invite Howard Hughes to bring his fortune to the state in order to "clean things up" or, more appropriately, help "clean up" the state's image and the image of its leading industry.

Demaris picks up the tale of "Las Vegas casinos and the Mob" twenty-five years later in Atlantic City. Actually, he presents considerable background information suggesting that the Mob was in Atlantic City a long time before the casinos came in 1978. Demaris looks at the campaigns for casinos in 1974 and 1976 and at the 1977 legislation providing for the casino regulatory framework. He looks at the promises about the differences casinos would make: jobs, urban renewal, prosperity for the poor and elderly, a revitalization of tourism. And the promise that there would be no Mob. Gov. Brendan Byrne said these words on the day he signed the 1977 legislation setting up the rules the casinos would live by: "I've said it before and I will repeat it again to organized crime: keep your filthy hands off Atlantic City Keep the hell out of our state" (Mahon 1980, 136). The theme of this sequel is that the chickens were given to the foxes. The casinos were handed to the Mob.

After providing the background materials, the author looks at the first casino and how it got its temporary license. Because the state was so committed to starting the economic miracle, a temporary license was given to Resorts International even though the state knew of many past wrongs and bad associations of the company's executives. Even after the company engaged in many practices considered to be against the interests of integrity after the casino opened, nonetheless the state gave it a permanent license because to do otherwise would destroy "the dream."

And so the pattern was set for licensing eight other casinos before Demaris's book was written. But the dream was not realized. Not by 1986 in any regard. Atlantic City was still a slum. The poor were still poor. Unemployment had not ended. Tourism had not returned. Gamers came in droves, but they were the poor and elderly who could not afford the twenty-three trips they made each year (on average). The state's treasury was not blessed by gambling taxes. The taxes were much less than the take from the state lottery. Crime had increased. Atlantic City had become the Boardwalk Jungle.

The books are written to be sensational. They are not written for researchers, as neither uses notes, cites authority in the text, or provides bibliographies. The very skewed anticasino point of view in each makes the lack of sources a critical shortfall.

Rose, I. Nelson. 1986. *Gambling and the Law.* Hollywood, CA: Gambling Times Press. 304 pp.

Over the past two decades, I. Nelson Rose has emerged as the leading academic authority on the law of gambling. He teaches gambling law, torts, property, and other such mundane legal things at the Whittier Law School in Costa Mesa, California. He is also a legal practitioner. *Gambling and the Law* is the first volume that has been especially devoted to gambling law. Unfortunately, it was not organized as a legal textbook but rather as a set of chapters that really do not hang well together, albeit they do have in many cases very good value separately. The chapters do not seem to be directed at the same audience, but then this difficulty is one that was inevitable given the author's stated purpose. He did not want to advise the reader on his or her legal problems—lawyers, not books, give advice. Rather he wished to prepare a legal guide to educate the player as a player, the player as a taxpayer, the player as a debtor; the casino as a license holder, a lender, an entrepreneurial organization, a taxpayer, and accountant; and also the academic or the general publican interested in gaming of one sort or another. The overreach was just too much for the project.

The limitations being recognized, we can also find value in the chapters. There is a good discussion on the common law of gambling, on the right to advertise gambling products, on gambling taxation, and on gambling debts. Some chapters are limited in value to people in specific geographical areas—chapters on California poker rules, on Nevada casino licensing. And some chapters stray far from the subject at hand (which is gambling). There are chapters on how to hire a lawyer and how to find legal citations in a library. The book is well documented with notes both in the form of sources and in the form of commentary. There is no bibliography, however, and no index.

The true value of the book is probably found in the career of the author. *Gambling and the Law* helped launch Nelson Rose's continuing quests to expose the law, to explain the law, and to elaborate upon the law of gambling. The quest finds fruition in the many newsletters he publishes and in the many columns he writes for academic as well as trade journals of the gambling industry. The book certainly deserves a well-organized sequel, but alas when Rose set about that task he found it also to be too vast a project, and he settled upon a book entitled *Blackjack and the Law.*

Rosecrance, John. 1988. *Gambling without Guilt: The Legitimation of an American Pastime.* Pacific Grove, CA: Brooks-Cole. 174 pp.

John Rosecrance presents an overview of the development of gambling in the United States. He offers chapters on games in the nineteenth and twentieth centuries, taking a look at race betting, lotteries, and casinos during each era. The value of these chapters is that he has taken material utilized before and condensed it into a quick read. The value of the book overall, however, is in his later chapters. Here he focuses upon problem gamblers, the strategies such gamblers use to cope with losses, and treatment opportunities for those who abuse gambling activity. Rosecrance expands upon themes he first expressed in his 1985 book, *The Degenerates of Lake Tahoe.* In that work he described gamblers (who played at Tahoe casino race books) as a fraternity of normal individuals who at various times hit losing streaks or succumbed to bad information and gambled and lost excessively. These gamblers (among whom Rosecrance lists himself) were living in a parallel world. They were not deviant, nor were they psychotic. They were normal. After all, all of us have subcultures into which we retreat at times.

Rosecrance provides a strong argument against the notion that excessive gambling is in and of itself a disease to be fitted into some medical model. Treatment need not require total abstinence, for the essential behaviors are normal. Rather the excessive gambler must be counseled with information, educated, reeducated, and given strategies for coping. In a sense the cure involves behavior modification. The excessive gambler's train has become derailed, fallen from the tracks. But the train can be righted and placed back on the track, and the journey can proceed with the gambler on board. Many other scholars (e.g., see Michael Walker's *The Psychology of Gambling*) have followed a lead provided in Rosecrance's work as they have pursued explanations of problem gambling within the context of acceptable social behaviors, rather than as a disease or an impulse control disorder. The value of Rosecrance's two major books is in the influence and guidance they have provided for those in the academic professions who look at gambling as their object of study.

Ross, Gary. 1987. *No Limit: The Incredible Obsession of Brian Molony*. New York: William Morrow. 301 pp. (Published in Canada in 1987 as *Stung: The Incredible Obsession of Brian Molony*. Toronto: Stoddard Publishers. 301 pp.)

When Brian Molony was invited in 1988 to be the featured speaker for the first National Symposium on Lotteries and Gambling in Vancouver, British Columbia, one local casino company boycotted the program. They felt that Molony's presence would be used by the media to discredit the industry. But Molony did not speak harshly about casinos. He accepts commercial gambling as a legitimate leisure-time activity that the majority of people can enjoy without any problems. He is not one of the majority, however; he is a compulsive gambler.

Brian Molony is somewhat overweight, and his suit fits uncomfortably over his frame. His appearance belies any notion that he engages in his escapades for personal profit or social advantage. Molony is articulate as he gives his message, and he exudes sincerity. He has been "stung," and you feel it as you listen to him. But Molony does not blame others, certainly not his former employer or the casino industry. He takes responsibility for his past behavior, and he sees only one cure for the compulsion that consumed so much of his life—more treatment programs for compulsive gamblers.

I was puzzled that Molony's single plea was for government and industry support for these programs, especially after I read *No Limit*. Gary Ross's excellent description of the case history of Brian Molony penetrates the gambling industry in a way that suggests many other places where reforms are long overdue. In *No Limit*, Ross gives a detailed account of Molony's life as a gambler. As a child of ten, Molony was drawn to racetracks near Toronto. Soon he was a bookie for his schoolmates. In college, his early gambling successes turned to failure. He learned how to deceive his friends and family and how to conceal his gambling activity. He was bright and industrious, and extra work efforts could always give him funds to pay off his losses.

His outstanding record as a student won him a position with Canada's second largest bank—the Canadian Imperial Bank of Commerce (CIBC). He was put on the fast track; at age twenty-five he was promoted to be as-

sistant manager of one of the bank's largest branches in Toronto. There he was placed in charge of loan accounts. His work habits were exemplary, and he earned the admiration of all those about him. He was hooked on gambling, however, and he was a loser. After one disastrous weekend, Molony discovered that his bookie-creditors were demanding an immediate payment of $22,000, "or else." Actually, he was not in physical danger; the creditors would have gladly accepted smaller payments over time. The "or else" was a more psychologically devastating threat: "Pay up, or else we will take no more bets from you." But he had to bet. How else was he to "catch up"?

Molony could not be cut off from the action. As some criminology theorists might view it, he had a motive, he had a desire, and he had an opportunity. He seized the opportunity. To a pattern of excessive gambling he now attached a history of embezzlements of money from loan accounts he controlled (or created) at the CIBC branch. Within nineteen months, he had "borrowed" C$10,395,800 and US$5,081,000. Often Molony would borrow from one account to repay another, so the bottom-line embezzlement figure totaled US$10,200,000.

Molony's first $22,000 "loan" was just the initial step in a campaign of chasing losses with more gambling—a campaign that led Molony from local racetracks to the casinos of Las Vegas and Atlantic City. Brian Molony's banking activities constituted the "largest single-handed bank fraud in Canadian history," according to the cover of *No Limit*. Yet the story told inside the cover suggests that the frauds were anything but single-handed. Although unassisted, Molony was constantly aided by very lax standards and shoddy internal procedures at his bank. Gary Ross presents us not only with a true story that reads like a novel but also with a treatise on gambling behavior and the structure of two financial industries—casino gaming and banking.

The book climbed to the top rungs of Canadian best-seller lists. It should also find its way to popularity as required reading for college classes in criminology and sociology, psychology, political science, and business administration. That Ross writes well and without footnotes or bibliography (unfortunately also without an index) should not deter academics from seizing the opportunity to have Molony's story told in the classroom. Ross presents a cogent summary of suggested causes of compulsive gambling—from Freudian analyses to biochemical hypotheses. He examines processes of treatment and describes the program Molony joined after being "discovered." The low success rates of the treatment programs and Molony's statement to the symposium that he never would have accepted treatment before his frauds were discovered give pause to acceptance of his singular solution to the problem of compulsive gambling.

Even when Molony agreed to join a program, he insisted that his problem was not a "gambling problem" but a "financial problem." Molony was "discovered" because some hard-working vice squad policemen listened to months of telephone conversations of known bookies. At one off-guard moment, Molony used his real name, and the police began to track down this big-time gambler, convinced that he must be a drug dealer. When they found that he worked at CIBC, they knew that the game was embezzlement. But for the bank the game was embarrassment. Not only had the bank been "stung" (to the tune of US$10.2 million), but they were "stung" by their own structural incompetencies that prevented an internal discovery of ninety-three cases of fraud extending over a nineteen-month period. Now they would be "stung" by publicity.

We can almost sense that Molony would still be out there (or here) today placing bets if the bank had caught him first. Certainly the bank would not have desired to have a public prosecution. He would have resigned, Lloyd's would have covered the loss (which they—the biggest of those "stung"—did), and it would have been business as usual. After all, had the bank not lost much more with poorly secured loans to Third World countries? Instead, the bank was exposed by outsiders. So it went through a ritual of hand-wringing, firing several employees whose actions were unrelated to Molony's and permitting a graceful early retirement for Molony's immediate supervisor, a man who should have been much more vigilant. Molony's early mentor, a man who engineered his early promotion, was banned to a branch bank in western Canada. His disgrace was followed by a suicide. Pressures of adverse publicity caused some structural changes regarding responsibility and lines of authority in handling loans.

From the book we can sense that some executives at the Marina in Las Vegas might feel that they too were "stung." A low-level credit officer at the Marina refused to give Molony complimentary services because his financial transactions were not in accordance with detailed house rules. The casino lost his business while he was still gambling in the tens of thousands. The rejection by the Marina propelled Molony to higher ground. Soon he was the most prized customer of Caesars Boardwalk Casino in Atlantic City. Caesars sent its Lear jet to Toronto to bring Molony in for gaming weekends. The casino offered him fine meals and female friendships, but Molony wanted only ribs (without gravy), a big coke, and lady luck. He thought of gaming, never

personal pleasure. At home he drove an old car, dressed in untailored suits, skimped on his share of the rent for the apartment he shared with his girlfriend, and embezzled millions. Caesars had to know something was wrong. But they wanted his money so much that they actually sent casino officials to Toronto to open up the casino cage there in order to handle his financial transactions. They helped Molony dodge international money transfer rules as well as New Jersey gaming regulations.

In his speech, Molony said that one casino official, when asked about Brian's money, replied that he thought nothing was wrong because he assumed Molony was a drug dealer. Caesars got "stung." As a punishment from New Jersey authorities, the casino was closed for one day, incurring a million-dollar business loss (to compare with over $3 million won from Molony). No major executives were disciplined.

Molony served two and a half years in prison. In the process he rekindled close relationships with a very supportive family, a girlfriend (now his wife and mother of his children), and many friends who stood by him. He has agreed to a program of restitution and community service—which includes speeches such as the one made in Vancouver. He is struggling financially as he seeks another career niche, now working as a business consultant. He has avoided gambling in the years since being discovered in 1982. In addition to telling us the story of Brian Molony, *No Limit* tells us about an industry that overlooks illegal and immoral behavior in order to maximize profits. Ross portrays casino gaming as an illegitimate industry, something that Molony refuses to do. Ross shows how casinos use psychological tricks to win money: They furnish favors of the flesh; give alcoholic drinks that inhibit reasoned wagering; offer credit and allow higher table limits to players who are gambling beyond their means. Many reforms must come to the mind of the reader. We can have legitimate casinos that make profits without improper gaming inducements. Casinos in many jurisdictions require identifications of players and knowledge of their occupations. Governments receive this information. Certainly it is doubtful that Molony could have been a player for long in these casinos. Many casinos have table limits and restrict credit, thus prohibiting players from chasing small losses with bigger and bigger bets. Casinos in some countries prohibit drinking. Many have opening hours that break up playing binges. Many governments sponsor programs of treatment for compulsive gamblers. We can do better in this regard. Iowa commits 0.5 percent of its lottery win to programs. Nevada gives exactly zero. But more than treatment is necessary, if we want no more cases like Molony's. Until we get industry-wide reforms, society will continue to be "stung" by manipulative, uncontrolled commercial gambling.

The review of Ross's book was reprinted with permission from William N. Thompson. "Review." *Journal of Gambling Behavior,* 5, no. 2 (Summer) 1988.

Rubin, Max. 1994. *Comp City: A Guide to Free Las Vegas Vacations.* Las Vegas: Huntington Press. 246 pp.

Max Rubin is a self-proclaimed Comp Wizard. He plays a different kind of game in Las Vegas. He takes the reader through excruciating detail after detail in an exploration of everything that a player could get "free" from a casino—from parking validations, a drink, buffets, gourmet meals, to a show, boxing match, suite of rooms, or an airline ticket. This is a studied effort that must be designed for the student of casino gambling or the casino executive in training. Rubin explains the processes that casinos utilize in determining which players or nonplayers receive each kind of "comp," or free, item. He demonstrates that the system is flawed and that players and others can take advantage of the casinos. Some players who place the notion of getting some item or service as a gratuity above almost everything else will find the book valuable. They will learn they must sit at a gambling table and play very slowly and that they must always get a pit boss to see them as they are sitting down. They must lead with large bets and later lower their bet amounts after the pit boss has recorded them as high rollers. They should buy large amounts of chips in a noticeable manner, but then secretly slip them into their pockets so they do not have to risk them in bets. It is a game—a stupid game. The game is predicated on the notion that many of the tourists who come to Las Vegas are cheap pigs who do not place any value on their time. I must say that in my opinion the point of coming to Las Vegas is having fun and being entertained—hopefully winning some money, or at least not losing too much in the process. It is not being able to pig out on things a person would not otherwise want—such as excess fatty foods and desserts, or drink after drink. So although Rubin's book is fun to read and educational for one wanting to know how casinos think, I hope it is not used as a guide book for tourists. It really tells a person how to ruin what could otherwise be a very good vacation experience.

Scarne, John. 1986 *Scarne's New Complete Guide to Gambling.* Fireside Edition. New York: Simon and Schuster. 871 pp.

John Scarne has been recognized as being among the leading authorities on gambling in modern times. He has been called America's Hoyle by many people. His knowledge was commanded by the Kefauver Committee and by the Department of War, which called upon Scarne to go among the wartime troops to tell them about the nature of games and the structures of odds, as well as the many scams that crooked players could use. One source claimed that he saved GI's millions and millions of dollars. Legitimate casinos in Las Vegas and Reno also have used his help. Scarne has penned many thick volumes on games: *Scarne's Encyclopedia of Games, Scarne–25 New Kinds of Skill Games, Scarne on Card Tricks,* and *Scarne on Cards,* among many others. *Scarne's New Complete Guide to Gambling* has been his best-selling book. It was originally published in 1961, issued in a second edition in 1974, and then reprinted in a paperback version by Simon and Schuster in 1986. But even with the updated paperback version much material on the environment of games is very dated. For instance, he neglects the entire wave of government-run lotteries that has swept over North America since 1964. On the other hand, the detailed description given to the mathematics of games and the discussion of luck, chance, skill, odds, payoffs, and gambling systems are enduring. After his general introduction, Scarne presents thirty chapters on the major forms of gambling—horse racing, sports betting, lotteries (prior to the modern United States), the numbers game, bingo, and the many precomputerized table and machine games found in casinos. He also examines games not usually associated with heavy gambling—bridge, backgammon, and gin rummy. He gives extensive treatment to carnival games as well, in addition to punchboards, chain letters, and pyramid schemes. About the only games he neglects to discuss are chess, checkers, and the games they play on Wall Street. The book is capped off with a valuable glossary containing over 400 items. For the reader who wants a single volume on games, this has to be it.

Sifakis, Carl. 1990. *The Encyclopedia of Gambling.* New York: Facts on File. 340 pp.

Carl Sifakis has been a crime reporter for United Press International and the *Buffalo Evening News.* He has also been a freelance writer. His writings have gravitated toward the roles of criminal groups in the United States. In addition to this encyclopedia, he wrote *The Mafia Encyclopedia* and *The Encyclopedia of American Crime.* This encyclopedia does give many pages to the underworld connections of gambling. The book covers the subject of world wide gambling from A to Z. A concentrated attention is given to games, their odds, their rules, and ways in which they have been compromised by shady characters. His detailed attention to games finds him offering dozens of items on various games of poker, ten entries on gin games, seven on games of rummy. The detail that is presented on games must be the book's greatest asset. Sifakis also presents a description of gaming in almost every national and subnational jurisdiction in the world. Many of the offerings reflect personal travel experiences. They seem to be dated in many cases, however, and appear to be collections of observations that may or may not have been verified. He does sprinkle the book with many many interesting stories about famous gamblers—both nice people and rogues. On almost every page there is an entry that will be of interest to any reader who would relish knowing more about gambling. Did you know that archaeologists digging in Egypt found dice inside pyramids that dated back 4,000 years? And the dice were crooked! Did you know that the Earl of Sandwich—noted for the obvious—was a compulsive gambler? Fun reading. Unfortunately, the writer did not document his entries, so we must either trust him as "the source" or wonder. On the other hand, Sifakis does provide a bibliography that includes many of his sources. These limitations being noted, the material in the book is comprehensive and should have value to all interested readers. I turned to Sifakis over and over again as I was refining the entries in this encyclopedia.

Skolnick, Jerome H. 1978. *House of Cards: Legalization and Control of Casino Gambling.* Boston: Little, Brown. 382 pp.

House of Cards receives my nomination for the best book on casino gambling in the 1970s. Author Jerome H. Skolnick, a criminology professor at the University of California–Berkeley, made long on-site inspections of Las Vegas casinos and the regulatory processes in Nevada over a three-year period before putting pen to paper. He collected historical data, and he interviewed hundreds of participants in the Las Vegas scene. He went on inspection tours with gaming agents, and he rode in metropolitan police cars. He came to know his subject very well.

Skolnick wanted to know how an industry so tied to what was considered "sin" and "vice" could be controlled in the public interest. He starts by examining the broad subject of gambling and considering whether casino "action" is "play or pathology." He concludes that the exercise of gambling can have useful meaning for very normal people. A second chapter looks at the legalization of "sin" behavior in the United States—alcoholic drinking, drug use, sexual relationships. He then turns to the casino, first focusing on the people who form this peculiar social institution: players, dealers, hookers. Then he looks at the games that are played in the casino. Internal management and control are considered essential for maintaining the "house edge" with the odds. He examines surveillance and accounting procedures.

Three chapters written by Skolnick's graduate assistant—now professor—John Dombrink trace the rise of the casino industry in Nevada, its search for respectability through legitimate capital investment, and the emergence of corporate gambling. Skolnick then describes the development of the governmental structures for regulation—the Gaming Control Board, the Nevada Gaming Commission, and their subunits. Four chapters are devoted to issues concerned with licensing and the Nevada model of difficult entry and self-regulation with state monitoring. The final chapters consider this monitoring activity: patrolling the casino floor, discretion in enforcement, auditing, and finding hidden interests. In his concluding chapter the author contrasts Nevada with a widely different model of regulation, that found in Great Britain.

The book is thoroughly documented and well written. It concludes with the dilemma faced by all regulatory agencies. How can a business be promoted for the general economic good of the community and still held to strict regulatory standards to ensure ethical operations? The question remains unanswered today, twenty-three years after it was posed by Jerome Skolnick.

Sternlieb, George, and James W. Hughes. 1983. *The Atlantic City Gamble: A Twentieth Century Fund Report.* Cambridge: Harvard University Press. 215 pp.

In my coauthored book *The Last Resort* (John D. Dombrink and William N. Thompson, 1990), a tale is told of the successful 1976 campaign for casinos in New Jersey. The success and the opening of the first Atlantic City casino halls led to much speculation that large commercial casinos would soon be in more than half of the states. Then like dominos, new campaigns for casinos in state after state fell to defeat. Of course, after our book was published, a movement for Native American casinos and riverboat and limited stakes casinos changed the pattern of results. We concluded in 1990, however, that negative reaction to casinos manifested in the many defeats of propositions in the early 1980s was somehow tied to very negative experiences that followed the opening of casinos in Atlantic City.

George Sternlieb and James Hughes document many of those negative experiences in their book *The Atlantic City Gamble*. They provide a well-researched and thoroughly documented account of the New Jersey campaign leading up to the successful 1976 vote. They describe the struggle in the legislature for implementing legislation in 1977, and they chronicle the first signs of realism that came with the licensing process that was followed so that the doors of Resorts International could open on Memorial Day weekend in 1978 (a story told in much more sordid detail by Gigi Mahon in *The Company that Bought the Boardwalk*). Soon there were more casinos and soon there was an ABSCAM (a Federal Bureau of Investigation code name based on *Arab* and *scam*)—a bribery scandal that unseated a U.S. senator and exposed the licensing authorities as politicians not always operating above the tables. Political favors flourished in all directions.

Still there were hopes, for there had been many promises. Casinos meant jobs, and by the time Sternlieb and Hughes's book was written there were nine casinos with 30,000 employees. But not all was rosy on this front, either. The casinos drove existing businesses out of town, as local restaurants and shops could not compete with casino facilities. Also many of their local customers had lost their homes in the mass urban redevelopment called casino construction. It was another case of urban renewal becoming urban removal. It was estimated that 2,000 local residents lost jobs in businesses outside of the casinos. Unfortunately, the jobs inside the casinos did not all go to local residents. Typically the casino employee commuted from the suburbs or from even farther away. City unemployment rates did not diminish. City taxes were supposed to tumble, but they did not. Land was assessed at a higher value, and taxes went up to pay for additional city services—not for the residents but for the casinos and their many customers. Housing supplies decreased, and housing stock deteriorated as landlords refrained from upkeep in hopes of selling out to casino developers. Crime rates increased.

The authors identified an essential problem in the fact that the visitors to the casinos were not resort tourists like those Atlantic City had attracted fifty years earlier. Now the casinos attracted day-trippers on buses. And the day-trippers did not spend money outside of the casinos. In chapter after chapter one fact is piled upon another, all leading the authors to conclude in the final paragraph of the book that the costs of casinos development in Atlantic City outweighed the virtues.

Tanioka, Ichiro. 2000 (English ed.). *Pachinko and the Japanese Society.* Osaka, Japan: Institute of Amusement Industries, Osaka University of Commerce. 146 pp.

Dr. Ichiro Tanioka is the leading gambling scholar in Japan, having authored many books on the subject. This is the first of his books that has appeared in English. In this well-illustrated volume, he brings together many perspectives on the most prevalent type of gambling in Japan, play at the pachinko machine. Although gambling per se is illegal in Japan, pachinko is permitted by legal authorities, who maintain a fiction that the game is not gambling. They assert (and Professor Tanioka concurs) that it is basically a "skill" game, hence lacking the crucial gambling element of "chance." They also indicate that the machines are not gambling devices, because prizes are awarded not in cash but rather in merchandise. The authorities pretend not to notice that the merchandise is quickly exchanged for cash by the players outside of the pachinko parlors.

This facet of Japanese gambling law and other parts of the law are explored. So too is the subject of pachinko and pathological gambling. Tanioka examines many types of games, and he ranks the elements of the games such as excitement, expectations, speed of action, money limitations, and rules of play. He then concludes that pachinko is the leading game in terms of its allure for habitual players. He looks at the allure as it impacts various demographic groups in Japan—gender groups, age groups, and social classes. A wealth of statistics reveals the business implications of the pachinko parlors in Japan. Professor Tanioka, who holds his doctorate in sociology from the University of Southern California, ends the volume with a series of proposals aimed mostly at making the game more responsible by eliminating several of its aspects that attract pathological gamblers. This is the definitive English language book on gambling in Japan.

Thompson, William N. 1997. *Legalized Gambling: A Reference Handbook.* 2d ed. Santa Barbara, CA: ABC-CLIO. 298 pp.

This book is part of the ABC-CLIO World Issues series. The book treats the issue of gambling in the context of U.S. and Canadian developments. An initial chapter introduces gambling by exploring its history and political issues. There are discussions of forms of government regulation of gambling, the rationale for gambling behaviors, and social and religious perspectives on gambling activity. There is also a discussion of the positive and negative aspects of gambling that focuses upon economic impacts and the issue of problem gambling. The book also includes chapters offering a chronology of events, a selection of short biographies of leading figures in gambling history, a review of legislation of gambling, major court cases, several quotations on the subject, a glossary, and a directory of private and public gambling organizations. The book also reviews a wide selection of books and films that have a gambling focus.

Thompson, William N., and Michele Comeau. 1992. *Casino Customer Service = The WIN WIN Game.* New York: Gaming and Wagering Business. 332 pp.

Casinos face a major dilemma: how to take money from customers and send them away empty handed yet still desiring to return. The answer is to give them entertainment value and good experiences. Make them feel good through delivery of top customer service. This is the first volume to be written on the topic of customer service in the casino environment. The book takes a close look at the roles played by executives, supervisors, and frontline employees in the casino. Attention is given to defining just who the customer is, telling how to ascertain customers' wants and desires, and developing a customer service mission statement and objectives that can be measured. Supervisory skills and motivation techniques are examined as are topics such as dealing with the angry customer, recovery from bad situations, communication, and stress reduction for dealers. The book concludes with several case studies of both successful and unsuccessful efforts at customer satisfaction in casinos.

Thorpe, Edward O. 1962. *Beat the Dealer: A Winning Strategy for the Game of Twenty-One.* New York: Random House. 236 pp.

When Edward Thorpe wrote this classic on gambling strategy, he was an assistant professor of mathematics at New York State University. He had received a Ph.D. from the University of California, Los Angeles (UCLA), with research focused upon probability theory. *Beat the Dealer* has to be the most popular application of probability theory ever written. Before this book was written, craps was the most popular casino game. Before craps it was faro. After the book came out, all players who felt they had a brain that could function within a casino environment rushed to the blackjack tables. The casino could be beaten! And they did not have to cheat to beat the house.

Thorpe discusses the many rules of blackjack, and then he explains his winning system. The system is based upon counting cards that have already been played (dealt) and thereby assessing which cards remain to be dealt. If the remaining supply of cards includes an unusually large number of aces and ten-value (face and tens) cards, the probability of having a natural blackjack" dealt is much higher than otherwise. The natural blackjack consists of two cards—an ace and a ten-value card. The player is more likely to receive a blackjack and so is the dealer. If the dealer gets a blackjack and the player gets less than a twenty-one or goes bust (over twenty-one), the player loses his bet—say, for instance, two dollars. If the player gets the blackjack, the player keeps his two dollars and wins three dollars from the dealer. This advantage gives the player an odds advantage over the house.

Other advantages may also follow from being aware of the flow of the deck. These are discussed in detail, as are many intricacies of strategies depending on what the player is dealt and what card the dealer shows.

Thorpe also exposes flaws in other gambling systems, and he discusses strategies that casinos may use to keep their advantage—or to try to keep their advantage.

Thorpe was not a gambler when as a UCLA student he drove to Las Vegas for a short vacation over the Christmas break. He thought he would find sunshine and cheap accommodations in the gambling city. A fellow professor clued him into a blackjack strategy and urged him to try it out. He went to the tables, but he did not win with the system. But what he did do was discover the game, and he became fascinated with its possibilities. He returned to the university, and he gained access to the "high speed" computer of the day. He played hand after hand—hundreds of hands. Soon he had his system, the material for a book, and a new career, and Las Vegas had a lot more blackjack players.

Las Vegas also found that some of these Thorpe system players were winning. So Las Vegas started to ban "counters" from playing blackjack. Players known as "counters" began to use disguises, and cat-and-mouse games ensued for four decades—they are still going on. As a matter of law the Nevada courts allowed the casinos to expel the "counters," but the Atlantic City casinos were not able to ban them from the games. Instead, Atlantic City operators adjusted by adding decks of cards to the supply that could be dealt for a game, and they began to shuffle cards more often.

Thorpe stands today as a genius who in his quest to beat the house probably did more good for the casino gaming industry that could be imagined.

Turner, Wallace. 1965. *Gambler's Money: The New Force in American Life.* Boston: Houghton Mifflin. 306 pp.

Wallace Turner was a Pulitzer Prize–winning journalist with the *New York Times*. In his 1965 book *Gambler's Money*, he thoroughly attacks the integrity of Nevada casino gambling. He reserves favorable comments for only one operator in the state, Bill Harrah. He strongly suggests that the records of the others justified closing casino gambling down altogether in the state. He regretted that this would not be politically possible.

Turner presents detail after detail about crooked characters and crooked deals, skimming, laundering money, and that infamous Teamsters' union fund of Jimmy Hoffa's. A major theme of the book is that illegal gambling profits (either skimmed by the registered owners or funds given to illegal hidden owners) migrate toward other legitimate business. There the money is used to infect the corporate sector with illicit practices that somehow harm the good name of commerce. Turner laments that the southern bloc of U.S. senators is tightly linked to the notion of states' rights (because of the integration challenge), precluding wholesale federal action against the Nevada casino actions that are supported by the state government. Powerful senators such as Pat McCarren, Alan Bible, and Howard Cannon were influential in defending the state's interests. Turner applauded the efforts of the Kefauver Committee, the McClellan Committees, and the work of Robert Kennedy. Somehow he totally missed the connection between John F. Kennedy and his father, the Rat Pack, and their kindred Mafioso clan.

Turner's story is so skewed in one direction that it takes on a total appearance of overkill:

> By the social and ethical rules of American culture, gambling is immoral business, tainting those who operate it. . . . This is a *fact* of sociology, that when gamblers are given a foothold in legality, they rapidly expand it into a permanent bridgehead . . . working their changes on the pattern of American life. (283)

Reading his words, which came into print only shortly after Ed Reid and Ovid Demaris wrote *The Green Felt Jungle* (1963), we can understand the elation the good people must have felt in 1966 when Howard Hughes began to buy out the Mob. The book is interesting, fun to read, but the stories are old hat. Society has survived the expansion of casino gambling as a legal commodity into a majority of the states, lotteries into three-quarters of the states, and some form of betting into forty-eight states. Maybe we have all "gone to hell in a handbasket." If so, we seem to have enjoyed the journey.

Venturi, Robert, Denise Scott Brown, and Steven Izenour. 1993. *Learning from Las Vegas: The Forgotten Symbolism of Architectural Form.* 2d ed. (paperback). Cambridge: MIT Press. 188 pp. (First edition, 1972, 188 pp.).

The three authors of *Learning from Las Vegas* are all members of a Philadelphia architectural firm. They joined forces with a class of Yale architectural students and ventured off on a ten-day excursion into the southern Nevada desert and the Las Vegas Strip. They came in 1968. The authors present a defense of the ordinary, the gaudy, even the ugly (or what has been perceived by other architects to be ugly). They see art in the commercial business strip, and its epitome is represented by the casino Strip, otherwise known as Las Vegas Boulevard South. Pop art triumphs in their well-illustrated and diagrammed pages. Las Vegas is presented as a "model" for the commercial strip and supermarket parking lots everywhere.

Venturi, Brown, and Izenour examine the billboards and the large neon signs; the wedding chapels and the shape of the casino buildings, à la 1968; the traffic patterns; and the styles of life within the casinos. In their later chapters, they seek connections between what they find in Las Vegas and the rest of the United States. As they do so, they seek out the roots of Las Vegas architecture in the buildings and the utilization of space found in the ancient Roman Empire.

The authors are clearly seeking to shock by their iconoclastic rejection of what had been passing for conventional wisdom in the architectural fraternity of the 1960s. They clearly see buildings and structures as a response to people's needs, but also to their desires and to the patterns of their daily lives. The book represents a precursor to the central notion expressed in *Time Magazine*'s 1994 article, "All American City" (10 January)— that all of the United States is becoming like Las Vegas. And that, the authors claim, would not be all that bad, for to learn from popular culture would not deprive the architect of his or her status in high-culture society. But then it just may alter the high-culture society enough to make it more sympathetic to current desires.

The shorter 1993 revised edition in paperback offers a short preface and a bibliography of sources that incorporate criticisms and evaluations of the original book.

Walker, Michael B. 1992. *The Psychology of Gambling.* Oxford: Pergamon Press. 262 pp.

Michael Walker offers what I consider to be the best single volume of information on gambling behavior— normal and otherwise. The book is comprehensive in that it gives credence to all the major approaches to gambling phenomena. Nonetheless it is not without a decided point of view. Walker, as distinguished from many writers on gambling behavior that have preceded him, believes that gambling is a very normal activity, albeit subject to abuses. He starts with the premise that gamblers are normal and that they are thinking as they make decisions to play.

Walker's initial discussion focuses upon what he calls "everyday gambling." He looks at the context of play in major forms of games—horse racing, poker, blackjack, and bridge. He sees gamblers starting from a rational position but falling into several categories—part-time players, serious players, bustouts, and professionals. He considers the players' perceptions of luck and skill and their use of thinking strategies—for the most part faulty ones, but thinking ones nonetheless. Walker offers the notion that players are consciously trying to be rational while they play. He then considers games of "pure chance"—numbers, lottos, bingo, and slot machines.

After reviewing many of the theories of gambling (and providing very good descriptions of the theories), he presents the essential message of his book, his sociocognitive theory of gambling involvement. For many people—indeed most—gambling presents a challenge that can be conquered by knowledge and skill. In luck games, players feel that they have a chance, often expressing the notion that "someone has to win." As play progresses, however, the gambler can fall into a trap—not unlike that of any businessperson who has invested in a bad enterprise. As I read, I thought of the entrepreneur who was losing one dollar on each widget he produced and sold. His solution was simple—he had to work harder and increase sales. This line of thought leads to heavy gambling (by the gambler and the businessperson) and may progress to compulsive gambling.

Walker takes a close look at the measurements utilized to determine who is a problem gambler (South Oaks Gambling Screen, Gamblers Anonymous (GA) scale, *Diagnostic and Statistical Manual of Mental Disorders* (DSM) III, and (DSM) IV and also at the consequences of heavy gambling on the players as well as on the families of the players. He then rejects the disease model of problem gambling, and he rejects the notion that there is evidence to suggest that gambling is an addiction related to arousal disorders. He also examines a very wide range of treatment strategies for heavy gamblers—from GA steps to psychoanalysis and behavior modification. He concludes with a finding that money is the primary reason for gambling problems. The downfall of the heavy gambler is found in the debts incurred as the player forfeits rationality for irrational thoughts. The most effective treatment for most heavy problem gamblers, then, is to get them to return to rational thought processes. Only then can they correct their misguided behaviors. And then, with rationality restored, they may return to normal gambling behaviors.

Weinstein, David, and Lillian Deitch. 1974. *The Impact of Legalized Gambling: The Socioeconomic Consequences of Lotteries and Off-Track Betting.* New York: Praeger. 208 pp.

Within five years of the first mass market U.S. lotteries, Weinstein and Deitch tackled the social and economic questions about gambling that are still being studied. What is the effect of legalized gambling on government revenues, on taxpayers, on family life, and on illegal gambling?

The authors cover a wide range in this short book. They look at the origins of the lottery, lottery administration and marketing, sales experience of the lotteries, operating expenses, and net revenues and their distribution. They seek to measure the impact of lotteries on state finances, concluding that it is quite small. They also find that earmarking funds for programs is not effective unless the legal provisions are very specific. They find that lotteries do not deflect taxes that would otherwise come through sales of other goods. The authors examine the notion of regressivity of lottery taxes. They are inconclusive in their results, although they see that lottery participation is about equal across all income classes.

Chapters are devoted to foreign lotteries and also to offtrack betting in New York State. In a consideration of the social consequences of lotteries, the authors ask: "Is gambling rational?" They conclude that a lottery offers a chance for a big prize that would otherwise be out of reach of a player. For this chance the player need only offer a small consideration that will not affect lifestyle. Moreover, they see lotteries as offering a release from socially induced tensions. Lotteries may operate as safety valves for society. For the most part, they do not think that lottery play will lead to addictive behaviors and the negative social impacts that result—family disintegration, poor work habits, crime. The authors are uncertain about the effects that legal gambling has on illegal gambling enterprise.

The book also poses policy questions about the regulatory format for gambling games—whether they should be run by the government or by private groups. An appendix lists all the states with lotteries (as of

1974) and provides extensive information about the administration of the games. A very thorough bibliography of the early years of state lotteries is included.

David Weinstein and Lillian Deitch's book is now a quarter-century old. The questions asked then by the authors were the right questions. The nature of lotteries and other gambling has changed considerably since 1974, however. All games are faster, and gambling is more pervasive in society. It can be expected that the answers to the questions have changed as well. But then, that is why studies like theirs must continue.

BIBLIOGRAPHY

Abt, Vicki, James F. Smith, and Eugene Martin Christiansen. 1985. *The Business of Risk: Commercial Gambling in Mainstream America.* Lawrence: University Press of Kansas. 286 pp.

Adler, Bill. 1986. *The Lottery Book.* New York: William Morrow. 167 pp.

Aginsky, Burt W., and Ethel G. Aginsky. 1950. "The Pomo: A Profile of Gambling among Indians." In *Gambling* (special volume of *The Annals of the Academy of Political and Social Science*), edited by Morris Ploscowe and Edwin J. Lucas, 108–113. Philadelphia: The American Academy of Political and Social Science.

Ainslie, Tom. 1975. *Ainslie's Complete Hoyle.* New York: Simon and Schuster. 526 pp.

Ainslie, Tom. 1978. *Ainslie's Encyclopedia of Thoroughbred Handicapping.* New York: William Morrow. 320 pp.

Ainslie, Tom. 1979. *Ainslie's Complete Guide to Thoroughbred Racing.* New York: Simon and Schuster. 479 pp.

Albanese, Jay S. 1985. "The Effect of Casino Gambling on Crime." *Federal Probation* 49 (June): 39–44.

Alcamo, John. 1991. *Atlantic City: Behind the Tables.* Grand Rapids, MI: Gollehon. 233 pp.

Alfieri, Donald. 1994. "The Ontario Casino Project: A Case Study." In *Gambling in Canada: The Bottomline,* edited by Colin Campbell, 85–92. Burnaby, B.C.: Simon Fraser University.

Allen, David D. 1952. *The Nature of Gambling.* New York: Coward-McCann. 249 pp.

Alvarez, A. Alfred. 1983. *The Biggest Game in Town.* Boston: Houghton Mifflin. 185 pp.

American Gaming Association. 1996a. *Economic Impacts of Casino Gaming in the United States.* 2 vols. Las Vegas: Arthur Andersen.

American Gaming Association [AGA]. 1996b. *The Responsible Gaming Resource Guide.* Kansas City, MO: AGA. 111 pp.

American Psychiatric Association. 1980. *Diagnostic and Statistical Manual of Mental Disorders.* 3d ed. Washington, DC: American Psychiatric Association. 494 pp.

Anders, Gary C. 1998. "Indian Gaming: Financial and Regulatory Issues." In *Gambling: Socioeconomic Impacts and Public Policy* (special volume of *The Annals of the American Academy of Political and Social Science*), edited by James H. Frey, 98–108. Thousand Oaks, CA: Sage.

Andersen, Kurt. 1994. "Las Vegas: The New All-American City." *Time* 143 (10 January): 42–51.

Arcuri, Alan F., David Lister, and Franklin O. Smith. 1985. "Shaping Adolescent Gambling Behavior." *Adolescence* 20 (Winter): 935–938.

Arnold, Peter, ed. 1985. *The Book of Games.* New York: Exeter. 256 pp.

Asbury, Herbert. 1938. *Sucker's Progress: An Informal History of Gambling in America from the Colonies to Canfield.* New York: Dodd, Mead. 493 pp.

Atkins, Joe. 1991. "The States' Bad Bet." *Christianity Today* 35 (November): 16–18.

Balboni, Alan. 1999. "Moe Dalitz: Controversial Founding Father of Modern Las Vegas." In *The Maverick Spirit: Building the New Nevada,* edited by Richard O. Davies, 24–43. Reno: University of Nevada Press.

Banker, Lem, and Fred Klein. 1986. *Lem Banker's Book of Sports Betting.* New York: Dutton. 182 pp.

Barker, Thomas, and Marjie Britz. 2000. *Jokers Wild: Legalized Gambling in the Twenty-First Century.* Westport, CN: Praeger. 224 pp.

Barnhart, Russell T. 1978. *Casino Gambling: Why You Win, Why You Lose.* New York: Dutton. 221 pp.

Barnhart, Russell T. 1983. *Gamblers of Yesteryear.* Las Vegas: Gamblers Book Club. 239 pp.

Barrier, Michael. 1991. "How Bookmaking and Bookselling Came Together in Las Vegas." *Nations Business* 79 (November): 20.

Barthelme, Frederick, and Steven Barthelme. 1999. *Double Down: Reflections on Gambling and Loss.* Boston: Houghton-Mifflin. 198 pp.

Bates, Anna Louise. 1995. *Weeder in the Garden of the Lord: Anthony Comstock's Life and Career.* Lanham, MD: University Press of America. 216 pp.

Beal, George. 1975. *Playing-Cards and Their Story.* New York: Arco. 120 pp.

Bell, Raymond. 1976. "Moral Views on Gambling Promulgated by Major American Religious Bodies." In Appendix I of *Gambling in America*. Washington, DC: National Commission on the Policy of Gambling.

Berger, A. J., and Nancy Bruning. 1979. *Lady Luck's Companion: How to Play, How to Enjoy, How to Bet, How to Win*. New York: Harper and Row. 280 pp.

Bergler, Edmund. 1943. "The Gambler: The Misunderstood Neurotic." *Journal of Criminal Psychopathology* 4: 379–393.

Bergler, Edmund. 1957. *The Psychology of Gambling*. New York: Hill and Wang. 244 pp. Reprint, 1985. New York: International Universities Press. 224 pp.

Berman, Susan. 1981. *Easy Street: The True Story of a Mob Family*. New York: Dial Press. 214 pp.

Beyer, Andrew. 1978. *My $50,000 Year at the Races*. New York: Harcourt Brace Jovanovich. 163 pp.

Beyer, Andrew. 1993. *Beyer on Speed: New Strategies for Racetrack Betting*. Boston: Houghton Mifflin. 239 pp.

Bible, Paul A. 1986. "The Regulatory Structure of Gaming Control in Nevada: Suggestions for Reform." *Nevada Public Affairs Review* 2(2): 12–14.

Binion, Lester (Benny). 1973. *Some Recollections of a Texas and Las Vegas Gambling Operator*. Reno: University of Nevada Oral History Project. 95 pp.

Blaszczynski, A. P., A. C. Wilson, and N. McConaghy. 1986. "Sensation Seeking and Pathological Gambling." *British Journal of Addiction* 81 (February): 113–117.

Bloch, Herbert A. 1951. "The Sociology of Gambling." *American Journal of Sociology* 57 (November): 215–221.

Bloch, Herbert A. 1962. "The Gambling Business: An American Paradox." *Crime and Delinquency* 8, no. 4 (October): 355–364.

Blume, Sheila B. 1987. "Compulsive Gambling and the Medical Model." *Journal of Gambling Behavior* 3(4): 237–247.

Bolus, Jim. 1990. *The Insider's Pocket Guide to Horse Racing*. Dallas: Taylor Publishing. 150 pp.

Borg, Mary O., Paul M. Mason, and Stephen L. Shapiro. 1990 "An Economic Comparison of Gambling Behavior in Atlantic City and Las Vegas." *Public Finance Quarterly* 18 (July): 291–312.

Borg, Mary O, Paul M. Mason, and Stephen L. Shapiro. 1991. "The Incidence of Taxes on Casino Gambling: Exploiting the Tired and Poor." *American Journal of Economics and Sociology* 50 (July): 323–332.

Bortolin, Greg. 2000. "Grads in the Game." *Nevada Silver and Blue* (University of Nevada, Reno) (August): 12–30.

Bowen, John, Zheng Gu, and Vincent Eade. 1998. *The Hospitality Industry's Impact on the State of Nevada*. Las Vegas: International Gaming Institute, University of Nevada, Las Vegas. 71 pp.

Bowers, Michael W., and A. Constindina Titus. 1987. "Nevada's Black Book: The Constitutionality of Exclusion Lists in Casino Gaming Regulation." *Whittier Law Review* 9 (Spring): 313–330.

Bradshaw, Jon. 1975. *Fast Company*. New York: Harper Magazine Press. 239 pp.

Braidwaite, Larry. 1985. *Gambling: A Deadly Game*. Nashville, TN: Broadman Press. 220 pp.

Branigan, Cynthia A. 1997. *The Reign of the Greyhound*. New York: Howell Book House, Simon and Schuster. 193pp.

Brenner, Gabriel A. 1986. "Why Do People Gamble? Further Canadian Evidence." *Journal of Gambling Behavior* 2(2): 121–129.

Brenner, Reuven, and Gabrielle A. Brenner. 1990. *Gambling and Speculation: A Theory, a History, and a Future of Some Human Decisions*. New York: Cambridge University Press. 286 pp.

Brill, Steven. 1978. *The Teamsters*. New York: Simon and Schuster. 414 pp.

Broun, Heywood, and Margaret Leech. 1927. *Anthony Comstock, Boundsman of the Lord*. New York: A and C Boni. 285 pp.

Burbank, Jeff. 2000. *License to Steal: Nevada's Gaming Control System in the Megaresort Age*. Reno: University of Nevada Press. 263 pp.

Bybee, Shannon. 1988. "Problem Gambling: One View from the Gaming Industry Side." *Journal of Gambling Behavior* 4 (Winter): 301–308.

Cabot, Anthony N. 1996. *Casino Gaming: Policy, Economics, and Regulation*. Las Vegas: International Gaming Institute, University of Nevada, Las Vegas. 527 pp.

Cabot, Anthony N. 1999a. *Federal Gambling Law*. Las Vegas: Trace. 362 pp.

Cabot, Anthony N., ed. 1989. *Casino Credit and Collection Law*. Las Vegas: International Association of Gaming Attorneys. 170 pp.

Cabot, Anthony N., ed. 1999b. *Internet Gambling Report III*. Las Vegas: Trace. 400 pp.

Cabot, Anthony N., William N. Thompson, and Andrew Tottenham, eds. 1991. *International Casino Law*. 1st ed. Reno: Institute for the Study of Gambling, University of Nevada, Reno. 474 pp.

Cabot, Anthony N., William N. Thompson, and Andrew Tottenham, eds. 1993. *International Casino Law*. 2d ed. Reno: Institute for the Study of Gambling, University of Nevada, Reno. 565 pp.

Cabot, Anthony N., William N. Thompson, Andrew Tottenham, and Carl Braunlich, eds. 1999. *International*

Casino Law. 3d ed. Reno: Institute for the Study of Gambling, University of Nevada, Reno. 650 pp.

Campbell, Colin, ed. 1994. *Gambling in Canada: The Bottomline.* Burnaby, B.C.: Simon Fraser University. 198 pp.

Campbell, Colin, and John Lowman. 1989. "Gambling in Canada: Golden Goose or Trojan Horse?" In *Gambling in Canada: Golden Goose or Trojan Horse?* edited by Colin Campbell and John Lowman, xvii–xxxvii. Burnaby, B.C.: Simon Fraser University.

Campbell, Colin, and John Lowman, eds. 1989. *Gambling in Canada: Golden Goose or Trojan Horse?* Burnaby, B.C.: Simon Fraser University. 417 pp.

Campbell, Colin, and Garry Smith. 1988. "Canadian Gambling: Trends and Public Policy Issues." In *Gambling: Socioeconomic Impacts and Public Policy* (special volume of *The Annals of the American Academy of Political and Social Science*), edited by James H. Frey, 22–35. Thousand Oaks, CA: Sage.

Campbell, Felicia. 1973. "The Gambling Mystique: Mythologies and Typologies." Ph.D diss., Department of English, United States International University.

Campbell, Felicia. 1976a. "The Future of Gambling." *The Futurist,* 1 April, 84–90.

Campbell, Felicia. 1976b. "The Positive View of Gambling." In *Gambling and Society: Interdisciplinary Studies on the Subject of Gambling,* edited by William R. Eadington, 219–228. Springfield, IL: Thomas.

Cardano, Girolamo. 1961. *The Book on Games of Chance.* Translated by Sydney Henry Gould. New York: Holt, Rinehart, Winston. 57 pp.

Carroll, David. 1977. *Playboy's Illustrated Treasury of Gambling.* New York: Crown Publishers. 255 pp.

Carroll, Michael T., and Eddie Tafoya, eds. 2000. *Phenomenological Approaches to Popular Culture.* Bowling Green, OH: Bowling Green State University Popular Press. 269 pp.

Cashen, Henry C., and John C. Dill. 1992. "The Real Truth About Indian Gaming and the States." *State Legislatures* 18 (March): 23–25.

Chafetz, Henry. 1960. *Play the Devil: A History of Gambling in the United States from 1492 to 1955.* New York: Potter Publishers. 475 pp.

Chiricos, Ted. 1994. "Casinos and Crime: An Assessment of the Evidence." Manuscript.

Christiansen, Eugene Martin. 1998. "Gambling and the American Economy." In *Gambling: Socioeconomic Impacts and Public Policy* (special volume of *The Annals of the American Academy of Political and Social Science*), edited by James H. Frey, 36–52. Thousand Oaks, CA: Sage.

Christiansen, Eugene Martin. 1999. "The 1998 Gross Annual Wager." *International Gaming and Wagering Business* (August): 20ff.

Churchill, Peter. 1981. *Horse Racing.* Dorset, England: Blandford Press. 169 pp.

Clark, Thomas L. 1987. *The Dictionary of Gambling and Gaming.* Cold Spring, NY: Lexik House Publishers. 263 pp.

Clotfelter, Charles T. 1979. "On the Regressivity of State-Operated 'Number' Games." *National Tax Journal* 32: 543–547.

Clotfelter, Charles T., and Philip J. Cook. 1989. *Selling Hope: State Lotteries in America.* Cambridge: Harvard University Press. 323 pp.

Coggins, Ross, ed. 1966. *The Gambling Menace.* Nashville, TN: Broadman Press. 128 pp.

Cohen, John, and C. E. M. Hansel. 1958. "The Nature of Decisions in Gambling." *Acta Psychologica* 13 (December): 357–370.

Cohn and Wolfe. 1999. *The 1999 Industry Report: A Profile of America's Casino Gaming Industry.* Washington, DC: American Gaming Association. 97 pp.

Comings, David E. 1998. "The Molecular Genetics of Pathological Gambling." *CSN Spectrums* 6(1): 26–37.

Commission on the Review of the National Policy toward Gambling. 1976. *Gambling in America: Final Report.* Washington, DC: Government Printing Office. 1,397 pp.

Comstock, Anthony. 1967. *Traps for the Young.* Cambridge: The Belknap Press of Harvard University Press. 262 pp.

Corelli, Rae. 1994. "Betting on Casinos." *Maclean's* 107 (30 May): 26–29.

Cornell Law Project. 1977. *The Development of the Law of Gambling: 1776–1976.* Washington, DC: National Institute of Law Enforcement and Criminal Justice. 934 pp.

Culin, Stewart. 1907. *Games of the North American Indians.* Washington, DC: Government Printing Office. 846 pp.

Cullerton, Robert P. 1989. "The Prevalence Rates of Pathological Gambling: A Look at the Methods." *Journal of Gambling Behavior* 5(1): 22–41.

Current Biography. 1966, 1974, 1975, 1977, 1989. *Current Biography Yearbook.* New York: H. W. Wilson.

Custer, Robert, and Harry Milt. 1985. *When Luck Runs Out: Help for Compulsive Gamblers and Their Families.* New York: Facts on File. 239 pp.

Darder, Richard. 1991. "An Assessment of a Motivational Environment As Viewed by Dealers in the Casino Industry." M.A. Thesis, University of Nevada, Las Vegas.

David, Florence Nightingale. 1962. *Games, Gods, and Gambling: The Origins and History of Probability and Statistical Ideas from the Earliest Times to the Newtonian Era.* New York: Haefner Publishing. 275 pp.

Davies, Richard O., ed. 1999. *The Maverick Spirit: Building the New Nevada.* Reno: University of Nevada Press. 304 pp.

Davis, Berta. 1992. *Gambling in America: A Growth Industry.* New York: Franklin Watts. 112 pp.

Davis, John. 1988. *Mafia Kingfish: Carlos Marcellos and the Assassination of John F. Kennedy.* New York: McGraw-Hill. 580 pp.

Davis-Goff, Annabel, ed. 1996. *The Literary Companion to Gambling.* London: Sinclair-Stevenson. 246 pp.

DeArment, Robert K. 1982. *Knights of the Green Cloth: The Saga of Frontier Gamblers.* Norman: University of Oklahoma Press. 423 pp.

Demaris, Ovid. 1983. *The Vegas Legacy.* New York: Delacorte. 518 pp.

Demaris, Ovid. 1986. *Boardwalk Jungle: How Greed, Corruption and the Mafia Turned Atlantic City into the Boardwalk Jungle.* New York: Bantam Books. 436 pp.

Denton, Sally, and Roger Morris. 2001. *The Money and the Power: The Making of Las Vegas and Its Hold on America.* New York: Knopf. 479 pp.

Desmond, Gerald R. 1952. "Gambling among the Yakima." Ph.D. diss., Catholic University of America.

Devereux, Edward C. 1980. *Gambling and the Social Structure: A Sociological Study of Lotteries and Horse Racing in Contemporary America.* New York: Arno Press. 1,084 pp. Reprint, 1949. Ph.D. diss., Harvard University.

Devereux, George. 1950. "Psychodynamics of Mohave Gambling." *American Imago* 7, no. 1 (March): 55–65.

Devol, George H. 1887. *Forty Years a Gambler on the Mississippi.* Cincinnati: Devol and Haynes. 300 pp.

Dickerson, Mark G. 1984. *Compulsive Gamblers.* London: Longman. 156 pp.

Dixon, David. 1990. *From Prohibition to Regulation: Bookmaking, Anti Gambling and the Law.* Oxford: Clarendon Press. 408 pp.

Dombrink, John D. 1981. "Outlaw Businessmen: Organized Crime and the Legalization of Casino Gambling." Ph.D. diss., University of California, Berkeley. 362 pp.

Dombrink, John D., and William N. Thompson. 1986. "The Report of the 1986 Commission on Organized Crime and Its Implications for Commercial Gaming in America." *Nevada Public Affairs Review* 1986(2): 70–75.

Dombrink, John D., and William N. Thompson. 1990. *The Last Resort: Success and Failure in Campaigns for Casinos.* Reno: University of Nevada Press. 220 pp.

Don Passos, John R. 1904. "Gambling and Cognate Vices." *Yale Law Review* 14: 9–17.

Doocey, Paul. 1997. "A Mixed Forecast." *International Gaming and Wagering Business* 18, no. 12 (December): 1, 38–40.

Doocey, Paul. 1994. "Taking the Weakening Pulse of the Greyhound Industry." *International Gaming and Wagering Business* (July): 44–47, 60.

Dostoyevsky, Fyodor. 1972. *The Gambler.* Translated from the 1866 Russian edition by Victor Terras. Chicago: University of Chicago Press. 164 pp.

Douglass, William A. 1999. "William F. Harrah: Nevada Gaming Mogul." In *The Maverick Spirit: Building the New Nevada,* edited by Richard O. Davies, 58–73. Reno: University of Nevada Press.

Drosnin, Michael. 1985. *Citizen Hughes: In His Own Words—How Howard Hughes Tried to Buy America.* New York: Holt, Rinehart, and Winston. 532 pp.

Dunne, Joseph. 1985. "Increasing Public Awareness of Pathological Gambling Behavior: A History of the National Council on Compulsive Gambling." *Journal of Gambling Behavior* 1, no. 1 (Spring/Summer): 8–16.

Dunstan, Roger. 1997. *Gambling in California.* Sacramento: California Research Bureau, California State Library. Various pagings.

Eadington, William R. 1982. "The Evolution of Corporate Gambling in Nevada." *Nevada Review of Business and Economics* 6:1 (Summer): 13–22.

Eadington, William R. 1986. "Possible Effects of the California Lottery on Nevada's Casino Industry." *Nevada Public Affairs Review* 2: 7–11.

Eadington, William R. 1998. "Contributions of Casino Style Gambling to Local Economies." In *Gambling: Socioeconomic Impacts and Public Policy* (special volume of *The Annals of the American Academy of Political and Social Science*), edited by James H. Frey, 53–65. Thousand Oaks, CA: Sage.

Eadington, William R., ed. 1976. *Gambling and Society: Interdisciplinary Studies on the Subject of Gambling.* Springfield, IL: Thomas. 466 pp.

Eadington, William R., ed. 1982. *The Gambling Papers.* 13 vols. Reno: Bureau of Business and Economic Research, University of Nevada, Reno.

Eadington, William R., ed. 1985. *The Gambling Studies.* 5 vols. Reno: Bureau of Business and Economic Research, University of Nevada, Reno.

Eadington, William R., ed. 1988. *Gambling Research: Proceedings of the Seventh International Conference on Gambling and Risk Taking.* 5 vols. Reno: Bureau of Business and Economic Research, University of Nevada, Reno.

Eadington, William R., ed. 1990. *Indian Gaming and the Law.* Reno: Institute for the Study of Gambling, University of Nevada, Reno. 298 pp.

Eadington, William R., and Judy A. Cornelius, eds. 1991. *Gambling and Public Policy: International Perspectives.* Reno: Institute for the Study of Gambling, University of Nevada, Reno. 688 pp.

Eadington, William R., and Judy A. Cornelius, eds. 1992. *Gambling and Commercial Gaming: Essays in Business, Economics, Philosophy, and Science.* Reno: Institute of Gambling Research, University of Nevada, Reno. 656 pp.

Eadington, William R., and Judy A. Cornelius, eds. 1993. *Gambling Behavior and Problem Gambling.* Reno: Institute for the Study of Gambling, University of Nevada, Reno. 678 pp.

Eadington, William R., and James S. Hattori. 1978. "A Legislative History of Gambling in Nevada." *Nevada Review of Business and Economics* 2 (Spring): 13–17.

Eadington, William R., and John Rosecrance, eds. 1986. "Betting on the Future in Nevada and Elsewhere." Special issue of *Nevada Public Affairs Review* 2.

Earley, Pete. 2000. *Super Casino: Inside the "New" Las Vegas.* New York: Bantam Books. 386 pp.

Eder, Robert W. 1990. "Opening the Mirage: The Human Resources Challenge." *Cornell Hotel and Restaurant Administration Quarterly* 31 (August): 25–31.

Edwards, Jerome E. 1990. "From Back Alley to Main Street: Nevada's Acceptance of Gambling." *Nevada Historical Society Quarterly* 33 (Spring): 16–27.

Edwards, Jerome E. 1994. "Nevada Gambling: Just Another Business Enterprise." *Nevada Historical Society Quarterly* 37 (Summer): 101–114.

Edwards, Jerome E. 1999. "Grant Sawyer: A Liberal Governor for a Conservative State." In *The Maverick Spirit: Building the New Nevada,* edited by Richard O. Davies, 134–149. Reno: University of Nevada Press.

Eisenberg, Dennis, Uri Dan, and Eli Landau. 1978. *Meyer Lansky: Mogul of the Mob.* New York: Paddington Press. 346 pp.

Eisler, Kim Isaac. 2001. *Revenge of the Pequots: How a Small Native American Tribe Created the World's Most Profitable Casino.* New York: Simon and Schuster. 267 pp.

Elazar, Daniel. 1972. *American Federalism: A View from the States.* 2d ed. New York: Crowell. 256 pp.

Eliade, Mircea, ed. 1987. *The Encyclopedia of Religion.* 16 vols. New York: Macmillan.

Elliott, Gary. 1999. *The New Western Frontier: An Illustrated History of Las Vegas.* Carlsbad, CA: Heritage Media Corp. 232 pp.

The Evans Group. 1996. *A Study of the Economic Impact of the Gaming Industry through 2005.* Evanston, IL: The Evans Group. Various pagings.

Everson, R. C., and C. C. Jones. 1964. *The Way They Run.* Los Angeles: Techno-Graphic Publications. 209 pp.

Ezell, John S. 1960. *Fortune's Merry Wheel.* Cambridge: Harvard University Press. 331 pp.

Fabian, Ann Vincent. 1983. "Rascals and Gentlemen: The Meaning of American Gambling, 1820–1890." Ph.D. diss., Yale University. 383 pp.

Fabian, Ann Vincent. 1990. *Card Sharps, Dream Books & Bucket Shops: Gambling in 19th Century America.* Ithaca, NY: Cornell University Press. 250 pp.

Faiss, Robert D., and Anthony N. Cabot. 1986. "Gaming on the High Seas." *New York Law School Journal of International and Comparative Law* 8 (Winter): 105–107.

Farrell, Ronald A., and Carole Case. 1995. *The Black Book and the Mob: The Untold Story of the Control of Nevada's Casinos.* Madison: University of Wisconsin Press. 285 pp.

Fenich, George G., and Kathryn Hashimoto. 1996. *Casino Gaming Dictionary: Terms and Language for Managers.* Dubuque, IA: Kendall-Hunt. 105 pp.

Fey, Marshall. 1983. *Slot Machines: An Illustrated History of America's Most Popular Coin-Operated Device.* Las Vegas: Nevada Publications. 240 pp.

Findlay, John M. 1986. *People of Chance: Gambling in American Society from Jamestown to Las Vegas.* New York: Oxford University Press. 272 pp.

Flannery, Regina, and John M. Cooper. 1946. "Social Mechanisms in Gros Ventre Gambling." *Southwestern Journal of Anthropology* 2: 391–419.

Fleming, Alice M. 1978. *Something for Nothing: A History of Gambling.* New York: Delacorte Press. 149 pp.

Fortenay, Charles L. 1980. *Estes Kefauver: A Biography.* Knoxville: University of Tennessee Press. 424 pp.

France, Clemens J. 1902. "The Gambling Impulse." *American Journal of Psychology* 13 (July): 364–407.

Franckiewiez, Victor J. 1993. "The States Ante Up: An Analysis of Casino Gaming Statutes." *Loyola Law Review* 38 (Winter): 1123–1157.

Freud, Sigmund. 1974. "Dostoyevsky and Parricide." In *The Psychology of Gambling,* edited by Jon Halliday and Peter Fuller, 157–174. London: Allen Lane.

Frey, James H. 1992. "Gambling on Sport: Policy Issues." *Journal of Gambling Studies* 8(4): 351–360.

Frey, James H. 1998. "Federal Involvement in U.S. Gaming Regulation." In *Gambling: Socioeconomic Im-*

pacts and Public Policy (special volume of *The Annals of the American Academy of Political and Social Science*), edited by James H. Frey, 138–152. Thousand Oaks, CA: Sage.

Frey, James H., ed. 1998. *Gambling: Socioeconomic Impacts and Public Policy.* Special volume of *The Annals of the American Academy of Political and Social Science.* Thousand Oaks, CA: Sage. March. 240 pp.

Frey, James H., and Donald E. Carns. 1987. "The Work Environment of Gambling Casinos." *Anthropology of Work Review* 8, no. 4 (December): 38–42.

Frey, James H., and William R. Eadington, eds. 1984. *Gambling: Views from the Social Sciences.* Special volume of *The Annals of the American Academy of Political and Social Science.* Beverly Hills, CA: Sage. July. 233 pp.

Frey, James, Loren Reichert, and Kenneth Russell. 1981. "Prostitution, Business, and Police: The Maintenance of an Illegal Economy." Paper presented to the Pacific Sociological Association, July 1981, 239–249.

Friedman, Bill. 1982 Rev. ed. *Casino Management.* Secaucus, NJ: Lyle Stuart. 542 pp.

Friedman, Joseph, Simon Hakim, and J. Weinblatt. 1989. "Casino Gambling as a 'Growth Pole' Strategy and Its Effects on Crime." *Journal of Regional Science* 29 (November): 615–624.

Galliher, John, and John Cross. 1983. *Morals Legislation without Morality: The Case of Nevada.* New Brunswick, NJ: Rutgers University Press. 163 pp.

Galski, T., ed. 1987. *A Handbook on Pathological Gambling.* Springfield, IL: Charles C. Thomas. 211 pp.

Gamblers Anonymous. 1964. *The GA Group.* 2d ed. Los Angeles: Gamblers Anonymous. 14 pp.

Gamblers Anonymous. 1984. *Sharing Recovery through Gamblers Anonymous.* Los Angeles: Gamblers Anonymous. 241 pp.

"Gambling under Attack." 1996. *CQ Researcher* 6(33).

Gaminara, William. 1996. *According to Hoyle.* London: Nick Hern Books. 90 pp.

Gardiner, Alexander. 1930. *Canfield: The True Story of the Greatest Gambler.* Garden City, NY: Doubleday-Dornan. 350 pp.

Gardner, Jack. 1980. *Gambling: A Guide to Information Sources.* Detroit: Gale Research. 286 pp.

Garrison, Omar. 1970. *Howard Hughes in Las Vegas.* New York: Lyle Stuart. 293 pp.

Gazel, Ricardo. 1998. "The Economic Impacts of Casino Gambling at the State and Local Level." In *Gambling: Socioeconomic Impacts and Public Policy* (special volume of *The Annals of the American Academy of Political and Social Science),* edited by James H. Frey, 66–84. Thousand Oaks, CA: Sage.

Geis, Gilbert. 1979. *Not the Law's Business.* New York: Schocken. 262 pp.

General Conference of the United Methodist Church. 1984. *The Book of Discipline.* Nashville, TN: United Methodist Publishing. 769 pp.

Gertz, Clifford. 1972. "Deep Play: Notes on the Balinese Cockfight." *Daedalus* 10 (Winter): 1–37.

Giacopassi, David, and B. Grant Stitt. 1993. "Assessing the Impact of Casino Gambling on Crime in Mississippi." *American Journal of Criminal Justice* 18: 117–131.

Gibson, Walter. 1974. *Hoyle's Modern Encyclopedia of Card Games.* Garden City, NY: Doubleday. 398 pp.

Gold, Stephen D. 1994. "It's Not a Miracle, It's a Mirage." *State Legislatures* 20 (February): 28–31.

Goodall, Leonard E. 1994. "Marketing Behavior of Gaming Stocks: An Analysis of the First Twenty Years." *Journal of Gambling Studies* 10 (Winter): 323–337.

Goodman, Robert. 1995. *The Luck Business: The Devastating Consequences and Broken Promises of America's Gambling Explosion.* New York: Free Press. 273 pp.

Gorman, Joseph B. 1971. *Kefauver: A Political Biography.* New York: Oxford University Press. 434 pp.

Greenberg, Pam. 1991. "Midwest States Wager on Historic Riverboat Gambling." *State Legislatures* 17 (March): 17.

Greenberg, Pam, and Judy Zelio. 1992. "States and the Indian Gaming Regulatory Act." *State Legislative Report* 17 (July): 1–18.

Greenlees, E. Malcolm. 1988. *Casino Accounting and Financial Management.* Reno: University of Nevada Press. 378 pp.

Grinols, Earl L. 1994. "Bluff or Winning Hand? Riverboat Gambling and Regional Employment and Unemployment." *Illinois Business Review* 52 (Spring): 8–11.

Grinols, Earl L., and J. D. Omorov. 1996a. "Development or Dreamfield Delusions: Assessing Casino Gambling's Costs and Benefits." *Journal of Law and Commerce* 16 (Spring): 49–87.

Grinols, Earl, and J. D. Omorov. 1996b. "When Casinos Win, Who Loses?" *Illinois Business Review* 53, no. 1 (Spring): 7–11, 19.

Guild, Leo. 1973. *The World's Greatest Gambling Systems.* Los Angeles: Sirkay. 98 pp.

Hakim, Simon, and Andrew J. Buck. 1989. "Do Casinos Enhance Crime?" *Journal of Criminal Justice* 17(5): 409–416.

Halliday, Jon, and Peter Fuller, eds. 1974. *The Psychology of Gambling.* London: Allen Lane. 310 pp.

Harp, Lonnie. 1994. "States Bet on Riverboat Casinos for New Revenue." *Education Week* 13 (16 March): 13–16.

Hashimoto, Kathryn, Sheryl Fried Kline, and George Fenich, eds. 1998. *Casino Management: Past, Present, Future.* 2d ed. Dubuque, IA: Kendall-Hunt. 362 pp.

Hayano, D. M. 1982. *Poker Faces: The Life and Work of Professional Card Players.* Berkeley: University of California Press. 205 pp.

Haythorn, J. Denny. 1990. "Compulsive Gambling: A Selected, Annotated Bibliography." *Law Library Journal* 82 (Winter): 147–160.

Heineman, Mary. 1992. *Losing Your Shirt: Recovery for Compulsive Gamblers and Their Families.* Minneapolis: Compcare Publishers. 191 pp.

Henriksson, Lennart E. 1966. "Hardly a Quick Fix: Casino Gambling in Canada." *Canadian Public Policy* 22(2): 116–128.

Herald, George, and Edward Radin. 1963. *The Big Wheel: Monte Carlo's Opulent Century.* New York: Morrow. 247 pp.

Herman, Robert D. 1976. *Gamblers and Gambling: Motives, Institutions, and Controls.* Lexington, MA: D. C. Heath. 142 pp.

Herman, Robert D., ed. 1969. *Gambling.* New York: Harper and Row. 264 pp.

Hersh, Seymour. 1997. *The Darker Side of Camelot.* Boston: Little, Brown. 498 pp.

Herz, Howard, and Kregg Herz. 1995. *A Collector's Guide to Nevada Gaming Checks and Chips.* Racine, WI: Whitman Products. 288 pp.

Heubusch, Kevin. 1997. "Taking Chances on Casinos." *American Demographics* 19 (May): 35–40.

Hirshey, Gerri. 1994. "Gambling Nation." *New York Times Magazine,* 17 July, 34–44, 50–51, 53–54, 61.

Holden, Anthony. 1990. *Big Deal: A Year As a Professional Poker Player.* New York: Viking. 306 pp.

Hollingsworth, Kent. 1976. *The Kentucky Thoroughbred.* Lexington: University of Kentucky Press. 196 pp.

Holmes, William L. 1987. "Effect of Gambling Device Laws: Foreign and United States." Paper presented to the Seventh International Conference on Gambling and Risk Taking, 23 August, Reno, Nevada.

Hopkins, A. D. 1997a. "Benny Binion: He Who Has the Gold Makes the Rules." In *The Players: The Men Who Made Las Vegas,* edited by Jack Sheehan, 48–67. Reno: University of Nevada Press.

Hopkins, A. D. 1997b. "Jay Sarno: He Came to Play." In *The Players: The Men Who Made Las Vegas,* edited by Jack Sheehan, 92–103. Reno: University of Nevada Press.

Hopkins, A. D., and K. J. Evans. 1999. *The First 100: Portraits of the Men and Women Who Shaped Las Vegas.* Las Vegas: Huntington Press. 272 pp.

Hopkins, Samuel. 1835. *The Evils of Gambling: A Sermon.* Montpelier, VT: E. F. Walton and Son. 18 pp.

Hotaling, Edward. 1995. *They're Off! Horse Racing at Saratoga.* Syracuse, NY: Syracuse University Press. 368 pp.

Hoyle, Edmund. 1748. *A Short History on the Game of Whist.* London: T. Osborne.

Hsu, Cathy H. C., ed. 1999. *Legalized Gambling in the United States: The Economic and Social Impact.* New York: Haworth Hospitality Press. 264 pp.

Huizinga, Johan. 1955. *Homo Ludens: A Study of the Play-Element in Culture.* Boston: Beacon Press. 220 pp.

Hulse, James W. 1986. *Forty Years in the Wilderness.* Reno: University of Nevada Press. 141 pp.

Hulse, James W. 1991. *The Silver State.* Reno: University of Nevada Press.

Hulse, James W. 1997. "Nevada and the Twenty-First Century." In *Towards 2000: Public Policy in Nevada,* edited by Dennis L. Soden and Eric Herzik, 1–14. Dubuque, IA: Kendall-Hunt.

Ignatin, George. 1984. "Sports Betting." In *Gambling: Views from the Social Sciences* (special volume of *The Annals of the American Academy of Political and Social Science*), edited by James H. Frey and William R. Eadington, 168–177. Beverly Hills, CA: Sage.

Jackson, Richard, and Lloyd Hudman. 1987. "Border Towns, Gambling, and the Mormon Culture Region." *Journal of Cultural Geography* 8: 35–48.

Jackson, Stanley. 1975. *Inside Monte Carlo.* New York: Stein and Day. 278 pp.

Jacobs, Durand F. 1986. "A General Theory of Addictions: A New Theoretical Model." *Journal of Gambling Behavior* 2 (Spring): 15–31.

Jacobs, Louis. 1973. *What Does Judaism Say About . . .?* Jerusalem: Keter Publishing. 346 pp.

Jacoby, Oswald. 1947. *How to Figure the Odds.* Garden City, N Y: Doubleday. 215 pp.

Jacoby, Oswald. 1963. *Oswald Jacoby on Gambling.* Garden City, NY: Doubleday. 192 pp.

Jensen, Marten. 2000. *Secrets of the New Casino Games.* New York: Cardoza Publishing. 144 pp.

Johnson, Cathy M., and Kenneth J. Meier. 1990. "The Wages of Sin: Taxing America's Legal Vices." *Western Political Quarterly* 43 (September): 577–595.

Johnson, Spencer. 1998. *Who Moved My Cheese?* New York: G. P. Putnam. 94 pp.

Johnston, David. 1992. *Temples of Chance: How America Inc. Bought out Murder Inc. to Win Control of the Casino Business.* New York: Doubleday. 312 pp.

Jones, J. Philip. 1973. *Gambling: Yesterday, and Today, A Complete History.* Devon, England: David and Charles, 192 pp.

Kallick-Kaufman, Maureen. 1979. "The Micro and Macro Dimensions of Gambling in the United States." *Journal of Social Issues* 35(24): 7–26.

Kaplan, H. Roy. 1978. *Lottery Winners: How They Won and How Winning Changed Their Lives.* New York: Harper and Row. 173 pp.

Karcher, Alan. 1989. *Lotteries.* New Brunswick, NJ: Transaction Publishers. 116 pp.

Karlen, Neal. 1990. "Dice, Drinks and a Degree." *Rolling Stone* 588 (4 October): 144–145, 147–148.

Karlins, Marvin. 1983. *Psyching Out Vegas: Winning through Psychology in the Casinos of the World.* Van Nuys, CA: Gambling Times. 283 pp.

Katz, Jeffrey L. 1991. "Raising the Stakes on Legal Gambling." *Governing* 3 (February): 17, 19–20.

Keever, William R. 1984. *The Gambling Times Guide to Jai Alai.* Hollywood, CA: Gambling Times. 2–4 pp.

Kefauver, Estes. 1951. *Crime in America.* Garden City, NY: Doubleday. 333 pp.

Kelly, Joseph M. 2000. "Internet Gambling Law." *William Mitchell Law Review* 26: 118–177.

Kennedy, Robert. 1960. *The Enemy Within.* New York: Harper. 338 pp.

Kimball, Spencer, ed. 1982. *The Teachings of Spencer W. Kimball.* Salt Lake City, UT: Deseret Book Company. 664 pp.

Kindt, John. 1994. "Increased Crime and Legalized Gambling Operations." *Criminal Law Bulletin* 43: 538–539.

Kindt, John. 1995. "U.S. National Security and the Strategic Economic Base: The Business/Economic Impacts of the Legalization of Gambling Activities." *Saint Louis University Law Review* 39: 567–584.

Kindt, John. 1998. "Follow the Money: Gambling, Ethics and Subpoenas." In *Gambling: Socioeconomic Impacts and Public* Policy (special volume of *The Annals of the American Academy of Political and Social Science*), edited by James H. Frey, 86–97. Thousand Oaks, CA: Sage.

King, R. T., ed. 1992. *Playing the Cards That Are Dealt: Mead Dixon, the Law, and Casino Gambling.* Reno: University of Nevada Oral History Program. 276 pp.

King, R. T., ed. 1993. *Hang Tough! Grant Sawyer: An Activist in the Governor's Mansion.* Reno: University of Nevada Oral History Program. 256 pp.

King, R. T., ed. 1994. *Always Bet on the Butcher: Warren Nelson and Casino Gambling, 1930–1980.* Reno: University of Nevada Oral History Program. 242 pp.

King, Rufus. 1969. *Gambling and Organized Crime.* Washington, DC: Public Affairs Press. 239 pp.

Klein, Howard J., and Gary Selesner. 1983. "Results of the First Gallup Organization Study of Public Attitudes toward Legalized Gambling." *Gambling Business Magazine* 3, November 5–7; 48–49.

Kling, Dwayne. 2000. *The Rise of the Biggest Little City: An Encyclopedic History of Reno Gaming, 1931–1981.* Reno: University of Nevada Press. 226 pp.

Knapp, Bettina L. 2000. *Gambling, Game, and Psyche.* Albany: State University of New York Press. 308 pp.

Knapp, Terry. 1985. "Review of *The Chase.*" *Journal of Gambling Behavior* 3 (Winter): 288–291.

Knapp Commission. 1972. *The Knapp Commission Report on Police Corruption.* New York: George Braziller. 283 pp.

Konik, Michael. 1996. "The Grand Old Man." *Poker World,* February, 447.

Kurland, Gerald. 1972. *James Hoffa.* Charlotteville, NY: SamHar Press. 32 pp.

Kusyszyn, Igor, ed. 1972. *Studies in the Psychology of Gambling.* New York: Simon and Schuster. 172 pp.

Kusyszyn, Igor, and R. Rutter. 1985. "Personality Characteristics of Heavy Gamblers." *Journal of Gambling Behavior* 1: 59–63.

Lacey, Robert. 1991. *Little Man: Meyer Lansky and the Gangster Life.* Boston: Little, Brown. 547 pp.

Ladouceur, Robert. 1996. "The Prevalence of Pathological Gambling in Canada." *Journal of Gambling Studies* 12(2): 129–142.

Ladouceur, Robert, et al. 1987. "Risk Taking Behavior in Gamblers and Non-Gamblers During Prolonged Exposure." *Journal of Gambling Behavior* 3 (Summer): 115–122.

Ladouceur, Robert, et al. 1994. "Social Cost of Pathological Gambling." *Journal of Gambling Studies* 10 (Winter): 399–409.

La Fleur, Terri. 1992. "Charting the Growth of Video Lottery." *International Gaming and Wagering Business* (August-September): 1, 62, 64–65.

Lalli, Sergio. 1997. "Howard Hughes in Las Vegas." In *The Players: The Men Who Made Las Vegas,* edited by Jack Sheehan, 133–158. Reno: University of Nevada Press.

Land, Barbara, and Myrick Land. 1995. *A Short History of Reno.* Reno: University of Nevada Press. 130 pp.

Land, Barbara, and Myrick Land. 1999. 2d. *A Short History of Las Vegas.* Reno: University of Nevada Press. 240 pp.

Las Vegas Convention and Visitors Authority [LVCVA]. 1999. *1999 Visitor Profile.* Las Vegas: LVCVA. 83 pp.

Lee, Barbara A., and James Chelius. 1989. "Government Regulation of Labor-Management Corruption: The Casino Industry Experience in New Jersey." *Industrial and Labor Relations Review* 42 (July): 536–548.

Lehne, Richard. 1986. *Casino Policy.* New Brunswick, NJ: Rutgers University Press. 268 pp.

Lemmel, Maurice. 1966. *Gambling: Nevada Style.* Garden City, NY: Dolphin Books. 217 pp.

Lesieur, Henry R. 1979. "The Compulsive Gambler's Spiral of Options and Involvement." *Psychiatry* 42: 79–87.

Lesieur, Henry R. 1984. *The Chase: The Career of the Compulsive Gambler.* 2d ed. Cambridge, MA: Schenkman Publishing. 323 pp.

Lesieur, Henry R. 1992. "Compulsive Gambling." *Society,* May-June, 43–50.

Lesieur, Henry R. 1998. "Costs and Treatment of Pathological Gambling." In *Gambling: Socioeconomic Impacts and Public Policy* (special volume of *The Annals of the American Academy of Political and Social Science*), edited by James H. Frey, 153–171. Thousand Oaks, CA: Sage.

Lesieur, Henry R., and Sheila B. Blume. 1987. "The South Oaks Gambling Screen (SOGS)." *American Journal of Psychiatry* 144(9): 1184–1188.

Lesieur, Henry, and Robert L. Custer. 1984. "Pathological Gambling: Roots, Phases, and Treatment." In *Gambling: Views from the Social Sciences* (special volume of *The Annals of the American Academy of Political and Social Science*), edited by James H. Frey and William R. Eadington, 146–156. Beverly Hills, CA: Sage.

Lesieur, Henry R., and Kenneth Puig. 1987. "Insurance Problems and Pathological Gambling." *Journal of Gambling Behavior* 3(2): 123–136.

Lesieur, Henry R., and Richard J. Rosenthal. 1991. "Pathological Gambling: A Review of the Literature." *Journal of Gambling Studies* 7 (Spring): 5–39.

Lester, David, ed. 1979. *Gambling Today.* Springfield, IL: Thomas. 148 pp.

Levinson, David. 1996. *Religion: A Cross-Cultural Encyclopedia.* Santa Barbara, CA: ABC-CLIO. 288 pp.

Lionel, Sawyer, and Collins. 1995. *Nevada Gaming Law.* 2d ed. Las Vegas, NV: Lionel, Sawyer, and Collins. 442 pp.

Litsky, Frank. 1975. *Superstars.* Secaucus, NJ: Derbibooks. 351 pp.

Long, Patrick, Jo Clark, and Derick Liston. 1994. *Win, Lose, or Draw? Gambling with America's Small Towns.* Washington, DC: Aspen Institute. 97 pp.

Longstreet, Stephen. 1977. *Win or Lose: A Social History of Gambling in America.* Indianapolis, IN: Bobbs-Merrill. 268 pp.

Lorber, Leah L. 1993. "State Rights, Tribal Sovereignty, and the White Man's Firewater: State Prohibition of Gambling on New Indian Lands." *Indian Law Journal* 69 (Winter): 255–274.

Lorenz, Valerie C. 1987. "Family Dynamics of Pathological Gamblers." In *A Handbook on Pathological Gambling,* edited by T. Galski, 71–88. Springfield, IL: Charles C. Thomas.

Lorenz, Valerie C., and D. E. Shuttlesworth. 1988. "The Impact of Pathological Gambling on the Spouse of the Gambler." *Journal of Gambling Behavior* 4: 13–26.

Ludlow, Daniel H. 1992. *Encyclopedia of Mormonism.* 5 vols. New York: Macmillan.

Lutrin, Carl, and William N. Thompson. 2000. "A Tale of Two States: Political Cultures Converge around a Divisive Issue: California, Nevada, and Gambling." Paper prepared for the Western Political Science Association, 26 March, San Jose, California.

Lyons, Paul. 1999. *The Quotable Gambler.* New York: Lyons Press. 326 pp.

Maas, Peter. 1973. *Serpico.* New York: Viking Press. 314 pp.

MacDougal, Ernest D. 1936. *Speculation and Gambling.* Boston: Stratford. 252 pp.

Magnuson, Jon. 1994. "Casino Wars: Ethics and Economics in Indian Country." *Christian Century* 111 (16 February): 169–171.

Maheu, Robert, and Richard Hack. 1992. *Next to Hughes: Behind the Power and Tragic Downfall of Howard Hughes by His Closest Advisor.* New York: HarperCollins. 289 pp.

Mahon, Gigi. 1980. *The Company That Bought the Boardwalk.* New York: Random House. 262 pp.

Mandel, Leon. 1982. *William Fisk Harrah: The Life and Times of a Gambling Magnate.* Garden City, NY: Doubleday. 223 pp.

Mangalmurti, Sandeep, and Robert Allan Cooke. 1981. *State Lotteries: Seducing the Less Fortunate?* Heartland Policy Study 35). Chicago: Heartland Institute. 38 pp.

Mangione, Thomas W., and Floyd J. Fowler Jr. 1979. "Enforcing the Gambling Laws." *Journal of Social Issues* 35(3): 115–128.

Manness, Garth. 1989. "Views from the Regulators: Manitoba's Situation." In *Gambling in Canada: Golden Goose or Trojan Horse?* edited by Colin Campbell and John Lowman, 69–76. Burnaby, B.C.: Simon Fraser University.

Margolis, Jeremy D. 1997. *Casinos and Crime: An Analysis of the Evidence.* Washington, DC: American Gaming Association. 67 pp.

Martinez, Tomas M. 1983. *The Gambling Scene: Why People Gamble.* Springfield, IL: Charles C. Thomas. 231 pp.

McBride, Dennis. 1981. "Boulder City: How It Began." Manuscript. Special Collections Library, University of Nevada, Las Vegas. 106 pp.

McCall, William W. 1989. "Operational Review of Gaming in Alberta 1978 to 1987." In *Gambling in Canada: Golden Goose or Trojan Horse?* edited by Colin Campbell and John Lowman, 77–92. Burnaby, B.C.: Simon Fraser University.

McCulloch, Anne Merline. 1994. "The Politics of Indian Gaming: Tribe/State Relations and American Federalism." *Publius: The Journal of Federalism* 24 (Summer): 99–112.

McMillen, Jan. 1996. *Gambling Cultures: Studies in History and Interpretation.* London: Routledge. 321 pp.

Merchant, Larry. 1973. *The National Football Lottery.* New York: Holt, Rinehart and Winston. 325 pp.

Messick, Hank. 1971. *Lansky.* New York: Berkeley Medallion. 302 pp.

Midwest Hospitality Advisors. 1992. *Impact: Indian Gaming in the State of Minnesota.* Minneapolis, MN: Marquette Partners. 30 pp.

Miller, Len. 1983. *Gambling Times Guide to Casino Games.* Secaucus, NJ: Lyle Stuart. 168 pp.

Miller, William J., and Martin D. Schwartz. 1998. "Casino Gambling and Street Crime." In *Gambling: Socioeconomic Impacts and Public Policy* (special volume of *The Annals of the American Academy of Political and Social Science*), edited by James H. Frey, 124–137. Thousand Oaks, CA: Sage.

Millman, Chad. 2001. *The Odds: One Season, Three Gamblers, and the Death of Their Las Vegas.* New York: Public Affairs. 260 pp.

Minnesota State Lottery. 1994. *Gambling in Minnesota.* Roseville: Minnesota State Lottery. 46 pp.

Mirkovich, Thomas R., and Allison A. Cowgill. 1996. *Casino Gambling in the United States.* Lanham, MD: Scarecrow Press. 432 pp.

Mitler, Ernest A. *Legal and Administrative Problems in the Control of Legalized Gambling: A Comparative Study.* 1986. Ph.D. diss., Linacre College, Oxford University. 380 pp.

Moehring, Eugene P. 1989. *Resort City in the Sunset: Las Vegas 1930–1970.* Reno: University of Nevada Press. 359 pp.

Moehring, Eugene P. 2000. *Resort City in the Sunset: Las Vegas 1930–2000.* 2d ed. Reno: University of Nevada Press. 359 pp.

Mok, Waiman P., and Joseph Habra. 1991. "Age and Gambling Behavior: A Declining and Shifting Pattern of Participation." *Journal of Gambling Studies* 7, no. 4, (Winter): 313–336.

Moldea, Dan E. 1979. *Interference: How Organized Crime Influences Professional Football.* New York: William Morrow. 512 pp.

Moody, Bill, and A. D. Hopkins. 1997. "Jackie Gaughan: Keeping the Faith on Fremont Street." In *The Players: The Men Who Made Las Vegas,* edited by Jack Sheehan, 120–132. Reno: University of Nevada Press.

Moody, Eric N. 1994. "Nevada's Legalization of Casino Gambling in 1931: Purely a Business Proposition." *Nevada Historical Society Quarterly* 27 (Summer): 79–100.

Moody, Gordon E. 1990. *Quit Compulsive Gambling: The Action Plan for Gamblers and Their Families.* Wellingborough, Northhampton, England: Thorsons. 144 pp.

Moore, William Howard. 1974. *The Kefauver Committee and the Politics of Crime, 1950–1952.* Columbia: University of Missouri Press. 269 pp.

Morehead, Albert H., Richard L. Frey, and Geoffrey Mott-Smith. 1964. *The New Complete Hoyle.* Garden City, NY: Doubleday. 740 pp.

Morrison, Robert S. 1994. *High Stakes to High Risk: The Strange Story of Resorts International and the Taj Mahal.* Ashtabula, OH: Lake Erie Press. 378 pp.

National Collegiate Athletic Association [NCAA]. 1999. *Don't Bet on It: Don't Gamble on Your Future.* Indianapolis: NCAA. 16 pp.

National Gambling Impact Study Commission [NGISC]. 1999. *Final Report.* Washington, DC: NGISC. Various paging.

National Opinion Research Center. 1999. "Gambling Impact and Behavior Study." *Report to the National Gambling Impact Study Commission.*

National Research Council. 1999. *Pathological Gambling: A Critical Review.* Washington, DC: National Academy Press. 340 pp.

Navasky, Victor S. 1971. *Kennedy Justice.* New York: Antheneum Press. 482 pp.

The New Catholic Encyclopedia. 1967. 17 vols. New York: McGraw-Hill.

Newman, David, ed. 1962. *Esquire's Book of Gambling.* New York: Harper and Row. 333 pp.

Niebuhr, H. Richard. 1951. *Christ and Culture.* New York: Harper and Row. 259 pp.

O'Brien, Thomas. 1985. "Perspectives on the Regulation of Casino Gaming in Atlantic City, New Jersey." In *The Gambling Studies,* edited by William R. Eadington, vol. 1, 121–127. Reno: Bureau of Business and Economic Research, University of Nevada, Reno.

O'Brien, Timothy L. 1998. *Bad Bet: The Inside Story of the Glamour, Glitz, and Danger of America's Gambling Industry.* New York: Random House. 339 pp.

Ochrym, Ronald George, and Clifton Park. 1990. "Street Crime, Tourism and Casinos: An Empirical Comparison." *Journal of Gambling Studies* 6 (Summer): 127–138.

Odessky, Dick. 1999. *Fly on the Wall: Recollection of Las Vegas' Good Old, Bad Old Days.* Las Vegas: Huntington Press Publishing. 245 pp.

O'Donnell, John R., and James Rutherford. 1991. *Trumped: The Inside Story of the Real Donald Trump, His Cunning Rise & Spectacular Fall.* New York: Simon and Schuster. 348 pp.

Oldman, D. J. 1974. "Chance and Skill: A Study of Roulette." *Sociology* 8: 407–426.

Oldman, D. J. 1978. "Compulsive Gamblers." *Sociological Review* 26: 349–371.

Ortiz, Darwin. 1984. *Gambling Scams: How They Work, How to Detect Them, How to Protect Yourself.* New York: Dodd, Mead. 262 pp.

Osborne, Walter D. 1966. *Horseracing.* New York: Pocket Books. 96 pp.

Ostrander, Gilman. 1966. *Nevada: The Great Rotten Borough 1859–1964.* New York: Alfred A. Knopf. 247 pp.

Painton, Pricilla. 1989. "Boardwalk of Broken Dreams." *Time* 134 (29 September): 64–69.

Palermo, David. 1997. "Kerkorian: The Reticent Billionaire." In *The Players: The Men Who Made Las Vegas,* edited by Jack Sheehan, 159–167. Reno: University of Nevada Press.

Palermo, David. 1998. "The Secret Slot Market." *International Gaming and Wagering Business* (December): 1, 18–22.

Parmer, Charles B. 1939. *For Gold and Glory.* New York: Carrick and Evans. 352 pp.

Pasquaretta, Paul. 1994. "On the 'Indianness' of Bingo: Gambling and the Native American Community." *Critical Inquiry* 20 (Summer): 694–714.

Patterson, Jerry L., and Walter Jaye. 1983. *Casino Gambling.* New York: Putnam. 240 pp.

Patterson, Jerry L., and Jack Painter. 1985. *Sports Betting: A Winner's Handbook.* New York: Putnam. 251 pp.

Peterson, Virgil W. 1951. *Gambling: Should It Be Legalized?* Springfield, IL: Charles C. Thomas. 158 pp.

Peterson, Virgil W. 1965. "A Look at Legalized Gambling." *Christian Century* 82 (26 May): 667.

Ploscowe, Morris, and Edwin J. Lukas, eds. 1950. *Gambling* Special volume of *The Annals of the American Academy of Political and Social Science.* Philadelphia: The American Academy of Political and Social Science. 209 pp.

Politizer, Robert M., James S. Morrow, and Sandra B. Leavey. 1981. "Report on the Social Cost of Pathological Gambling and the Cost-Benefit Effectiveness of Treatment." Paper presented to the Fifth National Conference on Gambling and Risk Taking, 22 October, Reno, Nevada.

Pollock, Michael. 1987. *Hostage to Fortune: Atlantic City and Casino Gambling.* Princeton, NJ: Center for Analysis of Public Issues. 204 pp.

Ponting, J. Rick. 1994. "The Paradox of on Reserve Casino Gambling: Musings of a Nervous Sociologist." In *Gambling in Canada: The Bottomline,* edited by Colin Campbell, 57–68. Burnaby, B.C.: Simon Fraser University.

Popkin, James. 1993a. "Gambling with the Mob? Wise Guys Have Set Their Sights on the Booming Indian Casino Business." *U.S. News and World Report,* 115 (23 August): 30–32.

Popkin, James. 1993b. "Tricks of the Trade." *U.S. News and World Report,* 116 (14 March): 48–52.

Popkin, James, and Ketia Hetter. 1994. "America's Gambling Craze." *U.S. News and World Report,* 116 (14 March): 42–43, 46.

Powell, Colin. 1995. *My American Journey.* New York: Random House. 643 pp.

President's Commission on Law Enforcement and Administration of Justice. 1967. *The Challenge of Crime in a Free Society.* Washington, DC: U.S. Government Printing Office. 340 pp.

Presswood, Gary. 1992. "Howard Hughes: Alive and Well in Las Vegas." Manuscript. Las Vegas: University of Nevada, Las Vegas, Department of Public Administration.

Preston, Frederick W., Bo J. Bernhard, Robert E. Hunter, and Shannon L Bybee. 1998. "Gambling as Stigmatized Behavior and the Law." In *Gambling: Socioeconomic Impacts and Public Policy* (special volume of *The Annals of the American Academy of Political and Social Science*), edited by James H. Frey, 186–196. Thousand Oaks, CA: Sage.

Proffitt, T. D. 1994. *Tijuana: The History of a Mexican Metropolis.* San Diego, CA: San Diego State University Press. 411 pp.

Prowse, Peter. 1994. "An Operator's View." In *Gambling in Canada: The Bottomline,* edited by Colin Campbell, 105–110. Burnaby, B.C.: Simon Fraser University.

Puzo, Mario. 1977. *Inside Las Vegas.* New York: Gosset and Dunlap. 253 pp.

Reid, Ed, and Ovid Demaris. 1963. *The Green Felt Jungle.* New York: Trident Press. 242 pp. Reprint, 1994. New York: Pocket Books. 244 pp.

Rice, Cy. 1969. *Nick The Greek: King of the Gamblers.* New York: Funk and Wagnalls. 235 pp.

Rich, Wilbur C. 1990. "The Politics of Casino Gambling Detroit Style." *Urban Affairs Quarterly,* 26 (December): 274–298.

Roberts, John M., Malcolm Arth, and Robert R. Bush. 1959. "Games in Culture." *American Anthropologist* 61: 597–605.

Robertson, William H. P. 1964. *A History of Thoroughbred Racing in America.* Englewood Cliffs, NJ: Prentice-Hall. 621 pp.

Roehl, Wesley S. 1994. "Gambling as a Tourist Attraction: Trends and Issues for the 21st Century." In *Tourism: The State of the Art,* edited by A. V. Seaton, 155–168. Chichester, England: John Wiley. 867 pp.

Rombola, Ferde. 1984. *The Book on Bookmaking.* Hollywood, CA: Romford Press. 147 pp.

Romero, John. 1994. *Casino Marketing.* New York: International Gaming and Wagering Business. 268 pp.

Rose, I. Nelson. 1980. "The Legalization and Control of Casino Gambling." *Fordham Law Review,* 8: 245–300.

Rose, I. Nelson. 1986a. "Turning in the High Rollers: The Impact of the New Cash Regulations." *Nevada Public Affairs Review,* 2: 21–26.

Rose, I. Nelson. 1986b. *Gambling and the Law.* Hollywood, CA: Gambling Times Press. 304 pp.

Rose, I. Nelson. 1992. "The Future of Indian Gaming." *Journal of Gambling Studies* 8 (Winter): 383–399.

Rose, Pete, and Roger Kahn. 1989. *Pete Rose: My Story.* New York: Macmillan. 300 pp.

Rosecrance, John. 1985a. *The Degenerates of Lake Tahoe.* New York: Peter Lang. 169 pp.

Rosecrance, John. 1985b. "Compulsive Gambling and the Medicalization of Deviance." *Social Problems* 32: 275–284.

Rosecrance, John. 1986a. "Why Regular Gamblers Don't Quit: A Sociological Perspective." *Sociological Perspectives* 29: 357–378.

Rosecrance, John. 1986b. "The Next Best Thing: A Study of Problem Gambling." *The International Journal of the Addictions* 12: 1727–1739.

Rosecrance, John. 1988. *Gambling without Guilt: The Legitimation of an American Pastime.* Pacific Grove, CA: Brooks-Cole. 174 pp.

Rosen, Charles. 1978. *Scandals of '51: How Gamblers Almost Killed College Basketball.* New York: Henry Holt. 262 pp.

Rosenthal, R. J. 1992. "Pathological Gambling." *Psychiatric Annals* 22: 72–78.

Roske, Ralph J. 1990. "Gambling in Nevada: The Early Years, 1861–1931." *Nevada Historical Society Quarterly* 33 (Spring): 28–40.

Ross, Gary. 1987. *No Limit: The Incredible Obsession of Brian Molony.* New York: William Morrow. 301 pp. (Published in Canada in 1987 as *Stung: The Incredible Obsession of Brian Molony.* Toronto: Stoddart Publishers. 301 pp.)

Rowley, William D. 1984. *Reno, Hub of Washoe County.* Woodland Hills, CA: Windsor Publications. 128 pp.

Roxborough, Michael (Roxy), and Mike Rhoden. 1989. *Race and Sports Book Management.* Las Vegas: Gambler's Book Club. 128 pp.

Royden, Halsey L., Patrick Suppes, and Karol Walsh. 1959. "A Model for the Experimental Measurement of the Utility of Gambling." *Behavioral Science* 4: 11–18.

Rubin, Max. 1994. *Comp City: A Guide to Free Las Vegas Vacations.* Las Vegas: Huntington Press. 296 pp.

Samuelson, Paul A. 1976. *Economics.* 10th ed. New York: McGraw Hill. 917 pp.

Saskatchewan Tourism Authority [STA]. 1996. *Report on Casino Gambling.* Regina: STA. 16 pp.

Sasuly, Richard. 1982. *Bookies and Bettors: Two Hundred Years of Gambling.* New York: Henry Holt. 266 pp.

Scarne, John. 1978. *Scarne's Guide to Casino Gambling.* New York: Simon and Schuster. 352 pp.

Scarne, John. 1986. *Scarne's New Complete Guide to Gambling.* Fireside Edition. New York: Simon and Schuster. 871 pp.

Schacht, Joseph. 1964. *An Introduction to Islamic Law.* Oxford: Clarendon Press. 304 pp.

Schatzberg, Rufus. 1993. *Black Organized Crime in Harlem, 1820–1930.* New York: Garland Publishing. 157 pp.

Schatzberg, Rufus. 1996. *African American Organized Crime: A Social History.* New York: Garland Publishing. 264 pp.

Schlosser, Eric. 1997. "The Business of Pornography: Who's Making the Money." *U.S. News and World Report* 22, 10 February, 42–50.

Schrag, Peter. 1998. *Paradise Lost: California's Experience, America's Future.* New York: New Press. 344 pp.

Schwartz, Rosalie. 1997. *Pleasure Island: Tourism and Temptation in Cuba.* Lincoln: University of Nevada Press. 239 pp.

Schwer, Keith. 1989. "Why the Las Vegas Multiplier Is Less than 3." *Las Vegas Metropolitan Economic Indicators.* Las Vegas: Center for Business and Economic Research, University of Nevada, Las Vegas, 1–4.

Schwer, R. Keith, Charles Moseley, and William N. Thompson. 2001. "Gambling and the Elderly in Las Vegas," Draft Manuscript, Center for Business and Economic Research, University of Nevada, Las Vegas.

Scoblete, Frank. 1991. *Beat the Craps out of the Casinos: How to Play Craps and Win.* Chicago: Bonus Books. 162 pp.

Scott, Marvin B. 1968. *The Racing Game.* Chicago: Aldine. 186 pp.

Seal, Mark. 1997. "Steve Wynn: King of Wow." In *The Players: The Men Who Made Las Vegas,* edited by Jack Sheehan, 168–182. Reno: University of Nevada Press.

Shaffer, Howard J., Matthew N. Hall, and Joni Vander Bilt. 1997. *Estimating the Prevalence of Disordered Gambling Behavior in the United States and Canada: A Meta-analysis.* Boston: Harvard Medical School. 122 pp.

Shaffer, Howard J., Sharon A. Stein, Blase Gambino, and Thomas N. Cummings, eds. 1989. *Compulsive Gambling: Theory, Research, and Practice.* Lexington, MA: Lexington Books. 350 pp.

Shapiro, Joseph P. 1996. "America's Gambling Fever." *U.S. News and World Report,* v. 120: 15 January, 52–61.

Sheehan, Jack. 1997. "Sam Boyd's Quiet Legacy." In *The Players: The Men Who Made Las Vegas,* edited by Jack Sheehan, 104–119. Reno: University of Nevada Press.

Sheehan, Jack, ed. 1997. *The Players: The Men Who Made Las Vegas.* Reno: University of Nevada Press. 224 pp.

Sifakis, Carl. 1990. *The Encyclopedia of Gambling.* New York: Facts on File. 340 pp.

Silberstang, Edwin. 1972. *Playboy's Book of Games.* Chicago: Playboy Press. 511 pp.

Silberstang, Edwin. 1980. *Playboy's Guide to Casino Gambling.* Chicago: Playboy Press. 448 pp.

Silberstang, Edwin. 1985. *The Winner's Guide to Sports Betting.* New York: New American Library. 363 pp.

Simurda, Stephen J. 1994. "When Gambling Comes to Town." *Columbia Journalism Review* 32 (January): 36–38.

Skolnick, Jerome H. 1978. *House of Cards: Legalization and Control of Casino Gambling.* Boston: Little, Brown. 382 pp.

Skolnick, Jerome H. 1979. "The Social Risks of Casino Gambling." *Psychology Today,* July, 22–27.

Sloan, Jim. 1993. *Nevada: True Tales from the Neon Wilderness.* Salt Lake City: University of Utah Press. 209 pp.

Sloane, Arthur A. 1991. *Hoffa.* Cambridge: MIT Press. 430 pp.

Smith, Garry, and Tom Hinch. 1996. "Canadian Casinos as Tourist Attractions: Chasing the Pot of Gold." *Journal of Travel Research* 34(3): 37–45.

Smith, Garry, Bonnie Williams, and Robert Pitter. 1989. "How Alberta Amateur Sports Groups Prosper through Legalized Gambling." In *Gambling in Canada: Golden Goose or Trojan Horse?* edited by Colin Campbell and John Lowman, 323–333. Burnaby, B.C. Simon Fraser University.

Smith, Garry, and Harold Wynne. 1999. *Gambling and Crime in Western Canada: Exploring Myth and Reality.* Calgary, Alta.: Canada West Foundation. 128 pp.

Smith, Harold S. 1961. *I Want to Quit Winners.* Englewood Cliffs, NJ: Prentice-Hall. 336 pp.

Smith, John L. 1995. *Running Scared: The Life and Treacherous Times of Steven Wynn.* New York: Barricade Books. 352 pp.

Smith, John L. 1997a. "Moe Dalitz and the Desert." In *The Players: The Men Who Made Las Vegas,* edited by Jack Sheehan, 35–47. Reno: University of Nevada Press.

Smith, John L. 1997b. "The Ghost of Ben Siegel." In *The Players: The Men Who Made Las Vegas,* edited by Jack Sheehan, 81–91. Reno: University of Nevada Press.

Smith, Sharon B. 1998. *The Complete Idiot's Guide to Betting on Horses.* New York: Alpha Books. 268 pp.

Social Science Research Center, Mississippi State University. 1995. *The National Gambling Survey.* State College: Mississippi State University.

Soden, Dennis L., and Eric Herzik, eds. 1997. *Towards 2000: Public Policy in Nevada.* Dubuque, IA: Kendall-Hunt. 290 pp.

Sokolow, Gary. 1990. "The Future of Gambling in Indian Country." *American Indian Law Review* 15: 151–181.

Spanier, David. 1977. *Total Poker.* New York: Simon and Schuster. 255 pp.

Spanier, David. 1992. *Welcome to the Pleasuredome: Inside Las Vegas.* Reno: University of Nevada Press. 275 pp.

Spanier, David. 1994. *Inside the Gambler's Mind.* Reno: University of Nevada Press. 240 pp.

Spanier, David. 1995. "The Joy of Gambling." *Wilson Quarterly* 19: 34–40.

Spencer, Donald D. 1994. *Casino Chip Collecting.* Ormond Beach, FL: Camelot Publishing. 120 pp.

Starkey, L. M. 1964. *Money, Mania, and Morals.* New York: Abington Press. 128 pp.

Stein, Jean. 1970. *American Journey: The Times of Robert Kennedy.* New York: Harcourt Brace Jovanovich. 372 pp.

Sternlieb, George, and James W. Hughes. 1983. *The Atlantic City Gamble: A Twentieth Century Fund Report.* Cambridge: Harvard University Press. 215 pp.

Stinchfield, Randy, and Ken C. Winters. 1998. "Gambling and Problem Gambling among Youths." In *Gambling: Socioeconomic Impacts and Public Policy* (special volume of *The Annals of the American Academy of Political and Social Science*), edited by James H. Frey, 172–185. Tousand Oaks, CA: Sage.

Stokowski, Patricia A. 1992. "The Colorado Gambling Boom: An Experiment in Rural Community Development." *Small Town* 22 (May-June): 12–19.

Stowers, Carlton. 1982. *The Unsinkable Titanic Thompson*. Burnet, TX: Eakin Press. 234 pp.

Strachan, Mary Lou, and Robert Custer. 1989. "Female Compulsive Gamblers in Las Vegas." Paper presented to 4th International Conference on Compulsive Gambling, 19 October, Las Vegas, Nevada.

Strate, Larry D., and Ann M. Mayo. 1990. "Federal Control of Indian Lands v. State Control of Gaming: Cabazon Bingo and the Indian Gaming Regulatory Act." *Journal of Gambling Studies* 6 (Spring): 63–72.

Stuart, Lyle. 1979. *Casino Gambling for the Winner*. New York: Ballantine. 208 pp.

Stuart, Lyle. 1994. *Winning at Casino Gambling*. New York: Barricade Books. 320 pp.

Sugar, Bert Randolph. 1992. *Caesars Palace Sports Book of Betting*. New York: St. Martin's Press. 186 pp.

Suits, Daniel B. 1977. "Gambling Taxes: Regressivity and Revenue Potential." *National Tax Journal* 30(1): 43–61.

Sullivan, G. 1972. *By Chance a Winner: The History of Lotteries*. New York: Dodd Mead. 135 pp.

Swanson, Leslie Charles. 1989. *Riverboat Gamblers of History*. Moline, IL: L. C. Swanson. 60 pp.

Sylvester, Kathleen. 1992. "Casinomania: Jackpot Fever." *Governing* 6 (December): 22–26.

Taber, J. I. 1987. "Compulsive Gambling: An Examination of Relevant Models." *Journal of Gambling Behavior* 3: 219–223.

Tanioka, Ichiro. 2000 (English ed.) *Pachinko and the Japanese Society*. Osaka, Japan: Institute of Amusement Industries, Osaka University of Commerce. 146 pp.

Tegtmeier, Ralph. 1989. *Casinos*. New York: Vendome Press. 256 pp.

Teske, Paul, and Bela Sur. 1991. "Winners and Losers: Politics, Casino Gambling, and Development in Atlantic City." *Policy Studies Review* 10 (Spring-Summer): 130–137.

Teski, Marea, Robert Helsabeck, Franklin Smith, and Charles Yeager. 1983. *A City Revitalized: The Elderly Lose at Monopoly*. Lanham, MD: University Press of America. 191 pp.

Thomas, W. I. 1901. "The Gambling Instinct." *American Journal of Sociology* 6: 750–763.

Thomas, William V. 1979. "Gambling's New Respectablilty." *Editorial Research Reports* 2, no. 12 (September): 707–724.

Thompson, William N. 1985. "Patterns of Public Response to Lottery, Horserace, and Casino Gambling Issues." *Nevada Review of Business and Economics* 9 (Spring): 12–22.

Thompson, William N. 1989a. "Stung: The Incredible Story of Brian Molony by Gary Ross: A Review." *Journal of Gambling Behavior* 5, no. 2 (Summer): 153–157.

Thompson, William N. 1989b. "Puerto Rico: Heavy Taxes, Regs Burden Casinos." *Gaming and Wagering Business*, 15 September, 1, 73–76.

Thompson, William N. 1991. "Machismo: Manifestations of a Cultural Value in the Latin American Casino." *Journal of Gambling Studies* 7, no. 2 (Spring): 143–164.

Thompson, William N. 1994a. *Legalized Gambling: A Reference Handbook*. Santa Barbara, CA: ABC-CLIO. 209 pp.

Thompson, William N. 1994b. *Taxation and Casino Gambling*. Las Vegas: Mirage. 50pp.

Thompson, William N. 1996. *Native American Issues: A Reference Handbook*. Santa Barbara, CA: ABC-CLIO. 293 pp.

Thompson, William N. 1997. *Legalized Gambling: A Reference Handbook*. 2d ed. Santa Barbara, CA: ABC-CLIO. 298 pp.

Thompson, William N. 1998a. "Casinos de Juegos del Mundo: A Survey of World Gambling." In *Gambling: Socioeconomic Impacts and Public Policy* (special volume of *The Annals of the American Academy of Political and Social Science*), edited by James H. Frey, 11–21. Thousand Oaks, CA: Sage.

Thompson, William N. 1998b. "The Economics of Casino Gambling." In *Casino Management: Past, Present, Future*, 2d ed., edited by Kathryn Hashimoto, Sheryl Fried Kline, and George Fenich, 306–319. Dubuque, IA: Kendall-Hunt.

Thompson, William N. 1998c. "Gaming Issues for Nevada Policymaking." In *Towards 2000: Public Policy in Nevada*, edited by Dennis L. Soden and Eric Herzik, 111–120. Dubuque, IA: Kendall-Hunt.

Thompson, William N. 1998d. "Not Exactly the Best Gaming Venue: The Nevada Grocery Store Casino." *Gaming Law Review* 2, no. 5 (October): 459–461.

Thompson, William N. 1999a. "Casinos in Las Vegas: Where Impacts Are Not the Issue." In *Legalized Gambling in the United States: The Economic and Social Impact*, edited by Cathy H. C. Hsu, 93–112. New York: Haworth Hospitality Press.

Thompson, William N. 1999b. "History, Development, and Legislation of Native American Casino Gaming." In *Legalized Gambling in the United States: The Economic and Social Impact*, edited by Cathy H. C. Hsu, 41–61. New York: Haworth Hospitality Press.

Thompson, William N. 1999c. "Racinos and the Public Interest." *Gaming Law Review* 3, no. 5–6 (December): 283–286.

Thompson, William N. 1999d. "The South Carolina Bat-tlefield." *Gaming Law Review* 3, no. 1 (February): 5–8.

Thompson, William N. 1999e. "Steve Wynn: I Got the Message." In *The Maverick Spirit: Building the New Nevada,* edited by Richard O. Davies, 194–210. Reno: University of Nevada Press.

Thompson, William N., and Michele Comeau. 1992. *Casino Customer Service = The WIN WIN Game.* New York: Gaming and Wagering Business. 332 pp.

Thompson, William N., and Diana R. Dever. 1994a. "A Sovereignty Checklist for Indian Gaming." Parts 1 and 2. *Indian Gaming* 4 (April): 5–7; 4 (May): 8–9.

Thompson, William N., and Diana R. Dever. 1994b. "The Sovereign Games of North America: An Exploratory Study of First Nations' Gambling." In *Gambling in Canada: The Bottomline,* edited by Colin Campbell, 69–87. Burnaby, B.C.: Simon Fraser University.

Thompson, William N., and Diana R. Dever. 1997. Edited by Eadington and Cornelius, 295–315.

Thompson, William N., and Ricardo Gazel. 1995. "The Last Resort Revisited." *Journal of Gambling Studies* 12, no. 3 (Fall): 335–339.

Thompson, William N., and Ricardo Gazel. 1996. *The Economics of Casino Gambling in Illinois.* Chicago: Chicago Better Government Association. 25 pp.

Thompson, William N., Ricardo Gazel, and Dan Rick-man. 1995. *The Economic Impact of Native American Gaming in Wisconsin.* Milwaukee: Wisconsin Policy Research Institute. 50 pp.

Thompson, William N., Ricardo Gazel, and Dan Rick-man. 1996a. *The Social Costs of Gambling in Wiscon-sin.* Mequon, WI: Wisconsin Policy Research Insti-tute. 43 pp.

Thompson, William N., Ricardo Gazel, and Dan Rick-man. 1996b. *Casinos and Crime: What's the Connec-tion?* Mequon, WI: Wisconsin Policy Research Insti-tute. 30 pp.

Thompson, William N., and J. Kent Pinney. 1990. "The Mismarketing of Dutch Casinos." *Journal of Gam-bling Behavior* 6, no. 3 (Fall): 205–221.

Thompson, William N., J. Kent Pinney, and Jack Schi-browski. 1996. "The Family that Gambles Together: Business and Social Concerns." *Journal of Travel Re-search* 34, no. 3 (Winter): 70–75.

Thompson, William N,. and Frank Quinn. 2000. "South Carolina Saga: Death Comes to Video Machine Gam-bling: An Impact Analysis." Paper presented to the National Conference on Problem Gambling, 6 Octo-ber, Philadelphia.

Thorpe, Edward O. 1962. *Beat the Dealer: A Winning Strategy for the Game of Twenty One.* New York: Ran-dom House. 236 pp.

Thorpe, Edward O. 1984. *The Mathematics of Gambling.* Secaucus, NJ: Gambling Times. 161 pp.

Tilley, Roger. 1973. *A History of Playing Cards.* New York: Potter. 192 pp.

Time-Life, Inc. 1978. *The Gamblers.* The Old West Se-ries. Alexandria, VA: Time-Life Books. 240 pp.

Tosches, Mike, ed. 1995. *Literary Las Vegas: The Best Writing about America's Most Fabulous City.* New York: Henry Holt. 358 pp.

Trump, Donald, and Tony Schwartz. 1987. *Trump: The Art of the Deal.* New York: Random House. 246 pp.

Tuccille, Jerome. 1987. *Trump.* 3d ed. New York: D. I.Fine. 272 pp.

Turner, Wallace. 1965. *Gambler's Money: The New Force in American Life.* Boston: Houghton Mifflin. 306 pp.

Twain, Mark. 1872. *Roughing It.* Hartford, CT: American Publishing. 591 pp.

University of Nevada, Las Vegas [UNLV]. 1999. *Gradu-ate Catalog.* Las Vegas: UNLV. 280 pp.

U.S. Senate Committee on Government Operations. 1962. *Gambling and Organized Crime—Report.* Washington, DC: U.S. Government Printing Office. 48 pp.

Van Der Slik, Jack. 1990. "Legalized Gambling: Preda-tory Policy." *Illinois Issues* (March): 10.

Venturi, Robert, Denise Scott Brown, and Steven Izenour. 1993. *Learning from Las Vegas: The Forgot-ten Symbolism of Architectural Form.* 2d ed. Cam-bridge: MIT Press. 188 pp.

Vinson, Barney. 1986 and 1988. *Las Vegas: Behind the Tables.* 2 vols. Grand Rapids, MI: Gollehon. 229 pp.

Vizenor, Gerald. 1992. "Gambling with Sovereignty." *American Indian Quarterly* 16 (Summer): 411–413.

Vogel, Harold L. 1994. *Entertainment Industry Econom-ics: A Guide for Financial Analysis.* New York: Press Syndicate of the University of Cambridge. 446 pp.

Volberg, Rachael A. 1996. "Prevalence Studies of Prob-lem Gambling in the United States." *Journal of Gam-bling Studies* 12(2): 111–128.

Volberg, Rachael A., and H. J. Steadman. 1989. "Preva-lence Estimates of Pathological Gambling in New Jersey and Maryland." *American Journal of Psychia-try* 146: 1618–1619.

Wacker, R. F., and W. N. Thompson. 1997. "The Michi-gan Question: A Legal Quandary." *Gaming Law Re-view* 1 (Winter): 501–510.

Wagenaar, Willem Albert. 1988. *Paradoxes of Gambling Behaviour: Essays in Cognitive Psychology.* Hillsdale, NJ: Erlbaum. 126 pp.

Wagenaar, Willem Albert, and G. Keren. 1988. "Chance and Luck Are the Same." *Journal of Behavioral Deci-sion Making* 1: 65–75.

Wagman, Robert. 1986. *Instant Millionaires*. Washington, DC: Woodbine House. 298 pp.

Wagner, Walter. 1972. *To Gamble, or Not to Gamble*. New York: World Publishing. 370 pp.

Walker, Michael B. 1992. *The Psychology of Gambling*. Oxford: Pergamon Press. 262 pp.

Walker, Michael B., ed. 1987. *Faces of Gambling*. Sydney, Australia: National Association for Gambling Studies. 315 pp.

Walsh, Thomas. 1991. *Greyhound Racing for Fun and Profit*. Deerfield Beach, FL: Liberty Publishing. 145 pp.

Watson, Tom. 1987. *Don't Bet on It*. Ventura, CA: Regal Books. 249 pp.

WEFA Group (with ICR Research Group, Henry Lesieur, and William Thompson). 1997. *A Study Concerning the Effects of Legalized Gambling on the Citizens of the State of Connecticut*. Eddystone, PA: WEFA Group. Various pagings.

Weinstein, David, and Lillian Deitch. 1974. *The Impact of Legalized Gambling: The Socioeconomic Consequences of Lotteries and Off-Track Betting*. New York: Praeger. 208 pp.

Weisbroat, Irwin. 1991. "A Tribute to Robert L. Custer, MD." *Journal of Gambling Studies* 7, no. 1 (Spring): 3–4.

Weiss, Ann E. 1991. *Lotteries: Who Wins, Who Loses?* Hillside, NJ: Enslow. 112 pp.

Welles, Chris. 1989. "America's Gambling Fever: Everybody Wants a Piece of the Action—But Is It Good for Us?" *Business Week*, 24 April, 112–115, 118, 120.

Werblowsky, R. J. Z., and Geoffrey Wigoder, eds. 1966. *The Encyclopedia of the Jewish Religion*. New York: Holt, Rinehart, Winston. 415 pp.

Wigoder, Geoffrey. 1989. *The Encyclopedia of Judaism*. New York: Macmillan. 768 pp.

Windsor Police. 1995. *Crime and Casino Gambling: A Report*. Windsor, Ont.: Windsor Police Department. 50 pp.

Wolf, John D. 1990. "Taking a Gamble on the Casino Industry." *Christian Century*, 107, 17 January, 36–38.

Wolfgang, Ann K. 1988. "Gambling as a Function of Gender and Sensation Seeking." *Journal of Gambling Behavior* 4(2): 71–78.

Worsnop, Richard L. 1990. "Lucrative Lure of Lotteries and Gambling." *Editorial Research Reports* 1 (9 November): 634–647.

Worsnop, Richard L. 1994. "Gambling Boom: Will the Gambling Industry's Growth Hurt Society?" *CQ Researcher* 4 (November): 241–264.

Wortman, James F. 1999. "Personal Recollections of the New Jersey Gambling 'Experiment' in Atlantic City." In *Legalized Gambling in the United States: The Economic and Social Impact*, edited by Cathy H. C. Hsu, 25–39. New York: Haworth Hospitality Press.

Wykes, Alan. 1964. *The Complete Illustrated Guide to Gambling*. Garden City, NY: Doubleday. 352 pp.

Zola, J. K. 1963. "Observations on Gambling in a Lower Class Setting." *Social Problems* 10: 353–361.

CONTRIBUTORS

Bo Bernhard

Bo Bernhard, a Las Vegas native, received his B.A. from Harvard and his M.A. from the University of Nevada, Las Vegas, where he is a Ph.D. candidate in sociology. Bernhard serves as the director of operations for Problem Gambling Consultants, a nonprofit gambling treatment center.

Carl Braunlich

Carl Braunlich is an associate professor in hospitality and tourism at Purdue University. He was formerly in casino management in New Jersey, the Bahamas, and Las Vegas. He is a coeditor of *International Casino Law*.

Sergio Buth

Sergio Buth is a citizen of Suriname and a graduate student in the School of Hospitality Management at Florida International University.

Shannon Bybee

Shannon Bybee is the director of the International Gaming Institute at the University of Nevada, Las Vegas. He has served on the Gaming Control Board in Nevada and also in management with Alliance Gaming, the Claridge Casino, and Golden Nugget, Inc.

Anthony Cabot

Anthony Cabot is a partner in the law firm of Lionel, Sawyer, and Collins in Las Vegas. His many books include *The Internet Gambling Report, Federal Gambling Law,* and *Casino Gaming: Public Policy, Economics and Regulation*. He is a coeditor of *International Casino Law*.

Felicia Campbell

Felicia Campbell is a professor of English at the University of Nevada, Las Vegas. She received her B.A. and M.A. from the University of Wisconsin and her Ph.D. from United States International University. She is the editor of *Popular Culture Review*.

James Dallas

James Dallas is a retired United Methodist minister, having served congregations in Nevada and California.

He received his B.A. from Occidental College and his Ph.D. in theology from Claremont University. He teaches at Victor Valley College.

Larry Dandurand

Larry Dandurand is a professor of marketing at the University of Nevada, Las Vegas. He received his B.A. from the University of Minnesota and his Ph.D. from the University of Missouri in Columbia. He served in the Peace Corps in Panama and also taught in several countries as a Fulbright Scholar.

Diana Dever

Diana Dever is a professor of social sciences at Mohave College in Arizona. She received her B.A. from Wayne State University, her M.A. from Michigan, and her Ph.D. in history from the University of Nevada, Las Vegas.

John Dombrink

John Dombrink is a professor of criminology at the University of California, Irvine. His undergraduate education was at the University of San Francisco, and he received his Ph.D. from the University of California, Berkeley. He is coauthor of *The Last Resort: Success and Failure in Campaigns for Casinos*.

Robert Faiss

Robert Faiss is a senior partner with Lionel, Sawyer, and Collins law firm in Las Vegas. He has been recognized as the "premier gaming attorney" in the United States and one of "the 100 most influential lawyers in America" by the *National Law Journal*. He received his undergraduate education at the University of Nevada, Reno, and his legal education at American University in Washington, D.C.

Bonnie Galloway

Bonnie Galloway works as a private investment consultant. She has taught business and sociology as an adjunct professor at Rider University, Mercer County Community College, Coker College, and Francis Marion University. She received her B.A. from Hillsdale College, her M.B.A. from Wayne State, and her Ph.D. from Western Michigan University.

Ricardo Gazel
Ricardo Gazel is a research economist with the Inter-American Bank. He was formerly on the staff of the Federal Reserve Bank in Kansas City and the Center for Business and Economic Research at the University of Nevada, Las Vegas. His Ph.D. in economics was awarded by the University of Illinois in Champaign.

William Holmes
William Holmes is the president of Bill Holmes and Associates, an Annandale, Virginia, consulting firm. He was formerly a supervisory special agent with the Laboratory Division of the Federal Bureau of Investigation. He serves as treasurer of the Harbour Center treatment facility for compulsive gamblers in Baltimore, Maryland.

Carl Lutrin
Carl Lutrin is a professor of political science at California Polytechnic State University. He is coauthor of *American Public Administration*. His B.A. is from Adelphi, his M.A. is from Wisconsin, and his Ph.D. is from the University of Missouri, Columbia.

Patricia Maguire
Patricia Maguire is a professor of tourism at Central Washington University. She has also taught in the School of Hospitality Management at Florida International University.

Christian Marfels
Christian Marfels is a professor of economics at Dalhousie University in Halifax, Nova Scotia. He received his doctorate from the Free University of Berlin, and he specializes in industrial and antitrust economics, with a focus on the gambling industry.

Eugene Moehring
Eugene Moehring is a professor of history at the University of Nevada, Las Vegas. He received his undergraduate education at Queens College, where he also received an M.A. degree. His Ph.D. is from the City University of New York. Moehring is the author of *Resort City in the Sunbelt*.

David Nichols
David Nichols received his undergraduate education at the University of Nevada, Las Vegas. He has worked in the hospitality industry in Colorado, Puerto Rico, and

Costa Rica. He is a graduate student at the University of Texas, El Paso.

Frank Quinn
Frank Quinn is a psychologist with the Carolina Psychiatric Services in Columbia, South Carolina. His undergraduate degree is from the University of North Carolina in Chapel Hill, and he received his doctorate from the University of South Carolina.

Dan Rickman
Dan Rickman is a professor of economics at Oklahoma State University. He received his B.A., M. S., and Ph.D degrees from the University of Wyoming.

I. Nelson Rose
I. Nelson Rose received his undergraduate degree from the University of California, Los Angeles, and his law degree from Harvard University. He is the author of *Gambling and the Law* and *Blackjack and the Law*.

Robert Schmidt
Robert Schmidt is a social research analyst and adjunct professor at the University of Nevada, Las Vegas. He received his undergraduate degree from the University of Chicago and his Ph.D. in sociology from the University of Nevada, Las Vegas.

Garry Smith
Garry Smith is a retired professor of physical education and sports studies at the University of Alberta in Edmonton. He currently works with the Institute for Business Development at the university and also is a gambling research associate with the Canada West Foundation.

Dina Titus
Dina Titus is a professor of political science at the University of Nevada, Las Vegas, and also a member of the Nevada state Senate. She is the author of *Bombs in Their Backyards*. Her B.A. is from William and Mary, her M.A. from the University of Georgia, and her Ph.D. from Florida State University.

Andrew Tottenham
Andrew Tottenham is the head of the gaming consultant firm, Tottenham and Company, in London. He has worked many years in the casino industry. He is the coeditor of *International Casino Law*.

Elizabeth Vercher
Elizabeth Vercher is a native of Lyon, France, where she has been educated. She conducted research on the

French gambling industry while working at the Medias and Identities Center at the University of Lyon. Her Ph.D. was awarded by the University of Lyon.

R. Fred Wacker
R. Fred Wacker is a professor of history at Wayne State University and an adjunct professor in the Honors College at the University of Michigan. His B.A. is from Harvard, and his J.D. and Ph.D. are from the University of Michigan.

Sidney Watson
Sidney Watson is the supervisor of the Curriculum Materials Library of the University of Nevada, Las Vegas. She received her B.A. from the University of California,

Santa Barbara, and her master's in public administration from the University of Nevada, Las Vegas.

Maria White
Maria White is the head of circulations for the Lied Library at the University of Nevada, Las Vegas. She received her bachelor's and master's degrees in public administration from the University of Nevada, Las Vegas.

Bradley Wimmer
Bradley Wimmer is an associate professor of economics at the University of Nevada, Las Vegas. He has served as an economist with the Federal Communications Commission. His B.A. is from Coe College and his Ph.D. from the University of Kentucky.

INDEX

ABOUT THE AUTHOR

William N. Thompson is a professor of public administration at the University of Nevada, Las Vegas. His previous books with ABC-CLIO include *Legalized Gambling: A Reference Handbook* and *Native American Issues: A Reference Handbook*. He has also coauthored or coedited *International Casino Law, Casino Customer Service = The WIN WIN Game,* and *The Last Resort: Success and Failure in Campaigns for Casinos*. Prior to coming to the University of Nevada, he taught at Western Michigan University and Southeast Missouri State University, as well as serving as the elected supervisor of Kalamazoo Township in Michigan. His B.A. and M.A. degrees were awarded by Michigan State University, and his Ph.D. in political science is from the University of Missouri, Columbia.